The American Left, 1955-1970

THE AMERICAN LEFT, 1955-1970

A National Union
Catalog of Pamphlets
Published in the
United States
and Canada

‡

Edited and Compiled by
Ned Kehde

Greenwood Press
Westport, Connecticut • London, England

Library of Congress Cataloging in Publication Data

Kehde, Ned.
    The American left, 1955-1970.

    1. Radicalism—United States—Bibliography—Union lists.
2. Liberalism—United States—Bibliography—Union lists.
3. Radicalism—Canada—Bibliography—Union lists. 4. Liberalism—
Canada—Bibliography—Union lists. I. Title.
Z7165.U5K43   016.3205'13'0973   76-8002
ISBN 0-8371-8282-4

Library of Congress Catalog Card Number: 76-8002
ISBN: 0-8371-8282-4

First published in 1976

Greenwood Press, a division of Williamhouse-Regency Inc.
51 Riverside Avenue, Westport, Connecticut 06880

Printed in the United States of America

Contents

✝

Acknowledgments

✝

This work necessitated the invaluable assistance of a number of dedicated and gracious people. Theodora Hiles provided unexcelled research assistance in the odious task of searching through the *National Union Catalog*. The assistance of Mary Hanfelt and Kathy Hill was essential and always accurate. I cannot measure my indebtedness to my wife, Martha; her assistance and love were, as always, perfect and unlimited. I thank the following librarians and archivists: Dorothy Swason of the New York University Taimiment Library; Gerda Maskaleris, J.R.K. Kantor, and Gerald Simerman of the University of California at Berkeley Bancroft Library; John Glinka, George Griffin, Alexandra Mason, and John Nugent of the University of Kansas, David Heron of the University of California, Santa Cruz; Russ Benedict of the University of Nevada, Reno; Ed Weber of the University of Michigan Labadie Collection; James P. Danky, Eleanor McKay, Charles Shelter, and Josephine L. Harper of the State Hitorical Society of Wisconsin; Dick Akeryod of the Connecticut State Library. The financial aid from the University of Kansas General Research Fund made it possible to travel across the country in pursuit of the 4018 pamphlets I had to catalog and record, and it also paid Theodora Hiles' salary.

Introduction

Of all the materials which historians use in their efforts to reconstruct the past, pamphlets offer the greatest range of information and throw the clearest light upon the "mental furniture of the ordinary man." Especially does the historian interested in the "winds of doctrine" and the "climates of opinion" regard them highly, because unlike even correspondence and diaries, pamphlets reflect the attitude and opinions not only of their writers but also of their readers. . . . Every effort to facilitate the exploitation of pamphlets deserves the consideration of librarians no less than that of historians and other students whose searches carry them into the past.

CHARLES F. MULLETT, 1935[1]

This is a national union catalog of left-wing pamphlets published in the United States and Canada from 1955 through 1970. It is a national union catalog to the extent that I undertook the task of cataloging the pamphlets in the Labadie Collection of the University of Michigan, Bancroft Library of the University of California at Berkeley, Kansas Collection of the University of Kansas, Tamiment Library of New York University, Division of Archives and Manuscripts of the State Historical Society of Wisconsin, and others. In addition, I have listed the pamphlet entries from the *National Union Catalog* and from the card catalogs of the New York Public Library and the Library of the State Historical Society of Wisconsin.

There are 4,018 pamphlets listed, all of which are cataloged according to Anglo-American cataloging rules, with the exception of the entries from the *National Union Catalog* and the card catalogs of the New York Public Library and the Library of the State Historical Society of Wisconsin. These exceptions have been adapted to be as compatible as possible with the rest. All of the pamphlets have been subject-analyzed and assigned subject headings taken from the Library of Congress, 7th edition, *Subject Headings.* At the end of each entry there are alphabetic symbols (e.g., CU-B, Mo-U, Whi-A) indicating the library or libraries that own the pamphlet. The index provides access to all subjects, joint authors, writers of forewords, and publishers. Finally, the catalog can also be used in a number of instances as an index to underground newspapers and left-wing periodicals.

A definition of left-wing is necessary: Americans for Democratic Action was my level of measure in determining what was left-wing. I included any pamphlet published by the Americans for Democratic Action or by any person or group to the left of that organization. In regard to Canada, any person or organization to the left of the New Democratic Party was included. The events of the late 1960s politicalized or radicalized some traditionally nonpolitical and non-left-wing groups. Therefore, some publications of homosexual and homophile organizations, as well as some drug, utopian, mystical, and quasi-religious organizations (Feraferia, a collective, eco-religious settlement, is a prime example), have been included. In short, any pamphlet written by an individual or a political or social organization advocating a liberal to radical position was within my purview.

In his introduction to the first volume of *British Pamphleteers* (1948), George Orwell grappled with the difficult task of providing a clear definition of the pamphlet. He explained that there are definite characteristics which separate pamphlets from leaflets, manifestos, brochures, memorials, instructional manuals, circular letters, religious tracts, and the like. I appreciate Orwell's distinctions, and I tried to follow them as strictly as possible. However, I did deviate by including significant leaflets such as DuBois [W.E.B.] Clubs of America, *We Demand Massive Federal Intervention Now*), brochures (such as Student Peace Union, *An Introduction*), instructional manuals (such as Linda Borenstein, *Patching Up the Movement; A First Aid Manual*), manifestos (such as Students for a Democratic Society, *Constitution*), and religious tracts (such as James H. Johnson, *Religion Is a Gigantic Fraud*).

It was no arbitrary decision to set 1955 as the beginning date of this work. In 1955 the *Village Voice* began publication. By 1955 *I. F. Stone's Weekly*, founded two years earlier, had begun to wield some inspirational clout. In that same year the Student League for Industrial Democracy was inspired enough to trumpet that it was "a national liberal campus group, educating for increased democracy." It was a pivotal year for the nascent civil-rights movement following the Supreme Court decision of *Brown v. Board of Education of Topeka* in May 1954, which set the stage for the bus boycott in Montgomery, Alabama, beginning on December 5, 1955. It was just five short years before the Student League for Industrial Democracy would metamorphose into the Students for a Democratic Society, and in those intervening years the groundwork was laid for the New Left: SLATE was formed at Berkeley, the Student Peace Union was formed, Paul Goodman's *Growing Up Absurd* was published, and publication of *Studies on the Left* was begun.

The New Left had a few minor palpitations of life in 1971 and 1972— witnessed by the May Day extravaganza of 1971, the sporadic protests against the war in Southeast Asia, and the seriocomic activities at the Republican National Convention at Miami in the summer of 1972. The old left (Communist Party, Socialist Workers' Party, etc.) will never die. Although its fervor has diminished, the old left continues to publish pamphlets. Foreign students erupted on U.S. college campuses around 1971 to form a movement which produced numerous pamphlets. Since 1970 pamphleteers of the gay liberation movement and the women's rights movement have been most prolific. The Native American movement has gained momentum since 1970. The left is indomitable, and pamphleteering and the left are inseparable. It was an uncomfortable decision to end the catalog in 1970, and consequently, there are thousands of pamphlets for some enterprising bibliographer to tangle with—a supplement to this catalog is already in order.

---

1. Charles F. Mullett, "The Historians and the Use of the Pamphlets," *The Library Quarterly*, 5 (1935), 301.

Sample Entries and Explanation

B108[1]
The Black uprisings, Newark—Detroit, 1967.[2] Introduction by Paul Boutelle. [New York, Merit Publishers, 1969][3]
30p. illus. 22cm.[4]
Cover title.[5]
1. Negroes—Detroit. 2. Negroes—Newark. 3. Detroit—Riots, 1967. 4. Newark—Riots, 1067.[6] I. Boutelle, Paul. II. Merit Publishers.[7] KU-RH, MoU, WHi-L, MsSM, NUC 70-28048[8]

1. Entry number
2. Title
3. Place of publication, publisher, and date of publication
4. Number of pages, illustrations, size of the pamphlet
5. Indication that the title was taken from the cover of the pamphlet
6. Arabic numerals, indication of the subjects
7. Roman numerals, indication of added entries for publishers, joint authors, etc.
8. Indicates the libraries that own the pamphlet

B269[1]
Burt, Eric.[2]
Eyes on Washington. A program for people's legislation; what labor and the people can do to influence Congress in 1956[3]. [New York, New Century Publishers, 1955][4]
15p. 19cm.[5]
Cover title.
1. U.S. 84th Cong., 2d sess. 1956. 2. Taxation. 3. Rayburn, Sam Tallaferro, 1882-1966. 4. Johnson, Lyndon Baines, Pres., U.S., 1908-1976.[6] I. New Century Publishers.[7] KU-J, B7538[8]

1. Entry number
2. Author
3. Title
4. Place of publication, publisher, and date of publication
5. Number of pages and size
6. Subjects
7. Entry note added by publisher
8. Library symbol and the bibliographic number of the listing in Joel L. Seidman's *Communism in the United States; A Bibliography*, Ithaca, N.Y., Cornell University Press, 1969.

List of Libraries and Library Symbols

AAP—Auburn University, Auburn, Ala.

ArU—University of Arkansas, Fayetteville

C—California State Library, Sacramento

CaBVaU—University of British Columbia, Vancouver

CaBViP—Provincial Library, Victoria

CaOTP—Toronto Public Library, Metropolitan Bibliographic Centre

CaOTU—University of Toronto

CLL—Los Angeles County Law Library, Los Angeles

CLO—Occidental College, Los Angeles

CLSU—University of Southern California, Los Angeles

CLU—University of California at Los Angeles

CNoS—San Fernando Valley State College, Northridge, Calif.

CoU—University of Colorado, Boulder

CSaT—San Francisco Theological Seminary, San Anselmo, Calif.

CSf—San Francisco Public LIbrary

CSSR—Southern California Library for Social Studies and Research, Los Angeles

CSt—Stanford University Libraries

CSt-H—Stanford University Libraries, Hoover Institution on War, Revolution and Peace

CSt-L—Stanford University Libraries, Lane Medical Library

CtU—University of Connecticut, Storrs

CtY—Yale University, New Haven, Conn.

CtY-D—Yale University, New Haven, Conn., Divinity School Library

CU—University of California, Berkeley

CU-B—University of California, Berkeley, Bancroft Library

CU-SB—University of California, Santa Barbara

DeU—University of Delaware, Newark

DHHF. *See* DHUD

DHUD—U.S. Dept. of Housing and Urban Development Library

DLC—Library of Congress

DNLM—U.S. National Library of Medicine, Bethesda, Md.

DPU—Pan American Union Library Washington, D.C.

DS—U.S. Department of State Library

FMU—University of Miami, Coral Gables

FU—University of Florida, Gainesville

GA—Atlanta Public Library

GASC—Georgia State College, Atlanta

GAT—Georgia Institute of Technology, Atlanta

GAU—Atlanta University, Atlanta

GU—University of Georgia, Athens

IaU—University of Iowa, Iowa City

ICU—University of Chicago

IdU—University of Idaho, Moscow

IEds—Southern Illinois University, Edwardsville campus

IEN—Northwestern University, Evanston, Ill.

InU—Indiana University, Bloomington

IU—University of Illinois, Urbana

KMK—Kansas State University, Manhattan

KU—University of Kansas, Lawrence

KU-A—University of Kansas, Lawrence, University Archives

KU-J—University of Kansas, Lawrence, Josephson Collection (Department of Special Collection)

KU-RH—University of Kansas, Lawrence, Kansas Collection

KyU—University of Kentucky, Lexington

LLafS—University of Southwestern Louisiana, Lafayette

LN—New Orleans Public Library

LNHT—Tulane University Library, New Orleans

MB—Boston Public Library

MeB—Bowdoin College, Brunswick, Maine

MeBa—Bangor Public Library, Bangor, Maine

MH—Harvard University, Cambridge, Mass.

MH-AH—Harvard University, Cambridge, Mass., Andover-Harvard Theological Library

MH-BA—Harvard University, Cambridge, Mass., Graduate School of Business Administration Library

MH-IR—Harvard University, Cambridge, Mass., Industrial Relations Library

MH-L—Harvard University, Cambridge, Mass., Law School Library

MH-PA—Harvard University, Cambridge, Mass., Graduate School of Public Administration

MiDW—Wayne State Unviersity, Detroit

MiEM—Michigan State Unviersity, East Lansing

MiU—University of Michigan, Ann Arbor (95 percent of the entries are from the Labadie collection)

MiU-H—University of Michigan, Ann Arbor, Michigan Historical Collections

MiU-L—University of Michigan, Ann Arbor, Law School Library

MNS—Smith College, Northampton, Mass.

MnU—University of Minnesota, Minneapolis

MoKU—University of Missouri at Kansas City

MoSW—Washington University, St. Louis

MoU—University of Missouri, Columbia

MsSM—Mississippi State University, State College

MsU—University of Mississippi, University

N—New York State Library, Albany

NB—Brooklyn Public LIbrary

NBC—Brooklyn College

NbU—University of Nebraska, Lincoln

NBuU—State University of New York at Buffalo

NcD—Duke University, Durham

NcGU—University of North Carolina at Greensboro

NcGW—obsolete: See NcGU

NcRS—North Carolina State University at Raleigh

NcU—University of North Carolina, Chapel Hill

NcWsW—Wake Forest College, Winston-Salem, N.C.

NhU—University of New Hampshire, Durham

NIC—Cornell University, Ithaca, N.Y.

NjP——Princeton University, Princeton, N.J.

NjR—Rutgers, the State University, New Brunswick, N.J.

NN—New York Public Library

NNC—Columbia University, New York

NNC-L—Columbia University, Law Library, New York

NNJef—Jefferson School of Social Science, New York (defunct)

NNU—New York University, New York

NNU-T—New York University Libraries, New York, Taminent Library

NRU—University of Rochester, N.Y.

NUC 66-71619—National Union Catalog card number

OCIW—Case Western Reserve University, Cleveland

ODW—Ohio Wesleyan University, Delaware

OkU—University of Oklahoma, Norman

OO—Oberlin College, Oberlin, Ohio

OOxM—Miami University, Oxford, Ohio

Or—Oregon State Library, Salem

OrCS—Oregon State University Library, Corvallis

OrU—University of Oregon, Eugene

OU—Ohio State University, Columbus

P—Pennsylvania State Library, Harrisburg

PCamA—Alliance College, Cambridge Springs, Pa.

PP—Free Library of Philadelphia

PPBMR—Pennsylvania Economy League (Eastern Division)

PPCPC—Philadelphia City Planning Commission

PPD—Drexel Institute of Technology, Philadelphia

PPFr—Friends' Free Library of Germantown, Philadelphia

PPiU—University of Pittsburgh

PPT—Temple University, Philadelphia

PPULC—Union Library Catalogue of Pennsylvania, Philadelphia

PSC—Swarthmore College, Swarth-Pa.

PSC-Hi—Swarthmore College, Swarthmore, Pa., Friends Historical Library

RPB—Brown Unviersity, Providence, R.I.

ScCleU—Clemson University, Clemson, S.C.

TNJ—Joint University Libraries (Vanderbilt University, George Peabody College for Teachers and Scarritt College), Nashville, Tenn.

TU—University of Tennessee, Knoxville

TxDaM—Southern Methodist University, Dallas

TxFTC—Texas Christian University, Forth Worth

TxU—University of Texas, Austin

UU—University of Utah, Salt Lake City

ViRUT—Union Theological Seminary, Richmond, Va.

ViU—University of Virginia, Charlottesville

ViU-L—University of Virginia, Charlottesville, Law Library

Wa—Washington State Library, Olympia

WaT—Tacoma Public Library, Tacoma, Washington

WaU-L—University of Washington, Seattle, School of Law

WHi-A—State Historical Society of Wisconsin, Madison, Division of Archives and Manuscripts

WHi-L—State Historical Society of Wisconsin, Madison, Library

WU—University of Wisconsin, Madison

WvU—West Virginia University, Morgantown

Union Catalog
of Pamphlets

A

A1
A. Philip Randolph at 80--tributes
    and recollections.   [New York,
    A. Philip Randolph Institute,
    1969?]
  31p. illus.
  Excerpts from speeches made at
  the 80th birthday dinner, May 6,
  1969.
  1. Negroes. 2. Randolph, Asa
  Philip, 1889-   I. Randolph
  (A. Philip) Institute.
  WHi-L

A2
Aaron Dixon Defense Fund.
  Hands off Aaron Dixon, captain,
  Seattle Black Panther Party.
  [Seattle, 1968]
  15p. illus. 22cm.
  Cover title.
  1. Dixon, Aaron. 2. Negroes--
  Politics and suffrage. 3. Black
  Panther Party.
  WHi-L, MiU

A3
Aber, Joel.
  Germ warfare research for
  Vietnam. Project spicerack on
  the Pennsylvania campus, by Joel
  Aber, Jules Benjamin [and] Robin
  Martin. [Philadelphia, Philadelphia Area Committee to End
  the War in Vietnam, 1966]
  30p. illus. 22cm.
  Cover title.
  1. Pennsylvania. University.
  Institute for Cooperative
  Research. 2. Biological warfare. 3. Vietnamese conflict,
  1961-1975. I. Benjamin, Jules,
  jt. auth. II. Martin, Robin,
  jt. auth. III. Philadelphia

Area Committee to End the War
in Vietnam.
MoU, WHi-L

A4
Aberle, Kathleen Gough, 1925-
  Anthropology and imperialism.
  Ann Arbor, Radical Education
  Project [196]
  6p. 28cm.
  Cover title.
  1. Imperialism. 2. Anthropo-
  logy. 3. U.S.--Foreign policy.
  I. Radical Education Project.
  KU-RH, MoU

A5
Aberle, Kathleen Gough, 1925-
  The decline of the state and
  the coming of world society:
  an optimist's view of the
  future. [Detroit, Correspondence Publishing Co., c1962]
  31p. 19cm. (Correspondence
  pamphlet 4)
  Cover title.
  1. International organization.
  I. Correspondence Publishing
  Co.
  KU-RH

A6
Aberle, Kathleen Gough, 1925-
  The Indian revolutionary
  potential. Boston, New England
  Free Press [1969?]
  [23]-35p. 22cm.
  Cover title.
  Reprinted from Monthly Review,
  Feb. 1969.
  1. India--Pol. & govt.
  2. Revolutions--India. I. New
  England Free Press.
  MiU, KU-RH

A7
Aberle, Kathleen Gough, 1925-
  The struggle at Simon Fraser
  University. West Vancouver
  [College Printers Ltd., 1970]
  16p. 22cm.
  Cover title.
  Reprinted from Monthly Review,
  May 1970.
  1. Student movements--Canada.
  2. Simon Fraser University.
  KU-RH

A8
Aberle, Kathleen Gough, 1925-
  When the saints go marching in;
  an account of the ban-the-bomb
  movement in Britain. [Detroit,
  Correspondence Publishing Co.,
  1961]
  31p. 19cm. (Correspondence
  pamphlet 3)
  Cover title.
  1. Campaign for Nuclear Disarmament. 2. Atomic weapons and
  disarmament. I. Correspondence
  Publishing Co.
  KU-RH, MiU

A9
Abernathy, Ralph David.
  To preach the gospel to the poor.
  [Atlanta, Southern Christian
  Leadership Conference, 1969?]
  [7]p. 22cm.
  Cover title.
  At head of title: Letter from a
  Charleston jail.
  1. Poor. 2. Poor People's
  Campaign. I. Southern Christian
  Leadership Conference.
  MiU

A10
Abrams, Arnold.
  Watch on the Mekong. [Ithaca,
  N.Y., Glad Day Press, 1970?]
  [4]p. map, illus. 28cm.
  Caption title.
  Reprinted from Far Eastern
  Economic Review, May 14, 1970.
  1. Cambodia. 2. Vietnamese
  conflict, 1961-1975. I. Glad
  Day Press.
  NNU-T

A11
Abt, John J.
  Verdict first, trial after.
  [Los Angeles, Constitutional
  Liberties Information Center,
  196]
  24p.
  Cover title.
  1. Healey, Dorothy. 2. Anti-
  communist movements--Califor-
  nia. 3. Internal security.
  I. Constitutional Liberties
  Information Center.
  MiU

A12
Abt, John J.
  "Which side are you on?" [New
  York, New Outlook Publishers,
  1968]
  7p.
  Cover title.
  1. Anti-communist movements.
  2. Communism. 3. Internal
  security. I. New Outlook
  Publishers.
  MiU, NNU-T

A13
Acheson, Dean Gooderham, 1893-
  U.S. relations with China.
  Toronto, Research, Information,
  and Publications, Student Union
  for Peace Action [196]
  10p. 28cm.
  Cover title.
  1. U.S.--For. rel.--China
  (People's Republic of China,
  1949-   ) 2. China (People's
  Republic of China, 1949-   )
  --For. rel.--U.S. I. Student
  Union for Peace Action.
  WHi-A

A14
Achkar, Marof.
  Racism in South Africa; a call
  for international action.
  [New York] American Committee
  on Africa [1965]
  48p. port. 27cm.
  Cover title.
  Includes bibliography.
  1. Africa, South--Race question.
  I. American Committee on

Africa.
IEN, NUC66-71619

A15
Ad Hoc Committee for Christmas
    Week Vigil to Free All Politi-
    cal Prisoners.
What has happened to the Panthers
nationally. [Washington, New
Mobilization Committee, 1969]
[2]p. 36cm.
Caption title.
"Reprinted from a report by the
Ad Hoc Committee for Christmas
Week Vigil to Free All Political
Prisoners."
1. Black Panther Party. I. New
Mobilization Committee to End
the War in Vietnam.
KU-RH

A16
Ad Hoc Committee on the Human
    Rights and Genocide Treaties.
Is the U.S. a lost leader?
[New York, 1966?]
folder.
1. U.S.--Foreign policy.
WHi-L

A17
Ad Hoc Committee on the Triple
    Revolution.
The triple revolution: an ap-
praisal of the major U.S. crisis
and proposals for action. [New
York, Distributed by Students for
a Democratic Society, and Econ-
omic Research and Action Project,
196]
14p. 28cm.
Caption title.
1. Cybernetics. 2. Negroes--
Civil rights. 3. Atomic weapons.
I. Students for a Democratic
Society. II. Title.
KU-RH, WHi-L

A18
Ad Hoc Committee on the Triple
    Revolution.
Triple revolution, together with
commentary by Dave Dellinger and
growing up absorbed [by] Paul
Goodman. [New York, Liberation,
1964?]

11 [1]p. 28cm.
Caption title.
Reprinted from Liberation.
April 1964.
1. Cybernetics. 2. Negroes--
Civil rights. 3. Atomic wea-
pons. 4. Education. I. Dellin-
ger, Dave. II. Goodman, Paul,
1917-1972.
NNUT, KU-RH, WHi-A, NUC65-60082

A19
Adams, Frederick C.
The Kore, [Altadena, Calif.,
Feraferia, Inc., 1969]
3 leaves. 28cm.
Caption title.
1. Mysticism. I. Feraferia.
MoU

A20
Adams, Frederick C.
Paradisal sanctuary. [Altadena,
Calif., Feraferia, Inc. c1969]
2 leaves. 28cm.
Caption title.
1. Mysticism. 2. Collective
settlements. I. Feraferia.
MoU

A21
Adams, Jane.
Function of a regional organi-
zation. Iowa City [1965]
2p. 36cm.
1. Students for a Democratic
Society.
KU-RH

A22
Adelman, Bob.
Birth of a voter. [New York,
CORE, 196]
[4]p. 28cm.
Caption title.
1. Negroes--Politics and suf-
frage. 2. Louisiana--Race
question. I. Congress of Racial
Equality.
CU-B

A23
Adickes, Sandra.
My seven years (h)itch: a ramb-
ling, discursive, anecdotal

history of the evolution of a
radical teacher. Ann Arbor,
Conference on Radicals in the
Professions, 1967.
10p. 28cm.
Cover title.
1. Teachers. 2. Education--New
York (State)--New York (City)
3. Student movements. I. Conference on Radicals in the Professions.
MiU-H

A24
Adler, Jo.
   Tenant organizing techniques.
New York, Congress of Racial
Equality [196]
5 leaves. 28cm.
Cover title.
1. Landlord and tenant. 2. Tene-
ment-houses. I. Congress of
Racial Equality.
WHi-A

A25
Afanasenko, E.I.
   Report at the All-Russian teachers congress: the school at the
current stage of building communism. New York, International
Arts and Sciences Press [1960]
20-41p.
Reprinted from English translation in Soviet Education, v.
2, no. 9; 1960.
1. Education--Russia. I. International Arts and Sciences Press.
CLU

A26
Afanasenko, E.I.
   The school in new conditions;
the new man grows up in work.
New York, International Arts
and Sciences Press [1960]
8 leaves.
Reprinted from English translation in Soviet Education,
v. 2, no. 6; 1960.
1. Education--Russia. I. International Arts and Sciences Press.
KU-J, CLU

A27
Africa Fund.

Occupied Africa: facts the U.S.
needs to know. [New York, 1969]
6 [1] leaves. 28cm. (Africa
Fund bulletin number 1)
Caption title.
1. Cabinda Gulf Oil. 2. Petroleum industry and trade--Angola.
3. Petroleum industry and trade--
Mozambique.
KU-RH

A28
Africa Fund.
   Rhodesia or Zimbabwe; no middle
ground. New York, Africa Fund
associated with the American
Committee on Africa, 1969.
10p. 26cm.
Cover title.
1. Rhodesia--Pol. & govt.
2. Zimbabwe, Mashonaland.
I. American Committee on Africa.
KU-RH

A29
Africa Research Group.
   Africa retort; a tribal analysis
of U.S. Africanists. Who they
are; why to fight them. Cambridge, Mass., 1970.
93p. illus., ports. 28cm.
An extensive revision of a
pamphlet entitled African
studies in America.
1. African studies.
CSt-H, NUC72-99304

A30
Africa Research Group.
   David and Goliath collaborate
in Africa. [Boston, New
England Free Press, 1969?]
17p. 22cm.
Cover title.
Reprinted from Leviathan,
Sept. 1969.
1. Israel--Relations (general)
with Africa. 2. Africa--Rela-
tions (general) with Israel.
I. New England Free Press.
KU-RH

A31
Africa Research Group.
   International dependency in the
1970's: how America under-

develops the world; a state of
the empire report. [Cambridge,
Mass., 1970]
62p. illus. 28cm.
Cover title.
"Written on the occasion of the
International Development Conference, held in Washington, D.C.
on February 24-26, 1970."
1. Economic assistance, American.
2. Investments, American.
3. Underdeveloped areas. 4. U.S.
--Foreign policy.
DLC 72-192122, KU-RH, MiU, WHi-L

A32
Africa Research Group.
  Israel: imperialist mission in
  Africa. [n.p.] Tricontinental
  Publishers [1970?]
  [26]p. 20cm.
On cover: 2nd World Conference on
Palestine, Amman, 2-6 September,
1970. General Union of Palestine
Students.
1. Israel--For. rel.--Africa.
2. Africa--For. rel.--Israel.
I. Tricontinental Publishers.
NIC, MB, NUC 72-99278

A33
Africa Research Group.
  The other side of Nigeria's civil
  war. [Cambridge, Mass., 1970]
  29p. illus. 28cm.
Cover title.
1. Nigeria--Pol. & govt.
2. Nigeria--Econ. condit.
3. Nigeria--History--Civil War,
1967.
KU-RH, IU

A34
Africa Research Group.
  Radical study group. [Cambridge,
  Mass., 1969?]
  38p. illus. 28cm.
1. Africa--Pol. & govt.--Bibl.
2. Nationalism--Africa--Bibl.
DLC 70-286112, WvU

A35
Africa Research Group.
  Southern Africa. [Cambridge,
  Mass., 1970]
  12p. illus. 28cm.

1. Africa, South--Race question.
2. Nationalism--Africa, Southern.
DLC 70-284623

A36
African Freedom Day Action Against
  Apartheid, Washington, D.C.,
  1964.
  Conference working papers.
  [Oberlin, Ohio, 1964]
  1v. 28cm.
Cover title.
1. Africa, South--Race question.
WHi-A

A37
African studies in America--the
  extended family. A tribal
  analysis of U.S. Africanists:
  who they are; why to fight
  them. [Cambridge, Mass.]
  Africa Research Group [1970]
  93p. illus. 28cm.
1. African studies. 2. U.S.--
Relations (general) with Africa.
I. Africa Research Group.
KU-RH

A38
Agenda for a generation: a new
  left statement of values.
  Montreal, Our Generation
  [196]
  8 [1]p. 28cm.
Cover title.
1. Student movements. 2. Youth
--Political activity. I. Our
Generation.
NNU-T

A39
Agrarian work project. [n.p.,
  [196]
  [2]p. 28cm.
Caption title.
1. Agricultural laborers--
Southern States. 2. Southern
Student Organizing Committee.
3. Agricultural and Allied
Workers Union. 4. Mitchell,
H.L.
KU-RH

A40
Aguilar, Alonso.
  Latin America and the Alliance

for progress. Translated from
the Spanish by Ursula Wasserman.
New York, Monthly Review Press
1963.
36p. 22cm. (Monthly Review
pamphlet series, no. 24)
1. Alliance for Progress.
2. Latin America--Economic policy.
I. Monthly Review Press.
KU-RH, MiU, DLC 63-21962

A41
Ahmad, Eqbal.
  Revolutionary warfare. [Chicago,
  Students for a Democratic Soc-
  iety, 196]
  18p. 21cm.
  Cover title.
  1. Guerrilla warfare. 2. Revo-
  lutions. I. Students for a
  Democratic Society.
  MiU

A42
Ahmad, Eqbal.
  Revolutionary warfare; how to
  tell when the rebels have won.
  [Boston, New England Free Press,
  196]
  [4]p. illus. 28cm.
  Caption title.
  1. Guerrilla warfare. 2. Revo-
  lutions. I. New England Free
  Press.
  KU-RH

A43
Ahmad, Eqbal.
  Revolutionary warefare; how to
  tell when the rebels have won.
  [Ithaca, N.Y., Glad Day Press,
  196]
  [95-102]p. 28cm.
  Caption title.
  1. Guerrilla warfare. 2. Revolutions. I. Glad Day Press.
  MoU

A44
Air War Action Committee.
  The air war; the myth of de-
  escalation. [San Francisco,
  197]
  [8]p. illus. 22cm.
  Cover title.
  1. Vietnamese conflict, 1961-

1975. 2. U.S.--Military
policy.
KU-RH

A45
Alabama Christian Movement for
  Human Rights.
  Birmingham: people in motion.
  [Birmingham, Ala., Alabama
  Christian Movement for Human
  Rights, in cooperation with the
  Southern Conference Educational
  Fund, 196]
  [28]p. illus. 22cm.
  Cover title.
  1. Negroes--Civil rights.
  2. Birmingham, Ala.--Race
  question. 3. Negroes--Birming-
  ham, Ala. I. Southern Confer-
  ence Educational Fund.
  KU-RH, MiU, WHi-L

A46
Alabama Christian Movement for
  Human Rights.
  Nine years of progress of the
  Alabama Christian Movement for
  Human Rights, Birmingham,
  Alabama, nineteen hundred
  fifty-six through sixty-five.
  Birmingham [1965?]
  74p. illus.
  1. Alabama--Race question.
  2. Negroes--Alabama.
  WHi-L

A47
Alavi, Hamza.
  Imperialism, old and new.
  Boston, New England Free Press
  [196]
  [104]-126p. 22cm.
  Cover title.
  Reprinted from Socialist Regis-
  ter, 1964.
  1. Imperialism. I. New England
  Free Press.
  KU-RH, MoU

A48
Alavi, Hamza.
  Pakistan: the burden of US aid
  [by] Hamza Alavi & Amir Khusro.
  Boston, New England Free Press
  [196]
  14-48p. 22cm.

Cover title.
Reprinted from New University
Thought, autumn 1962.
1. Pakistan--Relations (general)
with the U.S.   2. Economic as-
sistance, American.   I. Khusro,
Amir, jt. auth.   II. New England
Free Press.
KU-RH, MoU

A49
Alavi, Hamza.
  Peasants & revolution.   Ann
  Arbor, Radical Education Project
  [196]
  37p. illus. 22cm.
  Cover title.
  Reprinted from the Socialist
  Register, 1965.
  1. Peasantry--India. 2. Peasant-
  ry--China. 3. Revolutions--Asia.
  I. Radical Education Project.
  KU-RH

A50
Alcock, Norman Z.
  The bridge of reason.   [Toronto,
  Canadian Peace Research Insti-
  tute, 196]
  40p. 22cm.
  1. Peace. I. Canadian Peace
  Research Institute.
  WHi-A

A51
Alert.
  The draft: a burning issue.
  [New York, University Christian
  Movement and Youth, National
  Council of Churches, 1968?]
  15p. illus. 28cm.
  Cover title.
  1. Military service, Compulsory.
  MoU

A52
Alfred, Helen L., ed.
  Worldwide trade for peace; an
  appeal for international econo-
  mic unity, by Holland Roberts,
  Victor Perlo [and] Mary Van
  Kleeck. San Francisco, Peace
  Publications Committee [1964]
  47p. 23cm.
  Cover title.
  Includes excerpts from addresses,

etc., by U Thant and others.
1. International economic inte-
gration. 2. Peace. I. Roberts,
Holland De Witte, 1895-
II. Perlo, Victor. III. Van
Kleeck, Mary. IV. Peace Publi-
cations Committee.
DLC 64-20566

A53
All power to the people; join the
  common conspiracy: an introduction to the Black Panther
  Party, Young Lords Organization, Young Patriots Organization. [n.p., 1969?]
  [4]p. 22cm.
  Cover title.
  1. Black Panther Party.
  2. Young Lords Organization.
  3. Young Patriots Organization.
  CU-B

A54
Allen, Bruce.
  Build the year-round work-in
  [by Bruce Allen, Carol Schik,
  Henry Illian. n.p., 1969?]
  [3]p. 36cm.
  Caption title.
  1. Students for a Democratic
  Society. 2. Labor and laboring
  classes.
  WHi-L

A55
Allen, Charles Russell, 1926-
  Concentration camps, U.S.A.,
  by Charles R. Allen, Jr. [New
  York, Marzani & Munsell, c1966]
  60p. illus. 21cm.
  Prepared for the Citizens Com-
  mittee for Constitutional Lib-
  erties.
  1. Concentration camps. 2. In-
  ternal security. I. Citizens
  Committee for Constitutional
  Liberties. II. Marzani and
  Munsell.
  MiU, MH-L, KU-RH, DLC 67-7011

A56
Allen, Charles Russell, 1926-
  Journey to the Soviet trade
  unions: an American eyewitness.
  [New York] Marzani & Munsell

[c1965]
64p. illus. 20cm.
1. Labor and laboring classes--
Russia. 2. Trade-unions--Russia.
I. Marzani and Munsell.
MiU, KU-RH

A57
Allen, Charles Russell, 1926-
  [Untitled. Newark, New Jersey
  Associates of the Emergency Civil
  Liberties Committee, 1955?]
  30p. 28cm.
  1. U.S. Congress. House. Com-
  mittee on Un-American Activities.
  2. Anti-communist movements.
  I. Emergency Civil Liberties
  Committee, New Jersey Associates.
  KU-J

A58
Allen, Donna.
  The economic necessity to dis-
  arm: a challenge to the old
  assumption, by Donna Allen, Wo-
  men Strike for Peace [and]
  Women's International League for
  Peace and Freedom. [n.p., 1964]
  10p. 28cm.
  Caption title.
  Delivered to the 2nd Internation-
  al Arms Control and Disarmament
  Symposium, Ann Arbor, Michigan,
  Jan. 23, 1964.
  1. Disarmament. I. Women Strike
  for Peace, Washington, D.C.
  II. Women's International League
  for Peace and Freedom. III. In-
  ternational Arms Control and
  Disarmament Symposium, Ann Arbor,
  Mich., 2d., 1964.
  WHi-A

A59
Allen, Donna.
  HUAC faces the new spirit. [New
  York, Liberation, 196]
  folder (6p.) 28cm.
  Caption title.
  Reprinted from Liberation, Oct.
  1966.
  1. U.S. Congress. House. Com-
  mittee on Un-American Activit-
  ies. I. Liberation.
  KU-RH

A60
Allen, Donna.
  So you think you have a free
  Press? [Louisville, Southern
  Conference Educational Fund,
  1969?]
  10p. 22cm.
  Cover title.
  1. Press. I. Southern Confer-
  ence Educational Fund.
  KU-RH

A61
Allen, Donna.
  What's wrong with war in Vietnam? Prepared by Donna Allen
  and Al Uhrie. [Washington, 196]
  [11]p. illus. 28cm.
  Cover title.
  1. Negroes--Civil rights.
  2. Vietnamese conflict, 1961-
  1975. I. Uhrie, Al, jt. ath.
  CU-B, WHi-L

A62
Allen, Duane.
  Where do we go from here? Some
  concrete suggestions for regional coordination as the key
  to summer action. [n.p., National Coordinating Committee to
  End the War in Vietnam, 1966]
  5p. 28cm.
  1. National Coordinating Committee to End the War in Vietnam. 2. Vietnamese conflict,
  1961-1975.
  WHi-A

A63
Allen, James Stewart, 1906-
  The lessons of Cuba. [New
  York, New Century Publishers,
  1961]
  31p. 19cm.
  Cover title.
  1. Cuba--History--1959-
  2. Communism--Cuba. I. New
  Century Publishers.
  WHi-L, MiU, CSt, TxU, NjP

A64
Allen, James Stewart, 1906-
  The United States and the

common market. New York, New
Century Publishers, 1962.
36p. 20cm.
Cover subtitle: Marxist view of
the new "free trade" policy.
1. European Economic Community.
2. U.S.--Foreign economic relations. 3. Foreign trade regulations. I. New Century Publishers.
IaU, NNU-T, MiU-L

A65
Allen, Pamela.
Free space; a perspective on the
small group in women's libera-
tion. [New York, Times Change
Press, 1970]
63p. illus. 18cm.
1. Women's Liberation Movement.
I. Times Change Press.
CtU, WHi-L

A66
Allen, Robert I.
Dialectics of black power.
[Boston, New England Free Press,
c1968]
33p. illus. 18cm. (A Guardian
pamphlet)
Cover title.
1. Negroes--Civil rights. I. New
England Free Press.
KU-RH

A67
Allen, Robert I.
Dialectics of black power. [New
York, Weekly Guardian Associates,
c1968]
32p. illus. 22cm. (A Guardian
pamphlet, 102)
Cover title.
1. Negroes--Civil rights.
I. Weekly Guardian Associates.
WU, NNU-T, KU-RH, WHi-L, MiU,
NUC 70-18335

A68
Allen, William.
Two socialists view the new left,
by William Allen & Paul Feldman.
[New York, Socialist Party USA,
196]
25p. 28cm.
Cover title.
1. Socialism. 2. Youth--Politi-

cal activity. I. Feldman, Paul,
jt. auth. II. Socialist Party
(U.S.)
CU-B

A69
Allman, T.D.
Anatomy of a coup. [Ithaca,
N.Y., Glad Day Press, 1970?]
17-22 [1]p. illus. 28cm.
Caption title.
Reprinted from Far Eastern Eco-
nomic Review, Ap. 9, 1970.
1. Revolutions--Cambodia.
2. Cambodia--Pol. & govt.
I. Glad Day Press.
NNU-T

A70
Allman, T.D.
Better dead than red. [Ithaca,
N.Y., Glad Day Press, 1970]
[4]p. illus. 28cm.
Caption title.
1. Cambodia--Pol. & govt.
2. U.S.--Military policy.
I. Glad Day Press.
NNU-T

A71
Alman, Emily.
Prisoner on our conscience; the
story of Morton Sobell, by
Emily and David Alman. [New
York, Committee to Secure Jus-
tice for Morton Sobell, 195]
43p. 22cm.
Cover title.
1. Sobell, Morton. I. Commit-
tee to Secure Justice for Morton
Sobell. II. Alman, David, jt.
auth.
MiU

A72
Altbach, Philip G.
The American peace movement,
1900-1962: a critical analysis
[by] Philip G. Altbach, nation-
al chairman, Student Peace
Union. [n.p., 196]
88 leaves. 28cm.
Cover title.
1. Peace.
I. Student Peace Union.
WHi-A

A73
Altbach, Philip G.
  The pacifist ethic and humanism.
  [2d. rev. Chicago, 1960]
  15p. 22cm.
  1. Pacifism.
  CU-B

A74
Alternative Perspectives on Vietnam.
  A statement of assumptions and a
  call for an international conference. [Ann Arbor, 196]
  11p. 28cm.
  Cover title.
  1. Vietnamese conflict, 1961-1975.
  CU-B

A75
Alternative Perspectives on Vietnam.
  A statement of assumptions and a
  call for an international confer-
  ence. [Ypsilanti, Mich., Huron
  Press, 1965]
  20p. 22cm.
  Cover title.
  1. Vietnamese conflict, 1961-1975.
  KU-RH

A76
Alvarado, Roger.
  La raza! Why a chicano party?
  Why chicano studies? By Roger
  Alvarado [and others] New York,
  Pathfinder Press, 1970.
  15p.
  1. Mexicans in the U.S. I. Path-
  finder Press.
  WHi-L

A77
Amalric, Jacques.
  Chicago and black power. [Bos-
  ton, New England Free Press, 196]
  22p. illus. 22cm.
  Cover title.
  Reprinted from Le Monde, Feb.
  1968.
  Translated by Denise Bordet and
  John Heckman.
  1. Negroes--Civil rights.
  2. Chicago--Race question.
  3. Detroit--Race question.
  I. New England Free Press.
  MoU

A78
American Committee for Protection
  of Foreign Born.
  Concentration camps, USA: it
  has happened here; it could happen again--to you. [New York,
  196]
  9p. 22cm.
  Cover title.
  1. Concentration camps. 2. Internal security.
  MiU, KU-RH

A79
American Committee for Protection
    of Foreign Born.
  End exile. [New York, 196]
  15p. 22cm.
  Cover title.
  1. Deportation. 2. Exiles.
  3. Aliens.
  KU-J, MiU

A80
American Committee for Protection
    of Foreign Born.
  Happy endings. [New York, 196]
  folder. 22x9cm.
  Cover title.
  1. Emigration and immigration.
  KU-RH

A81
American Committee for Protection
    of Foreign Born.
  The legacy of Abner Green; a
  memorial journal. [New York,
  1959]
  36p. illus. 25cm.
  Cover title.
  1. Green, Abner. 2. Aliens.
  KU-J

A82
American Committee for Protection
    of Foreign Born.
  Our badge of infamy; a petition
  to the United Nations on the
  treatment of the Mexican immigrants. [New York, 1959]
  46p. 19cm.
  Cover title.
  1. Mexicans in the U.S.
  2. Emigration and immigration

law.
KU-RH

A83
American Committee for Protection
of Foreign Born.
Statement on the struggle against
a police state. New York [196]
[1] leaf. 22cm.
Caption title.
1. Internal security.
KU-RH

A84
American Committee for Protection
of Foreign Born.
30th anniversary. November 3,
1963, Town Hall, New York City.
[New York, 1963?]
[80]p. ports. 22cm.
Cover title.
1. Aliens.
WHi-L, NUC 67-21015

A85
American Committee for Protection
of Foreign Born.
What is the American Committee
for Protection of Foreign Born.
New York [196]
[4]p. illus. 22cm.
Cover title.
KU-RH

A86
American Committee on Africa.
Act now for Robert Sobukwe's
release. [New York, 196]
3 leaves. 28cm.
Caption title.
1. Sobukwe, Robert Mangaliso.
2. Africa, South--race question.
KU-RH

A87
American Committee on Africa.
Action against apartheid: what
you can do about racial discrimination in South Africa. [New
York? 1960]
16p.
1. Africa, South--Race question.
2. U.S.--Relations (general)
with Africa, South. 3. Investments, American--Africa, South.
MiU, KU-RH

A88
American Committee on Africa.
American corporate investments
in South Africa. [New York,
1969]
10 leaves, 28cm.
Caption title.
1. Africa, South--Econ. condit.
2. U.S.--Relations (general)
with Africa, South. 3. Investments, American--Africa, South.
KU-RH

A89
American Committee on Africa.
More American bases in Portugal: at what price? [New York,
1969]
3 leaves. 28cm.
1. U.S.--For. rel.--Portugal.
2. Portugal--For. rel.--Africa.
3. Africa--Colonization.
KU-RH

A90
American Committee on Africa.
South Africa scores again as
South African airways bids for
U.S. tourists. [New York,
1969]
3 [1] leaves. 28cm.
Caption title.
1. Tourist trade--Africa, South.
2. Africa, South--Econ. condit.
KU-RH

A91
American Committee on Africa.
Southern Africa: crisis for
American policy. [New York,
196]
5 leaves. 28cm.
Caption title.
1. U.S.--For. rel.--Africa,
South. 2. Africa, South.
KU-RH

A92
American Committee on Africa.
Southwest Africa: information
sheet. New York, 1967.
[8]p. 28cm.
Caption title.
1. Africa, Southwest.
KU-RH

A93
American Committee on Africa.
  Southwest Africa: the UN's step-
  child. [New York, 1959]
  26p. illus. 22cm.
  1. Africa, Southwest. 2. United
  Nations.
  TxU, MNS

A94
American Committee on Africa.
  South West Africa: the UN's
  stepchild [edited by Winifred
  Courtney. 2d ed. New York,
  1960]
  26p. illus. 22cm.
  1. Africa, Southwest. 2. United
  Nations. I. Winifred, Courtney,
  ed.
  CSt-H, MiU

A95
American Committee on Africa.
  U.S. policy and Portuguese colonialism: the United Nations
  facade. [New York? 1969]
  8 [1] leaves. 28cm. (ACOA
  background paper)
  Caption title.
  1. Africa--Colonization.
  2. U.S.--For. rel.--Portugal.
  3. Portugal--For. rel.--Africa.
  4. United Nations.
  KU-RH

A96
American Committee on Africa.
  The U.S. should end the South
  African sugar quota and stop
  buying from South Africa. [New
  York, 196]
  [4]p. 28cm. (Priority action
  project, no. 2)
  Caption title.
  1. Africa, South--Relations
  (general) with U.S.
  KU-RH

A97
American Committee on Africa.
  U.S. subsidy to South Africa:
  the sugar quota. New York
  [196]
  15p. 23x10cm.
  Cover title.
  1. Africa, South--Relations

(general) with U.S.
  KU-RH

A98
American Committee on Africa.
  Africa Defense and Aid Fund.
  Aid victims of South Africa's
  racism. [New York, 196]
  folder. illus. 21x9cm.
  Cover title.
  1. Africa, South--Race question.
  KU-RH

A99
American Committee on Africa.
  Africa Defense and Aid Fund.
  Aid victims of Southern Africa's
  rule of terror. [New York,
  196]
  folder. illus. 22x10cm.
  Cover title.
  1. Africa, South--Race question.
  2. Africa, South--Pol. & govt.
  KU-RH

A100
American-European Seminar on the
    U.S.S.R.
  Report; including their interview with Khrushchev in the
  Kremlin. West Haven, Conn.,
  Printed by Promoting Enduring
  Peace [1957?]
  24p. map. 21cm.
  1. Russia--Descr. & trav.--
  1945-   2. Russia--Social
  conditions--1945-   I. Khrushchev, Nikita Sergeevich,
  1894-   II. Promoting Enduring Peace.
  WvU

A101
American Federation of Labor and
    Congress of Industrial Organi-
    zations. Research Dept.
  A background paper on the
  national economy. Introduction
  by Michael Harrington. New
  York, League for Industrial Democracy, 1966.
  8 [2]p. illus. 28cm. (Looking forward [no. 7])
  Cover title.
  1. U.S.--Econ. condit.

I. Harrington, Michael. II. League for Industrial Democracy.
NNU-T

A102
American Federation of Labor and
    Congress of International Or-
    ganizations. Research Dept.
The fantastic rise in corporate
profits. [Boston, New England
Free Press, 196]
[4]p. illus. 28cm.
Caption title.
Reprinted from AFL-CIO American
federationist.
1. Corporations. 2. Profit.
I. New England Free Press.
KU-RH, MiU

A103
American Humanist Association.
The humanist position and organization. [Yellow Springs, Ohio,
196]
[8]p. 21x10cm.
Cover title.
1. Humanism.
KU-RH

A104
American Humanist Association.
A humanist resolution on world
disarmament. [Sacramento,
1961?]
3 leaves. 28cm.
Caption title.
1. Disarmament. 2. Humanism.
KU-RH

A105
American Humanist Association.
Purposes and program of the
American Humanist Association.
[Yellow Spring, Ohio, 196]
[8]p. 22x10cm. (AHA publi-
cation no. 1)
1. Humanism.
KU-RH

A106
American Russian Institute for
    Cultural Relations with the
    Soviet Union, San Francisco.
The story of a long friendship,
1931-1956. The first 25 years
of the American Russian Institute of San Francisco, building
cultural relations and understanding between the United
States and the Soviet Union.
[San Francisco, 1956]
23p. illus., ports.
1. U.S.--Relations (general)
with Russia. 2. Russia--Rela-
tions (general) with the U.S.
NNC

A107
American Servicemen's Union.
Ft. Dix rebellion. [New York,
196]
[2]p. 28cm.
Caption title.
1. Soldiers. 2. Civil rights.
KU-RH

A108
American Servicemen's Union.
This pamphlet is your personal
property. It cannot be taken
from you for any reason. This
information may be very valuable
to you. Hold on to it. [New
York, 196]
[8]p. 28cm.
Cover title.
1. Soldiers. 2. U.S. Army--
Military life.
KU-RH

Americans for Democratic Action
see also
Campus Americans for Democratic
    Action.

A109
Americans for Democratic Action.
A legislative program for the
92nd congress. Washington
[1970?]
12p. 22cm.
Cover title.
1. U.S. 92d Cong., 1970-1972.
2. Liberalism.
KU-RH

A110
Americans for Democratic Action.
A liberal legislative action
program for 1970. Washington
[1970?]
folder. 22x9cm.

Cover title.
1. Liberalism.   2. U.S.   92d
Cong., 1970-1972.
KU-RH

A111
Americans for Democratic Action.
  1970 senatorial elections.
  Washington [1970]
  1v. (unpaged)   28cm.
  Cover title.
  1. U.S.   Congress.   Senate.
  2. Elections.
  KU-RH

A112
Americans for Democratic Action.
  Program for Americans '67.
  [Washington, 1967]
  40p.   illus.   23cm.
  Cover title.
  NcD, NUC69-97793

A113
Americans for Democratic Action.
  Proposed code of ethics for
  governmental personnel of the
  city of Philadelphia.   Philadelphia, 1961.
  22p.
  1. Philadelphia--Officials and
  employees.   2. Civil service
  ethics.
  PPBMR, PPULC, NUC67, 76537

A114
Americans for Democratic Action.
  Voting guide, 1956; how to make
  your vote count.   Foreward by
  Elmer Davis.   Washington [1956]
  128p.   illus.   20cm.
  1. Campaign literature, 1956.
  2. U.S.--Pol. & govt.--1953-
  PP, Wa, WaT, CU, FU, DLC 56-9301

A115
Americans for Democratic Action.
  What have you done about your
  convictions lately?   [Washington,
  196]
  folder.   22x9cm.
  Cover title.
  1. Liberalism.
  KU-RH

A116
Americans for Democratic Action.
  Massachusetts Chapter.
  Report on metropolitan problems,
  by Bernard J. Frieden and Mel-
  vin F. Levine.   Boston, 1957.
  8p.   illus., map.
  1. Metropolitan areas--Boston,
  Mass.   2. Cities and towns--
  Growth.   I. Frieden, Bernard J.,
  jt. auth.   II. Levine, Melvin
  F., jt. auth.
  MH-PA, IU

A117
Americans for Democratic Action.
  Southeastern Pennsylvania
  Chapter.
  A study of public school budgets and budgeting procedures
  in our larger cities [compared
  with Philadelphia]   Philadelphia, 1960.
  20p.
  1. Education--Finance.   2. Public schools--Pennsylvania.
  PPCPC

A118
Amin, Samir.
  The class struggle in Africa.
  [Cambridge, Mass.] Africa Re-
  search Group [196]
  46p.   22cm. (Reprint 2)
  Cover title.
  Reprinted from Revolution, 1964.
  1. Socialism in Africa.
  2. Social classes--Africa.
  3. Africa--Pol. & govt.--1960-
      I. Africa Research Group.
  KU-RH, MoU

A119
Analavage, Robert.
  Black and white divided; Laurel
  strike is broken.   [Boston, New
  England Free Press, 196]
  [4]p.   illus.   28cm.
  Caption title.
  Reprinted from the Southern
  Patriot.
  1. Grass Roots Organizing Work.
  2. Masonite Corporation.   3. In-
  ternational Woodworkers of

America, Local 5-443. 4. Ne-
groes--Employment. 5. Labor and
laboring classes--Mississippi.
I. New England Free Press.
KU-RH

A120
Analavage, Robert
Labor and the South, Laurel,
Mississippi. Black workers set
against white--strike broken.
Ann Arbor, Radical Education
Project [196]
[6]p. illus. 28cm.
Cover title.
Reprinted from Southern Patriot,
Jan. 1968.
1. Labor and laboring classes--
Mississippi. 2. Negroes--Em-
ployment. 3. Strikes and lock-
outs. 4. Mississippi--Race
questions. 5. Negroes--Missis-
sippi. I. Radical Education
Project.
WHi-L, MoU, MiU

A121
Analavage, Robert.
The lessons of Laurel: grass-
roots organizing in the South
[by Robert Analavage and Dottie
Zellner. Louisville, Ky.,
Southern Conference Educational
Fund, 1970?]
12p. illus. 28cm.
Cover title.
1. Grass Roots Organizing Work.
2. Laurel, Miss.--Pol. & govt.
3. Negroes--Civil rights.
4. Labor and laboring classes--
Mississippi. I. Zellner, Dottie,
jt. auth. II. Southern Conference Educational Fund.
KU-RH, Whi-L

A122
Analvage, Robert.
A new movement in the white
south. [Louisville, Ky.,
Southern Conference Educational
Fund, 196]
15p. illus. 22cm.
1. Grass Roots Organizing Work.
2. Labor and laboring classes--
Southern States. 3. Negroes--

Civil rights.
MoU

A123
Analysis of the strike, October
18-23. [n.p., 196]
61p. 22cm.
1. Student movements--Univer-
sity of Wisconsin. 2. Wisconsin. University.
NNU-T

A124
Anarchos.
Listen, Marxist. [New York,
1969]
30p. 22cm.
Cover title.
1. Students for a Democratic
Society. 2. Progressive Labor
Party. 3. Socialism. 4. Com-
munism--Russia.
MiU

A125
Anderson, Henry P.
To build a union: comments on
the organization of agricultural workers. [Stockton, Calif.?]
1961.
iv, 68p. 28cm.
1. Trade-unions--California.
2. Agricultural laborers--Cali-
fornia.
IU

A126
Anderson, Robert E.
Atlanta churches in crisis.
Atlanta, Southern Regional
Council [1969]
38p.
Caption title.
1. Church and race problems--
Atlanta. I. Southern Regional
Council.
NcU, NUC 70-112541

A127
Andrade, Joaquin.
Cuba: the Christians and the
new human being. Toronto,
Latin American Working Group
[1970?]
6p. illus. 28cm.

Caption title.
Reprinted from Direct from Cuba.
1. Cuba--Religion. I. Latin
American Working Group.
KU-RH

A128
Andreas, Carol.
  Notes on the liberation of
  women. [Seattle? Radical Women?
  196]
  15 leaves. 28cm.
  Caption title.
  1. Woman--Rights of women.
  I. Radical Women.
  WHi-L

A129
Anthony, Carl.
  Negro militancy in the north,
  talks by Carl Anthony and Peter
  Countryman, delivered in New
  Haven, Conn., October 21, 1962.
  New Haven, Northern Student
  Movement [1962?]
  [8]p. 28cm.
  Cover title.
  1. Negroes. 2. Violence.
  I. Countryman, Peter, jt. auth.
  II. Northern Student Movement.
  WHi-A

A130
Anti-expansion, Anti-ROTC Strike
    Steering Committee, Harvard
    University.
  Cambridge--the transformation of
  a working class city. Harvard
  and M.I.T. create imperial city.
  Boston, New England Free Press
  [1969?]
  20p. 21cm.
  Cover title.
  1. Cambridge, Mass. 2. Harvard
  University. 3. Massachusetts
  Institute of Technology. 4. Stu-
  dent movements--Boston. I. New
  England Free Press.
  KU-RH

A131
Anti-imperialist Coalition.
  March against war--but beware of
  hawks in doves clothing. [Oak-
  land, 1969]
  [2]p. 36cm.

Caption title.
1. Vietnamese conflict, 1961-
1975.
CU-B

A132
Anti-Mass.
  The anti-mass: methods of or-
  ganization of collectives.
  [New Haven, 1970]
  56p. illus.
  Cover title.
  1. Anarchism and anarchists.
  MiU

A133
Apostolic collaboration:
    Canada--Latin America.
    [Toronto? Latin American
    Working Group? 196]
  3 leaves. 28cm.
  Caption title.
  Reprinted from Mensaje, Jan.
  1966 and CIF reports, Aug. 16,
  1966.
  1. Canadian Catholic Conference.
  Office for Latin America.
  2. Canada--Relations (general)
  with Latin America. 3. Latin
  America--Relations (general)
  with Canada. 4. Catholics in
  Canada. I. Latin American
  Working Group.
  KU-RH

A134
Appalachian Committee for Full
    Employment.
  Statement of the Appalachian
  Committee for Full Employment,
  Hazard, Ky., to the Student-
  Miners Conference on Poverty
  and Unemployment. [n.p., 196]
  2 leaves. 28cm.
  Caption title.
  1. Strip mining. 2. Coal mines
  and mining--Kentucky.
  MiU

A135
Appalachian Committee for Full
    Employment.
  Voices for jobs and justice,
  prepared for Cleveland Community People's Conference Feb-
  19-21, 1965. [n.p., 1965?]

15 leaves. 28cm.
Cover title.
1. Poor--Hazard, Ky. 2. Ken-
tucky--Econ. condit.
WHi-A

A136
Appalachian People's Meeting,
    Charleston, W. Va., 1968.
  Report. [n.p., 196]
  14 leaves. 28cm.
  Cover title.
  1. Poor--Appalachian Mountains.
  2. Appalachian Mountains--Race
  question.
  WHi-L

A137
Appelbaum, David.
  The case for abolishing ROTC
  [by David Appelbaum and others
  of NUC. Boston, New England
  Free Press, 1970?]
  20p. illus. 22cm.
  Cover title.
  1. U.S. Army. Reserve Officers'
  Training Corps. I. New Universi-
  ty Conference. II. New England
  Free Press.
  KU-RH

A138
Aptheker, Bettina.
  Big business and the American
  university. New York, New Outlook Publishers, 1966.
  34p. illus. 21cm.
  1. Universities and colleges--
  Administration. 2. Universities
  and colleges--Finance. 3. Student movements. I. New Outlook
  Publishers.
  IU, KU-RH, NNU-T, NUC 67-78839

A139
Aptheker, Bettina.
  Columbia, inc. New York, W.E.B.
  DuBois Clubs of America [1968]
  35p.
  1. Columbia University.
  2. Student movements--Columbia
  University. I. DuBois (W.E.B.)
  Clubs of America
  WHi-L

A140
Aptheker, Bettina
  FSM: the Free Speech Movement
  at Berkeley. An historical
  narrative by Bettina Aptheker.
  An interpretive essay by Robert
  Kaufman and Michael Fosom. San
  Francisco, W.E.B. DuBois Clubs
  of America [1965]
  52p. illus. 22cm.
  1. Free Speech Movement.
  2. Student movements--Berkeley,
  Calif. I. Kaufman, Robert, jt.
  auth. II. Fosom, Michael, jt.
  auth. III. DuBois (W.E.B.)
  Clubs of America.
  C, CU-B, NNU-T

A141
Aptheker, Bettina.
  Higher education and the stu-
  dent rebellion in the United
  States, 1960-1969; a biblio-
  graphy. [New York, American
  Institute for Marxist Studies]
  1969.
  50p. 29cm. (Bibliographical
  series, no. 6)
  Cover title.
  1. Education, Higher--Bibl.
  2. Student movements--Bibl.
  I. American Institute for
  Marxist Studies.
  KU-RH, DLC

A142
Aptheker, Herbert, 1915-
  The American civil war. New
  York, International Publishers
  [c1961]
  22p. 20cm.
  1. U.S.--History--Civil War.
  I. International Publishers.
  MiU, NNU-T

A143
Aptheker, Herbert, 1915-
  Class consciousness in the
  United States. New York,
  Jefferson Bookshop, 1959.
  8p.
  Cover title.
  Reprinted from the New Times,
  no. 44 and 47.

1. Capitalism. 2. Communism.
3. Social classes. I. Jefferson
Bookshop.
WHi-L, NNU-T

A144
Aptheker, Herbert, 1915-
  Communism: menace or promise?
  New York, New Century Publishers,
  1963.
  24p. 19cm.
  1. Communism. I. New Century
  Publishers.
  WHi-L, NNU-T

A145
Aptheker, Herbert, 1915-   ed.
  Disarmament and the American
  economy: a symposium [by] James
  S. Allen [and others] New York,
  New Century Publishers, 1960.
  64p. 20cm.
  1. Disarmament. I. Allen, James
  Stewart, 1906-   II. New Cen-
  tury Publishers.
  RPB, IU, MH, OCL, WHi-L, A249,
  DLC60-4894

A146
Aptheker, Herbert, 1915-
  Dr. Martin Luther King, Vietnam
  and civil rights. [New York,
  New Outlook Publishers, 1967]
  14p.
  1. King, Martin Luther, 1929-
  1968. I. New Outlook Publishers.
  MoSW, NNU-T, WHi-L, MiU, NUC69-
  107944

A147
Aptheker, Herbert, 1915-
  The fraud of "Soviet anti-
  Semitism." New York, New
  Century Publishers, 1962.
  24p. 19cm.
  1. Antisemitism--Russia. I. New
  Century Publishers.
  NcD, OrU, NNU-T, MiU, NUC63-
  66531

A148
Aptheker, Herbert, 1915-
  John Brown: American martyr.
  New York, New Century Publish-
  ers, 1960.

24p.
1. Brown, John, 1800-1859.
I. New Century Publishers.
GAU, NNU-T, MiU

A149
Aptheker, Herbert, 1915-
  The labor movement in the
  South during slavery. New
  York, International Publish-
  ers [n.d.]
  24p.
  Cover title.
  1. Labor and laboring classes--
  Southern States. I. Internat-
  ional Publishers.
  NNU-T

A150
Aptheker, Herbert, 1915-
  The nature of revolution: the
  Marxist theory of social
  change. Based on a series of
  broadcasts made over station
  KPFA, Berkeley, California,
  February-April, 1959. New
  York, New Century Publishers,
  1959.
  31p. 19cm.
  Cover title: On the nature of
  revolution.
  1. Revolutions. 2. Socialism.
  I. New Century Publishers.
  NRU

A151
Aptheker, Herbert, 1915-
  Negro history; its lessons for
  our time. New York, New Century
  Publishers, 1956.
  23p. 19cm.
  1. Negroes--History. I. New
  Century Publishers.
  NNU-T, MiU

A152
Aptheker, Herbert, 1915-
  Negro slave revolts. [Nash-
  ville, Southern Student Organizing Committee, 196]
  4p. 28cm.
  Cover title.
  1. Slavery in the U.S.
  II. Southern Student Organizing Committee.
  MiU.

A153
Aptheker, Herbert, 1915-
  The Negro today. New York, Mar-
zani & Munsell [1962]
  62p. 23cm.
  1. Negroes--Civil rights.
  I. Marzani and Munsell.
  NNU-T, KU-RH

A154
Aptheker, Herbert, 1915-
  On the nature of freedom; the
Marxist view. Based on a series
of broadcasts made over station
KPFA, Berkeley, California, May-
July, 1959. New York, New Cen-
tury Publishers, 1960.
  32p. 20cm.
  1. Liberty. I. New Century
Publishers, 1960.
  NN, NNU-T, CSt-H, P, GU, DLC 60-
1960

A155
Aptheker, Herbert, 1915-
  On the nature of revolution; the
Marxist theory of social change.
New York, New Century Publishers,
1959.
  31p. 19cm.
  1. Revolutions. I. New Century
Publishers.
  MiU

A156
Aptheker, Herbert, 1915-
  Reality and mythology in today's
Japan. New York, New Century
Publishers, 1961.
  22p. 20cm.
  1. Japan--Pol. & govt.--1945-
        I. New Century Publishers.
  NN, NNU-T, NUC63-67460

A157
Aptheker, Herbert, 1915-
  Riding to freedom. New York,
New Century Publishers, 1961.
  14p. 20cm.
  1. Negroes--Civil rights.
  2. Alabama--Race question.
  I. New Century Publishers.
  WHi-L, NNU-T, MiU

A158
Aptheker, Herbert, 1915-

  Since Sputnik: how Americans
view the Soviet Union. New
York, New Century Publishers,
1959.
  32p. 20cm.
  1. Russia. 2. Artificial
satellites, Russian. I. New
Century Publishers.
  NN, MH

A159
Aptheker, Herbert, 1915-
  The United States and China:
peace or war? [New York, New
Century Publishers, 1958]
  23p. 21cm. (A political af-
fairs pamphlet)
  Reprinted, with some additions
by the author, from Political
Affairs, Oct., 1958.
  1. U.S.--For. rel.--China.
  2. China--For. rel.--U.S.
  I. New Century Publishers.
  NN, NNU-T, NcD

A160
Are men the enemy? [n.p., 1970?]
  [3]p. 28cm.
  Caption title.
  1. Woman--History and condition of women.
  KU-RH

A161
Armed struggle in South Africa.
      [Cambridge, Mass., Africa
    Research Group, 1969]
  14p. illus, 28cm.
  Cover title.
  1. Africa, South--Race question.
  2. Africa, South--Pol. & govt.
  I. Africa Research Group.
  KU-RH, MoU

A162
Arnold, David.
  Vietnam: symptom of a world
malaise. Ann Arbor, Peace
Research and Education Project
of Students for a Democratic
Society [1964?]
  [8]p. 28cm.
  Cover title.
  Reprinted from Fellowship, May
1964.
  1. Vietnamese conflict, 1961-

1975. 1. Students for a Democratic Society. Peace Research
and Education Project.
CU-B, WHi-L

A163
Arnold, David.
  Vietnam: symptom of a world
  malaise. New York, Students
  for a Democratic Society and its
  Peace Research and Education
  Project [196]
  7p. 28cm.
  Cover title.
  Reprinted from Fellowship, May
  1964.
  1. Vietnamese conflict, 1961-
  1975. I. Students for a Democratic Society. Peace Research
  and Education Project.
  WHi-A

A164
Arnolds, Edward B.
  A plea from Delano. [n.p., 196]
  [2]p. 28cm.
  Caption title.
  1. Agricultural laborers--Cali-
  fornia--Delano. 2. United Farm
  Workers.
  CU-B

Aronowitz, Stanley.
  Working papers for Nyack confer-
  ence...
    see also
Students for a Democratic Society.
  Working papers for Nyack confer-
  ence...

A165
Aronowitz, Stanley.
  Working papers for Nyack conference on unemployment & social
  change [by Stanley Aronowitz and
  others] New York, Students for
  a Democratic Society, 1963.
  [18]p. 28cm.
  Cover title.
  1. Negroes--Civil rights.
  2. U.S.--Econ. condit.
  3. Student movements. 4. Poverty. I. Students for a Democratic Society.
  KU-RH

A166
Aronson, Ronald.
  The new left in historical perspective: the movement and its
  critics. Montreal, Our Generation [196]
  11p. 28cm.
  Cover title.
  1. Student movements. I. Our
  Generation.
  NNU-T

A167
Aronson, Ronald.
  The new left in the United
  States [by] Ronald Aronson and
  John C. Cowley. [Montreal, Our
  Generation, 196]
  73-90p.
  Caption title.
  Reprinted from Socialist Regis-
  ter, 1967.
  1. Student movements. I. Cow-
  ley, John C., jt. auth. I. Our
  Generation.
  NNU-T

A168
Arrighi, Giovanni.
  Socialist development in
  Africa [by Giovanni Arrighi,
  John S. Saul, Glyn Hughes.
  Cambridge, Mass., Africa Re-
  search Group, 1970?]
  12-21, 11-30p. 22cm. (Reprint
  7)
  Cover title.
  1. Socialism in Africa.
  2. Africa--Pol. & govt.
  I. Africa Research Group
  MiU

A169
Arrow, Jeanne.
  Dangers in pro-women line and
  consciousness-raising. [New
  York, The Feminists, 1969?]
  13p. 28cm.
  Caption title.
  1. Woman--Rights of women.
  I. Feminists
  KU-RH

A170
Asian-African Conference, 1st,
  Bandung, Indonesia, 1955.

Texts of selected speeches and
final communique of the Asian-
African Conference, Bandung,
Indonesia, April 18-24, 1955.
With additional report on the
conference by Premier Chou En-
lai of the People's Republic of
China to the Standing Committee
of the National People's Congress in Peking. [New York, Far
East Reporter, 1955?]
63p. illus.
1. Asia--Pol. & govt.
2. Africa--Pol. & govt.
I. Chou, En-lai, 1898-
II. Far East Reporter.
KU-J, MiU, NIC, CU, NA

A171
Asimov, Isaac, 1920-
  Uncertain, coy, and hard to
  please. Boston, New England
  Free Press [1970?]
  [232]-246p. 21cm.
  Cover title.
  Reprinted from Asimov's The
  solar system and back.
  1. Woman. I. New England Free
  Press.
  KU-RH, WHi-A

A172
Atkins, Martha
  The hidden history of the female; the early feminist movement in the United States.
  [Boston, New England Free Press,
  197 ?]
  13p. 28cm.
  Cover title.
  1. Woman--Rights of women.
  2. Woman--History and condition
  of women. I. New England Free
  Press.
  MiU

A173
Atkinson, Ti-Grace.
  The institution of sexual inter-
  course. New York, The Feminists
  [1968]
  8 leaves. 28cm.
  Caption title.
  1. Sex. 2. Vagina. I. Feminists.
  WHi-L

A174
Atkinson, Ti-Grace.
  The institution of sexual inter-
  course. New York, The Femin-
  ists [1968]
  [10]p. 28cm.
  Caption title.
  1. Sex. 2. Vagina.
  I. Feminists.
  KU-RH

A175
Atkinson, Ti-Grace.
  Radical feminism. [New York,
  The Feminists, 1969]
  8 leaves. 28cm.
  Caption title.
  1. Woman--Rights of women.
  I. Feminists.
  KU-RH, WHi-L

A176
Atkinson, Ti-Grace.
  Radical feminism and love.
  New York, The Feminists [1969]
  4 leaves. 28cm.
  Cover title.
  1. Woman--Rights of women.
  2. Love. I. Feminists.
  WHi-L

A177
Atkinson, Ti-Grace.
  Vaginal orgasm as a hysterical
  survival response. New York,
  The Feminists [1968]
  3 leaves. 28cm.
  Caption title.
  1. Sex. 2. Woman. 3. Vagina.
  I. Feminists.
  KU-RH, WHi-L

A178
Authoritarian conditioning. [Van
    Nuys, Calif., SRAF Print
    Co-op] 1970.
  [26]p. 22cm.
  Cover title.
  At head of title: Solidarity
  group.
  Reprinted from Solidarity pam-
  phlet no. 33.
  Partial contents--On the whole-
  someness of honest toil, by
  Louise Crowley.
  1. Family. 2. Sex.

3. Authoritarianism. I. SRAF
Print Co-op.
Mi-U

A179
Ayers, Bill.
  Education: an American problem.
  Ann Arbor, Radical Education
  Project [196]
  10p. 28cm.
  Cover title.
  I. Education--Bibl. I. Radical

Education Project.
MoU

A180
Ayers, Bill.
  Education: an American problem.
  Boston New England Free Press
  [196]
  10p. 28cm.
  Cover title.
  1. Education--Bibl. I. New
  England Free Press.
  KU-RH

‡

B

‡

B1
Babcox, Peter.
  A day in the life of the conspiracy, Oct. 30, 1969. [Chi-
  cago, Chicago Area Draft Resisters, 1969?]
  8p. 22cm.
  1. Government, Resistance to.
  2. Chicago--Riots, August, 1968.
  3. Democratic Party. National
  Convention, Chicago, 1968.
  I. Chicago Area Draft Resisters.
  CU-B

B2
Bacheller, Don.
  On Regis Debray. New York, Independent Socialist Clubs of America [196]
  9 leaves. 28cm.
  Cover title.
  1. Debray, Regis. I. Independent Socialist Clubs of America.
  MiU-H

B3
Background of the South West
    Africa cases. [n.p., 196]
  9p. 28cm.
  Caption title.
  1. Africa, Southwest--Pol. &
  govt.
  KU-RH

B4
Bagdikian, Ben H.

The black immigrants. [New
York, National Sharecroppers
Fund] 1967.
unpaged illus.
1. Negroes--Employment.
I. National Sharecroppers Fund.
WHi-L

B5
Bailey, Elsa.
  Protest. [Philadelphia] American Friends Service Committee
  [c1963]
  (unpaged) illus. 15cm.
  1. Government, Resistance to.
  I. Friends, Society of. American Friends Service Committee.
  KU-RH

B6
Baker, Horace.
  The federal retreat in school
  desegregation. Atlanta,
  Southern Regional Council,
  1969.
  iv, 70p.
  1. Negroes--Education. 2. Segregation in education.
  I. Southern Regional Council.
  WHi-L

Baltimore Union for Jobs or
    Income Now
  see
Jobs or Income Now Community
    Union, Baltimore.

B7
Bancroft, Nancy.
  The Christian peace concern.
  New York, Students for a Demo-
  cratic Society and its Peace
  Research and Education Project
  [1963?].
  7p. 28cm.
  Cover title.
  1. Peace. 2. War and religion.
  I. Students for a Democratic
  Society. Peace Research and
  Education Project.
  MiU

B8
Banda, Michael.
  The Chinese communist party and
  the Hungarian revolution. [New
  York] Pioneer Publishers [1957?]
  21p. 17cm. (Pioneer pocket
  library no. 6)
  Cover title.
  1. Communism--China (People's
  Republic of China, 1949-   ).
  2. Chung-kuo Kung Ch'an Tang.
  3. Hungary--History--Revolution,
  1956. I. Pioneer Publishers.
  KU-RH

B9
Bang, Gustav.
  Crises in European history,
  translated from Danish by
  Arnold Petersen. New York, New
  York Labor News Co., 1961.
  98p. 19cm.
  1. Europe--History. I. New York
  Labor News Co.
  MiU

B10
Banner, Bruce.
  Writing--off checkoff: another
  mistake. [Berkeley? International Socialists? 1970].
  4p. 28cm.
  Caption title.
  1. Trade-unions. I. International Socialists.
  CU-B

B11
Baran, Paul A.
  The absorption of surplus; the
  sales effort [by] Paul Baran

[and] Paul Sweezy. [Boston,
New England Free Press, 196]
112-141p. 21cm.
Cover title.
1. Surplus commodities. 2. Ad-
vertising. I. Sweezy, Paul
Marlor, 1910-   , jt. auth.
II. New England Free Press.
KU-RH, MiU

B12
Baran, Paul A.
  The economics of racism, by
  Paul Baran and Paul Sweezy.
  [Boston, New England Free
  Press, c1966]
  32p. 22cm.
  Cover title.
  1. Capitalism. 2. Negroes--
  Civil rights. I. Sweezy, Paul
  Marlor, 1910-   , jt. auth.
  I. New England Free Press.
  MiU

B13
Baran, Paul A.
  Marxism and psychoanalysis.
  Comments: Aron Krich [and
  others]. Reply: Paul A. Baran.
  Appendix: the Soviet view of
  psychoanalysis, by D. Fedotov.
  Comment: Norman Reider. [New
  York, Monthly Review Press,
  1969]
  64p. 22cm. (Monthly review
  pamphlet series, no. 14)
  1. Communism. I. Monthly Re-
  view Press.
  MH, WU, OClW, CU, CSt, DNLM,
  KU-RH, MiU, DLC 60-3069

B14
Baran, Paul A.
  Paul Baran on Marxism--crisis
  of Marxism?--on the nature of
  Marxism. Boston, New England
  Free Press [196]
  224-[234], 259-268p. 22cm.
  Cover title.
  Reprinted from Monthly Review
  Oct. & Nov. 1958.
  1. Socialism. I. New England
  Free Press.
  KU-RH

B15
Baran, Paul A.
  Reflections on the Cuba revolu-
tion. New York, Monthly Review
Press, 1961.
  28p. 21cm. (Monthly review
pamphlet series, no. 18)
  Reprinted from Monthly Review,
Jan. & Feb. 1961.
  1. Cuba--Pol. & govt.--1933-1959.
  2. Cuba--Pol. & govt.--1959-
  3. Castro, Fidel, 1927-
  I. Monthly Review Press.
  MH, CSt, TNJ, CSt-H, KU-RH

B16
Baran, Paul A.
  Reflections on the Cuban revolution. [2d. ed. with new material added]. New York, Monthly
Review Press, 1961.
  45p. 21cm. (Monthly review
pamphlet series, no. 18)
  Reprinted from Monthly Review,
Jan. & Feb. 1961.
  1. Cuba--Pol. & govt.--1933-1959.
  2. Cuba--Social conditions.
  3. Cuba--Pol. & govt.--1959-
  I. Monthly Review Press.
  CSt, TxU, CU, KU-RH

B17
Barndt, Joseph R.
  Eradicating white racism. [n.p.
1968?]
  6p. 28cm.
  Caption title.
  Reprinted from Catholic Worker,
July 17, 1968.
  1. Negroes--Civil rights.
  2. Race discrimination.
  I. Catholic Worker.
  CU-B

B18
Barnet, Richard J.
  President Nixon's choices: the
way out of Vietnam. [New York,
Clergy and Laymen Concerned
about Vietnam, 196]
  [2]p. 28cm.
  Caption title.
  1. Vietnamese conflict, 1961-
1975. I. Clergy and Laymen Concerned About Vietnam.
  KU-RH

B19
Barnett, Donald L.
  Notes toward a strategy for
North American revolutionaries.
[Vancouver] Liberation Sup-
port Movement [1970]
  20p. 22cm. (International
liberation series 1)
  Cover title.
  1. Revolutions. 2. Radicalism.
  I. Liberation Support Movement.
  MiU

B20
Barnett, Donald L.
  Toward an international stra-
tegy. [Seattle, Liberation
Support Movement, 1970?]
  22p. 22cm.
  Cover title.
  1. Capitalism. 2. Socialism.
  I. Liberation Support Movement.
  MiU

B21
Barnett, Donald L.
  With the guerrillas in Angola.
[Oakland] Liberation Support
Movement [1970]
  34p. 22cm.
  Cover title.
  1. Guerrilas--Angola.
  2. Angola--Pol. & govt.
  3. Movimento Popular de Libertacao de Angola. I. Liberation Support Movement.
  MiU

B22
Barry, Kathleen.
  A view from the doll corner.
[Seattle? Radical Women? 196]
  6p. 28cm.
  Caption title.
  1. Education of women. 2. Edu-
cation. 3. Girls. I. Radical
Women.
  WHi-L

B23
Barton, Anthony.
  The chocolate children. [Bos-
ton, New England Free Press,
1970]
  9p. 22cm.
  Cover title.

Reprinted from This Magazine Is
About Schools, summer 1969.
1. Education--Pennsylvania--
Hershey. 2. Milton Hershey
School. I. New England Free
Press.
KU-RH

B24
Baton Rouge Committee on Registra-
    tion Education.   .
  Negro voting in Louisiana. 1st.
  ed. [n.p., 196]
  15p. 28cm.
  Cover title.
  1. Negroes--Civil rights.
  2. Negroes--Louisiana.
  CU-B

B25
Bax, Ernest Belfort, 1854-1926.
  The story of the French revolu-
  tion. With pref. to the Ameri-
  can ed. by Daniel De Leon. New
  York Labor News Co., 1956.
  xi, 120p. illus. 21cm.
  1. France--History--Revolution.
  I. New York Labor News Co.
  NIC, ICU

B26
Bay, Christian.
  Political and apolitical stu-
  dents. [Montreal, Our Genera-
  tion, 196]
  41-[59]p.
  Cover title.
  At head of title: Facts in
  search of theory.
  1. Student movements. 2. Youth--
  Political activity. I. Our
  Generation.
  NNU-T

B27
Bay, Christian.
  Student political activism.
  [Montreal, Our Generation, 196]
  50-73p.
  Caption title.
  1. Student movements.
  2. Youth--Political activity.
  I. Our Generation.
  NNU-T

B28
Bay, Noel.
  The freedom movement in Massa-
  chusetts. New York, Students
  for a Democratic Society and
  its Economic Research and Action
  Project [196]
  19p.
  Cover title.
  1. Negroes--Civil rights.
  2. Massachusetts--Race question.
  I. Students for a Democratic
  Society. Economic Research and
  Action Project.
  WHi-L

Bay Area National Lawyers Guild
  see also
National Lawyers Guild.

B29
Bay Area National Lawyers Guild.
  Legal first aid, written by the
  regional office of the Bay Area
  National Lawyers Guild. [San
  Francisco, Peoples Press, 1970?]
  27[1]p. illus. 22cm.
  1. Law enforcement. 2. Legal
  aid. I. Peoples Press.
  MiU

Bay Area Radical Education Project
  see also
Radical Education Project.

B30
Bay Area Radical Education Pro-
    ject.
  Empire and revolution. [San
  Francisco?] 1969.
  8p. 28cm. (REP review of
  literature no. 2)
  Caption title.
  1. U.S.--Foreign policy--Bibl.
  2. Revolutions--Bibl.
  CU-B

B31
Bay Area Radical Education Pro-
    ject.
  How now the empire? [San Francisco?] 1969.
  11 leaves. 28cm. (REP review

of literature 1)
Caption title.
1. Radicalism--Bibl.
CU-B

B32
Bay Area Radical Education Pro-
    ject.
Imperialism and revolution in
East Asia.   [San Francisco?]
1969.
10p.   28cm.   (Bay Area REP review of literature 3)
Caption title.
1. Revolutions--Asia--Bibl.
2. Imperialism--Bibl.
CU-B

B33
Bay Area Radical Education Pro-
    ject.
On the black worker's revolt.
[San Francisco, 1970]
4 leaves.   28cm.
Caption title.
1. Negroes--Civil rights.
2. Dodge Revolutionary Union
Movement.   3. League of Revolu-
tionary Black Workers.   4. Auto-
mobile industry workers.
CU-B

B34
Bay Area Revolutionary Union.
How can we deal with the pigs?
San Francisco [1969?]
[1] leaf.   36cm.
Caption title.
1. Police.
CU-B

B35
Bay Area Revolutionary Union.
Revolutionary youth and the road
to the proletariat.   [San Francisco, Bay Area Radical Education Project [1969?]
14p.   illus.   28cm.
Cover title.
1. Students for a Democratic
Society.   2. Labor and laboring
classes.   I. Bay Area Radical
Education Project.
MiU

B36
Bay Area Revolutionary Union.
We will fight and fight from
this generation to the next.
[San Francisco, 1969?]
[1] leaf.   36cm.
Caption title.
1. People's Park, Berkeley,
Calif.
CU-B

B37
Bay Area Revolutionary Union.
    Central Committee.
The red papers 3: women fight
for liberation [by Bob Avakian
and others for the Central
Committee of the Bay Area Revolutionary Union.   San Francisco, 1970?]
60p.   illus.   28cm.
Cover title.
1. Woman--Rights of women.
I. Avakian, Bob.
KU-RH

B38
Bay Area Revolutionary Union.
    Correspondence Committee.
The red papers.   [Correspon-
dence committee: Bob Avakian,
Bruce Franklin, Steve Hamilton.
San Francisco, 1969?]
30p.   illus.   28cm.
Cover title.
1. Communism.   2. Socialism.
3. Youth--Political activity.
4. Progressive Labor Party.
I. Avakian, Bob, jt. auth.
II. Franklin, Bruce, jt. auth.
III. Hamilton, Steve, jt. auth.
KU-RH, MoU

B39
Bay Area Revolutionary Union.
    Correspondence Committee.
The red papers 2.   [San Fran-
cisco, 1961?]
47p.   illus.   28cm.
Cover title.
Correspondence committee in-
cludes Bob Avakian, Bruce
Franklin and Steve Hamilton.
1. Imperialism.   2. Proletariat.

3. Youth--Political activity.
I. Avakian, Bob, jt. auth.
II. Franklin, Bruce, jt. auth.
III. Hamilton, Steve, jt. auth.
KU-RH

B40
Bay Area Spartacist.
  Whose national interest?
  [Berkeley, 1965]
  [2]p. 28cm.
  Caption title.
  1. Vietnamese conflict, 1961-
  1975.
  CU-B

B41
Bay Area Spartacist Committee.
  Neither a Korea nor Laos but a
  workers state. Berkeley, 1965.
  [1] leaf. 28cm.
  Caption title.
  1. Vietnamese conflict, 1961-
  1975.
  CU-B

Bay Area Spartacist League.
  see also
New York City Spartacist League.
Spartacist League.
Campus Spartacist Club, Berkeley,
    Calif.
Philadelphia Spartacist League.

B42
Bay Area Spartacist League.
  After the army, what. [Berkeley,
  1968?]
  [2]p. 28cm.
  Caption title.
  1. U.S. Army. 2. Vietnamese
  conflict, 1961-1975.
  CU-B

B43
Bay Area Spartacist League.
  Anti-war sellout. [Berkeley,
  1967?]
  [2]p. 36cm.
  Caption title.
  1. Socialist Workers Party.
  2. Vietnamese conflict, 1961-
  1975.
  CU-B

B44
Bay Area Spartacist League.
  Beyond phrase-mongering;
  position paper on the "Cleaver
  controversy." [Berkeley, 1968]
  [2]p. 28cm.
  Caption title.
  1. Negroes--Civil rights.
  2. Cleaver, Eldridge, 1935-
  CU-B

B45
Bay Area Spartacist League.
  Defend the movement, but change
  it. Berkeley, 1967.
  [1] leaf. 28cm.
  Caption title.
  1. Student movements.
  CU-B

B46
Bay Area Spartacist League.
  Does the Soviet nuclear shield
  cover Hanoi? An open letter to
  Attache Rogochov. [Berkeley?]
  1966.
  [1] leaf. 28cm.
  Caption title.
  1. Vietnamese conflict, 1961-
  1975. 2. Russia--Foreign policy. 3. Russia--Military policy.
  CU-B

B47
Bay Area Spartacist League.
  The fight for women's libera-
  tion. [Berkeley, 1970?]
  [2]p. 28cm.
  Caption title.
  1. Woman--Rights of women.
  CU-B

B48
Bay Area Spartacist League.
  Guevara's guerrillas--or work-
  er's revolutions? Rev.
  Berkeley, 1968.
  [1] leaf. 36cm.
  Caption title.
  1. Guerillas. 2. Revolutions.
  3. Labor and laboring classes.
  CU-B

B49
Bay Area Spartacist League.
  Is there an alternative to

futile demonstrations?
[Berkeley, 1968?]
Caption title.
1. Vietnamese conflict, 1961-
1975.   2. Demonstrations.
CU-B

B50
Bay Area Spartacist League.
  Jail or Canada? Hell no. If
  the army wants radicals, we will
  go. [Berkeley, 1967]
  [2]p. 36cm.
  Caption title.
  1. Military service, Compulsory.
  CU-B

B51
Bay Area Spartacist League.
  Letter to the Panthers.
  Berkeley, 1970.
  [1] leaf. 28cm.
  Caption title.
  1. Black Panther Party.
  CU-B

B52
Bay Area Spartacist League.
  One more march, a step forward?
  [Berkeley, 1967?]
  [2]p. 36cm.
  Caption title.
  1. Student movements.
  CU-B

B53
Bay Area Spartacist League.
  Out of the swamp; the left in
  the Berkeley election. [Berke-
  ley, 1967]
  [2]p. 36cm.
  Caption title.
  1. Berkeley, Calif.--Pol. &
  govt.
  CU-B

B54
Bay Area Spartacist League.
  The park and the revolution.
  Berkeley [1969?]
  [1] leaf. 28cm.
  Caption title.
  1. People's Park, Berkeley,
  Calif.
  CU-B

B55
Bay Area Spartacist League.
  SDS & revolution; student power
  or workers power? [Berkeley,
  196]
  [2]p. 36cm.
  Caption title.
  1. Students for a Democratic
  Society. 2. Labor and laboring
  classes.
  CU-B

B56
Bay Area Spartacist League.
  Terror in Latin America.
  Berkeley, 1967.
  [1] leaf. 28cm.
  Caption title.
  1. Political prisoners--Latin
  America. 2. Latin America--
  Pol. & govt.
  CU-B

B57
Bay Area Spartacist League.
  Victory for the French working
  class. [Berkeley, 1968]
  [2]p. 28cm.
  Cover title.
  1. Labor and laboring classes--
  France.
  CU-B

B58
Bay Area Spartacist League.
  When will we ever learn?
  [Berkeley, 1968]
  [2]p. 28cm.
  Caption title.
  1. Vietnamese conflict, 1961-
  1975. 2. Student movements.
  3. Stop the Draft Week, Berkeley, Calif.
  CU-B

B59
Bay Area Student Committee for
    Abolition of the House Com-
    mittee on Un-American Acti-
    vities.
  In search of the truth: an
  analysis of the H.C.U.A. propaganda film "operation abolition". Berkeley, Calif. [196]
  [8]p. 28cm.

Cover title.
1. U.S. Congress. House. Committee on Un-American Activities.
KU-RH

B60
Bazaar, Mona, ed.
  Black fury. [Los Angeles?
  196 ?]
  [82]p. illus.
  1. Negroes--Civil rights.
  MiU

B61
Beach, Mary, ed.
  Liberty or death, edited by Mary
  Beach. Freaked out & zapped out
  by Claude Pelieu. San Francisco, City Lights Books [196]
  1v. (unpaged) illus. 28cm.
  Cover title: Liberty or death;
  international protest & special
  Chicago section by Jeffery
  Blankfort.
  1. Student movements--France.
  2. Youth--Political activity.
  3. Chicago--Riots, August, 1968.
  I. Pelieu, Claude. II. Blankfort, Jeffery.
  KU-RH

B62
Beal, Francis M.
  Double jeopardy: to be black &
  female. [Detroit, Radical Education Project, 1970?]
  13p. illus. 22cm.
  Cover title.
  1. Negroes--Civil rights.
  2. Woman--Rights of women.
  I. Radical Education Project.
  MiU

B63
Beal, Francis M.
  Double jeopardy: to be black and
  female. [New York, Redstockings,
  196]
  [3] leaves. illus. 28cm.
  Caption title.
  1. Negroes--Civil rights.
  2. Woman--Rights of women.
  I. Redstockings of the Women's
  Liberation Movement.
  MiU

B64
Belden, Jack.
  Gold flower's story. [Boston,
  New England Free Press, 196]
  42p. illus. 28cm.
  Cover title.
  Reprinted from Jack Belden's
  China shakes the world.
  1. Woman--Rights of women.
  2. China (People's Republic of
  China, 1949-   ). 3. China--
  Pol. & govt.--1937-1949.
  I. New England Free Press.
  KU-RH

B65
Bell, Colin W.
  A considered comment on select-
  ive service from executive sec-
  retary of the American Friends
  Service Committee. [Philadel-
  phia? American Friends Service
  Committee? 1966?]
  [4]p. 28cm.
  Cover title.
  1. Military service, Compul-
  sory. 2. U.S. Selective Ser-
  vice System. I. Friends,
  Society of. American Friends
  Service Committee.
  KU-RH

B66
Bell, Daniel.
  The subversion of collective
  bargaining. Boston, New England Free Press [196]
  697-714p. 21cm.
  Cover title.
  Reprinted from Commentary, Mar.
  1960.
  1. Collective bargaining.
  2. Trade-unions.
  I. New England Free Press.
  MoU, KU-RH

B67
Bell, Daniel.
  Work and its discontents. New
  York, League for Industrial
  Democracy, 1970.
  [8] 56p. 22cm.
  Cover subtitle: The cult of
  efficiency in America.
  1. Labor and laboring classes.

I. League for Industrial Democracy.
WHi-L, NNU-T

B68
Bell, Patricia.
  Puerto Rico: island paradise of
  U.S. imperialism. [New York,
  New Outlook Publishers, 1967]
  31p. 22cm.
  Cover title.
  1. Puerto Rico. 2. Imperialism.
  I. New Outlook Publishers.
  MiU

B69
Bem, Sandra L.
  Training the woman to know her
  place, by Sandra L. Bem and
  Daryl J. Bem. [n.p., 1969?]
  6 leaves. 28cm.
  Caption title.
  1. Woman--Rights of women.
  2. Civil rights. I. Bem,
  Daryl J., jt. auth.
  KU-RH

B70
Beneson, Hal.
  The new left (draft). [Ann
  Arbor] Radical Education Project
  [1966?]
  10p. 28cm. (Study guide 2)
  Cover title.
  1. Student movements. 2. Youth--
  Political activity. I. Radical
  Education Project.
  MiU-H

B71
Bennett, John C.
  The place of civil disobedience.
  [New York, Clergy and Laymen
  Concerned About Vietnam, 196]
  [2]p. 28cm.
  Caption title.
  1. Government, Resistance to.
  I. Clergy and Laymen Concerned
  About Vietnam.
  KU-RH

B72
Bennett, Samuel.
  My last words on structure.
  [n.p., Students for a Democratic
  Society? 196]

[2]p. 28cm.
Caption title.
1. Students for a Democratic
Society. I. Students for a
Democratic Society.
CU-B

B73
Benson, H. W.
  The Communist Party at the
  crossroads; toward democratic
  socialism or back to Stalinism.
  [New York, New International
  Publishing Co., 1957?]
  40p.
  Published for the Independent
  Socialist League.
  1. Communist Party of the United
  States of America. I. Indepen-
  dent Socialist League. II. New
  International Publishing Co.
  MiEM, KU-J, NUC 66-80675

B74
Benston, Margaret.
  The political economy of
  women's liberation. Boston,
  New England Free Press [1970?]
  13-26p. 21cm.
  Cover title.
  Reprinted from Monthly Review,
  Sept. 1969.
  1. Woman--Rights of women.
  2. Woman--Employment. I. New
  England Free Press.
  KU-RH

B75
Benston, Margaret.
  The political economy of
  women's liberation. [Detroit,
  Radical Education Project,
  1970?]
  15 [1]p. illus. 22cm.
  Cover title.
  Reprinted from Monthly Review,
  Sept. 1969.
  1. Woman--Employment.
  2. Woman--Rights of women.
  I. Radical Education Project.
  KU-RH

B76
Benston, Margaret.
  The political economy of
  women's liberation. San Fran-

cisco, Bay Area Radical Education
Project [196]
15p. 22cm.
Cover title.
Reprinted from Monthly Review,
Sept. 1969.
1. Woman--Employment.
2. Woman--Rights of women.
I. Bay Area Radical Education
Project.
CU-B

B77
Benton, Nicholas.
God and my gay soul. Berkeley,
Calif., Committee of Concern for
Homosexuals [1970]
11p. 28cm.
Cover title.
1. Homosexuality. 2. Religion.
I. Committee of Concern for
Homosexuals.
KU-RH

B78
Bergmann, Frithjof.
Why do we fight in Vietnam?
[n.p., 196]
5p. 28cm.
Caption title.
1. Vietnamese conflict, 1961-
1975.
KU-RH

B79
Berkeley liberation program.
    [Berkeley? 1969?]
[8]p. 22cm.
Cover title.
1. Berkeley, Calif.
CU-B

B80
Berkeley--Oakland Woman for Peace.
Your draft-age son: a message
for peaceful parents. Berkeley,
1968.
27p. 21cm.
Cover title.
1. Military service, Compulsory.
CU-B

B81
Berkelhammer, Mathew, ed.

An investigation into the war
in Vietnam, prepared by a group
of students at the City College
of New York. Editors: Mathew
Berkelhammer [and others. New
York] 1965.
13 leaves. 28cm.
Cover title.
1. Vietnamese conflict, 1961-
1975.
WHi-A

B82
Bernick, Kitty.
Marxism: a syllabus designed for
a women's course (may also be
used by men). Boston, New
England Free Press [1970?]
[4]p. 28cm.
Caption title.
1. Socialism--Bibl. 2. Woman--
Bibl. I. New England Free
Press.
MiU

B83
Bernstein, Judi.
Sisters, brothers, lovers
listen [by] Judi Bernstein [and
others] Boston, New England
Free Press [196]
7p. 28cm.
Cover title.
Written for Student Union for
Peace Action membership confer-
ence.
1. Woman--Rights of women.
I. New England Free Press.
II. Student Union for Peace
Action.
KU-RH

B84
Berrigan, Daniel.
In peaceable conflict. [Nyack,
N.Y., Catholic Peace Fellow-
ship, 196]
[2]p. 28cm.
Cover title.
An address delivered Feb. 18,
1966 in the Community Church,
New York.
1. Peace. 2. Vietnamese con-
flict, 1961-1975. I. Catholic
Peace Fellowship.
KU-RH

B85
Berrigan, Philip.
  Berrigan: dialogue with doubt.
  Nyack, N.Y., Fellowship Publications (1960]
  8p. 28cm.
  Caption title.
  Reprinted from Liberation, Feb.
  1969.
  1. Nonviolence. 2. Students for
  a Democratic Society. 3. Revolutions. I. Fellowship Publications.
  KU-RH

B86
Bertelson, David.
  A comparative approach to the
  meaning of gay liberation.
  [Berkeley, Calif., Gay Switch-
  board, c1970]
  20p. 28cm.
  Caption title.
  1. Homosexuality. I. Gay
  Switchboard.
  KU-RH

B87
Best, Ruth.
  Oh, what a beautiful city.
  [Nyack, N.Y.? Fellowship Publi-
  cations? 1968?]
  [3]p. 28cm.
  Caption title.
  Reprinted from Fellowship, Sept.
  1968.
  1. Poverty. 2. Resurrection
  City. I. Fellowship Publica-
  tions.
  KU-RH

B88
Bevel, James.
  A movement to end mass murder.
  [n.p., 196]
  9p. 28cm.
  Caption title.
  1. Peace. 2. Negroes.
  MoU

B89
Bhoodan Center of Inquiry, Oak-
    hurst, Calif.
  Handbook. [Oakhurst, Calif.,
  1969]
  16 leaves. 28cm.

Cover title.
1. Communes.
KU-RH

B90
Binh, Nguyen Thi.
  Letter from a Vietnamese sister.
  [New Orleans, Southern Female
  Rights Union? 1970]
  [2]p. 28cm.
  Caption title.
  1. Vietnamese conflict, 1961-
  1975. I. Southern Female
  Rights Union.
  KU-RH

B91
Bishop, Gloria.
  Oasis in Birmingham. [New
  York, Liberation, 196 ?]
  [3]p.
  Reprinted from Liberation.
  1. Birmingham--Race question.
  2. Negroes--Civil rights.
  I. Liberation
  WHi-L

B92
Bittner, Lee.
  The educational system; "a
  student's view"... [Fresno,
  Calif., Resistance, 1969?]
  [2]p. 28cm.
  Caption title.
  1. Student movements. 2. High
  schools. I. Resistance.
  KU-RH

B93
Black, Edie.
  The Hanna industrial complex,
  by Edie Black and Fred Goff.
  New York, North American Con-
  gress on Latin America [c1969]
  16p. illus. 28cm.
  Cover title.
  1. Hanna Mining Co.
  2. Chrysler Corp. 3. National
  Steel Corp. 4. Consolidated
  Coal Co. 5. Republican Party.
  6. Brazil--Relations (general)
  with the U.S. I. Goff, Fred,
  jt. auth. II. North
  American Congress on Latin
  America.
  KU-RH

B94
Black, Edie.
  How to select targets to disrupt
  the empire [by Edie Black and
  Louis Reivich] Nashville, Tenn.,
  Southern Student Organizing Com-
  mittee [196]
  8p. 28cm.
  Cover title.
  1. Imperialism. I. Southern
  Student Organizing Committee.
  II. Reivich, Louis, jt. auth.
  MoU

B95
Black, Edie.
  A new look at the U.S. investments in Latin America. Ann
  Arbor, Radical Education Project
  [196]
  6p.
  Cover title.
  1. U.S.--Relations (general)
  with Latin America. 2. Investments, American--Latin America.
  3. Latin America--Econ. condit.
  I. Radical Education Project.
  WHi-L

B96
Black, Edie.
  The new strategy for U.S. in-
  vestment in Latin America.
  Boston, New England Free Press
  [196]
  [4]p. 28cm.
  Caption title.
  Reprinted from Viet-Report,
  April-May 1968.
  1. U.S.--Relations (general)
  with Latin America. 2. Invest-
  ments, American--Latin America.
  3. Latin America--Econ. condit.
  I. New England Free Press.
  KU-RH

B97
Black, Hugo Lafayette, 1886-
  Dissents in the United States
  Supreme Court by Justice Hugo
  Black, with Justice Warren and
  Justice Douglas concurring and
  by Mr. Justice Brennan. Lloyd
  Barenblatt, petitioner v.
  United States of America,
  June 8, 1959. [New York,

Emergency Civil Liberties Committee, 1959]
  33p. 22cm.
  1. Civil rights. I. Emergency
  Civil Liberties Committee.
  N, KU-J

B98
Black, Hugo Lafayette, 1886-
  A fateful moment in our history,
  dissenting opinion of Hugo L.
  Black in the McCarran Act deci-
  sion. [New York, Citizen's
  Committee for Constitutional
  Liberties, 196]
  31p.
  Cover title.
  1. U.S. Laws, statutes, etc.
  Internal Security Act of 1950.
  2. Civil rights. I. Citizen's
  Committee for Constitutional
  Liberties.
  MiU, KU-J

B99
Black and white construction
    workers divided by the bosses.
    Boston, New England Free
    Press [1970?]
  50-55p. illus. 28cm.
  Cover title.
  Reprinted from PL, Feb. 1970.
  "PLP Trade Union Section flyer,
  1969."
  1. Negroes--Employment. 2. Con-
  struction workers. 3. Dis-
  crimination in employment.
  I. Progressive Labor Party.
  Trade Union Section. II. New
  England Free Press.
  KU-RH

B100
Black nationalism & Marxist
    theory. [new ed. New York,
    Bulletin Publications, 1967]
  30 [2]p. 28cm.
  Cover title.
  At head of title: Open letter
  to SNCC.
  1. Negroes. 2. Socialism.
  3. Socialist Workers Party.
  4. Student Nonviolent Coordinating Committee. I. Bulletin

Publications.
MiU

B101
Black Panther Party.
  Black Panther Party platform and
  program. What we want; what we
  believe. [n.p.] 1966.
  [4]p. 22cm.
  Cover title.
  1. Black Panther Party.
  2. Negroes--Civil rights.
  CU-B

B102
Black Panther Party.
  Control your local police [co-
  sponsored by Black Panther
  Party & Peace and Freedom.
  Berkeley, Oakland, 196]
  [4]p. 28cm.
  Caption title.
  1. Law enforcement. 2. Police.
  I. Peace and Freedom Party.
  CU-B

B103
Black Panther Party.
  Position of the Black Panther
  Party for self defense on the
  seventh congressional district
  election and the candidacy of
  John George in the Democratic
  Party. Kathleen Cleaver, com-
  munication secretary, presented
  to the Alameda County Peace and
  Freedom Party meeting, Berkeley,
  Calif., Jan. 31, 1968. [Oak-
  land, 1968?]
  [4]p. 22cm. (Ministry of infor-
  mation black paper)
  Caption title.
  At head of title: Black Panther
  Party for Self-defense.
  I. Negroes--Politics and suf-
  frage. I. Cleaver, Kathleen.
  MoU

B104
Black Panther Party.
  Ten (10) point platform and program of the Black Panther Party.
  [n.p., 196]
  2 leaves. 36cm.
  Caption title.

1. Negroes--Civil rights.
KU-RH

B105
Black Panther Party. Central
  Headquarters.
  Rules of the Black Panther
  Party. Oakland [196]
  [1] leaf. 36cm.
  Caption title.
  KU-RH

B106
Black-Red Conference, Detroit,
  1969.
  A report on Black-Red Confer-
  ence, Detroit, Mich., Jan. 12,
  1969. Detroit, News & Letters,
  [1969]
  2, 7, 7p. 28cm.
  Contents--Welcome by Charles
  Benby. Presentation by Raya
  Dunayevskaya.
  1. Negroes--Politics and suf-
  frage. 2. Communism. I. Denby,
  Charles. II. Dunayevakaya,
  Raya. III. News & Letters.
  KU-RH, MoU

B107
Black Student Union.
  B.S.U. platform and program:
  what we want; what we believe.
  [Oakland? Black Panther Party?
  196]
  [4]p. 22cm.
  Cover title.
  1. Negroes--Education. 2. Student movements. I. Black Panther Party.
  KU-RH

B108
The Black uprisings, Newark--
  Detroit, 1967. Introduction
  by Paul Boutelle. [New York,
  Merit Publishers, 1969]
  30p. illus. 22cm.
  Cover title.
  1. Negroes--Detroit.
  2. Negroes--Newark.
  3. Detroit--Riots, 1967.
  4. Newark--Riots, 1967.
  I. Boutelle, Paul. II. Merit
  Publishers.

KU-RH, MoU, WHi-L, MsSM,
NUC 70-28048

B109
Blackett, P.M.S.
  The military background to dis-
armament, with an introduction
by Carl Marzani and a postscript
by Leo Huberman and Paul M.
Sweezy. [New York] Marzani &
Munsell [196]
13 [1]p. 24cm.
Cover title.
1. Disarmament. I. Huberman,
Leo, 1903-   . II. Sweezy,
Paul Marlor, 1910-   .
III. Marzani, Carl. IV. Marzani
and Munsell.
KU-J

B110
Blackman, Allan.
  Face to face with your draft
board, a guide to personal ap-
pearances. [Berkeley] World
Without War Council [1969]
98p. 22cm.
1. Military service, Compulsory.
2. Conscientious objectors.
I. World Without War Council.
CNoS, WHi-L, NUC 70-93494

B111
Block, Ashen.
  The Jewish tradition of peace.
[Nyack, N.Y., Jewish Peace Fel-
lowship, 196]
[9]p. 22cm.
Cover title.
Reprinted from Fellowship, Feb.
1953.
1. Jews. 2. Peace. I. Jewish
Peace Fellowship.
CU-B

B112
Bloice, Carl.
  The war on poverty and socialist
action orientation [by Carl
Bloice and Bob Kaufman. n.p.,
W.E.B. DuBois Clubs of America?
196]
7p. 28cm.
Caption title.
1. Poverty. 2. Socialism.
3. U.S. Office of Economic

Opportunity. I. Kaufman,
Robert, jt. auth. II. DuBois
(W.E.B.) Clubs of America.
WHi-A

B113
Bloomberg, Warner.
  The age of automation; its
effects on human welfare. New
York, League for Industrial
Democracy [c1955]
39p. 22cm.
Cover title.
1. Automation. I. League for
Industrial Democracy.
WHi-A

B114
Blossom, Frederick A.
  What can I do to break through
the color wall? [New Orleans,
Southern Conference Educational
Fund, 196]
folder. 22x10cm.
Cover title.
1. Negroes--Civil rights.
I. Southern Conference Educa-
tional Fund.
KU-RH

B115
Bluestone, Barry.
  Note on campus program. [Ann
Arbor, 196]
5p. 28cm.
Caption title.
1. Student movements--Univer-
sity of Michigan. 2. University of Michigan Student Employers Union. 3. Student employment.
WHi-A

B116
Blum, Shelley.
  University reform. New York,
Students for a Democratic
Society [196]
4p. 28cm.
Cover title.
1. Universities and colleges.
2. Student movements.
I. Students for a Democratic
Society.
MiU, WHi-A

B117
Boardman, Richard M.
  Letter from Richard M. Boardman
  to local board no. 114. [Chi-
  cago, American Friends Service
  Committee and Chicago Area Draft
  Resisters, 196]
  8p. 22cm.
  Caption title.
  1. Military service, Compulsory.
  2. Conscientious objectors.
  I. Chicago Area Draft Resisters.
  II. Friends, Society of. Ameri-
  can Friends Service Committee.
  KU-RH

B118
Boardman, Richard M.
  Resistance is. Chicago, Chicago
  Area Draft Resisters [1970?]
  13p. 28cm.
  Cover title.
  1. Resistance. 2. Military ser-
  vice, Compulsory. 3. Government,
  Resistance to. I. Chicago Area
  Draft Resisters.
  KU-RH

B119
The Bobby Hutton tribunal commit-
    tee. [Berkeley, Tribunal
    Committee, 1968]
  v, [38] leaves. 28cm.
  Cover title.
  Copyrighted by Len Holt.
  1. Hutton, Bobby. 2. Black
  Panther Party. I. Holt, Len.
  MiU

B120
Bodenheimer, Susanne.
  The hidden invaders: our civilian takeover in the Dominican
  Republic. [Ithaca? Cornell Committee on U.S.--Latin American
  Relations, 196]
  [4]p. 28cm.
  Caption title.
  Reprinted from Liberation, Feb.
  1967.
  1. Dominican Republic--Pol. &
  govt. 2. U.S.--For. rel.--Domi-
  nican Republic. I. Cornell Committee on U.S.--Latin American
  Relations.
  KU-RH

B121
Bodenheimer, Susanne.
  Peru: the foreign managers, by
  Susanne Bodenheimer and Alex
  Georgiadis. [San Francisco?
  Leviathan? 1969?]
  [6]p. 28cm.
  Cover title.
  Reprinted from Leviathan, Jy./
  Aug. 1969.
  1. Imperialism. 2. Peru--Pol.
  & govt. 3. U.S.--Relations
  (general) with Peru. I. Levia-
  than. II. Georgiadis, Alex,
  jt. auth.
  KU-RH

B122
Boggs, James.
  Manifesto for a Black revolutionary party. [Philadelphia,
  Pacesetters Publishing House,
  196]
  40p. 22cm.
  Cover title.
  1. Negroes--Politics and suffrage. 2. Negroes--Civil
  rights.
  MiU

B123
Boggs, James.
  Uprooting racism and racists in
  the United States, by James and
  Grace Lee Boggs. [Detroit, Ra-
  dical Education Project, c1970]
  16p. illus. 22cm.
  Cover title.
  1. Negroes--Civil rights.
  I. Boggs, Grace Lee, jt. auth.
  II. Radical Education Project.
  MiU

B124
Boletzer, Lilli A.
  Farm and migrant workers: a
  discussion paper. [Ann Arbor?]
  Voice Political Party, 1962.
  7 leaves. 28cm.
  Cover title.
  Originally written for Students
  for a Democratic Society, Aug.
  1961.
  1. Agricultural laborers.
  2. Mexicans in the U.S.
  I. Voice Political Party--

Students for a Democratic Society, Ann Arbor.
WHi-A

B125
Bolioli, Oscar L.
   The younger generation in Latin
America. [Toronto? Latin Ameri-
can Working Group? 196]
10p. 29cm.
Caption title.
Reprinted from Risk, v. 2, no.
2; 1966.
1. Youth--Latin America.
2. Latin America--Pol. & govt.
I. Latin American Working Group.
KU-RH

B126
Bollens, John.
   The broken shield; a look at the
anti-missile missile and Amer-
ica's military defense [by John
Bollens, Bradford Lyttle and
Kate Williams. Chicago? Peace
Education Program, American
Friends Service Committee? 196]
24p. 28cm.
1. U.S.--Military policy.
2. Antimissile missiles.
I. Lyttle, Bradford, jt. auth.
II. Williams, Kate, jt. auth.
III. Friends, Society of.
American Friends Service Commit-
tee.
WHi-A

B127
Bollinger, Betty.
   Report on tuition, written by
Betty Bollinger [and] Leif
Johnson. [n.p.] Campus Divi-
sion, Americans for Democratic
Action for the Liberal Study
Group [1962]
[5]p. 36cm.
Cover title.
"Presented by the National
Student Association Committee of
the Queens College Student As-
sociation."
1. University and colleges--
Finance. I. Johnson, Leif, jt.
auth. II. Liberal Study Group.
II. Americans for Democratic

Action, Campus Division.
MiU

B128
Bond, Julian, 1940-
   Black candidates: Southern cam-
paign experiences. Atlanta,
Voter Education Project, South-
ern Regional Council [1969]
57p. illus., ports.
Cover title.
Summary by Marvin Wall.
1. Negroes--Politics and suf-
frage. 2. Elections--Southern
States. I. Wall, Marvin.
II. Southern Regional Council.
WHi-L, MU, MH, MiU, NjP,
NUC 71-87858

B129
Bonnell, Victoria.
   Workers and the American econ-
omy; data on the labor force,
by Victoria Bonnell and Michael
Reich. [Boston? New England
Free Press, c1969?]
24p. 28cm.
Cover title.
1. Labor and laboring classes--
Statistics. I. Reich, Michael,
jt. auth. II. New England Free
Press.
KU-RH

B130
Bonpane, Blase.
   Our Latin Vietnam. Woodmont,
Conn., Promoting Enduring
Peace [196]
[2]p. 28cm.
Cover title.
1. Latin America--Relations
(general) with the U.S.
2. U.S.--Relations (general)
with Latin America. I. Promoting Enduring Peace.
KU-RH

Bookchin, Murray
   see also
Herber, Lewis

B131
Bookchin, Murray.
   Anarchy and organization [by]
Murray Bookchin. Anarchism,

terrorism and individualism [by]
Bob Dickens. Buffalo, N.Y.,
Friends of Malatesta, 196]
7p. 22cm.
1. Anarchism and anarchists.
I. Dickens, Bob, jt. auth.
II. Friends of Malatesta.
MiU

B132
Bookchin, Murray.
  Desire and need. [Montreal, Our
  Generation, 196]
  33-41 leaves.
  Caption title.
  1. Anarchism and anarchists.
  2. Revolutions. 3. Economics.
  I. Our Generation.
  NNU-T

B133
Bookchin, Murray.
  Ecology and revolutionary thought
  [by] Lewis Herber [pseudo]
  [Montreal, Our Generation, 196]
  13-32 leaves.
  Caption title.
  1. Environmental policy.
  2. Anarchism and anarchists.
  I. Our Generation.
  NNU-T, WHi-L

B134
Bookchin, Murray.
  Forms of freedom. [Montreal?
  Our Generation? 1968]
  23-[41]p.
  Cover title.
  1. Revolutions--History.
  2. Anarchism and anarchists.
  I. Our Generation.
  NNU-T

B135
Bookchin, Murray.
  Post-scarcity anarchy. [New
  York, Anarchos, 196]
  22p. 22cm.
  Cover title.
  1. Anarchism and anarchists.
  I. Anarchos.
  MiU

B136
Bookchin, Murray.
  Toward an ecological solution.

[Ithaca, N.Y., Glad Day Press,
1970?]
[6]p. illus. 28cm.
Caption title.
1. Environmental policy.
2. Anarchism and anarchists.
I. Glad Day Press.
NNU-T

B137
Bookchin, Murray.
  Towards a liberatory technology
  [by] Lewis Herber [pseudo.]
  [Montreal, Our Generation, 196]
  [49]-67 leaves.
  Caption title.
  1. Technocracy. I. Our Genera-
  tion.
  NNU-T

B138
Boorstein, Edward.
  Cuba and imperialism: the pre-
  revolutionary background. Boston, New England Free Press
  [c1968]
  16p. 22cm.
  Cover title.
  1. Cuba--Relations (general)
  with U.S. 2. Imperialism.
  I. New England Free Press.
  MiU

B139
Boorstein, Edward.
  Cuba vs. U.S. imperialism.
  [Chicago, Students for a Democratic Society, 196]
  folder (8p.) illus. 22cm.
  Cover title.
  1. Cuba--Relations (general)
  with U.S. 2. U.S.--Relations
  (general) with Cuba. 3. Imperialism. I. Students for a
  Democratic Society.
  MoU, KU-RH

B140
Booth, Heather.
  Toward a radical movement [by]
  Heather Booth, Evi Goldfield
  [and] Sue Munaker. Boston, New
  England Free Press [1968]
  [4]p. 28cm.
  Caption title.
  1. Woman--Rights of women.

I. Goldfield, Evi, jt. auth.
II. Munaker, Sue, jt. auth.
III. New England Free Press.
KU-RH, MoU

B141
Booth, Paul Robert.
  A basis for university reform.
  New York, Students for a Democratic Society [1964?]
  4p. 28cm.
  Cover title.
  1. Universities and colleges.
  2. Education. 3. Student movements. I. Students for a Democratic Society.
  WHi-A, MiU

B142
Booth, Paul Robert.
  Converting America. New York,
  Students for a Democratic
  Society [196]
  7 [1]p. 28cm.
  Cover title.
  1. Peace. 2. U.S.--Military
  policy. 3. Poverty. 4. U.S.--
  Econ. condit. I. Students for a
  Democratic Society.
  WHi-A

B143
Booth, Paul Robert.
  Economic conversion and the war
  on poverty. New York, Peace Research and Education Project of
  Students for a Democratic Society
  for the Liberal Study Group
  [196]
  7 [1]p. 28cm.
  Cover title.
  1. Peace. 2. U.S.--Military
  policy. 3. U.S.--Econ. condit.
  4. Poverty. I. Students for a
  Democratic Society. Peace Research and Education Project.
  II. Liberal Study Group.
  MiU, WHi-A, CU-B

B144
Booth, Paul Robert.
  Military and social spending--
  how are they related? [Chicago,
  Students for a Democratic Society, 1964?]
  [2]p. 28cm.

Caption title.
Reprinted from War/Peace Report,
Aug. 1964.
1. U.S.--Military policy.
2. Social change. I. Students
for a Democratic Society.
WHi-A, CU-B

B145
Booth, Paul Robert.
  Peace politics; a study of the
  American peace movement and the
  politics of the 1962 congress-
  ional elections. Sponsored by
  the Swarthmore College Peace
  Research Committee. Ann Arbor,
  Mich., Peace Research and Edu-
  cation Project, 1964.
  84 leaves. 28cm.
  1. Peace. 2. U.S.--Pol. &
  govt.--1959-   . I. Students
  for a Democratic Society.
  Peace Research and Education
  Project.
  PPULC, PSC, NUC 66-78623,
  MiU

B146
Booth, Paul Robert.
  Peace politics, 1962. [n.p.,
  1963?]
  [5] leaves. 28cm.
  Caption title.
  Speech delivered to Delaware
  Co., Penn. Sane, Mar. 1, 1963.
  1. Peace. 2. U.S.--Pol. &
  govt.--1959-
  WHi-A

B147
Booth, Paul Robert.
  Politics and the academic com-
  munity. [n.p.] Students for a
  Democratic Society [196]
  4p. 28cm.
  Cover title.
  1. Politics, Practical.
  2. Universities and colleges.
  I. Students for a Democratic
  Society.
  WHi-A

B148
Booth, Paul Robert.
  Politics and the university
  community. [n.p.] Students

for a Democratic Society [for
the] Liberal Study Group [196]
4p. 28cm.
1. Politics, Practical. 2. Universities and colleges. I. Students for a Democratic Society.
II. Liberal Study Group.
MiU

B149
Booth, Paul Robert.
  A strategy for university reform.
  Chicago, Students for a Democratic Society [196]
  7p. 28cm.
  Cover title.
  1. Universities and colleges.
  2. Student movements. 3. Education. I. Students for a Democratic Society.
  MoU, CU-B, WHi-L

B150
Booth, Paul Robert.
  Students work to convert Amer-
  ica. Ann Arbor, Students for a
  Democratic Society [196]
  3 leaves. 28cm.
  Caption title.
  1. Students for a Democratic
  Society. Peace Research and
  Education Project. I. Students
  for a Democratic Society.
  KU-RH, WHi-A

B151
Booth, Paul Robert.
  Working papers--summer projects.
  [n.p., Students for a Democratic
  Society, 1966?]
  [9]p. 28cm.
  Caption title.
  1. Students for a Democratic
  Society. I. Students for a
  Democratic Society.
  KU-RH, WHi-A

B152
Borenstein, Linda.
  Patching up the movement; a
  first aid manual [by] Linda
  Borenstein, John Johansson
  [and] Richard Winklestern.
  [Boston, New England Free Press,
  1970?]
  8p. 28cm.

Cover title.
1. First aid in illness and in-
jury. I. Johansson, John, jt.
auth. II. Winkelstern, Richard,
jt. auth. III. New England Free
Press.
KU-RH

B153
Boskey, Jill.
  The class background and orientation of the new left; some
  questions arising from the split
  at the Liberated Guardian.
  Boston, New England Free Press
  [1970?]
  7 [1]p. 28cm.
  Caption title.
  At head of title: Toward a
  working class politics.
  1. Guardian. 2. Student movements. 3. Social classes.
  I. New England Free Press.
  MiU

Boston Committee for Nonviolent
    Action.
  see also
Committee for Nonviolent Action.

B154
Boston Committee for Nonviolent
    Action.
  Why we walk. [Boston, 196]
  folder. 22x9cm.
  1. Nonviolence.
  CU-B

B155
Boud, Seam.
  The economics of apartheid: the
  facts are a challenge to the
  conscience of America. New
  York, Students for a Democratic
  Society [196]
  6 leaves. 28cm.
  Caption title.
  Reprinted from Worldview, Aug.
  1960.
  1. South Africa--Race question.
  WHi-A

B156
Boudin, Cathy.
  A guide to the grand jury [by]
  Cathy Boudin and Brian Glick.

[Boston, New England Free Press,
1970?]
[4]p. 28cm.
Caption title.
Reprinted from Liberation, June
1969.
1. Grand jury. I. Glock, Brian,
jt. auth. II. New England Free
Press.
KU-RH

B157
Boulding, Kenneth E.
  The impact of the draft on the
  legitimacy of the national state.
  Nyack, N.Y., Fellowship Publica-
  tions. [196]
  [4]p. 28cm.
  Caption title.
  Reprinted from Fellowship, July
  1968.
  1. Military service, Compulsory.
  I. Fellowship Publications.
  KU-RH

B158
Boulding, Kenneth E.
  The peace research movement.
  [n.p., 196]
  8p. 28cm.
  Cover title.
  1. Peace.
  WHi-A

B159
Boutelle, Paul.
  Murder in Memphis: Martin Luther
  King and the future of the black
  liberation struggle, by Paul Boutelle (and others. New York,
  Merit Publishers, 1968]
  15p. 22cm.
  Cover title.
  1. Negroes--Civil rights.
  2. King, Martin Luther, 1929-
  1968. I. Merit Publishers.
  KU-RH, WHi-L, MoU, MiU

B160
Bowman, Joan.
  Report from SNCC field secretary: the freedom ballot for
  governor. Jackson, Miss., 1963.
  5 leaves. 28cm.
  Caption title

1. Mississippi--Race question.
2. Mississippi--Pol. & govt.
3. Negroes--Mississippi.
I. Student Nonviolent Coordinating Committee.
CU-B

B161
Bowman, Le Roy Edward, 1887-
  Youth and delinquency in an in-
  adequate society: a League for
  Industrial Democracy statement.
  New York, League for Industrial
  Democracy [1960]
  47p. 22cm.
  1. Juvenile delinquency.
  I. League for Industrial Demo-
  cracy.
  WHi-A, OrU, IU, MiU, CU, NNU-T,
  CtY, DLC 60-4476

B162
Boyte, Harry.
  Poor whites: on the move [by]
  Harry [and Richard Landerman]
  Nashville, Southern Student
  Organizing Committee [196]
  3 [1]p. 28cm.
  Cover title.
  1. Labor and laboring classess--
  Durham, N.C. 2. Poor--Durham,
  N.C. I. Landerman, Richard,
  jt. auth. II. Southern Student
  Organizing Committee.
  KU-RH, CU-B

B163
Braden, Anne, 1924-
  Civil liberties and free speech
  as essential weapons in the
  struggle for civil rights. A
  discussion paper for considera-
  tion by the Civil Liberties
  Workshop at the Conference of
  Student Nonviolent Coordinating
  Committee in Atlanta, April 27-
  29, 1962. Prepared by Anne and
  Carl Braden. [n.p., 1962]
  11 leaves. 28cm.
  Caption title.
  1. Negroes--Civil rights.
  I. Student Nonviolent Coordina-
  ting Committee.
  II. Braden, Carl, jt. auth.
  MiU

B164
Braden, Anne, 1924-
  House Un-American Activities
  Committee: bulwark of segrega-
  tion. [Los Angeles, National
  Committee to Abolish the House
  Un-American Activities Committee,
  1963?]
  49p. illus. 22cm.
  1. Negroes--Segregation. 2. U.S.
  Congress. Committee on Un-Ameri-
  can Activities. I. National Com-
  mittee to Abolish the House Un-
  American Activities Committee.
  MiU, WHi-L, KU-RH

B165
Braden, Anne, 1924-
  Is there a significant place for
  the white southerner in the integration struggle? (A discussion paper for consideration of
  Student Conference at Chapel
  Hill, N.C., May 4, 1962. Prepared by Anne and Carl Braden)
  [n.p., Southern Conference Educational Fund? 1962?]
  [9] leaves. 28cm.
  Caption title.
  1. Southern states--Race question. 2. Negroes--Civil rights.
  I. Southern Conference Educational Fund.
  WHi-A

B166
Braden, Anne, 1924-
  Lessons of Louisville; a white
  community response to black
  rebellion. [Louisville, Ky.,
  Southern Conference Educational
  Fund, 1970?]
  23p. illus. 28cm.
  Cover title.
  1. Negroes--Louisville.
  2. Louisville--Race question.
  I. Southern Conference Educa-
  tional Fund.
  KU-RH, WHi-L

B167
Braden, Carl.
  How the inquisition affects you.
  How legislative inquisitions
  stifle integration and social
  progress. [New Orleans, South-

ern Conference Educational Fund,
1961]
20p.
Cover title.
1. U.S. Congress. Committee
on Un-American Activities.
2. Negroes--Segregation.
I. Southern Conference Educational Fund.
WHi-L

B168
Brainwashing and women: the psychological attack [by a Redstockings sister. New York,
  Redstockings, 196]
  4p. 28cm.
  Caption title.
  1. Woman. I. Redstockings of
  the Women's Liberation Movement.
  MoU

B169
Brandon, Peter.
  A brief history of Duke employees local 77, AFSCME, AFL-CIO,
  by Peter Brandon and Nancy
  Park. Nashville, Tenn., Southern Student Organizing Committee [1966?]
  5p. 28cm.
  1. Duke University, Durham,
  N.C. 2. Labor and laboring
  classes--Duke University,
  Durham, N.C. I. Park, Nancy,
  jt. auth. I. Southern Student
  Organizing Committee.
  WHi-L, MoU

B170
Brant, Irving.
  Congressional investigations
  and bills of attainder. [New
  Yorl] Emergency Civil Liberties
  Committee [1959?]
  14p. 22cm.
  Cover title.
  1. U.S. Congress. House.
  Committee on Un-American Acti-
  vities. I. Emergency Civil
  Liberties Committee.
  MiU, WHi-L, KU-RH

B171
Bras, Jaun Mari.
  The new struggle for Puerto

Rico's independence. Boston,
New England Free Press [1970?]
7p. 28cm.
Cover title.
Transcript of a speech delivered
at Harvard, April 1969.
1. Puerto Rico--Relations (general) with the U.S. 2. Puerto
Rico--Pol. & govt. I. New England Free Press.
KU-RH, MiU

B172
Bravo, Douglas.
   Douglas Bravo speaks: interview
with Venezuelan guerrilla lead-
er [includes a speech by Fidel
Castro. New York, Pathfinder
Press, 1970]
23p.
Cover title.
1. Cuba--Pol. & govt. 2. Vene-
zuela--Pol. & govt. I. Castro,
Fidel, 1927-   . II. Pathfinder
Press.
MiU

B173
Brecher, Jeremy.
   An economic crisis plan. [n.p.,
1965]
2p. 28cm.
Caption title.
At head of title: "1965 SDS
National Convention--working
paper."
1. U.S.--Econ. condit. 2. Economics. I. Students for a Democratic Society. National Convention, 1965.
WHi-A, KU-RH

B174
Brecher, Jeremy.
   On west coast organizing. [n.p.
1964?]
[4]p. 28cm.
Caption title.
1. Students for a Democratic
Society. 2. Student movements--
The West.
WHi-A

B175
Brecher, Jeremy.
   SDS foreign policy. [n.p.,

1965]
3p. 28cm.
Caption title.
At head of title: "1965 SDS
National Convention--working
paper."
1. U.S.--Foreign policy.
2. Underdeveloped areas.
3. Students for a Democratic
Society. I. Students for a
Democratic Society. National
Convention, 1965.
KU-RH, WHi-A

B176
Brecher, Jeremy.
   To radical politics '66. [n.p.,
Students for a Democratic Society? 196]
[2]p. 28cm.
Caption title.
1. U.S.--Pol. & govt.--1963-
  . 2. Radicalism. I. Students for a Democratic Society.
CU-B

B177
Breines, Paul.
   Would you believe? An introductory critique of the true
believer, by Paul Breines; and
Eric Hoffer and cold war ideology, by Peter Wiley. Ann
Arbor, Radical Education Project [196]
10p. illus. 22cm.
Cover title.
1. Hoffer, Eric. The true
believer. I. Wiley, Peter, jt.
auth. II. Radical Education
Project.
KU-RH

B178
Breines, Paul.
   Would you believe? An introductory critique of the true
believer, by Paul Breines; and
Eric Hoffer and cold war ideology, by Peter Wiley. Madison,
Wis., Madison Students for a
Democratic Society [196]
14p. 22cm.
Cover title.
1. Hoffer, Eric. The true
believer. I. Wiley, Peter, jt.

auth. I. Students for a Democratic Society, Madison, Wis.
KU-RH

B179
Breitbart, Vicki.
  Child care--who cares? Boston,
  Distributed by Female Liberation
  [1970?]
  7p. 28cm.
  Cover title.
  1. Children--Care and hygiene.
  2. Day nurseries. I. Female
  Liberation.
  KU-RH

B180
Breitbart, Vicki.
  Day care, who cares? Corporate
  and government child care plans.
  Boston, New England Free Press
  [1970?]
  [8]p. illus. 28cm.
  Cover title.
  1. Children--Care and hygiene.
  2. Day nurseries. I. New England Free Press.
  MiU

B181
Breitbart, Vicki.
  Day care who cares? Corporate
  and government child care plans.
  [Detroit, Radical Education Pro-
  ject, 1970?]
  7p. illus. 28cm.
  Cover title.
  Reprinted from Leviathan.
  1. Children--Care and hygiene.
  2. Woman--Rights of women.
  3. Day nurseries. I. Radical
  Education Project.
  WHi-L, KU-RH

B182
Breitman, George.
  Anti-negro prejudice; when it
  began, when it will end. [New
  York] Pioneer Publishers [1960]
  10p. 22cm.
  Cover title.
  Reprinted from Fourth Interna-
  tional, Sept. 1954.
  1. Negroes--Civil rights.
  I. Pioneer Publishers.
  MiU

B183
Breitman, George.
  The assassination of Malcolm X
  [by] George Breitman [and] Her-
  man Porter. [New York, Merit
  Publishers, 1969]
  31p. 22cm.
  Cover title.
  1. Little, Malcolm, 1925-1965.
  I. Merit Publishers. II. Por-
  ter, Herman, jt. auth.
  CU-B, MiU, KU-RH

B184
Breitman, George.
  Black nationalism and social-
  ism, by George Breitman [and]
  George Novack. [New York, Merit
  Publishers, 1969]
  31p. 22cm.
  Cover title.
  1. Little, Malcolm, 1925-1965.
  2. Negroes--Politics and suf-
  frage. 3. Socialism. I. Nov-
  ack, George Edward, jt. auth.
  II. Merit Publishers.
  KU-RH, KMK, WHi-L

B185
Breitman, George.
  How a minority can change society. [New York] Young Socialist Forum [196]
  27p.
  1. Negroes--Civil rights.
  2. Socialism. I. Young Socialist Forum.
  MiU

B186
Breitman, George.
  How a minority can change society. 2d. ed. [New York, Merit
  Publishers, 1966]
  24p.
  1. Negroes--Civil rights.
  2. Socialsim. I. Merit Publishers.
  WHi-L

B187
Breitman, George.
  How a minority can change soci-
  ety; the real potential of the
  Afro-American struggle [speech
  given in January 1964 at Mid-

west Educational Conference of
the Young Socialist Alliance in
Chicago. New York, Merit Publishers, 1968]
30p. illus. 21cm.
Cover title.
1. Negroes--Civil rights.
2. Socialism. I. Young Socialist Alliance. II. Merit Publishers.
KMK, CSt-H, NUC 70-68446

B188
Breitman, George.
  Malcolm X; the man and his ideas.
  New York, Merit Publishers, 1965.
  22p. 22cm.
  1. Little, Malcolm, 1925-1965.
  I. Merit Publishers.
  WHi-L, MU, NUC 70-4619

B189
Breitman, George.
  Malcolm X; the man and his ideas.
  [New York, Merit Publishers,
  1967]
  22p. 21cm.
  Cover title.
  1. Little, Malcolm, 1925-1965.
  I. Merit Publishers.
  CU-B

B190
Breitman, George.
  Malcolm X; the man and his ideas.
  [New York, Pathfinder Press,
  1970]
  22p. 22cm. (A Merit pamphlet)
  Cover title.
  1. Little, Malcolm, 1925-1965.
  I. Pathfinder Press.
  MiU, KU-RH

B191
Brewer, Tom.
  A call for creation of an American radical socialist party.
  [San Francisco, 196]
  2p. 36cm.
  Caption title.
  1. Socialism. 2. U.S.--Foreign
  policy. 3. Negroes--Civil
  rights.
  KU-RH

B192
Brewer, Tom.
  The non-violence of anger: a
  revolutionary political tactic
  for the United States in the
  twentieth century. [San Francisco, 196]
  8p. 36cm.
  Caption title.
  1. Williams, Robert Franklin,
  1925-   . 2. U.S.--Military
  policy. 3. Socialism.
  4. Peace.
  KU-RH

B193
Brick, Allan.
  The campus protest against
  ROTC. [Nashville, Tenn.,
  Southern Student Organizing
  Committee, 196]
  18p. 28cm.
  Cover title.
  1. Student movements. 2. U.S.
  Army. Reserve Officers Train-
  ing Corps. I. Southern Student
  Organizing Committee.
  MoU

B194
Brick, Allan.
  The campus protest against
  ROTC. Philadelphia [American
  Friends Service Committee,
  Peace Education Division, 1960?]
  Cover title.
  1. Student movements. I. U.S.
  Army. Reserve Officers' Train-
  ing Corps. I. Friends, Society
  of. American Friends Service
  Committee.
  WHi-L

B195
Brick, Allan.
  Repeal the draft: but how?
  [Washington, National Council
  to Repeal the Draft, 1969?]
  [2]p. 28cm.
  Caption title.
  Reprinted from Fellowship Magazine, May 1969.
  1. Military service, Compulsory. I. National Council to

Repeal the Draft.
KU-RH

B196
Brick, Allan
What is nonviolence today. [n.
p., 196]
5p. 28cm.
Caption title.
At head of title: Report on the
Catonsville nine.
1. Catonsville (Md.) Nine.
2. Government, Resistance to.
3. Nonviolence.
MoU

B197
Brinton, Howard Haines, 1884-
Guide to Quaker practice. Wallingford, Pa., Pendle Hill
[1955]
64p. 20cm. (Pendle Hill pamphlets no. 20)
1. Friends, Society of--Govern-
ment. I. Pendle Hill.
DLC 55-11311

B198
Brinton, Howard Haines, 1884-
The peace testimony of the
Society of Friends. [Philadel-
phia] American Friends Service
Committee [1958]
15p.
1. Friends, Society of. American Friends Service Committee.
2. Peace.
CtY

B199
Brinton, Howard Haines, 1884-
Quakerism and other religions.
Wallingford, Pa., Pendle Hill
[1957]
40p. 19cm. (Pendle Hill pam-
phlet, no. 93)
1. Friends, Society of.
I. Pendle Hill.
NcD, MiU, CtY, CU, DLC 57-10748

B200
Bristol, James E., 1912-
About meditation. [Philadelphia,
American Friends Service Commit-
tee, 1963?]
15p. 21x11cm.

1. Meditation. I. Friends,
Society of. American Friends
Service Committee.
NIC

B201
Bristol, James E., 1912-
James E. Bristol speaks on non-
violence as a positive concept.
[Philadelphia, American Friends
Service Committee, Peace Educa-
tion Division, 1963]
11p. 23x10cm.
1. Pacifism. 2. Nonviolence.
I. Friends, Society of. Ameri-
can Friends Service Committee.
MoU, KU-RH, NNC-L, NUC 66-89309

B202
Bristol, James E., 1912-
Our own worst enemies. [Nyack,
N.Y., Fellowship of Reconcilia-
tion, 196]
7p. 11cm.
Caption title.
1. Fellowship of Reconciliation.
KU-RH

B203
Bristol, James E., 1912-
Primer on pacificism. Phila-
delphia, Peace Education Divi-
sion, American Friends Service
Committee, 1966.
[8]p. 20cm.
Cover title.
1. Pacifism. I. Friends,
Society of. American Friends
Service Committee.
KU-RH

B204
Bristol, James E., 1912-
Stand fast in liberty. [Wal-
lingford, Pa., Pendle Hill,
1961]
24p. 20cm. (Pendle Hill pamphlet 119)
1. Anti-communist movements.
2. Liberty. I. Pendle Hill.
DLC 61-18784

B205
Bristol, William.
Let's talk about Cuba; Cuba and
the United States. [Philadel-

phia, Pa.] American Friends Service Committee, 1963.
33p.   22cm.
1. Cuba--For. rel.--U.S.
2. U.S.--For. rel.--Cuba.
I. Friends, Society of.   American Friends Service Committee.
CSt-H, NUC 68-82715

B206
Bromley, Dorothy Dunbar, comp.
 Eugene J. McCarthy on the re-
 cord, excerpts from his writings
 and speeches.   [1st ed.] Com-
 piled by Dorothy Dunbar Bromley
 and Ruth Gage-Colby.   New York,
 Coalition for a Democratic Al-
 ternative [c1968]
 36p.
 I. McCarthy, Eugene J., 1916-
   .   II. Gage-Colby, Ruth.
 III. Coalition for a Democratic
 Alternative.
 WHi-L

B207
Bronston, William.
 A treatise on reformation: the
 student health movement, by
 William Bronston and Michael
 McGarvey.   Ann Arbor, Conference
 on Radicals in the Professions,
 1967.
 9p.   28cm.
 Cover title.
 1. Student movements.   2. Medical care.   I. McGarvey, Michael,
 jt. auth.   II. Conference on
 Radicals in the Professions.
 MiU-H

B208
Brookes, Edgar Harry.
 America in travail.   [Walling-
 ford, Pa., Pendle Hill, 1968]
 24p.   (Pendle Hill pamphlet
 159)
 Cover title.
 1. Negroes--Civil rights.
 I. Pendle Hill.
 WHi-L

B209
Brooks, Thomas R.
 Are demonstrations self-defeat-
 ing?   [New York, CORE, 1962]

3p.   28cm.
 Caption title.
 1. Negroes--Civil rights.
 2. Demonstrations.   I. Congress
 of Racial Equality.
 CU-B

B210
Brooks, Thomas R.
 Black builders: a job program
 that works; the story of the
 Joint Apprenticeship Program
 of the Workers Defense League
 and the A. Philip Randolph Education Fund.   [New York, League
 for Industrial Democracy, 1970]
 56p.   illus.
 1. Randolph (A. Philip) Educational Fund.   2. Workers Defense League.   3. Negroes--Em-
 ployment.   I. League for Industrial Democracy.
 NNU-T

B211
Brooks, Thomas R.
 To build a new world; a brief
 history of American labor.   New
 York, League for Industrial
 Democracy, 1965.
 30p.   22cm.
 1. Labor and laboring classes--
 History.   I. League for Indus-
 trial Democracy.
 CSt-H, NNU-T, KU-RH,
 NUC 66-80156

B212
Brooks, Thomas R.
 Tragedy at Ocean Hill; teachers,
 community, children.   New York,
 League for Industrial Democra-
 cy [1969]
 [13]p.   22cm.   (Looking forward
 no. 13)
 Cover title.
 1. Education--New York (State)
 --New York (City).   2. New York
 (City)--Public schools.
 I. League of Industrial Demo-
 cracy.
 NNU-T

B213
Brown, Connie.
 Cambridge, Maryland: a case

study. [n.p., 1963?]
14p. 28cm.
Caption title.
1. Poor--Cambridge, Md.
2. Negroes--Cambridge, Md.
3. Cambridge, Md.--Race question.
WHi-A

B214
Brown, George E.
  For an all-volunteer military.
[Washington, National Council to
Repeal the Draft, C1969]
[3]p. illus. 28cm.
Caption title.
1. Military service, Compulsory.
I. National Council to Repeal
the Draft.
KU-RH

B215
Brown, H. Rap.
  Who are the real outlaws. [San
Francisco, Independent Action
Movement, 1967]
[4]p. 22cm.
Cover title.
1. Law enforcement. 2. Negroes
--Civil rights. I. Independent
Action Movement.
CU-B

B216
Brown, Ray.
  Our crisis economy. Rev. ed.
New York, Students for a Democratic Society [1964]
9p.
Cover title.
1. U.S.--Econ. condit.
2. Automation. I. Students for
a Democratic Society.
WHi-L, WHi-A

B217
Brown, Ray.
  Our crisis economy: the end of
the boom. [n.p., Students for
a Democratic Society? 196]
5p. 28cm.
Caption title.
1. U.S.--Econ. condit. I. Students for a Democratic Society.
WHi-A

B218
Brown, Ray.
  Our crisis economy: the end of
the boom. New York, Students
for a Democratic Society and
its Economic Research and Action
Project [196]
[5]p. 28cm.
Cover title.
1. U.S.--Econ. condit. I. Stu-
dents for a Democratic Society.
Economic Research and Action
Project.
KU-RH, MiU

B219
Brown, Ray.
  Our economic crisis. Chicago,
Students for a Democratic
Society [1964?]
12p. 22cm.
Cover title.
Revised edition.
1. U.S.--Econ. condit.
2. Automation. I. Students for
a Democratic Society.
KU-RH, WHi-L

B220
Brown, Rita Mae.
  Coitus interrupts. [n.p., Gay
Women's Liberation, 196]
3 leaves. 28cm.
Cover title.
1. Homosexuality. I. Gay
Women's Liberation.
CU-B

B221
Brown, Robert McAfee, 1920-
  The freedom riders: a clergy-
man's view. The freedom
riders: an historian's view, by
Frank Randall. [New York, Con-
gress of Racial Equality,
1961?]
[12]p. illus. 22cm.
Reprinted from Amherst College
Alumni News.
1. Negroes--Civil rights.
I. Randall, Frank, jt. auth.
II. Congress of Racial Equal-
ity.
WHi-A, CU-B, NUC 63-25999

B222
Brown, Robert McAfee.
  Two declarations on the draft
  [by] Robert McAfee Brown [and
  William Sloane Coffin. New York,
  Clergy and Laymen Concerned
  About Vietnam, 196]
  [4]p. 28cm.
  Caption title.
  1. Military service, Compulsory.
  I. Clergy and Laymen Concerned
  About Vietnam. II. Coffin, Wil-
  liam Sloane.
  KU-RH

B223
Browne, Robert S.
  The civil war in Vietnam. [New
  York, Turn Toward Peace, 196]
  [4]p. 28cm.
  Caption title.
  1. Vietnamese conflict, 1961-
  1975. I. Turn Toward Peace.
  WHi-A

B224
Browne, Robert S.
  Should the U.S. be partitioned
  into two separate and indepen-
  dent nations--one a homeland for
  black Americans. A symposium by
  Robert S. Browne and Robert
  Vernon. [New York, 1968]
  30p. 21cm.
  Cover title.
  1. Black nationalism. I. Ver-
  non, Robert, jt. auth.
  II. Merit Publishers.
  MiU, WHi-L, MoU, KU-RH

B225
Browning, Frank.
  From rumble to revolution: the
  Young Lords. [Ithaca, N.Y.,
  Glad Day Press, 1970?]
  7p. illus. 28cm.
  Caption title.
  Reprinted from Ramparts, Oct.
  1970.
  1. Puerto Ricans in the U.S.
  2. Young Lords. I. Glad Day
  Press.
  NNU-T

B226
Bruland, Mike.

Mississippi economics and
Mississippi's "new image"? Prepared for the Freedom Democratic Party by Mike Bruland.
Nashville, Southern Student Organizing Committee [196]
7 [1]p. 28cm.
Cover title.
1. Mississippi--Econ. condit.
2. Poor--Mississippi. 3. Ne-
groes--Mississippi. I. Mississippi Freedom Democratic Party.
II. Southern Student Organizing
Committee.
MiU

B227
Buch, Peter.
  Burning issues of the mideast
  crisis. [New York, Merit Publishers, 196]
  29p. 22cm.
  Cover title.
  1. Israel-Arab War, 1967-
  2. Near East--Pol. & govt.
  I. Merit Publishers.
  MiU, KU-RH

B228
Buchanan, Keith.
  The third world--its emergence
  and contours. Ann Arbor, Radi-
  cal Education Project [196]
  18p. 22cm.
  Cover title.
  1. Underdeveloped areas.
  I. Radical Education Project.
  CU-B

B229
Buck, Tim.
  Canada and the Russian Revolution; the impact of the world's
  first socialist revolution on
  labor and politics in Canada.
  Toronto, Progress Books, 1967.
  98p. 21cm.
  1. Labor and laboring classes--
  Canada. 2. Russia--History--
  Revolution, 1917-1921--Influ-
  ences. 3. Communism. I. Progress Books.
  ViU, WHi-L, InU, DeU, ICU,
  DLC 68-96912

B230
Buck, Tim.
Canada in the world crisis.
[Toronto, Progress Books, 1958]
29p. 20cm.
1. Canada--For. rel. 2. Labor-
Progressive Party (Canada)
I. Progress Books.
CaBVaU

B231
Buck, Tim.
Neutrality now; Canada can stay
out of war. [Toronto, Published
for the Communist Party of Canada by Progress Books, 1960]
21p.
Cover title.
1. Peace. 2. Canada--For. rel.
I. Progress Books.
CaOTU, NUC 64-6333

B232
Buck, Tim.
1917-1957, forty years of great
change; Canada and the great
Russian Revolution. [Toronto,
Progress Books, 1957]
44p.
Cover title.
1. Russia--History--Revolution,
1917-1921--Influences. 2. Com-
munism--Canada. I. Progress
Books.
CaOTU, NUC 63-7311

B233
Buck, Tim.
Power; the key to the future.
[Toronto, Published for the Com-
munist Party by Progress Books,
1963]
23p.
Cover title.
1. Power resources--Canada.
I. Progress Books.
CaOTU, NUC 65-53765

B234
Buck, Tim.
Put monopoly under control; a
new economic policy for Canada.
Toronto, Progress Books, 1964.
78p. 21cm.
1. Canada--Economic policy.

I. Progress Books.
CtY, CaOTU, DLC 66-44136

B235
Buck, Tim.
Victory through unity; report
to the constituent convention
of the Labor-Progressive Party.
[Toronto, Eveready Printers,
196]
64p.
1. Labor-Progressive Party
(Canada). 2. Socialism in
Canada.
MiEM, NUC 67-6656

B236
Buck, Tim.
Vietnam: eyewitness report, by
Tim Buck, Rae Murphy and Maurice Rush. [Toronto, Communist
Party of Canada, 1966]
19p. illus.
1. Vietnamese conflict, 1961-
1975. I. Communist Party of
Canada. II. Murphy, Rae, jt.
auth. III. Rush, Maurice, jt.
auth.
MH, NUC 68-81934

B237
Buckley, Neil.
Burning questions of our movement, a position paper for the
1965 SDS National Convention.
[n.p., 1968]
10p. 36cm.
Caption title.
1. Students for a Democratic
Society.
WHi-L

B238
Buddeberg, Manfred.
The new left in Germany and
Japan [by Manfred Buddeberg and
Ken Cloke] Nashville, Southern
Student Organizing Committee
[196]
20p. 28cm.
Cover title.
Reprinted from International
Socialism and New Left Notes.
1. Student movements--Germany.
2. Student movements--Japan.

I. Cloke, Ken, jt. auth.
II. Southern Student Organizing
Committee.
MoU

B239
Budish, Jacob M., 1886-
  The changing structure of the
  working class. In collaboration
  with Labor Research Association.
  New York, International Publish-
  ers [1962]
  64p. 20cm.
  1. Labor and laboring classes.
  I. International Publishers.
  II. Labor Research Association.
  DLC 62-16301

B240
Budish, Jacob M., 1886-
  People's capitalism; stock ownership and production. In collaboration with Labor Research
  Association. New York, International Publishers [1958]
  64p. 21cm.
  1. Capitalism. 2. Stock ownership. I. International Publishers. II. Labor Research Association.
  KU-J, OkU, MH-BA, CSt, ViU,
  DLC 59-284

B241
Bulganin, Nikolai Aleksandrovich,
  1895-
  Visit to Burma and Afganistan;
  speeches and interviews by N.A.
  Bulganin and N.S. Khrushchev together with text of joint Sov-
  iet-Burmese and Soviet-Afghan
  statements, communiques and
  treaties. [New York, New Century Publishers, 1956]
  46p.
  Cover title.
  1. Russia--For. rel.--Afghani-
  stan. 2. Russia--For. rel.--
  Burma. I. Khrushchev, Nikita
  Sergeevich, 1894- . jt.
  auth. I. New Century Publishers.
  KU-J

B242
Bulganin, Nikolai Aleksandrovich,
  1895-

Visit to India; speeches and
interviews by N.A. Bulganin and
N.S. Khrushchev together with
text of joint Soviet-Indian
statements and communiques.
New York, New Century Publishers [1956]
48p.
1. Russia--For. rel.--India.
I. Khrushchev, Nikita Sergeevich, 1894- , jt. auth.
II. New Century Publishers.
UU, NcD

B243
Bull, Jenny.
  High school women: oppression
  & liberation. Boston, Published for Resist by New England
  Free Press [1970?]
  5p. illus. 28cm.
  Reprinted from Women: A Journal
  of Liberation, 1970.
  1. Woman--Rights of women.
  2. High schools. 3. Education
  of women. I. New England Free
  Press. II. Resist.
  KU-RH

B244
Bundy, Jim.
  Philadelphia project closes.
  [n.p., Students for a Democratic Society, Economic Research
  and Action Project? 196]
  [2]p. 28cm.
  Caption title.
  1. Poor--Philadelphia.
  2. Philadelphia--Econ. condit.
  3. Student movements--Philadel-
  phia. I. Students for a Democratic Society. Economic Research and Action Project.
  KU-RH

B245
Bunnell, Fred.
  A unifying theme [by Fred Bun-
  nell and Cliff Humphrey. Al-
  bany, Calif., Peace and Freedom
  Party Ecology Action, 196]
  3 leaves. 28cm.
  1. Environmental policy.
  I. Humphrey, Cliff, jt. auth.
  II. Peace and Freedom Party
  Ecology Action.
  CU-B

B246
Burchett, Wilfred.
From chapter 1 of Again Korea?
Chicago, Distributed by Students
for a Democratic Society [196]
2p. 28cm.
Caption title.
1. Korea (Democratic People's
Republic, 1948-   ) 2. Japan--
For. rel.--Korea (Democratic
People's Republic, 1948-   )
3. U.S.--For. rel.--Korea (Demo-
cratic People's Republic,
1948-   ) I. Students for a
Democratic Society.
KU-RH

B247
Burchett, Wilfred.
Who controls Vietnam? [Chicago,
Students for a Democratic Soc-
iety] 1968.
[3] 9p. 22cm.
Reprinted from Guardian.
1. Vietnamese conflict, 1961-
1975. I. Students for a Democratic Society.
CU-B, WHi-L

B248
Burchill, Charles S.
Chinese aggression, myth or
menace? [Nashville] Southern
Student Organizing Committee
[1966?]
11p.
Cover title.
1. China (People's Republic of
China, 1949-   )--Foreign
policy. 2. United Nations.
I. Southern Student Organizing
Committee.
WHi-L

B249
Burchill, Charles S.
Chinese aggression; myth or
menace? Vancouver, the Study
Group on China Policy [196]
8p. 28cm.
Cover title.
Distributed by Radical Education
Project.
1. China (People's Republic of
China, 1949-   )--Foreign

policy. I. Study Group on China
Policy. II. Radical Education
Project.
WHi-A, KU-RH

B250
Burlage, Robb K.
The American planned economy:
a critique. New York, Students
for a Democratic Society and its
Economic Research and Action
Project [196]
8p. 28cm.
Cover title.
1. U.S.--Econ. condit. 2. Economics. I. Students for a Democratic Society. Economic Research and Action Project.
CU-B, MiU, WHi-L, KU-RH

B251
Burlage, Robb K.
A brief, critical bibliography
for the beginning to understand
the south. Columbus, O., Students for a Democratic Society
for the Liberal Study Group,
1962.
4p. 28cm.
Caption title.
1. Southern States--Bibl.
I. Students for a Democratic
Society. II. Liberal Study
Group.
KU-RH

B252
Burlage, Robb K.
For Dixie with love and squalor;
prospectus and introduction for
an SDS pamphlet. New York,
Students for a Democratic Society [196]
27p. 28cm.
Cover title.
1. Southern States--Race question. 2. Southern States--
Pol. & govt. 3. Negroes--Civil
rights. I. Students for a Democratic Society.
WHi-A

B253
Burlage, Robb K.
Johnson with eyes open, by Robb
Burlage, edited by Douglas

Ireland and the PEP staff. New
York, Political Education Pro-
ject [196]
18 [2]p. 28cm.
Cover title.
1. Johnson, Lyndon Baines, Pres.,
U.S., 1908-1973. 2. U.S.--Pol.
& govt.--1963-1968. I. Ireland,
Douglas, ed. II. Students for a
Democratic Society. Political
Education Project.
KU-RH, MiU

B254
Burlage, Robb K.
  The New York City affiliation
  plan; a case study of public
  entrepreneurship. Prepared for
  May 3, 1966 session of the Semi-
  nar on Health Policy, Institute
  for Policy Studies. Washington,
  Institute for Policy Studies
  [1966]
  17 leaves. 28cm.
  Caption title.
  1. Hygiene, Public--New York
  (City) 2. New York (City)--
  Hospitals. I. Institute for
  Policy Studies.
  NIC, NUC 69-24513

B255
Burlage, Robb K.
  The south as an underdeveloped
  country. [n.p.] Distributed by
  Students for a Democratic Soc-
  iety for the Liberal Study Group
  [1962]
  8p. 28cm.
  Cover title.
  1. Southern States--Econ. condit.
  I. Students for a Democratic
  Society. II. Liberal Study
  Group.
  WHi-A, MiU

B256
Burlage, Robb K.
  The south as an underdeveloped
  country. [n.p., Students for a
  Democratic Society? 196]
  8p. 28cm. (Working paper no. 6)
  Caption title.
  1. Southern States--Econ. condit.
  I. Students for a Democratic

Society.
WHi-A

B257
Burlage, Robb K.
  The south as an underdeveloped
  country. Nashville, Southern
  Student Organizing Committee
  [196]
  8p. 28cm.
  1. Southern States--Econ.
  condit. I. Southern Student
  Organizing Committee.
  MiU

B258
Burlage, Robb K.
  The south as an underdeveloped
  country. New York, Students
  for a Democratic Society [196]
  8p. 28cm.
  Cover title.
  1. Negroes--Civil rights.
  2. Southern States--Econ.
  condit. I. Students for a
  Democratic Society.
  MiU, CU-B, WHi-L

B259
Burlage, Robb K.
  This is war? An analysis of
  the war on poverty with special
  emphasis on Appalachia. New
  York, Students for a Democratic
  Society [196]
  22 [2]p. illus. 22cm.
  1. Poverty. 2. U.S. Office of
  Economic Opportunity. 3. Ap-
  palachian Mountains--Econ.
  condit. I. Students for a
  Democratic Society.
  MiU, WHi-A

B260
Burlage, Robb K.
  This is war? Nashville, South-
  ern Student Organizing Commit-
  tee [196]
  18p. 28cm.
  Cover title.
  1. Poverty. 2. U.S. Office of
  Economic Opportunity.
  I. Southern Student Organizing
  Committee.
  MoU

B261
Burlage, Robb K.
  This is war? Poverty in America
  with a study of Appalachia. New
  York, Students for a Democratic
  Society and its Economic Research
  and Action Project [1964?]
  22p.
  Cover title.
  1. Poverty. 2. U.S. Office of
  Economic Opportunity. 3. Appala-
  chian Mountains--Econ. condit.
  I. Students for a Democratic
  Society. Economic Research and
  Action Project.
  WHi-L

B262
Burlage, Robb K.
  The war on poverty; this is war?
  [Montreal, Our Generation, 196]
  18p. 28cm.
  Caption title.
  1. Poverty. 2. U.S. Office of
  Economic Opportunity. I. Our
  Generation.
  NNU-T

B263
Burnett, James T.
  Vietnam as opportunity. Prepared by James T. Burnett after
  discussions with Robert Pickus
  and Alex Garber. [Berkeley,
  World Without War Council, Policy Proposal Service, 1966]
  2p. 28cm.
  Caption title.
  1. Vietnamese conflict, 1961-
  1975. I. World Without War
  Council. II. Pickus, Robert.
  III. Garber, Alex.
  CU-B

B264
Burnham, Louis.
  Behind the lynching of Emmet
  Louis Till. [New York, Freedom
  Associates, 1955]
  15p.
  Cover title.
  1. Till, Emmet Louis.
  2. Mississippi--Race question.
  I. Freedom Associates.
  MiU, KU-J, WHi-L

B265
Burns, Emile, 1889-
  What is Marxism? New York, In-
  ternational Publishers [1957]
  91p. 21cm.
  1. Socialism. 2. Communism.
  I. Marx, Karl, 1818-1883.
  II. International Publishers.
  MoU, WU, NN, MiU, DLC 57-14973

B266
Burnstein, Malcolm S.
  The Un-American committee in
  San Francisco. [n.p., National
  Student Committee for Civil
  Liberties, 196]
  [16]p. 21cm.
  Caption title.
  Reprinted from New University
  Thought.
  1. Internal security. 2. U.S.
  Congress. House. Committee on
  Un-American Activities. I. Nat-
  ional Student Committee for
  Civil Liberties.
  KU-RH, MiU

B267
Burris, Barbara.
  What is women's liberation?
  [Seattle? Radical Women?] 1969.
  4p. 28cm.
  Cover title.
  1. Woman--Rights of women.
  I. Radical Women.
  WHi-L

B268
Burros, Robert Joseph.
  Horror of the future; an essay
  and three novelets viewing the
  terrible possibilities of nuclear tests and use of atomic
  weapons. [New York, Banner-
  Social Press, 1959]
  34p. 23cm. (Banner Social
  book)
  Cover title.
  1. Atomic weapons and disarmament.
  IEN, KU-J

B269
Burt, Eric.
  Eyes on Washington. A program

for people's legislation; what
labor and the people can do to
influence Congress in 1956.
[New York, New Century Publishers, 1955]
15p. 19cm.
Cover title.
1. U.S. 84th Cong., 2d. sess.
1956. 2. Taxation. 3. Rayburn,
Sam Tallaferro, 1882-196 .
4. Johnson, Lyndon Baines, Pres.,
U.S., 1908-1973. I. New Century
Publishers.
KU-J, B753

B270
Burton, Bernard.
  How to keep your job. [New York,
  New Century Publishers, 1955]
  15p. 19cm.
  Cover title.
  1. U.S.--Econ. condit. 2. Depressions. 3. War--Economic
  aspects. I. New Century Publishers.
  MiU, KU-J

B271
Business Executives Move for
  Vietnam Peace.
  Ten myths about Vietnam. [Des
  Moines, American Friends Ser-
  vice Committee, 1970]
  folder. 22x8cm.

Cover title.
1. Vietnamese conflict, 1961-
1975. I. Friends, Society of.
American Friends Service Committee.
KU-RH

B272
The bust book. [New York, Legal
    Rap; distributed by New York
    Regional S.D.S. and other or-
    ganizations, 1969]
    73p. illus.
    Cover title.
    1. Arrest (Police methods).
    2. Criminal procedure. 3. Pol-
    itical prisoners. I. Students
    for a Democratic Society, New
    York Regional.
    MoSW, WHi-L, NUC 70-9475

B273
Butler, Willis P.
    Cuba's revolutionary medicine.
    [Boston, New England Free
    Press, 196]
    [4]p. 28cm.
    Caption title.
    Reprinted from Ramparts.
    1. Medical care--Cuba.
    I. New England Free Press.
    KU-RH

C

CADRE
  see
Chicago Area Draft Resisters.

CORE
  see
Congress of Racial Equality

C1
CORE goes slumming. [New York,
    CORE, 196]
    [4]p. 28cm.
    Caption title.
    1. Negroes--Housing. I. Con-

gress of Racial Equality.
CU-B

C2
Cabral, Amilcar.
    The struggle in Guinea. [Cam-
    bridge, Africa Research Group,
    1969?]
    [429]-445p. 22cm.
    Cover title.
    Reprinted from International
    Socialist Journal.
    1. Guinea, Portuguese--Pol. &
    govt. 2. Portugal--Relations

(general) with Guinea, Portuguese. I. Africa Research Group.
KU-RH

C3
Cagle, Tom.
  Life in an auto plant. [New
  York, Pathfinder Press, 1970]
  23p. 21x9cm. (A Merit pamphlet)
  Cover title.
  1. International union, united
  automobile, aircraft and agricultural implement workers of
  America. 2. General Motors Corporation. 3. Automobile industry and trade. 4. Automobile
  industry workers. I. Pathfinder
  Press.
  CU-B, KU-RH, WHi-L

C4
Caldwell, Malcolm
  The coup d'etat in Cambodia.
  [Philadelphia, American Friends
  Service Committee, 196]
  [2]p. illus. 39cm.
  Caption title.
  1. Cambodia--Relations (general)
  with the U.S. I. Friends,
  Society of. American Friends
  Service Committee.
  KU-RH

C5
The Californian.
  Black Friday. [Berkeley, Dis-
  tributed by Bay Area Student
  Committee for the Abolition of
  the House Committee on Un-Ameri-
  can Activities, 1960?]
  [7]p. 28cm.
  Caption title.
  Reprinted from The Californian,
  July 1960.
  1. U.S. Congress. House.
  Committee on Un-American Acti-
  vities. I. Bay Area Student
  Committee for the Abolition of
  the House Committee on Un-Ameri-
  can Activities.
  KU-RH

C6
A call to found a revolutionary
  working class youth organization. [New York, Temporary
  Organizing Committee for a New

Marxist-Leninist Youth Organization, 196]
[5] leaves. illus. 35cm.
Cover title.
1. Youth--Political activity.
2. Labor and laboring classes.
3. Communism. I. Temporary
Organizing Committee for a New
Marxist-Leninist Youth Organization.
KU-RH

C7
Caloren, Fred.
  Nationalism in Quebec, 1967.
  [n.p., 196]
  913-918p.
  Caption title.
  1. Nationalism--Quebec.
  2. French in Quebec.
  NNU-T

C8
Calvert, Gregory.
  In white America: radical con-
  sciousness and social change.
  [San Francisco, Resistance and
  Radical Education Project, 196]
  5p. 36cm.
  Caption title.
  1. Students for a Democratic
  Society. I. Resistance.
  II. Radical Education Project.
  KU-RH

C9
Calvert, Gregory.
  In white America: S.D.S. & radi-
  cal consciousness, by Greg Cal-
  vert & Carl Davidson. Ann Arbor,
  Radical Education Project [196]
  8p. illus. 28cm.
  Cover title.
  Reprinted from Guardian.
  1. Students for a Democratic
  Society. 2. Student movements.
  I. Davidson, Carl, jt. auth.
  I. Radical Education Project.
  MoU, MiU

C10
Calvert, Gregory.
  The new left [by] Greg Calvert
  & Carol Neiman. Ann Arbor,
  Radical Education Project
  [196]
  15p. illus. 22cm.

Cover title.
1. Student movements. I. Neiman,
Carol, jt. auth. II. Radical
Education Project.
MoU

C11
Calvert, Gregory.
Participatory democracy, collect-
ive leadership and political re-
sponsibility. [n.p., 196]
4p. 28cm.
Caption title.
1. Students for a Democratic
Society.
KU-RH

C12
Camejo, Antonio.
Why we oppose tuition. [San
Francisco, Socialist Workers
California Campaign, 1970?]
[8]p. 23cm.
Caption title.
1. Universities and colleges--
California. I. Socialist Work-
ers California Campaign.
CU-B

C13
Camejo, Peter.
Full support to the workers and
students of France. [Berkeley?
Socialist Workers Party? 1968?]
[1] leaf. 36cm.
Caption title.
1. Revolutions--France. 2. Stu-
dent movements--France. 3. La-
bor and laboring classes--
France. I. Socialist Workers
Party.
CU-B

C14
Camejo, Peter.
How to make a revolution in the
U.S. [New York] Merit Publish-
ers [1969]
23p. 21x9cm.
Cover title.
1.Socialism. I. Merit Publish-
ers.
CU-B

C15
Camejo, Peter.

How to make a revolution in the
U.S. [New York, Pathfinder
Press, 1970]
23p. 22x9cm. (A Merit pamphlet)
1. Socialism. 2. Young Socialist Alliance. I. Pathfinder
Press.
KU-RH

C16
Camejo, Peter.
Liberalism, ultraleftism or
mass action. [New York, Path-
finder Press, 1970]
15p. illus. 21cm.
Cover title.
1. Radicalism. 2. Socialist
Workers Party. I. Pathfinder
Press.
MiU

C17
Camejo, Peter.
PFP or SWP in '68; a critical
history of new politics in
Berkeley. [Berkeley] California Young Socialist for Halstead and Boutelle [1968]
20 leaves. 28cm.
Cover title.
1. Peace and Freedom Party.
2. Socialist Workers Party.
3. Berkeley, Calif.--Pol. &
govt. I. California Young
Socialist for Halstead and
Boutelle.
CU-B

Campus Americans for Democratic
    Action.
    see also
Americans for Democratic Action.

C18
Campus Americans for Democratic
    Action.
    Bill of rights for academic
    community. New York [196]
    5 leaves 28cm.
    1. Student movements
    CU-B

C19
Campus Americans for Democratic
    Action.

Why stand we here idle? [New
York, 196]
folder.
Cover title.
1. Student movements.
WHi-A

C20
Campus Americans for Democratic
    Action. National Board.
    A call to student action. [n.p.,
    1965?]
    [7] leaves. 28cm.
    Cover title.
    1. Student movements.
    CU-B, WHi-A

C21
Campus Draft Opposition.
    Facing the draft; your rights;
    your alternatives; your deci-
    sions. Berkeley [196]
    [16]p. 22cm.
    Caption title.
    1. Military service, Compulsory.
    CU-B

Campus Spartacist Club, Berkeley,
    Calif.
    see also
Philadelphia Spartacist League.
Bay Area Spartacist League.
Spartacist League.
New York City Spartacist League.

C22
Campus Spartacist Club, Berkeley,
    Calif.
    What is the Spartacist League?
    [Berkeley? 1968?]
    [1] leaf. 28cm.
    Caption title.
    1. Socialism. 2. Spartacist
    League.
    CU-B

C23
Camus, Albert, 1913-1960.
    Neither victims nor execution-
    ers. Preface by Robert Pickus.
    [Berkeley, World Without War
    Council, c1968]
    19p. 21cm.
    Cover title.
    1. Peace. 2. Political ethics.
    I. Pickus, Robert.   II. World

Without War Council.
    KU-RH

C24
Camus, Albert, 1913-1960.
    Neither victims nor execution-
    ers. [Trans. by Dwight Mac-
    donald] Intro. by Waldo Frank.
    [New York, Liberation, 1960]
    Cover title.
    Reprinted from Liberation, Feb.
    1960.
    1. Peace. 2. Political ethics.
    I. Macdonald, Dwight. II. Lib-
    eration. III. Frank, Waldo.
    MiEM, MoU

C25
Canada and Latin America: a sum-
    mary. [Toronto? Latin Ameri-
    can Working Group, 196]
    5 leaves. 28cm.
    Caption title.
    1. Canada--Relations (general)
    with Latin America. 2. Latin
    America--Relations (general)
    with Canada. I. Latin American
    Working Group.
    KU-RH

C26
Canadian Peace Congress.
    Rally for peace and disarmament.
    [Toronto] 1960.
    23p. 23cm.
    Cover title.
    1. Peace. 2. Disarmament.
    KU-RH

C27
Cannon, James Patrick, 1890-
    The Debs centennial; written on
    the 100th anniversary of the
    birth of Eugene V. Debs. New
    York, Pioneer Publishers [1956]
    40p. (Pioneer pocket library,
    no. 5)
    1. Debs, Eugene Victor, 1855-
    1926. 2. Socialism. I. Pio-
    neer Publishers.
    WHi-L, CLU

C28
Cannon, James Patrick, 1890-
    E.V. Debs; the socialist move-
    ment of his time--its meaning

for today. [2d ed. New York,
Merit Publishers, 1967]
30p. illus. 22cm.
Cover title.
Reprinted from Fourth Interna-
tional, Winter 1956.
1. Debs, Eugene Victor, 1855-
1926. 2. Socialism. I. Merit
Publishers.
KU-RH, CU-B, MoU

C29
Cannon, James Patrick, 1890-
  The I.W.W.; on the fiftieth anniversary of the founding convention. New York, Pioneer Publishers [1956]
  41p. ports. 18cm.
  Cover title: The I.W.W., the
  great anticipation.
  Reprinted from Fourth International, Summer 1955.
  1. Industrial Workers of the
  World. I. Pioneer Publishers.
  KU-J, NN, WHi-L

C30
Cannon, James Patrick, 1890-
  The I.W.W. [2d. ed. New York,
  Merit Publishers, 1967]
  31p. port. 22cm.
  Reprinted from Fourth Interna-
  tional, Summer 1955.
  1. Industrial Workers of the
  World. I. Merit Publishers.
  KU-RH, DLC 67-4535

C31
Cannon, James Patrick, 1890-
  Peace politics vs. revolutionary politics; Henry Wallace and
  the 1948 presidential campaign.
  New York, Young Socialist Alliance [1968]
  26 leaves. 28cm.
  Cover title.
  1. Peace. 2. Socialism.
  3. Wallace, Henry Agard, 1888-
    . I. Young Socialist Alli-
  ance.
  CU-B

C32
Cannon, James Patrick, 1890-
  Socialism and democracy. New
  York, Pioneer Publishers [1959]

21p. 17cm.
Speech given at the West Coast
Vacation School, Sept. 1, 1957.
1. Socialism. 2. Democracy.
I. Pioneer Publishers.
KU-RH

C33
Cannon, James Patrick, 1890-
  Socialist election policy in
  1958. [New York] Pioneer
  Publishers [1958]
  11p. 21cm.
  Cover title.
  1. U.S.--Pol. & govt.--1959-
    . 2. Socialist Labor Party.
  I. Pioneer Publishers.
  KU-J

C34
Cannon, Terry.
  All power to the people; the
  story of the Black Panther
  Party. [San Francisco, Peo-
  ple's Press, c1970]
  45p. illus. 26cm.
  Cover title.
  1. Black Panther Party.
  2. Negroes--Civil rights.
  I. People's Press.
  MiU, KU-RH

C35
Cannon, Terry.
  Vietnam; a thousand years of
  struggle. [San Francisco,
  People's Press, c1969]
  47p. illus., map. 28cm.
  Cover title.
  1. Vietnam--History. 2. Viet-
  namese conflict, 1961-1975.
  I. People's Press.
  KU-RH, DLC

C36
Cantarow, Ellen.
  I am furious (female) [by Ellen
  Cantarow and others] Detroit,
  Radical Education Project [196]
  20p. illus. 22cm.
  Cover title.
  Reprinted from RIPSAW.
  "An attempt to formulate per-
  spectives for the Women's Cau-
  cus of the New University Con-
  ference."

1. Woman--Rights of women.
2. Capitalism. I. Radical Education Project. II. New University Conference. Women's Caucus.
KU-RH, WHi-L

C37
Canter, David S.
  MLF--force or farce? Chicago,
  Domino Publications, 1965.
  40p. 22cm.
  1. U.S.--Military policy.
  2. North Atlantic Treaty Organi-
  zation. 3. Atomic weapons.
  I. Domino Publications.
  WHi-L

C38
Cantrel, Callie.
  Southern mountain tradition,
  by Callie Cantrel & Luke Larmon.
  Folk heroes and protest, by D.T.
  Nashville, Southern Student Or-
  ganizing Committee [196]
  [3] 6p. 28cm.
  Cover title.
  1. Folk-lore--Southern States.
  2. Folk-songs--Southern States.
  I. Larmon, Luke, jt. auth.
  II. Southern Student Organizing
  Committee.
  MoU

C39
Capper, Charles.
  The case for the third party; a
  critique of American liberalism,
  by Charles Capper and Kim Moody.
  Prepared for the 1964 national
  convention of Students for a
  Democratic Society. [n.p.] 1964.
  10p. 28cm.
  Cover title.
  1. Liberalism. 2. U.S.--Pol. &
  govt.--1963-   . 3. Political
  parties. I. Moody, Kimberly,
  jt. auth. II. Students for a
  Democratic Society.
  WHi-A

C40
Cardinal, Andre.
  Quebec and the intellectuals.
  [Montreal, Our Generation, 196]
  6-14 leaves.
  Caption title.

1. Quebec. 2. Intellectuals--
Quebec. I. Our Generation.
NNU-T

C41
Carey, Gordon R.
  The city of "progress." [New
  York, CORE, 196]
  [4]p. 28cm.
  Caption title.
  1. Negroes--Civil rights.
  2. Statesville, N.C.--Race ques-
  tion. 3. Negroes--Statesville,
  N.C. I. Congress of Racial
  Equality.
  CU-B

C42
Carlisle, Harry.
  The evolution of the immigration
  and national law. [Los Angeles,
  Los Angeles Committee for the
  Protection of Foreign Born,
  1958?]
  7 [1]p. illus.
  Caption title.
  1. U.S. Laws, statutes, etc.
  Immigration and Nationality Law
  of 1952. 2. U.S. Laws, statutes, etc. Alien Registration
  Act of 1940. 3. U.S. Laws,
  statutes, etc. Internal Security Act of 1950. 4. Emigration
  and immigration law. I. Los
  Angeles Committee for the Protection of Foreign Born.
  MiU

C43
Carmichael, Stokely.
  Black power and the third world.
  [n.p., 1967?]
  10p. 29cm.
  Speech given at a meeting of the
  Organization of Latin American
  Solidarity, Havana, 1967.
  1. Underdeveloped areas.
  2. Negroes--Civil rights.
  I. Organization of Latin Ameri-
  can Solidarity, Havana, 1967.
  CSaT, NUC 70-14133

C44
Carmichael, Stokely.
  Black power and the third world.
  Nashville, Southern Student Or-

ganizing Committee [196]
10p. 28cm.
Cover title.
1. Underdeveloped areas.
2. Negroes--Civil rights.
I. Southern Student Organizing
Committee.
MoU

C45
Carmichael, Stokely.
  Power & racism. Nashville,
Southern Student Organizing
Committee [196]
8 [1]p. 28cm.
Cover title.
1. Negroes--Civil rights.
I. Southern Student Organizing
Committee.
MoU

C46
Carmichael, Stokely.
  Power and racism: what we want.
[Boston, New England Free Press,
c1966]
[4]p. 28cm.
Caption title.
Reprinted from New York Review
of Books.
1. Negroes--Civil rights.
2. Student Nonviolent Coordina-
ting Committee.
I. New England Free Press.
KU-RH, MoU

C47
Carmichael, Stokely.
  Stokely Carmichael key-note
statement at Arab student convention. [n.p., 1968?]
10p. 28cm.
Caption title.
1. Negroes--Civil rights.
CU-B

C48
Carmichael, Stokely.
  Toward black liberation. [New
York, Student Nonviolent Coor-
dinating Committee, 196]
[16]p. 22cm.
Cover title.
1. Negroes--Civil rights.
I. Student Nonviolent Coordina-
ting Committee.
CU-B

C49
Carmichael, Stokely.
  Toward black liberation. [New
York, Student Nonviolent Coor-
dinating Committee, c1966]
[13]p.
Reprinted from Massachusetts
Review, autumn 1966.
1. Negroes--Civil rights.
I. Student Nonviolent Coordina-
ting Committee.
WHi-L

C50
Carner, Lucy P.
  From vision to reality. Philadelphia, Women's International
League for Peace and Freedom,
1965.
19p. 20cm.
Cover title.
1. Peace. 2. Disarmament.
3. Civil rights. I. Women's
International League for Peace
and Freedom.
KU-RH, MoU

C51
Carner, Lucy P.
  Tax refusal: a statement for the
Women's International League for
Peace and Freedom. Philadelphia,
Women's International League for
Peace and Freedom [196]
4p. 28cm.
Caption title.
1. Taxation. 2. Government,
Resistance to. I. Women's Inter-
national League for Peace and
Freedom.
MoU

C52
Carstens, Kenneth.
  The "Bantustan" or "separate
development" policy. [New York,
American Committee on Africa,
196]
[2]p. 28cm.
Caption title.
1. Africa, South--Race question.
I. American Committee on Africa.
KU-RH

C53
Carter, Alprentice "Bunchy".

The genius of Huey Newton.
[n.p., 196]
[2] leaves. 28cm.
Caption title.
1. Newton, Huey P. 2. Negroes--
Civil rights. 3. Black Panther
Party.
KU-RH

C54
The case for abolishing ROTC.
   [Produced with the assistance
   of Joan Primeau and others.
   n.p., 1970?]
8p. 22cm.
Cover title.
1. U.S. Army. Reserve Officers'
Training Corps. I. Primeau,
Joan.
CU-B

C55
The case for civil disobedience,
   [n.p., 196]
[2]p. 28cm.
Caption title.
1. Government, Resistance to.
KU-RH

C56
The case of Bill Epton. [New
   York, Committee to Defend
   Resistance to Ghetto Life,
   196]
[8]p. illus. 28cm.
Cover title.
1. Epton, Bill. 2. Negroes--
New York (City). 3. Law en-
forcement--New York (City).
I. Committee to Defend Resist-
ance to Ghetto Life.
KU-RH

C57
Casey, Robert D.
   The last Indian was. [Tacoma,
Wash., Survival of the American
Indian Association, 196]
[16]p.
Cover title.
Reprinted from Catholic Worker,
June 1966.
1. Indians of North America--
Government relations. 2. In-
dians of North America--Claims.
I. Survival of the American

Indian Association.
WHi-L

C58
Caspary, William.
   American economic imperialism;
   a survey of the literature.
   [Ann Arbor, Radical Education
   Project, 196]
30p. 28cm.
Cover title.
1. Imperialism--Bibl. 2. U.S.--
Foreign policy--Bibl. 3. U.S.--
Foreign economic relations.
I. Radical Education Project.
CU-B

C59
Caspary, William.
   American economic imperialism;
   a survey of the literature.
   Detroit, Radical Education Pro-
   ject [1970?]
23p. 28cm.
Cover title.
1. Imperialism--Bibl. 2. U.S.--
Foreign policy--Bibl. 3. U.S.--
Foreign economic relations.
I. Radical Education Project.
KU-RH, MoU

C60
Castro, David.
   American Documentary Films:
   profile of art in revolution
   [by David Castro and Jerry
   Stoll. San Francisco, Ameri-
   can Documentary Films, c1967]
[8]p. 23x10cm.
Cover title.
1. Moving-pictures, Documentary.
I. American Documentary Films.
II. Stoll, Jerry
KU-RH

C61
Castro, Fidel, 1927-
   Castro speaks on unemployment.
   [New York, Young Socialist Forum,
   196]
24p. 22cm.
Cover title.
Translated by Bob Verney.
1. Unemployed--Cuba. 2. Cuba--
For. rel.--U.S. 3. U.S.--For.
rel.--Cuba. I. Young Socialist

Forum.
MiU, MoU

C62
Castro, Fidel, 1927-
  Cuba confronts the future, five
  years of the revolution. [Toron-
  to, Fair Play for Cuba Committee,
  1964]
  24p. 21cm.
  Cover title.
  1. Cuba--Pol. & govt.--1959-
  I. Fair Play for Cuba Committee.
  FU, NUC 65-79150

C63
Castro, Fidel, 1927-
  Cuba confronts the future; five
  years of the revolution, a speech
  by Fidel Castro, Jan. 2, 1964.
  [Toronto, Fair Play for Cuba
  Committee, 196]
  24p. 22cm.
  Cover title.
  1. Cuba--Pol. & govt.--1959-
  2. Socialism in Cuba. I. Fair
  Play for Cuba Committee.
  MoU

C64
Castro, Fidel, 1927-
  Cuba's agrarian reform; a speech
  [given at the closing of the
  National Congress of Cane Co-
  Operatives, August 18, 1962.
  Toronto, Fair Play for Cuba
  Committee, 1963]
  16p. 22cm.
  Cover title.
  1. Land tenure--Cuba. 2. Agri-
  culture and state--Cuba.
  I. Fair Play for Cuba Committee.
  NcD, NUC 64-62502, MoU

C65
Castro, Fidel, 1927-
  Cuba's socialist destiny. [New
  York, Fair Play for Cuba Commit-
  tee, 1961?]
  18 [1]p. 22cm.
  Cover title.
  Translation of a speech deliver-
  ed July 26, 1961.
  1. Cuba--Pol. & govt.--1959-
  2. Socialsim in Cuba. I. Fair
  Play for Cuba Committee.
  MoU, LNHT, KU-J

C66
Castro, Fidel, 1927-
  Declaration of Santiago, July
  26, 1964. [Toronto, Fair Play
  for Cuba Committee, 1964]
  36p. 22cm.
  1. Cuba--Pol. & govt.--1959-
  2. Organization of American
  States. I. Fair Play for Cuba
  Committee.
  MiU, MoU, FU, CSt-H, NUC 67-13171

C67
Castro, Fidel, 1927-
  Division in the face of the
  enemy was never a revolutionary
  or intelligent strategy. Speech
  delivered by the prime minister
  of Cuban revolutionary government,...Fidel Castro at the University of Havana, on March 13,
  1965. [Toronto? Fair Play for
  Cuba Committee? 196]
  14p. 21x10cm.
  Cover title.
  1. Cuba--Pol. & govt.--1959-
  I. Fair Play for Cuba Committee.
  MoU

C68
Castro, Fidel, 1927-
  Fidel Castro addresses Congress
  of American Women [assembled in
  Havana, January 15, 1963. Tor-
  onto, The Worker Vanguard Pub-
  lishing Association, 1963?]
  23 [1]p. 14cm.
  Cover title.
  1. Women in Cuba. I. Worker
  Vanguard Publishing Association.
  II. Congress of American Women.
  FU, NUC 66-61360

C69
Castro, Fidel, 1927-
  Fidel Castro denounces bureaucracy and sectarianism (speech
  of March 26, 1962) New York,
  Pioneer Publishers, 1962.
  40p. 21cm.
  1. Revolutions--Cuba.
  2. Cuba--Pol. & govt.--1954-
  3. Bureaucracy.
  4. Communism--Cuba
  I. Pioneer Publishers.
  KU-RH, NN, CLU, NcD
  NUC 64-66353

C70
Castro, Fidel, 1927-
  Fidel Castro denounces bureaucracy and sectarianism; speech
  of March 26, 1962. [2d. ed.
  New York, Merit Publishers,
  1968]
  40cm. 22cm.
  1. Cuba--Pol. & govt.--1959-
  2. Revolutions--Cuba. 3. Bureaucracy. 4. Communism--Cuba.
  I. Merit Publishers.
  KU-RH, MoU

C71
Castro, Fidel, 1927-
  Fidel Castro: May day speech.
  Che Guevara: economic planning
  in Cuba. [New York, Fair Play
  for Cuba Committee, 196]
  19p.
  Cover title.
  1. Cuba--Pol. & govt.--1959-
  2. Cuba--Economic policy.
  3. Cuba--For.rel.--U.S.
  4. Socialism in Cuba. I. Guevara, Ernesto, 1920-1967.
  II. Fair Play for Cuba Committee.
  MiU

C72
Castro, Fidel, 1927-
  Fidel Castro speaks on Marxism-
  Leninism. [New York] Fair Play
  for Cuba Committee [196]
  82 [1]p.
  Cover title.
  1. Socialsim. I. Fair Play for
  Cuba Committee.
  MH, MiU, NN

C73
Castro, Fidel, 1927-
  Fidel Castro speaks to the child-
  ren. [n.p., Distributed by Fair
  Play for Cuba Committee, 196 ?]
  28 [1]p. illus. 22cm.
  Cover title.
  1. Children. I. Fair Play for
  Cuba Committee.
  KU-J

C74
Castro, Fidel, 1927-
  Fidel Castro's tribute to Che
  Guevara. [New York, Merit

Publishers, 1967]
  14p. illus. 22cm.
  Cover title.
  1. Guerara, Ernesto, 1920-1967.
  MoU

C75
Castro, Fidel, 1927-
  History will absolve me. Translation from the Spanish of a
  defense plea. [n.p., c1961,
  1968]
  79p. 22cm.
  1. Cuba--Pol. & govt.--1933-1959.
  MoU

C76
Castro, Fidel, 1927-
  Labor day address about the
  destiny of Cuba. New York, Fair
  Play for Cuba [1960]
  19p. 28cm.
  Cover title.
  Speech delivered May 1, 1960.
  1. Soldiers--Cuba. 2. Cuba--
  History. I. Fair Play for Cuba
  Committee.
  MiU

C77
Castro, Fidel, 1927-
  May day speech [by] Fidel Castro.
  Economic planning in Cuba [by]
  Che Guevara. Berkeley, Calif.,
  Fair Play for Cuba Committee
  [1961]
  19, 19p. 22cm.
  1. Cuba--Pol. & govt.--1959-
  2. Cuba--Economic policy.
  3. Cuba--For. rel.--U.S.
  4. Socialism in Cuba. I. Guevara, Ernesto, 1920-1967.
  II. Fair Play for Cuba Committee.
  NcD

C78
Castro, Fidel, 1927-
  A new stage in the advance of
  Cuban socialism. [New York]
  Merit [1968?]
  48p. 18cm.
  1. Socialism in Cuba. 2. Cuba--
  Pol. & govt.--1959.
  3. Underdeveloped areas.
  I. Merit Publishers.
  MU, NUC 70-28543

C79
Castro, Fidel, 1927-
  Our line is the line of consist-
  ent anti-imperialism, a speech
  by Fidel Castro, delivered on
  September 28 '63 to a mass rally
  celebrating the 3rd anniversary
  of the organization of the committees for the defense of the
  revolution. [Toronto, Fair Play
  for Cuba Committee, 1963?]
  12p. 22cm.
  Cover title.
  1. U.S.--For. rel.--Cuba.
  2. Cuba--For. rel.--U.S.
  I. Fair Play for Cuba Committee.
  MiU

C80
Castro, Fidel, 1927-
  The revolution must be a school
  of unfettered thought. Text of
  a speech by Fidel Castro at the
  University of Havana, March 13,
  1962. [New York, Merit Publishers, 1969]
  14p. 22cm.
  1. Cuba--Pol. & govt.--1959-
  2. Revolutions. I. Merit Publishers.
  MoU

C81
Castro, Fidel, 1927-
  The revolution must be a school
  of unfettered thought. Text of
  a speech by Fidel Castro at the
  University of of [sic] Havana
  March 13, 1962. New York, Pioneer Publishers, 1962.
  14p. 22cm.
  1. Cuba--Pol. & govt.--1959-
  2. Revolutions. I. Pioneer
  Publishers.
  CLU, NcD, NUC 64-66351

C82
Castro, Fidel, 1927-
  The road to revolution in Latin
  America; speech delivered in
  Havana July 26, 1963, celebrat-
  ing tenth anniversary of attack
  of Moncada Barracks. New York,
  Pioneer Publishers [1963]
  32p.
  1. Cuba--Pol. & govt.--1959-

I. Pioneer Publishers.
MiU, NUC 64-62512

C83
Castro, Fidel, 1927-
  The second declaration of Havana. New York, Pioneer Publishers, 1962.
  23p. 22cm.
  Cover subtitle: Cuba's answer
  to the OAS.
  1. Organization of American
  States. 2. Cuba--Pol. & govt.--
  1959-   . I. Pioneer Publishers.
  MiU, MoU, CLU, MH-L,
  NUC 64-9796Rev.

C84
Castro, Fidel, 1927-
  Speech at the United Nations,
  General Assembly session, September 26, 1960. [New York,
  Fair Play for Cuba Committee,
  1960?]
  30p. 28cm.
  1. Cuba--For. rel.--U.S.
  2. U.S.--For. rel.--Cuba.
  3. World politics--1955-
  I. Fair Play for Cuba Committee.
  TxU, MiU, WHi-L, ViU, LU

C85
Castro, Fidel, 1927-
  A speech to Soviet technicians.
  New York, Fair Play for Cuba
  Committee [196]
  [4]p. 23cm.
  1. Cuba--Pol. & govt.--1959-
  2. Russia--For. rel.--Cuba.
  3. Cuba--For. rel.--Russia.
  I. Fair Play for Cuba Committee.
  FU, MiU, NUC 67-20739

C86
Castro, Fidel, 1927-
  Speech to the women. Jan. 15,
  1963. [New York, Fair Play for
  Cuba Committee, 1963]
  33p. 13x21cm.
  1. Woman. 2. Women in Cuba.
  3. Cuba--Pol. & govt.--1959-
  I. Fair Play for Cuba Committee.
  FU, NcD, NIC, NUC 64-66354

C87
Castro, Fidel, 1927-
  Those who are not revolutionary
  fighters cannot be called communists; March 13, 1967 speech.
  New York, Merit Publishers, 1968.
  72p. 19cm.
  1. Communism--Venezuela.
  2. Venezuela--For. rel.--Cuba.
  I. Merit Publishers.
  MU, MoU, KU-RH

C88
Castro, Fidel, 1927-
  Tribute to Che Guevara [text of
  speech in memory of Ernesto Che
  Guevara at the Plaza of the Revolution, Havana, on Oct. 18,
  1967. New York, Merit] 1967.
  14p. ports. 22cm.
  1. Guevara, Ernesto, 1920-1967.
  2. Cuba--History--1959-
  I. Merit Publishers.
  CSt-H, KU-RH, NUC 69-70291

C89
Castro, Fidel, 1927-
  26th of July, 1963. [Excerpts
  from a speech delivered on the
  occasion of the tenth anniversary celebration of 26th of
  July, Cuba's revolutionary holi-
  day. New York, Fair Play for
  Cuba Committee, 1963]
  24p. 27cm.
  Cover title.
  1. Cuba--Pol. & govt.--1959-
  I. Fair Play for Cuba Committee.
  NcD, NUC 64-62511

C90
Castro, Fidel, 1927-
  26 of July speech, given at
  Havana celebrations, July 26,
  1961. Translated by Rolando
  Nunez. Toronto, Canadian Fair
  Play for Cuba Committee [1961]
  35p.
  Cover title.
  1. Cuba--Pol. & govt.--1959-
  I. Canadian Fair Play for Cuba
  Committee.
  CaOTU

C91
Castro, Fidel, 1927-

Women & the Cuban revolution,
  speeches by Fidel Castro, arti-
  cles by Linda Jenness. [New
  York, Pathfinder Press, 1970]
  15p. 22cm.
  Cover title.
  1. Woman. 2. Women in Cuba.
  I. Jenness, Linda, jt. auth.
  II. Pathfinder Press.
  MiU, CU-B

C92
The catastrophe in Indonesia.
  Three articles on the fatal
  consequences of Communist
  party policy [by Ernest Mandel,
  United Secretariat of the
  Fourth International and T.
  Soedarso. Introduction by
  Joseph Hansen. New York,
  Merit Publishers, 1966]
  47p. 22cm.
  Cover title.
  1. Indonesia--Pol. & govt.--
  1950-   2. Communism--Indo-
  nesia. I. Mandel, Ernest.
  II. Soedarso, T. III. Hansen,
  Joseph. IV. Merit Publishers.
  KU-RH

C93
Catholic Peace Fellowship
  Peacemakers. [New York, 196]
  folder. 28x11cm.
  Cover title.
  1. Vietnamese conflict, 1961-
  1975. 2. Peace.
  CU-B

C94
Catholic Worker.
  Some facts about Vietnam [by
  Catholic Worker and others.
  New York, 196]
  folder. 22cm.
  Cover title.
  1. Vietnamese conflict, 1961-
  1975.
  CU-B

C95
Catholic Worker.
  Tragic conflict; the United
  States war in Vietnam [by Catho-
  lic Worker and others. New York,
  196]

[2]p.   28cm.
Caption title.
1. Vietnamese conflict, 1961-
1975.
CU-B

C96
Catonsville and Milwaukee.   Nyack,
    N.Y., Fellowship Publications
    [1968?]
    1 leaf. 28cm.
    Caption title.
    Reprinted from Fellowship, Nov.
    1968.
    1. Pacifism. 2. Government,
    Resistance to. I. Fellowship
    Publications.
    KU-RH

C97
Catonsville Nine--Milwaukee Four-
    teen Defense Committee.
    Delivered into resistance: the
    Catonsville Nine--Milwaukee
    Fourteen Defense Committee. New
    Haven, Conn., Advocate Press
    [c1969]
    78p.
    1. Government, Resistance to.
    2. Military service, Compulsory.
    3. Catonsville (Md.) Nine.
    4. Milwaukee Fourteen.
    WHi-L

C98
    Caudill, Harry M., 1922-
    Misdeal in Appalachia. New
    Orleans, Southern Conference
    Education Fund, 1965.
    folder.
    Reprinted from the Atlantic
    Monthly.
    1. Appalachian Mountains--Econ.
    condit. I. Southern Conference
    Educational Fund.
    WHi-L.

C99
    Caudill, Harry M., 1922-
    Poverty and affluence: Appala-
    chian wonderland, by Harry M.
    Caudill and William C. Blizzard.
    Charleston, W.Va., Appalachian
    South [1966]
    16p. illus. 28cm.
    1. Poverty. 2. Appalachian

Mountains--Econ. condit.
    I. Blizzard, William C.
    MoU, WHi-L

C100
Central Committee for Conscient-
    ious Objectors, Philadelphia.
    Are you a conscientious objector
    to war? Philadelphia, 1965.
    [1] leaf. 28cm.
    Caption title.
    1. Conscientious objectors.
    KU-RH

C101
Central Committee for Conscient-
    ious Objectors, Philadelphia.
    The CCCO draft counselor and the
    law. Philadelphia [196]
    6p. 28cm.
    Caption title.
    1. Military service, Compulsory.
    KU-RH

C102
Central Committee for Conscient-
    ious Objectors, Philadelphia.
    CCCO draft counselor's manual.
    [Chicago, Midwest Committee for
    Draft Counseling, 1969]
    1v. (various paging) 28cm.
    Cover title.
    1. Military service, Compulsory.
    KU-RH

C103
Central Committee for Conscient-
    ious Objectors, Philadelphia.
    The chaplain's guide to consci-
    entious objectors in the armed
    forces. Rev. Philadelphia,
    Central Committee for Conscient-
    ious Objectors [and] National
    Service Board for Religious Ob-
    jectors, 1961.
    11p. 22x9cm.
    1. Conscientious objectors.
    I. National Service Board for
    Religious Objectors.
    KU-RH, TxFTC, NUC 63-2632

C104
Central Committee for Conscient-
    ious Objectors, Philadelphia.
    The conscientious objector and
    the armed forces. Philadelphia

[1968?]
12 [2]p. 28cm.
Caption title.
1. Conscientious objectors.
MoU

C105
Central Committee for Conscient-
    ious Objectors, Philadelphia.
The conscientious objector and
the Reserve Officers Training
Corps. Philadelphia [1959]
11p.
Cover title.
1. Conscientious objectors.
2. U.S. Army. Reserve Officers' Training Corps.
WHi-A

C106
Central Committee for Conscient-
    ious Objectors, Philadelphia.
Emigration to Canada; notes for
draft age. Philadelphia [196]
4p. 28cm.
Caption title.
1. Military service, Compulsory.
2. Emigration and immigration
law--Canada.
KU-RH

C107
Central Committee for Conscient-
    ious Objectors, Philadelphia.
Handbook for conscientious objectors. 3d. ed. Philadelphia,
1957.
108p. 20cm.
1. Conscientious objectors.
CtY, ViU-L, MH-L, WaU-L

C108
Central Committee for Conscient-
    ious Objectors, Philadelphia.
Handbook for conscientious objectors, edited by George Willoughby, 5th ed. Philadelphia,
1962.
112p. 22cm.
1. Conscientious objectors.
I. Willoughby, George, ed.
KU-RH

C109
Central Committee for Conscient-
    ious Objectors, Philadelphia.

Handbook for conscientious objectors, edited by Arlo Tatum.
Philadelphia, 1968.
100p. 22cm.
1. Conscientious objectors.
I. Tatum, Arlo.
KU-RH

C110
Central Committee for Conscient-
    ious Objectors, Philadelphia.
The non-cooperator and the
draft. Philadelphia [1963]
11p. 22cm.
Cover title.
1. Conscientious objectors.
MoU, CU-B

C111
Cerve, John.
On individualism. Drugs: lib-
erator or oppressor? By John
Cerve. From personal to social
rebellion, by Jake Rosen. [New
York, Progressive Labor Party,
196]
13p. 28cm.
Cover title.
1. Narcotics. 2. Debray, Regis.
I. Rosen, Jake, jt. auth.
II. Progressive Labor Party.
WHi-L

C112
Chabot, Joe.
Chabot-Max draft for the new SDS
organizational brochure [by Joe
Chabot and Steve Max. n.p.,
196]
[4]p. 28cm.
Caption title.
1. Students for a Democratic
Society. I. Max, Steve, jt.
auth.
WHi-A

C113
Challenge--Desafio.
G.I.'s in Vietnam say: "get the
hell out!" [n.p., 196]
8p. illus.
Cover title.
1. Vietnamese conflict, 1961-
1975.
WHi-A

C114
Chambers, Val.
  Past and future activities of
  Chester, prepared for the Cleve-
  land Community People's Confer-
  ence. [n.p., 1965]
  6 leaves. 28cm.
  Cover title.
  1. Poor--Chester, Pa. 2. Ches-
  ter, Pa.--Econ. condit.
  I. Cleveland Community People's
  Conference.
  WHi-A

C115
Chand, Gyan, 1893-
  Democracy in China. Boston, New
  England Free Press [196]
  [384]-418p. 22cm.
  Cover title.
  Reprinted from Chand's The new
  economy of China.
  1. China (People's Republic of
  China, 1949-   )--Econ.
  condit. 2. Democracy. I. New
  England Free Press.
  MoU, KU-RH

C116
Chand, Gyan, 1893-
  Democracy in China. Toronto,
  Research, Information, and
  Publications Project, Student
  Union for Peace Action [196]
  13p. 28cm.
  Cover title.
  1. China (People's Republic of
  China, 1949-   )--Econ.
  condit. 2. Democracy. I. Stu-
  dent Union for Peace Action.
  WHi-A

C117
Chandler, Christopher.
  Black Panther killings in Chicago. Nyack, N.Y., Fellowship
  Publications [1970?]
  [4]p. 28cm.
  Caption title.
  At head of title: A conspiracy
  by whom, against whom?
  Reprinted from New York, Jan.
  10, 1970.
  1. Black Panther Party. 2. Pol-
  ice--Illinois--Chicago.

  I. Fellowship Publications.
  KU-RH

C118
Charter Group for a Pledge of
    Conscience.
  The Black Panther Party and the
  case of the New York 21. [New
  York, 1970?]
  29p. 22cm.
  Cover title.
  1. Black Panther Party.
  MiU, NNU-T, MiU

C119
Chasan, Dan.
  All about CORE. [New York, Con-
  gress of Racial Equality, 196]
  [20]p. illus. 21x10cm.
  Cover title.
  1. Congress of Racial Equality.
  2. Negroes--Civil rights.
  I. Congress of Racial Equality.
  WHi-A, CU-B, KU-RH

C120
Chase, Wilda.
  The twig benders. New York, The
  Feminists [1969?]
  6p. 28cm.
  Caption title.
  1. Woman--History and condition
  of women. I. Feminists.
  KU-RH

C121
Chasse, Robert.
  A field study in the dwindling
  force of cognition, where it is
  least expected. A critique of
  the Situationist International
  as a revolutionary organization
  [by Robert Chasse and Bruce
  Elwell. New York? 1970?]
  46p.
  Cover title.
  1. Situationist International.
  I. Elwell, Bruce, jt. auth.
  MiU

C122
Chavez, Cesar Estrada.
  The grape boycott; why it has to
  be. [Delano, Calif., United
  Farm Workers Organizing Commit-

tee, 196]
[4]p. 22cm.
Caption title.
1. Agricultural laborers--Calif.
--Delano. 2. Mexicans in the
U.S. I. United Farm Workers Or-
ganizing Committee.
KU-RH

C123
Chavez, Cesar Estrada.
"Right to work" laws--a trap for
America's minorities, by Cesar
E. Chavez and Bayard Rustin.
[New York, A. Philip Randolph
Institute and United Farm Work-
ers, AFL-CIO, 196]
20p. illus. 23cm.
Cover title.
Text in English and Spanish.
1. Mexicans in the U.S. 2. La-
bor laws and legislation.
I. Randolph (A. Philip) Insti-
tute. II. United Farm Workers.
III. Rustin, Bayard, 1910-
jt. auth.
KU-RH

C124
Cherkoss, Steve.
The Scheer campaign in the
Democratic primary. People
secondary. [Berkeley, Pro-
gressive Labor Party, Student
Club, 196]
[3]p. 28cm.
Caption title.
1. Scheer, Robert. 2. Demo-
cratic Party. 3. Politics, Prac-
tical. I. Progressive Labor
Party.
WHi-A

C125
Chertkov, Lynn.
Chemical and biological warfare.
[Washington, Mid-Atlantic Com-
mittee on Ft. Detrick, 196]
[2]p. 36cm.
Caption title.
1. Biological warfare.
2. Chemical warfare.
I. Mid-Atlantic Committee on
Ft. Detrick.
CU-B

C126
Chesler, Mark.
Student reactions to the Cuban
crisis and public dissent [by]
Mark Chesler and Richard Schmuck.
[Ann Arbor[Peace Research and
Education Project [196]
34 [9] leaves. 28cm.
Caption title.
1. U.S.--For. rel.--Russia.
2. Cuba--For. rel.--Russia.
3. Russia--For. rel.--Cuba.
4. Russia--For. rel.--U.S.
I. Students for a Democratic
Society. Peace Research and
Education Project. II. Schmuck,
Richard, jt. auth.
WHi-A

C127
Chesler, Mark.
Tutorials: a strategy for edu-
cational reform. New York,
Northern Student Movement.
[196]
22p. 28cm.
Cover title.
1. Education. 2. Negroes--Edu-
cation. I. Northern Student
Movement.
MiU

C128
Chester, Eric.
The Cuba economy: a discussion
paper. Ann Arbor [Independent
Socialist Clubs of America,
196]
7p. 28cm.
Caption title.
1. Cuba--Econ. condit. I. In-
dependent Socialist Clubs of
America.
MiU-H

Chicago Area Draft Resisters.
CADRE

C129
Chicago Area Draft Resisters.
Behind bars; a prison anthology.
Chicago [1968]
26p. 28cm.
Cover title.

1. Prisons.
KU-RH

C130
Chicago Committee for Equal Education.
Equal education for all. Chicago [1962]
[10]p. 22cm.
Cover title.
1. Negroes--Education.
MiU

C131
Chicago Committee to Defend Democratic Rights.
Freedom or enforced conformity:
the Supreme court review of the
Smith and McCarran acts. [Chi-
cago, 1960?]
8p. illus. 22cm.
Cover title.
1. Communism. 2. U.S. Laws,
statutes, etc. Internal Security Act of 1950.
MH-L, NUC 64-61523

C132
Chicago Committee to Defend the
Bill of Rights.
Goldwater--HUAC and the ultra-
right. [Chicago, 1964]
8p.
1. Goldwater, Barry Morris,
1909-   . 2. U.S. Congress.
House. Committee on Un-American
Activities.
WHi-L

C133
The Chicago conspiracy trial. The
Chicago conspiracy vs. the
Washington kangaroos. Offi-
cial pogrom. [Editors: Chris-
topher Cerf and Michael Frith.
New York] Domesday Book;
Grove Press special [1969]
24p. illus. 28cm.
Cover title.
1. Chicago--Riots, August, 1968.
2. Democratic Party. National
Convention, Chicago, 1968.
3. Government, Resistance to.
KU-RH ₋ₙₘₑₙₜ, Resistance to.
KU-RH

C134
China: voices of revolt. Detroit,
News & Letters [196]
10p. 28cm.
Cover title.
Reprinted from Survey of China
Mainland Press.
1. Human Provincial Proletarian
Revolutionary Great Alliance
Committee. 2. China (People's
Republic of China, 1949-   )
--Pol. & govt. 3. China (Peo-
ple's Republic of China, 1949-
)--Intellectual life.
I. News & Letters.
NNU-T, KU-RH

C135
China's view of the international
Communist dispute; difference
between comrade Togliatti and
us; a key article reprinted
from Peking Review. Together
with a series of searching an-
alytical articles written for
Workers World by Sam March.
[New York, Workers World,
196]
67p.
Cover title.
1. China (People's Republic of
China, 1949-   )--Foreign
policy. 2. China (People's Republic of China, 1949-   )
4. Communism. I. Marcy, Sam.
II. Workers World.
MiU

C136
Chomsky, Noam.
After Pinkville. [Boston, New
England Free Press, 196]
12p. 28cm.
Cover title.
1. Vietnamese conflict, 1961-
1975. I. New England Free Press.
KU-RH

C137
Chomsky, Noam.
Cambodia. [Ithaca, N.Y., Glad
Day Press, 1970?]
15p. illus. 28cm.
Cover title.
Reprinted from New York Review

of Books, June 4, 1970.
1. Cambodia. I. Glad Day Press.
NNU-T

C138
Church Peace Union.
   The moral dilemma of nuclear weapons. Essays from Worldview, a
   journal of religion and international affairs. [New York,
   c1961]
   78p. 23cm.
   1. Atomic weapons. 2. War and
   religion.
   WHi-A

C139
Cieciorka, Bobbi.
   Negroes in American history; a
   freedom primer. [rev. ed.]
   Text by Bobbi Cieciorka [and]
   Frank Cieciorka. Drawings [by]
   Frank Cieciorka. [Atlanta, Ga.,
   The Student Voice, 1966]
   63p.
   1. Negroes--Civil rights.
   I. Student Voice. II. Cieciorka,
   Frank, jt. auth.
   WHi-L

C140
Cieciorka, Bobbi.
   Negroes in American history; a
   freedom primer. Text [by] Bobbi
   Cieciorka [and] Frank Cieciorka.
   [Atlanta, Student Voice, 1965]
   51p. illus. 28cm.
   1. Negroes--History. 2. Ne-
   groes--Civil rights. I. Cie-
   ciorka, Frank, jt. auth.
   II. Student Voice.
   MiU

C141
Cisler, Lucinda.
   Women: a bibliography. New
   York, C1968, c1969.
   11p. 28cm.
   Caption title.
   1. Woman--Bibl.
   MoU

C142
Cisler, Lucinda.
   Women: a bibliography. 5th ed.,
   rev., enl. New York, 1969.

11p. 28cm.
Caption title.
1. Woman--Bibl.
MoU

C142
Cisler, Lucinda.
   Women: a bibliography. 5th ed.,
   rev., enl. New York, 1969.
   16p. 28cm.
   1. Woman--Bibl.
   KyU, MiU, NUC 70-59765

C143
Citizens Committee for Constitut-
      ional Liberties.
   End McCarranism; on this we
   stand together. Speeches made
   at June 7 rally, Manhattan Center, New York [by] Clark Foreman [and others. New York,
   1962?]
   38p. ports. 21cm.
   1. McCarthy, Joseph Raymond,
   1909-1957. 2. Communism.
   TxU, NcD, NUC 64-61881

C144
Citizens Committee for Constitut-
      ional Liberties.
   Voices for liberty. Stop Mc-
   Carransim; today's McCarthyism.
   [New York, 196]
   30p. 22cm.
   Cover title.
   1. Anti-communist movements.
   2. Civil rights. 3. U.S. Laws,
   statutes, etc. Internal Secur-
   ity Act of 1950.
   MiU, WHi-A

C145
Citizens Committee for Constitut-
      ional Liberties. Youth Com-
      mittee.
   Free speech victory. [New York,
   196]
   16p. illus.
   Cover title.
   1. Student movements. 2. Liberty
   of speech.
   MiU

C146
Citizens United for Adequate
      Welfare.

CUFAW speaks for itself, prepared for the Cleveland Community
People's Conference, February 19-
21, 1965. [n.p., 1965?]
12 leaves. 28cm.
Cover title.
1. Public welfare.
WHi-A

C147
Civil Rights Congress.
The crimes of Claude Lightfoot
and Junius Scales. [New York,
1955]
15p. illus.
1. Negroes. 2. Communism.
3. Lightfoot, Claude M., 1910-
        . 4. Scales, Junius.
WHi-L

C148
Civil Rights Congress.
The Nelson case: state sedition
laws are weapons of anti-labor,
anti-negro, anti-semitic repression. New York, 1955.
1. Nelson, Steve. 2. Communism.
3. Negroes--Civil rights.
4. Jews. 5. Labor and laboring
classes.
WHi-L

C149
Civil Rights Congress. National
    Leadership Conference, New
    York, 1955.
Keynote address; report of deli-
berations. New York [1955?]
23 leaves. 28cm.
Cover title.
1. McCarthy, Joseph Raymond,
1909-1957. 2. Civil rights.
3. Subversive activities.
KU-J

C150
Clamage, Dena.
Proposed national SDS activity
[by Dena Clamage and Mel McDonald. n.p., 196]
2 leaves. 28cm.
Caption title.
1. Vietnamese conflict, 1961-
1975. 2. Students for a Democratic Society. I. McDonald,

Mel, jt. auth.
WHi-A

C151
Clapp, Gordon Rufus, 1905-
TVA and its critics. New York,
League for Industrial Democracy
[c1955, 1956]
14p. illus. 22cm.
1. Tennessee Valley Authority.
2. League for Industrial Democracy.
WHi-A, DLC 55-4844

C152
Clark, Ed.
The two worlds of Carl Oglesby.
[n.p., 1968?]
[6]p. 28cm.
Caption title.
1. Oglesby, Carl.
CU-B

C153
Clark, George.
Students for a Democratic Soci-
ety. [Montreal, Our Generation,
196]
30-39 leaves.
Caption title.
1. Students for a Democratic
Society.
NNU-T

C154
Clark, Joseph, 1913-
Geneva: road to peace. [New
York, New Century Publishers,
1955]
15p. 19cm.
Cover title.
1. U.S.--For. rel.--Russia.
2. Russia--For. rel.--U.S.
3. Geneva. Conference, 1954.
I. New Century Publishers.
KU-J

C155
Clark, Kenneth Bancroft, 1914-
The present dilemma of the
negro. [n.p., 1967?]
11p.
Cover title.
"Address before the annual meet-
ing of the Southern Regional

Council, Nov. 2, 1967."
1. Negroes--Civil rights.
I. Southern Regional Council.
WHi-L

C156
Clark, Kenneth Bancroft, 1914-
The present dilemma of the
negro. An address before the
annual meeting of the Southern
Regional Council, November 2,
1967. [Detroit? People Against
Racism, 1968?]
17p. 28cm.
Cover title.
1. Negroes--Civil rights.
I. Southern Regional Council.
II. People Against Racism.
KU-RH

C157
Clarke, Nelson.
Berlin: peace of war? [Toronto,
Published by Progress Books for
the Labor-Progressive Party,
1959]
23p.
1. Berlin question (1945-   )
I. Labor-Progressive Party
(Canada) II. Progress Books.
CaOTU

C158
Clayton, Edward Taylor, 1921-
    1966.
The SCLS story. [Atlanta,
Southern Christian Leadership
Conference, c1964]
63p. illus.
1. Southern Christian Leader-
ship Conference. I. Southern
Christian Leadership Conference.
WHi-L

C159
Clayton, James L.
The usury of war. Vietnam: the
200-year mortgage. [Woodmont,
Conn., Promoting Enduring Peace,
1969?]
[2]p. 28cm.
Caption title.
Reprinted from The Nation, May
26, 1969.
1. Vietnamese Conflict, 1961-
1975. I. Promoting Enduring

Peace.
KU-RH

C160
Cleage, Albert B.
Myths about Malcolm X. Two
views: Rev. Albert Cleage [and]
George Breitman. [New York,
Merit Publishers, 1968]
30p. 22cm.
Cover title.
1. Little, Malcolm, 1925-1965.
2. Negroes--Civil rights.
I. Breitman, George, jt. auth.
II. Merit Publishers.
CU-B, WHi-L, MsSM, NUC 70-25161

C161
Cleage, Albert B.
Myths about Malcolm X: two views
[by] Rev. Albert Cleage and Geo-
rge Breitman. [New York, Merit
Publishers, 1969]
30p. 22cm.
Cover title.
1. Little, Malcolm, 1925-1965.
2. Negroes--Civil rights.
I. Breitman, George, jt. auth.
I. Merit Publishers.
KU-RH

C162
Cleary, Josephine.
Notes from the lower classes II.
New York, The Feminists, 1969.
[1] leaf. 28cm.
Caption title.
1. Social classes. I. Feminists.
KU-RH, WHi-L

C163
Cleaver, Eldridge, 1935-
The black man's stake in Vietnam.
[n.p., 1970?]
[4]p. illus.
Cover title.
1. Vietnamese conflict, 1961-
1975. 2. Negroes.
NNU-T

C164
Cleaver, Eldridge, 1935-
Eldridge Cleaver is free [ad-
dress given at Berkeley Community
Center, Nov. 1, 1968. Berkeley,
White Panther Party, Bay Area,

1969]
[8]p. port. 22cm.
Cover title.
1. Negroes--Civil rights.
2. Black Panther Party.
I. White Panther Party.
CU-B

C165
Cleaver, Eldridge, 1935-
The fascists have already decided in advance to murder
chairman Bobby Seale in the
electric chair. San Francisco,
Black Panther Party Legal Defense Fund [1970?]
[1] leaf. 44cm.
Caption title.
1. Seale, Bobby. 2. Black
Panther Party. 3. Law Enforcement. I. Black Panther Party.
Legal Defense Fund.
CU-B

C166
Cleaver, Eldridge, 1935-
A letter from Eldridge Cleaver.
[Los Angeles, Peace and Freedom
Party, Cleaver for President
Campaign, 1968?]
[2]p. 36cm.
Caption title.
1. Peace and Freedom Party.
I. Cleaver for President Cam-
paign.
CU-B

C167
Cleaver, Eldridge, 1935-
On the constitution. [n.p.,
Black Panther Party, 1970?]
[4]p. 45cm.
Caption title.
Contents--Message to America by
the Black Panther Party; Towards
a new constitution, by Huey P.
Newton.
1. Negroes--Civil rights.
2. Black Panther Party. I. New-
ton, Huey P. II. Black Panther
Party.
CU-B, NNU-T

C168
Cleaver, Eldridge, 1935-
On the ideology of the Black
Panther Party. [n.p., 196]

11p.
1.Black Panther Party.
WHi-L

C169
Cleaver, Eldridge, 1935-
On the ideology of the Black
Panther Party. [San Francisco,
196]
11 [3]p. 26cm.
Cover title.
1. Black Panther Party.
MiU

C170
Cleaver, Eldridge, 1935-
Revolution and education. [n.p.,
196 ?]
[8]p. 21cm.
Cover title.
1. Student movements. 2. Universities and colleges.
MiU, CU-B

C171
Cleaver, Eldridge, 1935-
Revolution in the white mother
country and national liberation
in the black colony. [Oakland,
Black Panther Party for Self-
Defense, 1968?]
[4]p. 22cm.
Caption title.
1. Peace and Freedom Party.
2. Black Panther Party.
3. U.S.--Race question.
I. Black Panther Party.
CU-B

C172
Cleaver, Eldridge, 1935-
Revolution in the white mother
country and national liberation
in the black colony. Presented
to the Peace and Freedom founding convention, Richmond, California, March 16, 1968. [San
Francisco, Black Panther Party,
196]
[4]p. 22cm.
Caption title.
1. Peace and Freedom Party.
2. Black Panther Party. 3. U.S.
--Race question. I. Black Panther Party.
NNU-T, MoU.

C173
Cleaver, Harry.
  Counterinsurgency research in
  Thailand. [East Palo Alto,
  Calif.] Pacific Studies Center
  [1970?]
  109 leaves. 28cm.
  Cover title.
  1. U.S. Advanced Research Projects Agency. 2. Military research. 3. Thailand--Relations
  (general) with the U.S. I. Pacific Studies Center.
  KU-RH

C174
Cleaver, Harry.
  Preliminary bibliography on
  direct investment and the multi-
  national corporation. E. Palo
  Alto, Calif., Pacific Studies
  Center, 1969.
  20 leaves. 28cm. (Pacific
  Studies Center bibliographical
  center no. 1)
  1. U.S.--Foreign economic relations. 2. Corporations.
  3. International economic relations. I. Pacific Studies
  Center.
  KU-RH

C175
Cleaver, Kathleen.
  Position of the Black Panther
  Party for Self Defense on the
  seventh congressional district
  election and the candidacy of
  John George in the Democratic
  Party. [Oakland, Black Panther
  Party, 1968?]
  [4]p. 22cm.
  Caption title.
  1. Black Panther Party.
  2. Negroes--Politics and suffrage. 3. Democratic Party.
  4. George, John. I. Black Panther Party.
  CU-B

C176
Cleaver, Kathleen.
  Release Eldridge Cleaver. An
  appeal for letters demanding
  justice from the California
  adult authority. [Oakland,

Black Panther Party, 1968]
  [4]p. 22cm.
  Caption title.
  1. Cleaver, Eldridge, 1935-
  I. Black Panther Party.
  CU-B

C177
Cleaver, Kathleen.
  Transcript of press conference
  held May 13, 1968, announcing
  the candidacy of Eldridge Cleaver for the Peace and Freedom
  nomination for the president of
  the U.S. Prepared statements
  [by] Kathleen Cleaver [and
  others. n.p., 1968?]
  3p. 36 cm.
  Caption title.
  1. Cleaver, Eldridge, 1935-
  2. Social changes. 3. Black
  Panther Party. 4. Peace and
  Freedom Party.
  CU-B

C178
Cleaver for President Committee.
  Why Peace & Freedom should no-
  minate Eldridge Cleaver for
  president. [San Francisco?
  1968?]
  7p. 24cm.
  Caption title.
  1. Cleaver, Eldridge, 1935-
  2. Peace and Freedom Party.
  CU-B

C179
Clecak, Peter.
  The limits of university reform. [Montreal, Our Generation, 196]
  74-84 leaves.
  Caption title.
  1. Universities and colleges.
  2. Student movements. I. Our
  Generation.
  NNU-T

C180
Clergy and Laymen Concerned About
    Vietnam.
  A call for amnesty and reconcil-
  iation. [An open letter to the
  American people, by Richard A.
  Falk. New York, 196]

2p. 36cm.
Caption title.
1. Amnesty. 2. Vietnamese con-
flict, 1961-1975. I. Falk,
Richard A.
KU-RH

C181
Clergy and Laymen Concerned About
    Vietnam.
Clergy and Laymen Concerned
About Vietnam. [New York,
1969?]
folder. 22x9cm.
Cover title.
1. Vietnamese conflict, 1961-
1975.
KU-RH

C182
Clergy and Laymen Concerned About
    Vietnam.
Conscience and conscription.
[New York, 1967?]
[2]p. 28cm.
Caption title.
1. Military service, Compulsory.
KU-RH

C183
Clergy and Laymen Concerned About
    Vietnam.
Crisis of conscience. [New
York, 1967]
[12]p.
1. Vietnamese conflict, 1961-
1975.
WHi-L

C184
Clergy and Laymen Concerned About
    Vietnam.
Deserters in exile. [New York,
1968?]
15p.
1. Vietnamese conflict, 1961-
1975. 2. Desertion, Military.
WHi-L

C185
Clergy and Laymen Concerned About
    Vietnam.
Dr. Martin Luther King, Jr.,
Dr. John C. Bennett, Dr. Henry
Steele Commager, Rabbi Abraham
Herschel speak on the war in

Vietnam. [New York, 1967]
31p.
1. Vietnamese conflict, 1961-
1975. I. King, Martin Luther,
1929-1968. II. Bennett, John
C. III. Commager, Henry Steele.
IV. Herschel, Abraham.
WHi-L

C186
Clergy and Laymen Concerned About
    Vietnam.
In whose name? [New York, 1967?]
19p. 28cm.
1. Vietnamese conflict, 1961-
1975.
MoU, KU-RH

C187
Clergy and Laymen Concerned About
    Vietnam.
The religious community and Am-
erican politics. A statement
prepared for Vietnam sabbath,
November 2-3, 1968.
[New York, 1968?]
[2]p. 36cm.
Caption title.
1. Vietnamese conflict, 1961-
1975.
KU-RH

C188
Clergy and Laymen Concerned About
    Vietnam.
Who's right? Who's wrong?--on
Vietnam. [New York, 196]
10p. 35cm.
1. Vietnamese conflict, 1961-
1975..
WHi-L, KU-RH

C189
Cleveland Radical Women's Group.
Sweet 16 to saggy 36; saga of
American womanhood. [Cleveland,
1969?]
19p. illus. 22cm.
Cover title.
1. Woman--Rights of women.
KU-RH

C190
Clifford, Clark McAdams, 1906-
A Viet Nam reappraisal. Wood-
mont, Conn., Promoting Enduring
Peace [1969?]

[2]p. 28cm. (No. 151)
Caption title.
Excerpted from Foreign Affairs,
July 1969.
1. Vietnamese conflict, 1961-
1975. I. Promoting Enduring
Peace.
KU-RH

C191
Cloke, Ken.
  Law and the radical lawyer. Ann
Arbor, Conference on Radicals
in the Professions, 1967.
7p. 28cm.
Cover title.
1. Lawyers. 2. Radicalism.
I. Conference on Radicals in the
Professions.
MiU-H

C192
Cloke, Ken.
  Law and the radical lawyers.
Boston, New England Free Press
[196]
28-36p. 22cm.
Cover title.
Reprinted from Our Generation.
1. Lawyers. 2. Radicalism.
I. New England Free Press.
KU-RH, MiU

C193
Cloke, Ken.
  A pocket manual on draft resistance. [New York, Weekly Guardian Associates, c1968]
43p. 22x11cm.
Cover title.
1. Military service, Compulsory.
CU-B, WHi-A

C194
Clowen, Richard.
  Ghetto redevelopment: corporate
imperialism for the poor [by]
Richard Clowen [and] Frances
Piven. Ann Arbor, Radical Edu-
cation Project [1969?]
365-367p. illus. 28cm.
Cover title.
Reprinted from The Nation, Oct.
16, 1967.
1. Urban renewal. I. Piven,
Frances, jt. auth. II. Radical

Education Project.
KU-RH

C195
Coalition of American Indian
  Citizens.
  Poor people's campaign. [Den-
ver, Coalition of American In-
dian Citizens, Western Poor
People's Campaign, 1968]
15p. illus. 28cm.
1. Indians of North America.
2. Poor. I. Western Poor
People's Campaign.
WHi-L

C196
Coatsworth, John H.
  Walt W. Rostow: the stages of
economic stagnation. Ann Arbor,
Radical Education Project
[1969?]
21p. illus. 22cm.
Cover title.
1. Rostow, Walt Whitman, 1916-
     . Stages of Economic
Growth, a Non-Communist Mani-
festo. I. Radical Education
Project.
MoU, KU-RH

C197
Cobb, Charles.
  Prospectus for summer freedom
school program, originally submitted by Charles Cobb. [Jack-
son, Miss.? Council of Federated
Organizations? 1964]
5 leaves. 28cm.
Caption title.
1. Negroes--Education. 2. Mis-
sissippi--Race question.
I. Council of Federated Organizations.
WHi-A

C198
Coffin, Jerry.
  Local organizing--a discussion.
[New York, War Resisters League,
1970?]
5 leaves. 28cm.
Cover title.
1. Peace--Societies, etc.
2. War Resisters League.
KU-RH

C199
Coffin, William Sloane.
  The ministry of reconciliation
  between Marxists and Christians.
  [Woodmont, Conn., Promoting En-
  during Peace, 196]
  2p. 28cm.
  Caption title.
  "A sermon given in Battell Cha-
  pel...at the ordination service
  for Jay Stoner, Oct. 22, 1967."
  1. Socialsim, Christian.
  I. Promoting Enduring Peace.
  KU-RH

C200
Coffin, William Sloane.
  Why are the clergy concerned
  about Vietnam? [New York, Cler-
  gy and Laymen Concerned About
  Vietnam, 196]
  6p. 28cm.
  Caption title.
  1. Vietnamese conflict, 1961-
  1975. I. Clergy and Laymen
  Concerned About Vietnam.
  KU-RH

C201
Cogley, John.
  Deserters in exile [by] John
  Cogley [and others. New York,
  Clergy and Laymen Concerned
  About Vietnam, 1968?]
  15p. 28cm.
  Cover title.
  1. Vietnamese conflict, 1961-
  1975. 2. Destruction, Military.
  I. Clergy and Laymen Concerned
  About Vietnam.
  KU-RH

C202
Cohen, Dan.
  The target is man. The story
  of chemical, biological, radio-
  logical warfare. [Chicago,
  Shahn-ti Sena Publishers and
  Student Peace Union, 196]
  24p. 22cm.
  Cover title.
  1. Biological warfare. 2. Chem-
  ical warfare. 3. Atomic weapons.
  I. Student Peace Union.
  II. Shahn-ti Sena Publishers.
  WHi-A

C203
Cohen, David.
  Foreign policy papers: order and
  honor, by David Cohen. Foreign
  aid by Barry Smoler. [n.p.]
  Campus Division, Americans for
  Democratic Action on behalf of
  the Liberal Study Group [1962]
  2, 3p. 36cm.
  1. U.S.--Foreign policy.
  I. Americans for Democratic Ac-
  tion. Campus Division.
  II. Liberal Study Group.
  III. Smoler, Barry, jt. auth.
  WHi-A

C204
Cohen, Fred.
  Big business and urban stagnation, by Fred Cohen and Marc
  Weiss. San Francisco, Bay Area
  Radical Education Project [196]
  18p. 22cm.
  Cover title.
  Reprinted from Pacific Research
  and World Empire Telegram, vol.
  1, no. 2.
  1. Corporations. 2. Business
  and politics. 3. Cities and
  towns. I. Bay Area Radical Education Project. II. Weiss,
  Mark, jt. auth.
  CU-B

C205
Cohen, Fred.
  Private power and the new Indochina war. [Detroit, Radical
  Education Project, 1970?]
  14p. illus. 22cm.
  Cover title.
  1. U.S.--Foreign policy.
  2. Business and politics.
  3. U.S.--Foreign economic relations. I. Radical Education
  Project.
  KU-RH

C206
Cohen, Joel I.
  Hughes for senate: a campaign
  history. [Cambridge, Mass.,
  Massachusetts Political Action
  for Peace, c1964]
  iii, 49p. illus. 28cm.
  1. Hughes, Henry Stuart, 1916-

2. U.S. Congress.
Senate--Elections. I. Massachu-
setts Political Action for Peace.
KU-RH

C207
Cohen, Matt.
How the university has survived.
Toronto, Research, Information
and Publications Project, Stu-
dent Union for Peace Action
[196]
4p. 28cm.
Speech given at Waterloo, Dec.
5, 1965.
Cover title.
1. Universities and colleges.
I. Student Union for Peace
Action.
WHi-A

C208
Cohen, Matt.
Ideas on the university. Tor-
onto, Research, Information and
Publications Project, Student
Union for Peace Action [196]
5p. 28cm.
Speech given at McMaster Univer-
sity, Oct. 1965.
Cover title.
1.Free schools. 2. Universities
and colleges. I. Student Union
for Peace Action.
WHi-A

C209
Cohen, Stan.
Notes on dentention centers [by]
Stan Cohen. Approved school:
how does it feel? [by] Ian Tay-
lor. Montreal, Our Generation
[196]
unpaged.
Cover title.
Reprinted from Anarchy.
1. Taylor, Ian, jt. auth.
II. Our Generation.
NNU-T

C210
Cohn-Bendit, Gabriel.
Anarchism in the May movement
in France [interviews with Gab-
riel Cohn-Bendit and Daniel
Cohn-Bendit. Mountain View,

Calif., SRAFPRINT, 196]
[20]p. 22cm.
Cover title.
1. Anarchism and anarchists--
France. 2. Student movements--
France. I. Cohen-Bendit, Dan-
iel. II. SRAFPRINT Co-Op.
MiU

C211
Coleman, Leslie, 1901-
Youth will organize for freedom.
[Chicago, Students for a Demo-
cratic Society, 1968]
11p.
1. Students for a Democratic
Society. 2. Military service,
Compulsory. 3. Negroes--Civil
rights. I. Students for a Demo-
cratic Society.
WHi-L, NUC 69-73248

C212
Coles, Robert.
The migrant farmer. Atlanta,
Southern Regional Council, 1965.
32p.
1. Agricultural laborers.
I. Southern Regional Council.
WHi-L

C213
Coles, Robert.
Southern children under desegregation; a report to be presented
to the American Psychiatric Association at its annual meeting,
May 6, 1963. [Atlanta, Southern
Regional Council, 1963?]
46p.
1. Negroes--Education. 2. Edu-
cation--Southern States.
3. Segregation in education.
I. Southern Regional Council.
GAU, NUC 67-47852

C214
Colon, Clara.
Enter fighting: today's woman,
a Marxist-Leninist view. [New
York, New Outlook Publishers,
1970]
95p. 22cm.
Cover title.
1. Woman--Rights of women.
2. Communism. I. New Outlook

Publishers.
MiU

C215
Columbia Strike Committee.
  Why we strike. [New York, 1968?]
  19p.
  Cover title.
  1. Student movements--Columbia
  University.
  WHi-L

C216
Combined Universities Campaign for
    Nuclear Disarmament.
  Prospectus for North Bay '64.
  [n.p., 1964]
  5 leaves. 28cm.
  Cover title.
  1. North Bay, Ontario. 2. Disarmament.
  WHi-A

C217
Come out!; selections from the
    radical gay liberation news-
    paper. [New York, Times
    Change Press, 1970]
  62p. illus. 18cm.
  1. Homosexuality. I. Times
  Change Press.
  CtU

C218
Commager, Henry Steele.
  1918-1968: is the world safer
  for anything? [Woodmont, Conn.,
  Promoting Enduring Peace, c1968]
  [4]p. 28cm.
  Caption title.
  Reprinted from Saturday Review.
  1. War. 2. Peace. I. Promoting
  Enduring Peace.
  KU-RH

C219
Commager, Henry Steele.
  On the way to 1984. [Nashville]
  Southern Student Organizing Com-
  mittee [196]
  5 [1]p. 28cm.
  Cover title.
  1. U.S. Central Intelligence
  Agency. 2. Vietnamese conflict,
  1961-1975. I. Southern Student

Organizing Committee.
MiU

C220
Commager, Henry Steele.
  Why the students revolt; a noted
  historian takes a look at the
  turmoil on our campus. Philadelphia, Women's International
  League for Peace and Freedom,
  1968.
  6p. 28cm.
  Cover title.
  Reprinted from Philadelphia Evening Bulletin.
  1. Student movements. I. Women's
  International League for Peace
  and Freedom.
  KU-RH

C221
Committee for a Labor Party.
  This is not an open group. Albany, Calif. [1970]
  [1] leaf. 36cm.
  Caption title.
  1. Progressive Labor Party.
  2. Bay Area Strike Support Committee. 3. General Electric
  Company. 4. Strike and lockouts.
  CU-B

C222
Committee for Economic Alterna-
    tives, Davis, Calif.
  Economic measures against the
  war. [Davis, Calif.? 196]
  [2] leaves. 28cm.
  Caption title.
  1. Vietnamese conflict, 1961-
  1975.
  KU-RH

C223
Committee for Free Assembly and
    Political Expression on
    Campus.
  A fight for democratic rights;
  support the right of the Young
  Socialist Alliance to gain re-
  cognition on Florida state campuses. [Tallahassee, Fld.,
  1972?]
  folder. 22x9cm.
  Cover title.

1. Student movements--Florida.
2. Young Socialist Alliance.
KU-RH

C224
Committee for GI Rights.
    Soldiers' against the war; the
    story of Pvt. Andrew Stapp and
    the Fort Sill GI's. [New York]
    1967.
    7p. illus.
    Caption title.
    1. Vietnamese conflict, 1961-
    1975. 2. Stapp, Andrew.
    3. Soldiers.
    WHi-L

C225
Committee for Lowndes County.
    Support the Lowndes County Free-
    dom Organization. [Berkeley,
    196]
    folder. 22x10cm.
    Cover title.
    1. Lowndes County, Ala.--Race
    question. 2. Negroes--Lowndes
    County, Ala.
    CU-B

C226
Committee for Miners.
    Working papers on poverty in
    Eastern Kentucky. Hazard, Ken-
    tucky Conference, sponsors:
    Committee for Miners [and] Eco-
    nomic Research and Action Pro-
    ject of Students for a Democra-
    tic Society. Ann Arbor, Econo-
    mic Research and Action Project
    [1964]
    1v. 28cm.
    Cover title.
    1. Poor--Kentucky. 2. Kentucky
    --Economic conditions. I. Stu-
    dents for a Democratic Action.
    Economic Research and Action
    Project.
    WHi-A

C227
Committee for Nonviolent Action.
    Act now for freedom to travel.
    [New York, Committee for Non-
    Violent Action, 1964?]
    [2]p. 28cm.
    Caption title.

1. Travel. 2. International
travel regulations.
CU-B

C228
Committee for Nonviolent Action.
    The continuing Cuban crisis;
    policy statement of the Quebec-
    Washington-Guantanamo walk for
    peace sponsored by the National
    Committee for Nonviolent Action.
    [New York, 196]
    [4]p. 28cm.
    Caption title.
    1. Cuba.
    CU-B

C229
Committee for Nonviolent Action.
    The Cuban crisis; policy state-
    ment of the National Committee
    for Nonviolent Action. [New
    York, 196]
    folder.
    Caption title.
    1. U.S.--For. rel.--Russia.
    2. Russia--For. rel.--U.S.
    3. Cuba--For. rel.--Russia.
    WHi-A

C230
Committee for Nonviolent Action.
    Quebec-Washington-Guantanamo
    walk for peace. [New York,
    196]
    [4]p. illus. 28cm.
    1. Peace. I. Title.
    WHi-A

C231
Committee for Nonviolent Action.
    Some facts about Vietnam. [New
    York, 196]
    folder 21x10cm.
    Cover title.
    1. Vietnamese conflict, 1961-
    1975.
    CU-B

C232
Committee for Nonviolent Action.
    Victims and executioners. [New
    York, 196]
    [2]p. 28cm.
    Caption title.
    1. Vietnamese conflict,

1961-1975.
CU-B, KU-RH

C233
Committee for Nonviolent Action.
  What is CNVA. [New York, 196]
  folder.
  1. Peace--Societies, etc.
  WHi-A

C234
Committee for One Society.
  Inventory of racism: how to look
  for institutional racism. Chicago, 1968.
  5p. 28cm.
  Cover title.
  1. Race discrimination.
  CU-B

C235
Committee for One Society.
  Racism in the United States; who
  is responsible? [Chicago?
  196 ?]
  [12] leaves. 28cm.
  Caption title.
  1. Negroes--Civil rights.
  2. Race discrimination.
  CU-B

C236
Committee for One Society.
  The YMCA of metropolitan Chicago; an action research project. Chicago, 1968.
  9 leaves. 28cm.
  Caption title.
  1. Negroes--Civil rights.
  CU-B

C237
Committee for Peaceful Alterna-
    tives, Chicago.
  Guide to disarmament. [Chicago,
  195]
  24p.
  Cover title.
  1. Atomic weapons and disarmament.
  WHi-L

C238
Committee for Political Studies.
  Hope for the future. New York
  [1969?]

9 leaves. 28cm.
1. Socialism. 2. Revolutions.
KU-RH

C239
Committee for Political Studies.
  The road to power; a catalogue
  of revolutionary literature.
  [New York? 196]
  2 leaves. 28cm.
  Cover title.
  1. Socialism--Bibliography.
  KU-RH

C240
Committee for Political Studies.
  Winning the masses for United
  States revolution; a discussion
  pamphlet for people interested
  in socialism, dealing with the
  question that is uppermost; is
  there a revolutionary future for
  the people of the United States?
  New York [1967]
  15 leaves. 28cm.
  "2nd revised edition."
  1. Revolutions. 2. Socialism.
  KU-RH

C241
Committee for the Distribution of
    the Mississippi Story.
  Mississippi violence vs human
  rights. Atlanta [196]
  [16]p. illus. 22cm.
  Cover title.
  1. Mississippi--Race question.
  MiU

C242
Committee for Traditional Indian
    Land and Life.
  The black mesa crisis. Rev.
  Los Angeles, Calif., 1970.
  9p. 28cm.
  1. Indians of North America--
  Government relations. 2. Na-
  vaho Indians. 3. Hopi Indians.
  KU-RH

C243
Committee for World Development
    and World Disarmament.
  The challenge of peace. New
  York [1957]
  28p. 28cm. (Louis Pink lec-

tures, 1956-1957)
1. Peace.   2. International cooperation.
MiU-L, NNC-L

C244
Committee for World Development
    and World Disarmament.
Disarmament and nuclear weapons
tests; a compilation of organizational statements, policies &
resolutions on disarmament and
nuclear weapons testing and
some related foreign policy
issues. New York [196]
37p. 28cm.
Cover title.
1. Atomic weapons and disarmament. 2. U.S.--Foreign policy.
WHi-A

C245
Committee for World Development
    and World Disarmament.
The economics of disarmament;
a discussion and survey. New
York, 1959.
[4]p. (1st fact sheet)
1. U.S.--Military policy.
2. U.S.--Econ. condit. 3. Disarmament.
DS

C246
Committee of Concerned Asian
    Scholars.
Arguments & counter arguments
concerning the U.S. involvement
in Indo-China. [Berkeley, 1970]
5p. 36cm.
Caption title.
1. Indochina, French--For. rel.
--U.S.
CU-B

C247
Committee of Concerned Asian
    Scholars.
Do you still believe in the
war? [Berkeley, 1970?]
[2]p. 28cm.
Caption title.
1. Vietnamese conflict, 1961-
1975.
CU-B

C248
Committee of Concerned Asian
    Scholars.
The North Vietnamese agression
argument. [Berkeley, 1970?]
[2]p. 28cm.
Caption title.
1. Vietnamese conflict, 1961-
1975.
CU-B

C249
Committee of Concerned Asian
    Scholars, Cornell University.
Fact sheet on Cambodia. [Ith-
aca, N.Y., Glad Day Press,
196]
[4]p. 28cm.
Caption title.
1. Cambodia. I. Glad Day Press.
NNU-T

C250
Committee of Concerned Asian
    Scholars, Cornell University.
Fact sheet on Vietnam. [Ithaca,
N.Y., Glad Day Press, 196]
[2]p. 28cm.
Caption title.
1. Vietnam. I. Glad Day Press.
NNU-T

C251
Committee of Concerned Asian
    Scholars, Cornell University.
Laotian fact sheet. [Ithaca,
N.Y., Glad Day Press, 196]
[2]p. 28cm.
Caption title.
1. Laos. I. Glad Day Press.
NNU-T

C252
Committee of Concerned Asian
    Scholars, Harvard Chapter.
Fact sheets on the Indochina
war. [Cambridge, Mass, 1969?]
(unpaged) 28cm.
Cover title.
1. U.S.--Military policy.
2. Indochina, French--For. rel.
--U.S.
KU-RH

C253
Committee of Correspondence.

A statement. [New York, 1960?]
[8]p. 24x10cm.
Cover title.
1. Social change. 2. Peace.
CU-B

C254
Committee of First Amendment
    Defendants.
Behind the bars for the first
amendment; the story of 36 Americans, four of them already
in jail, and the rest facing
the possibility of imprisonment
because they believe the first
amendment to the constitution
means what it says. [New York,
1960]
32p. illus. 21cm.
1. Civil rights. 2. U.S. Constitution. 1st amendment.
MH, OrU, MiU, KU-J, WHi-L

C255
Committee of Inquiry into the Ad-
    ministration of Justice in the
    Freedom Struggle.
Justice. [New York, Congress
of Racial Equality, 1962]
33p. illus. 23cm.
Cover title.
1. Negroes--Civil rights.
2. Student Nonviolent Coordinating Committee.
MiU, WHi-L, NUC 64-66858

C256
Committee of Responsibility to
    Save War-Burned and War-
    Injured Vietnamese Children.
Six who survived. [New York,
c1968]
[20]p. 23cm.
Cover title.
1. Vietnamese conflict, 1961-
1975. 2. Children.
CU-B

C257
Committee of Returned Volunteers.
Committee of Returned Volun-
teers: position paper on the
Peace Corps. [Chicago, 1970?]
[2]p. 28cm.
Caption title.

1. U.S. Peace Corps.
KU-RH

C258
Committee of Returned Volunteers.
Cutler-Hammer: global understanding through electronic
warfare. [Milwaukee, 196]
[4]p. illus. 28cm.
Caption title.
1. Cutler-Hammer Corporation.
2. Africa, South--Race question.
KU-RH

C259
Committee of Returned Volunteers.
If the Peace Corps appeals to
you maybe Chase Manhattan can,
too. [Milwaukee, 1970?]
26p. 22cm.
Cover title.
1. U.S. Peace Corps. 2. U.S.--
Foreign policy.
KU-RH

C260
Committee of Returned Volunteers.
Luta struggle: voices of African liberation. [New York,
1970?]
29p. illus. 28cm.
Cover title.
1. Africa, South--Race question.
KU-RH

C261
Committee of Returned Volunteers.
Volunteer? [Chicago, 1970?]
32p. 28cm.
Cover title.
1. U.S. Peace Corps. 2. Un-
derdeveloped areas. 3. U.S.--
Foreign policy.
KU-RH

C262
Committee of Returned Volunteers,
    Milwaukee Chapter.
Peru: discovering imperialism.
2d ed. [Milwaukee] 1970.
54p. map. 28cm.
1. Imperialism. 2. U.S.--Rela-
tions (general) with Peru.
3. Peru--Relations (general)
with the U.S. 4. Peru--Pol.

& govt.
KU-RH

C263
Committee of Returned Volunteers.
    National Office.
CRV political position paper.
Chicago [1970?]
[2]p. 28cm.
Caption title.
1. U.S.--Foreign policy.
2. Underdeveloped area.
KU-RH

C264
Committee of Returned Volunteers,
    New York.
1970: a year of decision in
Japan--U.S. security treaty.
[New York, 1970?]
6p. 28cm.
Caption title.
1. U.S.--Foreign relations--
Japan. 2. Japan--Foreign rela-
tions--U.S.
KU-RH

C265
Committee of Returned Volunteers,
    New York. Africa Committee.
Mozambique will be free. [New
York, c1969]
44p. illus. 28cm.
Cover title.
1. Mozambique--Pol. & govt.
2. Portugal--Relations (general)
with Mozambique.
KU-RH

C266
Committee of Returned Volunteers.
    New York. Africa Group.
Gulf Oil Corporation: a study
in exploitation. [New York,
1971]
47p. illus. 26cm.
1. Gulf Oil Corporation.
2. Petroleum industry and trade.
KU-RH

C267
Committee of Returned Volunteers,
    San Francisco.
Thailand [an information kit.
San Francisco, 1970?]
1v. (unpaged) illus., map.

31cm.
1. Thailand--Pol. & govt.
2. U.S.--Relations (general)
with Thailand.
KU-RH

C268
Committee on Racial Equality,
    Syracuse.
Syracuse: how far from Birmingham? [Syracuse, N.Y., 1963]
24p. illus.
1. Syracuse, N.Y.--Race question.
2. New York (State)--Race question. 3. Negroes--Syracuse,
N.Y.
WHi-L

C269
Committee to Aid the Bloomington
    Students.
The Indiana "subversion" speech.
[New York, 196]
26p. 22cm.
Cover title.
1. Young Socialist Alliance.
2. Student movements--Indiana.
3. Anti-communist movements--
Indiana.
WHi-L

C270
Committee to Defend Francisco
    Molina.
The case of Francisco Molina,
political prisoner. [New York,
196]
15p. illus.
Cover title.
1. Political prisoners.
2. Cuba. 3. U.S.--For. rel.--
Cuba. 4. Molina, Francisco.
MiU

C271
Committee to Defend the French
    Students.
France: the struggle continues.
[New York, 1968]
31p. illus.
Cover title.
1. Paris--Riots, 1968. 2. Stu-
dent movements--France.
MiU

C272
Committee to Defend the Rights of
    Pfc. Petrick.
  Free speech for GIs; the case of
  Pfc. Howard Petrick, a soldier
  opposed to the Vietnam war.
  [New York, 1967]
  23p. illus. 28cm.
  Cover title.
  1. Vietnamese conflict, 1961-
  1975. 2. Soldiers. 3. Civil
  rights. 4. Petrick, Howard.
  CU-B, MoU, WHi-L

C273
Committee to End Sedition Laws.
  State sedition laws, the Nelson
  case and the threat to labor,
  the negro people, academic and
  religious circles. Pittsburg
  [1955?]
  9 [1] leaf. 28cm.
  Cover title.
  At head of title: Facts.
  1. Nelson, Steve. 2. Negroes--
  Civil rights. 3. Sedition.
  4. Subversive activities.
  KU-J

C274
Committee to Oppose the Deporta-
    tion of Joseph Johnson.
  Anti-war cartoons, by Eric
  [James Erickson. Minneapolis]
  1967.
  31p.
  1. Vietnamese conflict, 1961-
  1975. 2. Johnson, Joseph.
  WHi-L

C275
Committee to Support Resistance.
  A call to resist illegitimate
  authority; to the young men of
  America, to the whole of the
  American people, and to all men
  of good will everywhere. [St.
  Louis, 196]
  2 [2] leaves. 28cm.
  Caption title.
  1. Government, Resistance to.
  2. Vietnamese conflict, 1961-
  1975.
  KU-RH

C276
Commonweal.
  Red, white and blue fascism?
  Woodmont, Conn., Promoting
  Enduring Peace [1969]
  [1] leaf. 28cm. (No. 147)
  Caption title.
  Reprinted from Commonweal, June
  20, 1969.
  1. Fascism. I. Promoting En-
  during Peace.
  KU-RH

C277
Communist Party of Canada.
  Program of the Labor Progressive
  Party. [Toronto, Eveready
  Printers, n.d.]
  46p.
  Cover title.
  1. Labor-Progressive Party
  (Canada) 2. Communism--Canada.
  CaOTC, NUC 69-80466

C278
Communist Party of Canada.
  The road to socialism in Canada;
  the program of the Communist
  Party of Canada. [Toronto,
  1967?]
  32p.
  Cover title.
  1. Socialism in Canada.
  MiU

C279
Communist Party of Canada.
  Submission of the Labor-Progres-
  sive Party to the Royal Commis-
  sion on Canada's Economic Pros-
  pects, January 1956. [Toronto,
  Progress Pub., 1956]
  48p.
  Cover title: Canada's future:
  what the Labor-Progressive
  Party proposed to the Royal
  Commission on Canada's Economic
  Prospects.
  1. Canada--Econ. condit.
  2. Communism--Canada
  I. Labor-Progressive
  Party (Canada)
  CaOTC; NUC 69-80722

C280
Communist Party of Canada. <u>Nat-</u>
    <u>ional Executive Committee</u>.
Socialism and you.   [Toronto,
Progress Books, 1959]
28p.
Cover title.
1. Socialism in Canada.
I. Progress Books.
CaOTC

C281
Communist Party of Canada.
    <u>20th Convention</u>, <u>1969</u>.
The 20th convention Communist
Party of Canada, April 4-6,
1969; resolutions, reports,
policy statements.   [Toronto,
1969?]
102p.
Cover title.
1. Communism--Canada.
MiU

C282
Communist Party of the United
    States of America.
The challenge to labor; resolu-
tion adopted by the 17th Nation-
al Convention of the Communist
Party, U.S.A.   [New York, New
Century Publishers, 1960]
18p.
Cover title.
1. Labor and laboring classes.
2. Communism.   I. New Century
Publishers.
MiU

C283
Communist Party of the United
    States of America.
Constitution of the Communist
Party of the United States of
America.   [New York, New Cen-
tury Publishers, 1957]
24p.   17cm.
Text...adopted by the 16th
National Convention--February
9-12, 1957.
1. Communism.
NcD, MiU, MiDW, WHi-L, KU-RH

C284
Communist Party of the United
    States of America.

Constitution of the Communist
Party, U.S.A.; adopted by the
16th National Convention,
February 9-12, 1957. [n.p.,
1957]
7 leaves. 26cm.
Cover title.
1. Communism.
KU-J

C285
Communist Party of the United
    States of America.
Draft resolution for the 16th
national convention of the
Communist Party, U.S.A., New
York, New Century Publishers,
1956.
62p.   19cm.
"Adopted Sept. 13, 1956"
1. Communism.
KU-J

C286
Communist Party of the United
    States of America.
Main political resolution
adopted by the 16th annual
convention of the Communist
Party, U.S.A., February 7-12,
1957. New York, New Century
Publishers, 1957.
81p.
1. U.S.--Pol. & govt.--1953-
        . I. New Century
Publishers.
KU-J

C287
Communist Party of the United
    States of America.
New program of the Communist
Party, U.S.A.; a draft. New
York, Political Affairs Pub-
lishers [1966]
127p.   22cm.
1. Communism.   I. Political
Affairs Publishers.
NBuU, InU, OU, NIC, IaU, N,
NcD, 66-19254

C288
Communist Party of the United
    States of America.
New program of the Communist
Party, U.S.A.; second draft.

New York, 1968.
1 v.
1. Communism.
WHi-L, MiU, NUC 70-61075

C289
Communist Party of the United
    States of America.
New program of the Communist
Party, U.S.A. New York, New
Outlook Publishers, 1970.
128p. 22cm.
1. New Outlook Publishers.
LC 79-127023

C290
Communist Party of the United
    States of America.
Notes and proposals for the
coming convention of the Communist Party. Submitted by a
group of communist intellectuals. [n.p., 1957?]
16 leaves. 36cm.
Caption title.
1. Communism.
KU-J

C291
Communist Party of the United
    States of America.
Passage to progress. The 1964
election mandate and the road
ahead. New York, New Century
Publishers, 1964.
13p.
1. U.S.--Pol. & govt.--1963-
     . 2. Johnson, Lyndon
Baines, Pres., U.S., 1908-1973.
I. New Century Publishers.
CSSR

C292
Communist Party of the United
    States of America.
S.D.S. at the crossroads [by
Communist Party--W.E.B. Du-
Bois Club Caucus. Chicago,
1969]
[2]p. 36cm.
Caption title.
1. Students for a Democratic
Society. I. DuBois (W.E.B.)
Clubs of America.
WHi-L

C293
Communist Party of the United
    States of America.
To end poverty and unemployment
in the U.S.: economic program
of the Communist Party, U.S.A.
[New York, 1964]
[8]p. illus. 28cm.
Caption title.
At head of title: An American
people's program.
1. Poverty. 2. Negroes--Employ-
ment. 3. U.S.--Econ. condit.
KU-RH

C294
Communist Party of the United
    States of America.
Unite for peace, Negro freedom,
labor's advance, socialism;
resolutions of the 18th national
convention of the Communist Party, U.S.A. New York, New Outlook Publishers, 1967.
120p.
1. Communism. I. New Outlook
Publishers.
MiU, NUC 69-136238

C295
Communist Party of the United
    States of America.
The United States in crisis;
the communist solution. New
York, New Outlook Publishers,
1969.
91p. 19cm.
"Main political resolution
adopted by the 19th National
Convention of the Communist
Party, U.S.A., May 3, 1969."
1. U.S.--Pol. & govt.--1969-
          I. New Outlook Publishers.
ICU, IU, DLC, 78-283494,
WHi-L, AAP

C296
Communist Party of the United
    States of America. Connect-
    icut.
The economy of Connecticut;
problems and program. [Bridge-
port, Conn., 1958]
35p. 23cm.
Cover title.

1. Connecticut--Econ. condit.
KU-J, WHi-L

C297
Communist Party of the United
    States of America. 18th
    Convention, New York, 1966.
For life with purpose. [n.p.,
1966?]
49p.
1. Communism.
WHi-L

C298
Communist Party of the United
    States of America. Minnesota.
Are you paying their taxes? A
study with action recommendations, by the Minnesota Communist Party. Minneapolis,
1970.
20 leaves. 28cm.
Caption title.
1. Taxation--Minnesota.
KU-RH

C299
Communist Party of the United
    States of America. National
    Committee.
Draft resolution for the 16th
national convention of the
Communist Party, USA (adopted
13 Sept. 1956) New York, New
Century Publishers, 1956.
62p.
I. New Century Publishers.
NNJef, MH-PA, DLC, ViU, DS,
NcD, CtY, WHi-L

C300
Communist Party of the United
    States of America. National
    Convention.
An open letter to Pres. Johnson
and an appeal to the American
people, black and white. [New
York, 1968?]
7p. ports. 23cm.
1. Johnson, Lyndon Baines,
Pres., U.S. 1908-1973.
2. Negroes.
CoU

C301
Communist Party of the United
    States of America. National
    Committee.
Peace, jobs, democracy; a pro-
gram for 86th Congress. [New
York, n.d.]
[4]p. illus. 28cm.
Caption title.
1. Peace. 2. Communism.
WHi-L, NUC 64-63207

C302
Communist Party of the United
    States of America. National
    Committee.
A policy for American labor.
[New York, New Century Pub-
lishers, 1958]
19p. 20cm. (A Political
Affairs pamphlet)
Cover title.
1. Labor and laboring classes.
I. New Century Publishers.
KU-RH

C303
Communist Party of the United
    States of America. National
    Committee.
Theoretical aspects of the
Negro question in the United
States. New York [1959?]
39p. illus.
"Supplement to Party Affairs,
February, 1959"
1. Negroes. 2. U.S.--Race
question. 3. Communism.
MiU, KU-J, NUC 70-4537

C304
Communist Party of the United
    States of America. National
    Farm Commission.
The farm crisis; a program for
farmer-labor unity to meet the
problems confronting agriculture in the United States today.
New York [New Century Publish-
ers] 1955.
23p.
Cover title.
1. Agriculture. I. New

Century Publishers.
WHi-L, KU-J

C305
Communist Party of the United
    States of America. National
    Resolutions Committee.
Resolution on social democracy,
submitted by the National Resolution Committee for Action at
the National Convention. [n.p.,
195]
3 leaves. 36cm.
Caption title.
1. Socialism. 2. Liberalism.
KU-J

C306
Communist Party of the United
    States of America. National
    Veterans Committee.
On the struggle against re-
visionism. New York, 1956.
112p. 20cm.
Partial contents--William Z.
Foster on Earl Browder.
1. Browder, Earl Russell,
1891-   I. Foster, William
Zebulon, 1881-
RPB

C307
Communist Party of the United
    States of America. New York
    District. Educational Dept.
A manual of self study. [New
York, 195]
35p. 21cm.
Cover title.
1. Communism.
NIC, NUC 64-63310

C308
Communist Party of the United
    States of America. New York
    (State)
The democratic way of the crisis
in education; a program for re-
solving the crisis in the New
York City public school system.
[New York, 1964]
71p. 23cm.
1. Negroes--Education. 2. New
York (City)--Public schools.
N, WHi-L, NUC 65-54154

C309
Communist Party of the United
    States of America. New York
    (State)
Subways are for sitting; [a ten
year plan to meet New York
City's subway crisis. New York,
1963?]
19 leaves. map. 28cm.
Cover title.
1. Subways--New York (City)
NN, NUC 64-63208

C310
Communist Party of the United
    States of America. 17th Con-
    vention, New York, 1959.
Main political resolution. On
trade union problems. On the
negro question in the U.S.
[New York, New Century Publish-
ers] 1960.
97p. 20cm. (Political Affairs,
v. 39, no. 2, Feb., 1960)
"Special enlarged issue."
1. Negroes--Civil rights.
2. Trade-unions. I. New Century Publishers.
NIC

C311
Communist Party of the United
    States of America. 17th Con-
    vention, New York, 1959.
The negro question in the U.S.
A.; resolution adopted by the
17th national convention of the
Communist Party, U.S.A., to-
gether with the address to the
convention by Claude Lightfoot.
[New York, New Century Publish-
ers, 1960]
23p. 20cm.
1. Negroes--Civil rights.
2. Communism. I. Lightfoot,
Claude M. 1910-   II. New
Century Publishers.
ICU

C312
Communist Party of the United
    States of America. 17th Con-
    vention, New York, 1959.
Our sights to the future; key-
note report and concluding re-

marks by Gus Hall.   [New York,
New Century Publishers, 1960]
30p.   20cm.
1. Campaign literature, 1960,
Communist.   I. Hall, Gus.
II. New Century Publishers.
N, DLC, NUC 63-4624

C313
Communist Party of the United
    States of America. 16th Con-
    vention, New York, 1957.
Main political resolution
adopted by the 16th annual con-
vention of the Communist Party,
U.S.A., Feb. 9-12, 1957. New
York, New Century Publishers,
1957.
81p.
I. New Century Publishers.
MH, NN, CtY, KU-S

C314
Communist Party of the United
    States of America. 16th Con-
    vention, New York, 1957.
Resolution adopted by the 16th
national convention, CPUSA,
February 9-12, 1957. [New York?
1957?
24 leaves. 36cm.
Cover title.
NIC, NUC 69-60788

C315
Communist Party of the United
    States of America. Southern
    California.
A municipal program for Los
Angeles. [Los Angeles, 1959]
15p. 22cm.
1. Los Angeles--Pol. & govt.
CU-B, NUC 66-55431

C316
Communist Party of the United
    States of America. Southern
    California.
Telling it as it is; twenty
questions on the war in Vietnam.
[Los Angeles, 1966?]
folder (8p.) 21x10cm.
Caption title.
1. Vietnamese conflict, 1961-
1975.
CU-B

C317
Communist Party of the United
    States of America (Marxist-
    Leninist)
Declaration of the Communist
Party USA (Marxist-Leninist)
[San Pedro, Calif., 196 ?]
7 [1]p. 22cm. (Political
pamphlet 1)
Cover title.
MiU

C318
Compean, Mario.
La raza unida party in Texas.
Speeches by Mario Compean and
Jose Angel Gutierrez. [New
York, Pathfinder Press, 1970]
15p.
1. Mexicans in the U.S. 2. La
Raza Unida Party. I. Gutierrez,
Jose Angel, jt. auth. II. Path-
finder Press.
WHi-L

C319
Computer People for Peace.
Clark Squire and the Panther 21.
[New York, 197]
[20] leaves. 28cm.
Cover title.
1. Black Panther Party.
2. Squire, Clark.
NNU-T

C320
Condit, Wid.
The administration monster.
[Berkeley, Young People's
Socialist League, 1965]
9p.
1. Free Speech Movement.
I. Young People's Socialist
League.
CU-B

C321
Conference on Poverty and the
    Economy, University of Illi-
    nois, 1964.
[Working papers. n.p., Univer-
sity of Illinois Young Democrats
and Students for a Democratic
Society, 1964?]
1v. 28cm.
Cover title.

1. Poverty. 2. U.S.--Econ.
condit. I. Students for a Democratic Society.
WHi-A

C322
Congress of Racial Equality.
  A brief history of the Congress
  of Racial Equality, 1942-1969.
  New York, 1969.
  6 leaves. 28cm.
  Cover title.
  1. Negroes--Civil rights.
  CU-B

C323
Congress of Racial Equality.
  CORE offers an answer. [New
  York, 196]
  [4]p. illus. 21x9cm.
  Cover title: Where is democracy.
  1. Negroes--Civil rights.
  KU-RH

C324
Congress of Racial Equality.
  CORE rules for action. New
  York [196 ?]
  folder. 22x9cm.
  Cover title.
  1. Negroes--Civil rights.
  CU-B

C325
Congress of Racial Equality.
  Calendar of coercion. New
  York [196]
  [12]p. illus.
  1. Negroes--Civil rights.
  MiU

C326
Congress of Racial Equality.
  Justice? [New York., 1962]
  33p. illus.
  1. Negroes--Civil rights.
  MH-IR, NUC 64-63388

C327
Congress of Racial Equality.
  Rent strikes. [New York?
  196 ?]
  5 leaves. 28cm.
  Caption title.
  1. Negroes--Civil rights.
  2. Negroes--Housing.
  CU-B

C328
Congress of Racial Equality.
  Sit ins; the students report.
  [Compiled and edited by Jim
  Peck. New York, c1960]
  [16]p. illus. 21cm.
  1. Student movements.
  2. Negroes--Civil rights.
  I. Peck, James.
  NjR, DLC, MNS, NcD

C329
Congress of Racial Equality.
  This is CORE. New York [196]
  folder 21x10cm.
  Cover title.
  1. Negroes--Civil rights.
  CU-B

C330
Congress of Racial Equality,
  Berkeley, Calif. Chapter.
  Presentation to the Berkeley
  Board of Education on de facto
  segregated schools. [Berkeley?]
  1962.
  6p. 36cm.
  Caption title.
  1. Berkeley, Calif.--Race quest-
  ion. 2. Negroes--Berkeley,
  Calif.
  CU-B

C331
Congress of Racial Equality,
  Cleveland.
  Proposal for creating a move-
  ment of unemployed in Cleveland
  [by] Cleveland CORE and the
  Cleveland Community Project of
  SDS. Ann Arbor, Students for a
  Democratic Society and its Eco-
  nomic Research and Action Pro-
  ject [196]
  8p. 28cm.
  Cover title.
  1. Poor--Cleveland. 2. Cleve-
  land--Econ. condit. 3. Ne-
  groes--Civil rights. I. Stu-
  dents for a Democratic Society,
  Cleveland. II. Students for a
  Democratic Society. Economic
  Research and Action Project.
  MiU, WHi-A

C332
Congress of Racial Equality.

Legal Dept.
The 1965 civil rights law; a hard
hard look. [n.p., 1965?]
19 leaves. 29cm.
1. Negroes--Civil rights.
C, NUC 69-66080

C333
Congress of Racial Equality,
    Los Angeles.
Our proposal to make a dream
come true. Los Angeles [196 ?]
[24]p. 11x16cm.
Cover title.
1. Negroes--Civil rights.
CU-B

C334
Congress of Racial Equality.
    Tallahassee, Fld.
White student hunger-strikes
against segregated lunch
counters. Tallahassee [1961?]
[1] leaf. 36cm.
Caption title.
1. Student movements.
2. Negroes--Civil rights.
CU-B

C335
Connecticut War Tax Resisters'
    Fund for Life.
Statement opening the fund for
life. Voluntown, Conn., 1971.
[1] leaf. 28cm.
Caption title.
1. Vietnamese conflict, 1961-
1975. 2. Tax evasion.
KU-RH

C336
Connections.
California's prisoners: victims
of the adult authority. [San
Francisco, 196]
[4]p. 21cm.
1. Prisoners--California.
KU-RH

C337
Connections.
Connections. [San Francisco,
196]
[4]p. 22cm.
1. Prisons.
KU-RH

C338
Connections.
Connections [and excerpts from
a correspondence between a
prison widow and a columnist of
the San Quentin news. San
Francisco, 196]
[4]p. 22cm.
1. Prisons.
KU-RH

C339
The conscience of the Senate on
    the Vietnam war. Introduct-
    ion: McNamara's war, by Carl
    Marzani. [New York] Marzani
    & Munsell [196]
23p. 23cm.
Cover title.
1. Vietnamese conflict, 1961-
1975. 2. U.S. Congress.
Senate. I. Marzani, Carl.
II. Marzani and Munsell.
WHi-A

C340
Conscription and conscience;
    letters from draft resisters
    to the selective service
    system, December 4, 1967.
    [Ann Arbor, 1967?]
[9] leaves. 28cm.
Cover title.
1. Military service, Compulsory.
MiU-H

C341
Conspiracy.
Conspiracy. [Chicago, 1970?]
[6]p. 29x22cm.
Cover title.
1. Chicago--Riots, August, 1968.
2. Democratic Party. National
Convention, Chicago, 1968.
3. Government, Resistance to.
KU-RH

C342
Conspiracy.
Join the conspiracy. [Chicago,
1969?]
8p. 21cm.
Cover title.
1. Chicago--Riot, August 1968.
2. Democratic Party. National
Convention, Chicago, 1968.

3. Government, Resistance to.
KU-RH

C343
Constitutional Liberties Infor-
    mation Center.
  Verdict first, trial after.
  [Los Angeles, 196]
  24p. 21x9cm.
  Partial contents--Opening state-
  ment of John J. Abt.
  1. Healey, Dorothy. 2. Commun-
  ism. 3. Internal security.
  I. Abt, John J.
  KU-RH

C344
Continental Congress for Solid-
    arity with Cuba, Niteroi,
    Brazil, 1963.
  Complete resolutions. New York,
  Fair Play for Cuba Committee
  [1963?]
  13 leaves. 28cm.
  Cover title.
  1. Cuba--For. rel.--Latin Amer-
  ica. 2. U.S.--For. rel.--Latin
  America. 3. Latin America--For.
  rel.--Cuba. I. Fair Play for
  Cuba Committee.
  FU, MiU, NUC 6613693

C345
Converse, Elizabeth, ed.
  Alternative perspectives on
  Vietnam: report on an inter-
  national conference, edited by
  Elizabeth Converse, Herbert C.
  Kelman and Edward Vandenberg.
  Ithaca, N.Y., Inter-University
  Committee for Debate of Foreign
  Policy [1966]
  82p. 28cm.
  1. Vietnamese conflict, 1961-
  1975. I. Kelman, Herbert C.
  II. Vandenberg, Edward.
  III. Inter-University Committee
  for Debate of Foreign Policy.
  WHi-A

C346
Conyers, James E.
  Black youth in a southern metro-
  polis. [Atlanta, Southern Regional Council, 1968]
  31p.

1. Youth--Atlanta. 2. Negroes--
Atlanta. 3. Atlanta--Race ques-
tion. I. Southern Regional
Council.
WHi-L

C347
Cook, Ann.
  Federal aid to education. [n.
  p.] Campus Division, Americans
  for Democratic Action [1963]
  11p. 36cm.
  Cover title.
  1. Federal aid to education.
  I. Americans for Democratic
  Action, Campus Division.
  MiU

C348
Cooke, Joanne.
  Here's to you, Mrs. Robinson.
  [n.p., 1969?]
  4 leaves. 28cm.
  Caption title.
  Reprinted from Motive, Mar.-
  Ap. 1969.
  1. Woman--Rights of women.
  KU-RH

C349
Cooperative High School Indepen-
    dent Press.
  A directory of high school
  underground papers, compiled
  by CHIPS. [Naperville, Ill.,
  1970]
  [10]p. 22cm.
  Cover title.
  1. Underground literature.
  KU-RH

C350
Copeland, Vincent.
  Expanding empire: the global
  war drive of big business and
  the forces that will stop it.
  [3d ed.] New York, Workers
  World Press [1971]
  62p. 22cm.
  1. U.S.--Econ. condit.
  2. U.S.--Foreign policy.
  3. Capitalism.
  4. Imperialism. I. Workers
  World Press.
  MiU, KU-RH

C351
Corretjer, Juan Antonio.
  Albizu Campos and the Ponce massacre. [New York, World Viet
  Publishers, 1965]
  24p. illus. 22cm.
  Cover title.
  1. Albizu Campos, Pedro, 1891-
      2. Puerto Rico--History--
  1898-1952. I. World View Publishers.
  MiU, KU-RH

C352
Cota, Kathie.
  Reflections on collectives, by
  the sisters in the collective
  that has no name [by] Kathie
  Cota [and others. Minneapolis,
  Women's Counseling Service
  1970?]
  8p. 22cm.
  Caption title.
  1. Woman--Rights of women.
  I. Women's Counseling Service,
  Minneapolis.
  KU-RH

C353
Cote, Michal.
  Canada and the O.A.S.: vision
  or mirage? [Toronto?] Latin
  American Working Group, 1969.
  40p. 28cm.
  Caption title.
  1. Organization of American
  States. 2. Canada--Relations
  (general) with Latin America.
  I. Latin American Working Group.
  KU-RH

C354
Coughlin, Richard J.
  Vietnam: lost opportunities for
  American policy. [Nashville]
  Southern Student Organizing
  Committee [196]
  4 [1]p. 28cm.
  Cover title.
  Reprinted from New South Stu-
  dent, Ap. 1967.
  1. Vietnamese conflict, 1961-
  1975. I. Southern Student
  Organizing Committee.
  MiU, WHi-L

C355
Council for a Livable World.
  ABM: point of no return? A
  critique of the Nike-X anti-
  ballistic missile system.
  [Washington, c1967]
  28p. 21cm.
  1. Antimissile missiles.
  KU-RH

C356
Council for a Volunteer Military.
  A volunteer military; the alternative to conscription. [Chi-
  cago, 196]
  10p. 22cm.
  Cover title.
  1. Military service, Compulsory.
  KU-RH

C357
Council for a World Without War.
  Vietnam kit. [Berkeley, 196]
  1v. illus. 36cm.
  1. Vietnamese conflict, 1961-
  1975.
  MoU

C358
Council of Federated Organizations.
  COFO political program. [Jack-
  son, Miss., 1964]
  3p. 28cm.
  Caption title.
  1. Negroes--Politics and suffrage. 2. Mississippi--Race
  questions. 3. Democratic Party.
  WHi-A

C359
Council of Federated Organizations.
  Freedom school data. Jackson,
  Miss. [1964?]
  5 [3] leaves. 28cm.
  Caption title.
  Partial contents--The house of
  liberty, by Joyce Brown.
  1. Negroes--Education. I. Brown,
  Joyce.
  WHi-A

C360
Council of Federated Organizations.
  Our powerless government.
  [Jackson, Miss.? 1964?]

[2] leaves. 36cm.
Caption title.
1. Mississippi--Race question.
WHi-A

C361
Council on Religion and the Homo-
    sexual.
  A brief of injustices; an in-
  dictment of our society in its
  treatment of the homosexual.
  San Francisco [196]
  12p. 28cm.
  1. Homosexuality.
  CU-B

C362
Council on Religion and the Homo-
    sexual.
  CRH: 1964/1968. [San Francisco,
  196]
  15p. 22cm. (Essays on homosexuality. Essay number 3)
  1. Homosexuality.
  MiU, KU-RH

C363
Council on Religion and the Homo-
    sexual.
  The challenge and progress of
  homosexual law reform. [San
  Francisco] 1968.
  72p. 22cm. (Essays on homosexuality, Essay number 2)
  1. Homosexuality.
  MiU

C364
Council on Religion and the Homo-
    sexual.
  A compendium of opinion of
  churches and church organizations. San Francisco, 1967.
  10p. 23cm.
  1. Homosexuality.
  CU-B

C365
Cousins, Andrea.
  Harlem: the neighborhood and
  social change. New York, Distributed by Students for a
  Democratic Society and its Economic Research and Action Project [196]
  15p. 28cm.

Cover title.
1. Harlem, New York (City).
2. Negroes--Harlem, New York
(City) I. Students for a Democratic Society. Economic Research and Action Project.
MiU, WHi-A

C366
Cowan, Paul.
  Schools of a revolution: seeing
  past the uniforms. [Chicago?
  Committee of Returned Volunteers? 196]
  6p. 28cm.
  Caption title.
  1. Cuba. I. Committee of Returned Volunteers.
  KU-RH

C367
Cowley, Joyce.
  Pioneers of women's liberation.
  [New York, Pathfinder Press,
  1969, 1971]
  15p. 22cm. (A Merit pamphlet)
  1. Woman--Rights of women.
  I. Pathfinder Press.
  CU-B, KU-RH

C368
Cowley, Joyce.
  The Santana case; tragedy of a
  Puerto Rican youth. [New York]
  Pioneer Publishers [1957]
  16 [2]p. illus. 22cm.
  Cover title.
  1. Puerto Ricans in the U.S.
  2. Santana, Frank. I. Pioneer
  Publishers.
  MiU

C369
Cox, Cedric.
  A report by four Canadians on
  Cuba as they saw it [by Cedric
  Cox and others] Toronto, Fair
  Play for Cuba Committee [196]
  31p.
  1. Cuba. I. Fair Play for Cuba
  Committee.
  MiU

C370
Cox, Harvey.
  Preventive war against the

Black Panthers. Nyack, N.Y.,
Fellowship Publications [1970?]
1 leaf. 28cm.
Caption title.
1. Black Panther Party. I. Fellowship Publications.
KU-RH

C371
Critical reactions to the Warren
    report. [New York] Marzani
    & Munsell [1964?]
64p. 22cm.
Cover title.
1. U.S. Warren Commission.
2. Kennedy, John Fitzgerald,
Pres. U.S., 1917-1963--Assasi-
nation. I. Marzani and Munsell.
KU-RH

C372
Crompton, Louis.
Homosexuality and the sickness
theory: a critique. [Berkeley,
Calif.? Committee of Concern
for Homosexuals? 1970?]
10p. 28cm.
Caption title.
1. Homosexuality. I. Committee
of Concern for Homosexuals.
KU-RH

C373
Cromwell, Niram A.
Life doesn't have to be this
way in the U.S.A. El Monte,
Calif., Foundation for Human
Advancement [196]
1v. (unpaged) 36cm.
1. Social change. 2. U.S.--So-
cial conditions. 3. U.S.--Econ.
condit.
MiU

C374
Cronan, Sheila.
Marriage. New York, The Feminists [196]
8p. 28cm.
Caption title.
1. Marriage. 2. Woman--Rights
of women. I. Feminists.
WHi-L

C375
Crosby, Alexander L.

The rape of the first amendment.
[New York, Emergency Civil Liberties Committee, 1961?]
20p. illus. 23cm.
Cover title.
1. U.S. Laws, statutes, etc.
Internal Security Act of 1950.
2. Communism. 3. Internal
security. I. Emergency Civil
Liberties Committee.
MiU, WHi-A, KU-RH

C376
Crosby, H. Ashton.
NATO tomorrow; its future as
adjunct of European and U.S.
security. [Washington, Council
for a Livable World, 1965]
[4]p. 28cm.
Caption title.
1. North Atlantic Treaty
Organization. 2. U.S.--Military
policy. I. Council for a Livable World.
KU-RH

C377
Crowell, Suzanne.
Appalachian history book (first
draft) Louisville, Ky.,
Southern Conference Educational
Fund [196]
39 [8]p. 28cm.
1. Appalachian Mountains--His-
tory. I. Southern Conference
Educational Fund.
WHi-L

C378
Crowley, George.
Post-utopian anarchy [by]
George & Louise Crowley.
Seattle, 1964.
22 leaves. 28cm.
Cover title.
1. Anarchism and anarchists.
I. Crowley, Louise, jt. auth.
MiU

C379
Crowley, George.
The urban school--a proposal to
Seattle. [Seattle, Seattle
Group, 196]
15 leaves. illus. 36cm. (Sea-
ttle Group pamphlet number 1)

1. Seattle--Schools. 2. Negroes
--Education. I. Seattle Group.
MiU

C380
Cruse, Harold.
  Marxism and the Negro struggle,
  articles by Harold Cruse,
  George Breitman, Clifton De-
  Berry. New York, Pioneer Pub-
  lishers [1965]
  48p. 22cm.
  1. Negroes--Civil rights.
  2. Socialism. I. Breitman,
  George, jt. auth. II. DeBerry,
  Clifton, jt. auth. III. Pioneer
  Publishers.
  MiU

C381
Cruse, Harold.
  Marxism and the Negro struggle,
  articles by Harold Cruse,
  George Breitman [and] Clifton
  DeBerry. [New York, Merit
  Publishers, 1968]
  46p. 22cm.
  Cover title.
  1. Negroes--Civil rights.
  2. Socialism. I. Breitman,
  George, jt. auth. II. DeBerry,
  Clifton, jt. auth. III. Merit
  Publishers.
  CSt-H, MoU, KU-RH, NUC 70-49472

C382
Cuba fights bureaucracy. [Ithaca,
    N.Y., Glad Day Press & Nia-
    gara Region SDS, 1967?]
  23p. 22cm.
  Cover title.
  1. Cuba--Pol. & govt.--1959-
    I. Glad Day Press.
  II. Students for a Democratic
  Society, Niagara Region.
  CU-B

C383
Cusick, Patrick A.
  Field secretary's report. [n.
  p., 1964]
  5p. 28cm.
  Caption title.
  At head of title: SPU national
  convention 1964.
  1. Student Peace Union.
  CU-B

C384
Czechoslovakia: revolution and
    counter revolution. [Detroit,
    News & Letters Committee and
  Marxist Humanist Group, 1968]
  62p. illus. 18cm.
  Cover title.
  1. Revolutions--Czechoslovak
  Republic. 2. Czechoslovak
  Republc--Pol. & govt. I. News
  & Letters.
  MoU

D

D1
Dady, Bill.
  Background information for the
  SDS Louisville project. [New
  York] Students for a Democratic
  Society and Economic Research
  and Action Project [196]
  [4]p. 28cm.
  1. Louisville--Race question.
  2. Student movements--Louisville.
  I. Students for a Democratic
  Society. Economic Research and
  Action Project.
  MiU

D2
Dalto, Ken.
  Guardian seeks false unity, by
  Ken Dalto and Phil Alkana.
  [Chicago, 1969]
  [2]p. 28cm.
  Caption title.
  1. Guardian. 2. Students for a
  Democratic Society. I. Alkana,
  Phil, jt. auth.
  WHi-L

D3
Dann, Jimm.

In the great depression, 1930-
1940 communists try to organize
factories in the fields; organizing California migrant workers. Boston, New England Free
Press [196]
72-96p. illus. 28cm.
Cover title.
Reprinted from PL, Feb. 1969.
1. Communist Party of the United
States of America. 2. Migrant
labor--California. I. New England Free Press.
KU-RH

D4
David Orton Defense Committee.
A case study of repression; the
political persecution of Professor David Orton at Sir
George Williams University, 1967
-1969. [Montreal, 1969]
81p. 28cm.
Cover title.
1. Orton, David. 2. Political
rights--Sir George Williams
University.
MiU

D5
Davidowincz, Peter.
Prospectus for the Baltimore
Research and Action Project; a
summer program in the organization of the unemployed, by
Peter Davidowincz and Kimberly
Moody. [Baltimore?] Baltimore
Students for a Democratic Society and the Economic Research
and Action Project of Students
for a Democratic Society, 1964.
17p. 28cm.
Cover title.
1. Baltimore--Race question.
2. Poor--Baltimore. I. Students
for a Democratic Society, Baltimore. II. Moody, Kimberly,
jt. auth.
MiU, WHi-A

D6
Davidson, Carl.
How will whites overcome skin
privilege? [Letter to editor
by Carl Davidson and Harry
Ring, in reply. New York, The

Militant, 1970?]
[2]p. 26cm.
Caption title.
1. Negroes--Civil rights.
2. Labor and laboring classes.
3. Capitalism. I. Ring, Harry,
jt. auth. II. The Militant.
KU-RH

D7
Davidson, Carl.
An internal education proposal,
or what we gotta do to get
smart. [n.p., Students for a
Democratic Society? 1965?]
6 leaves. 36cm.
Caption title.
I. Students for a Democratic
Society.
CU-B

D8
Davidson, Carl.
The multiversity: crucible of
the new working class; long-
range strategies for student
power movements. [n.p., 196]
18p.
1. Student movements. 2. Universities and colleges.
WHi-L

D9
Davidson, Carl.
The multiversity: crucible of
the new working class; long-
range strategies for student
power movements. Nashville,
Southern Student Organizing
Committee [196]
27p. 28cm.
Cover title.
1. Student movements. 2. Uni-
versities and colleges.
I. Southern Student Organizing
Committee.
MoU

D10
Davidson, Carl.
The new radicals and the multiversity. [Montreal, Our Generation, 196]
3-32p.
Caption title.
1. Student movements. 2. Uni-

versities and colleges. I. Our
Generation.
NNU-T

D11
Davidson, Carl.
The new radicals in the multi-
versity. An analysis and stra-
tegy for the student movement.
[Chicago, Students for a Demo-
cratic Society] 1968.
37p. illus. 22cm.
Cover title.
1. Student movements. 2. Uni-
versities and colleges.
I. Students for a Democratic
Society.
MoU, CU-B, WHi-L

D12
Davidson, Carl.
Our fight is here; essays on
draft resistance [by] Carl Dav-
idson [and others] Chicago,
Students for a Democratic Soc-
iety [196]
20p. illus. 28cm.
Cover title.
1. Military service, Compulsory.
2. Government, Resistance to.
I. Students for a Democratic
Society.
MiU

D13
Davidson, Carl.
Toward a student syndicalist
movement. New York, Radical
Education Project [196]
[4]p. 28cm.
Cover title.
Subtitle: University reform
revisited.
1. Student movements. 2. Uni-
versities and colleges.
I. Radical Education Project.
NNU-T

D14
Davidson, Carl.
Toward a student syndicalists
movement or university reform
revisited. Nashville, Southern Student Organizing Committee [196]
8p. 28cm.

Cover title.
1. Student movements. 2. Uni-
versities and colleges.
I. Southern Student Organizing
Committee.
MoU, WHi-L

D15
Davidson, Carl.
Toward student syndicalism.
[n.p., Students for a Democratic
Society, 196]
[6]p. 22cm.
Cover title.
1. Universities and colleges.
2. Student movements. I. Students for a Democratic Society.
CU-B

D16
Davidson, Carl.
Towards a movement of student
syndicalism. Montreal, Our
Generation [196]
102-[111]p.
Cover title.
1. Student movements. 2. Uni-
versities and colleges. I. Our
Generation.
NNU-T

D17
Davis, Benjamin Jefferson, 1903-
1964.
Ben Davis on the McCarran Act
at the Harvard Law Forum. [New
York, Gus Hall-Benjamin J.
Davis Defense Committee, 196]
19p. illus. 22cm.
Cover title.
1. U.S. Laws, statutes, etc.
Internal security act of 1950.
2. Communist Party of the
United States of America.
I. Gus Hall-Benjamin J. Davis
Defense Committee.
MiU, WHi-L, KU-J

D18
Davis, Benjamin Jefferson, 1903-
1964.
Must Negro-Americans wait
another hundred years for freedom? Against tokenism and grad-
ualism. [New York, New Century
Publishers, 1963]

15p.
Reprinted from Political Affairs,
Feb. 1963.
1. Negroes--Civil rights.
I. New Century Publishers.
MiEM, WHi-L, MiU, NUC 67-86886

D19
Davis, Benjamin Jefferson, 1903-
    1964.
The Negro people on the march.
New York, New Century Publish-
ers, 1956.
48p.
1. Negroes--Civil rights.
I. New Century Publishers.
MiU, KU-J, D59

D20
Davis, Benjamin Jefferson, 1903-
    1964.
On the struggle for peace and
freedom, with an introduction
by Harry K. Wells. Excerpts
from published writings, issued
on the occasion Negro history
week, 1956. New York, Jefferson School of Social Science,
1956.
22 leaves. 28cm.
Cover title.
1. Negroes--Civil rights.
I. Jefferson School of Social
Science. II. Wells, Harry K.
KU-J

D21
Davis, Benjamin Jefferson, 1903-
    1964.
The path of Negro liberation.
[New York, New Century Publish-
ers, 1957]
22p. 19cm.
Cover title.
Contains resolution on Negro
rights adopted by the Communist
Party of the United States at
the plenary session of the
National Committee, New York,
December 3-5, 1946 plus excerpts
from the discussion.
1. Negroes--Civil rights.
I. Communist Party of the United
States of America. National
Committee. II. New Century
Publishers.
CoU, NUC 72-10785

D22
Davis, Benjamin Jefferson, 1903-
    1964.
Upsurge in the south. The
negro people fight for freedom.
[New York, New Century Publishers, 1960]
23p. 22cm.
Cover title.
1. Negroes--Civil rights.
2. Southern States--Race question. I. New Century Publishers.
WHi-L, MiU

D23
Davis, Dennis.
G.I. Joe's a red. Boston, New
England Free Press [1970?]
48-56p. illus. 28cm.
Cover title.
Reprinted from PL, August 1968.
1. Military offenses.
2. Soldiers. I. New England
Free Press.
KU-RH

D24
Davis, Jerome.
Profits for war, profits for
peace. [Woodmont, Conn., Promoting Enduring Peace, 1969?]
[2]p. 28cm.
Caption title.
1. Peace. 2. U.S.--Military
policy. 3. War--Economic aspects. I. Promoting Enduring
Peace.
KU-RH

D25
Davis, Jerome.
Why complete and total disarma-
ment? [Woodmont, Conn., Pro-
moting Enduring Peace, 196]
[8]p. 21cm.
Cover title.
1. Disarmament. I. Promoting
Enduring Peace.
MoU

D26
Davis, Michael M.
National health insurance; what
is it? How would it work? Why
is it needed? Alternatives?
New York, League for Industrial
Democracy [c1956]

19p. 22cm.
Cover title.
1. Insurance, Health. I. League
for Industrial Democracy.
MiU, NNU-T

Davis, Rennard
  xDavis, Rennie.

D27
Davis, Rennard.
  Campus political parties: an
  illiberal projection by Rennard
  Davis and Bruce Payne. [n.p.]
  Distributed for the Liberal
  Study Group by Students for a
  Democratic Society [1962]
  6, 2p. 28cm.
  Cover title.
  1. Student movements. 2. Uni-
  versities and colleges. I. Stu-
  dents for a Democratic Society.
  II. Liberal Study Group.
  III. Payne, Bruce, jt. auth.
  MiU

D28
Davis, Rennard.
  Some ideas for campus work to
  strengthen the SDS community
  program. [Ann Arbor, ERAP]
  1964.
  [3] leaves. 28cm.
  Caption title.
  1. Community organization.
  I. Students for a Democratic
  Society. Economic Research and
  Action Project.
  KU-RH

D29
Davis, Rennard.
  The war on poverty: notes on
  insurgent response. New York,
  Students for a Democratic
  Society [1965?]
  11p. 28cm.
  Cover title.
  1. U.S. Laws, statutes, etc.
  Economic Opportunity Act of
  1964. 2. U.S. Office of Econo-
  mic Opportunity. 3. Poverty.
  I. Students for a Democratic
  Society.
  KU-RH

Davis, Rennie
  see
Davis, Rennard.

D30
Day, Noel.
  The American left: post-election
  prospects and problems. [New
  York, Distributed by Students
  for a Democratic Society, 196]
  [4]p. 28cm.
  Caption title.
  Reprinted from National Guardian.
  1. Liberalism. 2. U.S.--Pol. &
  govt.--1963-   I. Students
  for a Democratic Society.
  WHi-A, CU-B, KU-RH

D31
Day, Noel.
  The freedom movement in Massa-
  chusetts. New York, Students
  for a Democratic Society and its
  Economic Research and Action
  Project [196]
  19p. 28cm.
  Cover title.
  1. Negroes--Boston. 2. Boston--
  Race question. I. Students for
  a Democratic Society. Economic
  Research and Action Project.
  WHi-A

D32
Day, Noel.
  A white America in a non-white
  world. New York, Students for
  a Democratic Society, 1962.
  9p.
  Cover title.
  Edited version of a speech given
  at an SDS conference in Cambridge, Mass., Dec. 1962.
  1. Negroes. I. Students for a
  Democratic Society.
  WHi-L, NUC 69-88204

D33
Dean, Heather.
  On passing two whores and a nun.
  Toronto, Research, Information
  and Publications Project, Student Union for Peace Action
  [196]
  8p. 28cm.

Cover title.
At head of title: the sexual
caste system.
1. Woman--History and condition
of women.   I. Student Union for
Peace Action.
WHi-A

D34
Dean, Heather.
  Scarce resources: the dynamic of
American imperialism.   Ann Arbor, Radical Education Project
[196]
  9p.   28cm.
  Cover title.
  1. Imperialism.   2. U.S.--For-
eign policy.   I. Radical Education Project.
  KU-RH

D35
Dean, Heather.
  Scarce resources: the dynamic of
American imperialism.   [Nash-
ville, Southern Student Organizing Committee, 1966]
  12 [1]p.
  1. Imperialism.   2. U.S.--For-
eign policy.   I. Southern Student Organizing Committee.
  WHi-L

D36
Dean, Heather.
  Scarce resources: the dynamic of
American imperialism.   [Toronto]
Research, Information and Publications Project, Student Union
for Peace Action, 1966.
  11p.   28cm.
  Cover title.
  1. Imperialism.   2. U.S.--For-
eign policy.   I. Student Union
for Peace Action.
  KU-RH, WHi-A

D37
Dean, Heather.
  The sexual caste system; on
passing two whores and a nun.
Revised by Minneapolis Female
Liberation Group.   [n.p., 1969?]
  7p.   28cm.
  Cover title.
  1. Woman--Rights of women.

I. Minneapolis Female Liberation
Group.
  KU-RH

D38
Deane, Hugh.
  The war in Vietnam.   New York,
Monthly Review Press, 1963.
  32p.   22cm.   (Monthly review
pamphlet series, no. 23)
  1. Vietnamese conflict, 1961-
1975.   I. Monthly Review Press.
  KU-RH, DLC 63-19862

D39
Debate within SDS: RYM II vs.
    Weatherman.   Detroit, Radical
    Education Project [1969]
  43p.   illus.   28cm.
  Cover title.
  1. Students for a Democratic
Society.
  MoU

D40
Debord, Guy.
  Society of the spectacle.
Detroit [Black & Red] 1970.
  1v. (unpaged)   illus.   22cm.
  I. Black & Red.
  MoU

D41
Debray, Regis.
  The long march in Latin America.
Guerrilla movements: theory and
practice.   Ann Arbor, Radical
Education Project [196]
  17-58p.   map.   22cm.
  Cover title.
  1. Guerillas.   2. Revolutions--
Latin America.   I. Radical Edu-
cation Project.
  MoU

D42
Declaration of communist and
    worker's parties of socialist
    countries.   [New York, New
    Century Publishers, 1957]
  15p.   20cm.
  Caption title.
  1. U.S.--Foreign policy.
  2. Communism.
  I. New Century Publisher.
  KU-J

D43
Declaration of conscience against
    the war in Vietnam. New York,
    Catholic Worker [etc., 196]
    [1] leaf. 28cm.
    Caption title.
    1. Vietnamese conflict, 1961-
    1975. I. Catholic Worker.
    KU-RH

D44
Decornoy, Jacques.
    Laos: the forgotten war. [Bos-
    ton, New England Free Press,
    1969?]
    23p. 21cm.
    Cover title.
    Reprinted from Le Monde, July 3,
    1968.
    1. Laos--Pol. & govt. 2. Laos--
    Foreign relations--U.S. I. New
    England Free Press.
    KU-RH, MiU

D45
De Leon, Daniel, 1852-1914.
    Abolition of poverty; socialism
    versus ultramontane economics
    and politics. New York, New
    York Labor News Co., 1962.
    68p. 19cm.
    "Seventh printing."
    1. Poverty. 2. Socialism.
    3. Catholics. 4. Gasson,
    Thomas Ignatius, 1859-1930.
    I. New York Labor News Co.
    KU-RH

D46
De Leon, Daniel, 1852-1914.
    As to politics, and a discussion
    upon the relative importance of
    political action and of class
    conscious economic action, and
    the urgent necessity of both.
    New York, New York Labor News
    Co., 1956.
    x, 117p. 18cm.
    "Sixth printing."
    1. Socialism. 2. Industrial
    Workers of the World. 3. Soc-
    ialist Labor Party. I. New York
    Labor News Co.
    CU-B, KU-RH

D47
De Leon, Daniel, 1852-1914.
    The burning question of trade
    unionism. A lecture delivered
    at Newark, N.Y., April 24,
    1904. New York, 1960.
    43p. 19cm.
    1. Socialism. 2. Trade-unions.
    KU-RH, McB, NUC 65-7500

D48
De Leon, Daniel, 1852-1914.
    Capitalism vs. socialism. New
    York, New York Labor News Co.,
    1963.
    62p. 19cm.
    "New edition."
    Partial contents--speeches by
    William H. Berry.
    1. Socialism. 2. Capitalism.
    I. Berry, William Harvey, 1852-
    1928. I. New York Labor News
    Co.
    KU-RH

D49
De Leon, Daniel, 1852-1914.
    Fifteen questions answered by
    Daniel De Leon. Socialist an-
    swers to fifteen questions
    asked by Providence, R.I.,
    "visitor," representing Roman
    Catholic political machine.
    New York, New York Labor News
    Co., 1961.
    121p. 19cm.
    "Thirteenth edition, 1961."
    1. Socialism. I. New York
    Labor News Co.
    KU-RH

D50
De Leon, Daniel, 1852-1914.
    Industrial unionism; selected
    editorials. New York, New York
    Labor News Co., 1963.
    79p. 19cm.
    "Fifth printing."
    1. Socialism. 2. Trade-unions.
    I. New York Labor News Co.
    KU-RH, MeB, NUC 64-69466

D51
De Leon, Daniel, 1852-1914.
    Marxian science and the colleges.

[New ed.] Brooklyn, New York
Labor News, 1966.
96p. 19cm.
1. Socialism. 2. Universities
and colleges. I. New York Labor
News Co.
MU, NUC 69-63136

D52
De Leon, Daniel, 1852-1914.
  Party ownership of the press.
  Historic documents relating to
  the establishing of the princi-
  ples involved. [New York[New
  York Labor News Co., 1931.
  32p. 24cm.
  1. Socialism. 2. Socialist
  Labor Party. I. New York Labor
  News Co.
  KU-RH

D53
De Leon, Daniel, 1852-1914.
  Reform or revolution. New York,
  New York Labor News Co., 1961.
  ix, 32p. 19cm.
  Address delivered on January 26,
  1896, at Well's Memorial Hall,
  Boston, Mass.
  1. Socialism. 2. Revolutions.
  3. Social change. 4. Reforms.
  I. New York Labor News Co.
  MeB, CU-B, KU-J, KU-RH,
  NUC 65-7833

D54
De Leon, Daniel, 1852-1914.
  Socialism versus anarchism; an
  address. New York, New York
  Labor News, 1962.
  79p. 19cm.
  "First ed. ...1901...Amplified
  ed. with Lafargue essay and
  Socialist Industrial Unionism
  statement...1962."
  1. Socialism. 2. Anarchism and
  anarchists. I. Lafargue, Paul,
  1842-1911. II. New York Labor
  News Co.
  KU, NUC 67-86263

D55
De Leon, Daniel, 1852-1914.
  Socialism vs. 'individualism';
  debate: Daniel De Leon vs.
  Thomas F. Carmody. New York,

New York Labor News Co., 1955.
46p. 18cm.
New edition, 1942.
Second printing, 1955.
I. Socialism. I. Carmody,
Thomas, 1859-1922, jt. auth.
II. New York Labor News Co.
KU-RH

D56
De Leon, Daniel, 1852-1914.
  Socialist reconstruction of
  society; the industrial vote.
  New York, New York Labor News
  Co., 1963.
  79p. 19cm.
  1. Socialism. 2. Industrial
  Workers of the World. 3. Labor
  and laboring classes. I. New
  York Labor News Co.
  KU-RH, MeB, CU-B, NUC 65-5924

D57
De Leon, Daniel, 1852-1914.
  Socialist vs. capitalist economics (Marx on Mallock) New York,
  New York Labor News Co., 1963.
  47p. 19cm.
  1. Capitalism. 2. Socialism.
  3. Mallock, William Hurrell,
  1849-1923.
  KU-RH

D58
De Leon, Daniel, 1852-1914.
  Ten canons of the proletarian
  revolution; a revolutionary de-
  calogue. New York, New York
  Labor News Co., 1955.
  31p. 19cm.
  1. Socialism. I. New York Labor
  News Co.
  KU-RH

D59
De Leon, Daniel, 1852-1914.
  Two pages from Roman history:
  plebs leaders and labor leaders
  and the warning of the Gracchi.
  New York, New York Labor News
  Co., 1959.
  105p. port. 19cm.
  1. Labor and laboring classes--
  Rome. 2. Socialism. I. New
  York Labor News Co.
  NN, KU-J

D60
De Leon, Daniel, 1852-1914.
  The Vatican in politics; ultra-
  montanism. [The Roman Catholic
  political machine in action.
  Editorials] New York, New York
  Labor News, 1962.
  79p. 19cm.
  1. Catholic Church. 2. Poli-
  tics, Practical. I. New York
  Labor News Co.
  KU, NUC 67-87271

D61
De Leon, Daniel, 1852-1914.
  What means this strike? New
  York, New York Labor News Co.,
  1958.
  x, 37p. illus. 19cm.
  Address delivered at New Bed-
  ford, Mass., Feb. 11, 1898.
  New introduction by Arnold
  Petersen.
  New enlarged edition.
  Seventh printing.
  1. Socialism. 2. Strikes and
  lockouts. I. Petersen, Arnold,
  1885-   II. New York Labor
  News Co.
  WHi-L, KU-J

D62
De Leon, Daniel, 1852-1914.
  What means this strike? [New
  introduction by Arnold Petersen]
  New York, New York Labor News
  Co., 1960.
  x, 37p. 19cm.
  Eighth printing.
  1. Socialism. 2. Strikes and
  lockouts. I. Petersen, Arnold,
  1885-   II. New York Labor
  News Co.
  CU-B, KU-RH

D63
Dellinger, Dave.
  America's lost plantation. In-
  troduction by Waldo Frank. [New
  York, Liberation, 196]
  56p. illus. 22cm.
  Cover title.
  Reprinted from Liberation,
  Dec. 1960; Jan. & Mar. 1961.
  1. Cuba--Pol. & govt.--1959-
        I. Frank, Waldo.

II. Liberation.
MiU, NcD

D64
Dellinger, Dave.
  Cuba: the revolution not seen.
  [Nashville] Southern Student
  Organizing Committee [196]
  5p. Cover title.
  1. Cuba--For. rel.--U.S.
  2. U.S.--For. rel.--Cuba.
  3. Pacifism. I. Southern
  Student Organizing Committee.
  WHi-L

D65
Dellinger, Dave.
  The new nonviolence. Nashville,
  Southern Student Organizing Com-
  mittee [196]
  6p. 28cm.
  Cover title.
  Reprinted from Win, June 11,
  1966.
  1. Nonviolence. 2. Negroes--
  Civil rights. I. Southern Stu-
  dent Organizing Committee.
  WHi-L, MoU

D66
Dellinger, Dave.
  On the new nonviolence. [New
  York WIN Magazine, 196]
  [4]p. 28cm.
  Caption title.
  Speech given to the New York
  Workshop in Nonviolence, Ap.
  23-24, 1966. Reprinted from
  WIN Magazine, v. II, no. 10.
  1. Nonviolence. 2. Negroes--
  Civil rights. I. New York
  Workshop in Nonviolence.
  II. War Resistance League.
  KU-RH

D67
Dellinger, Dave.
  Political realism and moral
  disaster. [New York, 1966]
  16-19p.
  Reprinted from the Feb. 1966
  Liberation.
  1. Vietnamese conflict, 1961-
  1975.
  WHi-L

D68
Dellinger, Dave.
  Report from revolutionary China.
  [Boston? New England Free Press,
  196]
  7p. illus. 28cm.
  Cover title.
  Reprinted from Liberation, Jan.
  1967.
  1. China (People's Republic of
  China, 1949-   )--Intellectual
  life. I. New England Free
  Press.
  KU-RH

D69
Dellinger, Dave.
  A report on China's cultural
  revolution. Toronto, Research,
  Information, and Publications
  Project, Student Union for Peace
  Action [196]
  11p. 28cm.
  Cover title.
  Reprinted from Liberation, Jan.
  1967.
  1. China (People's Republic of
  China, 1949-   )--Intellectual
  life. I. Student Union for Peace
  Action.
  WHi-A

D70
Dellinger, Dave.
  The revolution not seen. New
  York, Students for a Democratic
  Society [196]
  3p. 28cm.
  Cover title.
  Reprinted from New Politics,
  Fall 1962.
  1. Cuba--Pol. & govt.--1959-
       2. U.S.--For. rel.--
  Cuba. 3. Cuba--For. rel.--U.S.
  I. Students for a Democratic
  Society.
  WHi-A, CU-B

D71
Dellinger, Dave.
  What is Cuba really like? [New
  York, Liberation, 1964]
  23p. illus. 28cm.
  Reprinted from Liberation, June,
  July and August 1964.
  1. Cuba--Pol. & govt.--1959-

       I. Liberation.
  MNS, NUC 65-76901

D72
Dellinger, Patchen.
  Seeds of liberation. [New
  York? Liberation? 196]
  [1] leaf. 28cm.
  Caption title.
  1. Students for a Democratic
  Society. Economic Research
  and Action Project. 2. Jobs
  or Income Now Community Union.
  I. Liberation.
  KU-RH

D73
De Marco, Gordon.
  Support the Vietnamese workers
  and peasants and the international working class--build an
  anti-imperialist, anti-racist
  movement. A draft. [n.p.,
  1969?]
  [6]p. 36cm.
  Caption title.
  1. Students for a Democratic
  Society. 2. Imperialism.
  3. Vietnamese conflict, 1961-
  1975.
  WHi-L

D74
Deming, Barbara.
  On revolution and equalibrium.
  Palo Alto, Institute for Study
  of Nonviolence [196]
  13p. 28cm.
  Cover title.
  1. Revolutions. 2. Pacifism.
  I. Institute for Study of
  Nonviolence.
  CU-B

D75
Deming, Barbara.
  Revolution: violent and non-
  violent. Two documents: on
  revolution and equalibrium [by]
  Barbara Deming [and] declaration
  at his court martial [by] Regis
  Debray. [New York, Liberation,
  196]
  28p. illus. 28cm.
  Caption title.
  Reprinted from Liberation,

Feb. 1968.
1. Revolutions.   2. Pacifism.
3. Guevara, Ernesto, 1920-1967.
4. Guerillas--Bolivia.   I. Debray, Regis, jt. auth.   II. Liberation.
KU-RH, NNU-T

D76
De Muth, Jerry.
  G.E.: profile of a corporation.
Ann Arbor, Radical Education
Project [196]
[502]-512p.   22cm.
Cover title.
Reprinted from Dissent, July-
Aug. 1967.
1. General Electric Corporation.
I. Radical Education Project.
MoU, WHi-L

D77
De Muth, Jerry.
  G.E.: profile of a corporation.
Boston, New England Free Press
[196]
503-512p.   22cm.
Cover title.
Reprinted from Dissent, July-
Aug. 1967.
1. General Electric Corporation.
I. New England Free Press.
KU-RH, MiU

D78
De Muth, Jerry.
  Tired of being sick and tried.
[Atlanta, Student Nonviolent
Coordinating Committee, 196]
[2]p.   36cm.
Caption title.
Reprinted from The Nation,
June 1, 1964.
1. Negroes--Civil rights.
2. Mississippi--Race question.
I. Student Nonviolent Coordina-
ting Committee.
WHi-A

D79
Denby, Charles.
  Where we stand on the negro
struggle, by Charles Denby and
Andy Phillips. Detroit, News
& Letters [196 ?]
6 leaves.   28cm.

Cover title.
At head of title: draft chapter.
1. Negroes--Civil rights.
2. Socialism. I. Phillips,
Andy, jt. auth.   II. News &
Letters.
MiU

D80
Denby, Charles.
  Workers battle automation.
[Detroit, News & Letters, 1960]
62p. illus. 17cm.
Cover title.
1. Automation.   2. Labor and
laboring classes. I. News &
Letters.
MoU, WHi-L, MiU-H, MH-IR,
NUC 63-8428.

C81
Dennis, Eugene, 1905?-
  The communist take a new look.
New York, New Century Publish-
ers, 1956.
48p. 19cm.
Report to a meeting of the
national committee, CPUSA.
1. Communist Party of the
United States of America.
2. U.S.--Pol. & govt.--1953-
          I. New Century Publishers.
MiU, NNJef, WHi-L, KU-J

D82
Dennis, Eugene, 1905?-
  Letters from prison. Selected
by Peggy Dennis. New York, In-
ternational Publishers [1956]
157p. illus. 21cm.
1. Communism. I. International
Publishers. II. Dennis, Peggy.
KU-J, KyU, WaU-L, CU, ICU, NN,
NcD, IU, DLC 562531

D83
Dennis, Eugene, 1905?-
  On uniting and strengthening
the party and its mass work.
(Resolution submitted by E.
Dennis) Adopted by National
Committee--Feb. 15, 1958.
[n.p., 1958?]
4 leaves. 36cm.
Caption title.
1. Communist Party of the

United States of America.
KU-J

D84
Dennis, Eugene, 1905?-
  Report of Eugene Dennis on
  behalf of the national board to
  the meeting of the national
  committee, April 28, 1956.
  [n.p., 1956]
  21 leaves. 36cm.
  Caption title.
  1. U.S.--Pol. & govt.--1953-
        2. Communist Party of
  the United States of America.
  KU-J

D85
Dennis, Eugene, 1905?-
  Text of keynote address by
  Eugene Dennis to the sixteenth
  national convention of the
  C.P.U.S.A. [n.p., 1957?]
  Caption title.
  1. Communist Party of the United
  States of America.
  KU-J

D86
Dennis, Eugene, 1905?-
  Toward the 1960 elections.
  [New York, New Century Publishers, 1959]
  16p. 20cm. (A political
  affair pamphlet)
  Cover title.
  1. U.S.--Pol. & govt.--1959-
        I. New Century Publish-
  ers.
  KU-RH, NRU

D87
Dennis, Eugene, 1905?-
  What America needs; a communist
  view, by Eugene Dennis and John
  Gates. [New York, New Century
  Publishers, 1956]
  23p. 19cm.
  1. Communism. I. Gates, John,
  jt. auth. II. New Century
  Publishers.
  NN, KU-J

D88
Dennison, George.
  The first street school. Ann

Arbor, Radical Education Project
[196]
19p. 28cm.
Cover title.
Reprinted from Liberation, July
1966.
1. First Street School. 2. Edu-
cation--New York (State)--New
York (City) 3. Free schools--
New York (City) I. Radical
Education Project.
MoU

D89
Dennison, George.
  The first street school. Boston, New England Free Press
  [196]
  11p. 28cm.
  Caption title.
  Reprinted from Liberation, July
  1966.
  1. First Street School.
  2. Education--New York (State)--
  New York (City). 3. Free
  schools--New York (City)
  I. New England Free Press.
  KU-RH

D90
Densmore, Dana.
  Sex roles and female oppression:
  a collection of articles. [Bos-
  ton, New England Free Press,
  1969?]
  29p. 22cm.
  Cover title.
  Reprinted from No More Fun and
  Games.
  1. Woman--Rights of women.
  I. New England Free Press.
  WHi-L, MiU, KU-RH

de Rivera, Alice
  see
Rivera, Alice de

D91
Dertz, Laura.
  Women's liberation and the
  fight against the war [by
  Laura Dertz, Ruth Getts, Jac-
  quiline Rice. n.p., 1970?]
  2p. 28cm.
  At head of title: position
  paper.
  1. Vietnamese conflict, 1961-

1975.   2. Woman--Rights of wo-
men.   I. Getts, Ruth, jt. auth.
II. Rice, Jackquiline, jt. auth.
KU-RH

De Santa Anna, Julio
    see
Santa Anna, Julio De

D92
Deutscher, Isaac, 1907-
  Myths of the cold war. Ann
  Arbor, Radical Education Project
  [196]
  13p. 22cm.
  Cover title.
  1. World politics--1955-
  I. Radical Education Project.
  CU-B

D93
Deutscher, Isaac, 1907-
  On socialist man. [New York,
  Merit Publishers, c1967, 1969]
  2p. 22cm.
  Cover title.
  1. Socialism. I. Merit Pub-
  lishers.
  KU-RH

D94
Dewart, Leslie.
  A Catholic speaks on Cuba.
  Toronto, Fair Play for Cuba
  [1961?]
  6p. 22cm.
  Caption title.
  1. Cuba. 2. Catholics.
  I. Fair Play for Cuba Committee.
  MiU

D95
Dewart, Leslie.
  Education & political values;
  the dilemma of liberal democracy. [Montreal? Our Generation? 196]
  16p.
  Cover title.
  1. Education. 2. Politics,
  Practical. I. Our Generation.
  NNU-T

D96
Dewart, Leslie.
  Education & political values;

the dilemma of liberal demo-
cracy. Toronto, Research,
Information and Publications
Project, Student Union for
Peace Action [19]65.
16p. 28cm.
Cover title.
1. Education. 2. Politics,
Practical. 3. Democracy.
I. Student Union for Peace
Action.
WHi-A

D97
Diamant, Gregory.
  SDS, elections, and the summer
  program [by Gregory Diamant and
  others. n.p., 1969]
  3p. 28cm.
  Caption title.
  1. Students for a Democratic
  Society.
  WHi-L

D98
Dibble, Vernon K.
  The garrison society. Ann
  Arbor, Radical Education Pro-
  ject [196]
  106-115p. 22cm.
  Cover title.
  Reprinted from New University
  Thought, v. 5, no. 1-2.
  1. U.S.--Military policy.
  2. Militarism. 3. Law enforce-
  ment. I. Radical Education
  Project.
  MiU, WHi-L, CU-B

D99
Dick Gregory Committee
  Dick Gregory for president in
  1968. Berkeley, 1968.
  2p. 26cm.
  Caption title.
  1. Gregory, Dick. 2. Peace and
  Freedom Party.
  CU-B

D100
Dickens, Bob.
  The parts are all around us.
  [Buffalo, N.Y., Friends of Mala-
  testa, 196]
  12p. 22cm.
  Cover title.

1. Anarchism and anarchists.
I. Friends of Malatesta.
MiU

D101
DiGia, Ralph.
 A report to telephone tax re-
fusers, by Ralph DiGia and Maris
Cakars. New York, War Resisters
League and Committee for Nonvio-
lent Action [1966?]
[1] leaf. 28cm.
Caption title.
1. Taxation. 2. Tax evasion.
I. War Resisters League.
II. Committee for Nonviolent
Action. III. Cakars, Maris,
jt. auth.
CU-B

C102
Diner, Helen.
 The story of the amazons. New
York, The Feminists [196]
2p. 28cm.
Caption title.
1. Women--History and condition
of women. I. Feminists.
WHi-L, KU-RH

D103
Dinh, Tran Van.
 Fear of a bloodbath. [New
York, Clergy and Laymen Concern-
ed About Vietnam, 1969]
[2]p. 28cm.
Caption title.
Reprinted from New Republic,
Dec. 6, 1969.
1. Vietnamese conflict, 1961-
1975. I. Clergy and Laymen
Concerned About Vietnam.
KU-RH

D104
Dix, Keith.
 Mother Jones in Appalachia.
Detroit, Radical Education
Project [1970?]
7p. illus. 28cm.
Cover title.
Reprinted from People's Appala-
chia, June-July 1970.
1. Labor and laboring classes--
Appalachian Mountains. 2. Har-
ris, Mary, 1830-

3. Appalachian Mountains.
I. Radical Education Project.
MiU

D105
Dixon, Marlene.
 Why women's liberation? San
Francisco, Bay Area Radical
Education Project [1970?]
14 [1]p. illus. 22cm.
Cover title.
Reprinted from Ramparts, Dec.
1969 and Women, Fall 1969.
1. Woman--Rights of women.
I. Bay Area Radical Education
Project.
MiU

D106
Dobbs, Farrell.
 Recent trends in labor movement.
[New York, Militant Publishing
Association, 1967?]
31p. 28cm.
Cover title.
1. Trade-unions. 2. Labor and
laboring classes. 3. Youth--
Political activity. I. Mili-
tant Publishing Association.
CU-B

D107
Documents on the Negro struggle,
 including the texts of discussions with Leon Trotsky,
1933 and 1939, and Socialist
Workers Party convention
resolutions, 1939 and 1948.
New York, Pioneer Publishers
[1961?]
42p. (Bulletin of Marxist
studies, 4)
1. Negroes--Civil rights.
2. Socialist Labor Party.
I. Trotskii, Lev, 1879-1940.
II. Pioneer Publishers.
MH-NUC 65-43771

D108
Domhoff, William.
 Researching the governing class
of America. Boston, New England
Free Press [1969?]
7p. 28cm.
Cover title.
1. U.S.--Pol. & govt--Bibl.

2. Power (Social science)--Bibl.
I. New England Free Press.
KU-RH

D109
Donahue, Bill.
Sabotage [by] Bill Donahue [and]
Neil Mclay. [n.p., Student
Peace Union, National Convention,
1964]
[2] leaves. 28cm.
Caption title.
1. Peace. 2. Sabotage.
I. Student Peace Union. Nation-
al Convention, 1964.
CU-B

D110
Don't mourn--organize. [San
    Francisco, The Movement Press,
    1968]
35p. illus. 22x28cm.
Cover title.
1. Student movements. 2. Poverty. 3. Community organizations. I. Movement Press.
CU-B, WHi-L

D111
Dorticos Torrado, Osvaldo, Pres.
    Cuba, 1919-
Cuba will not capitulate. New
York, Fair Play for Cuba Commit-
tee [1962?]
[24]p.
Cover title.
1. Cuba--Pol. & govt.--1959-
        I. Fair Play for Cuba
Committee.
MiU

D112
Dorticos Torrado, Osvaldo, Pres.
    Cuba, 1919-
The institutional and political
changes made by the Cuban revol-
ution. [New York[Fair Play for
Cuba Committee [1961]
[5]p.
Cover title.
Reprinted from Cuba, Nov. 1961.
1. Cuba--Pol. & govt., 1959-
        I. Fair Play for Cuba
Committee.
MiU

D113
Doucet, Paul.
Quebec: secular and free.
[Montreal? Our Generation?
196]
910-[913] leaves. 28cm.
Caption title.
1. Quebec--Pol. & govt. I. Our
Generation.
NNU-T

D114
Dowd, Douglas.
The economic history of the
United States in the twentieth
century. [Cambridge, Mass.]
Union for Radical Political
Economics, 1969.
9-23p. 27cm. (Union for Radi-
cal Political Economics. Oc-
casional papers, no. 2)
1. U.S.--Econ. condit.
I. Union for Radical Political
Economics.
CtU

D115
Dowson, Ross.
The power & dilemma of the trade
unions. [Toronto, Workers Van-
guard, 1967]
14 [1]p. 22cm.
Cover title.
1. Trade-unions. I. Workers
Vanguard.
MoU, WHi-L

D116
Dowty, Janet.
Movement speakers guide. Ann
Arbor, Radical Education Pro-
ject [1967]
24p. 28cm.
Cover title.
I. Radical Education Project.
NNU-T

D117
Dowty, Stu.
The academic quagmire. Ann
Arbor, Radical Education Pro-
ject [196]
7p. 28cm.
Cover title.
Reprinted from the Radicals in

the Professions Newsletter.
1. Education.   2. Universities
and colleges.   I. Radical Education Project.
MoU

D118
Draft counseling centers.   Nash-
    ville, Southern Student Organ-
    izing Committee [196]
15 [2]p.   28cm.
Cover title.
1. Military service, Compulsory.
I. Southern Student Organizing
Committee.
CU-B, MiU

D119
Draft Help.
    Homosexuality: the draft &
    armed forces.   [San Francisco,
    196]
6p.   28cm.
Caption title.
1. Homosexuality.   2. Military
service, Compulsory.
KU-RH

D120
The draft is in trouble; up
    against it with Nixon and the
    draft.   [Chicago? Chicago
    Area Draft Resisters? 197]
1 leaf.   illus.   36cm.
Caption title.
1. Military service, Compulsory.
I. Chicago Area Draft Resisters.
KU-RH

D121
Drake, St. Clair.
    Our urban poor; promises to
    keep and miles to go.   Intro-
    duction by Bayard Rustin.
    [New York, A. Philip Randolph
    Educational Fund, 1966?]
24p.   (A. Philip Randolph
educational fund, 3)
1. Negroes--Civil rights.
2. Slums.   3. Poverty.   I. Randolph (A. Philip) Education
Fund.
WHi-L

D122
Draper, Anne.

The dirt on California agri-
    business and the university
    [by] Anne Draper [and] Hal
    Draper.   [Berkeley, Independent
    Socialist Clubs of America,
    c1968]
32p.   28cm.
Cover title.
1. Agriculture--California.
2. California.   University.
I. Draper, Hal, jt. auth.
II. Independent Socialist Clubs
of America.
WHi-L, MiU

D123
Draper, Hal.
    Clark Kerr: the liberal as
    proto-fascist.   Ann Arbor,
    Radical Education Project
    [196]
10p.   28cm.
Cover title.
1. Kerr, Clark, 1911-
2. Universities and colleges--
Administration.   I. Radical
Education Project.
MiU

D124
Draper, Hal.
    The fight for independence in
    Vietnam [by Hal Draper and Kim
    Moody.   Berkeley] Independent
    Socialist Club [1966]
12p.   24cm.
Cover title.
1. Vietnamese conflict, 1961-
1975.   I. Moody, Kimberly, jt.
auth.   II. Independent Socialist Clubs of America.
CU-B

D125
Draper, Hal.
    Independent socialism; a per-
    spective for the left.   [Ber-
    keley, Calif.] Independent
    Socialist Committee [c1964]
23p.   22cm.
Cover title.
1. Socialism.   I. Independent
Socialist Committee.
KU-RH

D126
Draper, Hal., ed.
  Introduction to independent soc-
  ialism, selected articles from
  Labor Action, edited by Hal
  Draper. Berkeley, Independent
  Socialist Press [c1963?]
  242p. 24cm.
  1. Socialism. I. Labor Action.
  II. Independent Socialist Press.
  KU-J

D127
Draper, Hal.
  The mind of Clark Kerr. [Berke-
  ley, Calif.] Independent Social-
  ist Club [c1964]
  14p. 22cm.
  Cover title.
  At head of title: Behind the
  battle of Berkeley.
  1. Kerr, Clark, 1911-
  2. Universities and colleges--
  Administration. I. Independent
  Socialist Club.
  CU-B, KU-RH

D128
Draper, Hal.
  The mind of Clark Kerr; his
  view of the university factory
  & the "new slavery". Boston,
  New England Free Press [1968]
  iii, 11 [1]p. 22cm.
  Cover title.
  Second edition.
  1. Kerr, Clark, 1911-
  2. Universities and colleges--
  Administration. I. New England
  Free Press.
  KU-RH

D129
Draper, Hal.
  The mind of Clark Kerr. [2d.
  ed.] Ann Arbor, Radical Edu-
  cation Project [1968]
  iv, 11p. 22cm.
  Cover title.
  1. Kerr, Clark, 1911-
  2. Universities and colleges--
  Administration. I. Radical
  Education Project.
  WHi-L

D130
Draper, Hal.
  The two souls of socialism.
  [Rev. ed.] Highland Park,
  Mich., International Socialists
  [c1966, 1970]
  30 [2]p. 21cm.
  1. Socialism. I. International
  Socialists.
  KU-RH

D131
Draper, Hal.
  The two souls of socialism.
  [Rev. ed.] New York, Indepen-
  dent Socialist Clubs of America
  [c1966, 1968]
  30p. 22cm.
  1. Socialism. I. Independent
  Socialist Clubs of America.
  KU-RH

D132
Draper, Hal.
  The two souls of socialism:
  socialism from below v. social-
  ism from above. [New York]
  Young People's Socialist League
  [1963]
  31p. 22cm.
  Cover title.
  Reprinted from the Anvil, 1960.
  1. Socialism. I. Young People's
  Socialist League.
  KU-RH

D133
Draper, Theodore, 1912-
  The roots of the Dominican
  crisis. New York, League for
  Industrial Democracy [1965?]
  15p. 28cm. (Looking forward
  no. 3)
  Cover title.
  Reprinted from New Leader,
  May 24, 1965.
  1. Dominican Republic--Pol. &
  govt. 2. Bosch, Juan.
  I. League for Industrial
  Democracy.
  WHi-A, WHi-L

D134
Drushka, Ken.

An approach to student reform.
Toronto, Student Union for Peace
Action [19] 65.
10p. 28cm.
Cover title.
1. Universities and colleges.
2. Student movements. I. Student Union for Peace Action.
WHi-A

D135
Dubois, Ellen.
Struggling into existence the
feminism of Sarah and Angelina
Grimke. Boston, New England
Free Press [1970?]
10 [1]p. 28cm.
Cover title.
Reprinted from Women: a journal
of liberation, Sp. 1970.
1. Woman--Rights of women.
I. New England Free Press.
MiU

D136
DuBois, William Edward Burghardt,
    1868-
Back toward slavery; excerpts
from Black reconstruction in
America. [Boston, New England
Free Press, 1970?]
53p. 22cm.
Cover title.
1. Negroes--Civil rights.
I. New England Free Press.
MiU

D137
DuBois (W.E.B.) Clubs of America.
Civil liberties. [n.p., 196]
4p. 28cm.
Caption title.
1. Civil rights.
WHi-A

D138
DuBois, (W.E.B.) Clubs of America.
Civil rights in the north.
[n.p., 196]
5p. 28cm.
Caption title.
1. Negroes--Civil rights.
WHi-A

D139
DuBois (W.E.B.) Clubs of America.

Civil rights in the south.
[n.p., 196]
2p. 28cm.
Caption title.
1. Negroes--Civil rights.
2. Southern states--Race
question.
WHi-A

D140
DuBois, (W.E.B.) Clubs of America.
Civil rights working papers.
6,4,3,5,8,[1] 11, 9 leaves,
28cm.
Cover title.
1. Negroes--Civil rights.
CU-B

D141
DuBois, (W.E.B.) Clubs of America.
Constitution [adopted in San
Francisco, June 21, 1964, n.p.,
1964]
8p. 28cm.
Cover title.
1. Student movements.
CU-B, WHi-A

D142
DuBois (W.E.B.) Clubs of America.
Culture and education: convention report. [San Francisco,
1964?]
24p. 22cm.
Cover title.
1. Art. 2. Education.
WHi-A

D143
DuBois (W.E.B.) Clubs of America.
Dominican news blackout. San
Francisco [196]
2 leaves. 28cm.
Caption title.
1. Dominican Republic--For.
rel.--U.S. 2. U.S.--For. rel.--
Dominican Republic. 3. News-
papers. 4. Television broad-
casting of news.
WHi-A

D144
DuBois (W.E.B.) Clubs of America.
DuBois vs. SACE [New York,
196]
folder.

Cover title.
1. U.S. Subversive Activities
Board. 2. Internal security.
WHi-L

D145
DuBois (W.E.B.) Clubs of America.
Election issues: 1964. Presen-
tation to the Democratic Party
convention platform committee,
Atlantic City August 1964.
[San Francisco, 1964]
5, 5p. 28cm. (Spur supplement)
1. Negroes--Civil rights.
2. U.S.--Foreign policy.
3. U.S.--Pol. & govt.--1963-
        4. Democratic Party.
National Convention, Atlantic
City, 1964.
WHi-A

D146
DuBois (W.E.B.) Clubs of America.
Founding convention resolutions,
June 21, 1964. San Francisco
[1964?]
1v. (Various pagings) 28cm.
Cover title.
CU-B

D147
DuBois (W.E.B.) Clubs of America.
The ghetto rebellions. [New
York? 1968?]
5p.
1. Negroes--Civil rights.
2. Riots. 3. Slums.
WHi-L

D148
DuBois (W.E.B.) Clubs of America.
Labor and unemployment. [n.p.,
196]
3p. 28cm.
Caption title.
1. Labor and laboring classes.
2. Employment (Economic theory)
WHi-A

D149
DuBois (W.E.B.) Clubs of America.
"My fight is in the ghettos of
Philadelphia--not in Viet-Nam."
Pvt. Ronald Lockman. [n.p.]
1967.
7p.

1. Vietnamese conflict, 1961-
1975. 2. Lockman, Ronald.
3. Philadelphia--Race question.
4. Negroes--Philadelphia.
WHi-L

D150
DuBois (W.E.B.) Clubs of America.
National conference on new
politics: an analysis. New
York [1968?]
5p.
1. Politics, Practical.
2. Liberalism.
WHi-L

D151
DuBois (W.E.B.) Clubs of America.
Peace activity: general state-
ment. [n.p., 196]
11p. 28cm.
Caption title.
1. Peace--Societies, etc.
WHi-A

D152
DuBois (W.E.B.) Clubs of America.
Political perspectives. [n.p.,
196]
6p. 28cm.
Caption title.
1. Socialism.
WHi-A

D153
DuBois (W.E.B.) Clubs of America.
Report and resolutions on cul-
ture and education. Adopted at
the founding convention, San
Francisco, 21, June 1964.
[San Francisco, 1964]
24p. 22cm.
Caption title.
1. Education. 2. Universities
and colleges.
CU-B

D154
DuBois (W.E.B.) Clubs of America.
A statement. [New York, 1964]
2 leaves. 28cm.
Caption title.
1. Fascism.
2. Goldwater, Barry Morris,
1909-
WHi-A

D155
DuBois (W.E.B.) Clubs of America.
  Statement on the House Committee
  on Un-American Activities and
  its pending investigation of
  the Ku Klux Klan. [San Francis-
  co] 1965.
  3 leaves. 28cm.
  Caption title.
  1. Ku Klux Klan. 2. U.S.
  Congress. House. Committee on
  Un-American Activities.
  WHi-A

D156
DuBois (W.E.B.) Clubs of America.
  The W.E.B. DuBois Clubs. [Chi-
  cago, 196]
  folder. 28cm.
  CU-B

D157
DuBois (W.E.B.) Clubs of America.
  W.E.B. DuBois Clubs of America.
  [San Francisco, 196]
  folder.
  WHi-A

D158
DuBois (W.E.B.) Clubs of America,
  Chicago.
  We demand massive federal in-
  tervention now. [Chicago, 196]
  [1] leaf. 28cm.
  Caption title.
  1. Southern States--Race ques-
  tion. 2. Negroes--Civil rights.
  WHi-A

D159
DuBois (W.E.B.) Clubs of America,
  Chicago.
  Youth's stake in the 1964
  elections. Chicago [1964?]
  4p. 28cm.
  Cover title.
  1. Goldwater, Barry Morris,
  1909-   2. Youth--Political
  activity.
  WHi-A

D160
DuBois (W.E.B.) Clubs of America.
  Committee on Urban and Rural
  Problems.
  Resolutions of the committee on

urban and rural problems. [n.
p., 196]
5p. 28cm.
Caption title.
1. Minorities. 2. Poverty.
3. Socialism.
WHi-A

D161
DuBois (W.E.B.) Clubs of America.
  National Education and Re-
  search Committee.
  Teaching guide. [n.p., 1965]
  3p. 28cm.
  1. Teaching.
  CU-B

D162
DuBois (W.E.B.) Clubs of America.
  New York (State)
  New York State conference,
  December 12-13, 1964; report
  on education. [n.p., 1964?]
  5p. 28cm.
  Caption title.
  1. Education.
  CU-B

D163
DuBois (W.E.B.) Clubs of America.
  New York (State)
  W.E.B. DuBois Club--state-wide
  conference; perspectives for
  action. [n.p., 1964?]
  7p. 28cm.
  1. Student movements.
  CU-B

D164
DuBois (W.E.B.) Clubs of America.
  New York (State) Conference,
  1964.
  Report on education. [n.p.,
  1964?]
  Caption title.
  1. Education. 2. Student
  movements.
  WHi-A

D165
DuBrul, Paul.
  The student and the vote, a dis-
  cussion paper by Paul DuBrul.
  [n.p.] Students for a Democratic
  Society for the Liberal Study
  Group [196]

3p. 28cm.
Cover title.
1. Student movements.
2. Politics, Practical. I. Students for a Democratic Society.
II. Liberal Study Group.
MiU

D166
Dubuc, Alfred.
   Economic problems of confedera-
tion. Toronto, Research, Infor-
mation and Publication Project,
Student Union for Peace Action
[196]
5p. 28cm.
1. Canada--Econ. condit.
I. Student Union for Peace
Action.
WHi-A

D167
Duc, Ngo Cong.
   Ngo Cong Duc: the new politics
in Saigon that Nixon ignores.
[The statement of Ngo Cong Duc,
and the way to end the war, by
Rennie Davis and others.
Ithaca, N.Y., Glad Day Press,
1970]
3-[7]p. illus. 28cm.
Cover title.
Reprinted from New York Review
of Books, Nov. 5, 1970.
1. Vietnamese conflict, 1961-
1975. I. Davis, Rennard, jt.
auth. II. Glad Day Press.
NNU-T

D168
Dudnick, Robert.
   Black workers in revolt; how
Detroit's new black revolutionary workers are changing the
face of American trade unionism. [Detroit, Radical Education Project, 1969?]
14p. illus. 22cm.
Cover title.
Partially reprinted from Guardian, February 15, 1969.
1. Negroes--Employment.
2. Trade-unions. 3. Negroes--
Detroit. I. Radical Education
Project.
KU-RH, CU-B

D169
Dudnick, Robert.
   Black workers in revolt. How
Detroit's new black revolutionary workers are changing the
face of American trade unionism. [New York, Guardian,
1969?]
15p. illus.
Cover title.
1. Negroes--Employment.
2. Negroes--Detroit. 3. Labor
and laboring classes--Detroit.
4. Trade-unions. I. Guardian.
MiU

D170
Duff, Edward.
   There is a conspiracy. Lawn-
dale, Calif., Catholic Council
on Civil Liberties [196 ?]
[7]p.
Cover title.
1. Anti-communist movements.
2. Communism. I. Catholic
Council on Civil Liberties.
MiU

D171
Dumais, Mario.
   Social classes in Quebec.
[Montreal] Our Generation
[196]
9p. 22cm.
Cover title.
1. Social classes--Quebec.
2. Quebec--Social conditions.
I. Our Generation.
NNU-T

D172
Dumas, Evelyn.
   The new labour left in Quebec.
[Montreal, Our Generation, 196]
85-102p. 22cm.
Caption title.
1. Labor and laboring classes--
Quebec. I. Our Generation.
NNU-T

D173
Dunayevskaya, Raya.
   The Arab-Israeli collision, the
world powers, and the struggle
for the minds of men. Detroit,
News & Letters [19]67.

8p. 28cm.
Cover title.
1. Israel-Arab War, 1967.
2. Socialism. I. News & Letters.
MiU, KU-RH

D174
Dunayevskaya, Raya.
  China, Russia, USA--state capit-
  alism and Marx humanism or
  philosophy and revolution.
  [Detroit, News & Letters, 1967]
  63p. illus. 18cm.
  Cover title.
  1. China (People's Republic of
  China, 1949-   ) 2. Commun-
  ism. 3. Russia. I. News &
  Letters.
  MiU-H

D175
Dunayevskaya, Raya.
  Czechoslovakia: revolution and
  counter revolution. [Detroit]
  News & Letters [1968]
  62p. illus., maps. 18cm.
  1. Czechoslovak Republic--Re-
  lations (general) with Russia.
  2. Russia--Relations (general)
  with Czechoslovak Republic.
  I. News & Letters.
  MiU-H

D176
Dunayevskaya, Raya.
  Do Mao's and De Gaulle's pre-
  tensions to new world roles
  change the international
  balance of power? The state of
  the world economy and the theory
  of retrogression. Detroit, News
  & Letters, 1966.
  8p. 28cm.
  Caption title.
  1. World politics--1955-
  2. China (People's Republic of
  China, 1949-   )--Foreign
  policy. 3. France--Foreign
  policy. I. News & Letters.
  CU-B

D177
Dunayevskaya, Raya.
  Lenin on Hegel's science of
  logic; for "the materialist
  friends of the Hegelian

dialectic." Detroit, News &
Letters [196]
21p. 28cm.
Cover title.
At head of title: Notes on a
series of lectures.
1. Hegel, Georg Wihelm Fried-
rich, 1770-1831. 2. Lenin,
Vladimir Illich, 1870-1924.
I. News & Letters.
MiU

D178
Dunayevskaya, Raya.
  Mao's China and the "proletar-
  ian cultural revolution".
  [Detroit] News & Letters
  [1969?]
  13p. 28cm.
  Cover title.
  Reprinted from New Politics,
  V. 6, no. 2; 1968.
  1. China (People's Republic of
  China, 1949-   )--Intellect-
  ual life. I. News & Letters.
  NNU-T, KU-RH

D179
Dunayevskaya, Raya.
  Marxist-humanism; its origin
  and development in America,
  1941 to 1969. [Detroit, News
  & Letters, 1969?]
  14p. 28cm.
  Cover title.
  At head of title: The Raya
  Dunayevskaya collection.
  1. Socialism--Bibl. I. News &
  Letters.
  MiU

D180
Dunayevskaya, Raya.
  The missing link. Detroit,
  News & Letters, 1968.
  18p. 28cm. (Post-convention
  bulletin no. 2)
  Cover title.
  At head of title: Report to the
  convention of News & Letters.
  1. China (People's Republic of
  China, 1949-   )--Intellectual
  life. 2. Czechoslovak Republic
  --Pol. & govt. I. News &
  Letters.
  MiU

D181
Dunayevskaya, Raya.
  Nationalism, communism, Marxist-
  humanism and the Afro-Asian re-
  volution. [Detroit, News &
  Letters, 1959]
  28p. 19cm.
  1. Communism. 2. Revolutions--
  Africa. 3. Revolutions--Asia.
  I. News & Letters.
  NN, NUC 67-9739

D182
Dunayevskaya, Raya.
  The needed American revolution.
  Detroit, News & Letters, 1969.
  21p. 28cm.
  Cover title.
  1. Negroes--Civil rights.
  2. Socialism. 3. Revolutions.
  I. News & Letters.
  KU-RH, MoU

D183
Dunayevskaya, Raya.
  Perspectives: 1966-1967 and
  excerpt from the discussion by
  John. [Detroit, News & Letters]
  1966.
  19, 2p. 28cm. (News & Letters
  post-convention bulletin no. 2)
  At head of title: Convention
  report by Raya Dunayevskaya.
  1. Socialism. 2. Negroes--
  Civil rights. 3. Youth--Politi-
  cal activity. I. News &
  Letters.
  MiU

D184
Dunayevskaya, Raya.
  State-capitalism and Marx's
  humanism; or, philosophy and
  revolution. Includes also as
  appendix analysis of Rosa Luxem-
  burg's accumulation of capital.
  [Detroit, News & Letters, 1967]
  63p. illus., ports. 18cm.
  Cover title.
  At head of title: China, Russia,
  USA.
  1. China (People's Republic of
  China, 1949-   ) 2. Communism. 3. Luxemberg, Rosa, 1870-
  1919. Die Akkumulation des
  Kapitals. 4. Russia. I. News

& Letters.
MH-PA, LU, MiD, WHi-L, DLC
68-1012

D185
Dunayevskaya, Raya.
  U.S. and Russia enter Middle
  East cockpit. Detroit, News &
  Letters [196]
  5, 8p. 28cm.
  Cover title.
  At head of title: Two articles
  on new emerging forces.
  1. Russia--For. rel.--Near East.
  2. U.S.--For. rel.--Near East.
  3. Israel-Arab War, 1967.
  I. News & Letters.
  NNU-T

D186
Dunayevskaya, Raya.
  What is theory? or "history and
  its process". Detroit, News &
  Letters, 1970.
  17p. 28cm.
  Cover title.
  1. History. I. News & Letters.
  NNU-T

D187
Dunbar, Anthony.
  The will to survive; a study of
  a Mississippi plantation community; based on the words of its
  citizens, with an introduction
  by Charles H. Percy. Atlanta
  [Southern Regional Council]
  1969.
  iv, 64p.
  1. Negroes--Mississippi.
  2. Mississippi--Race question.
  I. Southern Regional Council.
  MiU, WHi-L

D188
Dunbar, Roxanne.
  Female liberation as the basis
  for social revolution. [Nash-
  ville, Southern Student Organi-
  zing Committee, 196]
  5p. 28cm.
  Cover title.
  1. Woman--Rights of women.
  I. Southern Student Organizing
  Committee.
  KU-RH

D189
Dunbar, Roxanne.
  Female liberation as the basis
  for social revolution--2. [New
  Orleans, Southern Female Rights
  Union] 1970.
  7 [1]p. 28cm.
  Caption title.
  1. Woman--Rights of women.
  I. Southern Female Rights
  Union, New Orleans.
  WHi-L, KU-RH

D190
Dunbar, Roxanne.
  Poor white women. Boston, New
  England Free Press [1969?]
  [2]p. 28cm.
  Caption title.
  1. Woman. 2. Poor. I. New
  England Free Press.
  KU-RH

D191
Dunbar, Roxanne.
  Students and revolutions, by
  Roxanne Dunbar and Vernon
  Grizzard. Cambridge, Mass.
  [196]
  9p. 28cm.
  Cover title.
  1. Student movements.
  2. Revolutions. I. Grizzard,
  Vernon, jt. auth.
  MiU

D192
Duncan, Donald.
  Don Duncan speaks out. [Berke-
  ley, Calif., Women for Peace,
  196]
  8p. 22cm.
  Cover title.
  Reprint of speech given at a
  VDC rally Nov. 20, 1965.
  1. Vietnamese conflict, 1961-
  1975. I. Women for Peace.
  CU-B

D193
Duncan, Donald.
  A "Green Beret" blas the war.
  [Chicago, Distributed by Students for a Democratic Society,
  196]
  [10]p. illus. 28cm.

  Caption title.
  Reprinted from Ramparts, Feb.
  1966.
  1. Vietnamese conflict, 1961-
  1975. I. Students for a Democratic Society.
  KU-RH, MiU-H, WHi-L

D194
Duncan, Donald.
  Support our soldiers: reject
  Humphrey-Nixon-Wallace. [New
  York, National Mobilization
  Committee to End the War in
  Vietnam, 1968?]
  [2]p. 28cm.
  Caption title.
  1. Vietnamese conflict, 1961-
  1975. 2. Wallace, George
  Corley, 1919-   3. Humphrey,
  Hubert Horatio, 1911-
  4. Nixon, Richard Milhous,
  Pres., U.S., 1913-
  I. National Mobilization Com-
  mittee to End the War in
  Vietnam.
  KU-RH

D195
Duncan, Donald.
  "The whole thing was a lie."
  [n.p., 196]
  13-24p. 28cm.
  Caption title.
  Reprinted from Ramparts.
  1. Vietnamese conflict, 1961-
  1975.
  KU-RH

D196
Dundas, Malcolm.
  An examination of the byways of
  prisons. [Palo Alto, Calif.,
  Palo Alto Resistance, 196]
  20p. 22cm.
  Cover title.
  1. Prisons. I. Resistance,
  Palo Alto, Calif.
  KU-RH, MoU

D197
Dungan, Margaret.
  The prospect of overcoming
  world hunger. Philadelphia,
  Women's International League
  for Peace and Freedom, 1968.

6p. 28cm.
Cover title.
1. Hunger. 2. Underdeveloped
areas. I. Women's International League for Peace and Freedom.
MoU, KU-RH

D198
Dunham, Barrows.
  Thinkers and treasures. New
York, Monthly Review Press, 1960.
47p. 22cm. (Monthly Review
pamphlet series, no. 15)
I. Monthly Review Press.
KU-J, MiU

D199
Durr, Clifford J.
  Jesus as a free speech victim;
trial by terror 2000 years ago.
[New York, Emergency Civil
Liberties Committee, 196]
10p. 21cm.
Cover title.
Reprinted from The Churchman,
July-Aug. 1960.
1. Civil rights. 2. Liberty
of speech. I. Emergency Civil

Liberties Committee.
WHi-A

D200
Dutt, Rajani Palme, 1896-
  Whither China? With an introduction by Gus Hall. New York,
New Outlook Publishers, 1967.
37p. 22cm.
1. China (People's Republic
of China, 1949-   )--Pol. &
govt. I. Hall, Gus.
II. New Outlook Publishers.
KU-RH, MiU, WHi-A

D201
Dynamics of world revolution
      today. [Toronto, Workers
      Vanguard Publishing, 1964]
44p. 22cm.
Cover title.
1. Revolutions. 2. Communism.
I. Workers Vanguard Publishing.
MoU

E

E1
East coast conspiracy to save
      lives. [Ithaca, N.Y., Glad
      Day Press, 1970?]
[4]p. 28cm.
Caption title.
1. Vietnamese conflict, 1961-
1975. 2. Peace. I. Glad Day
Press.
KU-RH

E2
Eccles, Marriner S.
  Statement of U.S. position in
Vietnam. Salt Lake City, 1965.
6 leaves. 28cm.
Cover title.
1. Vietnamese conflict, 1961-
1975.
KU-RH

E3
Ecology Action Educational
      Institute.
  But what can I do? Berkeley,
Calif. [1969?]
[2]p. 28cm.
Caption title.
1. Pollution. 2. Environmental
policy.
KU-RH

E4
Economic Action for Peace.
  Economic Action for Peace.
[Berkeley, 1970?]
[2]p. 28cm.
Caption title.
1. Vietnamese conflict, 1961-
1975.
CU-B

Economic Research and Action
    Project.
  see
Students for a Democratic Society.
  Economic Research and Action
  Project.

E6
Edelman, Irwin.
  There is a third side to the
  Rosenberg-Sobell case. [New
  York, 1958?]
  [6]p.
  Cover title.
  1. Sobell, Martin. 2. Jews.
  3. Communism. 4. Fascism.
  5. Rosenberg, Julius, 1918-
  1953. 6. Rosenberg, Ethel
  Greenglass, 1916-1953.
  WHi-L

E7
Edelman, Judy.
  Women on the job: a Marxist-
  Leninist view. [New York,
  New Outlook Publishers, 1970]
  21p. 19cm.
  Cover title.
  1. Woman--Rights of women.
  I. New Outlook Publishers.
  MiU

E8
Edelestein, Joel.
  Rent strike: what, when, how.
  New York, Students for a
  Democratic Society [196]
  5p. 28cm.
  Cover title.
  1. Negroes--Housing. 2. Rent.
  3. Landlord and tenant.
  I. Students for a Democratic
  Society.
  WHi-A

E9
Edelstein, Helen J.
  Health care for the aged.
  [n.p.] Campus Division, Americans for Democratic Action on
  behalf of the Liberal Study
  Group [1962]
  4 leaves. 36cm.
  Caption title.
  1. Aged--Medical care. I. Americans for Democratic Action.

Campus Division. I. Liberal
  Study Group.
  WHi-A

E10
Edgren, John.
  Influence or power [by John
  Edgren and others. Ann Arbor?
  Voice-SDS? 1966?]
  [4]p. 36cm.
  Caption title.
  1. Student movements--Ann
  Arbor. I. Voice Political
  Party-Students for a Democratic
  Society, Ann Arbor.
  MiU-H

E11
Edwards, Richard C.
  A radical approach to economic;
  basis for a new curriculum, by
  Richard C. Edwards, Arthur
  MacEwan and the staff of social
  science 125. Boston, New Eng-
  land Free Press [1970]
  12p. 28cm.
  Cover title.
  Reprinted from American Economic
  Review, May 1970.
  1. Economics--Study and teach-
  ing. I. MacEwan, Arthur, jt.
  auth. I. New England Free
  Press.
  KU-RH

E12
Edwards, Theodore.
  Marxism and Christianity: are
  they compatible? A debate
  between Theodore Edwards and
  Rev. Blase Bonpane. [New York,
  Pathfinder Press, 1970]
  21p. 22cm. (A Merit pamphlet)
  Cover title.
  1. Socialism and Religion.
  I. Bonpane, Blase. I. Path-
  finder Press.
  KU-RH

E13
Egleson, Nick.
  Changes in our thinking. [n.p.,
  Students for a Democratic Soci-
  ety? 196]
  7p. 28cm.
  Caption title.

1. Student movements. I. Students for a Democratic Society.
CU-B

E14
Egleson, Nick.
  Letter to the movement: re-cre-
  ation, self transformation and
  revolutionary consciousness.
  Boston, New England Free Press
  [196]
  4p. 28cm.
  Caption title.
  Reprinted from Liberation.
  1. Student movements. I. New
  England Free Press.
  MiU

E15
Egleson, Nick.
  Philadelphia Research and Action
  Project prospectus. Ann Arbor,
  Economic Research and Action
  Project [196]
  6p. 28cm.
  Cover title.
  1. Philadelphia--Econ. condit.
  2. Poor--Philadelphia. I. Stu-
  dents for a Democratic Society.
  Economic Research and Action
  Project.
  MiU, WHi-A

E16
Egleson, Nick.
  The survey and community organization. Nashville, Southern Student Organizing Committee [196]
  5 [5]p. 28cm.
  1. Surveys. 2. Community organization. I. Southern Student
  Organizing Committee.
  MoU

E17
Egleson, Nick.
  The survey and community organization. New York, Students for
  a Democratic Society and its Economic Research and Action Project [196]
  [13]p.
  Cover title.
  1. Surveys. 2. Community organization. I. Students for a Democratic Society. Economic

Research and Action Project.
WHi-L

E18
Eisan, Arlene.
  Bibliography on the labor move-
  ment. New York, Students for a
  Democratic Society [196]
  7p. 28cm.
  Cover title.
  1. Labor and laboring classes--
  Bibl. I. Students for a Demo-
  cratic Society.
  WHi-A, KU-RH

E19
Eldon Avenue Revolutionary Union
    Movement.
  The 1970 U.A.W. contract settlements. [Detroit? 1970?]
  [4]p.
  Caption title.
  1. Negroes--Civil rights.
  2. Automobile industry workers.
  3. International Union, United
  Automobile, Aircraft and Agricultural Implement Workers of America.
  MiU

E20
Eldridge Cleaver Election Committee.
  Eldridge Cleaver for Prisident
  [n.p., 1968?]
  [2]p.]8cm.
  Caption title.
  1. Cleaver,
  CU-B

E21
Elkus, Ben.
  The Huey Newton case, prepared
  by Ben Elken and Aidan Kelly.
  [n.p., 196 ?]
  1. Negroes--Cifil rights. 2. New
  2. Newton, Huey
  Aidan
  CU-B

E22
Ellison, Ralph
  The city in crisis [by] Ralph Ellison, Whitney Young, Jr., Herbert Gans with an introduction by
  Bayard Rustin. [New York, A. P
  Philip Randolph Educational Fund
  1966
  60p. illus. (A. Philip Ran-

colph Educational Fund 4)
1. Cities and towns. 2. Poverty.
3. Negroes--Civil rights.
I. Gans, Herbert J., jt. auth.
II. Young, Whitney, jt. auth.
III. Rustin, Ralph, 1910-
IV. Randolph (A. Philip) Edu-
cational Fund.
WHi-L

E23
El-Messiri, Abdel-Wahab M.
   Israel: base of western imperialism. [New York, Committee to
   Support Middle East Liberation,
   1970]
   24p. 22cm.
   1. Israel-Arab War, 1967.
   2. Israel--Foreign policy.
   3. Imperialism. I. Committee
   to Support Middle East Liberation.
   KU-RH

E24
Emel ianov, Vasilii Semenovich,
      1901-
   A scientist's responsibility.
   New York, Crosscurrents Press
   [1963]
   39p. 22cm.
   1. Atomic warfare--Moral and
   religious aspects. 2. Political
   ethics. 3. Atomic weapons and
   disarmament. I. Crosscurrents
   Press.
   DLC 63-21035

E25
Emergency Civil Liberties Com-
      mittee.
   Prospect for a great American
   Society. [New York, 1964]
   [4]p. 23x10cm.
   1. Civil rights.
   KU-RH

D26
Emergency Civil Liberties Com-
      mittee.
   The Smith act; its origin, use,
   poison. [New York, 1956]
   [12]p.
   Cover title.
   1. Smith, Howard Worth, 1883-
         2. U.S. Laws, statutes,

etc. Alien Registration Act
of 1940. 3. Communist Party of
the United States of America.
MiEM, KU-J, MiU, WHi-L,
NUC 67-32629

E27
Emergency Civil Liberties Com-
      mittee.
   "A would-be murder walks the
   streets of Louisville." [New
   York, 1955?]
   Cover title.
   1. Louisville--Race question.
   2. Negroes--Louisville.
   WHi-L

E28
Emerson, Thomas I.
   Dialogue on the constitutional-
   ity of the Committee on Un-
   American Activities of the
   House of Representatives 89th
   Congress [by] Thomas I. Emerson
   v. Francis J. McNamara. [Los
   Angeles, National Committee to
   Abolish the House Un-American
   Activities Committee, 196]
   56p. 22cm.
   Cover title.
   1. U.S. Congress. House. Com-
   mittee on Un-American Activities.
   I. McNamara, Francis J., jt.
   auth. II. National Committee to
   Abolish the House Un-American
   Activities Committee.
   KU-RH

E29
Emigration to Canada: legal notes
      for draft age men; plus a
      summary and analysis of the
      new immigration regulations
      [by the Toronto Anti-Draft
      Programme] Nashville, South-
      ern Student Organizing Com-
      mittee [1967?]
   6p. [3] leaves. 28cm.
   Cover title.
   1. Military service, Compulsory.
   2. Emigration and immigration
   law--Canada. I. Toronto Anti-
   Draft Programme. II. Southern
   Student Organizing Committee.
   MiU, CU-B

E30
End McCarranism: on this we stand
    together. [New York, Citizens
    Committee for Constitutional
    Liberties, 196]
  38p.
  Cover title.
  1. U.S. Laws, statutes, etc.
  Internal Security Act of 1950.
  2. Communism. 3. Anti-commun-
  ist movements. I. Citizens
  Committee for Constitutional
  Liberties.
  MiU

E31
Engels, Friedrich, 1820-1895.
  The origin of the family.
  [Boston, New England Free Press,
  1970?]
  19-74p. 25cm.
  Cover title.
  1. Family. I. New England Free
  Press.
  KU-RH

E32
Engels, Friedrich, 1820-1895.
  Principles of communism. A new
  translation by Paul M. Sweezy.
  [New York? Monthly Review, 1963]
  23p. 22cm. (Monthly review
  pamphlet series, no. 4)
  1. Communism. I. Sweezy, Paul
  Marlor, 1910-   I. Monthly
  Review Press.
  KU-RH

E33
Episcopal Peace Fellowship.
  Cross before flag: Epispocal
  statements on war and peace.
  [New York, 196]
  16p. 23x10cm.
  Cover title.
  1. Peace. 2. War.
  KU-RH

E34
Epton, Bill.
  We accuse: Bill Epton speaks
  to the court. [Brooklyn, Progressive Labor Party, 1966]
  [40]p. 23cm.
  Cover title.
  1. Harlem, New York (City)--

Riots. 2. Negroes--Harlem,
New York (City) I. Progressive
Labor Party.
WHi-L, MiU

E35
Ethiopian Students Union in North
    America.
  Repressions in Ethiopia. [Cam-
  bridge, Mass.] Africa Research
  Group [1971]
  12p. 22cm.
  Cover title.
  1. Ethiopia--Pol. & govt.
  I. Africa Research Group.
  KU-RH

E36
Eubanks, Carolyn.
  The fight for women's liberation
  is basic to defeating imperialism [by Carolyn Eubanks and
  others. n.p., 1969]
  6p. 36cm.
  Caption title.
  1. Woman--Rights of women.
  2. Students for a Democratic
  Society.
  WHi-L

E37
Eugene Victor Debs (1855-1955)--
    the centennial year. [New
    York] Debs Centennial Com-
    mittee [and] Socialist Soci-
    ety, USA, 1956.
  53p. 23cm.
  1. Socialism. 2. Debs, Eugene
  Victor, 1855-1926. I. Debs
  Centennial Committee.
  II. Socialist Society.
  KU-J

E38
Evansohn, John.
  Literature on the American
  working class [by] John Evansohn
  [and others] Boston, New England
  Free Press [1969?]
  [32]-55p. 22cm.
  Cover title.
  Reprinted from Radical America,
  Ap. 1969.
  1. Labor and laboring classes.
  2. Labor and laboring classes
  in literature. I. New England

Free Press.
KU-RH

E39
Every cook can govern: a study of
    democracy in ancient Greece.
    Also: Negro Americans and
    American politics. [Detroit,

Correspondence Publishing
    Co., 1956]
22p. 21cm. (Correspondence
pamphlet [no.] 2)
1. Democracy. 2. Negroes--Civil
rights. I. Correspondence
Publishing Co.
MiU

F

F1
FTA
    Steve Gilbert: soldier in the
    freedom army. [Louisville, 196]
    folder. illus.
    1. Gilbert, Steve. 2. Soldiers.
    WHi-L

F2
Facing Reality Publishing
    Committee.
    Detroit: the July days. [De-
    troit, 1967?]
    4p. 22cm.
    Caption title.
    1. Negroes--Detroit. 2. De-
    troit--Race question. 3. De-
    troit--Riots, 1967.
    MiU

F3
Facing Reality Publishing
    Committee.
    Negro Americans take lead: a
    statement in American civili-
    zation. Detroit [1964]
    44p. 22cm.
    1. Negroes--Civil rights.
    MiU, CU-B

F4
Facts on Huey P. Newton's legal
    defense in court. Berkeley,
    Calif., Huey P. Newton De-
    fense Fund [196]
    5 [1]p. 22cm.
    Caption title.
    1. Newton, Huey P. I. Huey P.
    Newton Defense Fund.
    NNU-T

F5
Fahey, Joseph J.
    Peace, war and the Christian
    conscience. [New York, The
    Christopers, 196]
    20p. 23x10cm.
    Cover title.
    1. Peace. 2. War and religion.
    KU-RH

F6
Fair Housing Council of Metro-
    politan Washington.
    Negro military servicemen and
    racial discrimination in hous-
    ing. Washington, Metropolitan
    Washington Housing Program of
    the American Friends Service
    Committee, 1966.
    12p.
    1. Negroes--Housing. I. Friends,
    Society of. American Friends
    Service Committee.
    DHHF, DLC, NUC 68-107646

F7
Fair Play for Cuba Committee.
    Canadian students in Cuba.
    [Toronto, 1965]
    59p. illus. 22cm.
    Includes some text in French.
    1. Cuba--Descr. & trav.--1961-
        2. Cuba--Foreign opinion,
    Canadian. 3. Canadian students
    in Cuba.
    Cst-H, FU, CaOTU, WHi-L,
    MoU, DLC 67-110260

F8
Fair Play for Cuba Committee.

Fair Play for Cuba Committee,
summer '64. Featuring a report
on the Canadian students' work
tour to Cuba, a poem by Al Purdy
[and] impressions by Dorothy
Steeves. Including excerpts
from Castro's May Day speech
'64. [Toronto, 1964]
36p. 22cm.
F.P.C.C. Bulletin, summer 1964.
1. Cuba--Descr. & trav.--1961-
        2. Cuba--Foreign opinion,
Canadian. 3. Canadian students
in Cuba.
TxU

F9
Fair Play for Cuba Committee.
  The real Cuba: an interview with
  Michael Chartrand; a contribution by Vernel Olson; a contribution by John Riddell. Toronto [1964]
  36p. 22cm.
  1. Cuba. I. Chartrand, Michael.
  II. Olson, Vernel. III. Riddell, John.
  MoU, FU, CSt-H, NUC 67-43655

F10
Fair Play for Cuba Committee.
  A report by four Canadians on
  Cuba as they saw it. Toronto
  [1963]
  31p.
  1. Cuba--Descr. & trav.--1961-
        2. Cuba--Foreign opinion,
  Canadian.
  CaOTU, NUC 64-43210

F11
Fall, Bernard B., 1926-
  Blitz in Vietnam. [Berkeley,
  Turn Toward Peace, 196]
  7p. 28cm.
  Caption title.
  Reprinted from New Republic,
  Oct. 9, 1965.
  1. Vietnamese conflict, 1961-
  1975. I. Turn Toward Peace.
  CU-B

F12
Far East Reporter.
  The China-India conflict. [New
  York, 196]

47p. map. 20cm.
Cover title.
1. China (People's Republic of
China, 1949-   )--For. rel.--
India. 2. India--For. rel.--
China (People's Republic of
China, 1949-   )
KU-J, NIC, CSt-H, NUC 68-80732

F13
Far East Reporter.
  China's path to her new society.
  [New York, 1959?]
  16p.
  Cover title.
  1. China (People's Republic of
  China, 1949-   )
  CLU, NUC 67--4039

F14
Far East Reporter.
  The impact of current United
  States policy on Philippine
  "independence". [New York?
  Maud Russell, 1965]
  42p. map. 22cm.
  Cover title.
  1. U.S.--For. rel.--Philippine
  Islands. 2. Philippine Islands
  --For. rel.--U.S.
  NIC, NUC 66-77311

F15
Far East Reporter.
  Letters from China, written by
  a seventeen year old girl, her
  Chinese father, her American
  mother, an American woman in
  Shanghai [and] an English woman
  in Peking. [New York, 1956?]
  63p.
  1. China (People's Republic of
  China, 1949-   )--Social conditions.
  MiU, NUC 67-87623

F16
Far East Reporter.
  The "new era" in the Philippines.
  [New York, 1962?]
  12p. 21cm.
  Cover title.
  1. Philippine Islands--Pol. &
  govt.
  NIC, NUC 64-31551

F17
Farber, Jerry.
  The student as nigger. Boston,
  New England Free Press [196]
  6p. 22cm.
  Cover title.
  1. Students. 2. Education.
  I. New England Free Press.
  KU-RH

F18
Farber, Jerry.
  Student as nigger. [Pasadena,
  Calif., The Resistance, 196]
  [4]p. 28cm.
  Caption title.
  1. Students. 2. Education.
  I. Resistance.
  KU-RH

F19
Farber, Jerry.
  The student as nigger. Illus.
  by Nick Thorkelson. [Madison,
  Wis., Connections] 1968.
  [7]p. (Connections reprint
  no. 1)
  Cover title.
  1. Students. 2. Education.
  I. Connections.
  WHi-L

F20
Farber, Jerry.
The student as nigger. Illus. by
  Nick Thorkelson. [Montreal]
  Our Generation [196]
  [10]p. illus. 22cm.
  Cover title.
  1. Students. 2. Education.
  I. Our Generation.
  NNU-T

F21
Farber, Sam.
  A statement on the state of the
  YPSL. [Berkeley, Calif., 1964]
  2p. 28cm.
  Caption title.
  1. Young People's Socialist
  League.
  KU-RH

F22
Farmer, James.
  Louisiana story, 1963. [New

York, Congress of Racial Equality, 1963]
[10]p. illus. 22cm.
1. Negroes--Louisiana.
2. Louisiana--Race question.
I. Congress of Racial Equality.
KU-RH, CU-B

F23
Farren, Patrick.
  The war has taxed us enough;
  why I won't pay for the war no
  more. [Boston, New England
  Free Press, 197]
  folder. 22x10cm.
  1. Vietnamese conflict, 1961-
  1975. 2. Tax evasion. I. New
  England Free Press.
  KU-RH

F24
Fasulo, G.
  The powers behind apartheid.
  [Boston, New England Free Press,
  1970?]
  22p. map. 22cm. (Africa Research Group. Reprint 3)
  Cover title.
  1. Africa, South--Econ. condit.--
  1918-1961. 2. Africa, South--
  Econ. condit.--1961-
  3. Africa, South--Pol. & govt.--
  1948-   I. New England Free
  Press.
  DLC 77-29444

F25
Fasulo, G.
  The powers behind apartheid.
  [Cambridge, Mass.] Africa Re-
  search Group [196]
  22p. illus. 22cm. (Reprint 3)
  Cover title.
  1. Africa, South--Race question.
  2. Africa, South--Econ. condit.
  I. Africa Research Group.
  MoU, KU-RH

Fath
  see
Palestine National Liberation
    Movement

F26
Favreau, Robert.
  The quandary of L' Union

Generale des Etudiants du Que
bec. [Montreal, Our Generation,
196]
93-101 leaves.
Caption title.
1. Student movements--Quebec.
2. L'Union Generale des Etudiants du Quebec. I. Our Genera-·
tion.
NNU-T

F27
Federation of Communities in
    Service.
Don't go 'way. [Knoxville,
Tenn., c1969]
[20]p. illus. 18x18cm.
Cover title.
1. Art and society. 2. Art--
Appalachian Mountains. 3. Ap-
palachian Mountains--Econ.
condit.
KU-RH

F28
Feiffer, Jules.
Feiffer on Vietnam. [New York,
Student Peace Union, 196]
13p. illus. 22cm.
Cover title.
1. Vietnamese conflict, 1961-
1975. I. Student Peace Union.
WHi-L, KU-RH

F29
Fein, Ollie.
Notes on alternatives facing the
radicals in medicine, by Ollie
and Charlotte Fein. Ann Arbor,
Conference on Radicals in the
Professions, 1967.
3p. 28cm.
Cover title.
1. Poor. 2. Medical care.
3. Radicalism. I. Conference
on Radicals in the Professions.
I. Fein, Charlotte, jt. auth.
MiU-H

F30
Feinberg, Abraham L.
Vietnam and civil disobedience.
[n.p., Fellowship, 196]
[1] leaf. 36cm.
Caption title.
1. Vietnamese conflict, 1961-

1975. 2. Government, Resistance
to. I. Fellowship.
CU-B

F31
Feingold, Eugene.
Politics 1964; corporations and
crisis, by Eugene Feingold &
Tom Hayden. [New York] Students
for a Democratic Society and its
Economic Research and Action
Project [196]
13p. 28cm.
1. Corporations. 2. Business
and politics. 3. Democratic
Party--Southern States. I. Stu-
dents for a Democratic Society.
Economic Research and Action
Project. II. Hayden, Thomas,
jt. auth.
MiU, WHi-A

F32
Feingold, Eugene.
Politics 1965--corporation and
crisis by Eugene Feingold and
Tom Hayden. [Chicago, Students
for a Democratic Society, 1965?]
13p. 28cm.
1. Corporations. 2. Business
and politics. I. Students for
a Democratic Society. II. Hayden, Thomas, jt. auth.
CU-B

F33
Feld, Bernard T.
Preventing the further prolifer-
ation of nuclear weapons. [Wash-
ington] Council for a Livable
World, 1965.
[4]p. 28cm. (Study paper)
Caption title.
1. Atomic weapons and disarma-
ment. I. Council for a Livable
World.
KU-RH

F34
Feld, Bernard T.
A program for arms control, es-
pecially in central Europe.
Washington, Council for a Liv-
able World, 1965.
[4]p. 28cm. (Study paper)
Caption title.

1. U.S.--Military policy.
2. Atomic weapons. I. Council
for a Livable World.
KU-RH

F35
Feldman, Paul.
  The pathos of "black power".
  New York, League for Industrial
  Democracy [1967?]
  [12]p. 22cm. (Looking forward
  no. 8)
  Cover title.
  Reprinted from Dissent, Jan.-
  Feb., 1967.
  1. Negroes--Civil rights.
  I. League for Industrial Demo-
  cracy.
  NNU-T, WHi-L

F36
Feldman, Sandra.
  Decentralization and the city
  schools. [New York, League for
  Industrial Democracy, 196]
  [16]p. 22cm. (Looking forward
  no. 12)
  1. Negroes--Education. 2. Edu-
  cation--New York (State)--New
  York (City) I. League for Industrial Democracy.
  WHi-L, KU-RH, NNU-T

F37
Fellowship House.
  The third way [Philadelphia,
  196]
  [12]p. 22cm.
  Cover title.
  1. Negroes--Civil rights.
  KU-RH

F38
Fellowship of Reconciliation
    (United States)
  Chaos in Saigon: comments on
  the precarious state of civil
  peace in South Vietnam and the
  prospects for real peace in
  Vietnam. [New York, 1968]
  folder.
  1. Vietnamese conflict, 1961-
  1975.
  WHi-L

F39
Fellowship of Reconciliation
    (United States)
  The Fellowship of Reconciliation;
  what it is; what it does. [Ny-
  ack, N.Y., 196]
  [8]p. 23x9cm.
  Cover title.
  KU-RH

F40
Fellowship of Reconciliation
    (United States)
  It's your choice. [Nyack, N.Y.,
  196]
  folder. 22x9cm.
  Cover title.
  1. Military service, Compulsory.
  KU-RH

F41
Fellowship of Reconciliation
    (United States)
  Martin Luther King and the
  Montgomery story: how 50,000
  Negroes found a new way to end
  racial discrimination. [Nyack,
  N.Y., 1957]
  [16]p. illus. 27cm.
  Cover title.
  1. King, Martin Luther, 1929-
  1968. 2. Negroes--Alabama.
  3. Alabama--Race question.
  NN

F42
Fellowship of Reconciliation
    (United States)
  Next steps on Cuba and Latin
  America. Nyack, N.Y. [1962?]
  7 leaves. 28cm.
  1. Cuba--For. rel.--Latin Ameri-
  ca. 2. Cuba--For. rel.--U.S.
  3. Latin America--For. rel.--
  Cuba. 4. U.S.--For. rel.--Cuba.
  FU, NUC 65-8184

F43
Fellowship of Reconciliation
    (United States)
  To the end of the war and beyond.
  [Nyack, N.Y., 197]
  folder, 21cm.
  1. Vietnamese conflict, 1961-

1975.
KU-RH

F44
Fellowship of Reconciliation
     (United States). Clergymen's
     Emergency Committee for Viet-
     nam.
   A report from Vietnam. Berkeley, Turn Toward Peace [1965]
   3p. 28cm.
   Caption title.
   1. Vietnamese conflict, 1961-
   1975. I. Turn Towards Peace.
   CU-B

F45
Female liberation, a joint state-
     ment by six female liberation
     groups in Chapel Hill and
     Durham, N.C. [n.p., 197]
   4p. 28cm.
   Caption title.
   1. Woman--Rights of women.
   KU-RH

F46
Feminists.
   Dangers in the pro-women line
   and consciousnes-rasing. [New
   York, 196]
   13p. 28cm.
   Caption title.
   1. Woman--Rights of women.
   WHi-L

F47
Feminists.
   History of the Feminists. [New
   York, 1970]
   2p. 28cm.
   1. Woman.
   WHi-L

F48
Feminists.
   Organizational principles and
   structure. New York [1969?]
   10p. 28cm.
   Caption title.
   1. Woman--Rights of women.
   WHi-L, KU-RH

F49
Fenster, Leo.
   At twice the price; Mexican

auto swindle. [Toronto? Latin
American Working Group? 1970?]
[6]p. 28cm.
Caption title.
Reprinted from The Nation,
June 2, 1969.
1. Automobile industry and
trade--Mexico. 2. Automobile
industry and trade--Latin Ameri-
ca. I. Latin America Working
Group.
KU-RH

F50
Feraferia.
The historical perspective of
Feraferia; psycho-ecological
evolution. Altadena, Calif.
[c1969]
2 leaves. 28cm.
1. Mysticism. 2. Collective
settlements.
MoU

F51
Feraferia.
Topocosmic mandala of the sacred
land sky love year. [Altadena,
Calif., c1969]
3 leaves. illus. 28cm.
Caption title.
1. Mysticism.
MoU

F52
Ferber, Mike.
Be realistic: demand the impos-
sible [by] Mike Ferber. I find
no more honorable position in
America than that of the criminal
[by] Dave Harris. [New York,
War Resisters League, 196]
[16]p. 23x11cm.
Cover title.
1. Military service, Compulsory.
2. Government, Resistance to.
I. Harris, David, jt. auth.
II. War Resisters League.
CU-B

F53
Ferber, Mike.
On the Resistance [by] Mike Ferber [and] Dave Harris. [n.p.,
196]
10p. 22cm.

Cover title.
1. Military service, Compulsory.
2. Resistance. 3. Government,
Resistance to. I. Harris, David,
jt. auth.
KU-RH

F54
Ferber, Mile.
On the Resistance [by] Mike
Ferber [and] Dave Harris. [Palo
Alto, Calif., Institute for the
Study of Nonviolence, 1970?]
16 [1]p. 22cm.
"Excerpts from remarks made by
Michael Ferber and Dave Harris
at the 21st Annual Student Con-
gress at Kansas State Univer-
sity, August 21, 1968."
1. Military service, Compulsory.
2. Resistance. 3. Government,
Resistance to. I. Harris, Da-
vid, jt. auth. II. Institute
for the Study of Nonviolence.
KU-RH

F55
Ferry, W.H.
Disarm to parley: a case for
unilateral disarmament.
[Philadelphia, Peace Education
Program, American Friends Ser-
vice Committee, 1961]
16p. 22cm.
Cover title.
"Originally delivered as an
address entitled The case for
unilateral disarmament, on
Dec. 2, 1960 before the America
Association for the United
Nations in Santa Barbara,
Calif."
1. Disarmament. 2. U.S.--Mili-
tary policy. I. Friends, Soc-
iety of. American Friends
Committee.
MoU, DS

F56
Ferry, W.H.
Toward a moral economy, a pre-
consultation paper by W.H.
Ferry. [n.p., Fellowship Pub-
lications, 196]
6p. 36cm.
Cover title.

At head of title: Peace on
earth: moral and technological
implications.
1. Economics. 2. Cybernetics.
3. Peace. I. Fellowship Publications.
MoU

F57
Ferry, W.H.
What price for peace. Des
Moines, World Peace Broadcasting
Foundation [196]
10p. 28cm.
Cover title.
1. Peace. I. World Peace Broad-
casting Foundation.
WHi-A

F58
Fifth Avenue Vietnam Peace
    Parage Committee.
In the teeth of war; photogra-
phic documentary of the March
26th, 1966, New York City demonstration against the war in
Vietnam. Photos. by Martin
Berman [and others] Introd. by
Dave Dellinger. Additional
text from speeches at the
demonstration by Juan Mari Bras
[and others New York] 1966.
64p. illus. 28cm.
1. Vietnamese conflict, 1961-
1975. I. Berman, Martin.
II. Dellinger, Dave.
CU-B, MB, NRU, OrU, DLC 67-
17651

F59
Finberg, Howard.
Crisis at San Francisco State.
San Francisco, Insight Publi-
cations, 1969.
51p. illus. 28cm.
Cover title: An interpretive
look at...San Francisco State
College crisis.
1. California, State College,
San Francisco. 2. Student
movements--San Francisco.
I. Insight Publications.
CSf, NUC 70-10360

F60
Finnerty, Daniel, ed.

Exiled: handbook for the draft
age emigrant, edited by Daniel
Finnerty [and] Charles Funnell.
[Philadelphia, Philadelphia Resistance, 1968]
59, iii, ip. 22cm.
1. Military service, Compulsory.
I. Funnell, Charles. II. Resistance, Philadelphia.
MoU

F61
"The first step in the procurement
   of military manpower is registration". [n.p., Resistance,
   196 ?]
[12]p. 22cm.
Cover title.
1. Military service, Compulsory.
I. Resistance.
CU-B

F62
Fisher, Margaret.
  Fair housing handbook. [Rev.
  ed. Philadelphia] American
  Friends Service Committee and
  the National Committee Against
  Discrimination in Housing [1965,
  c1964]
  ii, 42p. illus.
  1. Negroes--Housing. I. Friends,
  Society of. American Friends
  Service Committee. II. National Committee Against Discrimination in Housing.
  WHi-L

F63
Fisher, William.
  A housing program developed by
  the 1961 CORE Housing Institute.
  Revised and distributed by the
  Program Department. New York,
  CORE [1961?]
  6p. 28cm.
  Caption title.
  1. Negroes--Housing. I. Con-
  gress of Racial Equality.
  CU-B

F64
Fisk, Alfred G.
  Peace through disarmament.
  [New York, Committee for World
  Development & World Disarmament,

1961?]
10p. 22cm.
1. Disarmament. I. Committee
for World Development and World
Disarmament.
NN

F65
Fitch, Robert.
  A Galbraith reappraisal: the
  ideologue as gadfly. Ann
  Arbor, Radical Education Pro-
  ject [1969?]
  9p. 22cm.
  Cover title.
  Reprinted from Ramparts, May
  1968.
  1. Galbraith, John Kenneth,
  1908-   I. Radical Education
  Project.
  MiU, MoU, KU-RH

F66
Flacks, Richard.
  A campus peace research and education program. Ann Arbor, Students for a Democratic Society
  and its Peace Research and Education Project [196]
  6p. 28cm.
  Cover title.
  1. Students for a Democratic
  Society. Peace Research and
  Education Project. 2. Student
  movements. 3. Peace.
  WHi-A

F67
Flacks, Richard.
  Chicago: organizing the unem-
  ployed. New York, Students for
  a Democratic Society and its
  Economic Research and Action
  Project [196]
  10p. 28cm.
  Cover title.
  1. Poor--Chicago. 2. Jobs or
  Income Now Community Union.
  3. Chicago--Econ. condit.
  I. Students for a Democratic
  Society. Economic Research and
  Action Project.
  WHi-A

F68
Flacks, Richard.

The Chicago project. Ann Arbor,
Students for a Democratic Socie-
ty and its Economic Research and
Action Project [196]
10p. 28cm.
Cover title.
1. Jobs or Income Now Community
Action. 2. Poor--Chicago.
3. Chicago--Econ. action.
I. Students for a Democratic
Society. Economic Research and
Action Project.
WHi-A

F69
Flacks, Richard.
Some problems, issues, proposals.
[n.p., 1965]
5p. 28cm. (SDS national con-
vention--working papers)
Caption title.
At head of title: "1965 national
convention--work papers."
1. U.S.--Pol. & govt.--1961-
         2. U.S.--Foreign policy.
3. Youth--Political activity.
I. Students for a Democratic
Society. National Convention,
1965.
WHi-L, KU-RH

F70
Flacks, Richard.
Taking Goldwater seriously.
New York, Students for a Demo-
cratic Society and its Economic
Research and Action Project [196]
4p. 28cm.
Cover title.
1. Goldwater, Barry Morris,
1909-   I. Students for a
Democratic Society. Economic
Research and Action Project.
MiU

F71
Flake, Vivian E. (Miyasato)
A women dissenter speaks.
[Honolulu, Hawaii Resistance,
196 ?]
3 leaves. 28cm.
Caption title.
1. Vietnamese conflict, 1961-
1975. I. Hawaii Resistance.
CU-B

F72
Flaming, Karl H.
Who riots and why? Black and
white perspectives in Milwaukee.
[Milwaukee] Milwaukee Urban
League, 1968.
xii, 79p.
Cover title.
1. Milwaukee--Riots, 1967.
2. Milwaukee--Race question.
3. Negroes--Milwaukee.
WHi-L

F73
Fleming, Antony.
The machinery of conformity.
[Buffalo, N.Y., Friends of
Malatesta, 196]
[353]-364p. 22cm.
Cover title.
Reprinted from Anarchy
1. Anarchism and anarchists.
2. Conformity. I. Friends of
Malatesta.
MiU

F74
Fleming, Denna Frank, 1893-
Does deterrence deter? A study
and commentary. [Philadelphia,
Peace Literature Service of the
American Friends Service Committee, 1962]
28p. 22cm. (Beyond deterrence
series)
1. Deterrence (Strategy)
2. U.S.--Military policy.
3. World politics--1955-
I. Friends, Society of. American Friends Service Committee.
WHi-L, DLC 62-51083

F75
Fleming, Denna Frank, 1893-
Our fifty year failure to make
peace. [Winnipeg, Canadian Dimension, 196]
[5]p. 28cm.
Caption title.
Reprinted from Canadian Dimension.
1. U.S.--Foreign policy.
2. World Politics--1955-
I. Canadian Dimension.
KU-RH

F76
Fleming, Denna Frank, 1893-
  Vietnam and the crashing domi-
  noes. [New York, 1968]
  9p. 22cm.
  Cover title.
  Reprinted from New World Review,
  Summer 1968.
  1. Vietnamese conflict, 1961-
  1975. I. New World Review.
  KU-RH

F77
Fleming, Denna Frank, 1893-
  The western interventions in
  the Soviet Union 1918-1920.
  [New York, 196]
  13p. 21cm.
  Cover title.
  Reprinted from New World Re-
  view, Fall 1967.
  1. Russia--Foreign policy.
  2. U.S.--For. rel.--Russia.
  3. U.S.--Foreign policy.
  I. New World Review.
  KU-RH

F78
Flug, Mike.
  The Maryland Freedom Union:
  workers doing and thinking.
  Detroit, News & Letters [196]
  9p. 28cm.
  Cover title.
  1. Maryland--Race question.
  2. Negroes--Maryland. 3. Mary-
  land Freedom Union. I. News &
  Letters.
  NNU-T, MiU

F79
Flynn, Elizabeth Gurley.
  Freedom begins at home. [New
  York, New Century Publishers,
  1961]
  22p.
  1. Communism. 2. U.S. Laws,
  statutes, etc. Internal Security Act of 1950. I. New Century
  Publishers.
  MiEM, KU-J, NUC 67-97073

F80
Flynn, Eliza-eth Gurley.
  Horizons of the future for a
  socialist America. [New York,

Communist Party USA, 1959]
  46p. illus. 22cm.
  1. Socialism in the U.S.
  I. Communist Party of the United
  States of America.
  KU-J, WHi-L

F81
Flynn, Elizabeth Gurley.
  The McCarran act; fact and
  fancy. [New York, Gus Hall-
  Benjamin J. Davis Defense
  Committee, 1963?]
  28p. illus.
  1. U.S. Laws, statutes, etc.
  Internal Security Act of 1950.
  2. Communism. I. Gus Hall-Benjamin J. Davis Defense Committee.
  MiEM, NUC 67-90276

F82
Folsom, Michael B.
  Shakespeare: a Marxist bibliography. [New York, American
  Institute for Marxist Studies]
  1965.
  9p. 28cm. (Bibliographical
  series no. 2)
  Cover title.
  1. Shakespeare, William, 1564-
  1616--Political and social
  views--Bibl. I. American Institute for Marxist Studies.
  WHi-L

F83
Forbes, Allan.
  A critique of the safeguard
  ABM. [Washington] Council for
  a Livable World [c1969]
  36p. 23cm.
  1. Antimissile missiles.
  2. U.S.--Military policy.
  I. Council for a Livable World.
  KU-RH

F84
The Foreign Policy Association:
  50 years of successful imperialism. [New York, New York
  Regional SDS, 196]
  5p. illus. 28cm.
  Cover title.
  1. Foreign Policy Association.
  2. Imperialism. 3. U.S.--For-

eign policy. I. Students for a
Democratic Society, New York
Region.
NNU-T

F85
Foreman, Clark.
End McCarranism: on this we
stand together [by] Clark Fore-
man [and others. New York,
Citizens Committee for Constitu-
tional Liberties, 196]
38p. 21cm.
Cover title.
Speeches made at June 7 rally
Manhattan Center New York.
1. Internal security. 2. U.S.
Laws, statutes, etc. Internal
Security Act of 1950. I. Citi-
zens Committee for Constitution-
al Liberties.
KU-RH

F86
Forest, James H.
Catholics and conscientious
objection. [Nyack, N.Y.,
Catholic Peace Fellowship,
1967]
[12]p. 23x10cm.
1. Conscientious objectors.
2. Catholics. I. Catholic
Peace Fellowship.
KU-RH

F87
Forest, James H.
For those who sit in the warm
sunlight. [New York, Catholic
Peace Fellowship, 1965?]
[4]p. 28cm.
Caption title.
Reprinted from Fellowship Maga-
zine, Sept. 1965.
1. Catholic Worker. 2. Peace--
Period. 3. Catholics.
I. Catholic Peace Fellowship.
KU-RH

F88
Forman, James, 1928-
The direction of change for the
black liberation movement.
[Berkeley, Alliance for Black
Unity; San Jose Friends of
SNCC, 1967?]

18p. 22cm.
Cover title.
"A speech...keynoting the
Black Youth Conference held in
Los Angeles, California, Nov-
ember 1967."
1. Negroes--Civil rights.
I. Friends of Student Nonviolent
Coordinating Committee. II. Al-
liance for Black Unity.
CU-B

F89
Forman, James, 1928-
Liberation will come from a
black thing. [Chicago, Students
for a Democratic Society, 1968?]
15p. illus. 23cm.
Cover title.
Speech presented at the Western
Regional Black Youth Conference,
Los Angeles, Nov. 23, 1967.
1. Negroes--Civil rights.
I. Students for a Democratic
Society.
KU-RH, WHi-A, WHi-L, NcRS

F90
Forman, James, 1928-
United States: high tide of
black resistance. [Chicago,
Students for a Democratic
Society, 1969]
23p. illus.
Cover title.
1. Student movements.
2. Negroes--Civil rights.
I. Students for a Democratic
Society.
PPiU, NUC 70-83289

F91
Forman, James, 1928-
United States 1967: high tide
of black resistance. [Chicago,
Students for a Democratic Soc-
iety, 1969?]
folder (8p.) illus. 25cm.
Cover title.
1. Negroes--Civil rights.
I. Students for a Democratic
Society.
KU-RH

F92
Forman, Pat.

Advance under attack [by Pat Forman and others. n.p., Students
for a Democratic Society, 1969?]
3p. 28cm.
Cover title.
1. Law enforcement. 2. Student
movements. I. Students for a
Democratic Society.
KU-RH

F93
Fort Hood Three Defense Committee.
  The Fort Hood three: the case of
  the three G.I.'s who said "no"
  to the war in Vietnam. [New
  York, 1966]
  31p. illus. 22cm.
  Cover title.
  1. Vietnamese conflict, 1961-
  1975.
  WHi-L, MoU

F94
Foster, William Zebulon, 1881-
    1961.
  The historical advance of world
  socialism. New York, International Publishers [1960]
  48p. 21cm.
  1. Socialism. I. International
  Publishers.
  KU-J, KU-RH, F487

F95
Foster, William Zebulon, 1881-
    1961.
  Marxism-Leninism vs. revision-
  ism, by William Z. Foster [and
  others] Foreward by Max Weiss.
  New York, New Century Publish-
  ers [1956]
  111p.
  1. Communism. 2. Communist
  Party of the United States of
  America. 3. Socialism.
  I. New Century Publishers.
  KU-J

F96
Foster, William Zebulon, 1881-
    1961.
  Speech delivered...to 16th
  national convention of the
  Communist Party, February 9,
  1957. [n.p., 1957]
  5 leaves. 36cm.

Caption title.
1. Communist Party of the United
States of America.
KU-J

F97
Foster, William Zebulon, 1881-
    1961.
  The party crisis and the way
  out. [n.p., 1957?]
  17 leaves. 36cm.
  Caption title.
  1. Communist Party of the United
  States of America.
  KU-J

F98
Fourth International. Founding
    Conference, 1938.
  The death agony of capitalism
  and the task of the Fourth International; the transitional
  program adopted by the founding
  conference of the Fourth International; with statutes of the
  Fourth International. New York,
  Pioneer Publishers [c1964]
  64p. 18cm. (Pioneer pocket
  library no. 1)
  First printing May 1946.
  1. Socialism. 2. Communism--
  Russia. I. Pioneer Publishers.
  KU-RH

F99
Fourth International. United
    Secretariat.
  Khrushchev's downfall: a state-
  ment by the United Secretariat
  of the Fourth International.
  New deepening of the Sino-
  Soviet rift? by Joseph Hansen.
  New York, Pioneer Publishers
  [196]
  15p. 21cm.
  Cover title.
  1. Russia--Pol. & govt.
  2. Khrushchev, Nikita Sergee-
  vich, 1894-   3. Russia--
  For. rel.--China (People's
  Republic of China, 1949-   )
  4. China (People's Republic of
  China, 1949-   )--For. rel.--
  Russia. I. Pioneer Publishers.
  II. Hansen, Joseph.
  KU-RH, MoU

F100
Fourth International. <u>World
    Congress, April 1969</u>.
    The worldwide youth radicaliza-
    tion and the tasks of the Fourth
    International. [New York, Young
    Socialist Alliance, 1969]
    29p. 22cm. (A Young Socialist
    pamphlet)
    1. Youth--Political activity.
    2. Radicalism. I. Young Social-
    ist Alliance.
    CU-B, KU-RH

F101
The Fourth International and
    'Spartacist'. [New York,
    Bulletin of International
    Socialism, 1966]
    38p.
    Cover title.
    1. Socialism. 2. Fourth Inter-
    national. 3. Spartacist.
    I. Bulletin of International
    Socialism.
    WHi-L

F102
Fox, Stephen.
    The anti-war convention, Nov.
    25-28 and the YSA-SWP perspec-
    tive. [Los Angeles? 1965]
    5 leaves. 36cm.
    Caption title.
    1. Young Socialist Alliance.
    2. Socialist Workers Party.
    3. Vietnamese conflict, 1961-
    1975. 4. National Coordinating
    Committee to End the War in
    Vietnam.
    KU-RH

F103
Frank, Andre Gunder.
    The development of underdevel-
    opment. Boston, New England
    Free Press [196]
    17-31p. 22cm.
    Cover title.
    Reprinted from Monthly Review,
    Sept. 1966.
    1. Underdeveloped areas.
    2. Latin America--Econ. condit.
    I. New England Free Press.
    KU-RH, MoU

F104
Frank, Andre Gunder.
    Exploitation or aid? U.S.--
    Brazil economic relations: a
    case study of U.S. imperialism.
    Ann Arbor, Radical Education
    Project [196]
    318-[323]p. 28cm.
    Reprinted from The Nation,
    Nov. 16, 1963.
    1. Economic assistance, Ameri-
    can--Brazil. 2. Brazil--Rela-
    tions (general) with the U.S.
    3. Imperialism. I. Radical
    Education Project.
    MoU

F105
Frank, Andre Gunder.
    Exploitation or aid? U.S.--
    Brazil economic relations: a
    case study of U.S. imperialism.
    Boston, New England Free Press
    [196]
    318-[323]p. illus. 28cm.
    Cover title.
    Reprinted from The Nation,
    Nov. 16, 1963
    1. Economic assistance, Ameri-
    can--Brazil. 2. Brazil--Rela-
    tions (general) with the U.S.
    3. Imperialism. I. New England
    Free Press.
    KU-RH

F106
Frank, Andre Gunder.
    Exploitation or aid? U.S.--Bra-
    zil economic relations. New
    York, Students for a Democratic
    Society and its Peace Research
    and Education Project and its
    Economic Research and Action
    Project [1963?]
    13p. 28cm.
    Cover title.
    1. Economic assistance, Ameri-
    can--Brazil. 2. Brazil--Rela-
    tions (general) with the U.S.
    3. Imperialism. I. Students for
    a Democratic Society. Peace Re-
    search and Education Project.
    WHi-A, WHi-L, NNU-T

F107
Frank, Andre Gunder.
  Hugo Blanco must not die. An
  address to a meeting in solidarity with the imperilled Peruvian
  leader and the freedom struggle
  in Latin America, with introductory comments by Kenneth
  Golby. [Toronto, Robert Mc-
  Carthy, 196]
  16p. 22cm.
  Cover title.
  1. Peru--Pol. & govt. 2. Latin
  America--Pol. & govt. 3. Blanco, Hugo.
  MoU, MiU

F108
Frank, Andre Gunder.
  Hunger. [Ann Arbor, Radical
  Education Project, 196]
  6p. 28cm.
  Cover title.
  1. Food supply--Latin America.
  I. Radical Education Group.
  KU-RH, MoU

F109
Frank, Andre Gunder.
  Latin America: a decrepit capitalist castle with a feudal--
  seeming facade. Ann Arbor,
  Radical Education Project [196]
  468-[478]p. 22cm.
  Cover title.
  Reprinted from Monthly Review,
  Dec. 1963.
  1. Latin America--Econ. condit.
  2. Latin America--Pol. & govt.
  3. Capitalism. I. Radical Education Project.
  MiU

F110
Frank, Andre Gunder.
  Latin America: decrepit capitalist castle with a feudal--
  seeming facade. [Toronto, Distributed by the Latin American
  Working Group, 196]
  7p. 28cm.
  Reprinted from Monthly Review,
  Dec. 1963.
  1. Latin America--Econ. condit.
  2. Latin America--Pol. & govt.
  3. Capitalism. I. Latin

American Working Group.
KU-RH

F111
Frank, Andre Gunder.
  On the mechanisms of imperialism: the case of Brazil. Detroit, Radical Education Project
  [1970?]
  284-297p. 22cm.
  Cover title.
  Reprinted from Monthly Review,
  Sept. 1964.
  1. Imperialism. 2. U.S.--
  Relations (general) with Brazil.
  3. Brazil--Relations (general)
  with the U.S. I. Radical Education Project.
  KU-RH, MoU

F112
Frank, Andrew Gunder
  Rowtow's stages of economic
  growth through escalation to
  nuclear destruction. Ann Arbor,
  Radical Education Project [196]
  8p. 28cm.
  1. Rostow, Walt Whitman, 1916-
      The stages of economic
  growth; a non-communist manifesto. 2. War--Economic aspects
  I. Radical Education Project.
  KU-RH, MoU

F113
Frank, Andre Gunder.
  The varieties of land reform.
  [Toronto, Latin American Work-
  ing Group, 196]
  4p. 28cm.
  Caption title.
  1. Land reform--Latin America.
  I. Latin American Working
  Group.
  KU-RH

F114
Frank, Jerome David, 1909-
  The nuclear arms race--sanity
  and survival; address...to a
  public meeting sponsored by
  Psi Chi, the national psycholo-
  gical fraternity at George Wash-
  ington University, Washington,
  D.C. Des Moines, World Peace
  Broadcasting Foundation [1961?]

13p.
1. Atomic weapons. 2. U.S.--
Military policy. I. World Peace
Broadcasting Foundation.
DS

F115
Frank, Jerome David, 1909-
Sanity and survival: the non
violent alternative. [Berkeley,
Calif.] Acts for Peace [1960?]
16p. 21cm. (Fresh thoughts on
war series, no. 2)
Cover title.
1. Peace. 2. Disarmament.
3. Nonviolence. 4. U.S.--For.
rel.--Russia. I. Acts for
Peace.
CSt, WHi-A

F116
Frank, Mark.
Fallup; mankind's new atomic
danger. [Toronto, Progress
Books, 1962]
50p.
Cover title.
1. Radioactive waste disposal.
2. Atomic power. I. Progress
Books.
CaOTU, NUC 64-28711

F117
Frank, Mark.
Poison for the young: a major
reason for rising juvenile
delinquency. [Toronto, Progress
Books, 1962]
48p. illus. 20cm.
1. Juvenile delinquency--Canada.
2. Obscenity (Law)--Canada.
I. Progress Books.
IEN, CaOTU, NUC 64-68245

F118
Frank, Pierre.
Key problems of the transition
from capitalism to socialism;
3 articles by Pierre Frank,
George Novack [and] Ernest
Mandel. [New York, Merit
Publishers, 1969]
63p. 22cm.
Cover title.
1. Socialism. 2. Capitalism.
3. Marxian economics.

I. Novack, George Edward, jt.
auth. II. Mandel, Ernest, jt.
auth. III. Merit Publishers.
KU-RH, DLC 70-247955

F119
Frank, Pierre.
The worker-student uprising of
1968: first phase of the French
socialist revolution. [New
York, Merit Publishers, 1968]
48p. 22cm.
Reprinted from the International
Socialist Review, Sept.-Oct.
1968.
1. Student movements--France.
2. Paris--Riots, 1968.
I. Merit Publishers.
MiU, CtY, CU-B

F120
Franklin, Bruce.
The lumpenproletariat and the
Revolutionary Youth Movement.
Boston, New England Free Press
[1970?]
7p. 28cm. (Documents on SDS
and the split)
Cover title.
1. Youth--Political activity.
2. Students for a Democratic
Society. Revolutionary Youth
Movement. I. New England Free
Press.
KU-RH

F121
Frantz, Laurent B.
The McCarren Act: an analysis.
[Chicago, Chicago Committee to
Defend the Bill of Rights,
1962?]
12 [1]p.
Cover title.
1. U.S. Laws, statutes, etc.
Internal Security Act of 1950.
I. Chicago Committee to Defend
the Bill of Rights.
MiU

F122
Fraser, Clara.
Discussion draft for Radical
Women Conference, February 23,
1960. Which road towards wo-
men's liberation--the movement

as a radical vanguard or a sin-
gle issue coalition? Seattle,
Radical Women [1970?]
12 leaves. 28cm.
Caption title.
1. Woman--Rights of Women.
I. Radical Women.
WHi-L

F123
Fraser, Clara.
  The emancipation of women.
  Seattle, Seattle Radical Wo-
  men [196]
  6p. 28cm.
  Cover title.
  Reprinted from Revolutionary
  Age, v. 1, no. 3; 1968.
  1. Woman--Rights of women.
  I. Seattle Radical Women.
  WHi-L

F124
Fraser, R.S.
  For the materialist conception
  of the negro question. [New
  York, Spartacist, 1964]
  26 leaves. 28cm. (Marxist
  bulletin, no. 5)
  Cover title.
  1. Negroes. 2. Socialism.
  I. Spartacist.
  WHi-L

F125
Fraser, Steve.
  Economism or socialism?
  Socialist transitional program,
  by Steve Fraser & Tony Papert.
  (Part II) [New York? National
  Caucus of Labor Committees,
  1970]
  38p. 22cm.
  Cover title.
  1. Socialism. I. National
  Caucus of Labor Committees.
  II. Papert, Tony, jt. auth.
  KU-RH

F126
Free Bobby Seale; free the NY 21;
  understand the Black Panther
  Party. [n.p., 1970?]
  12 [1] leaf. 28cm.
  Cover title.
  1. Seale, Bobby.

2. Black Panther Party.
NNU-T, CU-B, MiU

F127
Free Speech Movement.
  FSM--declaration of independence.
  [Berkeley, 1965]
  [1] leaf.
  Caption title.
  1. Student movements--Berkeley,
  Calif.
  CU-B

F128
Free Speech Movement.
  The position of the Free Speech
  Movement in the obscenity case.
  [Berkeley, 1965?]
  [2]p.
  Caption title.
  1. Student movements--Berkeley,
  Calif.
  CU-B

F129
Free Speech Movement.
  Provisional platform of the
  Free Speech Movement. [Berke-
  ley, 1964?]
  [2]p. 28cm.
  1. Student movements--Berkeley,
  Calif.
  CU-B

F130
Free Speech Movement.
  The trial. [Berkeley] 1965.
  [4]p. 28cm.
  Caption title.
  1. Student movements--Berkeley,
  Calif.
  CU-B

F131
Free Speech Movement.
  We want a university. Dedicated
  to the 800. [Berkeley, 1964?]
  10p. 28cm.
  Cover title.
  1. Student movements--Berkeley,
  Calif.
  CU-B

F132
Free Speech Movement.
  We've been confronted. [Berk-

eley] 1965.
[1] leaf.
Caption title.
1. Student movements--Berkeley,
Calif.
CU-B

F133
Free Student Movement.
Why we have decided to begin to
exercise our rights. [Berkeley,
1964]
[2]p. 28cm.
Caption title.
1. Student movements--Berkeley,
Calif.
CU-B

F134
Free the Soledad Brothers.
[Ithaca, N.Y., Glad Day Press,
1970?]
8p. illus. 34cm.
Cover title.
Reprinted from Liberated
Guardian.
1. Negroes. 2. Prisoners.
I. Glad Day Press.
NNU-T

F135
Free University of Ann Arbor.
The Free University of Ann
Arbor. [Ann Arbor, 1966?]
18p.
Cover title.
1. Free schools--Ann Arbor,
Mich.
MiU-H

F136
Freedman, Samuel.
U of M & HUAC; a reply to the
Smith-Cutler report [signed:
Samuel Freedman, Lane Vander-
slice, Peter Steinberger.
Ann Arbor, VOICE Political
Party--SDS, 1966?]
4p.
Caption title.
1. Student movements--Ann
Arbor. 2. U.S. Congress.
House. Committee on Un-Ameri-
can Activities. I. Voice
Political Party--Students for
a Democratic Society, Ann

Arbor. II. Vanderslice, Lane,
jt. auth. III. Steinberger,
Peter, jt. auth.
MiU-H

F137
Freedom Democratic Clubs of
    Illinois.
A platform for freedom. Chicago [1964?]
16p. 28cm.
Cover title.
1. Negroes--Chicago.
2. Chicago--Race question.
WHi-A

F138
Freedom Democratic Clubs of
    Illinois.
Some questions and answers
about Freedom Democratic Clubs
of Illinois. [Chicago, 196]
3 leaves. 28cm.
Caption title.
1. Negroes--Civil rights.
2. Negroes--Illinois.
3. Illinois--Race question.
WHi-A

F139
Freedom Now for Lt. Howe
    Committee.
Do GIs have rights? The case
of Lt. Howe. Denver [196]
folder. 22x9cm.
1. Howe, Henry H. 2. Soldiers.
3. Vietnamese conflict, 1961-
1975.
KU-RH

F140
Freedom Socialist Party.
Introducing the Freedom Socialist Party. Seattle, 1967.
11p. 22cm.
1. Socialism.
CU-B

F141
Freeman, Jo.
Women's liberation front.
[n.p., 1969?]
4p. 28cm.
Caption title.
Reprinted from Moderator,
Nov. 1968.

1. Woman--History and condition
of women.
KU-RH

F142
Freeman, Michael.
  The Brazil coup: two views.
  Michael Freeman: End of the
  Alliance for Progress? Andre
  Gunder Frank: Brazil in per-
  spective. New York, Students
  for a Democratic Society and
  its Peace Research and Economic
  Project [1964?]
  2 [1] 5p. 28cm.
  Cover title.
  Reprinted from Peace News,
  Ap. 10, 1964; The Nation,
  Ap. 27, 1964.
  1. Brazil--Pol. & govt.
  2. Alliance for Progress.
  I. Frank, Andre Gunder, jt.
  auth. I. Students for a Demo-
  cratic Society. Peace Research
  and Economic Project.
  NNU-T, WHi-A, WHi-L

F143
Frey, Sofia.
  The truth about Jews in the
  Soviet Union, with a foreward
  by J.M. Budish. [New York,
  New Century Publishers, 1960]
  15p.
  At head of title: The letter
  Life refused to print.
  1. Jews in Russia. I. Budish,
  J.M. II. New Century Publish-
  ers.
  KU-J

F144
Freidenberg, Edgar Zodiag, 1921-
  Contemptuous hairdressers;
  ceremonies of humiliation in
  school. Ann Arbor, Radical
  Education Project [196]
  9-[18]p. 22cm.
  Cover title.
  1. Education. 2. Students.
  I. Radical Education Project.
  MoU, WHi-L

F145
Friedenberg, Edgar Zodiag, 1921-
  Our contemptuous hairdressers;

ceremonies of humiliation in
school. [Boston, New England
Free Press, 196]
8p. 21cm.
Caption title.
Reprinted from This Magazine
is About Schools.
1. Education. 2. Students.
I. New England Free Press.
KU-RH

F146
Friedman, David.
  Analysis and perspective for
  the national student strike
  [drafted by D. Friedman, based
  on a New School fraction meeting with Kim Moody and Bill
  Gerchaw. [New York? International Socialists, 1970]
  4 leaves. 28cm.
  Caption title.
  1. Student movements. 2. Vietnamese conflict, 1961-1975.
  3. Cambodia. I. Moody, Kimberly. II. Gerchaw, Bill.
  III. International Socialists.
  CU-B

F147
Friedman, David, ed.
  Crisis in the schools: teachers
  and the community. New York,
  Independent Socialist Clubs of
  America [196]
  68p. 28cm.
  1. Education--New York (State)--
  New York (City). 2. American
  Federation of Teachers.
  3. United Federation of Teach-
  ers. 4. New York (City)--
  Public schools. I. Independent
  Socialist Clubs of America.
  KU-RH

F148
Friedman, Linda.
  Community college [by Linda
  Friedman and others. Chicago,
  New University Conference,
  1970?]
  19p. 28cm.
  Caption title.
  1. Education. 2. Student
  movements. 3. Universities
  and colleges. I. New University

Conference.
KU-RH

F149
Friedman, Sam.
  Worrisome thoughts about commit-
ment in community projects. [n.
p., 1965]
  [1] leaf. 28cm. (SDS national
convention--working paper)
  Caption title.
  1. Community organization.
  I. Students for a Democratic
Society.
  KU-RH

F150
Friends, Society of. American
    Friends Service Committee.
  Books for friendship; a list of
books recommended for children.
3d ed. [Philadelphia, c1962]
63p. 23cm.
  First published in 1953 under
title: Books are bridges.
  1. Children's liberature--Bibl.
  TxDaM, DLC 63-2055

F151
Friends, Society of. American
    Friends Service Committee.
  Draft counseling and educational
centers [Philadelphia] CO Services, American Friends Service
Committee [1968]
20p. 22cm.
  Cover title.
  1. Military service, Compulsory.
  2. Conscientious objectors.
  MoU

F152
Friends, Society of. American
    Friends Service Committee.
  Durham survey 1959; report to
employers. [n.p., 1959?]
9 [1] leaf. 28cm.
  1. Durham, N.C.--Surveys.
  NcD, NUC 72-77905

F153
Friends, Society of. American
    Friends Service Committee.
  Equal opportunity in housing.
A report to the President.
AFSC (American Friends Service

Committee) experience and recommendations. re: Executive order
11063. Philadelphia, 1967.
44p.
  1. Negroes--Housing. 2. Discrimination in housing.
  DHUD, NUC 70-63862

F154
Friends, Society of. American
    Friends Service Committee.
  Escalation: a policy of failure.
[Prepared by American Friends
Service Committee and Friends
Committee on National Legisla-
tion. Philadelphia? 196]
36p. 22cm.
  Cover title.
  1. Vietnamese conflict, 1961-
1975. 2. U.S.--Military policy.
  I. Friends Committee on Nation-
al Legislation, Washington, D.C.
  KU-RH, MeB, NUC 70-87999

F155
Friends, Society of. American
    Friends Service Committee.
  Fair housing handbook; a practical manual for those who are
working to create and maintain
inclusive communities. [Phila-
delphia, 1964]
ii, 42p. illus. 23cm.
  1. Discrimination in housing.
  CU, DLC 64-23029

F156
Friends, Society of. American
    Friends Service Committee.
  Final report of the Farm Workers
Opportunity Project. Pasadena,
[1967]
130p. illus.
  1. Mexicans in the U.S.
  2. Migrant labor--California.
  3. Agricultural laborers--
California.
  InU, NUC 69-70415

F157
Friends, Society of. American
    Friends Service Committee.
  For peace in Vietnam. [Phila-
delphia, 196]
folder. 23x10cm.
  Caption title.

1. Vietnamese conflict, 1961-
1975.
KU-RH

F158
Friends, Society of. <u>American</u>
    <u>Friends Service Committee</u>.
Hiring conscientious objectors.
[Philadelphia, 196]
[4]p. 22x10cm.
Caption title.
1. Conscientious objectors.
KU-RH

F159
Friends, Society of. <u>American</u>
    <u>Friends Service Committee</u>.
In the wake of hurricane Cam-
ille; an analysis of the federal response. A report by the
American Friends Service Committee [and] the Southern Regional Council. [Philadelphia]
1969.
34 leaves.
1. Hurricanes. 2. Disaster
relief. I. Southern Regional
Council.
NcU, NUC 70-112558

F160
Friends, Society of. <u>American</u>
    <u>Friends Service Committee</u>.
Indians of California, past and
present. [San Francisco, 1955?]
36p. illus. 22cm.
1. Indians of North America--
California. 2. Indians of North
America--Government relations.
DLC 56-4134

F161
Friends, Society of. <u>American</u>
    <u>Friends Service Committee</u>.
Indians of California; past and
present. [Rev. ed. San Francisco, 1957]
36p. illus. 22cm.
1. Indians of North America--
Government relations.
CSt, DLC, NN

F162
Friends, Society of. <u>American</u>
    <u>Friends Service Committee</u>.
Journey through a wall; a

Quaker mission to a divided
Germany, Sept. 8-30, 1963.
[Philadelphia] American Friends
Service Committee, 1964.
71p. map. 23cm.
1. German reunification ques-
tion (1949-   )
PPULC, CSt, NUC 6513437

F163
Friends, Society of. <u>American</u>
    <u>Friends Service Committee</u>.
Meeting the Russians: American
Quakers visit the Soviet Union.
A report prepared by the dele-
gation, Wroe Alderson [& others]
Philadelphia, 1956.
94p. map. 23cm.
1. Russia--Desc. & trav.--1945-
        2. Russia--Soc. condit.--
1945-   I. Alderson, Wroe.
CSt-H, TxU, InU, CtY, NN, WaU,
ArU, RPB, DLC 57-6671

F164
Friends, Society of. <u>American</u>
    <u>Friends Service Committee</u>.
A new China policy; some Quaker
proposals. New Haven, Yale
University Press, 1965.
ix, 68p. map. 21cm.
A report prepared by members
of the working party on China
policy, American Friends Service
Committee, Sept. 1964-Feb. 1965,
for the committee.
1. U.S.--For. rel.--China, 1949-
) 2. China (People's Re-
public of China, 1949-   )--
For. rel.--U.S.
DS, FU, MH, NcD, WaU, CSt, TNJ,
DLC 65-15048

F165
Friends, Society of. <u>American</u>
    <u>Friends Service Committee</u>.
One American: books on race
relations for children. Graded
and annotated. Cambridge, Mass.,
The Committee [1964]
6p. 29cm.
Cover title.
1. Children's literature--Bibl.
2. Negroes--Civil Rights--
Bibl.
MH-AH, NUC 64-70667

F166
Friends, Society of. American
    Friends Service Committee.
Race relations; a bibliography,
with sections on housing, education, employment. Rev. ed.
Cambridge, Mass., The Committee,
1964.
26p. 28cm.
Cover title.
1. Negroes--Civil rights--Bibl.
MH-AH

F167
Friends, Society of. American
    Friends Service Committee.
Report on the implementation of
Title VI of the Civil Rights
Act of 1964 in regard to school
desegregation. Recommendations
for 1966-67 [by] American
Friends Service Committee [and]
NAACP Legal Defense and Educa-
tional Fund. [n.p.] 1965.
59 leaves. 28cm.
Caption title.
1. Negroes--Civil rights.
2. U.S. Laws, statutes, etc.
Civil Rights Acts of 1964.
I. National Association for the
Advancement of Colored People.
Legal Defense and Educational
Fund.
IaU, NUC 69-102179

F168
Friends, Society of. American
    Friends Service Committee.
A report to the President;
AFSC experience and recommenda-
tions Re: Executive order 11063
on equal opportunity in housing.
Philadelphia, 1967.
ii, 37, xxxi leaves. 28cm.
Cover title.
1. Negroes--Housing. 2. Discri-
mination in housing.
IU, DLC, NUC 69-75712

F169
Friends, Society of. American
    Friends Service Committee.
Search for peace in the Middle
East. A study prepared by a
working party, initiated by the
American Friends Service Com-

mittee and Canadian Friends
Service Committee. Philadelphia
[c1970]
vii, 75p. 23cm.
1. Israel-Arab war, 1967.
2. Near East--Pol. & govt.
I. Friends, Society of. Canadian Friends Service Committee.
KU-RH

F170
Friends, Society of. American
    Friends Service Committee.
Something's happening here to
the draft. [Des Moines, 1968?]
folder. 22x9cm.
Cover title.
1. Military service, Compulsory.
KU-RH

F171
Friends, Society of. American
    Friends Service Committee.
Speak truth to power, a Quaker
search for an alternative to
violence; a study of international conflict. [Philadelphia,
1955]
71p. 23cm.
1. Pacifism. 2. U.S.--For.
rel.--1945-
WU

F172
Friends, Society of. American
    Friends Service Committee.
Speak truth to power, a Quaker
search for an alternative to
violence. A study of international conflict prepared for the
American Friends Service Committee. [Philadelphia, 1961]
71p.
1. Pacifism. 2. U.S.--For. rel.
--1945-

F173
Friends, Society of. American
    Friends Service Committee.
Speak truth to power, a Quaker
search for an alternative to
violence. A study of international conflict prepared for
American Friends Service Committee. [Philadelphia? 1967?]
71p. 25cm.

1. Pacifism.   2. U.S.--For.
rel.--1945-
KU-RH

F174
Friends, Society of.   American
    Friends Service Committee.
The spirit they live in; a report on problems confronting
American Indians, their fellow
citizens and their government.
[n.p., 1956]
[19]p. illus.
1. Indians of North America.
Or, DLC, NN

F175
Friends, Society of.   American
    Friends Service Committee.
An uncommon controversey [sic];
an inquiry into the treaty-pro-
tected fishing rights of the
tribes of the Northwest coast.
[n.p.] National Congress of
American Indians [1967?]
3p., iv, 200 [38]p. illus.
28cm.
1. Indians of North America.
I. National Congress of American
Indians.
MH-L, CLL, NjR, MnU-L

F176
Friends, Society of.   American
    Friends Service Committee.
The U.S. in Vietnam; a critical
look at the basic arguments
supporting America's Vietnam
policy. [San Francisco, 1966]
29p. 23cm.
Cover title.
1. Vietnamese conflict, 1961-
1975.
CLO, NUC 67-92309

F177
Friends, Society of.   American
    Friends Service Committee.
Vietnam 1969; a condensation of
a documented American Friends
Service Committee white paper
on ending the war. [Seattle,
1969?]
[2] leaves. 28cm.
Caption title.
1. Vietnamese conflict, 1961-

1975.
KU-RH

F178
Friends, Society of.   American
    Friends Service Committee.
Vietnam, 1969; an American
Friends Service Committee white
paper on ending the war. [Des
Moines] 1969.
7p. 22cm.
Cover title.
1. Vietnamese conflict, 1961-
1975.
KU-RH

F179
Friends, Society of.   American
    Friends Service Committee.
You too have a stake in ending
war, poverty, injustice.
[Philadelphia, 196]
folder. 21x9cm.
Cover title.
1. Vietnamese conflict, 1961-
1975. 2. Social change.
KU-RH

F180
Friends, Society of.   American
    Friends Service Committee.
    Community Relations Program.
Integration of Washington
schools. [Washington, 195]
unpaged. 23cm.
1. Washington, D.C.--Public
schools. 2. Washington, D.C.--
Race question. 3. Negroes--
Washington, D.C.
DLC 55-20549

F181
Friends, Society of.   American
    Friends Service Committee.
    Community Relations Program.
They say that you say; the challenge of house and race. Philadelphia, 1955.
15p. illus.
Cover title.
1. Negroes--Housing.
WHi-L

F182
Friends, Society of.   American
    Friends Service Committee.

New England Region.
Nonviolence in theory and practice, outline and reading list
for a discussion seminar of 8
weekly two-hour sessions. Cambridge, 1962.
17p. 28cm.
Cover title.
1. Nonviolence.
WHi-A

F183
Friends, Society of. American
    Friends Service Committee.
    New York Metropolitan Region.
Making the draft an issue in
your community; a manual for
local draft counseling groups.
New York [196]
8p. 28cm.
Caption title.
1. Military service, Compulsory.
MoU

F184
Friends, Society of. American
    Friends Service Committee.
    Peace Education Division.
The position of the Society of
Friends with regard to war.
[Philadelphia, 1961]
[12]p. 15cm.
1. War.
PSC-Hi, NUC 69-119628

F185
Friends, Society of. American
    Friends Service Committee.
    Peace Education Program.
The triple revolution discus-
sion packet. New York, 1965.
unpaged.
NNC, NUC 69-10703

F186
Friends, Society of. American
    Friends Service Committee.
    Southeastern Office.
Intimidation, reprisal, and
violence in the South's racial
crisis. Published jointly by
Southeastern Office, American
Friends Service Committee, Dept.
of Racial and Cultural Relat-
ions, National Council of the
Churches of Christ in the

United States of America [and]
Southern Regional Council.
High Point, N.C., 1959.
30p. 28cm.
1. Segregation in education.
2. Southern States--Race question. 3. Negroes--Civil rights.
I. Southern Regional Council.
NNC, NcD, NN, PPFr, LC 59-2811

F187
Friends, Society of. Canadian
    Friends Service Committee.
Brief in response to the Indian
policy statement of the Cana-
dian government of June, 1969.
Toronto [1969]
8p.
1. Indians of North America--
Canada.
CaOTP, NUC 72-47112

F188
Friends, Society of. Canadian
    Friends Service Committee.
Let us try, then, what love can
do...a survey on the Indian
Canadian. [Toronto, 1960?]
23p. 28cm.
Cover title.
1. Indians of North America--
Canada.
CaBVaU

F189
Friends, Society of. Canadian
    Friends Service Committee.
The Quakers in Canada. [Toro-
nto, 196 ?]
8p. 16cm.
Cover title.
KU-RH

F190
Friends and Neighbors of David
    Hyun.
Exile: the story of David Hyun.
[Los Angeles, 1955?]
16p. illus. 22cm.
Cover title.
1. Hyun, David. 2. Exiles.
3. Emigration and immigration
law.
KU-J

F191
Friends Committee on Legislation
    of California.
  Capital punishment, a selected
  bibliography. San Francisco,
  1966.
  7 leaves. 28cm.
  Cover title.
  1. Capital punishment--Bibl.
  TxU, MH-L, NUC 69-121026

F192
Friends Committee on National
    Legislation, Washington, D.C.
  Beliefs into action; a guide
  to political education and
  action. [Rev. Washington,
  1963]
  13p. 21cm.
  Cover title.
  1. U.S.--Pol. & govt.--1961-
  KU-RH

F193
Friends Committee on National
    Legislation, Washington, D.C.
  Controversy over Cuba; staff
  study prepared by Frances E.
  Neely. Washington, 1961.
  26p. 28cm.
  1. Cuba--Relations (general)
  with the U.S. 2. Cuba--Pol.
  & govt.--1959-   I. Neely,
  Frances Elizabeth.
  TxU

F194
Friends Committee on National
    Legislation, Washington, D.C.
  The FCNL story: fifteen years
  of Quaker witness. Washington,
  1958.
  40p. illus. 22cm.
  KU-RH, PSC-Hi

F195
Friends Committee on National
    Legislation, Washington, D.C.
  Questions on disarmament and
  your job. [Washington, 1959?]
  15p. illus.
  Cover title.
  1. Disarmament. 2. U.S.--
  Econ. condit.
  CLU, KU-RH

F195A
Friends Committee on National
    Legislation, Washington, D.C.
  This life we take; the case
  against capital punishment.
  [Washington, 1959]
  23p. illus. 22cm.
  Cover title.
  1. Capital punishment.
  KU-RH, NN, NNC-L

F196
Friends Committee on National
    Legislation, Washington, D.C.
  U.S. government policy toward
  American Indians, a few basic
  facts. [Prepared by Mabel B.
  Ellis for Subcommittee on
  Indian Legislation, Friends
  Committee on Legislation] Rev.
  February 1, 1957. [Pasadena,
  Calif., 1957]
  24p. 23cm.
  1. Indians of North America--
  Government relations.
  MiU

F197
Friends Peace Committee,
    Philadelphia.
  ABC's about Vietnam. [Phila-
  delphia, 1965]
  [4]p. 22cm.
  Cover title.
  1. Vietnamese conflict, 1961-
  1975.
  WHi-A

F198
Friends Peace Committee,
    Philadelphia.
  The draft law and your choices.
  Philadelphia [196]
  folder. illus. 22x10cm.
  Cover title.
  1. Military service, Compulsory.
  KU-RH

F199
Friends Peace Committee,
    Philadelphia.
  A perspective on nonviolence.
  Philadelphia, 1957.
  32p. 20cm.
  1. Government, Resistance to.

2. Negroes--Civil rights.
3. Nonviolence.
KU-RH, MoU, N, NUC 68-61405

F200
Friends Peace Committee,
    Philadelphia.
A perspective on public witness.
[Philadelphia, 1962]
44p. 21cm.
Caption title.
1. Social change.
KU-RH

F201
Friends Peace Committee,
    Philadelphia.
Senator Fulbright on Vietnam:
a review of his book The arrogance of power. [Philadelphia,
196]
4p. 22cm.
Cover title.
1. Fulbright, James William,
1905-   The arrogance of
power.
KU-RH

F202
Friends Peace Committee,
    Philadelphia.
The use of force in international affairs. Philadelphia
[1961]
46p. 17cm.
Cover title.
1. World politics--1955-
KU-RH

F203
Friends Peace Committee,
    Philadelphia.
The use of force in international affairs. Philadelphia
[1961]
46p. 18cm.
1. International police.
2. United Nations.
CSt-H, NUC 64-27251

F204
From refugees to Palestinians;
    the birth of a revolution.
    [Washington, Middle East
    Research and Information
    Project, 1970?]

[4]p. illus. 28cm.
Cover title.
Reprinted from the Liberated
Guardian, Sept. 17, 1970.
1. Jewish-Arab relations.
2. Near East--Pol. & govt.
I. Middle East Research and
Information Project.
KU-RH

F205
Fromm, Erich, 1900-
    Different forms of violence.
    [Nyack, N.Y.? Fellowship Pub-
    lications? 1965?]
    [4]p. 36cm.
    Reprinted from Fellowship,
    March 1965.
    1. Violence. I. Fellowship
    Publications.
    KU-RH

F206
Fromm, Eric, 1900-
    Let man prevail; a socialist
    manifesto and program. New
    York, Call Association [Soc-
    ialist Party, 1962]
    36p. 23cm.
    1. Socialism. I. Call Asso-
    ciation. II. Socialist Party
    (U.S.)
    KU-RH

F207
Fromm, Erich, 1900-
    War within man, a psychological
    enquiry into the roots of des-
    tructiveness; a study and com-
    mentary. [Comments by Jerome
    Frank and others. Philadelphia,
    Peace Literature Service of
    the American Friends Service
    Committee, 1963]
    56p. 22cm. (Beyond deterrence
    series)
    1. War--Psychological aspects.
    2. Aggressiveness (Psychology)
    WaU, CSt-H, ODW, DS, DNLM,
    NcU, MiU, DLC 66-2253

F208
Fromm, Erich, 1900-
    Why is America violent? [n.p.,
    1968?]
    [1] leaf. 36cm.

Caption title.
Reprinted from National Catholic
Reporter, June 12, 1968.
1. Violence. I. National
Catholic Reporter.
KU-RH

F209
Fuchs, Jo Ann.
  Women say no to war and racism.
  Baltimore, Baltimore Women's
  Coalition for Women's Rights,
  1970?]
  2p. 36cm.
  Caption title.
  1. Vietnamese conflict, 1961-
  1975. 2. Woman--Rights of
  women. I. Baltimore Women's
  Coalition for Women's Rights.
  KU-RH

F210
Fuentes, Carlos.
  The argument of Latin America;
  words for North Americans.
  Ann Arbor, Radical Education
  Project [196]
  487-502p. 22cm.
  Cover title.
  Reprinted from Monthly Review,
  Jan. 1963.
  1. Latin America--Econ. condit.
  2. Latin America--Relations
  (general) with the U.S.
  1. Radical Education Project.
  MiU, MoU

F211
Fuentes, Carlos.
  The argument of Latin America:
  words for North Americans.
  Nashville, Southern Student
  Organizing Committee [196]

14p. 28cm.
Cover title.
Reprinted from Monthly Review,
Jan. 1963.
1. Latin America--Econ. condit.
2. Latin America--Relations
(general) with the U.S. I. Southern Student Organizing Committee.
MiU

F212
Fuentes, Carlos.
  The argument of Latin America:
  words for the North Americans.
  Toronto, Fair Play for Cuba
  Committee [1963?]
  13p. 22cm.
  Reprinted from Monthly Review,
  Jan. 1963.
  Cover title: A Latin American
  speaks to North Americans.
  1. Latin America--Econ. condit.
  2. Latin America--Soc. condit.
  I. Fair Play for Cuba Committee.
  CSt-H, NUC 67-89987

F213
Fusfeld, Daniel R.
  Fascist democracy in the
  United States. [Ann Arbor,
  Union for Radical Political
  Economics, 1968?]
  35p. 26cm. (Reprint no. 2)
  Cover title.
  Conference papers of the
  Union for Radical Political
  Economics, Dec. 1968.
  1. Fascism. 2. U.S.--Pol. &
  govt.--1963-   I. Union for
  Radical Political Economics.
  MiU

‡

G

‡

G1
GI Civil Liberties Defense
    Committee.
  Are soldiers citizens? [New
  York, 196]
  folder. illus. 21x9cm.

Caption title.
1. Soldiers. 2. Civil rights.
KU-RH

G2
Gabriner, Bob.

The Wisconsin Draft Resistance
Union; from conscience to class
[by] Bob Gabriner and Barbara
Baran. Boston, New England
Free Press [1969?]
7p. 21cm.
Cover title.
Reprinted from The Movement,
April 1969.
1. Wisconsin Draft Resistance
Union. 2. Student movements--
Wisconsin. 3. Military service,
Compulsory. I. Baran, Barbara,
jt. auth. II. New England Free
Press.
CU-B, KU-RH

G3
Gaither, Thomas.
Jailed-in. [New York, CORE,
1961?]
[16]p. 22cm.
Cover title.
1. Negroes--Civil rights.
2. Law enforcement. I. Congress
of Racial Equality.
CU-B

G4
Gaither, Thomas.
Jailed-in [edited by Jim Peck.
New York, League for Industrial
Democracy, 1961]
[16]p. 22cm.
Cover title.
1. Negroes--Civil rights.
2. Law enforcement. I. Peck,
James. I. League for Industrial
Democracy.
NNU-T, WHi-A

G5
Galambos, Eva.
The tax structure of the southern states: an analysis. Atlanta, Southern Regional Council,
1969.
18p. illus. (Resources development center. Publication no.
1)
1. Taxation--Southern States.
I. Southern Regional Council.
TU, IU, NIC, Wa, DHUD

G6
Galtung, Johan.

Reflections on non-violence.
[Montreal] Our Generation
[196]
26-33 leaves.
Caption title.
At head of title: Conflicts and
realities.
1. Nonviolence. I. Our
Generation.
NNU-T

G7
Gannett, Betty.
End the war in Vietnam. [New
York, New Outlook Publishers,
1965]
23p. maps. 20cm.
1. Vietnamese conflict, 1961-
1975. I. New Outlook Publishers.
WHi-L, NUC 67-98912

G8
Gans, Curtis.
Southern political education
project, by Gans and Haber.
[n.p., 196]
6 leaves. 28cm.
Caption title.
1. Southern States--Pol. &
govt. 2. Negroes--Southern
States. 3. Student movements--
Southern States. I. Haber,
Robert Alan, jt. auth.
WHi-A

G9
Gans, Herbert J.
The failure of urban renewal;
a critique and some proposals.
New York, League for Industrial
Democracy [1965?]
[9]p. 28cm. (Looking forward
no. 2)
Cover title.
Reprinted from Commentary,
April 1965.
1. Urban renewal. I. League for
Industrial Democracy.
KU-RH, NNU-T, WHi-L

G10
Garcia, Jose A.
THE O.A.S.--a creature of United
States interests. [Toronto]
Latin American Working Group,
1969.

6p.   28cm.   (Summer project
1969)
Caption title.
1. Organization of American
States. 2. U.S.--Relations
(general) with Latin America.
1. Latin American Working
Group.
KU-RH

G11
Gardner, Jennifer.
  False consciousness. [Berkeley,
  Calif., Tooth & Nail; New York,
  Redstockings, 196]
  [2]p. 28cm.
  Caption title.
  1. Woman--Rights of women.
  I. Tooth & Nail. II. Redstock-
  ings of the Women's Liberation
  Movement.
  MoU

G12
Gargan, Edward T.
  Radical Catholics of the right.
  [Omaha] Catholic Council on
  Civil Liberties [1962]
  [12]p. 22cm.
  Cover title.
  A paper delivered at the fifth
  National Catholic Social Action
  Conference.
  1. Catholics in the U.S.
  2. Conservatism. 3. John Birch
  Society. I. Catholic Council on
  Civil Liberties.
  MiU, KU-RH

G13
Garrett, Banning.
  The road to Phnom Penh; Cambodia
  takes up the gun. Boston, New
  England Free Press [1970?]
  7p. illus., map. 28cm.
  Caption title.
  Reprinted from Ramparts, Aug.
  1970.
  1. Cambodia--Pol. & govt.
  I. New England Free Press.
  KU-RH

G14
Garrett, Banning.
  The road to Phnom Penh; Cambodia
  takes up the gun. [Ithaca, N.Y.,

Glad Day Press, 1970?]
4p. illus. 28cm.
Cover title.
1. Cambodia--Pol. & govt.
I. Glad Day Press.
NNU-T

G15
Garrett, Banning.
  The Vietnamization of Laos.
  [Ithaca, N.Y., Glad Day Press,
  1970?]
  7p. map. 28cm.
  Caption title.
  Reprinted from Ramparts, June
  1970.
  1. Laos--For. rel.--U.S.
  I. Glad Day Press.
  NNU-T

G16
Garson, Barbara.
  MacBird. [Berkeley, Independent
  Socialist Club, c1966]
  30p.
  Cover title.
  I. Title. II. Independent
  Socialist Club.
  WHi-L

G17
Garson, David C.
  Comments on working with other
  groups. [n.p., 1965]
  2p. 28cm. (SDS 1965 national
  convention--working paper)
  Caption title.
  At head of title: SDS 1965
  national convention--working
  paper.
  1. Reformers. I. Students for
  a Democratic Society, National
  Convention, 1965.
  KU-RH

G18
Garson, David C.
  What is the free university?
  [Princeton, N.Y., Free Univer-
  sity Project, 1965?]
  [2]p. 28cm.
  Caption title.
  1. Free schools. 2. Universit-
  ies and colleges.
  WHi-A

G19
Garson, Marvin.
  The regents. [Berkeley] Inde-
  pendent Socialist Club [1967]
  25p. 21cm.
  Cover title.
  1. Free Speech Movement.
  2. California. University.
  I. Independent Socialist Club.
  CU-B

G20
Garson, Marvin.
  Statement of principles [by]
  Marvin Garson, amended by Mario
  Savio. [Berkeley? 196]
  [1] leaf. 28cm.
  1. Peace and Freedom Movement.
  2. Student movements--Berkeley,
  Calif. I. Savio, Mario.
  CU-B

G21
Gaspary, William.
  American economic imperialism:
  a survey of the literature.
  Ann Arbor, Radical Education
  Project [1967?]
  23p.
  1. Economic assistance, American.
  2. Underdeveloped areas.
  3. Imperialism. I. Radical Education Project.
  NNC, NUC 72-80984

G22
Gates, Albert.
  Democracy and revolution.
  Chicago, Young People's Social-
  ist League [1964]
  4p. 28cm.
  Reprinted from Labor Action,
  1953.
  1. Socialism. I. Young People's
  Socialist League.
  KU-RH, CU-B

G23
Gavi, Phillipe.
  Eruption in India. Boston, New
  England Free Press [196]
  [4]p. 28cm.
  Caption title.
  Reprinted from Ramparts.
  1. India--Pol. & govt.

  I. New England Free Press.
  KU-RH

G24
Gavi, Phillipe.
  Eruption in India. [Ithaca,
  N.Y., Glad Day Press, 1970?]
  [4]p. illus. 28cm.
  Caption title.
  Reprinted from Ramparts, April
  1970.
  1. India--Pol. & govt. I. Glad
  Day Press.
  NNU-T

G25
Gay Women's Liberation.
  Lesbians as bogey women.
  [Berkeley, San Francisco, 196 ?]
  2 leaves. 28cm.
  Caption title.
  1. Homosexuality. 2. Women.
  CU-B

G26
Gehman, Linford K.
  "Looking through a hole into
  hell"; two wars, two letters
  [by Linford K. Gehman and Roger
  D. Marshall. Des Moines,
  American Friends Service Com-
  mittee, 196]
  folder. 22x9cm.
  Cover title.
  1. Vietnamese conflict, 1961-
  1975. 2. Nigeria. I. Marshall,
  Roger D., jt. auth. II. Friends,
  Society of. American Friends
  Service Committee.
  KU-RH

G27
Genovese, Eugene D., 1930-
  The legacy of slavery and the
  roots of black nationalism.
  Boston, New England Free Press,
  1966.
  26p. 22cm.
  Caption title.
  Reprinted from Studies on the
  Left.
  1. Slavery in the U.S.
  2. Negroes--Civil rights.
  I. New England Free Press.
  KU-RH, WU

G28
Genovese, Eugene D., 1930-
  The legacy of slavery and the
  roots of black nationalism.
  Nashville, Southern Student Or-
  ganizing Committee [196]
  18p. 28cm.
  Cover title.
  1. Slavery in the U.S.
  2. Negroes--Civil rights.
  I. Southern Student Organizing
  Committee.
  MoU

G29
Genovese, Eugene D., 1930-
  War on two fronts. [Winnipeg,
  Canadian Dimension, 196]
  5p. 28cm.
  Caption title.
  1. U.S.--Pol. & govt.--1963-
       I. Canadian Dimension.
  MoU

G30
Genet, Jean, 1910-
  Here and now for Bobby Seale.
  [New York, Committee to Defend
  the Panthers, 196]
  [2]p. 28cm.
  Caption title.
  Translated by Judy Oringer.
  1. Seale, Bobby. 2. Black
  Panther Party. I. Committee
  to Defend the Panthers.
  KU-RH, NNU-T, CU-B

G31
Genet, Jean, 1910-
  Here and now for Bobby Seale.
  [San Francisco, Ministry of
  Information, Black Panther
  Party, 196]
  1. Seale, Bobby. 2. Black
  Panther Party. I. Black Panther
  Party.
  NNU-T

G32
Genet, Jean, 1910-
  May Day speech, description by
  Allen Ginsberg. [San Francisco]
  City Lights [c1970]
  25p.
  Speech delivered in 1970 at
  Yale University.

1. Race awareness. I. City
Lights.
MiU

G33
Gerassi, John.
  Latin America--the next Vietnam?
  [Toronto? Latin American Working
  Group? 196]
  6p. 28cm.
  Caption title.
  Reprinted from Viet-Report,
  v. 3, no. 1; 1967.
  1. Latin America--Pol. & govt.
  2. U.S.--Military policy.
  I. Latin American Working Group.
  KU-RH

G34
Gerassi, Marysa N.
  The Tupamaros; Uruguay's urban
  guerrillas. [Toronto? Latin
  American Working Group, 196]
  306-310p. illus. 28cm.
  Caption title.
  Reprinted from The Nation,
  Sept. 29, 1969.
  1. Guerrillas--Uruguay.
  2. Uruguay--Pol. & govt.
  I. Latin American Working Group.
  KU-RH

G35
Gerassi, Marysa N.
  Uruguay's urban guerrillas.
  [Boston, New England Free Press,
  1970?]
  7 [1]p. 22cm.
  Caption title.
  Reprinted from New Left Review,
  July-Aug. 1970.
  1. Guerrillas--Uruguay.
  2. Uruguay--Pol. & govt.
  I. New England Free Press.
  MiU

G36
Gershman, Carl.
  Protest persecution of Soviet
  Jewry. [New York, Young People's
  Socialist League, 197]
  [2]p. 28cm.
  Caption title.
  1. Jews in Russia. I. Young
  People's Socialist League.
  KU-RH

G37
Geyer, Alan.
  The just war and the selective
  objector. [n.p., 1966]
  199-210p. 28cm.
  Caption title.
  Reprinted from The Christian
  Century, Feb. 16, 1966.
  1. Conscientious objectors.
  2. War.
  KU-RH

G38
Geyer, Georgie Anne.
  The illusion dies. [Woodmont,
  Promoting Enduring Peace, 1969]
  [4]p. 28cm.
  Caption title.
  At head of title: Letter from
  Saigon.
  Reprinted from The Progressive,
  Feb. 1969.
  1. Vietnamese conflict, 1961-
  1975. I. Promoting Enduring
  Peace.
  KU-RH

G39
Gilbarg, Dan.
  Vietnam: U.S. imperialism and
  us. Strike. [Boston, New
  England Free Press, 1970?]
  40 [2]p. 21cm.
  1. Vietnamese conflict, 1961-
  1975. 2. Student movements--
  Harvard University. 3. U.S.--
  Foreign policy. 4. Imperialism.
  I. New England Free Press.
  KU-RH

G40
Gilbert, David.
  Consumption: domestic imperialism. A new left introduction to
  the political economy of American capitalism. [Ann Arbor,
  Radical Education Project,
  1969?]
  15p. 22cm.
  1. Capitalism. 2. Consumption
  (Economics) I. Radical Education Project.
  MoU, KU-RH

G41
Gilbert, David.

U.S. imperialism, by David
Gilbert and David Loud. [Chi-
cago, Students for a Democratic
Society, 1968]
25p. 22cm.
Cover title.
1. Imperialism. 2. U.S.--For-
eign policy. I. Loud, David,
jt. auth. II. Students for a
Democratic Society.
CU-B, WHi-A

G42
Gilly, Adolfo.
  Inside the Cuban revolution.
  Translated from the Spanish by
  Felix Gutierrez. New York,
  Monthly Review Press, 1964.
  vii, 88p. 22cm.
  Reprinted from Monthly Review,
  Oct. 1964.
  1. Cuba--History--1959-
  2. Cuba--Soc. condit. I. Mon-
  thly Review Press.
  DLC

G43
Ginger, Ann Fagan.
  The movement and the lawyer.
  Ann Arbor, Conference on Radicals in the Professions, 1967.
  4p. 28cm.
  1. Student movements. 2. Lawyers. I. Conference on Radicals in the Professions.
  MiU-H

G44
Ginger, Ann Fagan.
  Suffragettes and the selective
  service system (a lawyer mother
  of teenage sons views the draft)
  [Washington, Women's International League for Peace and
  Freedom, 1968]
  5p. 28cm.
  1. Military service, Compulsory.
  I. Women's International League
  for Peace and Freedom.
  CU-B

G45
Gintis, Herbett Malena.
  Neo-classical warfare economics
  and individual development.
  Cambridge, Mass., Union for

Radical Political Economics
[1970]
60p. 27cm. (Union for Radical
Political Economics. Occasional
papers, no. 3)
1. Welfare economics. 2. Individualism. I. Union for Radical
Political Economics.
CtU

G46
Gintis, Herbert Malena.
  Poverty economics. [Boston,
New England Free Press, 196]
34p. 22cm.
Cover title.
1. Poverty. 2. Capitalism.
3. Negroes--Civil rights.
I. New England Free Press.
MoU

G47
Gish, Tom.
  This is the war that is. The
failures of the poverty pro-
gram in eastern Kentucky.
Chicago, Students for a Demo-
cratic Society. [1965?]
5p. 28cm.
Cover title.
1. Public welfare. 2. U.S.
Office of Economic Opportunit-
ies. 3. Poor--Kentucky.
I. Students for a Democratic
Society.
CU-B

G48
Gish, Tom.
  This is the war that is; the
failures of the poverty program
in eastern Kentucky. New York,
Political Education Project
associated with Students for a
Democratic Society [1964]
6p.
Cover title.
1. Public welfare. 2. U.S.
Office of Economic Opportunit-
ies. 3. Poor--Kentucky.
4. Kentucky--Econ. condit.
I. Students for a Democratic
Society. Political Education
Project.
WHi-L, NNU-T

G49
Gitlin, Todd.
  Americans fight United States'
role in South Africa. Ann
Arbor, Students for a Democratic Society [196]
[3] leaves. 28cm.
Caption title.
1. U.S.--Relations (general)
with South Africa. 2. South
Africa--Relations (general) with
the U.S. 3. Chase Manhattan
Bank, New York. I. Students
for a Democratic Society.
KU-RH, WHi-A

G50
Gitlin, Todd.
  The battlefields and the war.
[n.p., 196]
8p. 28cm.
Cover title.
1. Student movements.
2. Organization.
MiU

G51
Gitlin, Todd.
  Bibliography of war/peace books.
New York, Students for a Demo-
cratic Society [196]
6p. 28cm.
Cover title.
1. War--Bibl. 2. Peace--Bibl.
I. Students for a Democratic
Society.
KU-RH

G52
Gitlin, Todd.
  Bibliography of war/peace books.
New York, Students for a Demo-
cratic Society and its Peace
Research and Education Project
[196]
8p.
Cover title.
1. Peace--Bibl. I. Students for
a Democratic Society. Peace
Research and Education Project.
WHi-L

G53
Gitlin, Todd.
  The CIA at college: into twi-

light and back, by Todd Gitlin
and Bob Ross.   [Chicago, Students for a Democratic Society,
196]
10p.
Cover title.
1. United States National Student Association. 2. U.S.
Central Intelligence Agency.
3. Universities and colleges.
I. Ross, Bob, jt. auth.
II. Students for a Democratic
Society.
WHi-A

G54
Gitlin, Todd.
  The CIA at college: into twi-
light and back, by Todd Gitlin
and Bob Ross. [New York: Lib-
eration Press; distributed by
Students for a Democratic Soci-
ety, 196]
10p. 21cm.
Cover title.
1. U.S. Central Intelligence
Agency. 2. United States Na-
tional Student Association.
3. Universities and colleges.
I. Ross, Bob, jt. auth.
II. Students for a Democratic
Society. Liberation Press.
KU-RH

G55
Gitlin, Todd.
  The case against the draft.
New York, Distributed by Stu-
dents for a Democratic Society
and College Young Christian
Students for the Liberal Study
Group [196]
12p. 28cm.
Cover title.
1. Military service, Compulsory.
I. Students for a Democratic
Society. II. College Young
Christian Students. III. Lib-
eral Study Group.
WHi-A

G56
Gitlin, Todd.
  The case against the draft.
New York, Students for a Demo-
cratic Society [1964?]

12p.
Cover title.
1. Military service, Compulsory.
I. Students for a Democratic
Society.
WHi-L, NNU-T, NUC 69-62825

G57
Gitlin, Todd.
  Cuba and the American movement.
[Ithaca, Glad Day Press, 1968?]
[12]p. 28cm.
Caption title.
Content--Cuba: the revolution-
ary society, by Dave Dellinger.
Reprinted from Liberation.
1. Cuba--Relations (general)
with the U.S. I. Dellinger,
Dave. II. Glad Day Press.
CU-B

G58
Gitlin, Todd.
  Deterrence and reality: where
nuclear strategy comes from.
New York, Students for a Democratic Society and its Peace
Research and Education Project
[1964?]
7p. 28cm.
Cover title.
1. U.S.--Military policy.
2. World politics--1955-
3. Atomic warfare. I. Students
for a Democratic Society. Peace
Research and Education Project.
WHi-L, MiU, NNU-T

G59
Gitlin, Todd.
  Local pluralism as theory and
ideology. [n.p., 1967]
22 leaves. 29cm.
Caption title.
1. Pluralism. 2. Local
government.
CSaT, NUC 68-92786

G60
Gitlin, Todd.
  Notes for national convention
foreign policy workshop [by Todd
Gitlin and Carl Oglesby. n.p.,
Students for a Democratic Soci-
ety, 196]
4p. 28cm.

Caption title.
1. U.S.--Foreign policy.
I. Oglesby, Carl, jt. auth.
II. Students for a Democratic
Society.
KU-RH

G61
Gitlin, Todd.
  Notes on arguing about Vietnam.
  [n.p., Students for a Democratic
  Society? 196]
  2p. 28cm.
  Cover title.
  1. Vietnamese conflict, 1961-
  1975. I. Students for a Democratic Society.
  KU-RH

G62
Gitlin, Todd.
  On organizing the poor in Ameri-
  ca. [n.p., 196]
  6p. 28cm.
  Caption title.
  1. Poor. 2. Organization.
  CU-B

G63
Gitlin, Todd.
  On organizing the poor in Ameri-
  ca. [Montreal, Our Generation,
  196]
  22-29 leaves.
  Caption title.
  1. Poor. 2. Organization.
  I. Our Generation.
  NNU-T

G64
Gitlin, Todd.
  The politics and vision of the
  new left. San Francisco, Clergy and Laymen [and] Radical Education Project [196]
  10 leaves. 28cm.
  Cover title.
  1. Student movements. 2. Politics, Practical. I. Radical
  Education Project.
  CU-B

G65
Gitlin, Todd.
  Student political action, 1960-
  1963: the view of a participant.

New York, Students for a Democratic Society [1963?]
17p. 28cm.
Cover title.
1. Student movements. I. Students for a Democratic Society.
WHi-L, KU-RH

G66
Gitlin, Todd.
  Vietnam; a selected bibliography. New York, Students for a
  Democratic Society and its Peace
  and Education Project [196]
  5p. 22cm.
  Cover title.
  1. Vietnamese conflict, 1961-
  1975--Bibl. I. Students for a
  Democratic Society. Peace Research and Education Project.
  KU-RH, WHi-A

G67
Gittings, John.
  China and the cold war. Boston,
  New England Free Press [196]
  [196]-208p. 21cm.
  Cover title.
  Reprinted from Survey, Jan.
  1966.
  1. China (People's Republic of
  China, 1949-   )--Foreign
  policy. 2. World politics--
  1955-   I. New England Free
  Press.
  KU-RH, MoU

G68
Gittings, John.
  China and the cold war. Toron-
  to, Research, Information and
  Publications Project, Student
  Union for Peace Action [1966?]
  [196]-208p. 22cm.
  Cover title.
  1. China (People's Republic of
  China, 1949-   )--Foreign pol-
  icy. 2. World politics--1955-
      I. Student Union for
  Peace Action.
  WHi-A

G69
Glaberman, Martin.
  "Be his payment high or low":
  the American working class in

the sixties. [Detroit] Facing
Reality Publishing Committee
[1966]
21p. 22cm.
Reprinted from International
Socialism, Summer 1965 and
Studies on the Left, Summer 1964.
1. Socialism. 2. Labor and la-
boring classes. 3. Trade-unions.
4. Automobile industry workers.
I. Facing Reality Publishing
Committee.
MiU

G70
Glaberman, Martin.
Theory and practice, introduc-
tion by C.L.R. James. Detroit
[Facing Reality Publishing Com-
mittee, 1969]
18p. 21cm.
1. Socialism. 2. Negroes--
Civil rights. 3. Revolutions.
I. James, Cyril Lionel Robert,
1901-   II. Facing Reality
Publishing Committee.
MiU, WHi-L

G71
Glasser, Ira.
Judgement at Fort Jackson: the
trial of Captain Howard Levy.
Nashville, Southern Student
Organizing Committee [196]
7 [1]p. 28cm.
Reprinted from Christianity and
Crisis, Aug. 7, 1967.
1. Levy, Howard. 2. Soldiers.
3. Vietnamese conflict, 1961-
1975. I. Southern Student Or-
ganizing Committee.
MiU

G72
Glasser, Ira.
Judgement at Fort Jackson: the
trial of Howard Levy, M.D.
Nashville, Southern Student Organizing Committee [196]
7p. 28cm.
Cover title.
Reprinted from Christianity
and Crisis, Aug. 7, 1967.
1. Levy, Howard. 2. Vietnamese
conflict, 1961-1975. 3. Soldiers. I. Southern Student

Organizing Committee.
CU-B

G73
Glick, Mike.
SDS 1969--where now: excerpts
from a position paper signed by
Mike Glick [and others. n.p.]
SDS Wisconsin State Conference
by Milwaukee Organizing Commit-
tee, 1969.
5 leaves. 28cm.
Cover title.
1. Students for a Democratic
Society.
WHi-L

G74
Glick, Mike.
SDS position paper [signed:
Mike Glick and others. n.p.,
1969?]
8p. 36cm.
Caption title.
1. Students for a Democratic
Society.
WHi-L

G75
Glotta, Ronald.
The radical lawyer and the dynamics of a rent strike. Ann
Arbor, Conference on Radicals in
the Professions, 1967.
4 [1]p. 28cm.
Cover title.
1. Landlord and tenant.
2. Rent. 3. Lawyers. I. Conference on Radicals in the Professions.
MiU-H

G76
Glusman, Paul.
One, two, three...many SDS's
(a symposium) [by] Paul Glusman,
David Horowitz [and] Todd Gitlin. [Cicero, Ill., Johnny
Appleseed Patriotic Publications, c1969]
[8]p. 28cm.
Cover title.
1. Students for a Democratic
Society. I. Horowitz, David,
jt. auth. II. Gitlin, Todd,
jt. auth. III. Johnny Appleseed

Patriotic Publications.
MoU

G77
Goff, Fred.
  The violence of domination: U.S.
  power and the Dominican Republic
  [by] Fred Goff and Michael Lock-
  er. [New York, North American
  Congress on Latin America] 1967.
  23p. 28cm.
  Cover title.
  1. Dominican Republic--Relations
  (general) with the U.S. I. Lock-
  er, Michael, jt. auth.
  II. North American Congress on
  Latin America.
  WHi-L

G78
Goldfield, Mike.
  Marxism: an introduction. [Ann
  Arbor, Radical Education Pro-
  ject, 196]
  10p. 28cm. (Study guide series)
  1. Socialism--Bibl. 2. Marx,
  Karl, 1818-1883. 3. Marxian
  economics--Bibl. I. Radical
  Education Project.
  CU-B

G79
Goldman, Emma, 1869-1940.
  Emma Goldman rebel. [Mountain
  View, Calif., Srafprint Co-op,
  1970?]
  35p. illus. 22cm.
  1. Communism--Russia.
  2. Russia--Pol. & govt.
  3. Most, Johann. I. Srafprint
  Co-op.
  MiU

G80
Goldman, Emma, 1869-1940.
  The traffic in women and other
  essays on feminism. [New York,
  Times Change Press, c1970]
  63p.
  1. Woman--Rights of women.
  I. Times Change Press.
  WHi-L

G81
Gompertz, Steve.
  The draft and you; your lights

and your alternatives. [Berke-
ley, Berkeley SDS Anti-Draft
Union? 196]
folder. 21x9cm.
Cover title.
1. Military service, Compulsory.
I. Students for a Democratic
Society, Berkeley, Calif.
Anti-Draft Union.
CU-B

G82
Gonick, Cyril Wolfe.
  Self-government in the multiversity. Winnipeg, Canadian Dimension [196]
  [2]p. 28cm.
  Caption title.
  1. Universities and colleges.
  2. Student movements. I. Canadian Dimension.
  MoU

G83
Gonick, Cyril Wolfe.
  What every Canadian can learn
  from Vietnam. [Winnipeg,
  Canadian Dimension, 1968]
  48p. illus.
  Cover title.
  1. Vietnamese conflict, 1961-
  1975. 2. Canada--Foreign policy. I. Canadian Dimension.
  CaOtc, CaBVaU, ClU, NUC 69-51414

G84
Gonze, Collin.
  South African crisis and United
  States policy [by] Collin Gonze,
  George M. Houser [and] Perry M.
  Sturges. New York, American
  Committee on Africa [c1962]
  63p. 21cm. (Africa today
  pamphlet, 5)
  1. Africa, South--Race question.
  2. U.S.--Relations (general)
  with Africa, South. 3. Africa,
  South--Relations (general) with
  the U.S. I. American Committee
  on Africa.
  KU-RH, MiU

G85
Goodman, Paul, 1911-1972.
  The black flag of anarchism.
  [Corinth, Vt., Black Mountain

Press, 1968?]
9 [1]p. 22cm.
Reprinted from New York Review
of Books, Nov. 21, 1968.
1. Anarchism and anarchists.
2. Students for a Democratic
Society. I. Black Mountain
Press.
KU-RH

G86
Goodman, Paul, 1911-1972.
  A causeries at the military-
  industrial. Palo Alto, Calif.,
  Institute for the Study of Nonviolence [196]
  [8]p. illus. 28cm.
  Reprinted from New York Review
  of Books, Nov. 23, 1967.
  1. U.S.--Military policy.
  2. Corporations. 3. Disarmament. I. Institute for the
  Study of Nonviolence.
  KU-RH

G87
Goodman, Paul, 1911-1972.
  Thoughts on Berkeley. [New
  York, Distributed by Students
  for a Democratic Society, 196]
  [4]p.
  Caption title.
  1. Student movements. I. Stu-
  dents for a Democratic Society.
  Whi-A

G88
Goodman, Percival.
  The decay of American cities;
  an alternative habitation for
  man; a plan for planning. Nashville, Southern Student Organizing Committee [196]
  9p. 28cm.
  1. Cities and towns--Planning.
  I. Southern Student Organizing
  Committee.
  MiU, WHi-L

G89
Goodman, Richard.
  The law & monopoly: the case of
  tetracyclene. Ann Arbor, Radical Education Project [196]
  45-49p. 22cm.
  1. Drug trade. I. Radical Education Project.
  MoU

G90
Goodman, Richard.
  The law & monopoly: the case tet-
  racyclene. Boston, New England
  Free Press [196]
  45-49p. 22cm.
  Reprinted from New University
  Thought, v. 3, no. 4; 1963.
  1. Drug trade. I. New England
  Free Press.
  MiU, KU-RH

G91
Gordon, Jerry.
  The right to distribute leaflets
  at high school. [n.p., 196]
  [5]p. 28cm.
  Reprinted from Student Mobiliser.
  Prepared for the Cleveland Area
  Peace Action Council.
  1. Student movements. 2. High
  schools.
  KU-RH

G92
Gordon, Jesse.
  A new look at Cuba: the chal-
  lenge to Kennedy, by Jesse Gor-
  don and Gen. Hugh B. Hester.
  New York, Fair Play for Cuba
  Committee [196]
  11p.
  Reprinted from New World Review,
  April 1961.
  1. Cuba--Pol. & govt.--1959-
          2. U.S.--For. rel.--Cuba.
  I. Hester, Hugh B. II. Fair
  Play for Cuba Committee.

G93
Gordon, Larry.
  Notes on development organization in the ghetto: Chester, Pa.,
  by Larry Gordon and Vernon
  Grizzard. [n.p.] Students for
  a Democratic Society and its
  Economic Research and Action
  Project [196]
  4p. 28cm.
  1. Chester, Pa.--Race question.
  2. Chester, Pa.--Econ. condit.
  3. Negroes--Chester, Pa.
  4. Poor--Chester, Pa. I. Grizzard, Vernon, jt. auth.
  II. Students for a Democratic
  Society. Economic Research
  and Action.

Project.
WHi-A, WHi-L

G94
Gordon, Linda.
  Families. [Cambridge, Mass.,
  Bread and Roses; Boston, New
  England Free Press, c1970]
  24p. illus. 25cm.
  Cover title.
  1. Family. 2. Woman--Rights of
  women. I. Bread and Roses.
  II. New England Free Press.
  KU-RH

G95
Gorgen, Carol Perry.
  Catholic conscientious objectors.
  [San Francisco? 196]
  64p. 22cm.
  1. Conscientious objectors.
  2. Catholics.
  KU-RH

G96
Gorson, Arthur.
  The road to a voice for jobs
  and justice. Ann Arbor, Students for a Democratic Society
  [196]
  3 leaves. 28cm.
  Caption title.
  1. Voice for Jobs and Justice.
  2. Newspapers--Kentucky.
  3. Appalachian Committee for
  Full Employment. 4. Miners--
  Hazard, Ky. I. Students for a
  Democratic Society.
  KU-RH

G97
Gott, Richard.
  Guevara, Debray and the CIA;
  report from Bolivia. Ann Arbor,
  Radical Education Project [196]
  521-530p. illus. 28cm.
  Cover title.
  1. Debray, Regis. 2. Guevara,
  Ernesto, 1920-1967. 3. U.S.
  Central Intelligence Agency.
  4. Guerrillas--Bolivia.
  I. Radical Education Project.
  MoU

G98
Gott, Richard.

Guevara, Debray and the CIA;
  report from Bolivia. Detroit,
  Radical Education Project [1970?]
  521-530p. illus. 28cm.
  Cover title.
  Reprinted from The Nation,
  Nov. 20, 1967.
  1. Debray, Regis. 2. Guevara,
  Ernesto, 1920-1967. 3. U.S.
  Central Intelligence Agency.
  4. Guerrillas--Bolivia.
  I. Radical Education Project.
  KU-RH

G99
Gottfried, Sue.
  What do you mean nonviolence?
  The story of wars with peaceful
  weapons. Illustrated by Elsa
  Bailey. Nyack, N.Y., Fellow-
  ship Publications [196]
  31p. 23cm.
  Cover title.
  1. Government, Resistance to.
  2. Nonviolence. I. Fellowship
  Publications.
  MoU

G100
Gottlieb, Bob.
  Consumption: domestic imperial-
  ism. A new left introduction
  to the political economy of Am-
  erican capitalism [by Bob Got-
  tlieb and Susan Sutheim. Bos-
  ton, New England Free Press,
  196]
  16p. 21cm. (MDS pamphlet
  no. 1)
  "This paper was developed with
  the Wisconsin Draft Resistance
  Union."
  Cover title.
  1. Consumption (Economics)
  I. Sutheim, Susan, jt. auth.
  II. New England Free Press.
  III. Movement for a Democratic
  Society. IV. Wisconsin Draft
  Resistance Union.
  KU-RH, MiU

G101
Gottlieb, Bob.
  Consumption: domestic imperialism; a new left introduction to
  the political economy of Ameri-

can capitalism [by Bob Gottlieb
and Susan Sutheim. New York,
Movement for a Democratic Soci-
ety, 196]
16p.
1. Consumption (Economics)
I. Sutheim, Susan, jt. auth.
II. Movement for a Democratic
Society.
WHi-L

G102
Gottlieb, Sanford.
   The case for Vietnamese neutra-
lization. New York, National
Committee for a Sane Nuclear
Policy [196]
2 leaves. 28cm.
Caption title.
1. Vietnamese conflict, 1961-
1975. I. National Committee
for a Sane Nuclear Policy.
WHi-L

G103
Gottlieb, Sanford.
   Peace and politics, by Sanford
Gottlieb and Norman Hunt. New
York, National Committee for a
Sane Nuclear Policy [196]
7 leaves. 28cm.
1. Peace. 2. U.S.--Foreign
policy. 3. Politics, Practical.
I. Hunt, Norman, jt. auth.
II. National Committee for a
Sane Nuclear Policy.
WHi-A

G104
Gottlieb, Sanford.
   Report on SANE mission to
Algiers, Paris and Vietnam.
[n.p., National Committee for
a Sane Nuclear Policy] 1965.
[8] leaves. 28cm.
1. Vietnamese conflict, 1961-
1975. I. National Committee
for a Sane Nuclear Policy.
WHi-L

Gough, Kathleen, 1925-
   see
Aberle, Kathleen Gough, 1925-

G105
Gould House Conference on the

Economics of Disarmament, New
   York, 1961.
Report of Gould House Conference
on Economics of Disarmament
[initiated by the Committee for
World Development and World
Disarmament and the Post War
World Council] Jan. 28-30, 1961.
[New York, 1961]
17, xiip.
1. Disarmament--Economic as-
pects. I. Committee for World
Development and World Disarma-
ment. II. Post War World
Council.
MH-PA, DS

G106
Gourley, Edward Drew.
   America's moral crisis. Des
Moines, The Farmers Association
[1964?]
[24]p. 17cm.
Cover title.
Reprinted from US Farm News.
1. U.S.--Foreign policy.
2. Communism. 3. Anti-communist
movements. I. Farmers Association.
KU-RH

G107
Graham, John.
   The American system. Toronto,
Research, Information & Publications Project, Student Union
for Peace Action [196]
[16]p. 28cm.
Cover title.
1. U.S.--Military policy.
2. U.S.--Foreign policy.
3. U.S.--Pol. & govt.--1961-
          I. Student Union for
Peace Action.
WHi-A

G108
Grahn, Judy.
   Lesbians as women. [San Francisco, Gay Women's Liberation,
196]
5 leaves. 28cm.
Caption title.
1. Homosexuality. 2. Woman.
3. Gay Women's Liberation.
CU-B

G109
Grahn, Judy.
　On the development of a purple
　fist.　[n.p., 1969]
　[5]p.　28cm.
　Caption title.
　1. Homosexuality.　2. Woman.
　CU-B

G110
Grambau, Hugh.
　The UMSEU and the future.　[Ann
　Arbor? 196]
　[2] leaves.　28cm.
　Caption title.
　1. University of Michigan Stu-
　dent Employees' Union.　2. Stu-
　dent movements--University of
　Michigan.
　WHi-A

G111
Granma.
　Cuba fights bureaucracy.
　[Ithaca, N.Y., Glad Day Press &
　Niagara Region SDS, 196]
　23p.　illus.　22cm.
　Cover title.
　1. Cuba--Pol. & govt.--1959-
　　　I. Glad Day Press.
　II. Students for a Democratic
　Society, Niagara Region.
　MoU

G112
Grant, Bess Myerson.
　You don't have to buy war, Mrs.
　Smith.　[Beverly Hills, Calif.,
　Another Mother for Peace, 1970]
　[4]p.　28cm.
　Caption title.
　An address at the World Mothers
　Day Assembly of Another Mother
　for Peace, San Francisco, May
　9, 1970.
　1. Vietnamese conflict, 1961-
　1975.　I. Another Mother for
　Peace.
　KU-RH

G113
Grass Roots Writing Collective,
　Palo Alto, Calif.
　The promised land: a Grass Roots
　report on mid-peninsula land
　use.　[2d. ed. Palo Alto, 1971?]

60p.　illus.　28cm.
Cover title.
1. Stanford University.　2. Palo
Alto, Calif.--Pol. & govt.
3. Military research.　4. Pol-
lution--Palo Alto, Calif.
5. Cities and towns--Planning--
Palo Alto, Calif.
KU-RH

G114
Gray, Jack.
　Agrarian policies.　Boston, New
　England Free Press [196]
　[32]-39p.　28cm.
　Caption title.
　Reprinted from Bulletin of
　Atomic Scientists, June 1966.
　1. Agriculture--China (People's
　Republic of China, 1949-　　)
　I. New England Free Press.
　KU-RH

G115
Gray, Jack.
　Agrarian policies.　Toronto,
　Research, Information, and Publ-
　lications, Student Union for
　Peace Action [196]
　[32]-39p.　28cm.
　Caption title.
　Reprinted from Bulletin of the
　Atomic Scientists, June 1966.
　1. Agriculture--China (People's
　Republic of China, 1949-　　)
　I. Student Union for Peace
　Action.
　WHi-A, MoU

G116
Gray, Victoria J.
　Testimony on proposed voting
　legislation in 89th Congress,
　by Mrs. Victoria J. Gray, for
　the Executive Committee, Missis-
　sippi Freedom Democratic Party
　before the House Committee on
　the Judiciary subcommittee [no.]
　5, March 25, 1965.　[n.p., 1965]
　4p.　36cm.
　Caption title.
　1. Negroes--Civil rights.
　I. Mississippi Freedom Demo-
　cratic Party.
　WHi-A

G117
Greater Washington "Don't Buy Cali-
   fornia Grapes" Committee.
   Where does the Roman Catholic
   Church stand on the "Delano
   grape strike?"
   [Washington, D.C., 1968]
   6p. 28cm.
   Caption title.
   1. Catholic Church in the U.S.
   2. Agricultural laborers--Calif.
   --Delano. 3. United Farm Work-
   ers Organizing Committee.
   KU-RH

G118
Greeman, Dick.
   In a crisis the center falls
   out: the role of the faculty in
   the Columbia strike. [Ann Arbor,
   Radical Education Project, 1969?]
   5p. illus. 28cm.
   Caption title.
   1. Columbia University. 2. Student movements--Columbia University. I. Radical Education
   Project.
   KU-RH, MoU

G119
Green, Donald Ross.
   Black belt schools: beyond de-
   segragation, by Donald Ross
   Green [and others] Atlanta,
   Southern Regional Council, 1965.
   40p. 22cm. (Southern Regional
   Council. Toward Regional Realism, no. 4)
   1. Education--Southern States.
   2. Negroes--Education. I. Southern Regional Council.
   MH-L, NcD, NUC 66-40691

G120
Green, Gil.
   Terrorism--is it revolutionary.
   New York, New Outlook Publish-
   ers, 1970.
   40p. 19cm.
   1. Terrorism. 2. Revolutions.
   I. New Outlook Publishers.
   MiU

G121
Green, Max.
   After the moratorium; a demo-
   cratic peace movement; politics,

not parades, by Max Green,
Steve Kelman [and] Josh Muravchik. [New York, Young People's
Socialist League, 1970?]
[4]p. 24cm.
Caption title.
1. Vietnamese conflict, 1961-
1975. 2. Peace. 3. Demonstrations. I. Young People's Socialist League. II. Kelman,
Steve, jt. auth. III. Muravchik,
Josh, jt. auth.
KU-RH

G122
Green, Philip.
   Political framework of decision-
   making; a course syllabus.
   Chicago, Students for a Democra-
   tic Society [196]
   4p. 28cm.
   1. U.S.--Pol. & govt.--Bibl.
   2. Political science--Bibl.
   I. Students for a Democratic
   Society.
   CU-B, MiU

G123
Greenberg, David F.
   Alternatives to the draft; a
   political analysis. [Chicago,
   Chicago Area Draft Resisters,
   196]
   4p. 28cm.
   Cover title.
   1. Military service, Compulsory.
   I. Chicago Area Draft Resisters.
   KU-RH

G124
Greenberg, David F.
   Alternatives to the draft: a
   political analysis. New York,
   Resistance [196]
   [8]p. 22cm.
   Caption title.
   1. Military service, Compulsory.
   I. Resistance.
   MoU

G125
Greenberg, David F.
   The problem of prisons. Chicago,
   Chicago Area Draft Resisters
   [1970?]
   18p. 28cm.

Cover title.
1. Prisons. I. Chicago Area
Draft Resisters.
KU-RH

G126
Greenberg, David F.
  Vietnam is not an accident.
Chicago, Chicago Area Draft Re-
sisters [196]
  9p. 28cm.
  Cover title.
  1. U.S.--Foreign policy.
  2. Vietnamese conflict, 1961-
  1975. I. Chicago Area Draft
  Resisters.
  KU-RH

G127
Greenberg, Richard.
  Problems relating to unemployment in the vicinity of Hazard,
Kentucky [substantially revised
and edited by ERAP staff for the
purposes of the Hazard conference. n.p., 1963?]
  17p. 28cm.
  Caption title.
  1. Poor--Hazard, Ky. 2. Hazard,
  Ky.--Econ. condit. I. Students
  for a Democratic Society. Economic Research and Action Project.
  MiU

G128
Greenblatt, Robert.
  Hanoi: a preliminary report.
[n.p., National Mobilization
Committee, 1968?]
  4p. 28cm.
  1. Hanoi 2. Vietnamese conflict, 1961-1975. I. National
  Mobilization Committee to end
  the war in Vietnam.
  CU-B

G129
Greene, Felix.
  As China sees United States
policy. "The Chinese case"; a
chapter from Awakened China by
Felix Greene, with book reviews
from New York Herald Tribune,
The National Guardian, The
Washington Post. [New York]

Far East Reporter [1963?]
  35p. illus. 21cm.
  Cover title.
  1. China (People's Republic of
  China, 1949-   )--For. rel.--
  U.S. 2. U.S.--Foreign policy.
  I. Far East Reporter.
  CSt-H, NUC 71-54045

G130
Greene, Felix.
  A divorce trial in China.
Ann Arbor, Radical Education
Project [196]
  [195]-207p. 18cm.
  Cover title.
  1. Divorce--China (People's Re-
  public of China, 1949-   )
  I. Radical Education Project.
  MoU

G131
Greene, Felix.
  A divorce trial in China. Bos-
ton, New England Free Press,
[196]
  [195]-207p. 17cm.
  Cover title.
  Reprinted from Felix Greene's
  Awakened China.
  1.Divorce--China (People's Re-
  public of China, 1949-   )
  I. New England Free Press.
  WHi-A, KU-RH

G132
Greene, Felix.
  Visit to a rural commune. Ann
Arbor, Radical Education Pro-
ject [196]
  26p. 22cm.
  Cover title.
  Reprinted from Felix Greene's
  Awakened China.
  1. Communes--China (People's Re-
  public of China, 1949-   )
  I. Radical Education Project.
  MoU

G133
Greene, Felix.
  Visit to a rural commune. Boston, New England Free Press
[196]
  [149]-171p. 18cm.
  Cover title.

Reprinted from Felix Greene's
Awakened China.
1. Communes--China (People's
Republic of China, 1949-   )
I. New England Free Press.
KU-RH

G134
Greene, Felix.
    Visit to a rural commune. Tor-
onto, Research, Information and
Publications Project, Student
Union for Peace Action [196]
[149]-171p.
1. Communes--China (People's
Republic of China, 1949-   )
I. Student Union for Peace Ac-
tion.
WHi-A

G135
Greene, Felix.
    What's really happening in
China? [San Francisco] City
Lights Books [c1959]
51p. 20cm.
1. China (People's Republic of
China, 1949-   ) I. City
Lights Books.
KU-RH

G136
Greer, Edward.
    Roadblock to revolution; a radi-
cal critique of the Progressive
Labor Party, by Edward Greer and
Charles Lengram. [Boston, New
England Free Press, c1969]
26p. 28cm.
Cover title.
1. Progressive Labor Party.
I. Lengram, Charles, jt. auth.
II. New England Free Press.
CU-B

C137
Grey, Stan.
    Politics and the dynamics of
social change [by] Stan Grey.
A response: community organizing
and social change [by] Pat Uhl.
Toronto, Research, Information
and Publications, Student Union
for Peace Action [1966?]
17p. 28cm.
1. Politics, Practical. 2. Soc-

ial change. 3. Community organ-
ization. I. Uhl, Pat, jt. auth.
II. Student Union for Peace
Action.
WHi-A

G138
Grier, Eunice.
    Discrimination in housing: a
handbook of facts, by Eunice
and George Grier. [New York,
Anti-Defamation League of
B'nai B'rith, c1960]
67p. (Freedom pamphlets)
1. Negroes--Housing. 2. Discrimination in housing.
I. Grier, George, jt. auth.
WHi-L

G139
Grissom, Tom.
    Bibliography on the integration
of education, science, the military and ideology in post-war
America. E. Palo Alto, Calif.,
Pacific Studies Center, 1970.
12 leaves. 28cm. (Pacific
Studies Center bibliography
series no. 2)
1. Military research. 2. Universities and colleges.
3. Federal aid to education.
4. U.S.--Foreign policy.
I. Pacific Studies Center.
KU-RH

G140
Griswold, Deirdre.
    Indonesia: the second greatest
crime of the century. New York,
World View Publishers [1970]
96p. 22cm.
"A Youth Against War & Fascism
pamphlet."
1. Indonesia--For. rel.--U.S.
2. U.S. Central Intelligence
Agency. I. World View Publishers. II. Youth Against War and
Fascism.
KU-RH

G141
Grizzard, Vernon.
    The masculine ideology and
police power [by Vernon Grizzard with Roxanne Dunbar. New

Orleans? Southern Female Rights
Union? 1969?]
[2]p. 28cm.
Caption title.
1. Police. I. Dunbar, Roxanne,
jt. auth. II. Southern Female
Rights Union, New Orleans.
KU-RH

G142
Guardian.
  Panthers! [New York, 1970]
  8p. illus. 33cm. (Special
  supplement)
  Caption title.
  1. Black Panther Party.
  KU-RH

G143
Guardian.
  Vietnam genocide. [New York,
  1969]
  8p. illus. 43cm. (A special
  supplement)
  Caption title.
  1. Vietnamese conflict, 1961-
  1975.
  KU-RH

G144
Guerin, Daniel, 1904-
  Negroes on the march: a French-
  man's report on the American
  Negro struggle. [Translated
  and edited by Duncan Ferguson]
  New York, Weissman [1956]
  190p. port.
  1. Negroes--Civil rights.
  NNC, MiU, NcD, MnU, WHi-L

G145
Guevara, Ernesto, 1920-1967.
  Charges the U.N. to meet the
  challenge of imperialism. [Tor-
  onto, Fair Play for Cuba Committee, 196]
  12p.
  Cover title.
  Reprinted from the Militant.
  1. U.S.--Foreign policy.
  2. Cuba--For. rel.--U.S.
  3. Imperialism. I. Fair Play
  for Cuba committee.
  MiU

G146
Guevara, Ernesto, 1920-1967.
  'Che' Guevara, Cuba's Minister
  of Industries, charges the U.N.
  to meet the challenge of imperialism. [Toronto, Fair Play
  for Cuba Committee, 196]
  12p. 21cm.
  Reprinted from the Militant.
  Speech delivered in the United
  Nations General Assembly.
  1. Cuba--For. rel.--U.S
  2. U.S.--For. rel.--Cuba
  I. Fair Play for Cuba Committee.
  FU, CSt-H, DPU, NUC 68-7925

G147
Guevara, Ernesto, 1920-1967.
  Che Guevara on Africa. [Toron-
  to, Fair Play for Cuba Committee, 1965?]
  8p. 22cm.
  Translations of two interviews
  with Che Guevara by Bodam Rouissi and Josie Fanon.
  1. Africa--For. rel.--Cuba.
  2. Cuba--For. rel.--Africa.
  3. Africa--Pol. & govt.
  I. Rouissi, Bodam. II. Fair
  Play for Cuba Committee.
  III. Fanon, Josie.
  FU, NUC 67-29913

G148
Guevara, Ernesto, 1920-1967.
  Che Guevara on Vietnam and
  world revolution. [New York,
  Merit Publishers, 1967?]
  15p. 22cm.
  1. Vietnamese conflict, 1961-
  1975. 2. World politics--1955-
      I. Merit Publishers.
  MoU

G149
Guevara, Ernesto, 1920-1967.
  Che Guevara speaks; selected
  speeches and writings. [Edited
  by George Lavan] New York, Merit
  Publishers [1967]
  159p. 23cm.
  1. Cuba--History--1959-
  2. World politics--1955-
  I. Lavan, George, ed.

II. Merit Publishers.
DLC 67-31739rev.

G150
Guevara, Ernesto, 1920-1967.
  Cuba and the "Kennedy plan".
  [New York] Fair Play for Cuba
  Committee [1961]
  [7]p.
  Cover title.
  1. Alliance for Progress.
  2. U.S.--Relations (general)
  with Latin America.
  I. Fair Play for Cuba Committee.
  MiU

G151
Guevara, Ernesto, 1920-1967.
  Man and socialism in Cuba.
  [Chicago? Students for a Demo-
  cratic Society, 1969?]
  24p. 22cm.
  Cover title.
  1. Cuba--Pol. & govt.--1959-
          2. Socialism in Cuba.
  I. Students for a Democratic
  Society.
  WHi-L

G152
Guevara, Ernesto, 1920-1967.
  May Day speech to labor--1963.
  [New York, Fair Play for Cuba
  Committee, 1963]
  23p. 22cm.
  1. Cuba--Pol. & govt.--1959-
          I. Fair Play for Cuba
  Committee.
  NcD, NUC 64-71295.

G153
Guevara, Ernesto, 1920-1967.
  Message to the Tri-continental
  Congress. Nashville, Southern
  Student Organizing Committee
  [196]
  16p. 28cm.
  Cover title.
  1. U.S.--Foreign policy.
  2. Vietnamese conflict, 1961-
  1975. I. Tricontinental Con-
  ference of African, Asian and
  Latin American Peoples, 1st,
  Havana, 1966. II. Southern
  Student Organizing Committee.
  MoU, MiU

G154
Guevara, Ernesto, 1920-1967.
  On Vietnam and world revolution.
  [New York, Merit Publishers,
  1967]
  15p. 22cm.
  1. Imperialism. 2. Vietnamese
  conflict, 1961-1975. I. Merit
  Publishers.
  DLC 67-7287

G155
Guevara, Ernesto, 1920-1967.
  Socialism and man. [New York,
  Young Socialist Alliance, 1969]
  22p. 22cm. (A Young Socialist
  pamphlet)
  Cover title.
  1. Communism--Cuba. 2. Cuba--
  Pol. & govt.--1959-
  I. Young Socialist Alliance.
  KU-RH

G156
Guevara, Ernesto, 1920-1967.
  Socialism and man. [Toronto?
  Fair Play for Cuba Committee]
  1966.
  23p. illus. 22cm.
  1. Socialism in Cuba. 2. Cuba--
  Pol. & govt.--1959-
  I. Fair Play for Cuba Committee.
  CSt-H, NUC 67-91317

C157
Guevara, Ernesto, 1920-1967.
  Socialism & man. [Toronto, Fair
  Play for Cuba Committee, 196]
  24p.
  Cover title.
  1. Communism--Cuba. 2. Cuba--
  Pol. & govt.--1959-
  I. Fair Play for Cuba Committee.
  MiU

G158
Guevara, Ernesto, 1920-1967.
  Vietnam & the third world. Ann
  Arbor, Radical Education Pro-
  ject [1969]
  13p. 21cm.
  Cover title.
  Reprinted from New Left Review,
  May-June 1967.
  1. Vietnamese conflict, 1961-
  1975. 2. Imperialism.

3. U.S.--Foreign policy.
I. Radical Education Project.
KU-RH

G159
Guide to conscientious objection.
[Chicago, Students for a Demo-
cratic Society, 196]
12p. 21cm.
Cover title.
1. Conscientious objectors.
I. Students for a Democratic
Society.
CU-B, KU-RH

G160
Gulf Action Project.
Spring offensive against Gulf
Oil. [Pittsburg, 1970?]
[4]p. 28cm.
Caption title.
1. Gulf Oil Corporation.
2. Student movements--Pittsburgh.
KU-RH

G161
Gurin, David.
City planning: professionals and
protestors. Ann Arbor, Confer-
ence on Radicals in the Profes-
sions, 1967.
6p. 28cm.
Cover title.
1. Cities and towns--Planning.
I. Conference on Radicals in the
Professions.
MiU-H

G162
Gus Hall-Benjamin J. Davis Defense
Committee.
The McCarran Act and the right
to travel. [New York, 196]
[12]p. illus.
Cover title.
1. Freedom of movement. 2. U.S.
Laws, statutes, etc. Internal
Security Act of 1950. 3. Apthe-
ker, Herbert, 1915-
4. Flynn, Elizabeth Gurley.
KU-J, MiU

G163
Gus Hall-Benjamin J. Davis Defense
Committee.
McCarran Act prosecutions must
be halted now. [New York, 196]
folder. 28cm.
Caption title.
1. U.S. Laws, statutes, etc.
Internal Security Act of 1950.
2. Anti-communist movements.
CU-B

G164
Gwynn, Betsy.
[Letter, by Betsy Gwynn and Cl
Nardi. n.p., 1970]
5 leaves. 28cm.
1. Woman--Rights of women.
I. Nardi, Cl, jt. auth.

H

H1
Haag, John.
A call to the movement: third
party--vehicle for organization.
[n.p., California Peace & Freedom Party, 196]
2 leaves. 28cm.
Caption title.
1. Peace and Freedom Party.
WHi-L

Haber, Al.
see
Haber, Robert Alan.

H2
Haber, Barbara.
Getting by with a little help
from our friends [by] Barbara
Haber and Al Haber, Ann Arbor,
Radical Education Project [196]

44-62p. 22cm.
Cover title.
1. Student movements. I. Radical Education Project. II. Haber, Robert Alan, jt. auth.
MoU

H3
Haber, Barbara.
   Getting by with a little help from our friends [by] Barbara Haber and Al Haber. Boston, New England Free Press [196]
   44-62p. 22cm.
   Cover title.
   Originally written for the Radicals in the Professions Conference, July 1967.
   1. Radicalism. I. New England Free Press. II. Haber, Robert Alan, jt. auth.
KU-RH

Haber, Robert Alan
   xHaber, Al.

H4
Haber, Robert Alan.
   The Baltimore anti-poverty program: a critique of the November 5, 1964 "final" corrected draft. [n.p., Students for a Democratic Society? 1965?]
   5p. 28cm.
   Cover title.
   1. Poor--Baltimore. 2. Baltimore Human Renewal Program.
   I. Students for a Democratic Society.
KU-RH

H5
Haber, Robert Alan.
   The "end of ideology" as ideology. [Chicago? Students for a Democratic Society? 196]
   16p. 28cm.
   Cover title.
   1. Bell, Daniel. The end of ideology. 2. Lipset, Seymour Martin. Political man.
   3. Shils, Edward Albert, 1911-
       I. Students for a Democratic Society.
CU-B

H6
Haber, Robert Alan.
   The end of ideology as ideology. [Montreal, Our Generation, 196]
   [51-68]p.
   Caption title.
   1. Bell, Daniel. The end of ideology. 2. Lipset, Seymour Martin. Political man.
   3. Shils, Edward Albert, 1911-
       I. Our Generation.
NNU-T

H7
Haber, Robert Alan.
   The end of ideology as ideology. San Francisco, Students for a Democratic Society [196]
   17p. 28cm.
   Cover title.
   1. Bell, Daniel. The end of ideology. 2. Ideology. I. Students for a Democratic Society.
MiU

H8
Haber, Robert Alan.
   Peace, power and the university, by Al Haber and Dick Flacks. Ann Arbor, Peace Research and Education Project, 1963.
   12p. 28cm.
   Cover title.
   1. Peace. 2. Student movements. I. Flacks, Richard, jt. auth. II. Students for a Democratic Society. Peace Research and Education Project.
WHi-A

H9
Haber, Robert Alan.
   Professionals and social change project. [n.p.] 1961.
   2 leaves. 28cm.
   Caption title.
   1. Students for a Democratic Society. 2. Social change.
WHi-A

H10
Haber, Robert Alan.
   Students and labor. [n.p., Students for a Democratic Society, 1962]

19p. 28cm.
Cover title.
1. Labor and laboring classes.
2. Student movements. I. Students for a Democratic Society.
WHi-A

H11
Haber, Robert Alan.
  Students and labor. Nashville,
  Southern Student Organizing
  Committee [196]
  20p. 28cm.
  Cover title.
  1. Labor and laboring classes.
  2. Student movements. I. South-
  ern Student Organizing Committee.
  CU-B

H12
Haber, Robert Alan.
  Students and labor. New York,
  Students for a Democratic Society [1962]
  19p.
  Cover title.
  1. Labor and laboring classes.
  2. Student movements. I. Students for a Democratic Society.
  WHi-L

H13
Haber, Robert Alan.
  Taking Johnson seriously; a re-
  sponse to Richard Flacks, by Al
  and Barbara Haber. [n.p., Stu-
  dents for a Democratic Society
  1964?]
  [2]p. 28cm.
  Caption title.
  1. Johnson, Lyndon Baines, Pres.
  U.S., 1908-1973. 2. Goldwater,
  Barry Morris, 1909-
  I. Haber, Barbara, jt. auth.
  II. Students for a Democratic
  Society.
  KU-RH

H14
Hagan, Roger.
  Counter-insurgency and the new
  foreign relations. New York,
  Students for a Democratic Society [1965?]
  [11]p. 22cm.

Cover title.
Reprinted from The Correspon-
dence, Autumn 1964.
1. U.S.--Foreign policy.
I. Students for a Democratic
Society.
CU-B, WHi-L

H15
Hagan, Roger.
  Counter-insurgency and the new
  foreign relations. New York,
  Students for a Democratic Soc-
  iety and its Peace Research
  and Education Project [196]
  [9]p. 22cm.
  Caption title.
  1. U.S.--Foreign policy.
  I. Students for a Democratic
  Society. Peace Research and
  Education Project.
  WHi-A

H16
Haggstrom, Warren C.
  The power of the poor. Ann
  Arbor, Students for a Democratic
  Society and its Economic Re-
  search and Action Project [196]
  14p. 28cm.
  Cover title.
  1. Poverty. I. Students for a
  Democratic Society. Economic
  Research and Action Project.
  WHi-L, WHi-A, MiU

H17
Haggstrom, Warren C.
  The power of the poor. Montreal,
  Our Generation [196]
  16p. 28cm.
  Cover title.
  "A revision of a paper prepared
  for the 71st annual American
  Psychology Association conven-
  tion, Sept. 1964.
  1. Poverty. I. Our Generation.
  NNU-T

H18
Haggstrom, Warren C.
  The power of the poor. Toronto,
  Research, Information and Publications Project, Student Union
  for Peace, 1965.
  16p. 28cm.

Cover title.
1. Poor.   I. Student Union for
Peace Action.
WHi-A

H19
Hahn, Al.
   Civil rights in the north: a dis-
cussion paper by Al Hahn and
Sandra Cason.   [New York] Stu-
dents for a Democratic Society
for the Liberal Study Group
[196]
7p.   28cm.
Cover title.
1. Negroes--Civil rights.
I. Students for a Democratic
Society.   II. Liberal Study
Group.
MiU, NNU-T

H20
Hahn, Lorna.
   War in Algeria: is confederation
the answer?   [New York] American
Committee on Africa [196]
32p.   22cm.   (Africa today pam-
phlet: 1)
Cover title.
1. Algeria--Pol. & govt.
2. Revolutions--Algeria.
I. American Committee on Africa.
MiU

H21
Hall, Gus.
   Catholics and communists: ele-
ments of a dialogue.   [New York,
Political Affairs Publishers,
1964]
31p.   22cm.
Cover title.
1. Catholics.   2. Communism and
religion.   I. Political Affairs
Publishers.
MiU, WHi-L, MH-AR, NUC 65-25838

H22
Hall, Gus.
   Czechoslovakia at the crossroads.
[Report to the meeting of the
National Committee of the Com-
munist Party, U.S.A. on August
31-September 2, 1968.   New York,
New Outlook Publishing, 1968]
36p.   22cm.

Cover title.
1. Czechoslovak Republic--Pol.
& govt.   I. New Outlook Publishers.   II. Communist Party of the
United States of America.   National Committee.
NcGU, NjR, CSt-H, NUC 69-76724

H23
Hall, Gus.
   The eleventh hour--defeat the
new fascist threat.   [New York,
New Currents Publishers, 1964]
22p.   22x10cm.
Cover title.
1. Presidents--U.S.--Elections--
1964.   2. Goldwater, Barry
Morris, 1909-   3. Republi-
can Party.   4. Fascism.   I. New
Currents Publishers.
KU-RH, MiEM, NN, H21, NUC 67-
95144

H24
Hall, Gus.
   The fight against the Nixon-
Agnew road to disaster.   [New
York, New Outlook Publishers,
1970]
43p.   19cm.
Cover title.
1. U.S.--Pol. & govt.--1969-
     2. Nixon, Richard Milhous,
Pres., U.S., 1913-   I. New
Outlook Publishers.
MiU

H25
Hall, Gus.
   For a meaningful alternative:
report to the June 10, 1967
meeting of the national committee of the Communist Party,
U.S.A.   New York, New Outlook
Publishers, 1967.
64p.
1. Communism.   2. U.S.--Pol. &
govt.--1963   I. New Outlook
Publishers.
CSSR, WHi-L

H26
Hall, Gus.
   For a radical change: the communist view.   Report and concluding remarks to the 18th

national convention, Communist
Party, U.S.A., June 22-26, 1966.
New York, New Outlook Publishers,
1966.
80p. illus. 22cm.
1. U.S.--Pol. & govt.--1945-
        I. Communist Party of the
United States of America. 18th
Convention, New York, 1966.
II. New Outlook Publishers.
WHi-L, NIC, CSSR, NUC 67-97894

H27
Hall, Gus.
    Free Americans from McCarran Act
danger. [New York, Gus Hall-Ben-
jamin Davis Defense Committee,
1962]
15p. 22x10cm.
Cover title.
1. U.S.--Laws, statutes, etc.
Internal Security Act of 1950.
2. Internal security. I. Gus
Hall-Benjamin Davis Defense
Committee.
MiU, KU-RH, MiEM, KU-J,
NUC 67-95116

H28
Hall, Gus.
    Hard hats and hard facts. New
York, New Outlook Publishers,
1970.
24p. 19cm.
1. Labor and laboring classes.
2. U.S.--Pol. & govt.--1969-
        I. New Outlook Publishers.
WHi-L, MiU

H29
Hall, Gus.
    How to shape history. [n.p.,
1969?]
7p.
Speech delivered to the national
party conference, Jan. 13,
1969.
1. Communism.
WHi-L

H30
Hall, Gus.
    Imperialist rivalries and the
world struggle for peace. [New
York, New Outlook Publishers,
1968]

23p. 22cm.
1. U.S.--Foreign policy.
I. New Outlook Publishers.
MiU

H31
Hall, Gus.
    Labor: key force for peace,
civil rights and economic security. New York, New Outlook
Publishers, 1966.
48p.
1. Labor and laboring classes.
2. Communism. 3. Civil rights.
I. New Outlook Publishers.
WHi-L

H32
Hall, Gus.
    Main report of Gus Hall, to the
meeting of the national committee in Chicago, March 25, 1960.
[Chicago, 1960]
13 leaves. 36cm.
Caption title.
1. U.S.--Pol. & govt.--1945-
        I. Communist Party of the
United States of America. National Committee.
NN, NUC 64-17473

H33
Hall, Gus.
    Main street to Wall Street: end
the cold war. New York, New
Century Publishers, 1962.
48p.
1. World politics--1955-
2. U.S.--Foreign policy. I. New
Century Publishers.
CSSR, WHi-A, NNC, NIC, OrU,
KU-J, NUC 63-17973

H34
Hall, Gus.
    Negro freedom is in the interest
of every American. [New York,
New Currents Publishers, 1964]
16p.
Cover title.
1. Negroes--Civil rights.
I. New Currents Publishers.
MiU

H35
Hall, Gus.

On course: the revolutionary
process; report to the 19th national convention of the Communist Party, U.S.A., by its general
secretary. New York, New Outlook Publishers, 1969.
96p. 19cm.
I. Communist Party of the United
States of America. 19th Convention, New York, 1969.
CtY, NUC 71-20125

H36
Hall, Gus.
The only choice: peaceful co-
existence. New York, New Century Publishers, 1963.
48p. 19cm.
1. U.S.--For. rel.--Russia.
2. Russia--For. rel.--U.S.
I. New Century Publishers.
OU, WHi-L, MoKU, KU-J, IU, TxU,
NcD, NIC, NUC 64-18890

H37
Hall, Gus.
An open letter to the Socialist
Party from Gus Hall. [New York,
Communist Party, U.S.A., 1962]
3p. 28cm.
1. Socialist Party (U.S.)
I. Communist Party of the United
States of America.
WHi-L, NUC 64-43599

H38
Hall, Gus.
Our country in crisis--the people
must act. [New York, New Outlook Publishers, 1970]
36p. 19cm.
Cover title.
1. U.S.--Pol. & govt.--1969-
    I. New Outlook Publishers.
MiU

H39
Hall, Gus.
Our sights to the future. [New
York, New Century Publishers,
1960]
30p.
1. Communism. I. New Century
Publishers.
WHi-L

H40
Hall, Gus.
The path to revolution, the
communist program. [New York,
New Outlook Publishers, 1968]
39p.
1. Communism. 2. Communist
Party of the United States of
America. I. New Outlook Pub-
lishers.
WHi-L

H41
Hall, Gus.
Stop war in Vietnam now. [New
York, The Worker, 1965?]
7p. 22x10cm.
Cover title.
"Address...delivered at Town
Hall in New York, March 26,
1965."
1. Vietnamese conflict, 1961-
1975.
CU-B, WHi-L

H42
Hall, Gus.
The summit failure: how peace
can be won. [New York, New
Century Publishers, 1960]
22p. 19cm.
Cover title.
1. U.S.--For. rel.--Russia.
2. Russia--For. rel.--U.S.
I. New Century Publishers.
WHi-L, MiU

H43
Hall, Gus.
Toward a peace ticket in 1968;
defeat the forces of war and
racism. New York, New Outlook
Publishers, 1967.
30p. 20cm.
1. Vietnamese conflict, 1961-
1975. 2. U.S.--Pol. & govt.--
1969-   3. Negroes--Civil
rights. I. New Outlook Publishers.
KU-RH, CSSR

H44
Hall, Gus.
The ultra-right, Kennedy, and
the role of the progressive.

For people's unity against big
business reaction and the war
danger. [New York? Communist
Party USA? 1961?]
folder. 28cm.
Caption title.
1. Fascism. 2. Kennedy, John
Fitzgerald, Pres. U.S., 1917-
1963. 3. Liberalism. I. Communist Party of the United
States of America.
KU-RH

H45
Hall, Gus.
  The United States in today's
  world. New York, New Century
  Publishers, 1961.
  62p. illus.
  At head of title: Report to the
  National Committee of the Com-
  munist Party, U.S.A.
  Cover title: What the communist
  stand for.
  1. U.S.--Foreign policy.
  2. U.S.--Pol. & govt.--1961-
        I. Communist Party of the
  United States of America.
  II. New Century Publishers.
  MiEM, WHi-L, KU-J, NUC 67-95115

H46
Hall, Gus.
  Which way U.S.A. 1964? The
  communist view. [New York,
  New Century Publishers, 1964]
  30p. port. 19cm.
  1. Communism. 2. U.S.--Pol. &
  govt.--1963-   I. New Century Publishers.
  WHi-L, CSt, NcD, OU, GU, KU-RH,
  DLC 76-22356

H47
Hall, Gus.
  Working-class approach to women's
  liberation. [New York, New Outlook Publishers, 1970]
  12p. 22cm.
  Cover title.
  1. Woman--Rights of women.
  2. Labor and laboring classes.
  I. New Outlook Publishers.
  MiU

H48
Hall, Gus.
  Your stake in the 1960 elections.
  [New York, New Century Publish-
  ers, 1960]
  31p. 19cm.
  Cover title.
  1. Presidents--U.S.--Election--
  1960. 2. Communist Party of the
  United States of America. I. New
  Century Publishers.
  KU-RH, MiU, NUC 67-95114

H49
Hall, Irving.
  The Meisenbach case; the FBI
  and HUAC convicted. [Berkeley,
  Calif., Bay Area Student Committee for the Abolition of the
  House Committee on Un-American
  Activities, 196]
  [16]p. 28cm.
  Cover title.
  1. U.S. Congress. House.
  Committee on Un-American Activities. 2. Meisenbach, Robert.
  3. U.S. Federal Bureau of Investigation. I. Bay Area Student Committee for the Abolition
  of the Committee on Un-American
  Activities.
  KU-RH

H50
Hall, Martin.
  The German Democratic Republic;
  most maligned of all of the
  people's republics of eastern
  Europe. [New York, New World
  Review, 1962]
  7p.
  1. Germany (Democratic Republic,
  1949-   ) I. New World Review.
  KU-J

H51
Halle, Louis J.
  The inhibiting effect of absol-
  ute weapons; is war obsolete?
  [Philadelphia, Peace Literature
  Service, American Friends Ser-
  vice Committee, 196]
  [12]p. 22x10cm.
  Cover title.

Reprinted from The New Republic,
April 2, 1962.
1. Atomic warfare and society.
2. War. 3. World politics--
1955-1965. I. Friends, Society
of. American Friends Service
Committee.
KU-RH

H52
Halonen, Kae.
  Man's world & welcome to it.
  Detroit, Radical Education
  Project [1970?]
  [8]p. illus. 22cm.
  Reprinted from Speak Out.
  1. Woman--Rights of women.
  I. Radical Education Project.
  KU-RH, MiU

H53
Halperin, Morton.
  China's foreign policy [by]
  Morton Halperin and Dwight
  Perkins. Toronto, Research,
  Information and Publications
  Project, Student Union for Peace
  Action [196]
  14p. 28cm.
  Cover title.
  1. China (People's Republic of
  China, 1949-   )--Foreign
  policy. I. Student Union for
  Peace Action. II. Perkins,
  Dwight, jt. auth.
  WHi-A

H54
Halperin, Morton.
  Chinese foreign policy [by]
  Morton Halperin [and] Dwight
  Perkins. Boston, New England
  Free Press [196]
  19p. 22cm.
  Cover title.
  1. China (People's Republic of
  China, 1949-   )--Foreign
  policy. I. New England Free
  Press. II. Perkins, Dwight,
  jt. auth.
  MoU

H55
Halstead, Fred.
  A further alarm signal from
  Chicago: an open letter from

Fred Halstead. [New York]
1969.
5p. 28cm.
1. Police--Illinois--Chicago.
MoU

H56
Halstead, Fred.
  A further alarm signal from
  Chicago: an open letter from
  Fred Halstead. [New York,
  Socialist Workers Party, 1969]
  4 [3]p. 28cm.
  Caption title.
  1. Police--Illinois--Chicago.
  I. Socialist Workers Party.
  WHi-L

H57
Halstead, Fred.
  If that be revolution, make the
  most of it. [New York, Socialist Workers Campaign Committee,
  1968?]
  [4]p. illus.
  Cover title.
  "Speech by Fred Halstead, Socialist Workers candidate for
  president, San Francisco Anti-
  war Rally, April 27, 1968."
  1. Vietnamese conflict, 1961-
  1975. I. Socialist Workers
  Campaign Committee.
  WHi-L

H58
Halstead, Fred.
  A letter to GI's on the '68
  elections. [New York, Socialist
  Workers Campaign Committee,
  1968?]
  folder. 22x9cm.
  Cover title.
  1. Vietnamese conflict, 1961-
  1975. 2. President--U.S.--El-
  ection--1968. I. Socialist
  Workers Campaign Committee.
  KU-RH

H59
Ham, Adolfo.
  Towards a theological interpretation of the Latin American
  social revolution. [n.p., 196]
  6 leaves. 28cm.
  Caption title.

Reprinted from Communio Viatorum,
v.8, no. 1; Sp. 1965.
1. Revolutions--Latin America.
2. Latin America--Pol. & govt.
3. Latin America--Social conditions.
KU-RH

H60
Hamer, Fanny Lou.
To praise our bridges: an auto-
biography. [Taped and edited by
Julius Lester and Mary Varela
of SNCC. Jackson, Miss., KIPCO,
196]
26p. illus. 28cm.
1. Mississippi--Race question.
2. Negroes--Mississippi.
I. Lester, Julius. II. Varela,
Mary. III. Student Non-violent
Coordinating Committee.
MiU

H61
Hamill, Robert H.
A just war, or just another war.
[Woodmont, Promoting Enduring
Peace, 196]
[4]p. 23cm.
Caption title.
1. Vietnamese conflict, 1961-
1975. I. Promoting Enduring
Peace.
KU-RH

H62
Hamilton, Mary.
Freedom riders speak for them-
selves [by] Mary Hanilton [and
others. Detroit, News & Letters,
1961]
62p. illus. 18cm.
1. Negroes--Civil rights.
2. Student movements--Southern
States. I. News & Letters.
NIC, IU, NUC 70-36598, NNU-T

H63
Hamilton, Richard.
The development of the American
political economy: a reading
list for radicals, compiled by
Professor Richard Hamilton,
James O'Brien [and] Peter Wiley.
[Madison, Wis.,] Madison Stu-
dents for a Democratic Society

[196]
13p.
Cover title.
1. U.S.--History--Bibl.
2. U.S.--Pol. & govt.--Bibl.
3. U.S.--Econ. condit--Bibl.
I. O'Brien, James, jt. auth.
II. Wiley, Peter, jt. auth.
III. Students for a Democratic
Society, Madison, Wis.
WHi-L

H64
Hammer & Steel.
Purge the ranks! Clarify the
program! [Mattapan, Mass.,
1969]
4p. 22cm.
Caption title.
1. Progressive Labor Party.
2. Students for a Democratic
Society.
WHi-L

H65
Hampton, Fred, 1948-1969.
You've got to make a commitment.
[Chicago, Black Panther Party?
1969?]
48p. illus. 22cm.
1. Negroes--Civil rights.
2. Black Panther Party.
KU-RH

H66
Handbook on ecological living,
    or how you can help. [Cam-
    bridge, Mass., American
    Friends Service Committee,
    New England Regional Office,
    196]
10p. 28cm.
Cover title.
1. Environmental policy.
I. Friends, Society of. Ameri-
can Friends Service Committee.
New England Regional Office.
KU-RH

H67
Hanley, George.
Bus stop: Alice's restaurant
revisited. Ann Arbor, Radical
Education Project [196]
folder (6p) 22cm.
Caption title.

Reprinted from Connections.
1. Military service, Compulsory.
I. Radical Education Project.
MoU

H68
Hansen, Beatrice, 1926-1969.
    A political biography of Walter
    Reuther: the record of an op-
    portunist. [1st. ed. New York,
    Merit Publishers, 1969]
    23p. 22cm.
    Cover title.
    1. Reuther, Walter Philip, 1907-
    1970. I. Merit Publishers.
    KU-RH, CU-B, WHi-L

H69
Hansen, Joseph.
    In defense of the Cuban revolu-
    tion: an answer to the State
    Department and Theodore Draper.
    [New York, Pioneer Publishers,
    1961.]
    30p. 20cm.
    1. Cuba--Pol. & govt.--1933-
    1959. 2. Draper, Theodore.
    3. U.S. Dept. of State.
    I. Pioneer Publishers.
    MiU, TNJ

H70
Hansen, Joseph,
    The "population explosion"; how
    socialist view it. [2d. ed.
    New York, Pathfinder Press,
    1970]
    47p. 22cm.
    Cover title.
    1. Population. 2. Socialism.
    I. Pathfinder Press.
    KU-RH

H71
Hansen, Joseph.
    The Socialist Workers Party;
    what it is--what it stands for.
    [Rev. ed. New York] Pioneer
    Publishers [1958]
    54p. 17cm.
    Cover title.
    1. Socialist Workers Party.
    I. Pioneer Publishers.
    KU-RH, LNHT, WHi-L

H72
Hansen, Joseph.
    The theory of the Cuban revolu-
    tion. [New York] Pioneer Pub-
    lishers [1962]
    30p. 22cm.
    1. Cuba--Pol. & govt.--1933-
    1959. I. Pioneer Publishers.
    TxU, DPU, MiU, NUC 64-17829

H73
Hansen, Joseph.
    Too many babies? [A Marxist
    answer to some frightening
    questions] New York, Pioneer
    Publishers [1961?]
    48p. 21cm.
    1. Population. 2. Socialism.
    I. Pioneer Publishers.
    OU, MoU

H74
Hansen, Joseph.
    Trotskyism and the Cuban
    revolution--an answer to Hoy.
    [New York, Pioneer Publishers,
    1962]
    14p. 21cm.
    Reprinted from The Militant,
    Oct, 1962.
    1. Communism--Cuba. 2. Cuba--
    Pol. & govt.--1959-
    3. Hoy (Havana) I. Pioneer
    Publishers.
    CSt-H, MiU, NUC 67-90267

H75
Hansen, Joseph.
    The truth about Cuba. New York,
    Pioneer Publishers [1960?]
    48p. 21cm.
    Reprinted from The Militant,
    May 9 to Aug. 22, 1960.
    1. Cuba--History--1933-1959.
    I. Pioneer Publishers.
    KU-RH, MiU, ICU, MH, NcU,
    CLSU, DLC 60-51926

H76
Hanson, Haldore.
    Partnership for freedom; pro-
    posals for world economic growth.
    Washington, UDA Educational Fund
    [1955]

52p. 23cm.
Distributed by Americans for
Democratic Action.
1. U.S.--Foreign policy.
2. Underdeveloped areas.
3. Russia--Foreign policy.
I. Union for Democratic Action.
Educational Fund. II. Americans
for Democratic Action.
KU-H

H77
Hanson, Haldore.
  Peace is positive. Washington
  [Union for Democratic Action,
  1956]
  38p. 22cm.
  1. Peace. 2. Russia--For. rel.
  --U.S. 3. U.S.--For. Rel.--
  Russia. I. Union for Democra-
  tic Action.
  WHi-A

H78
Hanson, Mary.
  The black colony in America, by
  Mary Hanson [and others. Chi-
  cago, Students for a Democratic
  Society, 196]
  12p.
  Cover title.
  1. Negroes--Civil rights.
  I. Students for a Democratic
  Society.
  WHi-L

H79
Hanson, Mary.
  Eritrea: the hidden war in East
  Africa. [Detroit, Radical Edu-
  cation Project, 1970?]
  9p. 22cm.
  Cover title.
  Reprinted from Pacific Research
  & World Empire Telegram.
  1. Ethiopia--Pol. & govt.
  2. Guerrillas--Ethiopia.
  3. Eritrea. I. Radical Educa-
  tion Project.
  KU-RH

H80
Harawitz, Elly.
  The welfare rights organization.
  [Oakland, Calif.? 196]
  7p. 28cm.

Cover title.
1. Public welfare.
WHi-A

H81
Harding, Jim.
  Canada's Indians: a powerless
  minority. [Toronto] Student
  Union for Peace Action [196]
  11p. 28cm.
  Cover title.
  1. Indians of North America--
  Canada. I. Student Union for
  Peace Action.
  WHi-A

H82
Harding, Jim.
  The strike at SFU. Drawings by
  Jerry Fuoco. [n.p., 1969]
  [8]p. illus. 28cm.
  Cover title.
  1. Student movements--San Fran-
  cisco. 2. San Francisco. Uni-
  versity. I. Fuoco, Jerry.
  NNU-T

H83
Harding, Jim.
  Toward a non-violent political
  philosophy. Toronto, Research,
  Information and Publications
  Project, Student Union for Peace
  Action, 1965.
  21p. 28cm.
  Cover title.
  1. Nonviolence. 2. Student
  Union for Peace Action.
  WHi-A

H84
Harding, Nina.
  Interrelationship of the black
  struggle and the woman question.
  Seattle, Radical Women [1970?]
  7 [1] leaf. 28cm.
  Caption title.
  At head of title: Discussion
  draft, Radical Women's Confer-
  ence, University of Washington,
  Feb. 23, 1970.
  1. Negroes--Civil rights.
  2. Women--Rights of women.
  I. Radical Women
  WHi-L

H85
Harlem Committee for the Panther
    21.
  The people will free the Panther
  21. [New York, 197]
  16 leaves. 28cm.
  Cover title.
  1. Black Panther Party.
  2. New York (State)--Race
  question.
  NNU-T

H86
Harlem Defense Council.
  Police terror in Harlem. [New
  York, CERGE, 196]
  12p. illus. 22cm.
  Cover title.
  1. Negroes--Harlem, New York
  (City) 2. Police--New York
  (State)--Harlem, New York (City)
  I. Committee to Defend Resist-
  ance to Ghetto Life.
  CU-B, MiU, KU-RH

H87
Harman, Chris.
  Party and class. [New York,
  International Socialists, 196]
  28p. 22cm.
  Reprinted from International
  Socialism.
  1. Socialism. 2. Political
  parties. 3. Social classes.
  I. International Socialists.
  KU-RH

H88
Harper, Kenneth.
  Inclusion and exclusion and the
  common denominator. [Seattle?
  Seattle Youth for Peace in Vietnam? 196]
  2p. 28cm.
  Caption title.
  1. Peace--Societies, etc.
  2. Vietnamese conflict, 1961-
  1975. I. Seattle Youth for
  Peace in Vietnam.
  WHi-A

H89
Harrington, Michael, 1928-
  American power in the twentieth
  century. New York, League for
  Industrial Democracy, 1957.

55p. 22cm.
Reprinted from Dissent.
1. Power (Social science)
2. U.S.--Soc. condit.--1945-
      3. U.S.--Econ. condit.--
1945-   I. League for Industrial Democracy.
NBuU, WaU, MiU, WHi-L, NUC 69-
73645

H90
Harrington, Michael, 1928-
  The American social order and
  American foreign policy. New
  York, Young People's Socialist
  League [1966?]
  12p.
  1. Social classes. 2. U.S.--
  Foreign policy. 3. U.S.--Soc.
  condit. I. Young People's
  Socialist League.
  WHi-L

H91
Harrington, Michael, 1928-
  The crisis in the German social
  democracy. New York, Young
  People's Socialist League [196]
  18p. 22cm.
  Cover title.
  1. Socialism in Germany (Fed-
  eral Republic, 1949-   )
  2. Germany (Federal Republic,
  1949-   )--Pol. & govt.
  I. Young People's Socialist
  League.
  CU-B

H92
Harrington, Michael, 1928-
  Does the peace movement need the
  communists? [Berkeley, Calif.,
  World Without War Council,
  1965?]
  [6]p.
  Reprinted from the Village
  Voice, Nov. 11, 1965.
  1. Vietnamese conflict, 1961-
  1975. 2. Communism. I. World
  Without War Council.
  WHi-L, NUC 69-91276

H93
Harrington, Michael, 1928-
  The economics of racism. [New
  York, Congress of Racial

Equality, 1963?]
6p. 28cm.
1. Negroes--Civil rights.
I. Congress of Racial Equality.
CU-B

H94
Harrington, Michael, 1928-
The new lost generation: jobless
youth. [New York, League for
Industrial Democracy, c1964]
[4]p. illus. 28cm.
Caption title.
Reprinted from New York Times
Magazine, May 24, 1964.
1. Youth. I. League for Indus-
trial Democracy.
KU-RH

H95
Harrington, Michael, 1928-
Oil and blood in Middle East.
[New York, Youth Committee for
Peace and Democracy in Middle
East, 1970?]
[4]p. illus. 22cm.
Cover title.
Reprinted from New America,
Feb. 26, 1970.
1. Near East--Pol. & govt.
2. Israel. I. Youth for Peace
and Democracy in the Middle
East.
KU-RH

H96
Harrington, Michael, 1928-
The politics of poverty. New
York, League for Industrial
Democracy, 1965.
24p.
1. Poverty. I. League for In-
dustrial Democracy.
NNC, CtY, N, OrU, NcD, NUC 67-
18163

H97
Harrington, Michael, 1928-
Poverty and politics. [n.p.,
Students for a Democratic Society? 196]
7p. 28cm. (Working paper no. 1)
Speech delivered at a Conference
on Poverty in Plenty at George-
town University, Jan. 23, 1964.
1. Poverty. 2. U.S.--Pol. &

govt.--1963-   I. Students
for a Democratic Society.
WHi-A

H98
Harrington, Michael, 1928-
The social-industrial complex.
[New York, League for Industrial
Democracy, 1968?]
13p. 23cm. (Looking forward
no. 10)
Cover title.
1. Corporations. 2. Business a
and politics. 3. Social change.
I. League for Industrial Demo-
cracy.
WHi-L, NNU-T, KU-RH, NUC 70-
103744

H99
Harrington, Michael, 1928-
Why I am a democratic socialist.
[New York] Young People's Soc-
ialist League [1967?]
15p. 23cm.
Speech delivered to the Young
People's Socialist League, Har-
vard-Radcliffe chapter, April
1967.
1. Socialism. I. Young People's
Socialist League.
KU-RH

H100
Harris, David.
On the necessity of revolution.
[Palo Alto, Calif., Institute
for the Study of Nonviolence,
1970?]
[8]p. illus. 28cm.
Cover title.
1. Revolutions. 2. Love.
I. Institute for the Study of
Nonviolence.
KU-RH

H101
Harris, Jon.
The Vietnam work-in II [by Jon
Harris and Jared Israel. n.p.,
1968]
[8]p. 28cm.
Caption title.
1. Vietnamese conflict, 1961-
1975. I. Israel, Jared, jt. auth.
WHi-L

H102
Harris, Lement.
    From peasantry to power farming:
    the story of Soviet agriculture.
    New York, International Publish-
    ers [c1968]
    63p. illus. 20cm.
    1. Agriculture--Russia.
    I. International Publishers.
    KU-RH

H103
Harris, Lement.
    From peasantry to power farming:
    the story of Soviet agriculture.
    [New York] National Council of
    American-Soviet Friendship,
    1968.
    63p. illus.
    1. Agriculture--Russia.
    I. National Council of American-
    Soviet Friendship.
    MiU

H104
Harris, Marvin.
    Portugal's African "wards": a
    first-hand report on labor and
    education in Mocambique. [New
    York] American Committee on
    Africa [1960]
    36p. 22cm. (Africa today pam-
    phlets: 2)
    Cover title.
    1. Labor and laboring classes--
    Mocambique. 2. Education--Mo-
    cambique. 3. Mocambique--Soc.
    condit. I. American Committee
    on Africa.
    MiU

H105
Harris, Mary, 1830-1930.
    Thoughts of Mother Jones, com-
    piled from her writings and
    speeches. [Huntington, W.V.,
    Appalachian Movement Press,
    1970]
    [8]p. 22cm.
    Cover title.
    1. Miners--Appalachian Mount-
    ains. 2. Capitalism. I. Appa-
    lachian Movement Press.
    MiU

H106
Harris, William Henry.
    Morality, moralism and Vietnam;
    analyzing the danger that ra-
    tionalization of 'why we are
    there' may lead to weakening of
    the nation's moral fiber.
    [Woodmont, Conn., Promoting En-
    during Peace, c1965.]
    [2]p. 28cm.
    Cover title.
    1. Vietnamese conflict, 1961-
    1975. I. Promoting Enduring
    Peace.
    KU-RH

H107
Hart Davalos, Armando.
    Education since the revolution.
    New York, Fair Play for Cuba
    Committee, 1963.
    10p. 28cm.
    1. Education--Cuba. I. Fair
    Play for Cuba Committee.
    FU, NcD, NUC 65-36873

H108
Hartman, Leon.
    The scandal of Consumers Union.
    4th ed. [n.p.] c1962.
    100p. illus. 17cm.
    Cover title.
    1. Consumer protection.
    2. Consumers Union.
    KU-RH

H109
Hartmire, Wayne C.
    Background information on the
    boycott of California table
    grapes. [n.p., 1968]
    [1] leaf. 28cm.
    Caption title.
    1. United Farm Workers Organi-
    zing Committee. 2. Agriculture
    laborers--Calif.--Delano.
    KU-RH

H110
Hartmire, Wayne C.
    The Delano grape strike: the
    farm worker's struggle for self
    determination. [Los Angeles,
    California Migrant Ministry,
    1969]

1969]
folder. 28cm.
Caption title.
1. Agriculture laborers--Calif.
--Delano. 2. Mexicans in the
U.S. 3. Chavez, Cesar Estrada.
4. United Farm Workers Organi-
zing Committee. I. California
Migrant Ministry.
KU-RH

H111
Harvey, Arthur.
Theory and practice of civil
disobedience. Canterbury, N.H.
[1967]
29p. 28cm.
Cover title.
1. Government, Resistance to.
KU-RH, MoU

H112
Harvey, Arthur.
Theory and practice of civil
disobedience. [Raymond, N.H.,
1961]
27p. 28cm.
1. Government, Resistance to.
NhU

H113
Harvey, Roy.
People's war in Angola; report
on the first Eastern Regional
Conference of the MPLA. [Oak-
land, 1970]
28p. illus. 22cm.
Cover title.
1. Angola--Pol. & govt.
2. Guerrillas--Angola.
3. Movimento Popular de Libertacao de Angola.
MiU

H114
Haslach, Henry.
U.S. policy toward China since
WW II. [Ann Arbor, Radical
Education Project, 196]
8p. 28cm. (Radical Education
Project study guide series)
Cover title.
1. U.S.--Relations (general)
with China (People's Republic
of China, 1949-   ) 2. China
(People's Republic of China,

1949-   )--Relations (general)
with the U.S. I. Radical Education Project.
MiU-H

H115
Hass, Eric.
The Americanism of socialism.
New York, New York Labor News
Co., 1962.
45p. 19cm.
"Tenth printing."
1. Socialism. I. New York Labor
News Co.
CU-B, KU-RH

H116
Hass, Eric.
Capitalism: breeder of race pre-
judice. New York, New York
Labor News Co., 1964.
46p. 19cm.
"First printing 1961."
1. Negroes--Civil rights.
2. Socialism. 3. Capitalism.
I. New York Labor News Co.
WHi-L, NUC 65-96679

H117
Hass, Eric.
Dave Beck, labor merchant; the
case history of a labor leader.
New York, New York Labor News
Co., 1955.
30p. 19cm.
1. Beck, Dave, 1894-
2. International Brotherhood
of Teamsters, Chauffeurs, Warehousemen and Helpers of America.
3. Labor and laboring classes.
I. New York Labor News Co.
DLC 55-13935

H118
Hass, Eric.
Militarism: labor's foes. [New
York, New York Labor News Co.,
1961]
16p. 18cm.
Cover title.
"Fourth printing."
1. Militariasm. 2. Labor and
laboring classes. 3. U.S.--
Military policy. I. New York
Labor News Co.
KU-RH

H119
Hass, Eric.
  Militarism: labor's foe. [New
  York] Socialist Labor Party
  [1955]
  16p. 19cm.
  Cover title.
  1. Militarism. 2. Labor and
  laboring classes. 3. Socialism.
  I. Socialist Labor Party.
  NN

H120
Hass, Eric.
  The reactionary right. New York,
  New York Labor News Co., 1963.
  78p. illus. 19cm.
  1. Fascism. 2. Militarism.
  I. New York Labor News Co.
  KU-RH, DLC 63-26075

H121
Hass, Eric.
  Socialism answers anti-semitism.
  New York, New York Labor News
  Co., 1960.
  48p. 19cm.
  1. Socialism. 2. Antisemitism.
  I. New York Labor News Co.
  KU-RH

H122
Hass, Eric.
  Socialist industrial unionism;
  the workers' power. Rev. ed.
  New York, New York Labor News
  Co., 1960.
  vi, 55p. 18cm.
  Thirteenth printing.
  1. Socialism. 2. Labor and
  laboring classes. I. New York
  Labor News Co.
  KU-RH

H123
Hass, Eric.
  Socialist industrial unionism;
  the workers' power. Rev. ed.
  New York, New York Labor News
  Co., 1967.
  vi, 55p.
  1. Socialism. I. New York Labor
  News Co.
  CU-B, MH-PA, NN

H124
Hass, Eric.
  What workers should know about
  automation...and what employers
  don't tell them, by Eric Hass
  and Stephen Emery. New York,
  New York Labor News Co., 1956.
  62p.
  1. Automation. I. Emery, Stephen, jt. auth. II. New York
  Labor News Co.
  CLU, LC, MiU, NN, WHi-L, KU-J

H125
Hassler, Alfred.
  Catonsville and Milwaukee.
  [Nyack, N.Y.? Fellowship Pub-
  lications? 196]
  [1] leaf. 28cm.
  Caption title.
  "An editorial in the November
  Fellowship."
  1. Government, Resistance to.
  2. Pacifism. 3. Catonsville
  (Md.) Nine. I. Fellowship
  Publications.
  KU-RH

H126
Hawaii Resistance.
  A chronology of the Crossroads
  sanctuary. [Honolulu, 196]
  8p. 28cm.
  Cover title.
  1. Vietnamese conflict, 1961-
  1975. 2. Desertion, Military.
  CU-B

H127
Hawaii Youth Congress, University
  of Hawaii, 1970.
  [Report of the Hawaii Youth
  Congress, 1970; an aquarian
  perspective on the year 2000.
  Honolulu? Vanguard Press, 1970]
  [28]p. illus. 24x25cm.
  1. Youth--Political activity.
  I. Vanguard Press.
  KU-RH

H128
Hayden, Thomas.
  All for Vietnam. [Ithaca, N.Y.,
  Glad Day Press, 1970?]

6p. illus. 28cm.
Caption title.
Reprinted from Ramparts, Sept.
1970.
1. Vietnamese conflict, 1961-
1975. I. Glad Day Press.
NNU-T

H129
Hayden, Thomas.
  Civil rights in the South: a dis-
cussion paper, by Tom Hayden and
Sandra Cason. [Ann Arbor] Voice
Political Party, 1962.
6 leaves. 28cm.
Cover title.
1. Negroes--Civil rights.
2. Negroes--Southern States.
I. Voice Political Party-
Students for a Democratic
Party, Ann Arbor. II. Cason,
Sandra, jt. auth.
MiU

H130
Hayden, Thomas.
  Civil rights in the South: a
discussion paper, by Tom Haydon
[sic] and Sandra Cason. [New
York?] Distributed by Students
for a Democratic Society for
the Liberal Study Group [196]
6 [1]p. 28cm.
Cover title.
1. Negroes--Civil rights.
2. Negroes--Southern States.
I. Students for a Democratic
Society. II. Liberal Study
Group. III. Cason, Sandra,
jt. auth.
NNU-T

H131
Hayden, Thomas.
  Civil rights in the United
States. New York, Students
for a Democratic Society [196]
4p. 28cm.
Cover title.
1. Negroes--Civil rights.
I. Students for a Democratic
Society.
WHi-L, MiU

H132
Hayden, Thomas.

The Dixiecrats and changing
southern power from Bourbon to
Bourbon [n.p.] 1963.
11 leaves.
Cover title.
Prepared for the Spring 1963
Conference of Student Nonviol-
ent Coordinating Committee in
Atlanta, Ga.
1. Democratic Party. 2. South-
ern States--Pol. & govt.
I. Student Nonviolent Coordina-
ting Committee.
WHi-L

H133
Hayden, Thomas.
  An interracial movement of the
poor? By Tom Hayden and Carl
Wittman. New York, Students
for a Democratic Society and its
Economic Research and Action
Project [196]
26p. 28cm.
Cover title.
1. Poor. 2. Negroes--Civil
rights. 3. Minorities. 4. Mex-
icans in the U.S. 5. Puerto
Ricans in the U.S. I. Wittam,
Carl, jt. auth. II. Students
for a Democratic Society.
Economic Research and Action
Project.
MiU, WHi-L, WHi-A, CU-B

H134
Hayden, Thomas.
  Liberal analysis and federal
power. New York, Students for
a Democratic Society [1964?]
[6]p.
Cover title.
1. Liberalism. 2. Negroes--
Civil rights. 3. Southern
States--Pol. & govt. 4. Power
(Social science) 5. Federal-
State controversies. I. Stu-
dents for a Democratic Society.
CU-B, WHi-L, NUC 69-62818

H135
Hayden, Thomas.
  Newark community union, by Tom
Hayden and Carl Wittman. New
York, Students for a Democratic
Society and its Economic Re-

search and Action Project [196]
7p. 28cm.
Cover title.
1. Newark, N.J.--Soc. condit.
2. Students for a Democratic
Society. 3. Poor--Newark, N.J.
4. Negroes--Newark, N.J.
I. Wittman, Carl, jt. auth.
II. Students for a Democratic
Society. Economic Research and
Action Project.
WHi-A, CU-B

H136
Hayden, Thomas.
Organizing the poor. Ann Arbor,
Students for a Democratic Soc-
iety [196]
5 leaves. 28cm.
Caption title.
1. Poor--Newark, N.J. 2. New-
ark, N.J.--Soc. condit.
I. Students for a Democratic
Society.
KU-RH, WHi-A

H137
Hayden, Thomas.
The peace movement: new possi-
bilities? By Tom Hayden and
Richard Flacks. New York, Stu-
dents for a Democratic Society
and Peace Research and Education
Project [196]
9 [1]p. 28cm.
Cover title.
1. Peace. I. Students for a
Democratic Society. Peace Re-
search and Education Project.
II. Flacks, Richard.
NNU-T, WHi-A, MiU

H138
Hayden, Thomas.
Perspectives on Democratic
National Convention [by] Tom
Hayden [and] Rennie Davis. [n.
p., 1968?]
17p. 28cm.
Cover title.
At head of title: rough draft,
not for publication.
1. Vietnamese conflict, 1961-
1975. 2. Democratic Party.
National Convention, Chicago,
1968. I. Davis, Rennard, jt.

auth.
WHi-L

H139
Hayden, Thomas.
Politics '65 [by] Thomas Hayden
[and] Eugene Feingold. [Chi-
cago, Students for a Democratic
Society, 196]
13p. 28cm.
Cover title.
1. U.S.--Pol. & govt.--1963-
          I. Feingold, Eugene, jt.
auth. II. Students for a Democratic Society.
WHi-L

H140
Hayden, Thomas.
The power of the Dixiecrats.
Nashville, Southern Student
Organizing Committee [196]
11p. 28cm.
Cover title.
1. Democratic Party--Southern
States. 2. Southern States--
Pol. & govt. I. Southern Stu-
dent Organizing Committee.
MoU

H141
Hayden, Thomas.
The power of the Dixiecrats.
New York, Students for a Demo-
cratic Society [1963?]
8 [3]p. 28cm.
Cover title.
Reprinted from New University
Thought.
Paper delivered to the SNCC
Conference in Atlanta, spring
1963.
1. Democratic Party--Southern
States. 2. Southern States--
Pol. & govt. I. Students for a
Democratic Society.
CU-B, WHi-L, NUC 69-61706

H142
Hayden, Thomas.
Report on McComb, Mississippi.
[n.p., 196]
15 leaves. 36cm.
Caption title.
1. Student Nonviolent Coordinating Committee. 2. McComb,

Miss.--Race question. 3. Negroes
--McComb, Miss.
WHi-A

H143
Hayden, Thomas.
  Revolution in Mississippi.
  [Introduction by Charles F.
  McDew. Foreward by Robert A.
  Haber and Harry Fleischman] New
  York, Students for a Democratic
  Society [c1962]
  28p. 22cm.
  1. Mississippi--Race question.
  2. Negroes--Mississippi.
  3. Student Nonviolent Coordina-
  ting Committee. 4. Moses,
  Robert. I. McDew, Charles F.
  II. Haber, Robert Alan.
  III. Fleischman, Harry.
  IV. Students for a Democratic
  Society.
  WHi-A, IU, IaU, OrU, NcD,
  NUC 63-18787

H144
Hayden, Thomas.
  Student social action. Chicago,
  Students for a Democratic Soc-
  iety [196]
  11p. 28cm.
  Cover title.
  1. Student movements. 2. Soc-
  ial change. I. Students for a
  Democratic Society.
  CU-B

H145
Hayden, Thomas.
  Student social action. Chicago,
  Students for a Democratic Soc-
  iety [196]
  [12]p. 28cm.
  Cover title.
  Printed by KFP publishing house,
  Lawrence, Kan.
  1. Student movements. 2. Soc-
  ial change. I. Students for a
  Democratic Society.
  WHi-A

H146
Hayden, Thomas.
  Student social action. Nashville, Southern Student Organizing Committee [196]

15p. 28cm.
  Cover title.
  1. Student movements. 2. Social change. I. Southern Student Organizing Committee.
  NNU-T

H147
Hayden, Thomas.
  Student social action. New
  York, Students for a Democratic
  Society [196]
  10p. 28cm.
  Cover title.
  1. Student movements. 2. Uni-
  versities and colleges.
  3. Education. I. Students for
  a Democratic Society.
  WHi-L, CU-B

H148
Hayden, Thomas.
  Student social action; from a
  speech delivered at Challenge,
  University of Michigan, March
  1962. New York, Students for a
  Democratic Society [196]
  [12]p. 28cm.
  Cover title.
  1. Student movements. I. Stu-
  dents for a Democratic Society.
  NNU-T

H149
Hayden, Thomas.
  Student social action: from
  liberation to community. [n.p.,
  1967]
  19p.
  Transcription of a talk given
  at the University of Michigan,
  spring 1962.
  I. Student movements.
  WHi-L

H150
Hayden, Thomas.
  Students and social action. New
  York, Students for a Democratic
  Society [196]
  10p. 28cm.
  Cover title.
  1. Student movements. 2. Social
  change. I. Students for a De-
  mocratic Society.
  KU-RH

H151
Hayden, Thomas.
  Who are the student boat-rockers?
  [n.p., c1961]
  Reprinted from Mademoiselle.
  1. Student movements.
  WHi-A

H152
Hayden, Thomas.
  Youth and conservatism: outline
  of an SDS pamphlet. [New York,
  Students for a Democratic Soc-
  iety, 1961]
  3 leaves. 28cm.
  Caption title.
  1. Conservatism. 2. Youth--
  Political activity. I. Students
  for a Democratic Society.
  WHi-A

H153
Hays, Samuel P.
  Municipal reform in the progressive era: whose class interest?
  Boston, New England Free Press
  [196]
  [148]-171p. 21cm.
  1. Municipal government. 2. Pro-
  gressivism (U.S. politics)
  3. Social classes. I. New England Free Press.
  MiU, KU-RH

H154
Healy, Dorothy.
  A communist speaks at a teach-
  in on Viet-Nam. [Los Angeles,
  Southern California Communist
  Party, 1966?]
  15p. 22x10cm.
  1. Vietnamese conflict, 1961-
  1975. I. Communist Party of the
  United States of America, Sou-
  thern California.
  CU-B, WHi-L, H157

H155
Healy, Dorothy.
  A communist talks to students.
  [Los Angeles, Southern California Communist Party, 1964]
  14p. 22x10cm.
  Speeches delivered at the University of California, Los Angeles; University of California,

Riverside; Cal-Tech and Occiden-
tal College.
1. Communism. I. Communist
Party of the United States of
America, Southern California.
MiEM, CU-B, NUC 67-102714

H156
Hearst, William Randolph.
  We stand for peaceful coexistence, interviews with N.S. Khrushchev, N.A. Bulganin [and] G.
  K. Zhukov, by William Randolph
  Hearst, Kingsburg Smith and
  Frank Conniff. New York, New
  Century Publishers, 1955.
  31p. 19cm.
  1. Russia--For. rel.--U.S.
  2. Peace. I. New Century Publishers. II. Khrushchev, Nikita Sergeevich, 1894-
  KU-J

H157
Hefner, William K.
  A new kind of politics, by
  William K. Hefner and Marshall
  R. Kaplan. [Greenfield, Mass.,
  Political Action for Peace,
  1962?]
  6p. 28cm.
  1. Peace. 2. Politics, Practical. I. Kaplan, Marshall R.,
  jt. auth. I. Political Action
  for Peace.
  WHi-A

H158
Heifitz, Robert.
  Eastern Kentucky: a draft program. New York, Students for a
  Democratic Society and its Economic Research and Action Project [196]
  6p. 28cm.
  1. Kentucky--Econ. condit.
  2. Coal mines and mining--Ken-
  tucky. I. Students for a Democratic Society. Economic Research and Action Project.
  MiU, WHi-L

H159
Heifitz, Robert.
  Proposals for an economic rede-
  velopment in eastern Kentucky.

[Revised and edited by ERAP
staff for the purposes of the
Hazard Conference. n.p., 1964?]
5p. 28cm.
1. Kentucky--Econ. condit.
I. Students for a Democratic
Society. Economic Research and
Action Project.
MiU

H160
Heilbroner, Robert L.
  Making a rational foreign pol-
  icy now. [Woodmont, Promoting
  Enduring Peace, 1968]
  64-71p. 28cm.
  Caption title.
  Reprinted from Harper's Maga-
  zine, Sept. 1968.
  1. U.S.--Foreign policy.
  I. Promoting Enduring Peace.
  KU-RH

H161
Heisler, Francis.
  The new conscientious objector.
  [Des Moines, American Friends
  Service Committee, 1968?]
  [4]p. 28cm.
  Caption title.
  Reprinted from Liberation, Jan.
  1967.
  1. Conscientious objectors.
  I. Friends, Society of. Ameri-
  can Friends Service Committee.
  KU-RH

H162
Heller, Abraham Aaron, 1874-
  American scientist no. 996: the
  story of Morton Sobell. [New
  York, 1955]
  23p. 22cm.
  1. Sobell, Morton. 2. Subversive activities.
  NH, NN

H163
Help us to organize for justice!
    [New York] American Service-
    men's Union [1969?]
  [4]p. 22cm.
  Caption title.
  1. U.S. Army--Military life.
  2. Soldiers. I. American Servicemen's Union.
  KU-RH

H164
Henig, Peter.
  Selective service system or, the
  manpower channelers. [Ithaca,
  N.Y., Glad Day Press, 1967?]
  [8]p. illus. 28cm.
  Caption title.
  Reprinted from New Left Notes,
  Jan. 20, 1967.
  1. U.S. Selective Service Sys-
  tem. 2. Military Service, Com-
  pulsory. I. Glad Day Press.
  MoU, KU-RH

H165
Henig, Peter.
  Selective service system or,
  the manpower channelers. Nashville, Southern Student Organizing Committee [196]
  13p. 28cm.
  1. U.S. Selective Service System. 2. Military service, Compulsory. I. Southern Student
  Organizing Committee.
  MoU, MiU

H166
Henner, Peter.
  Towards a radical student move-
  ment for the seventies. [New
  York, 1970?]
  [6] leaves. 36cm.
  Caption title.
  1. Student movements.
  KU-RH

H167
Henri, Ernst.
  The strategy of revenge; the
  new Blitz plan of the German
  General Staff. [New York, New
  Century Publishers, 1961]
  47p.
  1. Militarism--Germany (Federal
  Republic, 1949-   ) I. New
  Century Publishers.
  InU, KU-RH, KU-J, NUC 69-127686

H168
Henry, Jules.
  Capital's last frontier. [Bos-
  ton, New England Free Press,
  196]
  [4]p. 28cm.
  Caption title.

Reprinted from The Nation; Ap.
25, 1966.
1. U.S.--Foreign policy.
2. Vietnamese conflict, 1961-
1975. I. New England Free Press.
MoU, KU-RH

H169
Henry, Lyndon.
  A perspective for the YPSL left
wing. [New York? Young People's
Socialist League, 196]
5p. 28cm.
Caption title.
1. Socialism. 2. Youth--Politi-
cal activity. I. Young People's
Socialist League.
KU-RH

H170
Hentoff, Nat.
  On bringing democracy to Ameri-
ca. Woodmont, Conn., Promoting
Enduring Peace [c1969]
[4]p. 28cm.
Caption title.
Reprinted from Evergreen Review,
Aug. 1969.
1. Democracy. 2. Negroes--
Education. 3. Education--New
York (State)--New York (City)
I. Promoting Enduring Peace.
KU-RH

Herber, Lewis.
  see also
Bookchin, Murray.

H171
Herber, Lewis.
  Ecology and revolutionary
thought [by] Murray Bookchin
[pseud.] With the Ecology
Action East manifesto, and Toward an ecological solution.
[New York, Times Change Press,
1970]
63p. illus. 18cm.
1. Ecology. 2. Radicalism.
I. Times Change Press.
CtU

H172
Herman, Edward S.
  How to coo like a dove while
fighting to win: the public

relations on the Nixon policy
in Vietnam, by Edward S. Herman
and Richard B. Du Boff. 2d. ed.,
rev. [New York, Clergy and Laymen Concerned About Vietnam]
1969.
7 [1]p. 28cm.
Caption title.
1. Vietnamese conflict, 1961-
1975. I. Clergy and Laymen
Concerned About Vietnam.
II. Du Boff, Richard B., jt.
auth.
KU-RH

H173
Hersh, Barry.
  Resolution on political action,
by Barry Hersh, Ian McMahan
[and] Tom Barton. [n.p., Stu-
dent Peace Union, 1964?]
4p. 28cm.
Caption title.
1. Politics, Practical.
2. Peace. 3. Elections.
I. Student Peace Union.
II. McMahan, Ian, jt. auth.
III. Barton, Tom, jt. auth.
CU-B

H174
Hersh, Seymour.
  On uncovering the nerve gas
coverup. [Woodmont, Conn.,
Promoting Enduring Peace, 1969]
[3]p. 28cm.
Cover title.
Reprinted from Ramparts, 1969.
1. Gases, Asphyxiating and
poisonous--War use. 2. Biolo-
gical warfare. 3. Chemical
warfare. I. Promoting Enduring
Peace.
KU-RH

H175
Hersh, Seymour.
  Silent death. Woodmont, Conn.,
Promoting Enduring Peace [196]
[4]p. 28cm. (No. 144)
Caption title.
Reprinted from The Progressive,
May 1969.
1. Biological warfare. 2. Chem-
ical warfare. I. Promoting
Enduring Peace.
KU-RH

H176
Hertz, W.H.
  Where we stand on labor.
  Detroit, News & Letters [196 ?]
  7p. 28cm.
  Cover title.
  At head of title: draft chapter.
  1. Labor and laboring classes.
  2. Socialism. I. News &
  Letters.
  MiU

H177
Hicks, Judy.
  An anthropoligical approach to
  the position of women. [Louis-
  ville, Southern Conference Educational Fund, 1970?]
  folder. 22x9cm.
  Cover title.
  1. Woman--History and condition
  of women. I. Southern Conference Educational Fund.
  KU-RH

H178
Higginson, Thomas Wentworth.
  Nat Turner. [Los Angeles,
  Vanguard Society of America,
  1962]
  29p.
  Cover title.
  1. Negroes. 2. Turner, Nat.
  I. Vanguard Society of America.
  MiU

H179
Hill, Herbert, 1924-
  The ILGWU--fact or fiction.
  [n.p., NAACP? 196]
  23p. 22cm.
  Cover title.
  At head of title: a reply to
  Gus Hall.
  Reprinted from New Politics,
  1963.
  1. International Ladies Garment
  Workers' Union. 2. Negroes--
  Employment. 3. Puerto Ricans
  in the U.S. I. National Assoc-
  iation for the Advancement of
  Colored People.
  CU-B, WHi-L, MiU

H180
Hill, Herbert, 1924-

  The ILGWU today--the decay of a
  labor union. New York, National
  Association for the Advancement
  of Colored People [196]
  14p. 22cm.
  Cover title.
  Reprinted from New Politics.
  1. Negroes--Employment.
  2. Puerto Ricans in New York.
  3. International Ladies Garment
  Workers' Union. I. National
  Association for the Advancement
  of Colored People.
  WHi-L, MiU

H181
Hill, Herbert, 1924-
  Labor unions and the negro.
  [New York, National Association
  for the Advancement of Colored
  People, 1959]
  [9]p.
  Cover title.
  Reprinted from Commentary.
  1. Negroes--Employment.
  2. Trade-unions. I. National
  Association for the Advancement
  of Colored People.
  MiU

H182
Hills, Herbert, 1924-
  Racial inequality in employment:
  the patterns of discrimination.
  [New York, National Association
  for the Advancement of Colored
  People, 1965?]
  18p.
  1. Negroes--Employment.
  I. National Association for the
  Advancement of Colored People.
  WHi-L

H183
Hill, Herbert, 1924-
  The racial practices of organized labor in the age of Gompers
  and after. New York, National
  Association for the Advancement
  of Colored People [c1965]
  23p. 22cm.
  Cover title.
  Reprinted from New Politics.
  1. Trade-unions--History.
  2. Negroes--Employment--History.
  I. National Association for the

Advancement of Colored People.
MiU

H184
Hinton, William.
'Fanshen' re-examined in the
light of cultural revolution.
Boston, New England Free Press
[1969?]
97-112p. illus. 28cm.
Cover title.
Reprinted from PL, Feb. 1969.
1. China (People's Republic of
China, 1949-   )--Intellectual
life. I. New England Free
Press.
KU-RH

H185
Hip culture; 6 essays on its revolutionary potential. [New
York, Times Change Press,
1970]
62, [1]p. illus. 18cm.
1. U.S.--Soc. condit.--1960-
     2. Youth--Political ac-
tivity. 3. Radicalism.
I. Times Change Press.
CtU

H186
Hirsch, Carl.
Terror at Trumbull. [New York,
New Century Publishers, 1955]
15p. 19cm.
Cover title.
1. Chicago--Race question.
2. Negroes--Chicago. I. New
Century Publishers.
KU-J

H187
Hobson, Christopher Z.
Vietnam: any way out? [n.p.,
196]
12p. [1] leaf. 28cm.
Cover title.
1. Vietnamese conflict, 1961-
1975.
WHi-A

H188
Hobson, Christopher Z.
Vietnam: which way out? Ann
Arbor, Peace Research & Edu-
cation Project of Students for

a Democratic Society [196]
12 leaves. 28cm.
Cover title.
1. Vietnamese conflict, 1961-
1975. I. Students for a Democratic Society. Peace Research
and Education Project.
WHi-A, MiU

H189
Hochman, Larry.
Zionism and the Israeli state.
Ann Arbor, Radical Education
Project [196]
14p. 28cm.
Cover title.
1. Zionism. 2. Israel--Pol. &
govt. 3. Near East--Pol. &
govt. I. Radical Education
Project.
MoU, KU-RH

H190
Hochman, Larry.
Zionism and the Israeli state.
Boston, New England Free Press
[196]
14p. 28cm.
Cover title.
1. Zionism. 2. Israel--Pol.
& govt. 3. Near East--Pol. &
govt. I. New England Free
Press.
KU-RH

H191
Hodkinson, J. Raymond.
What is wrong with Negro col-
leges. Nashville, Southern Stu-
dent Organizing Committee [196]
5p. 28cm.
Reprinted from the New South
Student, Ap. 1966.
1. Negroes--Education.
I. Southern Student Organizing
Committee.
MiU, MoU, WHi-L

H194
Holden, Anna.
A first step toward school inte-
gration [foreword by Martin
Luther King. New York, Congress
for Racial Equality, 1958]
15 [2]p. illus. 23cm.
Cover title.

1. Negroes--Education. 2. Nash-
ville--Race question. I. Congress for Racial Equality.
II. King, Martin Luther, 1929-
1968.
CU-B, WHi-A

H195
Holmes County (Miss.) Freedom
    Democratic Party.
  Holmes County, Mississippi
  [taped recorded and edited by
  Mary Varela of SNCC. Jackson,
  Miss., KIPCO, 1967]
  38p. illus. 28cm.
  Cover title.
  1. Negroes--Holmes County, Miss.
  I. Student Nonviolent Coordina-
  ting Committee. II. Varela,
  Mary.
  MiU

H196
Holt, John.
  Notes on American education: the
  destruction of children. Boston,
  New England Free Press [196]
  55-60p. illus. 28cm.
  Cover title.
  Reprinted from Freelance, V. 6,
  no. 2
  Transcript of a speech delivered
  at Washington University, edited
  by David Glanz.
  1. Education. I. New England
  Free Press.
  KU-RH

H197
Hook, Charles.
  Attention: ex-SPU members and
  friends of peace. New York,
  1967.
  5 leaves. 28cm.
  Caption title.
  1. Peace. 2. Student Peace
  Union.
  CU-B

H198
Hook, Charles.
  The internationalist alternative: a basis for world peace
  and national unity. [New York,
  The International Perspective,
  1970]

45p. 23x10cm.
Cover title.
1. Internationalism. 2. World
politics--1965-   3. Peace.
I. International Perspective.
KU-RH

H199
Hook, Charles.
  Prospectus for the war corpor-
  ation. [New York, 1968?]
  36p. 28cm.
  Cover title.
  1. Peace. 2. War.
  KU-RH

H200
Hook, Charles.
  Why I support the National
  Liberation Front (Viet Cong)
  [New York? 196]
  4p. 28cm.
  Caption title.
  1. Viet Cong. 2. Vietnamese
  conflict, 1961-1975.
  KU-RH

H201
Hopper, Peggy.
  I don't want to change my life
  style--I want to change my life
  [by] Peggy Hopper and Steve
  Foldz. [Boston, New England
  Free Press, 1970?]
  [4]p. 28cm.
  Caption title.
  1. Woman--Rights of women.
  I. New England Free Press.
  MiU

H202
Horowitz, David.
  Corporations and the cold war.
  [Boston, New England Free
  Press, 1969?]
  36-50p. 21cm.
  Cover title.
  Reprinted from Horowitz's Cor-
  porations and the Cold War,
  Monthly Review Press, c1969.
  1. U.S.--Foreign policy.
  2. Corporations. 3. World
  politics--1955-   4. Busi-
  ness and politics. I. New
  England Free Press.
  MiU, KU-RH

H203
Horowitz, David.
  The rise of conglommerate corporations, by David Horowitz and
  Reese Erlich. Boston, New England Free Press [196]
  17p. illus. 28cm.
  Caption title.
  Reprinted from Ramparts, Nov.
  30 and Dec. 14-28, 1968.
  1. Corporations. 2. Business
  and politics. 3. U.S.--Econ.
  condit. I. Erlich, Reese, jt.
  auth. II. New England Free
  Press.
  KU-RH

H204
Horowitz, David.
  Sinews of empire. Boston, New
  England Free Press [196]
  33-42p. 28cm.
  Cover title.
  Reprinted from Ramparts.
  1. Universities and colleges.
  2. U.S.--Foreign policy.
  I. New England Free Press.
  KU-RH

H205
Horowitz, David.
  The universities and the ruling
  class: how wealth puts knowledge
  in its pocket. San Francisco,
  Bay Area Radical Education Pro-
  ject [1969?]
  17p. 28cm.
  Cover title.
  Reprinted from Ramparts.
  1. Universities and colleges.
  2. Power (Social science)
  I. Bay Area Radical Education
  Project.
  CU-B

H206
Horowitz, Gad.
  Nationalism, socialism and Cana-
  dian independence, essays by
  Gad Horowitz, Charles Taylor
  and C.W. Gonick. [Winnipeg,
  Canadian Dimension, 1967?]
  30p. illus.
  Cover title.
  Reprinted from Canadian Dimen-
  sion Magazine.

1. Socialism in Canada.
2. Nationalism--Canada.
I. Taylor, Charles, jt. auth.
II. Gonick, Cyril Wolfe, jt.
auth. III. Canadian Dimension.
CaOTU, NUC 70-41479

H207
Horowitz, Gus.
  Socialist and the anti-war
  movement. [New York? The
  Militant? 1969?]
  [5]p. 36cm.
  Caption title.
  Reprinted from the Militant,
  Oct. 1969.
  1. Socialist Workers Party.
  2. New Mobilization Committee to
  End the War in Vietnam. 3. Viet-
  namese conflict, 1961-1975.
  4. Peace--Societies, etc.
  I. The Militant.
  KU-RH

H208
Horowitz, Irving Louis.
  Games, strategies and peace.
  [Philadelphia, Peace Literature Service of the American
  Friends Service Committee,
  1963]
  64p. 22cm. (Beyond deterrence
  series)
  1. Atomic warfare. 2. Peace.
  I. Friends, Society of. American Friends Service Committee.
  CSt-H, MH, MoU, NUC 64-15799

H209
Houser, George M.
  Project: brotherhood. [New
  York, Congress of Racial Equal-
  ity, 196 ?]
  [4]p. 22cm.
  Caption title.
  At head of title: a report on
  last summer's workshop in the
  nation's capital, is.
  1. Negroes--Civil rights.
  I. Congress of Racial Equality.
  CU-B

H210
Houser, George M.
  A rationale for the protest
  against banks doing business

with South Africa, by George
M. Houser. New York, American
Committee on Africa, 1966.
6 leaves. 28cm.
Caption title.
1. South Africa--Race question.
2. U.S.--Relations (general)
with South Africa. 3. Banks
and banking--South Africa.
I. American Committee on Africa.
KU-RH

H211
Houser, George M.
  A report on a journey through
  rebel Angola. New York, American Committee on Africa [1962]
  11 leaves. 28cm.
  Caption title.
  1. Angola. I. American Committee on Africa.
  MNS, IEN, NUC 63-23349

H212
How Harvard rules. Being a total
  critique of Harvard University,
  including: new liberated documents, government research,
  the educational process ex-
  posed, strike posters, & free
  power chart. [Cambridge,
  Mass.] A.G.R. and The Old
  Mole [196]
  88p. illus. 28cm.
  Cover title.
  1. Harvard University. I. Africa Research Group. II. The
  Old Mole.
  KU-RH, WHi-L, DLC 79-284644

H213
How to start a high school underground. [Naperville, Ill.,
  John Schaller, 196]
  6p. 22cm.
  Cover title.
  1. Student movements. 2. High
  schools. I. Schaller, John.
  MoU, KU-RH

H214
Howard, Dick.
  SDS; present and future. [n.p.,
  196]
  8p. 28cm.
  Caption title.

1. Students for a Democratic
Society.
CU-B

H215
Howe, Florence.
  How the school system is rigged
  for failure [by] Florence Howe
  and Paul Lauter. [Boston, Pub-
  lished for Resist by New England
  Free Press, 1970?]
  5p. illus. 28cm.
  Cover title.
  Reprinted from New York Review,
  June 18, 1970.
  1. Education. I. Resist.
  II. New England Free Press.
  KU-RH

H216
Howe, Irving.
  New styles in leftism. [New
  York, League for Industrial
  Democracy, 196]
  31p. 23cm.
  Cover title.
  1. Student movements. I. Lea-
  gue for Industrial Democracy.
  CU-B

H217
Howe, Irving.
  On the nature of communism and
  relations with communists. New
  York, League for Industrial
  Democracy [196]
  15p. 28cm. (Looking forward
  no. 5)
  Cover title.
  1. Communism. 2. Students for
  a Democratic Society. 3. Anti-
  communist movements. I. League
  for Industrial Democracy.
  NcD, CU-B, NNU-T, KU-RH, H339,
  NUC 68-54534

H218
Hubbell, Charles.
  The weekly vigil for peace: suggestions for the conduct of re-
  current silent witness. Rev.
  Santa Barbara, Calif., 1967.
  25p. 19cm.
  1. Vietnamese conflict, 1961-
  1975. 2. Peace.
  MoU

H219
Huberman, Leo, 1903-1968.
  The ABC of socialism, by Leo
Huberman and Sybil H. May.
[New York, Monthly Review, c1952,
1962]
  64p.   22cm.   (Monthly review
pamphlet series, no. 7)
  Cover title.
  "Condensed from...The truth
about socialism [by L. Huberman]
edited by Sybil H. May."
  1. Socialism.   I. May, Sybil
H., 1893-   II. Monthly Re-
view Press.
  KU-RH

H220
Huberman, Leo, 1903-1968.
  The cultural revolution in
China: a socialist analysis [by]
Leo Huberman [and] Paul Sweezy.
Ann Arbor, Radical Education
Project [196]
  17p.   22cm.
  Cover title.
  Reprinted from Monthly Review,
Jan. 1967.
  1. China (People's Republic of
China, 1949-   )--Pol. & govt.
I. Radical Education Project.
II. Sweezy, Paul Marlor, 1910-
   , jt. auth.
  MoU

H221
Huberman, Leo, 1903-1968.
  The cultural revolution in
China: a socialist analysis
[by] Leo Huberman [and] Paul
Sweezy. Boston, New England
Free Press [1970?]
  17p.   21cm.
  Reprinted from Monthly Review,
Jan. 1967.
  1. China (People's Republic of
China, 1949-   )--Intellect-
ual life. 2. China (People's
Republic of China, 1949-   )
--Pol. & govt.   I. Sweezy, Paul
Marlor, 1910-   , jt. auth.
II. New England Free Press.
  KU-RH

H222
Huberman, Leo, 1903-1968.

  The cultural revolution in
China: a socialist analysis,
by Leo Huberman and Paul M.
Sweezy. San Francisco, Bay
Area Radical Education Project
[196]
  17p.   22cm.
  Cover title.
  Reprinted from Monthly Review,
Jan. 1967.
  1. China (People's Republic of
China, 1949-   )--Intellectual
life. I. Bay Area Radical Edu-
cation Project. II. Sweezy,
Paul Marlor, 1910-   , jt.
auth.
  CU-B

H223
Huberman, Leo, 1903-1968.
  The cultural revolution in
China: a socialist analysis [by]
Leo Huberman and Paul Sweezy.
Toronto, Research, Information,
and Publications Project, Stu-
dent Union for Peace Action
[196]
  11p.   28cm.
  Cover title.
  Reprinted from Monthly Review,
Jan. 196-.
  1. China (People's Republic of
China, 1949-   )--Intellect-
ual life. I. Student Union for
Peace Action. II. Sweezy, Paul
Marlor, 1910-   , jt. auth.
  WHi-A

H224
Huberman, Leo, 1903-1968.
  A fool's game: the China-India
border dispute [by] Leo Huber-
man [and] Paul Sweezy. Boston,
New England Free Press [1970?]
  465-486p.   22cm.
  Cover title.
  Reprinted from Monthly Review,
Jan. 1968.
  1. China (People's Republic of
China, 1949-   )--For. rel.--
India. 2. India--For. rel.--
China (People's Republic of
China, 1949-   ) I. Sweezy,
Paul Marlor, 1910-   , jt.
auth. II. New England Free Press.
  KU-RH

H225
Huberman, Leo, 1903-1968.
  Freedom under capitalism and
  socialism. [New York, Monthly
  Review Press, c1966]
  [20]p. illus. 22cm. (Monthly
  Review pamphlet series, no. 26)
  1. Capitalism. 2. Socialism.
  I. Monthly Review Press.
  WHi-L, MiU

H226
Huberman, Leo, 1903-1968.
  Notes on left propaganda. How
  to spread the word. Boston, New
  England Free Press [196]
  155-[160] 44-51p. 21cm.
  Cover title.
  Reprinted from Monthly Review,
  Sept. 1950; Dec. 1967.
  1. Propaganda. 2. Labor and
  laboring classes. 3. Teaching.
  4. Socialism. I. New England
  Free Press.
  KU-RH, MiU

H227
Huberman, Leo, 1903-1968.
  On segregation: the crisis in
  race relations. Two nations--
  white and black, by the editors
  of Monthly Review. New York,
  Monthly Review Press, 1956.
  31p. 22cm.
  1. Negroes--Civil rights.
  I. Monthly Review Press.
  KU-J, NcU, CLU, MiU

H228
Huberman, Leo.
  Revolution and counter revolution in the Dominican Republic;
  why the U.S. invaded [by] Leo
  Huberman [and] Paul Sweezy.
  Boston, New England Free Press
  [196]
  8p. 22cm.
  Cover title.
  1. Dominican Republic--Relat-
  ions (general) with the U.S.
  2. U.S.--Relations (general)
  with Dominican Republic.
  I. New England Free Press.
  II. Sweezy, Paul Marlor, 1910-
      , jt. auth.
  MiU

H229
Huberman, Leo, 1903-1968.
  Socialism is the only answer, by
  Leo Huberman and Paul M. Sweezy.
  [New York, Monthly Review, 1961]
  32p. 22cm. (Monthly review
  pamphlet series, no. 3)
  Cover title.
  1. Socialism. I. Sweezy, Paul
  Marlor, 1910-   , jt. auth.
  II. Monthly Review.
  KU-RH

H230
Huey Newton Defense Fund.
  Facts on Huey P. Newton's legal
  defense in court. Berkeley
  [196 ?]
  5p. 22cm.
  Caption title.
  1. Newton, Huey P.
  CU-B

H231
Hughes for Senate Committee.
  Stuart Hughes for senator: an
  open mind for an open future.
  [Cambridge, 196]
  folder. 23cm.
  Cover title.
  1. Hughes, Henry Stuart, 1916-

  KU-RH

H232
Hulett, John.
  The Black Panther Party, speech
  by John Hulett, interview with
  Stokely Carmichael, report from
  Lowndes County [by John Benson.
  New York, Merit Publishers,
  1966]
  30p. 22cm.
  1. Black Panther Party.
  2. Carmichael, Stokely.
  3. Lowndes County, Ala.--Race
  question. 4. Negroes--Civil
  rights. I. Merit Publishers.
  CU-B, WHi-L, MiU

H233
Humanity Guild.
  It can happen. [New York,
  196 ?]
  23p. 22x10cm.

1. Atomic warfare. 2. Peace.
3. Disarmament.
KU-RH

H234
Hutchinson, Dorothy.
  Proposal for an honorable peace
  in Vietnam. [Philadelphia] Wo-
  men's International League for
  Peace and Freedom [1968]
  8p. 23x10cm.
  Cover title.
  1. Vietnamese conflict, 1961-
  1975. I. Women's International
  League for Peace and Freedom.
  MoU, WHi-L, KU-RH

H235
Hutton, William R.
  The drug price scandal; testimony shows brand-name drugs are
  sold at exorbitant prices with
  tremendous variations. Boston,
  New England Free Press [196]
  [4]p. illus. 28cm.
  Caption title.
  1. Drugs--Price and sale.
  2. Drug trade. I. New England
  Free Press.
  KU-RH, MoU

H236
Huxley, Aldous Leonard, 1894-1963.
  Letter from Aldous Huxley to
  Anthony Brooks. [Montreal, Our
  Generation, 196]
  74-75 leaves.
  Caption title.
  1. Nonviolence. I. Our
  Generation.
  NNU-T

H237
Huxley, Julian Sorrell, 1887-
  Man, without god. [Yellow
  Springs, O., American Humanist
  Association, 196 ?]
  [10]p. 22x10cm.
  Cover title.
  1. Humanism. I. American
  Humanist Association.
  KU-RH

H238
Hymer, Bennett.
  The negro labor market in
  Chicago, 1966: conditions in
  employment and manpower train-
  ing. [Chicago, Chicago Urban
  League, 1966]
  16p.
  1. Negroes--Employment.
  2. Chicago--Race question.
  I. Chicago Urban League.
  WHi-L

H239
Hytten, Eyvind.
  Some experiences and consider-
  ations. [Montreal, Our Gener-
  ation, 196]
  42-[50]p.
  Caption title.
  At head of title: Nonviolence
  and development work.
  1. Nonviolence. I. Our
  Generation.
  NNU-T

I

I1
Ignatin, Noel.
  Which side are you on? U.S.
  history in perspective. [Chi-
  cago, Students for a Democratic
  Society, 196]
  folder (8p.) illus. 23cm.
  Cover title.

  1. Negroes--Civil rights.
  2. Labor and laboring classes.
  I. Students for a Democratic
  Society.
  KU-RH, WHi-A

I2
Ignatin, Noel.

White blindspot [by] Noel Ignatin. Can white radicals be
radicalized? [by] Ted Allen.
Detroit, Radical Education Project [1970?]
18p. illus. 28cm.
Cover title.
1. Negroes--Civil rights.
2. Labor and laboring classes.
3. Radicalism. I. Allen, Ted,
jt. auth. II. Radical Education
Project.
MiU, KU-RH

I3
Illich, Ivan.
  Celebration of awareness:
  excerpts. [Palo Alto, Institute for the Study of Nonviolence, 196 ?]
  [27]p. illus. 22cm.
  Cover title.
  1. Underdeveloped areas.
  2. Poor--Latin America.
  3. Latin America--Econ. condit.
  I. Institute for the Study of
  Nonviolence.
  KU-RH

I4
Immigration to Canada as an alter-
    native to the draft. Nash-
    ville, Southern Student Or-
    ganizing Committee [1967?]
  7 [7]p. 28cm.
  Cover title.
  Partial contents--A summary and
  analysis of the immigration regulations by the Toronto Anti-
  Draft Programme.
  1. Military service, Compulsory.
  2. Emigration and immigration
  law--Canada. I. Southern Student Organizing Committee.
  II. Toronto Anti-Draft Programme.
  MiU

I5
Immigration to Canada as an al-
    ternative to the draft. San
    Francisco, Students for a
    Democratic Society and the
    S.D.S. Storefront [1965?]
  8p. 28cm.
  Cover title.

  1. Military service, Compulsory.
  2. Emigration and immigration
  law--Canada. I. Students for a
  Democratic Society.
  MiU-H

I6
Independent Socialist Club.
  Platform proposals: black liberation, foreign policy, labor.
  Peace and Freedom Movement state
  convention, March 1968. [Ber-
  keley, 1968]
  [10]p. 28cm.
  Cover title.
  1. Negroes--Civil rights.
  2. U.S.--Foreign policy.
  3. Labor and laboring classes.
  4. Peace and Freedom Movement.
  CU-B

I7
Independent Socialist Club.
  Revolution and democracy.
  [n.p., 1969]
  2 leaves. 28cm.
  Caption title.
  1. Socialism. 2. Democracy.
  3. Revolutions.
  WHi-L

I8
Independent Socialist Clubs of
    America.
  A draft perspective on the
  international scene. [New York,
  196]
  23p. 28cm.
  Caption title.
  1. Military service, Compulsory.
  2. Capitalism.
  WHi-L

I9
Indians of All Tribes.
  Indians of All Tribe, Inc.,
  reply to counter-proposal of
  Robert Robertson for the U.S.A.
  [Berkeley?] 1970.
  3 leaves. 28cm.
  Caption title.
  1. Indians of North America--
  Government relations.
  CU-B

I10
Indonesia; the making of a

neo-colony. [Boston, New En-
gland Free Press, 1970?]
10p. illus., maps. 28cm.
Cover title.
"Originally published by the
Pacific Study Center in Pacific
Research and World Empire Tele-
gram."
1. Indonesia--Pol. & govt.
I. Pacific Study Center.
II. New England Free Press.
KU-RH

I11
Industrial Workers of the World.
  One big union of the Industrial
  Workers of the World. 5th rev.
  ed. Chicago, 1957.
  32p. 23cm.
  1. Socialism. 2. Labor and
  laboring classes. 3. Trade-
  unions.
  KU-RH, IdU, CU-B

I12
Industrial Workers of the World.
  Songs of the workers. 29th ed.
  Chicago, Industrial Workers of
  the World, 1956.
  64p. illus. 15cm.
  RPB, WHi-L, NUC 64-14537

I13
Industrial Workers of the World.
  Songs of the workers. 31st ed.
  Chicago, 1964.
  63 [1]p. illus. 15cm.
  WHi-L, RPB, NUC 67-41173

I14
Industrial Workers of the World.
  A union for all railroad workers. A candid statement of
  organization principles and
  structure, and also the tenta-
  tive demands for all railroad
  workers advanced by the rank
  and file to be acted and voted
  on by all railroad workers.
  [Chicago, 195 ?]
  32p. illus.
  1. Trade-unions. 2. Railroads--
  Employees.
  MH-IR, NUC 65-1363

I15
Institute for Policy Studies.
  Seminar on the United States
  and revolution in the non-revo-
  lutionary world. [Washington?
  196]
  5 leaves. 28cm.
  Caption title.
  1. Revolutions. 2. Underdeveloped areas. 3. U.S.--Foreign
  policy.
  WHi-A

I16
Institute for the Study of Non-
  violence.
  [Untitled pamphlet. Palo Alto,
  Calif., 196]
  [12]p. illus. 23cm.
  1. Military service, Compulsory.
  KU-RH

I17
International Committee of Conscience on Vietnam.
  Conscience on Vietnam. They are
  our brothers whom we kill.
  Berkeley, Turn Toward Peace
  [196]
  3p. 28cm.
  Caption title.
  1. Vietnamese conflict, 1961-
  1975. I. Turn Toward Peace.
  CU-B

I18
International Conference on Disarmament and Arms Control,
  Swarthmore College, 1962.
  Background papers. [Swarthmore,
  Pa., 1962]
  6v. 28cm.
- Cover title.
  1. U.S.--Military policy.
  2. U.S.--Foreign policy.
  3. Disarmament. 4. Student
  movements. 5. Peace.
  WHi-A

I19
International Liberation School.
  Firearms & self-defense: a
  handbook for radicals, revolutionaries and easy riders.

Produced by International Liberation School, with the help
of the Red Mountain Tribe] Detroit, Radical Education Project [1970?]
40p. illus. 25cm.
Cover title.
1. Firearms. I. Red Mountain
Tribe. II. Radical Education
Project.
WHi-L, KU-RH

I20
International Socialists.
  The International Socialists:
  an introduction. [Berkeley,
  196 ?]
  folder. 22x9cm.
  Cover title.
  1.Socialism.
  KU-RH

I21
International Socialists.
  International Socialists pro-
  gram in brief. [n.p., 196]
  3p. 28cm.
  Caption title.
  1. Socialism.
  KU-RH

I22
International Socialists.
  No politics as usual. [Ber-
  keley, 1969?]
  [2]p. 28cm.
  Caption title.
  1. U.S.--Pol. & govt.--1961-
       2. Imperialism.
  CU-B

I23
International Socialists.
  To reorient the I.S. [Berke-
  ley, 1970]
  27p. 28cm. (Reorient papers,
  no. 1)
  Cover title.
  1. Socialism.
  CU-B

I24
International union, united auto-
    mobile, aircraft and agri-
    cultural implement workers of
    America. Black Panther

Caucus, Fremont, Calif.
Building a rank-and-file caucus, by Black Panther Caucus,
U.A.W., Fremont, Calif. [Oak-
land, Black Panther Caucus,
1969?]
7p. 22cm.
Cover title.
1. Trade-unions. 2. Negroes--
Employment. 3. Automobile industry workers. I. Black Panther Caucus.
KU-RH

I25
Internationalist Perspective.
  Some questions and a message
  for the participants in the
  Cleveland anti-war conference
  of February 13-15, 1970. [New
  York, 1970?]
  [2]p. 28cm.
  Caption title.
  1. Vietnamese conflict, 1961-
  1975. 2. Peace. 3. Student
  Mobilization Committee to End
  the War in Vietnam.
  KU-RH

I26
Interracial Action Institute,
    Miami, 1959.
  Summary and evaluation [by
  Susan Bodan and James R. Robin-
  son] New York, CORE--Congress
  of Racial Equality [1960?]
  21p. 22cm.
  1. Negroes--Miami. 2. Miami--
  Race question. I. Boden, Susan,
  jt. auth. II. Robinson, James
  R., jt. auth. III. Congress of
  Racial Equality.
  NcD

I27
The invasion of Czechoslovakia.
    [New York, Merit Publishers,
    1969]
  47p. 22cm.
  Cover title.
  1. Czechoslovak Republic.
  2. Russia--For. rel.--Czechos-
  lovak Republic. I. Merit Publishers.
  KU-RH

I28
Ireland, Douglas.
  For a new coalition [by] Douglas
  Ireland & Steve Max. Chicago,
  Students for a Democratic Soc-
  iety [196]
  23p. 28cm.
  Cover title.
  1. Politics, Practical.
  2. Liberalism. I. Students for
  a Democratic Society. II. Max,
  Steve, jt. auth.
  MiU, CU-B

I29
Ireland, Douglas.
  SDS and '64--a tactical ap-
  proach [by] D. Ireland and S.
  Max. [n.p., 1964]
  [2]p. 28cm.
  Caption title.
  1. Politics, Practical.
  2. Students for a Democratic
  Society. I. Max, Steve, jt.
  auth.
  WHi-A

I30
Irons, Peter.
  Peace and politics, 1962, prepared by Peter Irons, Edward
  Knappman [and] Dawn Lander.
  Washington, Student Peace Union
  [1963?]
  39p. 28cm.
  Cover title.
  1. U.S.--Pol. & govt.--1961-
        2. Peace. 3. Disarma-
  ment. I. Knappman, Edward, jt.
  auth. II. Lander, Dawn, jt.
  auth. III. Student Peace Union.
  KU-RH

I31
The irrational in politics. [Van
  Nuys, Calif., SRAF Print Co-
  op] 1970.
  [13]p. 22cm.
  Cover title.
  Reprinted from Solidarity pamphlet no. 33
  At head of title: Solidarity
  group.
  1. Gt. Brit--Pol. & govt.
  2. Politics, Practical.
  I. SRAF Print Co-op.

II. Solidarity.
MiU

I32
Isely, Philip.
  Strategy for reclaiming earth
  for humanity; including plans
  for a peoples world parliament.
  [Denver, World Constitution and
  Parliament Association, c1970]
  40p. 22cm.
  Cover title.
  1. Environmental policy.
  2. Internationalism. 3. World
  politics--1965-   I. World
  Constitution and Parliament
  Association.
  KU-RH

I33
Israel, Jared.
  Less talk--more action; fight
  racism [by Jarel Israel and
  Mike Schwartz. n.p., 1969]
  [2]p. 36cm.
  Caption title.
  1. Negroes--Civil rights.
  2. Students for a Democratic
  Society.
  WHi-L

I34
Israeli Socialist Organization.
  The other Israel; a critique
  of Zionist history and policy.
  Detroit, Radical Education
  Project [1970?]
  10p. 28cm.
  Caption title.
  1. Israel-Arab War, 1967.
  2. Zionism. I. Radical Edu-
  cation Project.
  KU-RH, MiU

I35
Israeli Socialist Organization.
  The other Israel: Israeli
  critique of Zionist history and
  policy. [Van Nuys, Calif.
  SRAF Print Co-op] 1970.
  [10]p. 22cm.
  Cover title.
  1. Zionism. 2. Israel--
  History. I. SRAF Print Co-op.
  MiU

I36
Israeli Socialist Organization.
  The Palestine problem: Israel
  and imperialism. Boston, New
  England Free Press [1970]
  15p. 28cm.
  Cover title.
  Reprinted from International
  Socialism, no. 32; Sp. 1968.
  1. Jewish-Arab relations.
  2. Palestine. 3. Israel.
  1. New England Free Press.
  KU-RH, MiU

I37
Itkin, Michael Francis.
  Christ and the homosexual. A
  sermon preached during the mid-
  night celebration of the holy
  Eucharist, Christmas 1969, at
  the Community of Jesus Our
  Brother, and repeated at the
  Free Particle All-Gay Sympos-

ium--West Coast Gay Liberation
  Conference. Wesley Center,
  Berkeley, Calif. 26 December
  1969. [San Francisco, 197]
  5 leaves. 28cm.
  Caption title.
  1. Homosexuality.
  KU-RH

I38
Itkin, Michael Frances.
  Towards creative revolution.
  Presented at the Free Particle
  All-Gay Symposium--West Coast
  Gay Liberation Conference...,
  27 December 1969. San Fran-
  cisco [1970?]
  11 leaves. 36cm.
  Cover title.
  1. Revolutions. 2. Homosex-
  uality.
  KU-RH

✝
J
✝

JOIN
  see
Jobs or Income Now Community
    Union.

J1
Jack, Homer A.
  Angola: repression and revolt
  in Portugese Africa. [New
  York] American Committee in
  Africa [c1960]
  28p. 22cm.
  Cover title.
  1. Angola--Pol. & govt.
  2. Revolutions--Angola.
  I. American Committee on Africa.
  MiU

J2
Jackson, Bruce.
  Our prisons are criminal, by
  Bruce Jackson. [Inside North
  Carolina prisons, by Donald
  Hockaday] Nashville, Southern
  Student Organizing Committee
  [196]

8 [1] 3 [1]p. 28cm.
  Cover title.
  1. Prisons. I. Hockaday, Don-
  ald, jt. auth. II. Southern
  Student Organizing Committee.
  MoU

J3
Jackson, James E.
  The meaning of "black power",
  with an introduction by Henry
  Winston. New York, New Outlook
  Publishers, 1966]
  15p. 22cm.
  1. Negroes--Civil rights.
  I. Winston, Henry. II. New
  Outlook Publishers.
  CU-B, MiU

J4
Jackson, James E.
  The philosophy of communism.
  New York, New Century Publishers,
  1963.
  16p. 19cm.
  1. Communism. I. New Century

Publishers.
MiU, KU-J, KU-RH, WHi-L

J5
Jackson, James E.
  Some aspects of the. Negro
  question in the United States.
  [New York, Communist Party,
  U.S.A., 1959?]
  31p.
  Cover title.
  1. Negroes--Civil rights.
  I. Communist Party of the United
  States of America.
  MiU

J6
Jackson, James E.
  The South's new challenge. New
  York, New Century Publishers,
  1957.
  20p. 20cm.
  Reprinted from Political Affairs, Dec. 1957.
  1. Southern States--Race question. 2. Negroes--Southern
  States. I. New Century Publishers.
  NN, MiU, KU-J, CSSR

J7
Jackson, James E.
  3 brave men tell how freedom
  comes to an old south city--
  Nashville, Tenn. [New York,
  Publisher's New Press, 1963]
  27p. illus.
  Cover title.
  1. Nashville--Race question.
  2. Lewis, John Henry.
  3. Rollins, J. Metz. 4. Vivian, C. Tindell. 5. Negroes--
  Civil rights. I. Publisher's
  New Press.
  MiU, WHi-L

J8
Jackson, James E.
  A tribute in tears and a thrust
  for freedom. [New York, Publisher's Free Press, 1963]
  [24]p.
  Cover title.
  At head of title: At the fun-
  eral of Medgar Evers in Jackson, Mississippi.

1. Mississippi--Race question.
2. Negroes--Mississippi.
3. Evers, Medgar. I. Publisher's New Press.
MiU

J9
Jackson, James E.
  The view for here. New York,
  Publisher's New Press [1963]
  210p. illus.
  "A selection of editorials by
  James E. Jackson, editor of the
  Worker.
  1. Negroes. 2. Communism.
  I. Publisher's New Press.
  MiU, NUC 64-13413

J10
Jackson, Jim.
  Forces of progress in the
  south: workers, farmers and the
  negro people. New York, Jefferson School of Social Science.
  [1955]
  12 [1] leaf. 28cm.
  Cover title.
  1. Southern States--Race question. 2. Negroes--Southern
  States. I. Jefferson School of
  Social Science.
  KU-J

J11
Jacobs, Harold.
  Populist students and corporate
  society [by] Harold Jacobs
  [and] James Petras. [Montreal,
  Our Generation, 196]
  [143]-172 leaves.
  Caption title.
  1. Student movements. 2. Uni-
  versities and colleges.
  I. Petras, James, jt. auth.
  II. Our Generation.
  NNU-T

J12
Jacobs, James.
  Black workers set the pace.
  Boston, New England Free Press
  [1969?]
  7p. illus. 21cm.
  Cover title.
  Reprinted from The Movement,
  April 1969.

1. Negroes--Detroit. 2. Negroes
--Employment. 3. Automobile in-
dustry workers. 4. Eldon Avenue
Revolutionary Union Movement.
5. Trade-unions. I. New England
Free Press.
KU-RH

J13
Jacobs, James.
  The new rebels in industrial
America, by Jim Jacobs and
Larry Laskowski. San Francisco,
Bay Area Radical Education Pro-
ject [1969?]
18p. 22cm.
Cover title.
Reprinted from Leviathan,
Mar. 1969.
1. Youth--Political activity.
2. Negroes--Politics and suf-
frage. 3. Wallace, George
Corley, 1919-   4. Labor and
laboring classes. I. Bay Area
Radical Education Project.
I. Laskowski, Larry, jt. auth.
CU-B

J14
Jacobs, James.
  "Our thing is DRUM." The mid-
west and the League [by] Jim
Jacobs. An interview with Ken
Cockrel and Mike Hamlin of the
League for Revolutionary Work-
ers [by] Jim Jacobs and David
Wellman. Boston, New England
Free Press [1970?]
23p. 28cm.
Reprinted from Leviathan,
June 1970.
1. Automobile industry work-
ers--Detroit. 2. Negroes--
Employment. 3. Labor and
laboring classes. 4. Dodge
Revolutionary Union Movement.
I. Wellman, David, jt. auth.
II. Hamlin, Mike. III. Cock-
rel, Ken. IV. New England
Free Press.
MiU

J15
Jacobs, James.
  Power in American society.
[Ann Arbor, Radical Education

Project, 196]
7p. 28cm. (Radical Education
Project. Study guide series)
Cover title.
1. Power (Social science)--
Bibl. 2. U.S.--Pol. & govt.--
1961-   I. Radical Education Project.
WHi-L, KU-RH

J16
Jacobs, James.
  Power in American society.
[Boston, New England Free Press,
196]
7p. 28cm. (Radical Education
Project. Study Guide Series)
Cover title.
1. Power (Social science)--
Bibl. 2. U.S.--Pol. & govt.--
1961-   I. New England
Free Press.
KU-RH

J17
Jacobs, James.
  Power in American society
(draft) [Ann Arbor] Radical
Education Project [196]
10p. 28cm. (Study guide 1)
Cover title.
1. Power (Social science)--
Bibl. 2. U.S.--Pol. & govt.--
1961-   I. Radical Educa-
tion Project.
MiU-H

J18
Jacobs, James.
  S. M. Lipset: social scientist
of the smooth society. Ann
Arbor, Radical Education Pro-
ject [196]
15p. illus. 22cm.
Cover title.
1. Lipset, Seymour Martin.
Political Man. I. Radical
Education Project.
KU-RH

J19
Jacobs, James.
  S.M. Lipset: social scientist
of the smooth society. [Madi-
son, Wis.] Madison Students for
a Democratic Society [196]

17p. 22cm.
Cover title.
1. Lipset, Seymour Martin.
Political man. I. Students for
a Democratic Society, Madison,
Wis.
KU-RH, MiU, WHi-L, NUC 72-69969

J20
Jacobs, James.
  The U.A.W. settles with Ford,
  1967. Sellout and insurgency
  in the auto industry. Ann
  Arbor, Radical Education Project [1969?]
  7p. 28cm.
  Cover title.
  1. International union, united
  automobile, aircraft and agricultural implement workers of
  America. 2. Ford Motor Co.
  3. Automobile industry workers.
  I. Radical Education Project.
  MoU, KU-RH

J21
Jacobson, Julius.
  Third camp: the Independent
  Socialist view of war and peace
  policy, by Julius Jacobson and
  Hal Draper. [Berkeley, Calif.,
  Independent Socialist Committee,
  c1965]
  36p. 22cm.
  Cover title.
  1.Socialism. 2.War. 3. U.S.--
  Foreign policy. I. Draper,
  Hal, jt. auth. II. Independent
  Socialist Committee.
  KU-RH

J22
Jacobson, Tom.
  Unions and the working student.
  New York, Students for a Demo-
  cratic Society; Ann Arbor, Eco-
  nomic Research and Action Pro-
  ject [196]
  4p. 28cm.
  Cover title.
  1. Trade-unions. 2. Student
  movements. I. Students for a
  Democratic Society. Economic
  Research and Action Project.
  WHi-A, KU-RH, MiU

J23
Jailbreak. Boston, New England
  Free Press [1970?]
  7 [1]p. illus. 25cm.
  Cover title.
  1. Student movements--New York
  (City) 2. Negroes--Civil
  rights. I. New England Free
  Press.
  KU-RH

J24
James, Cyril Lionel Robert,
  1901-
  The case for West-Indian self
  government. [New York, University Place Book Shop, 1967]
  32p. 18cm.
  Cover title.
  1. West Indies--Pol. & govt.
  FU, CSt, CtY, NUC 69-55352

J25
James, Cyril Lionel Robert,
  1901-
  Education, propaganda, agita-
  tion. [2d. ed. Detroit, Facing Reality Publishing Commit-
  tee] 1968.
  35p. 28cm.
  1. Socialism. I. Facing Reality Publishing Committee.
  MiU

J26
James, Cyril Lionel Robert,
  1901-
  Every cook can govern: a study
  of democracy in ancient Greece.
  Also: Negro Americans and Ameri-
  can politics. [Highland Park,
  Mich., Facing Reality Book
  Service, 1956]
  22p. 21cm.
  Cover title.
  1. Negroes--Civil rights.
  2. Democracy. I. Facing
  Reality Book Service.
  CU-B

J27
James, Cyril Lionel Robert,
  1901-
  A history of Negro revolt. New
  York, Haskell House Publishers,

1969.
97p. 23cm.
Reprint of the 1938 ed.
1. Negroes--History. 2. Slavery in the United States--In-
surrections, etc.
DLC 75-101141

J28
James, Cyril Lionel Robert,
    1901-
Lenin, Trotsky and vanguard
party: a contemporary view.
Detroit, Facing Reality Pub.
Committee, 1964.
7p. 25cm.
1. Lenin, Vladimir Il'ich,
1870-1924. 2. Trotskii, Lev,
1879-1940. 3. Communism.
I. Facing Reality Publishing
Committee.
TxU, CU-B, MiU, NUC 70-13409

J29
James, Cyril Lionel Robert,
    1901-
Marxism for the sixties; based
on an address entitled "Marxism
1963", delivered in November
1963 to the Solidarity Group in
London, England. [Detroit,
1965]
23p. 23cm. (Speaking out;
bulletin of the Facing Reality
Publishing Committee, no. 2)
Cover title.
1. Communism. 2. Marx, Karl,
1818-1883. I. Facing Reality
Publishing Committee.
CSt, NUC 65-105456

J30
James, Cyril Lionel Robert,
    1901-
Notes on the life of George
Padmore. [n.p., 196]
62, x, iv leaves. 33cm.
1. Padmore, George, 1903-1959.
IEN, NUC 69-114132

J31
James, Cyril Lionel Robert,
    1901-
Perspectives and proposals.
[Detroit] Facing Reality, 1966.
46p. 28cm.

1. Socialism. 2. Leadership.
3. Lenin, Vladimir Il'ich,
1870-1924. I. Facing Reality
Publishing Committee.
MiU, CU-B

J32
James, Mike.
Break out & do it now. [Chi-
cago, Students for a Democratic
Society, 1968]
8p. 22cm.
Cover title.
1. Government, Resistance to.
I. Students for a Democratic
Society.
CU-B

J33
James, Mike.
Getting ready for the firing
line. [Chicago] JOIN Community
Union [196]
8p. 22cm.
Cover title.
1. Poor--Chicago. 2. Negroes--
Chicago. 3. Chicago--Econ.
condit. I. Jobs or Income Now
Community Union.
CU-B, WHi-L

J34
Jeffery, Sharon.
Prospectus for the Cleveland
community project. [New York]
Students for a Democratic
Society and Economic Research
and Action Project [196]
3p. 28cm.
Cover title.
1. Poor--Cleveland. 2. Negroes
--Cleveland. 3. Cleveland--
Econ. condit. I. Students for
a Democratic Society. Economic
Research and Action Project.
MiU, CU-B

J35
Jenner, Bill.
The new Chinese revolution.
San Francisco, Bay Area Radical
Education Project [196]
13p. 22cm.
Cover title.
Reprinted from New Left Review
no. 53

1. China (People's Republic of
China, 1949-   )--Intellectual
life. I. Bay Area Radical Education Project.
CU-B

J36
Jenness, Caroline.
  Immediate withdrawal vs. negotiations. Questions and answers on which way for the anti-
  war movement. [Cambridge,
  Mass., Bring the Troops Home
  Now Newsletter, 1966]
  14p. illus. 22cm.
  1. Vietnamese conflict, 1961-
  1975. I. Bring the Troops Home
  Now Newsletter.
  KU-RH, MoU, NIC, NUC 68-49582

J37
Jenness, Douglas.
  War and revolution in Vietnam.
  [New York, Young Socialist,
  1965]
  22p. 22cm.
  Cover title.
  1. Vietnamese conflict, 1961-
  1975. 2. Vietnam--History.
  I. Young Socialist.
  KU-RH, CU-B, WHi-L, NUC 68-
  103864

J38
Jenness, Douglas.
  The war in Vietnam [by Douglas
  Jenness and Robin Martin. New
  York, Young Socialist, 1965]
  15p. 22cm.
  Cover title.
  1. Vietnamese conflict, 1961-
  1975. I. Martin, Robin, jt.
  auth. II. Young Socialist.
  CU-B, MiU

J39
Jewish Peace Fellowship.
  Can a Jew be a conscientious
  objector? [Nyack, 1968?]
  folder. 23x9cm.
  Cover title.
  1. Conscientious objectors.
  2. Jews.
  KU-RH

J40
Jewish Peace Fellowship.
  Counselling young Jews about
  conscientious objection to military service. [Nyack, N.Y.?
  196]
  [4]p. 22x10cm.
  Caption title.
  1. Conscientious objectors.
  2. Jews.
  CU-B

J41
Jewish Peace Fellowship.
  Shalom: the program and philosophy of the Jewish Peace Fellowship. [New York, 196]
  folder. 23x10cm.
  Cover title.
  1. Jews. 2. Peace.
  CU-B

J42
Jobs or Income Now Community
    Union.
  If you can't find a job--read
  this. [Chicago? 196]
  6 leaves. 28cm.
  Cover title.
  1. Poverty. 2. Labor and
  laboring classes.
  WHi-A

J43
Jobs or Income Now Community
    Union.
  JOIN challenges Chicago's war
  on poverty. [Chicago, 1965]
  4 leaves. 28cm.
  Cover title.
  1. Chicago--Econ. condit.
  2. Poor--Chicago.
  WHi-A

J44
Jobs or Income Now Community
    Union.
  Vietnam. Chicago, SDS Liberation Press, 1968.
  13p. illus. 22cm.
  Cover title.
  1. Vietnamese conflict, 1961-
  1975. I. Students for a
  Democratic Society. Liberation

Press.
WHi-A

J45
Jobs or Income Now Community
     Union.
   Vietnam. [Nashville, Southern
   Student Organizing Committee,
   196]
   8p. 28cm.
   Cover title.
   1. Vietnam--History. I. Southern Student Organizing Committee.
   MoU

J46
Jobs or Income Now Community
     Union.
   What is JOIN? [Chicago? 196]
   [6] leaves. 28cm.
   Cover title.
   1. Poverty. 2. Employment
   (Economic theory)
   WHi-A

J47
Jobs or Income Now Community
     Union, Baltimore.
   Baltimore U-JOIN; the summer
   report. New York, Students for
   a Democratic Society and its
   Economic Research and Action
   Project [1964?]
   1v. (various pagings)
   Cover title.
   1. Poor--Baltimore. 2. Stu-
   dent movements--Baltimore.
   3. Baltimore--Econ. condit.
   I. Students for a Democratic
   Society. Economic Research
   and Action Project.
   WHi-L

J48
Jobs or Income Now Community
     Union, Baltimore.
   The summer report, prepared by
   the staff of the Baltimore
   Union for Jobs or Income Now.
   Ann Arbor, Economic Research
   and Action Project [196]
   9p. 28cm.
   Cover title.
   1. Unemployed--Baltimore.
   2. Baltimore--Econ. condit.

I. Students for a Democratic
Society. Economic Research and
Action Project.
KU-RH

J49
Jobs or Income Now Community
     Union, Chicago.
   JOIN and the presidential
   election. [Chicago, 1964]
   [2]p. 28cm.
   Caption title.
   1. Goldwater, Barry Morris,
   1909-   2. Johnson, Lyndon
   Baines, Pres. U.S., 1908-1973.
   3. Politics, Practical. 4. U.
   S.--Pol. & govt.--1963-
   WHi-A

J50
Jobs or Income Now Community
     Union, Chicago.
   JOIN community union; program
   for 1966. Chicago, 1966.
   65 leaves. 28cm.
   Caption title.
   1. Poor--Chicago. 2. Chicago--
   Econ. condit.
   WHi-A

J51
Jobs or Income Now Community
     Union, Chicago.
   Statement on urban progress
   centers. Presented to the
   Uptown Urban Progress Center
   on its opening day. [Chicago]
   1965.
   5 leaves. 28cm.
   Cover title.
   1. Poor--Chicago. 2. Chicago--
   Econ. condit.
   WHi-A

J52
Jobs or Income Now Community
     Union. Education Staff.
   The press. [Chicago, 1967]
   17p. 28cm.
   Cover title.
   1. Press.
   CU-B

J53
Jobs or Income Now Community
     Union. Education Staff.

Vietnam. Chicago, 1968.
13p. 22cm.
1. Vietnam--History. 2. U.S.--
For. rel.--Vietnam. 3. Vietnamese
conflict, 1961-1975.
CU-B

J54
Jobs or Income Now Community
    Union. Staff Education
    Committee.
Vietnam, prepared by the staff
education committee of JOIN
community union. Chicago [196]
15p. illus. 23cm.
Cover title.
1. Vietnamese conflict, 1961-
1975.
MoU, KU-RH

J55
Jobs or Income Now Community
    Union. Staff Education
    Committee.
Vietnam, prepared by the staff
education committee of JOIN
community union. [Chicago?]
SDS Liberation Press, 1968.
13p. illus. 22cm.
1. Vietnamese conflict, 1961-
1975. I. Students for a Democratic Society. Liberation
Press.
KU-RH

J56
Jobs or Income Now Community
    Union. Staff Education
    Committee.
Vietnam. [Madison, Wisconsin
Draft Resistance Union, 1968]
17p. illus.
Cover title.
1. Vietnamese conflict, 1961-
1975. I. Wisconsin Draft
Resistance Union.
WHi-L

J57
Jobs or Income Now Community
    Union. Staff Education
    Committee.
Who wants urban renewal.
[Chicago, 196]
21p. 28cm.

Cover title.
1. Urban renewal.
CU-B

J58
Joe Blatchford. Chicago, Commit-
    tee of Returned Volunteers
    [1970?]
9p. 28cm.
Caption title.
1. Blatchford, Joseph Hoffer,
1934-   2. U.S. Peace
Corps. I. Committee of Returned Volunteers.
KU-RH

J59
Joesten, Joachim.
The gaps in the Warren report.
[New York] Marzani & Munsell
[1964?]
159-206p. 21cm.
Cover title.
1. U.S. Warren Commission.
2. Kennedy, John Fitzgerald,
Pres. U.S., 1917-1963--Assassin-
ation. I. Marzani and Munsell.
KU-RH

J60
John Brown Society.
An introduction to the Black
Panther Party, written by John
Brown Society..., edited, with
new material by the Radical
Education Project. [Ann Arbor,
Radical Education Project]
1969.
25p. illus. 28cm.
Cover title.
1. Black Panther Party.
I. Radical Education Project.
MoU, KU-RH, MiU, WHi-L

J61
Johnny Appleseed Patriotic
    Publications.
For a party of the permanent
American revolution. Cicero
[1969?]
[1] leaf. 28cm.
Caption title.
1. Revolutions--U.S. 2. Soc-
ial change.
KU-RH

J62
Johnny Appleseed Patriotic
    Publications.
  Open letter to S.D.S. Cicero,
  Ill. [19]69
  [1] leaf. 28cm.
  Caption title.
  1. Students for a Democratic
  Society.
  CU-B, WHi-L

J63
Johnny Appleseed Patriotic
    Publications.
  An open letter to the American
  left. [Cicero, Ill., 1968?]
  [4]p. 28cm.
  Cover title.
  1. Patriotism.
  WHi-L, MoU

J64
Johnny Appleseed Patriotic
    Publications.
  Regis Debray: "the nation is of
  the essence of these times".
  Cicero [1969?]
  [1] leaf. 28cm.
  Caption title.
  1. Debray, Regis.
  KU-RH

J65
Johnny Appleseed Patriotic
    Publications.
  Toward a new patriotism.
  [Cicero, Ill., 196]
  folder (8p.) 22x10cm.
  Cover title.
  1. Patriotism. 2. Radicalism.
  MoU, KU-RH

J66
Johns, Major.
  It happened in Baton Rouge,
  U.S.A.; a real life drama of
  our deep South today, by Major
  Johns and Ronnie Moore.
  [edited by Jim Peck. New York,
  Congress of Racial Equality,
  196]
  [9]p. illus.
  Cover title.
  1. Baton Rouge, La.--Race quest-
  ion. 2. Negroes--Baton Rouge,
  La. I. Congress of Racial

Equality. II. Peck, James.
  III. Moore, Ronnie, jt. auth.
  MiU, WHi-L

J67
Johns, Major.
  It happened in Baton Rouge, U.
  S.A.; a real life drama of our
  deep South today, by Major
  Johns and Ronnie Moore. [New
  York, CORE, 196]
  [12]p. 22cm.
  Cover title.
  1. Baton Rouge, La.--Race
  question. 2. Negroes--Baton
  Rouge, La. I. Congress of
  Racial Equality. II. Moore,
  Ronnie, jt. auth.
  CU-B

J68
Johnson, D. Gale.
  Soviet agriculture. New York,
  Students for a Democratic Soc-
  iety and its Peace Research and
  Education Project [196]
  7p. 28cm.
  Cover title.
  Reprinted from Bulletin of the
  Atomic Scientists, Jan. 1964.
  1. Agriculture--Russia.
  2. Russia--Econ. condit.
  I. Students for a Democratic
  Society. Peace Research and
  Education Project.
  WHi-A

J69
Johnson, Eric.
  The threat of rank-and-file
  power and the assassination of
  Dow Wilson. Boston, New En-
  gland Free Press [196]
  [23]-33p. illus. 28cm.
  Cover title.
  Reprinted from PL, July-Aug.
  1967.
  1. Wilson, Dow. 2. Trade-
  unions. I. New England Free
  Press.
  KU-RH

J70
Johnson, J.R.
  Letters on organization. [De-
  troit] Facing Reality Publish-

ing Committee [1963?]
59 leaves.   28cm.
Cover title.
1. Socialism.   I. Facing Reality
Publishing Committee.
MiU

J71
Johnson, J.R.
  Marxism and the intellectuals:
  the working class and socialism
  in a review of two books by
  British socialist Raymond Williams; plus documentary material on the destruction of
  workers papers in the U.S.
  [Detroit] Facing Reality Publishing Committee [1962]
  32p.   20cm.
  1. Socialism.   2. Labor and
  laboring classes.   3. Williams,
  Raymond.   Culture and society.
  4. Williams, Raymond.   The long
  revolution.   I. Facing Reality
  Publishing Committee.
  CU-B, MiU

J72
Johnson, James Harvey.
  Religion is a gigantic fraud.
  [San Diego, Thinkers Club,
  196]
  [2]p.   22cm.
  Caption title.
  1. Religion.   2. Atheism.
  I. Thinkers Club.
  KU-RH

J73
Johnson, Joseph.
  "They have declared me a man
  without a country".   [Minnea-
  polis, Committee to Oppose the
  Deportation of Joseph Johnson,
  1966]
  22p.   port.   22cm.
  Cover title.
  1. Socialist Workers Party.
  2. Military service, Compulsory.
  3. Deportation.   I. Committee to
  Oppose the Deportation of
  Joseph Johnson.
  MoU

J74
Johnson, Oakley C.

The foreign agent: truth and
fiction.   New York, Gus Hall-
Benjamin J. Davis Defense
Committee, 1964.
48p.   19cm.
1. Communism.   2. Internal
security.   I. Gus Hall-Benjamin
J. Davis Defense Committee.
MiU, WHi-L

J75
Johnson, Oakley C.
  My grandson, Steve.   [New York,
  1970]
  11p.   22cm.
  Cover title.
  MiU

J76
Johnson, Peter.
  Palestinians fight a three-
  faced enemy.   [Washington, D.C.,
  Middle East Research and Infor-
  mation Project, 1970?]
  [4]p.   illus.   28cm.
  Caption title.
  1. Jewish-Arab relations.
  2. Near East--Pol. & govt.
  3. Israel-Arab war, 1967.
  I. Middle East Research and
  Information Project.
  KU-RH

J77
Johnson, Russell.
  The tangled Asian web.   [New
  York, Liberation, 1965?]
  folder.   28cm.
  Caption title.
  Reprinted from Liberation, Nov.
  1965.
  1. Asia--For. rel.--U.S.
  2. U.S.--For. rel.--Asia.
  I. Liberation.
  WHi-A

J78
Johnson, Steven.
  U.S. foreign policy & imperial-
  ism.   [Ann Arbor, Radical Edu-
  cation Project, 196]
  12p.   28cm.
  Cover title.
  1. U.S.--Foreign policy--Bibl.
  I. Radical Education Project.
  CU-B, WHi-L

J79
Johnson, Steven.
   U.S. foreign policy and imperial-
   ism. Ann Arbor, Radical Educa-
   tion Project [196]
   15 [1]p. 28cm. (Study guide 4)
   Cover title.
   1. U.S.--Foreign policy--Bibl.
   I. Radical Education Project.
   MiU

JOIN
   see
Jobs of Income Now Community
   Union.

J80
Joint Self Defense Committee.
   Record of Smith Act cases. New
   York, 1956.
   11 leaves. 28cm.
   Cover title.
   1. Anti-communist movements.
   KU-J

J81
A joint treaty of peace between
   the people of the United
   States, South Vietnam & North
   Vietnam. [Chicago, Volun-
   teer's Peace Treaty, 196]
   [2]p. 28cm.
   Caption title.
   1. Vietnamese conflict, 1961-
   1975. I. Volunteer's Peace
   Treaty.
   KU-RH

J82
Jolls, Shirley.
   Kangaroo court-martial: George
   Daniels and William Harvey, two
   black Marines who got 6 and 10
   years for opposing the Vietnam
   war. [New York] Committee for
   GI Rights [1969]
   14p. illus.
   1. Negroes. 2. Soldiers.
   3. Vietnamese conflict, 1961-
   1975. I. Committee for GI
   Rights.
   MiU

J83
Jones, Beverly.
   Toward a female liberation

movement, by Beverly Jones and
Judith Brown. Boston, New En-
gland Free Press [196]
37p. 28cm.
Cover title.
1. Woman--Rights of women.
I. Brown, Judith, jt. auth.
II. New England Free Press.
KU-RH, MiU

J84
Jones, Leroi.
   Cuba libre. New York, Fair Play
   for Cuba Committee [196]
   15p.
   Cover title.
   Reprinted from Evergreen Re-
   view, Nov.-Dec. 1960.
   1. Cuba. I. Fair Play for Cuba
   Committee.
   MiU

J85
Jones for Supervisor.
   Jones leads fight to end racism
   and poverty in Alameda County.
   [Berkeley, Calif., 1968]
   [4]p. 39cm.
   Caption title.
   Reprinted from Peace & Freedom
   News.
   1. Jones, Michael. 2. Negroes
   --Civil rights. 3. Alameda
   Co., Calif.--Pol. & govt.
   I. Peace and Freedom Party.
   CU-B

J86
Jordan, Joan.
   The place of American women;
   economic exploitation of women.
   Boston, New England Free Press
   [196]
   21p. 22cm.
   Cover title.
   Reprinted from Revolutionary
   Age, v.1. no. 3; 1968.
   1. Woman--Rights of women.
   I. New England Free Press.
   KU-RH

J87
Jordan, Joan.
   Protective laws. [Detroit,
   Radical Education Project,
   1970?]

22p. illus. 22cm.
Cover title.
1. Woman--Employment. I. Radical Education Project.
KU-RH, MiU

J88
Joreen.
  The 51o/o minority group: a statistical essay, by Joreen.
  [n.p., 1969?]
  5p. 28cm.
  Caption title.
  1. Woman--History and condition of women.
  KU-RH

J89
Josefowicz, Mike.
  Co-optation city (or, "Ford has a better idea") by Mike Josefowicz and Ted Gold. [New York] Teachers for a Democratic Society [196]
  10p. 28cm.
  1. Ford Foundation. 2. Education--New York (State).
  I. Gold, Mike, jt. auth.
  II. Teachers for a Democratic Society.
  CU-B

J90
Josephson, Leon.
  The individual in Soviet law. New York, New Century Publishers, 1957.
  24p. 20cm.
  1. Law--Russia. 2. Individualism. I. New Century Publishers.
  KU-J

J91
Joyce, Frank H.
  An analysis of American racism. Nashville, Southern Student Organizing Committee [196]
  7 [1]p. 28cm.
  Cover title.
  1. Negroes--Civil rights.
  I. Southern Student Organizing Committee.
  MoU

J92
Joyce, Frank H.

An analysis of American racism. Nashville, Southern Student Organizing Committee; Boston, New England Free Press [196]
  6p. 28cm.
  Cover title.
  1. Race discrimination.
  2. Negroes--Civil rights.
  I. Southern Student Organizing Committee. II. New England Free Press.
  KU-RH

J93
Joyce, Frank H.
  Introduction, definition and analysis. Detroit, People Against Racism [196]
  8p. 28cm.
  Caption title.
  1. Negroes--Civil rights.
  I. People Against Racism.
  CU-B

J94
Joyce, Frank H.
  People's victory at New Bethel: motor city cops lose their case. [Detroit?] Rep [1970?]
  [2]p. 28cm.
  Caption title.
  1. Police--Michigan--Detroit.
  I. Radical Education Project.
  KU-RH

J95
Joyce, Frank H.
  We have met the enemy and they are us. Excerpts from a speech delivered by Frank Joyce, executive secretary, People Against Racism, at Parkard Manse Boston, Mass., April 10, 1961. [Chicago? Committee for One, 1967?]
  [3] leaves. 28cm.
  Caption title.
  1. Negroes--Civil rights.
  I. People Against Racism.
  CU-B

J96
Joyce, James Avery.
  SEATO: false alibi. [Woodmont, Promoting Enduring Peace, c1967] folder. 22cm.

Caption title.
Reprinted from The Christian
Century, Nov. 8, 1967.
1. Southeast Asia Treaty Organization. 2. Vietnamese conflict,
1961-1975. I. Promoting Enduring Peace.
KU-RH

J97
Joye, Harlon.
   Will Negroes use guns? [n.p.]
Liberal Study Group, 1963.
[4]p. 28cm.
Cover title.
1. Negroes--Civil rights.
I. Liberal Study Group.
WHi-A

J98
Joye, Harlon.
   Will Negroes use guns? [n.p.]
Students for a Democratic Soc-
iety for the Liberal Study
Group [196]
6p. 28cm.
Cover title.
1. Negroes--Civil rights.
I. Students for a Democratic
Society. II. Liberal Study

Group.
MiU, WHi-L

J99
Junco, Sergio.
   Yanqui no! Castro no! Cuba si!
by a Cuban socialist--Sergio
Junco. [New York] Young Peo-
ples Socialist League [1962]
[13]p.
Cover title.
"Assisted by Nick Howard."
1. Socialism in Cuba. 2. Cuba--
History--1959-   I. Howard,
Nick. II. Young Peoples Soc-
ialist League.
MiU

J100
Junta of Militant Organizations.
   Crackdown in Florida. [Louis-
ville, Junta of Militant Organi-
zations and Southern Conference
Educational Fund, 1970?]
[16]p. illus. 22cm.
Cover title.
1. Police--Florida. 2. Florida
--Race question. 3. Negroes--
Florida. I. Southern Confer-
ence Educational Fund.
MiU

K

K1
Kagin, J.H.
   White blindspot. Brooklyn
[1967?]
25p. 21cm. (Osawatomie pamphlets no. 1)
Cover title.
"Letter to PL spring 1967."
1. Negroes. 2. Labor and
laboring classes.
MiU

K2
Kahin, George McTurnan.
   Address to the Inter-faith
Seminar for Clergy on Vietnam,
Boston University, October 1,
1965. [Ithaca, N.Y., Distri-

buted by the Division of Life
and Work, Ithaca Area Council
of Churches, 1965]
12p. 28cm.
1. Vietnam--Pol. & govt.
2. U.S.--For. rel.--Vietnam.
3. Vietnam--For. rel.--U.S.
NIC, NUC 67-37499

K3
Kahin, George McTurnan.
   The American involvement in
Vietnam, an address by George
McT. Kahin, Cornell University,
May 1970. [Ithaca, N.Y., Glad
Day Press, 1970?]
13p. 28cm.
Cover title.

1. Vietnamese conflict, 1961-
1975. I. Glad Day Press.
NNU-T

K4
Kahin, George McTurnan.
  Cambodia: the administration's
  version and the historical
  record. [Ithaca, N.Y., Glad
  Day Press, 1970?]
  13 [1]p. map. 28cm.
  1. Cambodia. I. Glad Day Press.
  NNU-T

K5
Kahin, George McTurnan.
  Consequences of the invasion
  of Cambodia. [Ithaca, N.Y.,
  Glad Day Press, 1970?]
  5p. map. 28cm.
  1. Cambodia. I. Glad Day Press.
  NNU-T

K6
Kahin, George McTurnan.
  Consequences of the invasion
  of Cambodia; plus Cambodia
  fact sheet. [Philadelphia]
  National Peace Literature Service, American Friends Service
  Committee [1970?]
  8p. 28cm.
  1. Cambodia--Pol. & govt.
  I. Friends, Society of. American Friends Service Committee.
  KU-RH

K7
Kahin, George McTurnan.
  Some questions relating to
  American policy in Vietnam:
  remarks delivered at the seminar on Southeast Asia of the
  Council for a Livable World.
  5 March 1965. Washington,
  Council for a Livable World,
  1965.
  [3]p. 28cm. (Study paper)
  1. Vietnamese conflict, 1961-
  1975. I. Council for a Livable
  World.
  KU-RH

K8
Kahin, George McTurnan.
  The United States in Vietnam
  [by] George McT. Kahin [and]

John W. Lewis. [n.p., 1965?]
28-40p. map.
Reprinted from the Bulletin of
the Atomic Scientists, Vol. 21,
no. 6; June 1965.
1. Vietnamese conflict, 1961-
1975. I. Lewis, John Wilson,
1930-   , jt. auth.
WHi-L, NUC 69-89906

K9
Kahin, George McTurnan.
  The United States in Vietnam
  [by] George McT. Kahin [and]
  John W. Lewis. [Ithaca, N.Y.,
  Glad Day Press, 196]
  [28-41]p. 28cm.
  1. Vietnamese conflict, 1961-
  1975. I. Lewis, John Wilson,
  1930-   , jt. auth.
  MoU

K10
Kahn, Bruce.
  The Elderfield report on classified research. [Ann Arbor?
  Voice Political Party-SDS?
  1968]
  10 leaves. 28cm.
  1. Military research. 2. Michigan. University. I. Voice
  Political Party--Students for a
  Democratic Society, Ann Arbor.

K11
Kahn, Tom.
  Civil rights: the true frontier,
  with a foreword by Bayard Rustin. [New York] Donald Press,
  1963.
  23p. 23cm.
  1. Negroes--Civil rights.
  I. Rustin, Bayard, 1910-
  CU-B

K12
Kahn, Tom.
  Economics of equality. [n.p.,
  196]
  [6] leaves. 28cm.
  1. Negroes--Civil rights.
  CU-B

K13
Kahn, Tom.

The economics of equality [fore-
word by A. Philip Randolph &
Michael Harrington] New York,
League for Industrial Democracy,
1964.
70p. 28cm.
1. Negroes--Civil rights.
2. Negroes--Econ. condit.
I. Randolph, Asa Philip, 1889-
      II. Harrington, Michael.
III. League for Industrial
Democracy.
WHi-A

K14
Kahn, Tom.
The economics of equality. New
York, League for Industrial
Democracy [distributed by the
Industrial Union Dept., American Federation of Labor, Congress of Industrial Organiza-
tions] 1964.
70p. illus. 23cm. (An L.I.D.
pamphlet)
1. Negroes--Econ. condit.
2. Negroes--Civil rights.
I. League for Industrial Democracy.
NjP, CtY, IU, CU, IaU, MiU,
NNU-T, DLC 65-2066

K15
Kahn, Tom.
Goldwater and the white backlash. New York, Political Education Project of Students for
a Democratic Society [196]
5p. 28cm.
Cover title.
1. Goldwater, Barry Morris,
1909-   2. U.S.--Pol. & govt.
govt.--1963-   3. Negroes--
Civil rights. I. Students for
a Democratic Society. Political Education Project.
KU-RH

K16
Kahn, Tom.
Let us live to make men free--
the negro in America democracy.
[New York, Young People's Soc-
ialist League, 196]
iv, 25p. 28cm.
Cover title.

1. Negroes--Civil rights.
I. Young People's Socialist
League.
WHi-A

K17
Kahn, Tom.
Let us live to make men free:
the negro in American democracy. [n.p., 1960?]
25 leaves.
1. Negroes--Civil rights.
MiU, NUC 63-40406

K18
Kahn, Tom.
The political significance of
the freedom rides. [n.p.] Dis-
tributed by Students for a
Democratic Society for the
Liberal Study Group [1962]
8p. 28cm.
Cover title.
1. Negroes--Civil rights.
2. Democratic Party.
I. Students for a Democratic
Society. II. Liberal Study
Group.
WHi-A

K19
Kahn, Tom.
The problem of the new left.
New York, League for Industrial
Democracy [1966?]
[12]p. 28cm. (Looking forward
no. 6)
Reprinted from Commentary,
July 1966.
1. Student movements. I. League
for Industrial Democracy.
NNU-T

K20
Kahn, Tom.
Random thoughts on the white
backlash. New York, Distributed
by Students for a Democratic
Society for the Liberal Study
Group. [196]
5p. 28cm.
Cover title.
1. Goldwater, Barry Morris,
1909-   2. Negroes--Civil
rights. I. Students for a
Democratic Society.

II. Liberal Study Group.
WHi-A

K21
Kahn, Tom.
Unfinished revolution. [With
forewords by Norman Thomas and
James Lawson] New York [Social-
ist Party-Social Democratic
Federation] 1960.
64p. illus. 24cm.
1. Negroes--Civil rights.
I. Socialist Party-Social
Democratic Federation.
II. Thomas, Norman. III. Law-
son, James.
MH, IaU, NIC, MiU, FU, MnU,
DLC 61-1039, WHi-A

K22
Kaiser, Ernest.
In defense of the people's
black & white history and
culture. [New York, 1970]
64p.
Reprinted from Freedomways,
v. 10, no. 1-3; 1970.
1. Negroes--Education.
WHi-L

K23
Kampf, Louis.
The open up schools. [Chicago,
New University Conference,
1970?]
16p. illus. 28cm.
Cover title.
1. Universities and colleges.
2. Education. I. New University Conference.
KU-RH

K24
Kansas University Civil Rights
Council. Research Committee.
Report of the research committee on fraternities and soroi-
ties. [Lawrence, KFP Publishing House, 1965]
34p. 28cm.
1. Negroes--Civil rights.
2. Greek letter societies.
I. Kansas Free Press.
KU-RH

K25
Kansas University Committee to
End the War in Vietnam.
Vietnam? What is the United
States doing? [Lawrence, Kan.,
1967?]
[9]p. illus. 28cm.
Cover title.
1. Vietnamese conflict, 1961-
1975.
KU-A

K26
Kaplan, Ralph.
American higher education--a
bibliography. [n.p.] Distri-
buted by Students for a Demo-
cratic Society for the Liberal
Study Group [1962?]
3p. 28cm.
Caption title.
1. Universities and colleges--
Bibl. I. Students for a Demo-
cratic Society. II. Liberal
Study Group.
KU-RH

K27
Kaplan, Ralph.
University reform bibliography.
[San Francisco, Students for a
Democratic Society, 1965]
5p. 28cm.
Cover title.
1. Universities and colleges--
Bibl. I. Students for a
Democratic Society.
MiU, CU-B

K28
Karim, Abdul Rahim.
Malaysia: an arena of inter-
national conflict. [New York,
Far East Reporter, 1964?]
9p. 22cm.
1. Malaysia--Pol. & govt.
2. Malaysia--For. rel.
I. Far East Reporter.
CSt-H, NUC 68-101943

K29
Karp, Nathan.
Crisis in America: a revolution
overdue. New York, New York

Labor News, 1970.
31p. 16cm.
Cover title.
1. Socialism. I. New York Labor
News Co.
MiU

K30
Karp, Nathan.
Unionism: fraudulent or gen-
iune? New York, New York Labor
News Co., 1958.
58p.
On cover: Socialist Labor
Party.
1. Trade-unions. I. New York
Labor News Co.
CLU, CU, NN, MiU, WHi, MH

K31
Karson, Marc.
The American Federation of
Labor and negro workers, 1894-
1949, by Marc Karson [and] Ronald Radosh. [Boston, New England Free Press, 1970?]
32p. 22cm.
1. Labor and laboring classes.
2. Negroes--Employment.
3. American Federation of
Labor. I. New England Free
Press. II. Radosh, Ronald, jt.
auth.
MiU

K32
Kashtan, William, 1909-
Automation and labor. [Toron-
to, Progress Books, 1964]
27p.
Cover title.
1. Automation. 2. Labor and
laboring classes. I. Progress
Books.
CaOTU, NUC66-80325

K33
Kashtan, William, 1909-
Say no to austerity. Full employment without inflation; a
reply to Mr. Trudeau. [Toron-
to, Progress Books, 196]
16p.
Cover title.
1. Unemployed--Canada. 2. Inflation (Finance)--Canada.

3. Canada--Econ. condit.
I. Progress Books.
MiU

K34
Kashtan, William, 1909-
Why Canada should quit NATO
[Toronto, Progress Books, 1969]
37p.
Cover title.
1. Canada--Foreign policy.
2. North Atlantic Treaty Organi-
zation. I. Progress Books.
MiU

K35
Kashtan, William, 1909-
Stop union raiding. [Toronto,
Published by Progress Books for
the Communist Party of Canada,
1962]
30p.
At head of title: Solidarity
forever.
1. Trade-unions--Canada.
I. Communist Party of Canada.
CaOTU, NUC 66-89162

K36
Kaslow, Andrew.
Drugs: enslaver--not liberator.
Fight individualism--serve the
people [by Andrew Kaslow and
others. n.p., 1969]
[2]p. 36cm.
Caption title.
1. Narcotics. 2. Students for
a Democratic Society.
WHi-L

K37
Kaufer, Katherine.
The political economy of male
chauvinism [by] Katherine Kau-
fer and Tom Christoffel. [Bos-
ton, New England Free Press,
1970?]
47-[54]p. 28cm.
Caption title.
Reprinted from PL
1. Woman--Rights of women.
I. Christoffel, Tom, jt. auth.
II. New England Free Press.
MiU

K38
Kearon, Pamela.
  Men-hating. New York, The
  Feminists [1969]
  3p. 28cm.
  Caption title.
  1. Woman--Rights of women.
  I. Feminists.
  KU-RH, WHi-L

K39
Kearon, Pamela.
  Power as a function of the
  group--some notes. New York,
  The Feminists [1969]
  4p. 28cm.
  Caption title.
  1. Woman. I. Feminists.
  KU-RH

K40
Kearon, Pamela.
  Power as a function of the
  group--some notes. New York,
  The Feminists [1969]
  3p. 28cm.
  Caption title.
  1. Woman. I. Feminists.
  WHi-L

K41
Kearon, Pamela.
  Rules and responsibility in a
  leaderless feminist revolutionary group. New York, The Feminists [1969]
  3p. 28cm.
  Caption title.
  1. Woman--Rights of Women.
  I. Feminists.
  KU-RH

K42
Kearon, Pamela.
  Rules and responsibility in a
  leaderless revolutionary (fem-
  inist) group. New York, The
  Feminists [1969]
  5 leaves. 28cm.
  Caption title.
  1. Woman. I. Feminists.
  WHi-L

K43
Kelly, Kathie.
  Civil liberties resolution, by

Kathie Kelly and Tom Barton.
  [n.p., Student Peace Union,
  1964]
  Caption title.
  1. Civil rights. 2. Young
  Socialist Alliance. 3. U.S.--
  Foreign relations--Russia.
  4. Russia--Foreign relations--
  U.S. I. Barton, Tom, jt. auth.
  II. Student Peace Union.
  CU-B

K44
Kelman, Herbert C.
  New departures in social action:
  the response of intellectuals
  to the Vietnam conflict, [n.p.,
  196]
  8 leaves. 28cm.
  Address delivered to the International Conference on Alternative Perspectives on Vietnam,
  Ann Arbor, 1965.
  1. Vietnamese conflict, 1961-
  1975. I. International Conference on Alternative Perspectives on Vietnam, Ann
  Arbor, 1965.
  CU-B

K45
Kelman, Steven.
  Beyond new leftism. [New York,
  Young People's Socialist
  League, 1969]
  21p. 19x8cm.
  Cover title.
  Reprinted from Commentary, Feb.
  1969.
  1. Student movements. 2. Youth
  --Political activity. I. Young
  People's Socialist League.
  WHi-L, KU-RH

K46
Kemble, Penn.
  Rediscovering American labor.
  [New York, League for Indus-
  trial Democracy, 1970?]
  10p. 28cm. (Looking forward
  no. 18)
  Cover title.
  1. Labor and laboring classes.
  I. League for Industrial
  Democracy.
  NNU-T

K47
Kemp, Stewart W.
  The military-civilian complex.
  [Washington, National Council
  to Repeal the Draft, 1970?]
  18-21p.   28cm.
  Caption title.
  1. Military service, Compulsory.
  I. National Council to Repeal
  the Draft.
  KU-RH

K48
Kempton, Murray.
  Panther 21: strangers to jus-
  tice, by Murray Kempton & David
  Shimkin.   [New York, Committee
  to Defend the Panther 21, c1970]
  [24]p.
  Cover title.
  1. Black Panther Party.
  I. Shimkin, David, jt. auth.
  II. Committee to Defend the
  Panther 21.
  NNU-T

K49
Kennan, George Frost, 1904-
  Berlin: disengagement revisited
  [introduction by Norman Thomas.
  n.p., National Committee for a
  Sane Nuclear Policy, 1961]
  [28]p.   22cm.
  Cover title.
  Reprinted from Foreign Affairs,
  Jan. 1959.
  1. Berlin question (1945-   )
  I. Thomas, Norman.   II. Nation-
  al Committee for a Sane Nuclear
  Policy.
  WHi-A

K50
Kentuckians Against Kentucky Un-
    American Activities Committee.
  If you have nothing to hide.
  [Louisville, 196]
  23p.   illus.
  Cover title.
  1. Anti-communist movements--
  Kentucky.   2. Internal security
  --Kentucky.   3. Civil rights--
  Kentucky.
  WHi-L

K51
Keyserling, Leon.
  Inflation and recession.   [New
  York, League for Industial De-
  mocracy, 1970]
  [7]p.   (Looking forward, no. 17)
  1. Inflation (Finance)   2. U.S.
  --Econ. condit.   I. League for
  Industrial Democracy.
  WHi-L

K52
Khrushchev, Nikita Sergeevich,
    1894-
  Khrushchev speaks to Moscow
  voters; speech at a meeting of
  the Kalinin Election District,
  March 16, 1962.   [New York]
  Crosscurrents Press [1962]
  32p.   22cm.   (Documents of current history, no. 23)
  1. Russia--Pol. & govt.--1953-
        I. Crosscurrents Press.
  DLC 62-16512

K53
Khrushchev, Nikita Sergeevich,
    1894-
  Khrushchev's tour of Asia; a
  report delivered by Nikita S.
  Khrushchev to a meeting in Moscow on March 5, 1960, on his
  trip to India, Burma, Indonesia,
  and Afghanistan, February 10 to
  March 5.   New York, Crosscurrents Press [1960]
  32p.   illus., ports.   22cm.
  1. Asia.   2. Visits of state--
  Asia.   I. Crosscurrents Press.
  NcD, DLC 61-4589

K54
Khrushchev, Nikita Sergeevich,
    1894-
  Mr. Khrushchev speaks; interview [with Daniel Schorr and
  others] broadcast over CBS
  Radio and Television network on
  June 2, 1957.   [New York, National Council of American-Soviet Friendship, 1957]
  16p.   23cm.
  1. Russia--Pol. & govt.--1953-
        2. Russia--For. rel.--

1945-   I. Schorr, Daniel
L.   II. National Council of
American-Soviet Friendship.
III. Columbia Broadcasting
System.
CSt-H, NN

K55
Khrushchev, Nikita Sergeevich,
    1894-
The new content of peaceful co-
existence in the nuclear age.
Speech by N.S. Khrushchev at
the 6th Congress of the Socialist Unity Party of Germany,
Berlin, January 16, 1963. New
York, Crosscurrents Press
[c1963]
48p. 22cm. (Documents of
current history, no. 29)
1. Russia--Foreign policy.
2. German reunification question
(1949-   ) I. Crosscurrents
Press.
KU-RH

K56
Khrushchev, Nikita Sergeevich,
    1894-
A peace treaty with Germany;
three speeches. [New York]
Crosscurrents Press [1961]
51p. 22cm. (Documents of
current history, no. 15)
Cover title.
1. German reunification quest-
ion (1949-   ) 2. Berlin
question (1945-   ) 3. U.S.
--For. rel.--Russia. 4. Russia
--For. rel.--U.S. I. Cross-
currents Press.
MiU, CSt-H, IEN, NIC FMU,
DLC 61-19935.

K57
Khrushchev, Nikita Sergeevich,
    1894-
The present international
situation and the foreign policy of the Soviet Union; report
to the USSR Supreme Soviet,
December 12, 1962. New York,
Crosscurrents Press [1963]
55p. 22cm. (Documents of current history, no. 27)
1. Russia--For. rel.--

1963-   2. World Politics--
1955-   I. Crosscurrents
Press.
MH, CtY, ICU, FMU, DLC 63-12760

K58
Khrushchev, Nikita Sergeevich,
    1894-
Proposals by the USSR; speech
[at the] fifteenth session of
the U.N. General Assembly,
Sept. 23, 1960. New York,
Crosscurrents Press [1960]
88p.
1. Disarmaments. 2. World
politics--1955-   3. Russia
--Foreign policy. I. Crosscurrents Press.
DS

K59
Khrushchev, Nikita Sergeevich,
    1894-
Raising the Soviet standard of
living: report by N.S. Khrushchev to the USSR Supreme Soviet, May 5, 1960; concluding
remarks, May 7; laws passed by
the Supreme Soviet, May 7.
New York, Crosscurrents Press
[1960]
101p. illus. 22cm.
1. Russia--Econ. condit.--1959-
        I. Crosscurrents Press.
CSt-H, KU, MoSW, MiU, NN,
DLC 60-4519

K60
Khrushchev, Nikita Sergeevich,
    1894-
Report on the program of the
Communist Party of the Soviet
Union, Oct. 17, 1961. New York,
Crosscurrents Press [1961]
183p. (Documents of current
history, 19)
1. Communism--Russia. 2. Kom-
munisticheskaia partiia Sovets-
kogo Soiuza. I. Crosscurrents
Press.
MH, KU-J

K61
Khrushchev, Nikita Sergeevich,
    1894-
Report to the Central Committee

of the CSPU to the 22nd Congress
of the Communist Party of the
Soviet Union and Khrushchev's
concluding speech to the 22nd
Congress, October 27, 1961.
New York, Crosscurrents Press
[c1961]
1. Communism--Russia. I. Kommunisticheskaia partiia Sovetskogo Soiuza. I. Crosscurrents
Press.
PCamA, NUC 65-4204, KU-J

K62
Khrushchev, Nikita Sergeevich,
    1894-
  The socialist way, national
  television address, Washington,
  D.C., September 27, 1959. [New
  York, New Century Publishers,
  1960]
  15p. 19cm.
  Cover title.
  1. Russia--Foreign policy.
  2. Communism--Russia. I. New
  Century Publishers.
  KU-J

K63
Khrushchev, Nikita Sergeevich,
    1894-
  Soviet policy in the current
  international situation; speech
  at the USSR Conference of
  Leaders in the Emulation Movement of Communist Work Teams
  and Shock Workers, May 28, 1960.
  New York, Crosscurrents Press
  [1960]
  59p. illus. 22cm. (Information series on the Soviet
  Union)
  1. Russia--For. rel.--1945-
        I. Crosscurrents Press.
  MiU, IU, CLU, MH, MoSW,
  DLC 60-50152

K64
Khrushchev, Nikita Sergeevich,
    1894-
  The Soviet stand on Germany.
  9 key documents including diplomatic papers and major
  speeches. Proposals for a
  German peace treaty, with a
  letter to the American people

from Nikita S. Khrushchev.
[New York] Crosscurrents Press
[c1961]
157p. 22cm.
1. German reunification question (1949-   ) 2. Berlin
question (1945-   ) 3. Russia
--For. rel.--U.S. 4. U.S.--
For. rel.--Russia. I. Crosscurrents Press.
KU-RH

K65
Khrushchev, Nikita Sergeevich,
    1894-
  Speech at the third Congress of
  the Rumanian Workers' Party,
  June 22, 1960. [New York,
  Crosscurrents Press, 1960]
  36p.
  1. Communism--Rumania.
  I. Crosscurrents Press.
  MH, FU, AAP, NIC, GU, NNC, NN

K66
Khrushchev, Nikita Sergeevich,
    1894-
  Speech by Nikita S. Khrushchev.
  Proposals by the USSR. Septem-
  ber 23, 1960. New York, Cross-
  currents Press [1960]
  88p. 22cm. (Information ser-
  ies on the Soviet Union)
  At head of title: Fifteenth
  session of the U.N. General
  Assembly.
  1. Russia--For. rel.--1945-
          2. World politics--1955-
          3. Disarmament.
  I. Crosscurrents Press.
  DS, IEN, NIC, NNC, NN, OCL,
  NNC-L, MB

K67
Khrushchev, Nikita Sergeevich,
    1894-
  Speeches. Pre-election address
  to his meeting in Budapest on
  the 13th anniversary of Hungary's liberation from fascism,
  Apr. 3, 1958. Ottawa Press
  office, USSR Embassy in Canada
  [1958]
  52p. 21cm.
  1. Russia--Pol. & govt.--1945-
          2. Russia--For. rel.--

1945-
NN

K68
Khrushchev, Nikita Sergeevich,
    1894-
    Statement and replies to quest-
ions, Gorky Park, Moscow, May
11, 1960: the U-2 Plane Incident. Photos. of the exhibit
on the U-2 Plane Incident at
Gorky Park, Moscow. Translated
from Pravda, May 13, 1960.
New York, Crosscurrents Press
[1960]
32p. illus. 22cm.
1. U-2 Incident, 1960.
I. Crosscurrents Press.
CSt-H, ICU, NNC, OCI,
DLC 60-50344

K69
Khrushchev, Nikita Sergeevich,
    1894-
    Three documents of current his-
tory. [New York] Crosscurrents
Press [1961]
36p. 21cm.
1. Atomic weapons and disarmament. 2. German reunification
question (1949-   ) 3. Rus-
sia--Foreign policy. I. Crosscurrents Press.
KU-RH, NcD, NNC, MH, FMU, NIC,
DLC 61-19197

K70
Khrushchev, Nikita Sergeevich,
    1894-
    Total disarmament in four
years; address before United
Nations, September 18, 1959
and text of Soviet proposals.
[New York, National Council of
American-Soviet Friendship,
1959]
30p. 22cm.
1. Disarmament. I. National
Council of American-Soviet
Friendship.
MH, GU, NIC, CLSU, DLC 60-204

K71
Khrushchev, Nikita Sergeevich,
    1894-
    World Congress for General

Disarmament and Peace; address,
July 10, 1962: general and complete disarmament--guarantee of
peace and security for all people. New York, Crosscurrents
Press [1962]
64p. 19cm. (Documents of current history, no. 25)
1. Disarmament. I. Crosscurrents Press.
DLC 62-6354

K72
Kifner, John.
    The story of the murder of Fred
Hampton (which the N.Y. Sunday
Times refused to print) [New
York, Committee to Defend the
Panthers, 1970]
[14]p. illus. 28cm.
Cover title.
1. Hampton, Fred, 1948-1969.
2. Black Panther Party.
I. Committee to Defend the
Panthers.
NNU-T

K73
King, Martin Luther, 1929-1968.
    America's greatest crisis.
[New York, Transport Workers
Union of America, AFL-CIO,
1961]
16p. port. 22cm.
"An address by Rev. Martin
Luther King to the 11th Consti-
tutional Convention, Transport
Workers Union of America, AFL-
CIO."
1. Negroes--Civil rights.
WHi-L, NUC 63-42531

K74
King, Martin Luther, 1929-1968.
    Beyond Vietnam; an address
sponsored by The Clergy and Lay-
men Concerned about Vietnam,
Riverside Church, New York
City, April 4, 1967. [Palo
Alto, Calif., Altoan Press,
1967]
12p. 25cm.
Caption title.
1. Vietnamese conflict, 1961-
1975. I. Clergy and Laymen
Concerned About Vietnam.
TxU, NUC 68-92175

K75
King, Martin Luther, 1929-1968.
  Conscience for change, by Martin
  Luther King, Jr. Canadian
  Broadcasting Co. [1967]
  46p. 20cm. (Massey lectures,
  7th ser.)
  1. Negroes--Civil rights.
  DLC 68-116325

K76
King, Martin Luther, 1929-1968.
  Declaration of independence
  from the war in Vietnam. Text
  of a speech delivered at the
  Riverside Church, April 4, 1967.
  [n.p., 196]
  6p. 28cm.
  Caption title.
  1. Vietnamese conflict, 1961-
  1975.
  KU-RH, WHi-L

K77
King, Martin Luther, 1929-1968.
  The domestic impact of the war
  in Vietnam [n.p., 196]
  4p. 28cm.
  Caption title.
  1. Vietnamese conflict, 1961-
  1975.
  CU-B, WHi-A

K78
King, Martin Luther, 1929-1968.
  I have a dream; speech at the
  March on Washington. [n.p.]
  c1963.
  6p. 23cm.
  Caption title.
  1. Negroes--Civil rights.
  DLC 63-25946

K79
King, Martin Luther, 1929-1968.
  In memoriam. The role of the
  behavioral scientist in the
  civil rights movements. [n.p.,
  1968?]
  7 leaves. 36cm.
  Caption title.
  1. Negroes--Civil rights.
  CU-B

K80
King, Martin Luther, 1929-1968.

  Letter from Birmingham city
  jail. [Philadelphia, American
  Friends Service Committee, 1963]
  15p. 23cm.
  Cover title.
  Addressed to Bishop C.C.J. Car-
  penter and seven other clergy-
  men.
  1. Negroes--Birmingham, Ala.
  2. Birmingham, Ala.--Race question. I. Friends, Society of.
  American Friends Service Committee.
  WHi-L, CU-B, CtY-D, NNC, IaU,
  NUC 65-3868

K81
King, Martin Luther, 1929-1968.
  The method of non-violence.
  [n.p., 1957?]
  [10] leaves. 29cm.
  Caption title.
  1. Nonviolence. 2. Negroes--
  Southern States. 3. Southern
  States--Race question.
  NN, NUC 65-4979

K82
King, Martin Luther, 1929-1968.
  Our struggle; the story of
  Montgomery. [New York, Congress
  of Racial Equality, 1957]
  [7]p. illus.
  Reprinted from Liberation,
  April 1956.
  1. Montgomery, Ala.--Race
  question. 2. Negroes--Mont-
  gomery, Ala. I. Congress of
  Racial Equality.
  WHi-L, NIC, NN, NcD, DLC

K83
King, Martin Luther, 1929-1968.
  Pilgrimage to nonviolence.
  [Nyack, N.Y., Fellowship Pub-
  lications, c1960]
  [4]p. 28cm.
  Caption title.
  Reprinted from Christian Century.
  1. Nonviolence. I. Fellowship
  Publications.
  KU-RH

K84
King, Martin Luther, 1929-1968.
  Showdown for nonviolence. [n.

p.] Cowles Communications, c1968.
[3]p. port.
Caption title.
Reprinted from Look, Ap. 16,
1968.
1. Nonviolence. 2. Negroes--
Civil rights.
WHi-L

K85
King, Martin Luther, 1929-1968.
A testament of hope. In his
final published statement; the
fallen civil rights leader
points the way out of America's
racial turmoil into the promised land of true equality.
[Nyack, N.Y.? Fellowship Publications? 1969?]
8p. illus. 28cm.
Caption title.
Reprinted from Playboy, Jan.
1969.
1. Negroes--Civil rights.
I. Fellowship Publications.
KU-RH

K86
King, Martin Luther, 1929-1968.
"Unwise and untimely". A letter from eight Alabama clergy-
men to Martin Luther King Jr.
and his reply to them on order
and common sense, the law and
justice, nonviolence and love.
[New York, Fellowship of Reconciliation, 196]
18 [4]p. 23x10cm.
Cover title.
Reprinted from Liberation, June
1963.
1. Negroes--Civil rights.
2. Nonviolence. I. Fellowship
Publications.
KU-RH, MoU

K87
King, Martin Luther, 1929-1968.
Vietnam is upon us. [n.p.,
1968]
4p. 28cm.
Caption title.
1. Vietnamese conflict, 1961-
1975.
WHi-A

K88
Kirk, Richard.
Crisis and leadership, by
Richard Kirk and Clara Kaye.
Seattle, Freedom Socialist
Publications, 1969.
76p. 21cm.
1. U.S.--Pol. & govt.--1963-
        2. Socialism. 3. World
politics--1965-   I. Kaye,
Clara, jt. auth. II. Freedom
Socialist Publications.
WHi-L, KU-RH

K89
Kirk, Richard.
Why we left the Socialist
Workers Party, by Richard Kirk
[and others. Seattle, Freedom
Socialist Party of Washington,
1966?]
8p. 22cm.
Caption title.
1. Socialist Workers Party.
I. Freedom Socialist Party.
CU-B

K90
Kissinger, C. Clark.
The Burns strike; a case study
in student participation in
labor. New York, Students for
a Democratic Society [196]
4p. 28cm.
1. Labor and laboring classes--
Madison, Wis. 2. Burns Garage,
Madison, Wis. 3. Student move-
ments--Madison, Wis. I. Students for a Democratic Society.
WHi-L, NNU-T

K91
Kissinger, C. Clark.
The S.D.S. chapter organizer's
handbook. [n.p.] Students for
a Democratic Society [196]
21p. 28cm.
Cover title.
1. Students for a Democratic
Society. 2. Organization.
I. Students for a Democratic
Society.
WHi-A

K92
Kissinger, C. Clark.

Why is there a SDS? The American student in the American society. [n.p., Students for a
Democratic Society? 196]
[6]p. 28cm.
Caption title.
1. Student movements. 2. Students for a Democratic Society.
WHi-A

K93
Kittredge, Jack.
  Chapter organizer's handbook.
  Chicago, Students for a Demo-
  cratic Society [196]
  19p. 28cm.
  Cover title.
  1. Organization. I. Students
  for a Democratic Society.
  MiU-H

K94
Klare, Michael T.
  A brief history of the New York
  Committee of Students for Peace
  in Vietnam. [New York, Friends
  of SPV, 1966]
  3 leaves. 36cm.
  Caption title.
  1. New York Committee of Students for Peace in Vietnam.
  2. Student movements--New York
  (City) 3. Vietnamese conflict,
  1961-1975.
  WHi-L

K95
Klare, Michael T.
  The great South Asian war: U.S.
  imperial strategy in Asia.
  [New York.] North American
  Congress on Latin America [1970]
  13p. illus. 28cm.
  Cover title.
  1. U.S.--Relations (general)
  with Asia, Southeastern.
  2. Imperialism. 3. Asia, South-
  eastern--Pol. & govt. 4. Viet-
  namese conflict, 1961-1975.
  I. North American Congress on
  Latin America.
  KU-RH, MiU

K96
Klare, Michael T.
  Some notes on high-school anti-

war organization. [n.p.] Summer Training Institute of the
National Coordinating Committee
to End the War in Vietnam, 1966.
[2] leaves. 36cm.
Caption title.
1. Student movements. 2. High
schools. I. National Coordinating Committee to End the War
in Vietnam. Summer Training
Institute.
WHi-L

K97
Klare, Michael T.
  The university-military complex:
  a directory and related documents. New York, North American Congress on Latin America
  [1968?]
  58p. illus. 28cm.
  1. Universities and colleges.
  2. Biological warfare. 3. Military research. 4. U.S.--Foreign
  policy. I. North American Congress on Latin America.
  WHi-L, KU-RH

K98
Klare, Michael T.
  The university-military-police
  complex: a directory and related
  documents. [New York] North
  American Congress on Latin
  America [c1970]
  88p. illus. 28cm.
  1. Universities and colleges.
  2. Police. 3. Military research. 4. Biological warfare.
  5. U.S.--Foreign policy.
  I. North American Congress on
  Latin America.
  KU-RH, CSt, DLC

K99
Klawitter, Robert.
  Degrading education [a proposal
  for abolishing the grading sys-
  tem. Chicago, New University
  Conference, 196 ?]
  12p. 28cm.
  Cover title.
  1. Grading and marking (Students)
  2. Universities and colleges.
  I. New University Conference.
  KU-RH

K100
Kleiman, Mark.
  High school reform: towards a
  student movement. Chicago,
  Students for a Democratic Society [196]
  10p. 22cm.
  Cover title.
  1. High schools. 2. Education.
  3. Student movements. I. Students for a Democratic Society.
  CU-B, KU-RH

K101
Kleiman, Mark.
  High school reform: towards a
  student movement. [Chicago,
  Students for a Democratic Society, 1967]
  13p. 22cm.
  Cover title.
  1. High schools. 2. Education.
  3. Student movements. I. Students for a Democratic Society.
  MiU

K102
Kleiman, Mark.
  High school reform: towards a
  student movement. [Nashville]
  Southern Student Organizing
  Committee [196]
  7p. 28cm.
  Cover title.
  1. High schools. 2. Education.
  3. Student movements. I. Southern Student Organizing Committee.
  KU-RH, MoU

K103
Klonsky, Mike.
  Revolutionary Youth Movement
  II, by Mike Klonsky [and others.
  Boston? New England Free Press?
  1970?]
  8p. illus. 28cm. (Documents
  on SDS and the SDS split)
  Cover title.
  Reprinted from RYM New Left
  Notes, July 8, 1969.
  1. Students for a Democratic
  Society. Revolutionary Youth
  Movement II. I. New England
  Free Press.
  KU-RH

K104
Knappman, Ed.
  A realistic approach to political action [by Ed Knappman
  and Peter Irons. n.p., 196]
  3p. 36cm.
  Caption title.
  1. Student Peace Union.
  2. Peace. I. Irons, Peter,
  jt. auth.
  WHi-A

K105
Knight, Bryan M.
  Poverty in Canada. [Montreal,
  Our Generation, 196]
  8-[22]p.
  Caption title.
  At head of title: An overview.
  1. Poor--Canada. I. Our
  Generation.
  NNU-T

K106
Knoll, Erwin.
  The military establishment
  rides high. [Woodmont, Promo-
  ting Enduring Peace, 196]
  [4]p. 23cm.
  Caption title.
  Reprinted from The Progressive,
  Feb. 1969.
  1. U.S.--Military policy.
  2. Corporations. I. Promoting
  Enduring Peace.
  KU-RH

K107
Knowledge and control: the issue
    of abortion. Boston, Female
    Liberation [1970]
  41p. 28cm.
  Cover title.
  1. Abortion. 2. Woman--Rights
  of women. I. Female Liberation.
  CU-B

K108
Koch, William H.
  The dual approach: an alternative in community development.
  [New York, Students for a Democratic Society and its Economic
  Research and Action Project,
  196]
  7p. 28cm.

Cover title.
1. Poverty. 2. Community or-
ganization. I. Students for a
Democratic Society. Economic
Research and Action Project.
WHi-A

K109
Koedt, Anne.
    The myth of the vaginal orgasm.
    Boston, New England Free Press
    [196]
    4 [1]p. 28cm.
    Cover title.
    1. Woman. 2. Sex. 3. Vagina.
    I. New England Free Press.
    KU-RH

K110
Kolko, Gabriel.
    The decline of American radi-
    calism in the Twentieth Century.
    Boston, New England Free Press
    [196]
    [9]-26p. 21cm.
    Cover title.
    Reprinted from Studies on the
    Left, Sept./Oct. 1966.
    1. Socialism. 2. Communism.
    I. New England Free Press.
    KU-RH

K111
Kolko, Gabriel.
    Taxation and inequality. Bos-
    ton, New England Free Press
    [196]
    [30]-45p. 21cm.
    Cover title.
    Reprinted from Kolko's The
    Triumph of Conservatism and
    Wealth and Power in America.
    1. Taxation. I. New England
    Free Press.
    KU-RH

K112
Komatsu, David.
    Mr. Johnson's little war on
    poverty. [Chicago, American
    Socialist Organizing Committee,
    196]
    28p. illus. 22cm.

Cover title.
1. Poverty. 2. U.S. Office of
Economic Opportunity. I. American Socialist Organizing Committee.
MiU

K113
Kommunisticheskaia partiia Sovets-
    kogo Soiuza.
    Program of the Communist Party
    of the Soviet Union (draft)
    New York, Crosscurrents Press
    [1961]
    128p. 22cm. (Documents of
    current no. 16)
    1. Communism--Russia. I. Cross-
    currents Press.
    KU-RH

K114
Kopkind, Andrew.
    The new generation of student
    organizers, or pulling the
    great society by its ears. Los
    Angeles, Students for a Demo-
    cratic Society [196]
    8p. 28cm.
    Reprinted from New Republic.
    1. Students for a Democratic
    Society.
    MiU-H

K115
Kopkind, Andrew.
    Of, by and for the poor; the
    new generation of student or-
    ganizers. [Chicago, Students
    for a Democratic Society, 196]
    [6]p. 28cm.
    Caption title.
    Reprinted from The New Republic,
    June 19, 1965.
    1. Students for a Democratic
    Society. 2. Student movements.
    3. Student Nonviolent Coordina-
    ting Committee. I. Students
    for a Democratic Society.
    WHi-L, KU-RH

K116
Kotelchuck, David.

Nashville, a prelimary study of
the power structure, by David
Kotelchuck and Ronda Stilley.
[Ann Arbor, Radical Education
Project, 196]
8p. 28cm.
Cover title.
1. Nashville--Pol. & govt.
2. Power (Social science)
I. Radical Education Project.
II. Stilley, Ronda, jt. auth.
WHi-A

K117
Kotelchuck, David.
Nashville, a preliminary study
of the power structure, by Dave
& Ronda Kotelchuck. Nashville,
Southern Student Organizing
Committee [196]
9p. 28cm.
Cover title.
1. Nashville--Pol. & govt.
2. Power (Social science)
I. Southern Student Organizing
Committee. II. Kotelchuck,
Ronda, jt. auth.
CU-B

K118
Krebs, Allen.
The university. Ann Arbor,
Radical Education Project
[196]
9p. illus. 28cm.
Cover title.
Reprinted from Treason, Summer
1967.
1. Student movements. 2. University and colleges. I. Radical Education Project.
MoU

K119
Krebs, Allen.
The university. Boston, New
England Free Press [196]
9p. illus. 28cm.
Cover title.
Reprinted from Treason, summer
1967.
1. Universities and colleges.
2. Student movements. I. New
England Free Press.
KU-RH

K120
Krebs, Sharon.
A history of the Cuban revolution: 1968-1959. [Chicago,
Students for a Democratic Society, 196]
folder (8p.) illus. 22cm.
Caption title.
1. Cuba--History. I. Students
for a Democratic Society.
MoU, KU-RH

K121
Krickus, Richard.
Peace research priorities, pre-
pared by Richard Krickus on the
basis of communications from
Kenneth Boulding, Bernard Feld,
Arthur Larson, Charles Osgood,
Ithiel Pool, Richard Snyder.
Washington, Peace Research In-
stitute, 1963.
13p. 28cm.
Cover title.
1. Disarmament. 2. Peace.
I. Peace Research Institute,
Washington, D.C.
MH-L, NUC 65-15163

K122
Krooth, Dick.
The people have a cause; join
together to be recognized. [n.
p., 1967?]
15p.
1. Mexicans in the U.S.
2. Minorities. 3. Labor and
laboring classes--Wisconsin.
WHi-L

K123
Kropotkin, Petr Alekseevich,
      Kniaz, 1842-1921.
The expropriation of dwellings.
[San Francisco, Friends of Dur-
ruti, 1969]
7p. 22cm.
Cover title.
Reprinted from Anarchy, Aug.
1969.
1. Housing. I. Friends of
Durruti.
CU-B

K124
Kropotkin, Petr Alekseevich,

Kniaz, 1848-1921.
Revolutionary government; a
pamphlet with special significance in the day of peace candidates and multi-racial leftist
slates. [Van Nuys, Calif.,
SRAF Print Co-op] 1970.
[20]p.   22cm.
Cover title.
1. Revolutions.   2. Anarchism
and anarchists.   I. SRAF Print
Co-op.
MiU

K125
Kubota, Stephen T.
  Roots of resistance.   [Honolulu]
  Hawaii Resistance, 1968.
  [1] leaf.   28cm.
  Caption title.
  1. Government, Resistance to.
  I. Hawaii Resistance.
  CU-B

K126
Kukich, George.
  Which way SDS [by George Kukich
  and others.   n.p., Students for
  a Democratic Society? 196]
  2 leaves.   28cm.
  Caption title.
  1. Students for a Democratic
  Society.   2. Socialism.
  I. Students for a Democratic
  Society.
  KU-RH

K127
Kunkin, Arthur.
  Realignment: one year after the
  party convention [signed by
  Arthur Kunkin and others.

Maywood, Calif., 1961?]
8 [2]leaves.   28cm.
Cover title.
1. Socialist Party (U.S.)
WHi-A

K128
Kunstler, William.
  In defense of Rap Brown.   [n.p.,
  Student Nonviolent Coordinating
  Committee? 1969?]
  [4] leaves.   28cm.
  Caption title.
  1. Brown, H. Rap.   I. Student
  Nonviolent Coordinating Com-
  mittee.
  KU-RH

K129
Kunstler, William.
  In defense of Rap Brown.   [New
  York, H. Rap Brown Defense Com-
  mittee, 1969]
  4 leaves.   28cm.
  Cover title: Let rap rap.
  1. Brown, H. Rap.   I. H. Rap
  Brown Defense Committee.
  WHi-L

K130
Kupferberg, Tuli.
  Sex & war.   [New York, Birth
  Press, c1962]
  vip.   28cm.   (Pedantic pamphlet
  number 2)
  Cover title.
  1. Sex.   2. War.   I. Birth
  Press.
  MiU

☦

L

☦

L1
Labor action.
  Introduction to independent
  socialism; selected articles
  from Labor action, edited by
  Hal Draper.   Berkeley, Calif.,
  Independent Socialist Press

[1963]
242p. illus. (Independent
socialist clippingbooks, no. 1)
"Articles from the annual 'pam-
phlet-issues' of...the weekly
published by the Independent
Socialist League...from 1950 on."

1. Socialism. 2. Communism.
I. Draper, Hal, ed. II. In-
dependent Socialist League.
MiU, IEB, NUC 69-17854

L2
Labor breakthrough in the south-
    ern classroom; University of
    Virginia. New York, League
    for Industrial Democracy,
    1968.
    44 [7]p. illus. 28cm.
    1. Labor and laboring classes--
    Virginia. I. League for Indus-
    trial Democracy.
    NNU-T

L3
Labor Committee for Peace in
    Vietnam.
    The unspeakable war. [New York,
    1966?]
    28p. illus. 22cm.
    Cover title.
    1. U.S.--Foreign relations--
    Vietnam. 2. U.S.--Military
    policy.
    WHi-L, MiU, NB, NUC 68-107479

L4
Labor Research Association.
    Apologists for monopoly. New
    York, International Publishers
    [1955]
    62p. 21cm.
    1. Monopolies. I. Internation-
    al Publishers.
    KU-J, DLC 55-1329

L5
Labor Research Association.
    The burden of taxes. New York,
    International Publishers [1956]
    47p. 20cm.
    1. Taxation. I. International
    Publishers.
    GA, CtY, KU-J, DLC 56-58255

L6
Labor Research Association.
    U.S. and the Philippines.
    [New York] International Pub-
    lishers [1958]
    64p. illus. 21cm.
    1. Philippine Islands--Pol. &

govt.--1946-   I. Inter-
national Publishers.
KU-J, NIC, CtY, MiU, CSt, NcD,
L31

L7
Labor Youth League. Education
    Dept.
    Learning about Marxism. [n.p.]
    1956.
    15 leaves. 28cm.
    Cover title.
    1. Socialism. 2. Marx, Karl,
    1818-1883.

L8
The Labyrinthine war, by a cor-
    respondent Vientiane. [Ith-
    aca, N.Y., Glad Day Press,
    1970?]
    [2]p. illus. 28cm.
    1. Laos. I. Glad Day Press.
    NNU-T

L9
Lacey, Fred.
    Memphis workers fight; the city
    sanitation workers' strike.
    Boston, New England Free Press
    [1969?]
    49-58p. illus. 28cm.
    Cover title.
    Reprinted from PL, Dec. 1968.
    1. Labor and laboring classes--
    Memphis, Tenn. 2. Memphis--
    Sanitation Workers Strike, 1968.
    I. New England Free Press.
    KU-RH

L10
La Feber, Walter.
    The Indochina war, a speech by
    Walter La Feber, Cornell Uni-
    versity, May 1970. [Ithaca,
    N.Y., Glad Day Press, 1970?]
    12p. 28cm.
    Cover title.
    1. Vietnamese conflict, 1961-
    1975. I. Glad Day Press.
    NNU-T

L11
Laidler, Harry Willington,
    1884-
    The Socialist Party, U.S.A.; its
    effect on social thought and

action. [New York? 196]
2p. 28cm.
Caption title.
1. Socialist Party (U.S.)
2. Social change.
KU-RH

L12
Lakey, George.
  They didn't call it nonviolence,
  but. Three cases of civilian
  insurrection in Latin America,
  by George Lakey and Patricia
  Parkman with the research assistance of Cynthia L. Adcock.
  Rev. Philadelphia, Quaker Action Group, 1969.
  8p. 28cm.
  Cover title.
  1. Nonviolence. 2. Revolutions
  --Latin America. I. Parkman,
  Patricia, jt. auth. II. Quaker Action Group.
  KU-RH

L13
Laliberte, Jean.
  Student social action. [Mon-
  treal, Our Generation, 196]
  [32-39]p. illus.
  Cover title.
  1. Student movement--Canada.
  I. Our Generation.
  NNU-T

L14
Lamb, Helen B.
  The tragedy of Vietnam; where
  do we go from here? [New York,
  Basic Pamphlets, c1964]
  49p. 14cm. (Basic pamphlets--
  17)
  Cover title.
  1. Vietnamese conflict, 1961-
  1975. I. Basic Pamphlets.
  MiU, KU-RH

L15
Lamb, Robert K.
  How to research your own hometown. Ann Arbor, Radical Education Project [196]
  8p. 28cm.
  Cover title.
  1. Community organization.

2. Cities and towns. I. Radical Education Project.
WHi-A

L16
Lamb, Robert K.
  Suggestions for a study of
  your hometown. [Nashville,
  Southern Student Organizing
  Committee [196]
  7p. 28cm.
  Cover title.
  1. Community organization.
  2. Power (Social science)
  3. Cities and towns. I. Southern Student Organizing Committee.
  CU-B, MiU

L17
Lamont, Corliss, 1902-
  The assault on academic freedom. [New York, Basic Pamphlets, c1955]
  38p. 15cm. (Basic pamphlet--
  9)
  Cover title.
  1. Teaching, Freedom of.
  I. Basic Pamphlets.
  MiU

L18
Lamont, Corliss, 1902-
  Back to the bill of rights.
  [New York, Basic Pamphlets,
  c1955]
  31p. 15cm. (Basic Pamphlets--
  5)
  Cover title.
  Fourth printing, 1955.
  1. U.S. Constitution. 1st-
  10th amendments. 2. Civil
  rights. I. Basic Pamphlets.
  MiU

L19
Lamont, Corliss, 1902-
  The crime against Cuba. [New
  York, 1961]
  39p. 15cm. (Basic pamphlets,
  14)
  Includes bibliography.
  1. Cuba--History--1959-
  2. Cuba--Relations (general)
  with the U.S. 3. U.S.--Rela-
  tions (general) with Cuba.

I. Basic Pamphlets.
TxU, MNS, MiU, KU

L20
Lamont, Corliss, 1902-
  The enduring impact of George
  Santayana. [New York, Basic
  Pamphlets, c1964]
  27p. (Basic pamphlets--16)
  1. Santayana, George, 1863-
  1952. I. Basic Pamphlets.
  MiU

L21
Lamont, Corliss, 1902-
  Humanism believes. [Yellow
  Springs, Ohio, American Human-
  ist Association, 196]
  [4]p. 22x10cm.
  Caption title.
  1. Humanism. I. American Human-
  ist Association.
  KU-RH

L22
Lamont, Corliss, 1902-   ed.
  A humanist symposium on metaphysics [by] J. Huxley [and
  others] Yellow Springs, Ohio,
  American Humanist Association
  [1960]
  39p. (Humanist pamphlet, 5)
  Originally appeared in the
  journal of philosophy, Jan.
  15, 1959.
  1. Metaphysics. I. Huxley,
  Sir Julian Sorrell, 1887-
  II. American Humanist Association.
  MH

L23
Lamont, Corliss, 1902-
  The humanist tradition. [New
  York, Basic Pamphlets, c1955]
  15p. (Basic pamphlets--3)
  Cover title.
  1. Humanism. I. Basic Pamph-
  lets.
  MiU

L24
Lamont, Corliss, 1902-
  A humanist's answer to the
  philosophic needs of today.
  [Yellow Springs, Ohio, Humanist

Press, c1957]
  16p. 23cm. (Humanist pamphlet,
  no. 2)
  Cover title.
  1. Humanism. I. Humanist Press.
  NN, NUC 63-31708

L25
Lamont, Corliss, 1902-
  My first sixty years. [New York,
  Basic Pamphlets, c1962]
  50p. 14cm. (Basic pamphlets--
  15)
  Cover title.
  Partial contents--An interview
  of Corliss Lamont by Casper
  Citron.
  1. Internal security. 2. Cuba.
  3. Communism. I. Basic Pam-
  phlets. II. Citron, Casper.
  KU-RH, MiU, MNS, NUC 63-31709

L26
Lamont, Corliss, 1902-
  My trip around the world. [New
  York, 1960]
  47p. 25cm. (Basic pamphlets,
  13)
  1. Voyages around the world.
  I. Basic pamphlets.
  MH, MiU, NUC 63-31710

L27
Lamont, Corliss, 1902-
  A peace program for the U.S.A.
  [New York, Basic Pamphlet, 1959]
  23p. (Basic pamphlet, 12)
  1. U.S.--For. rel.--1945-
  2. Peace. I. Basic Pamphlet.
  MiU, MU, NUC 63=311711

L28
Lamont, Corliss, 1902-
  The right to travel. [New York,
  Basic Pamphlets, 1957]
  41p. 14cm. (Basic pamphlets,
  10)
  1. Passports. 2. Travel.
  I. Basic Pamphlets.
  MH-L, NNC-L, MiU, WHi-L, DLC
  58-28519

L29
Lamont, Corliss, 1902-
  Soviet aggression: myth or
  reality? [New York, 195]

15p. 14cm.
Cover title.
1. Russia--Foreign policy.
WHi-L, CSSR

L30
Lamont, Corliss, 1902-
  To end nuclear bomb tests, by
  Corliss & Margaret Lamont.
  [2d. ed. New York, Basic Pam-
  phlets, 1958]
  47p. (Basic pamphlets, no. 11)
  Cover title.
  1. Atomic weapons and disarma-
  ment. I. Basic Pamphlets.
  II. Lamont, Margaret, jt. auth.
  InU, NNC, WHi-L

L31
Lamont, Corliss, 1902-
  Vietnam: Corliss Lamont vs. Am-
  bassador Lodge. [New York,
  1967]
  30p. 15cm. (Basic pamphlets,
  18)
  "Two open letters to Ambassa-
  dor Lodge."
  1. Lodge, Henry Cabot, 1902-
           2. Vietnamese conflict,
  1961-1975. I. Basic Pamphlets.
  MH, NNC, MiU, NUC 67-95723

L32
Land or death: Hugo Blanco and
    the peasant struggle in Peru.
    [New York, Young Socialist
    Alliance, 1967]
  22p. illus., ports. 22cm.
  Cover title.
  1. Blanco, Hugo. 2. Peasantry
  --Peru. 3. Peru--Pol. & govt.
  I. Young Socialist Alliance.
  KU-RH, TxU

L33
Landauer, Carl.
  Peace politics: the new left
  and the pity of it all, essays
  by Clark Landauer and Robert
  Pickus. [Berkeley, World Without War Council, 196]
  16p. 23cm.
  1. Peace--Societies, etc.
  2. Student movements. 3. Vietnamese conflict, 1961-1975.
  I. Pickus, Robert, jt. auth.

II. World Without War Council.
CU-B, WHi-L

L34
Lander, Dawn.
  An approach to the resolution
  on international conflict. [n.
  p., Student Peace Union, National Convention, 1964]
  [1] leaf. 28cm.
  Caption title.
  1. World politics--1955-
  2. Peace. I. Student Peace
  Union.
  CU-B

L35
Landy, Laurie.
  Women and the Chinese revolution. New York, International
  Socialists [196]
  50, vi [2]p. 22cm.
  1. Women in China. 2. Women
  in China (People's Republic of
  China, 1949-   ) I. International Socialists.
  KU-RH

L36
Landy, Sy.
  Black power, by Sy Landy and
  Charles Capper. [Berkeley]
  Independent Socialist Club
  [196]
  [4]p. 28cm.
  Cover title.
  1. Negroes--Civil rights.
  I. Independent Socialist Club.
  II. Capper, Charles, jt. auth.
  CU-B

L37
Landy, Sy.
  In defense of black power, by
  Sy Landy and Charles Capper.
  [n.p., 1966]
  11p. 28cm.
  "An SDS convention position
  paper."
  1. Negroes--Civil rights.
  I. Students for a Democratic
  Society. II. Capper, Charles,
  jt. auth.
  WHi-L

L38
Lange, Oscar Richard, 1904-

Economic development, planning,
and international cooperation.
New York, Monthly Review Press,
1963.
40p. 22cm. (Monthly Review
Press pamphlet series, no. 20)
1. Economic development.
2. Underdeveloped areas.
I. Monthly Review Press.
NNU-T, MiU, DLC 63-13434

L39
Langer, Elinor.
The Oakland seven. [n.p., 1969?]
[75]-82p. 28cm.
1. Stop the Draft Week. 2. Military service, Compulsory.
3. Vietnamese conflict, 1961-
1975. 4. Government, Resistance to.
KU-RH

L40
Langer, Elinor.
The women of the telephone com-
pany. [Boston, New England
Free Press, 1970?]
24p. 25cm.
Cover title.
Reprinted from New York Review
of Books, Mar. 1970.
1. Woman--Employment. 2. Ameri-
can Telephone and Telegraph
Company. I. New England Free
Press.
MiU

L41
Langhorst, Hilary.
"Motherhood" and the subordina-
tion of females and children.
[Somerville, Mass., Female
Liberation, 1970?]
[2]p. 28cm.
Caption title.
1. Woman--Rights of women.
2. Children. I. Female Liber-
ation.
KU-RH

L42
Larteguy, Jean.
Victory in Vietnam; what is the
price? [Berkeley, Calif.,
Vietnam Day Committee, 1965?]

[2]p. 28cm.
Caption title.
1. Vietnamese conflict, 1961-
1975. I. National Coordinating
Committee to End the War in
Vietnam. Vietnam Day Committee,
Berkeley.
CU-B

L43
Lauter, Paul.
The free university movement.
Nashville, Southern Student
Organizing Committee [196]
8p. 28cm.
1. Student movements. 2. Free
schools. I. Southern Student
Organizing Committee.
NNU-T, CU-B

L44
Lauter, Paul, comp.
Teaching about peace issues; a
peace education study kit.
[Philadelphia] National Peace
Literature Service of the Peace
Education Division of the Ameri-
can Friends Service Committee
[1965]
vii, 189p. 28cm.
Cover title.
1. Peace--Study and teaching.
I. Friends, Society of.
American Friends Service Com-
mittee.
IaU, NUC 70-44267

L45
Lawson, Elizabeth.
The gentleman from Mississippi;
our first negro congressman,
Hiram R. Revels. With an
introduction by William L. Patterson. [New York, 1960]
63p. 20cm.
1. Negroes--Politics and suffrage. 2. Revels, Hiram R.
3. Negroes--Mississippi.
KU-J

L46
Lawson, Elizabeth.
The people's almanac. Important
dates and events in the history
of the struggles of the peoples
of the USA. New York, New

Century Publishers, 1955.
64p. illus.
1. Social change. 2. U.S.--
History. I. New Century
Publishers.
KU-J, WHi-L, L139

L47
Lawson, W.T.
  Youth and violence. Victoria,
  B.C., Jim Lawson Memorial Fund.
  [1968]
  8p. 28cm.
  Cover title.
  1. Violence (Law) 2. Violence
  in mass media. 3. Youth.
  I. Jim Lawson Memorial Fund.
  KU-RH

L48
Lawyers Committee on American
    Policy Towards Vietnam.
  American policy vis-a-vis
  Vietnam. New York [196]
  43p. 20x8cm.
  Cover title.
  1. Vietnamese conflict, 1961-
  1975.
  KU-RH

L49
Lawyers Committee on American
    Policy Towards Vietnam.
  U.S. intervention in Vietnam is
  illegal. New York, 1967.
  Reprinted from New York Times,
  Jan. 15, 1967.
  1. Vietnamese conflict, 1961-
  1975.
  WHi-L

L50
Laxer, James.
  The student movement and Canadian independence. Winnipeg,
  Cannadian Dimension Magazine
  [196]
  16p. 28cm.
  Cover title.
  Reprinted from Canadian Dimension Magazine, v. 6, no. 3-4.
  1. Socialism. 2. Student move-
  ments--Canada. 3.Canada--Pol.
  & govt. I. Canadian Dimension
  Magazine.
  MoU, KU-RH

L51
Leadership Conference on Civil
    Rights.
  Call for a national campaign
  for a strong civil rights bill
  by Christmas. [New York,
  Leadership Conference on Civil
  Rights and March on Washington
  for Jobs & Freedom, 196]
  [4]p. 23x10cm.
  Cover title.
  1. Negroes--Civil rights.
  I. March on Washington for
  Jobs and Freedom.
  KU-RH

L52
Leadership Conference on Civil
    Rights.
  Program for civil rights--1960.
  [New York, 1960]
  14p.
  Cover title.
  1. Negroes--Civil rights.
  WHi-A

L53
League for Industrial Democracy.
  Constitution and by-laws of
  the League for Industrial Democracy, incorporated. [n.p.,
  1961?]
  3 leaves. 28cm.
  WHi-A

L54
League for Industrial Democracy.
  Down on the farm; the plight
  of agriculture labor. New York,
  League for Industrial Democracy
  and National Sharecroppers Fund
  [c1955]
  14p. 28cm.
  Cover title.
  1. Mexicans in the U.S.
  2. Agricultural laborers.
  I. National Sharecroppers Fund.
  KU-J

L55
League for Industrial Democracy.
  The forward march of American
  labor, a brief history of the
  American labor movement written
  for union members. [New rev.
  print.] New York [1956, c1945]
  32p. illus. 22cm. (L.I.D.

pamphlet series)
1. Trade-unions--History.
2. Labor and laboring classes--
History.
IU, DLC 56-45683

L56
League for Industrial Democracy.
Report: consultation on youth
and democratic change. New
York [196]
14 [2]p. 28cm.
1. Youth--Political activity.
2. Social change.
NNU-T

L57
League for Industrial Democracy.
The state of the student move-
ment, 1970. New York [1970]
26p. illus. 23cm.
Cover title.
1. Student movements.
NNU-T

L58
League for Industrial Democracy.
The urban school crisis: an
anthology of essays. New
York, 1966.
80p. illus.
1. Negroes--Education.
2. Education.
WHi-L

L59
League for Industrial Democracy.
What is the L.I.D.? [New York,
196]
folder. 23x11cm.
Caption title.
KU-RH, WHi-L

L60
League for Socialist Action.
Canada--U.S. relations [adopted
by the 1968 convention of the
League for Socialist Action/La
Ligue Socialiste Ouvriere]
Toronto, Vanguard Publications
[196]
5 [4]p. 22cm.
Cover title.
1. Canada--Relations (general)
with the U.S. I. Vanguard Pub-
lications.
MoU

L61
League for Socialist Action.
The status of women in Canada,
brief submitted to the Royal
Commission by the League for
Social Action/Ligue Socialiste
Ouvriere. Toronto, Vanguard
Publications [196]
16p. 15cm.
Cover title.
1. Women in Canada. I. Vanguard
Publications.
MoU

L62
League for Socialist Action.
Vive le Quebec libre: the socialist viewpoint statement of
the LSA-LSO. [Toronto, Vanguard Publications, 196]
1. Socialism in Canada.
2. Quebec--Pol. & govt.
I. Vanguard Publications.
MoU

L63
Lebeaux, Charles.
Life on A.D.C.: budgets of
despair. New York, Students
for a Democratic Society and
its Economic Research and
Action Project [196]
9p. 28cm.
Cover title.
Reprinted from New University
Thought, v. 3, no. 4.
1. Public welfare. I. Students
for a Democratic Society. Economic Research and Action Project.
WHi-L

L64
LeBlanc, Paul.
SDS: past, present, future.
[Pittsburgh, Pittsburgh Point,
1969]
7 leaves. 28cm.
Caption title.
1. Students for a Democratic
Society. I. Pittsburgh Point.
MoU

L65
Lechuga Hevia, Carlos.
Cuba's road to peace: a speech
to the United Nations by

delegate Carlos Lechuga. [Tor-
onto, Fair Play for Cuba Committee, 1963]
11 [1]p. 22cm.
Cover title.
1. Cuba--Pol. & govt.--1959-
        I. Fair Play for Cuba
Committee.
CSt-H, MiU, NUC 66-48795

L66
Ledda, Romano.
  Social classes and political
  struggle in Africa. Boston,
  New England Free Press [196]
  560-580p. 22cm.
  Cover title.
  Reprinted from International
  Socialist Journal, Aug. 1967.
  1. Social classes--Africa.
  2. Africa--Pol. & govt. I. New
  England Free Press.
  MiU

L67
Lee, Franz J.T.
  Anatomy of apartheid in south-
  ern Africa. [New York] Alex-
  ander Defense Committee [196]
  43p. illus. 22cm.
  Cover title.
  1. South Africa--Race question.
  I. Alexander Defense Committee.
  MiU

L68
Lee, V.T.
  Cuban counter-revolutionaries
  in the United States. Who are
  they? Who subsidizes them?
  How do they menace freedom in
  the U.S. as well as in Cuba?
  [New York] Fair Play for Cuba
  Committee [1962]
  [11]p. 22cm.
  Cover title.
  "An abridged version of a lec-
  ture delivered at a forum of
  the N.Y. chapter, FPCC on March
  12, 1962."
  1. Cuba--Relations (general)
  with the U.S. 2. U.S.--Rela-
  tions (general) with Cuba.
  3. Cubans in the U.S. I. Fair
  Play for Cuba Committee.
  MiU, FU, NUC 65-74142

L69
Lee, V.T.
  Drums of war. New York, Fair
  Play for Cuba Committee [196]
  7 [1]p.
  Caption title.
  1. U.S.--For. rel.--Cuba.
  2. Cuba--For. rel.--U.S.
  I. Fair Play for Cuba Committee.
  MiU

L70
Lee Otis Johnson Defense Com-
    mittee.
  Free Lee Otis Johnson, Houston's
  black political prisoners.
  [Houston, 1970?]
  folder. 21x9cm.
  Caption title.
  1. Johnson, Lee Otis.
  2. Negroes--Houston.
  CU-B

L71
Leghorn, Lisa.
  Child-care for the child.
  [Somerville, Mass., Female
  Liberation, 1970?]
  [2]p. 28cm.
  Caption title.
  1. Children--Care and hygiene.
  2. Woman--Rights of women.
  I. Female Liberation.
  KU-RH

L72
Lehmann, Jerry.
  We walked to Moscow. Raymond,
  N.H., Greenleaf Books, 1966.
  88p. illus., maps, facsims.
  30cm.
  1. Peace. 2. U.S.--For. rel.--
  Russia. 3. Russia--For. rel.--
  U.S. 4. San Francisco to Mos-
  cow Walk for Peace, 1960-1961.
  I. Greenleaf Books.
  NhU, MH, CSt-H, NUC 67-37551

L73
Leigh, Ruth.
  Man's right to life. [New York]
  Commission on Social Action of
  Reform Judaism [c1959]
  56p. 18cm.
  At head of title: Issue of
  conscience.

1. Capital punishment.
KU-RH

L74
Lemisch, Jesse.
  Towards a democratic history.
  [Ann Arbor] Radical Education
  Project [1967]
  [7]p. 28cm.
  1. Historiography. I. Radical
  Education Project.
  KU-RH, WHi-L, NNU-T, NUC 69-
  72617

L75
Lemoine, B. Roy.
  Quebec: a double revolution.
  Toronto, Research, Information
  and Publications Project, Student Union for Peace Action
  [196]
  4p. 28cm.
  Cover title.
  1. Quebec--Pol. & govt.
  2. French in Quebec. I. Student Union for Peace Action.
  WHi-A

L76
Lenin, Vladimir Il'ich, 1870-
    1924.
  The awakening of Asia; selected
  essays [1970]
  77p. 18cm. (Little new world
  paperbacks, LNW-22)
  1. Asia. I. International
  Publishers.
  DLC 76-130865

L77
Lenin, Vladimir Il'ich, 1870-
    1924.
  Imperialism, the highest stage
  of capitalism: a popular outline.
  New rev. translation. New
  York, International Publishers
  [1963, c1939]
  v, 128p. 20cm. (Little Lenin
  library)
  1. Capitalism. 2. Imperialism.
  I. International Publishers.
  CoU, MiU, NUC 65-95307

L78
Lenin, Vladimir Il'ich, 1870-
    1924.

"Left-wing" communism, an in-
  fantile disorder; a popular
  essay in Marxism strategy and
  tactics. New translation.
  New York, International Publishers.[1962]
  95p. 21cm. (Little Lenin
  Library, 20)
  1. Communism--Russia. 2. Communism. I. International
  Publishers.
  NjP, NUC 65-10139

L79
Lenin, Vladimir Il'ich, 1870-
    1924.
  Letter to American workers, introduction by Gus Hall. The
  story behind Lenin's letter
  to American worker [by] Art
  Shields. New York, New Outlook Publishers, 1970.
  39p. 23cm.
  1. Labor and laboring classes.
  2. Communism. I. Hall, Gus.
  II. Shields, Art. III. New
  Outlook Publishers.
  MiU

L80
Lenin, Vladimir Il'ich, 1870-
    1924.
  State and revolution. 2d. ed.
  New York, International Pub-
  lishers [1969]
  103p. 21cm.
  Third printing, 1969.
  1. Socialism. 2. Marx, Karl,
  1818-1883. 3. Revolutions.
  I. International Publishers.
  NBuU, MoSW, NUC70-69320

L81
Lenin, Vladimir Il'ich, 1870-
    1924.
  The teachings of Karl Marx.
  New York, International Publishers [1964]
  62p. 21cm. (Little Lenin
  library [new ser.])
  1. Marx, Karl, 1818-1883.
  2. Socialism. I. International
  Publishers.
  DLC 64-5216

L82
Lenin, Vladimir Il'ich, 1870-1924.
  Two tactics of social-democracy
  in the democracy revolution.
  New York, International Pub-
  lishers [1963]
  127p. (Little Lenin library)
  1. Revolutions. 2. Democracy.
  I. International Publishers.
  NNC, NBuU, NUC 65-28450

L83
Lens, Sidney.
  The mine mill conspiracy case.
  Introduction by Norman Thomas.
  [Denver, Mine-Mill Defense
  Committee, 1960?]
  [18]p. 23cm.
  I. Mine-Mill Defense Committee.
  II. Thomas, Norman.
  CSt

L84
Lens, Sidney.
  Questions for the left. Introduction by A.J. Muste. [New
  York, American Forum for Socialist Education, 1957]
  29p.
  Partial contents--Questions for
  the youth, by Tim Wohlforth.
  1. Socialism. 2. Youth--Poli-
  tical activity. I. Wohlforth,
  Tim. II. Muste, Abraham John,
  1885-   III. American Forum
  for Socialist Education.
  WHi-L

L85
Lens, Sidney.
  Revolution and cold war.
  [Philadelphia, American Friends
  Service Committee, c1962]
  64p. 22cm. (Beyong deterrence
  series)
  1. World politics--1955-
  2. Revolutions. 3. U.S.--For-
  eign policy. I. Friends, Society of. American Friends
  Service Committee.
  MoU, DS, MH, CSt-H, NUC 63-
  26378, KU-J

L86
Lens, Sidney.
  Revolution and you; the story

of the rising expectations of
the world's people. Nyack,
N.Y., Fellowship Publications
[196]
31p. illus. 22cm.
Cover title.
Illustrated by Jules Feiffer.
1. World politics--1955-
2. Revolutions. 3. U.S.--
Foreign policy. I. Fellowship
Publications. II. Feiffer,
Jules.
MoU

L87
Lerner, Eric.
  Why revolution? [New York?
  National Caucus of SDS Labor
  Committees, 1968]
  18p. (A Campaign publication)
  1. Revolutions. I. Students
  for a Democratic Society. Nat-
  ional Caucus. Labor Committee.
  WHi-L

L88
Lerner, Michael.
  Letter to the movement: con-
  spiracy in Seattle. [Ithaca,
  N.Y., Glad Day Press, 1970?]
  5p. 28cm.
  Caption title.
  1. Student movements--Seattle.
  I. Glad Day Press.
  NNU-T

L89
Lerner, Mike.
  Who's being fooled? [Berke-
  ley? Peace & Freedom Steering
  Committee, 1968?]
  [1] leaf. 36cm.
  1. Kennedy, Robert F., 1925-
  1968. I. Peace & Freedom
  Steering Committee.
  CU-B

L90
Lesnick, Henry.
  Guerrilla-street theatre. [n.
  p., Liberation News Service,
  c1970]
  69p. illus.
  1. Theater. 2. Drama. I. Liberation News Service.
  WHi-L

L91
Lester, Julius.
  The angry children of Malcolm X.
  Nashville, Southern Student Or-
  ganizing Committee, and New
  England Free Press [196]
  6 [1]p. 28cm.
  Cover title.
  Reprinted from Sing Out, Nov.
  1966.
  1. Negroes--Civil rights.
  I. Southern Student Organizing
  Committee.
  KU-RH

L92
Lester, Julius.
  The angry children of Malcom X.
  Nashville, Southern Student Or-
  ganizing Committee [c1966]
  9p. 28cm.
  Cover title.
  Reprinted from Sing Out, Nov.
  1966.
  1. Negroes--Civil rights.
  I. Southern Student Organizing
  Committee.
  KU-RH, MoU

L93
Lester, Julius.
  Perspective on the Atlanta
  rebellion. [San Francisco,
  Movement Press, c1967]
  [16]p. illus. 28cm.
  Cover title.
  1. Alabama--Race question.
  2. Negroes--Alabama. I. Movement Press.
  MiU

L94
Lester, Julius.
  Some revolutionary notes.
  [Palo Alto, Calif., Institute
  for the Study of Nonviolence,
  1970?]
  14p. 28cm.
  Cover title.
  1. Negroes--Civil rights.
  2. Youth--Political activity.
  3. Revolutions. I. Institute
  for the Study of Nonviolence.
  KU-RH, CU-B

L95
Let's build a dynamic and sus-
  tained student movement. [n.
  p., 196]
  3p. 38cm.
  Caption title.
  1. Student movements.
  KU-RH

L96
Letters from friends in China [by
  David Crook and others. New
  York] Far East Reporter [1965]
  16p. 22cm.
  Cover title.
  1. China (People's Republic of
  China, 1949-   ) I. Crook,
  David. II. Far East Reporter.
  CSt-H, NUC 70-19194

L97
Levertov, Denise, 1923-   comp.
  Out of the war shadow; an anthology of current poetry. New
  York, War Resisters League
  [c1967]
  1v. (unpaged) 21cm. (Peace
  calendar, v. 13)
  At head of title: 1968 peace
  calendar & appointment book.
  1. War Resisters League.
  NBuU, WU, MH, IEN, OCU, OrU,
  CLU, NUC 692112.

L98
Leviathan.
  Fight on to victory. Detroit's
  League speaks; an interview with
  Mike Hamlin and Ken Cockrel.
  Detroit, Radical Education Pro-
  ject [1969?]
  11p. 22cm.
  Cover title.
  1. Negroes--Detroit. 2. Dodge
  Revolutionary Union Movement.
  2. Automobile industry workers
  --Detroit. I. Hamlin, Mike.
  II. Cockrel, Ken. III. Radi-
  cal Education Project.
  MiU

L99
Levin, Alan.
  Political meddling and the

Florida Board of Regents. Nash-
ville, Southern Student Organi-
zing Committee [196]
7 [1] leaves. 28cm.
Cover title.
1. Universities and colleges--
Florida. 2. Education--Florida.
I. Southern Student Organizing
Committee.
MoU, WHi-L

L100
Levine, Bruce.
   Cuba; whose state. Ann Arbor,
   [Independent Socialist Club,
   196]
   9p. 28cm.
   Caption title.
   1. Socialism in Cuba. 2. Cuba--
   Pol. & govt.--1959-
   I. Independent Socialist Club.
   MiU-H

L101
Levine, Bruce.
   On student power. [Ann Arbor?
   Independent Socialist Club? 196]
   5p. 28cm.
   Caption title.
   1. Student movements. I. Inde-
   pendent Socialist Club.
   MiU-H

L102
Levine, Bruce.
   Some thoughts on classified research. [Ann Arbor? Voice Political Party--SDS? 1967]
   5p. 28cm.
   Caption title.
   1. Military research. 2. Universities and colleges.
   I. Voice Political Party-Students
   for a Democratic Society, Ann
   Arbor.
   MiU-H

L103
Levine, Eric.
   Berkeley free speech controversy.
   Chicago, Students for a Demo-
   cratic Society [1965]
   23p.
   1. Free Speech Movement.
   I. Students for a Democratic
   Society.
   CU-B

L104
Levine, Eric.
   The Berkeley free speech con-
   troversy. New York, Students
   for a Democratic Society.
   [196]
   23p. 28cm.
   Cover title.
   1. Free Speech Movement.
   I. Students for a Democratic
   Society.
   WHi-A, CU-B

L105
Lewack, Harold.
   The quiet revolution; a study
   of the Antigonish movement.
   New York, Student League for Industrial Democracy [c1955]
   20p. 21cm.
   1. Student movements--St. Francis Xavier University. 2. Catholics. I. Student League for
   Industrial Democracy.
   KU-J

L106
Lewis, Alan.
   First amendment on trial. [n.
   p., 1970?]
   [4]p. illus. 28cm.
   Caption title.
   Reprinted from Argus (College
   Park, Md.) v. 5, no. 2.
   1. Civil rights. 2. Soldiers.
   KU-RH

L107
Lewis, Alfred Baker, 1897-
   Why we have depressions and re-
   cessions. New York, League for
   Industrial Democracy [1962]
   31p. 22cm.
   Cover title.
   1. Depressions. 2. Business
   cycles. I. League for Indus-
   trial Democracy.
   IU, CSt, OrU, WHi-A, NNU-T,
   NUC 63-50855

L108
Lewis, W. Arthur.
   Racial competition: the key to
   survival. [New York, National
   Association for the Advancement
   of Colored People, 1969]
   11p. 22cm.

Cover title.
Reprinted from University: a
Princeton Quarterly.
1. Negroes--Civil rights.
I. National Association for the
Advancement of Colored People.
KU-RH

L109
Liberal Party of New York State.
State legislature program of the
Liberal Party of New York. New
York, 1963.
39p.
1. New York (State)--Pol. & govt.
WHi-L

L110
Liberation Support Movement.
Interview on Angola; commander
and member of MPLA comite direct-
or, Spartacus Monimambu. [Oak-
land, 1970]
34p. 22cm.
Cover title.
1. Angola--Pol. & govt. 2. Movi-
memto Popular de Libertacao de
Angola. I. Monimambu, Sparata-
cus.
MiU

L111
Liberation Support Movement.
Liberation Support Movement con-
stitution [ratified May 1970.
Seattle, 1970?]
4p. 22cm.
1. Revolutions.
MiU

L112
Liberation Support Movement.
Liberation Support Movement interview George Nyandoro, general
secretary, Zimbabwe African
People's Union [interviewed by
Don Barnett. Oakland, 1970]
12p. illus. 22cm.
1. Zimbabwe, Mashonaland--Pol.
& govt. 2. Zimbabwe African
People's Union. I. Barnett, Donald L. II. Nyandoro, George.
MiU

L113
Liberation Support Movement.

Liberation Support Movement interview sixth region commander
Seta Likambuild, Movimento Popular de Libertacao de Angola.
[Vancouver, 1970?]
35p. illus. 22cm.
Cover title.
Interviewed by Don Barnett.
1. Angola--Pol. & govt.
2. Guerrillas--Angola.
3. Movimento Popular de Libertacao de Angola. I. Barnett,
Donald L. II. Likambuild, Seta.
MiU

L114
Liberation Support Movement.
Liberation Support Movement interview [with] member of MPLA
comite director, Daniel Chipenda. [Seattle? 1969?]
22p. 22cm.
Cover title.
1. Movimento Popular Libertacao
de Angola. 2. Angola--Pol. &
govt. I. Chipenda, Daniel.
MiU

L115
Liberation Support Movement.
MPLA 1970. [Oakland, 1970]
28p. 26cm.
Cover title.
1. Movimento Popular de Liber-
tacao de Angola.
MiU

L116
Liberation Support Movement.
Memorandum of activities of
medical assistance service (S.
A.M.) of the Popular Movement
for the Liberation of Angola
(MPLA) in the liberated regions
of the eastern front--region
III. Interview with Dr. Americo
Boavida. [Oakland, 1970]
27p. 22cm.
Cover title.
1. Movimento Popular de Liber-
tacao de Angola. 2. Angola--
Pol. & govt. I. Boavida, Ameri-
co, 1922-1968.
MiU

L117
Lichtman, Richard.

The idealogical function of the
university. [Montreal, Our
Generation, 196]
14p. 28cm.
Caption title.
1. Universities and colleges.
I. Our Generation.
NNU-T

L118
Lieberman, E. James.
Non-violence vs pacifism: a psy-
chiatrist's view. [Montreal,
Our Generation, 196]
59-65 leaves.
Caption title.
1. Nonviolence. 2. Pacifism.
I. Our Generation.
NNU-T

L119
Liebert, Faith H.
Having a right--on baby. Detroit,
Radical Education Project [1970?]
18 [1]p. illus. 22cm.
Cover title.
1. Mothers. 2. Prenatal care.
3. Woman. I. Radical Education
Project.
MiU

L120
Light, Donald.
Income distribution: the first
stage in the consideration of
poverty. [Cambridge, Mass.]
Union for Radical Political Eco-
nomics, 1969]
8p. 27cm. (Union for Radical
Political Economics. Occasional
papers, no. 1)
1. Income. 2. Poverty.
I. Union for Radical Political
Economics.
CtU

L121
Light, Robert E.
Cuba versus CIA, by Robert E.
Light [and] Carl Marzani. New
York, Marzani & Munsell [c1961]
72p. illus. 24cm.
1. U.S. Central Intelligence
Agency. 2. Cuba--Pol. & govt.--
1959-   I. Marzani, Carl, jt.
auth. II. Marzani and Munsell.
KU-RH

L122
Lightfoot, Claude M., 1910-
Black America and the world
revolution. New York, New
Outlook Publishers, 1970.
94p.
1. Communism. 2. Negroes--
Civil rights. I. New Outlook
Publishers.
WHi-L

L123
Lightfoot, Claude M., 1910-
Black power and liberation: a
communist view. [New York, New
Outlook Publishers, 1967]
46p. 22cm.
Cover title.
1. Communism. 2. Negroes--
Civil rights. I. New Outlook
Publishers.
MiU

L125
Lightfoot, Claude M., 1910-
The challenge of the '56
elections. New York, New Cen-
tury Publishers, 1956.
24p.
Report to a meeting of the
National Committee, CPUSA,
April 1956.
1. Communist Party of the United
States of America. 2. Presi-
dents--U.S.--Election--1956.
I. New Century Publishers.
NNJef, KU-J, L239

L126
Lightfoot, Claude M., 1910-
The civil war and black libera-
tion today. [New York, New
Outlook Publishers, 1969]
15p.
Reprinted from Public Affairs,
Jan. 1969.
1. Negroes--Civil rights.
I. New Outlook Publishers.
WHi-L

L127
Lightfoot, Claude M., 1910-
"Not guilty." The case of
Claude Lightfoot. [New York,
New Century Publishers, 1955]
15p. 19cm.
Cover title.

1. Subversive activities.
2. Anti-communist movements.
I. New Century Publishers.
KU-J

L128
Lightfoot, Claude M., 1910-
   Review of electoral policies and
   tasks for 1956, report by Claude
   Lightfoot to National Committee
   meeting, April 29, 1956. [n.p.,
   1959]
   10p. 36cm.
   Caption title.
   1. Negroes--Civil rights.
   2. Communist Party of the United
   States of America. 3. Politics,
   Practical.
   KU-J

L129
Lightfoot, Claude M., 1910-
   Turning point in freedom road:
   the fight to end Jim Crow now.
   New York, New Century Publishers,
   1962.
   32p. 19cm.
   1. Negroes--Civil rights.
   I. New Century Publishers.
   WHi-L, MiU, NUC 65-25163

L130
Limpus, Layrel.
   Liberation of women; sexual re-
   pression & the family. [Boston,
   New England Free Press, 196]
   15p. 22cm.
   Cover title.
   Reprinted from This Magazine is
   About Schools.
   1. Woman--Rights of women.
   2. Family. I. New England Free
   Press.
   KU-RH

L131
Lin, Pao, 1908-
   Long live the victory of people's
   war, synopsized by Donald McKelvey. [Boston, New England Free
   Press, 1969?]
   [4]p. 28cm.
   Caption title.
   1. Guerrilla warfare. 2. Revolutions. 3. Communism--China.
   I. McKelvey, Donald. II. New

England Free Press.
KU-RH

L132
Lin, Pao, 1908-
   Long live the victory of people's
   war, a synopsis by Donald McKelvey. Toronto, Research, Information and Publications Project,
   Student Union for Peace Action
   [196]
   7p. 28cm.
   Cover title.
   Originally printed in (Peking)
   People's Daily, Sept. 3, 1965.
   1. Guerrilla warfare. 2. Revolutions. 3. Communism--China.
   I. McKelvey, Donald. II. Student Union for Peace Action.
   WHi-A

L133
Linder, Walter.
   Aftermath of the 1967 U.A.W.
   strike; sellout and insurgency
   in the auto industry. Boston,
   New England Free Press [1969?]
   26-32p. illus. 28cm.
   Cover title.
   Reprinted from PL, March-
   April 1968.
   1. Strikes and lockouts--Auto-
   mobile industry. 2. International union, united automobile,
   aircraft and agricultural workers of America. I. New England
   Free Press.
   KU-RH

L134
Linder, Walter.
   District 65, RWDSU, AFL-CIO; an
   analysis. [Boston, New England
   Free Press, 1970?]
   16p. illus. 22cm. (A Progres-
   sive Labor pamphlet)
   Cover title.
   1. Retail, Wholesale and Depart-
   ment Store Union, District 65.
   2. Trade-unions. I. New England
   Free Press. II. Progressive
   Labor Party.
   KU-RH

L135
Linder, Walter.

Dual unionism: outmoded strategy
or useful tactic? [By] Walter
Linder and Martin Stevens. Boston, New England Free Press [196]
[50-68]p. illus. 28cm.
Cover title.
Reprinted from PL, July-Aug. 1967.
1. Trade-unions. I. Stevens,
Martin, jt. auth. II. New England Free Press.
KU-RH

L136
Linder, Walter.
  The great Flint sit-down strike
  against G.M., 1936-37; how indus-
  trial unionism was won. Ann
  Arbor, Radical Education Project
  [196]
  [90]-123p. illus. 28cm.
  Reprinted from PL, Feb.-Mar. 1967.
  1. Strikes and lockouts--Automo-
  bile industry. 2. General Motors
  Corporation. 3. Trade-unions.
  I. Radical Education Project.
  KU-RH, MoU

L137
Linder, Walter.
  How industrial unionism was won:
  the great Flint sit-down strike
  against General Motors, 1936-37.
  [Brooklyn, Progressive Labor Par-
  ty, 196]
  [90]-123 [6]p. 28cm.
  Cover title.
  1. Strikes and lockouts--Automo-
  bile industry. 2. General Motors
  Corporation. 3. Trade-unions.
  I. Progressive Labor Party.
  CU-B

L138
Lipson, Laurie.
  Student power (addendum to student perspectives) [New York?
  Independent Socialist Club?
  196]
  5p. 28cm.
  Caption title.
  1. Student movements. I. Independent Socialist Club.
  MiU

L139
Listen, Marxist. [New York,

Anarchos, 1969]
30p.
1. Communism. 2. Anarchism and
anarchists. I. Anarchos.
WHi-L

L140
Little, Malcolm, 1925-1965.
  El Hajj Malik el Shabazz
  (Saint Malcolm) [Harlen, N.Y.,
  1968]
  [12]p.
  Cover title.
  1. Negroes.
  MiU

L141
Little, Malcolm, 1925-1965.
  Malcolm X on Afro-American his-
  tory. [1st ed. New York, Merit
  Publishers, 1967]
  48p. 22cm.
  Cover title.
  "Speech...from...a public meet-
  ing on January 24, 1965."
  1. Negroes--History. 2. Negroes
  in Africa--History. I. Merit
  Publishers.
  MoU, CU-B, MiU, MB, InU, ICU,
  DLC 67-3301

L142
Little, Malcolm, 1925-1965.
  Malcolm X on Afro-American history. Expanded and illustrated
  edition. New York, Pathfinder
  Press, 1970.
  74p. illus. 22cm.
  1. Negroes--History. 2. Negroes in Africa--History.
  I. Pathfinder Press.
  MiU

L143
Little, Malcolm, 1925-1965.
  Malcolm X talks to young people.
  [New York, Young Socialist Al-
  liance; distributed by Merit
  Publishers, 1969]
  36p. 22cm. (Young Socialist
  pamphlet)
  1. Negroes--Civil rights.
  2. Youth--Political activity.
  I. Young Socialist Alliance.
  OrU, KU-RH, MoU, CU-B, WHi-L,
  NUC 70-1707, MiU

L144
Little, Malcolm, 1925-1965.
  Two speeches by Malcolm X. [New
  York, Merit Publishers, 1969]
  31p. 22cm.
  Cover title.
  1. Negroes--Civil rights.
  I. Merit Publishers.
  OrU, MoU, KU-RH, NUC 69-112017

L145
Little, Malcolm, 1925-1965.
  Two speeches by Malcolm X [New
  York, Pioneer Publishers, 1965]
  31p. 22cm.
  Cover title.
  1. Negroes--Civil rights.
  I. Pioneer Publishers.
  MiU

L146
Lively, Walt.
  Resolution on civil rights [by
  Walt Liveley and Mary Gruzon.
  n.p., Student Peace Union, 1964]
  3p. 28cm.
  Caption title.
  1. Negroes--Civil rights.
  I. Student Peace Union, National
  Convention, 1964. II. Gruzon,
  Mary, jt. auth.
  CU-B

L147
Livingston, Gordon S.
  Letter from a Vietnam veteran.
  Woodmont, Conn., Promoting En-
  during Peace [1969?]
  [2]p. 28cm. (No. 158)
  Caption title.
  Reprinted from Saturday Review,
  Sept. 20, 1969.
  1. Vietnamese conflict, 1961-
  1975. 2. Medicine, Military.
  I. Promoting Enduring Peace.
  KU-RH

L148
Lockard, Roget.
  Resolution on electoral action
  [by] Roget Lockard and Gail Paradise. [n.p., Student Peace
  Union, 1964]
  [2]p. 28cm.
  Caption title.
  1. Politics, Practical. 2. U.S.

--Pol. & govt.--1963-
  3. Peace. I. Student Peace
  Union. II. Paradise, Gail, jt.
  auth.
  CU-B

L149
Lockshin, Larry.
  When in court: defend yourself.
  [Boston, New England Free Press,
  1970?]
  [4]p. 28cm.
  Cover title.
  Reprinted from The Movement,
  Oct. 1969.
  1. Courts. 2. Defense (Civil
  procedures) 3. Lawyers.
  I. New England Free Press.
  WHi-L, KU-RH

L150
Lonsdale, Kathleen (Yardley)
    1903-
  The spiritual sickness of the
  world today. [Philadelphia]
  Friends World Committee [Ameri-
  can Section and Fellowship
  Council] 1957.
  16p. 22cm.
  Cover title.
  Address given to the Confer-
  ence of Friends in the Americas,
  Wilmington College, Wilmington,
  Ohio, June 30, 1957.
  PPULS, PSC-Hi, NUC 65-28218

L151
Lonsdale, Kathleen (Yardley),
    1903-
  Three essays in social responsibility, by Kathleen Longsdale,
  Victor Paschkis [and] O.T. Benfey. [Bridgeport, Conn., Society for Social Responsibility
  in Science] 1956.
  30p. 19cm. (Pamphlet 3)
  Reprinted from the Bulletin of
  Atomic Scientists.
  1. Science--Social aspects.
  I. Society for Social Responsibility in Science. II. Paschkis, Victor, jt. auth.
  III. Benfey, O.T., jt. auth.
  MoU

L152
Look what's happening with women.

[Minneapolis? Women's Counseling
Service, 197]
[34]p. illus. 28cm.
Cover title.
1. Woman--Rights of women.
KU-RH

L153
Loomis, Mildred J.
  Clarifying the economics of
peace. [Brookville, Ohio, School
of Living, 196]
[6]p. illus. 28cm.
Caption title.
1. War--Economic aspects.
2. Peace. I. School of Living.
KU-RH

L154
Loomis, Mildred J.
  Go ahead and live. [Freeland,
Md., School of Living, 1968?]
[2]p.
Caption title.
Reprinted from Resurgence, Dec.
1967.
1. Social change. I. School of
Living.
WHi-L

L155
Louise Pettibone Smith Birthday
    Committee.
  Louise Pettibone Smith, diamond
jubilee, testimonial dinner, October 12, 1962. [New York, 1962]
[48]p. illus. 28cm.
Cover title.
1. U.S. Laws, statutes, etc.
Internal Security Act of 1950.
2. Smith, Louise Pettibone.
MiU

·L156
Love, Kennett.
  Tax resistance: hell, no--I won't
pay. [New York, War Tax Resis-
tance, c1969]
60-65p. 22cm.
Reprinted from The Washington
Monthly, Dec. 1969.
1. Tax evasion. 2. Government,
Resistance to. I. War Tax Re-
sistance.
KU-RH

L157
Lowe, Keith.
  Towards a black university.
Nashville, Southern Student Organizing Committee [196]
8 [1]p. 28cm.
Cover title.
1. Negroes--Education. I. Southern Student Organizing Committee.
MoU, WHi-L

L158
Lowinger, Paul.
  The doctor as a political acti-
vist: a progress report. Ann
Arbor, Conference on Radicals
in the Professions, 1967.
4 [1]p. 28cm.
Cover title.
1. Physicians. I. Conference
on Radicals in the Professions.
MiU-H

L159
Luce, Don.
  Torture in Saigon. [Berkeley,
Calif., Committee of Concerned
Asian Scholars, 196]
3 [1]p. 28cm.
Caption title.
Contents--Why I want peace, by
Chanh Trung.
1. Vietnamese conflict, 1961-
1975. I. Committee of Concern-
ed Asian Scholars.
CU-B

L160
Lumer, Hyman.
  Disarmament and American economy. Report to the 17th national convention of the Communist
Party, U.S.A. [New York, New
Century Publishers, 1960]
15p. 20cm.
Cover title.
1. Disarmament. 2. U.S.--Econ.
condit. I. New Century Publishers. II. Communist Party
of the United States of America.
KU-RH, WHi-L

L161
Lumer, Hyman.

The fight against Trotskyism.
[New York, New Outlook Publishers,
196]
13 [1]p. 22cm.
Cover title.
1. Socialist Workers Party.
2. Socialism. 3. Trotskii, Lev.,
1879-1940. I. New Outlook Publishers.
MiU

L162
Lumer, Hyman.
Is full employment possible?
New York, New Century Publishers, 1962.
128p. illus. 21cm.
1. Unemployed. 2. U.S.--Econ.
condit.--1945-   I. New Century Publishers.
KU-RH, L355, DLC 62-5408

L163
Lumer, Hyman.
The Middle East crisis. [New
York, New Outlook Publishers,
1967]
23p. 22cm.
Cover title.
1. Near East--Pol. & govt.
2. Israel-Arab War, 1967.
I. New Outlook Publishers.
MiU

L164
Lumer, Hyman.
The professional informer. [New
York, New Century Publishers,
1955]
23p. illus. 19cm.
1. Informers. 2. Internal security. 3. Anti-communist movements. I. New Century Publishers.
KU-J, L349, DLC 5621109

Lumer, Hyman.
The promise of automation and
how to realize it. [New York,
New Century Publishers, 1956]
23p. 19cm.
1. Automation--Social aspects.
I. New Century Publishers.
NN, CLU, KU-RH, L350, CSSR

L166
Lumer, Hyman.

Soviet anti-semitism: a cold-
war myth. [New York, Political
Affairs Publishers, 1964]
32p. 22cm.
Cover title.
1. Jews in Russia. 2. Antisemi-
tism--Russia. I. Political Affairs Publishers.
WHi-A, MiU

L167
Lumer, Hyman.
What are we doing in the Congo?
[New York, New Outlook Publishers, 1965]
23p.
Cover title.
1. U.S.--Relations (general)
with Congo (Leopoldville)
2. Congo (Leopoldville)--Rela-
tions (general) with the U.S.
MiU

L168
Lumer, Hyman.
Which way Israel? An eyewitness
account by a Marxist educator.
New York, New Outlook Publishers,
1966.
15p.
1. Israel--Pol. & govt. I. New
Outlook Publishers.
CSSR

L169
Lund, Caroline.
Women and the equal rights
amendment, by Caroline Lund and
Betsy Stone. [New York, Path-
finder Press, c1970]
15p. 22cm.
Cover title.
1. Woman--Rights of women.
I. Stone, Betsy, jt. auth.
II. Pathfinder Press.
MiU

L170
Lutheran Peace Fellowship.
The Lutheran Peace Fellowship.
[New York, 196]
folder. ports.
Cover title.
1. Peace--Societies, etc.
WHi-L

L171
Luxemberg, Rosa, 1870-1919.
  Reform or revolution. [New York,
  Pathfinder Press, 1970]
  53p. 22cm. (A Merit pamphlet)
  Cover title.
  1. Socialism. I. Pathfinder
  Press.
  CU-B, KU-RH

L172
Lydegraf, Clayton Van.
  Position paper on mass political
  action and election policy.
  [Seattle, Pacific Northwest Progressive Labor Party, 196]
  10p. 28cm.
  Caption title.
  1. Progressive Labor Party.
  2. U.S.--Pol. & govt.--1963-
  3. Elections. I. Progress Labor Party, Pacific Northwest.
  WHi-A

L173
Lydegraf, Clayton Van.
  U.S. imperialism and the fascist
  danger. [Seattle, Progressive
  Labor Party? 196]
  8p. 28cm.
  Cover title.
  1. Imperialism. 2. Fascism.
  3. U.S.--Military policy.
  I. Progressive Labor Party.
  WHi-A

L174
Lynd, Staughton.
  Coalition politics or nonviolent revolution? [New York, Liberation, 1965]
  [4]p.
  Reprinted from Liberation, June-
  July 1965.
  1. Negroes--Civil rights.
  2. Nonviolence. I. Liberation.
  WHi-L

L175
Lynd, Staughton.
  Jefferson and radicalism.
  [Nashville] Southern Student
  Organizing Committee [1967]
  5p. 28cm.
  Reprinted from New South Student,
  Oct. 1967.

1. Jefferson, Thomas, Pres. U.
S., 1743-1826. 2. Radicalism.
I. Southern Student Organizing
Committee.
MiU, WHi-L

L176
Lynd, Staughton.
  Intellectuals, the university
  and the movement. [Boston, New
  England Free Press, 196]
  [4]p. 28cm.
  Cover title.
  Speech delivered to the founding
  conference of New University
  Conference. Includes a reply
  by Jesse Lemisch.
  1. Universities and colleges.
  2. Student movements. 3. In-
  tellectuals. I. Lemisch,
  Jesse. II. New University Con-
  ference. III. New England Free
  Press.
  KU-RH

L177
Lynd, Staughton.
  Letter from jail: telling right
  from wrong. [n.p., 196]
  [3]p. 28cm.
  Caption title.
  Reprinted from Liberation, Dec.
  1968.
  1. Government, Resistance to.
  KU-RH

L178
Lynd, Staughton.
  The movement: a new beginning,
  by Staughton Lynd. A left wing
  alternative, by Greg Calvert.
  [New York, 1969?]
  [24]p. illus. 28cm.
  Cover title.
  Reprinted from Liberation, May
  1969.
  1. Student movements. 2. Stu-
  dents for a Democratic Society.
  I. Calvert, Gregory, jt. auth.
  KU-RH

L179
Lynd, Staughton.
  The movement: a new beginning,
  by Staughton Lynd. A left wing
  alternative, by Greg Calvert.

[Palo Alto? Institute for the
Study of Nonviolence, 1970?]
[26]p. 28cm.
1. Student movements. 2. Radi-
calism. 3. Military service,
Compulsory. 4. Students for a
Democratic Society. I. Calvert,
Gregory, jt. auth. II. Institute
for the Study of Nonviolence.
CU-B

L180
Lynd, Staughton.
  The new radicals and "participatory democracy". Chicago, Students for a Democratic Society
  [1965]
  10p. 22cm.
  Reprinted from Dissent, Summer
  1965.
  1. Democracy. 2. Student movements. 3. Youth--Political activity. I. Students for a Democratic Society.
  WHi-A, CU-B

L181
Lynd, Staughton.
  The new radicals & "participatory
  democracy". Los Angeles, Students for a Democratic Society
  [196]
  7p. 28cm.
  Cover title.
  Reprinted from Dissent.
  1. Democracy. 2. Student movements. 3. Student Nonviolent
  Coordinating Committee. 4. Ne-
  groes--Civil rights. I. Students
  for a Democratic Society.
  MiU-H

L182
Lynd, Staughton.
  SNCC: the beginning of ideology.
  [n.p., 196]
  3p. 36cm.
  Caption title.
  1. Student Nonviolent Coordina-
  ting Committee. 2. Negroes--
  Civil rights.
  WHi-A

L183
Lynn, Conrad J.
  Monroe, North Carolina, turning

point in American history. Two
speeches by Conrad J. Lynn,
foreword by James Boggs. [De-
troit, Correspondence Publishing
Co., c1962]
27p. 19cm.
Cover title.
1. Monroe, N.C.--Race question.
2. Negroes--Monroe, N.C.
3. Williams, Robert Franklin,
1925-   I. Correspondence
Publishing Co. II. Boggs,
James.
KU-RH

L184
Lynn, Conrad J.
  Turning point in American his-
  tory, two speeches by Conrad J.
  Lynn, foreword by James Bobbs.
  [Detroit, Correspondence Pub-
  lishing Co., c1962]
  27p. (Correspondence pamphlet
  5)
  Cover title.
  At head of title: Monroe, North
  Carolina.
  1. Monroe, N.C.--Race question.
  2. Negroes--Monroe, N.C.
  I. Correspondence Publishing
  Co. II. Boggs, James.
  WHi-L

L185
Lyons, Eve M.
  Basic facts on the Soviet Union.
  [New York, National Council of
  America-Soviet Friendship, 1961]
  63p. 23cm.
  Cover title.
  1. Russia. I. National Council
  of American-Soviet Friendship.
  KU-J

L186
Lyttle, Bradford.
  The importance of discipline in
  demonstrations for peace. [New
  York, Committee for Nonviolent
  Action, 196]
  2 leaves. 28cm.
  Caption title.
  1. Peace. 2. Nonviolence.
  3. Demonstrations. I. Commit-
  tee for Nonviolent Action.
  KU-RH

L187
Lyttle, Mary Suzuki.
  Minutemen attack on New England
  CNVA: a report. Voluntown, Conn.
  [1968]

4p. 28cm.
Cover title.
1. Minutemen. 2. Committee for
Nonviolent Action.
CU-B

‡

Mc

‡

Mc1
McAdoo, Bill.
  Pre-civil war black nationalism.
  [Brooklyn] Progressive Labor Party [196]
32p. illus. 28cm.
Cover title.
1. Negroes--History. 2. Black
nationalism--History. I. Progressive Labor Party.
MiU

Mc2
McAfee, Kathy.
  Black brothers have a better
  idea. Boston, New England Free
  Press [1970?]
[4]p. 28cm.
Caption title.
Reprinted from The Movement,
Aug. 1969.
1. Negroes--Employment. 2. Uni-
ted Black Brothers. 3. Students
for a Democratic Society. I. New
England Free Press.
KU-RH, MiU

Mc3
McAfee, Kathy.
  Bread & roses, by Kathy McAfee
  & Myrna Wood. [Detroit, Radical
  Education Project, 1969]
16p. illus. 22cm.
Cover title.
Reprinted from Leviathan, v. 1,
no. 3; Je. 1969.
1. Woman--Rights of women.
I. Radical Education Project.
II. Wood, Nyrna, jt. auth.
MiEM, MoU, MiU, WHi-L, KU-RH

Mc4
McAfee, Kathy.
  What is the revolutionary

potential of women's liberation?
[By] Kathy McAfee & Myrna Wood.
[Boston, New England Free Press,
1970?]
16p. 21cm.
Cover title.
Reprinted from Leviathan, v. 1,
no. 3; 1969; titled: Bread and
roses.
1. Woman--Rights of women.
I. New England Free Press.
II. Wood, Myrna, jt. auth.
KU-RH

Mc5
McBride, Jim.
  The black movement and white
  organizing [by Ron McBride and
  Jim O'Brien. n.p., Students
  for a Democratic Society? 196]
[4]p. 28cm.
Caption title.
1. Negroes--Civil rights.
I. O'Brien, James, jt. auth.
I. Students for a Democratic
Society.
CU-B

Mc6
McCain, James T.
  Guideline to political action.
  New York, Congress of Racial
  Equality [1966]
4 leaves.
1. Negroes--Civil rights.
2. Voters, Registration of.
I. Congress of Racial Equality.
NNC, NUC 67-105116

Mc7
McCain, James T.
  The right to vote. [New York,
  Congress of Racial Equality,
  1962]

1v. (unpaged) illus. 28cm.
Cover title.
1. Negroes--Politics and suffrage.
I. Congress of Racial Equality.
KU-RH, WHi-L, DLC

Mc8
McClaughry, John.
The voice of the dolphins.
[Washington, Council for a Liv-
able World, 196]
[4]p. 28cm.
Caption title.
Reprinted from the Progressive.
1. Szilard, Leo. 2. U.S.--Mili-
tary policy. 3. Council for a
Livable World. I. Council for a
Livable World.
KU-RH

Mc9
McCool, Maureen.
Canada and Latin America: trade
and development. [Toronto? Latin American Working Group] 1969.
18p. 28cm.
Caption title.
1. Canada--Relations (general)
with Latin America. 2. Latin
America--Relations (general)
with Canada. I. Latin American
Working Group.
KU-RH

Mc10
McCoy, Alfred.
Pan Am makes the going great,
by Alfred McCoy [and] Angus Mc-
Donald. [Boston, New England
Free Press, 1970?]
18p. 28cm.
Cover title.
Reprinted from Bulletin of Con-
cerned Asian Scholars, v.2, no.
2; Jan. 1970.
I. Pan American World Airway.
2. Vietnamese conflict, 1961-
1975. I. McDonald, Angus, jt.
auth. II. New England Free
Press.
KU-RH

Mc11
McCubbin, Bob.
Martin Sostre in court, edited
by Bob McCubbin. [Buffalo, Mar-

tin Sostre Defense Committee,
1969.
60p. illus. 22cm.
Cover title.
1. Sostre, Martin Gonzales,
1923-   2. Negroes--Civil
rights. 2. Police--New York
(State)--Buffalo. 3. Buffalo,
N.Y.--Race question.
MiU, CU-B

Mc12
McDermott, John.
Campus missionaries: the laying
on of culture. [Chicago, New
University Conference, 1969?]
7p. illus. 28cm.
Cover title.
Reprinted from The Nation,
Mar. 10, 1969.
1. Student movements. 2. Uni-
versities and colleges.
I. New University Conference.
KU-RH

Mc13
McDermott, John.
The laying on of culture. [Ith-
aca, N.Y., Glad Day Press, 196]
7p. illus. 28cm.
Cover title.
Reprinted from The Nation,
Mar. 10, 1969.
1. Student movements. 2. Uni-
versities and colleges.
I. Glad Day Press.
NNU-T

Mc14
McDermott, John.
A profile of Vietnamese history.
New York, Committee of Students
for Peace in Vietnam and Students for a Democratic Society,
New York Region [196]
25 [6]p. illus. 28cm.
Cover title.
1. Vietnamese conflict, 1961-
1975. I. Committee of Students
for Peace in Vietnam. II. Students for a Democratic Society,
New York Region.
WHi-L

Mc15
McDermott, John.

Thoughts on the movement; who
does the movement move? Ann
Arbor, Radical Education Project,
[196]
[4]p. illus. 28cm.
Reprinted from Viet-Report, Sept.
-Oct. 1967.
Cover title.
1. Vietnamese conflict, 1961-
1975. 2. Student movements.
I. Radical Education Project.
MoU

Mc16
McDermott, John.
Thoughts on the movement. Who
does the movement move? Boston,
New England Free Press [196]
[4]p. illus. 28cm.
Caption title.
Reprinted from Viet-Report, Sept.
-Oct. 1967.
1. Youth--Political activity.
2. Vietnamese conflict, 1961-
1975. I. New England Free Press.
KU-RH

Mc17
McDermott, John.
Welfare imperialism in Vietnam.
[n.p., 1966?]
76-88p.
Reprinted from The Nation,
July 25, 1966.
1. Vietnamese conflict, 1961-
1975.
WHi-L

Mc18
MacDonald, Dwight.
Our invisible poor. [New York,
Sidney Hillman Foundation, 196]
23p. 22x9cm.
Cover title.
1. Poverty.
KU-RH, WHi-L

Mc19
MacDonald, Dwight.
Why destroy draft cards? Berkeley, Calif., World Without War
Council [196]
3p. 28cm.
Caption title.
1. Government, Resistance to.
2. Military service, Compulsory.

I. World Without War Council.
CU-B

Mc20
MacDonald, Ray.
Corporate profits and the wage
gap, with an introd. by Michael
Harrington. New York, League
for Industrial Democracy [1968]
[6]p. tables (Looking forward,
no. 11)
Cover title.
Reprinted from AFL-CIO American
Federationist, July 1968.
1. U.S.--Econ. condit. 2. Pro-
fit. 3. Wages. I. Harrington,
Michael. II. League for Indus-
trial Democracy.
WHi-L, NNU-T

Mc21
McEldowney, Carol.
The radical and the welfare system. Ann Arbor, Conference on
Radicals in the Professions,
1967.
5p. 28cm.
1. Public welfare. 2. Radicalism. I. Conference on Radicals
in the Professions.
MiU

Mc22
McEldowney, Ken.
Disarmament and the American
economy. New York, Students
for a Democratic Society and its
Peace Research and Education
Project [1963?]
9p. 28cm.
Cover title.
1. Disarmament. 2. U.S.--Mili-
tary policy. I. Students for
a Democratic Society. Peace
Research and Education Project.
WHi-L, MiU, NUC 71-5280

Mc23
McEldowney, Ken.
Readings in poverty. Ann Arbor,
Economic Research and Action
Project of the Students for a
Democratic Society [196]
14p.
Cover title.
1. Poverty. 2. U.S.--Econ.

condit. I. Students for a Democratic Society. Economic Research and Action Project.
WHi-L, NUC 71-7473

Mc24
McEldowney, Ken.
  Readings on poverty. New York,
  Students for a Democratic Society [196]
  7p. 28cm.
  Cover title.
  1. Poverty. 2. U.S.--Econ.
  condit. I. Students for a Democratic Society.
  MiU

Mc25
McEldowney, Ken.
  Voice Political Party, by Ken
  and Carl McEldowney. [n.p.,
  1964?]
  [3]p. 28cm.
  Caption title.
  1. Student movements--Ann Arbor.
  2. Voice Political Party-Students
  for a Democratic Society, Ann
  Arbor. II. McEldowney, Carol,
  jt. auth.
  WHi-A

Mc26
McGill, Ralph.
  A human document. [Woodmont,
  Conn., Promoting Enduring Peace,
  196]
  [4]p. 22cm.
  Caption title.
  Reprinted from Atlanta Constitu-
  tion.
  1. Negroes--Civil rights.
  I. Promoting Enduring Peace.
  KU-RH

Mc27
McGovern, George Stanley, 1922-
  A conversation with Senator
  George McGovern. [Washington,
  Friends Committee on National
  Legislation, 196]
  [12]p. illus. 23cm.
  Cover title.
  1. U.S.--Pol. & govt.--1963-
  I. Friends Committee on Nation-
  al Legislation, Washington, D.C.
  KU-RH

Mc28
McKelvey, Donald.
  China. New York, Students for
  a Democratic Society and its
  Peace Research and Education
  Project [196]
  33p. 28cm.
  Cover title.
  Reprinted from SPU Discussion
  Bulletin.
  1. China (People's Republic of
  China, 1949-   ) I. Students
  for a Democratic Society. Peace
  Research and Education Project.
  WHi-A

Mc29
McKelvey, Donald.
  The doctrine of unfreedom, university reform, and campus political parties. New York, Students for a Democratic Society
  [196]
  6p. 28cm.
  Cover title.
  1. Student movements. 2. Universities and colleges.
  I. Students for a Democratic
  Society.
  MiU, WHi-A

Mc30
McKelvey, Donald.
  Economic development: the major
  power and peace. New York, Students for a Democratic Society
  and its Peace Research and Education Project [196]
  12p. 28cm.
  Cover title.
  1. Underdeveloped areas.
  2. World politics--1955-
  3. U.S.--Foreign policy.
  4. Russia--Foreign policy.
  5. China--Foreign policy.
  6. Power (Social science)
  7. Peace. I. Students for a
  Democratic Society. Peace Research and Education Project.
  WHi-L, MiU

Mc31
McKelvey, Donald.
  A practical utopia. New York,
  Students for a Democratic Soc-
  iety [196]

16p.   28cm.
Cover title.
1. Social change.   2. Sociology.
I. Students for a Democratic
Society.
MiU

Mc32
McKelvey, Donald.
  Socialist man and the Chinese
  revolution: the basis of the
  cultural revolution.   Boston,
  New England Free Press [196]
  4p.   28cm.
  Caption title.
  1. China (People's Republic of
  China, 1949-   )--Intellectual
  life.   2. Socialism.   I. New
  England Free Press.
  KU-RH, MoU

Mc33
McKelvey, Doanld.
  Socialist man and the Chinese
  revolution.   Toronto, Research,
  Information and Publications
  Project, Student Union for Peace
  Action [196]
  5p.   28cm
  Cover title.
  "Adapted from speeches at the
  1966 Socialist Scholars Confer-
  ence and a conference on China
  in spring 1967."
  1. China (People's Republic of
  China, 1949-   )--Intellectual
  life.   2. Socialism.   I. Student
  Union for Peace Action.
  WHi-A

Mc34
McKissick, Floyd B.
  Constructive militancy, a philo-
  sophy and a program.   New York,
  National Congress of Racial
  Equality [1966]
  14p.   22cm.
  Cover title.
  1. Radicalism.   2. Negroes--
  Civil rights.   I. Congress of
  Racial Equality.
  MiU

Mc35
McKissick, Floyd B.
  Genocide U.S.A.: a blueprint

for black survival, speech pre-
sented by Floyd B. McKissick.
New York, National Congress of
Racial Equality [1967?]
14p.   22cm.
Cover title.
1. Negroes--Civil rights.
2. Genocide.   I. Congress of
Racial Equality.
MiU

Mc36
McLaurin, Charles.
  Notes on organizing.   [Nash-
  ville] Southern Student Organizing Committee [196]
  3 leaves.   28cm.
  Cover title.
  1. Negroes--Civil rights.
  2. Student Nonviolent Coordinating Committee.   3. Community
  organization.   I. Southern Student Organizing Committee.
  WHi-L, MiU

Mc37
McMahan, Ian.
  International perspective: a
  draft perspective.   [New York]
  Independent Socialist Clubs of
  America [196]
  23p.   28cm.
  Cover title.
  1. Socialism.   I. Independent
  Socialist Clubs of America.
  CU-B

Mc38
McReynolds, David.
  Civilian defense: a discussion
  paper.   [n.p.] Distributed by
  Students for a Democratic Soc-
  iety for the Liberal Study
  Group [196]
  5p.   28cm.
  Cover title.
  1. Civilian defense.   I. Stu-
  dents for a Democratic Society.
  II. Liberal Study Group.
  WHi-L, MiU

Mc39
McReynolds, David.
  Statement by David McReynolds,
  issued November 6, 1965.   [New
  York, War Resisters League,

196]
[2]p. 28cm.
Caption title.
1. Vietnamese conflict, 1961-
1975. 2. Government, Resistance
to. I. War Resisters League.
KU-RH, CU-B

Mc40
McReynolds, David.
    Uptight with the draft? [New
    York? War Resisters League?
    1969?]
    [12]p. 22x10cm.
    Cover title.
    1. Military service, Compulsory.
    I. War Resisters League.
    KU-RH

Mc41
McSurely, Alan.
    Common group problems. [Louis-
    ville, Southern Conference Edu-
    cational Fund, c1967]
    8p. illus. 28cm. (Organizer's
    library series)
    Cover title.
    1. Organization. I. Southern
    Conference Education Fund.
    MoU, KU-RH

Mc42
McSurley, Alan.
    Getting and keeping people to-
    gether. [Louisville, Southern
    Conference Educational Fund,
    c1967]
    14p. illus. 22cm. (Organi-
    zer's library series)
    1. Organization. I. Southern
    Conference Educational Fund.
    KU-RH

Mc43
McSurely, Alan.
    Hang-ups: some common problems
    of people who organize other
    people into communities.
    [Louisville, Southern Conference
    Educational Fund, c1967]

15p. illus. 28cm. (Organizer's library series)
Cover title.
1. Reformers. 2. Organization.
I. Southern Conference Educational Fund.
MoU, KU-RH

Mc44
McSurely, Alan.
    How to negotiate. [Louisville,
    Southern Conference Educational
    Fund, c1967]
    9p. illus. 28cm. (Organi-
    zer's library series)
    Cover title.
    1. Negotiation. I. Southern
    Conference Educational Fund.
    KU-RH

Mc45
McSurely, Alan.
    How to put out a community news-
    paper. [Louisville, Southern
    Conference Educational Fund,
    c1967]
    [12]p. illus. 28cm. (Organi-
    zer's library series)
    Caption title.
    1. Newspapers. 2. Community
    organization. I. Southern
    Conference Educational Fund.
    KU-RH

Mc46
McSurely, Alan.
    A political fable: how the peo-
    ple of can-talk joined hands
    and quashed the quack-quacks.
    Louisville, Kentuckians Against
    Kentucky Un-American Activities
    Committee [196]
    8p. illus. 28cm.
    Cover title.
    1. Kentucky--Race question.
    2. Civil rights--Kentucky.
    3. Internal security--Kentucky.
    I. Kentuckians Against Kentucky
    Un-American Activities Committee.
    WHi-L

‡ M ‡

M1
Magdoff, Harry.
  Economic aspects of U.S. imperialism. Ann Arbor, Radical Education Project, c1966.
  31p. 21cm.
  Reprinted from Monthly Review,
Nov. 1966.
  1. Imperialism. 2. U.S.--For-
eign policy. 3. U.S.--Foreign
economic relations. I. Radical
Education Project.
  KU-RH

M2
Magdoff, Harry.
  Economic aspects of U.S. imperialism. New York, Monthly Review Press [c1966]
  31p. illus. 21cm. (Monthly
review series no. 27)
  Reprinted from Monthly Review,
No. 1966.
  1. Imperialism. 2. U.S.--For-
eign policy. 3. U.S.--Foreign
economic relations. I. Monthly
Review Press.
  MiU, KU-RH, WHi-L, NIC

M3
Magdoff, Harry.
  Problems of the United States
capitalism. [Ann Arbor, Radical Education Project, 1965]
  62-79p.
  Cover title.
  Reprinted from Socialist Register, 1965.
  1. Capitalism. 2. U.S.--Econ.
condit. I. Radical Education
Project.
  WHi-L

M4
Magdoff, Harry.
  Problems of U.S. capitalism.
Boston, New England Free Press
[196]
  [62]-79p. 22cm.

Cover title.
Reprinted from Socialist Register, 1965.
1. Capitalism. 2. U.S.--Econ.
condit. I. New England Free
Press.
MiU, KU-RH

M5
Magdoff, Harry.
  Problems of United States
capitalism. Detroit, Radical
Education Project [1970?]
  62-79p. 22cm.
  Cover title.
  Reprinted from Socialist Regis-
ter, 1965.
  1. Capitalism. 2. U.S.--Econ.
condit. I. Radical Education
Project.
  KU-RH

M6
Mage, Shane.
  The fight against war. [New
York] Young Socialist Forum
[1960]
  15 leaves. 28cm. (Educational
bulletin 4)
  1. U.S.--For. rel.--Russia.
  2. Russia--For. rel.--U.S.
  3. War. I. Young Socialist
Forum.
  MiU

M7
Mage, Shane.
  The Hungarian revolution. New
York, Young Socialist Forum,
1960
  iv, 35 [1] leaf. 28cm. (Educational bulletin 1)
  Cover title.
  1. Hungary--History--Revolution,
1956. I. Young Socialist Forum.
  MiU

M8
Magil, Abraham Bernard, 1905-

Which way Israel? New York, New
Century Publishers, 1956.
23p.
1. Israel--Foreign policy.
2. Near East--Pol. & govt.
I. New Century Publishers.
NNJeF, M36

M9
Magnuson, Bruce.
What to do about the crisis in
our cities? Is this our future.
Death of civil demoncracy?
Higher taxes forever. [Toronto,
Progress Books, 1969]
11p.
Cover title.
1. Taxation--Canada. 2. Demo-
cracy. 3. Cities and towns--
Canada. I. Progress Books.
MiU

M10
Mainardi, Pat.
The politics of housework.
Boston, New England Free Press
[1970?]
[4]p. illus. 28cm.
1. Woman--Rights of women.
I. New England Free Press.
KU-RH

M11
Mainardi, Pat.
The politics of housework. Rev.
[New York, Redstockings of the
Women's Liberation Movement]
1970.
[4]p. 28cm.
Caption title.
1. Woman--Rights of women.
I. Redstockings of the Women's
Liberation Movement.
MoU

M12
Mainardi, Pat.
The politics of housework.
[Somerville, Mass., Distributed
by Boston Female Liberation,
196]
3 [1]p. 28cm.
Cover title.
1. Woman--Rights of women.
I. Boston Female Liberation.
KU-RH

M13
Malatesta, Errico, 1853-1932.
The anarchist revolution. [Van
Nuys, Calif., SRAF Print, 196 ?]
[12]p. 22cm.
Cover title.
1. Anarchism and anarchists.
I. SRAF Print Co-op.
MiU

M14
Malatesta, Errico, 1853-1932.
Anarchy, with a biographical
note & a new appendix containing
Malatesta's statement on his
return to Italy in 1913. [Buf-
falo, Friends of Malatesta,
1970]
40p. 22cm.
Cover title.
1. Anarchism and anarchists.
I. Friends of Malatesta.
MiU

M15
Malatesta, Errico, 1853-1932.
Smash violence. [Mountain View,
SRAF Print Co-op, 197 ?]
[2]p. 22cm.
Cover title.
1. Fascism. 2. Anarchism and
anarchists. I. SRAF Print
Co-op.
MiU

M16
Malatesta, Errico, 1853-1932.
Vote what for? [3d. ed. New
York, Liberation League, 1959]
15p.
Cover title.
1. Anarchism and anarchists.
2. Politics, Practical.
I. Liberatarian League.
MiU

Malcolm X
  see
Little, Malcolm, 1925-1965.

M17
Malcolm X black hand society of
the world. [Chicago, 1968]
Cover title.
1. Negroes--Civil rights.
WHi-L

M18
Mallory, Mae.
  Letters from prison: the story of
  a frame up. [2d ed. Cleveland,
  Monroe Defense Committee, 196]
  70p.
  Cover title.
  1. Negroes--Civil rights.
  I. Monroe Defense Committee.
  MiU

M19
Manahar Cooperative Fellowship.
  Handbook. [Oakhurst, Calif.,
  1969]
  11 leaves. 28cm.
  Cover title.
  1. Collective settlements.
  KU-RH

M20
Mandel, Ernest.
  The catastrophe in Indonesia.
  Three articles on the fatal con-
  sequences of Communist party
  policy [by Ernest Mandel, United
  Secretariat of the Fourth Inter-
  national, and T. Soedarso. In-
  troduction by Joseph Hansen.
  New York, Merit Publishers, 1966]
  47p. 22cm.
  Cover title.
  1. Indonesia--Pol. & govt.
  2. Communism--Indonesia.
  I. Soedarso, T. II. Hansen,
  Joseph. I. Merit Publishers.
  MoU

M21
Mandel, Ernest.
  The common market: international
  capitalism and "supra-national-
  ity". Ann Arbor, Radical Education Project [196]
  27-41p. 22cm.
  Reprinted from Socialist Register, 1967.
  1. European Economic Community.
  2. Capitalism. I. Radical Education Project.
  MoU

M22
Mandel, Ernest.
  The common market: international
  capitalism and 'supra-national-

ity'. Boston, New England Free
Press [196]
[27]-41p. 21cm.
Reprinted from Socialist Register, 1967.
1. European Economic Community.
2. Capitalism. I. New England
Free Press.
KU-RH, MiU

M23
Mandel, Ernest.
  An introduction to Marxist eco-
  nomic theory. [New York, Young
  Socialist Alliance, 1967]
  78p.
  1. Marxian economics. I. Young
  Socialist Alliance.
  MiU, NUC 69-3294

M24
Mandel, Ernest.
  An introduction to Marxist eco-
  nomic theory. [New York, Merit
  Publishers, 1969]
  78p. 22cm.
  Translation of Initiation a la
  theorie economique marxists.
  1. Marxian economics. I. Merit
  Publishers.
  NBPol, NjP, MB, DLC 70-103695

M25
Mandel, Ernest.
  An introduction to Marxist economic theory. [New York] Pathfinder Press, 1970.
  78p. 22cm.
  Translation of Initiation a la
  theorie economique.
  1. Marxian economics. I. Pathfinder Press.
  PPT, NUC 72-65494

M26
Mandel, Ernest.
  The Marxist theory of alien-
  ation [by] Ernest Mandel and
  George Novack. [New York,
  Pathfinder Press, 1970]
  63p. 22cm. (A Merit pamphlet)
  Cover title.
  1. Socialism. 2. Alienation
  (Social psychology) 3. Com-
  munism and society. I. Novack,
  George Edward, jt. auth.

II. Pathfinder Press.
KU-RH, DLC 67-127845

M27
Mandel, Ernest.
On the revolutionary potential of
the working class [by] Ernest Mandel [and] George Novack. [New
York, Merit Publishers, 1969]
46p. 22cm.
1. Labor and laboring classes.
2. Socialism. I. Novack, George
Edward, jt. auth. II. Merit Publishers.
InU

M28
Mandel, Ernest.
On the revolutionary potential of
the working class [by] Ernest
Mandel [and] George Novack. [New
York, Pathfinder Press, 1970]
46p. 22cm. (A Merit pamphlet)
Cover title.
1. Labor and laboring classes.
2. Socialism. I. Novack, George
Edward, jt. auth. I. Pathfinder
Press.
KU-RH

M29
Mandel, Ernest.
On workers democracy. [New York]
Young Socialist Alliance [196]
[4]p. 28cm.
Caption title.
1. Labor and laboring classes.
2. Socialism. I. Young Social-
ist Alliance.
KU-RH

M30
Mandel, Ernest.
Peaceful coexistence and world
revolution. [New York, Pathfinder Press, 1970]
31p. 22cm. (A Merit pamphlet)
Cover title.
1. Russia--For. rel.--U.S.
2. World politics--1955-
3. Underdeveloped areas.
I. Pathfinder Press.
KU-RH

M31
Mandel, Ernest.

Revolutionary strategy in the
imperialist countries. [Intro-
duction by George Novack. New
York, Pathfinder Press, 1970]
15p. 22cm.
Cover title.
At head of title: The speech
Nixon & Mitchell tried to ban.
1. Socialism. 2. Revolutions.
I. Novack, George Edward.
I, Pathfinder Press.
KU-RH, MiU, InU

M32
Mandel, Erenst.
The revolutionary student movement: theory and practice. [New
York, Young Socialist Alliance;
distributed by Merit Publishers,
1969]
39p. 21cm. (A Young Socialist
pamphlet)
1. Student movements. I. Young
Socialist Alliance.
MoSW, CU-B, MiU, KU-RH,
NUC 69-136430

M33
Mandel, Ernest.
Vive Cuba: impressions de Cuba.
[Toronto, Fair Play for Cuba
Committee, 1965?]
13p. 22cm.
Cover title.
1. Cuba--Pol. & govt.--1959-
I. Fair Play for Cuba
Committee
CSt-H, NUC 72-25235

M34
Mandel, Ernest.
Where is America going? Bos-
ton, New England Free Press
[1970?]
15p. 21cm.
Cover title.
Reprinted from New Left Review,
March/April 1969.
1. U.S.--Econ. condit. 2. Ne-
groes--Employment. 3. Student
movements. I. New England Free
Press.
KU-RH

M35
Manifestations for peace; exper-

iences at Suffield, July 5,
1964 [and] Orcadi, November 28,
1964. [Grand Forks, B.C., Iskra Publications, 1965]
44p. 22cm.
Cover title.
1. Partial contents--A.J. Muste's
speech; John J. Verigin's speech;
Suffield manifestations by Anne
Rush.
1. Peace. 2. Disarmament.
I. Muste, Abraham John, 1885-
196 . I. Iskra Publications.
KU-RH

M36
Manitobasabi, Edna.
An Indian girl in the city.
[Buffalo, Friends of Malatesta,
197 ?]
17p. 22cm.
Cover title.
Reprinted from This Magazine is
About Schools, v. 4, no. 4.
1. Indians of North America--
Education. I. Friends of Mala-
testa.
MiU

M37
Mann, Eric.
The Columbia University insurrection: the problem of new left
tactics and strategy. [Montreal?
Our Generation? 196]
20 leaves.
Caption title.
1. Columbia University. 2. Student movements--Columbia University. I. Our Generation.
NNU-T

M38
Mann, Eric.
A new school for the ghetto.
Ann Arbor, Conference on Radicals in the Professions, 1967.
4p. 28cm.
Cover title.
1. Negroes--Education. I. Conference on Radicals in the Professions.
MiU-H

M39
Mann, Eric.

The Newark Community School.
[Boston, New England Free Press,
1968?]
7 [1]p. illus. 28cm.
Caption title.
Reprinted from Liberation, Aug.
1967.
1. Newark Community School.
2. Education--New Jersey--Ne-
wark. 3. Negroes--Education.
I. New England Free Press.
KU-RH

M40
Mann, Eric.
The Newark Community School.
[New York, Liberation, 196]
7p. illus. 28cm.
Caption title.
1. Education--New Jersey--
Newark. 2. Newark Community
School. 3. Negroes--Education.
I. Liberation.
MoU

M41
Manual for draft-age immigrants
to Canada. 5th ed. Revised
and edited by Byron Wall.
Toronto, House of Anansi, 1970.
105p. 20cm.
1. Military service, Compulsory.
2. Emigration and immigration
law--Canada. I. Wall, Byron,
ed.
KU-RH

M42
Mao, Tse-Tung, 1893-
Talks at the Yanan forum on
literature and art, May 1942.
Toronto, Research, Information,
and Publications Project, Stu-
dent Union for Peace Action
[196]
[24]p. 22cm.
Cover title.
1. Art. 2. Literature.
I. Student Union for Peace
Action.
WHi-A

M43
March against death: a Veitnam
memorial, Washington, D.C.,
November 13-16, 1969. [Wash-

ington, New Mobilization Committee to End the War in Vietnam, 1969]
[4]p. illus. 22cm.
Cover title.
1. Vietnamese conflict, 1961-
1975. I. New Mobilization Committee to End the War in Vietnam.
KU-RH

M44
March on Washington for Jobs and
    Freedom.
Organizational manual no. 1 New
York [1963]
8p. 21cm.
Caption title.
1. Negroes--Civil rights.
KU-RH

M45
Marcum, John.
Southern Africa and United States
policy: a consideration of alter-
natives. [n.p., 1967?]
[8]p. 28cm.
Caption title.
Reprinted from Africa Today, Oct.
1967.
1. U.S.--Relations (general) with
Africa, South. 2. Africa, South
--Relations (general) with U.S.
KU-RH

M46
Marcus, L.
The third stage of imperialism.
[New York] West Village Commit-
tee for Independent Political
Action [1967?]
46p. 22cm.
1. Imperialism. 2. U.S.--Econ.
condit. 3. Socialism. I. West
Village Committee Independent
Political Action.
KU-RH, MiU

M47
Marcus, L.
The mass strike. [New York,
Campaigner Publications] 1970.
13p. 22cm.
Cover title.
Reprinted from The Campaigner,
v. 1, no. 3; May-June 1968.
1. Student movements--Columbia

University. I. Campaigner
Publications.
KU-RH

M48
Marcuse, Herbert.
Radical perspectives 1969.
[Montreal, Our Generation, 196]
6p.
1. Radicalism. I. Our Genera-
tion.
NNU-T

M49
Marcy, Sam.
The subways belong to the people [by Sam Marcy, Deirdre Griswold and Pam Meyers] New York,
World View Publishers [1970?]
22p. illus. 22cm.
Reprinted from Workers World,
Jan. 10 and 29, 1970.
1. New York City Transit Authority. 2. Subways--New York
(City) I. Griswold, Dierdre,
jt. auth. II. Meyers, Pam,
jt. auth. III. World View Publishers.
KU-RH

M50
Mardiros, Anthony.
Socialism in Canada; is it
relevant? [Winnipeg, Canadian
Dimension, 196]
[3]p. illus. 28cm.
Caption title.
Reprinted from Canadian Dimen-
sion.
1. Socialism in Canada. I. Can-
adian Dimension.
KU-RH

M51
Markowitz, Gerald E.
Proposal for a radical presi-
dential campaign in 1968 [by]
Gerald E. Markowitz, Michael
Meeropol, Stephen C. Rankin.
[Madison? 1968?]
[8]p. 28cm.
Caption title.
1. Presidents--U.S.--Election--
1968. 2. U.S.--Pol. & govt.--
1963-   3. Radicalism.
I. Meeropol, Michael, jt. auth.

II. Rankin, Stephen C., jt. auth.
CU-B

M52
Martin, Bob.
  Radicalism and homosexuality.
  New York [Youth Committee of the
  North American Conference of
  Homophile Organizations] 1969.
  [2]p. 36cm.
  Caption title.
  1. Homosexuality. 2. Radicalism.
  I. North American Conference of
  Homophile Organizations. Youth
  Committee.
  KU-RH

M53
Martin, Gloria.
  Women in the revolutionary
  struggle. Seattle, Radical Wo-
  men [1970?]
  4 leaves. 28cm.
  Caption title.
  At head of title: Discussion
  draft for the Radical Women
  Conference, Feb. 23, 1970.
  1. Woman--Rights of women.
  I. Radical women.
  WHi-L

M54
Martin Luther King and the Mont-
    gomery story. [New York, Fel-
    lowship of Reconciliation,
    196 ?]
  [15]p.
  Cover title.
  1. King, Martin Luther, 1929-
  1968. 2. Montgomery, Ala.--
  Race question. 3. Negroes--
  Montgomery, Ala.
  WHi-L

M55
Marx, Karl, 1818-1883.
  On the labor party; selections
  from the writings of Karl Marx
  and Frederick Engels. [Toronto,
  Workers Vanguard Publishing
  Association, 1962]
  21p. 22cm.
  Caption title.
  Reprinted from the Labor Stan-
  dard 1881.
  1. Labor and laboring classes.

I. Workers Vanguard Publishing
Association. II. Engels, Fred-
erick, 1820-1895.
MoU

M56
Marzani, Carl.
  The shelter hoax and foreign
  policy [by] Carl Marzani [and
  others] New York, Marzani &
  Munsell, Inc. [196]
  96p. 23cm.
  1. U.S.--Foreign policy.
  2. Atomic bomb shelters.
  3. Russia--For. rel.--U.S.
  I. Marzani and Munsell.
  KU-RH, CSSR, DLC 62-2848

M57
Mason, Chick.
  Sources of our dilemma. [New
  York, Jefferson Book Shop,
  19]56-
  v. 28cm.
  Cover title.
  Contents--1. A rejection of
  the "right opportunist-left
  sectarian" explanation by our
  leadership.
  I. Communist Party of the United
  States of America.
  NIC

M58
Massachusetts Political Action
    for Peace.
  What are we tied to in Vietnam?
  [Cambridge, 196]
  folder. illus. 28cm.
  1. Vietnamese conflict, 1961-
  1975.
  KU-RH

M59
Massachusetts Smith Act Defen-
    dants' Committee.
  The Massachusetts Smith Act
  case: the facts, the law, the
  defendants. [Roxbury, Mass.,
  1956?]
  10p. illus. 21cm.
  Cover title.
  1. Internal security--Massa-
  chusetts. 2. Subversive acti-
  vities--Massachusetts.
  KU-J

M60
Max, Steve.
  The Mississippi Freedom Party:
  background and recent develop-
  ments. [New York, Political
  Education Project, 196]
  12 [2]p. 28cm.
  Caption title.
  Cover title: We shall over come:
  register-vote.
  1. Mississippi Freedom Democra-
  tic Party. 2. Mississippi--
  Race question. 3. Negroes--Mis-
  sissippi. I. Students for a
  Democratic Society. Political
  Education Project.
  KU-RH, CU-B

M61
Max, Steve.
  The Mississippi Freedom Democratic Party: background information
  for supportive campaigns by campus groups. [New York, Political
  Education Project, Students for a
  Democratic Society, 1964?]
  12p. 28cm.
  Cover title.
  1. Mississippi Freedom Democratic
  Party. 2. Student movements.
  3. Mississippi--Race question.
  4. Negroes--Mississippi. I. Students for a Democratic Society.
  Political Education Project.
  MiU

M62
Max, Steve.
  On the SDS conception of the
  positions on the left, the liberals and the right in America.
  [n.p., 196]
  4p. 28cm.
  Caption title.
  1. Assassination. 2. Liberalism.
  3. Conservatism. 4. Students for
  a Democratic Society.
  WHi-A

M63
Max, Steve.
  The rock-pile theory on SDS.
  [n.p., 196]
  3p. 28cm.
  1. Student movements.
  2. Students for a Democratic

Society.
WHi-A

M64
Max, Steve.
  Students for a Democratic Society and chapter organization,
  prepared by Steve Max [and
  others. n.p., 196]
  9p. 36cm.
  Caption title.
  1. Organization. 2. Students
  for a Democratic Society.
  WHi-A

M65
Max, Steve.
  Thoughts of sorts. [n.p., 196]
  [3]p. 28cm.
  Caption title.
  1. Student movements. 2. Stu-
  dents for a Democratic Society.
  WHi-A

M66
Max, Steve.
  Words butter no parsnips.
  [New York] Distributed by Stu-
  dents for a Democratic Society
  and its Economic Research and
  Action Project [196]
  3p. 28cm.
  Cover title.
  1. Radicalism. 2. Politics,
  Practical. 3. Community organi-
  zation. I. Students for a
  Democratic Society. Economic
  Research and Action Project.
  WHi-A

M67
Max-Neef, Manfred A.
  The Camelot project: U.S. in-
  tellectual intervention in
  South America. [Toronto? Latin
  American Working Group? 196]
  6p. 28cm.
  Caption title.
  1. U.S.--Relations (general)
  with Latin America. 2. Latin
  America--Relations (general)
  with U.S. I. Latin American
  Working Group.
  KU-RH

M68
May days--1970. [Van Nuys, Calif.,
    SRAF Print Co-op, 1970?]
    [25]p. illus. 22cm.
    Caption title.
    1. Student movements. I. SRAF
    Print Co-op.
    MiU

M69
May 2nd Committee, Harvard-
    Radcliffe.
    The significance of the state
    department white paper on Viet-
    nam. [Cambridge, 1965]
    11p. 26cm.
    Cover title.
    1. Vietnamese conflict, 1961-
    1975.
    CU-B, WHi-A, WHi-L, KU-RH

M70
May 2nd Movement.
    Attack & response. [n.p., 1965]
    [40]p. 28cm.
    Caption title.
    1. Vietnamese conflict, 1961-
    1975. 2. Military service,
    Compulsory.
    WHi-L

M71
May 2nd Movement.
    The Duffy Square arrests: pol-
    ice suppression of students who
    dissent. [New York, 1964?]
    [4]p. illus. 28cm.
    Caption title.
    1. Student movements. 2. Police
    --New York (State)--New York
    (City).
    WHi-L, KU-RH

M72
May 2nd Movement.
    Some comments on anti-draft
    unions. [New York, 196]
    [2]p. 36cm.
    Caption title.
    1. Military service, Compulsory.
    WHi-A

M73
May 2nd Movement.
    What is the May 2nd Movement?
    [New York, 1965]

4 leaves. 28cm.
    Cover title.
    1. Student movements.
    WHi-A

M74
Mayday Collective. Tactics and
    Logistics Section.
    May day tactical manual.
    [Washington, 1970?]
    24p. illus. 28cm.
    Cover title.
    1. Youth--Political activity.
    KU-RH

M75
Mayer, Milton.
    Milton Mayer speaks on the
    human crisis. [Philadelphia,
    Peace Education Division,
    American Friends Service Com-
    mittee, 1963]
    7p. 23x10cm.
    Cover title.
    1. Peace. 2. Social change.
    I. Friends, Society of.
    American Friends Service Com-
    mittee.
    MoU, KU-RH

M76
Mayer, Thomas F.
    The position and progress of
    black America: some pertinent
    statistics. Ann Arbor, Radi-
    cal Education Project [1968?]
    6 [1]p. 28cm.
    Cover title.
    Reprinted from the Bulletin of
    the Ann Arbor Citizens for New
    Politics, v. 1, no. 5, Nov.
    1967.
    1. Negroes--Statistics.
    I. Radical Education Project.
    MoU, WHi-L, KU-RH

M77
Meacham, Stewart.
    Labor and the cold war. Phila-
    delphia, American Friends Ser-
    vice Committee [1959]
    30p. 23cm.
    1. Labor and laboring classes.
    2. World politics--1955-
    3. U.S.--Econ. condit.
    I. Friends, Society of. Ameri-

can Friends Service Committee.
MoU, CLU, DS

M78
Meacham, Stewart.
   Resistance to the draft. [New
   York, Liberation, 196]
   [3]p. 28cm.
   Caption title.
   Reprinted from Liberation, Mar.
   1966.
   1. Military service, Compulsory.
   2. Government, Resistance to.
   I. Liberation.
   KU-RH

M79
Meeropol, Mike.
   Anti-imperialism. [n.p., Students for a Democratic Society,
   196]
   [2]p. 28cm.
   Cover title.
   1. Imperialism. 2. U.S.--Foreign
   policy. I. Students for a Democratic Society.
   CU-B

M80
Mehrhof, Barbara.
   An analysis of class in the wo-
   men's movement. New York, The
   Feminists [1969]
   5 leaves. 28cm.
   Caption title.
   1. Social classes. 2. Woman--
   Rights of women. I. Feminists.
   WHi-L

M81
Mehrhof, Barbara.
   Class structure in the women's
   movement. New York, The Feminists [1969]
   5p. 28cm.
   Caption title.
   1. Woman--Rights of women.
   2. Social classes. I. Feminists.
   KU-RH

M82
Mehrhof, Barbara.
   The rise of man; the origins of
   woman's oppression: one view,
   by Barbara Mehrhof and Sheila
   Cronan. [New York, The Feminists,

1969]
   6p. 28cm.
   Caption title.
   1. Woman--Rights of women.
   I. Cronan, Sheila, jt. auth.
   II. Feminists.
   KU-RH, WHi-L

M83
Meiklejohn, Alexander, 1872-
   The first amendment. [Chicago,
   Midwest Student Civil Liberties
   Coordinating Committee, 196]
   [4]p. 30cm.
   Caption title.
   Reprinted from I.F. Stone
   Weekly.
   1. U.S. Constitution. 1st
   Amendment. 2. Civil rights.
   I. Midwest Student Liberties
   Coordinating Committee.
   KU-RH

M84
Melman, Seymour.
   Business as usual: national
   suicide. [New York, Clergy and
   Laymen Concerned About Vietnam,
   196]
   folder (6p.) 28cm.
   Cover title.
   1. U.S.--Econ. condit. 2. U.S.
   --Military policy. I. Clergy
   and Laymen Concerned About
   Vietnam.
   KU-RH

M85
Melville, Thomas R.
   The church and reality in
   Guatemala. [Toronto, Distri-
   buted by the Latin American
   Working Group, 1969?]
   7p. 28cm.
   Caption title.
   "Excerpts from his CIDOC art-
   icle."
   1. Catholic Church in Guatemala.
   2. Guatemala--Religion. I. La-
   tin American Working Group.
   KU-RH

M86
Memorandum to the 15th session of
   the African Liberation Committee of the Organization of

African Unity. [Seattle, African Support Committee, 196]
6, 4p. 28cm.
Cover title.
1. Africa--Relations (general) with Portugal. 2. Portugal-- Relations (general) with Africa. I. African Support Committee.
CU-B

M87
Men and women living together; diagrams of some women's liberation discussions by a Bread & Roses member. [Minneapolis, Women's Liberation Center and Women's Counseling Service, 197]
[6]p. illus. 22cm.
1. Woman--Rights of women. I. Women's Counseling Service, Minneapolis. II. Women's Liberation Center, Minneapolis.
KU-RH

M88
Menuhin, Moshe.
Jews against Israel [by Moshe Menuhin and Valeri Rabinovich, Gravenhurst, Ontario, 196]
12p. 25cm.
Caption title.
1. Zionism. 2. Israel--Pol. & govt.
KU-RH

M89
Merton, Thomas, 1915-1968.
The black revolution. [Atlanta, Southern Christian Leadership Conference, 196]
[16]p. 22cm.
Cover title.
1. King, Martin Luther, 1929-1968. 2. Negroes--Civil rights. 3. Church and race problems. I. Southern Christian Leadership Conference.
WHi-L, MoSW, NUC 70-11512

M90
Merton, Thomas, 1915-1968.
Blessed are the meek: the Christian roots on nonviolence. [New York, Catholic Peace Fellowship, 1967]

[12]p. 22cm.
Caption title.
Reprinted from Fellowship, May 1967.
1. Nonviolence. I. Catholic Peace Fellowship.
MoU

M91
Merton, Thomas, 1915-1968.
An enemy of the state; review of in solitary witness. [n.p., 1964?]
8p. 28cm.
1. Zahn, Gordon, Charles, 1918-   In solitary witness.
KyU, NUC 67-48391

M92
Merton, Thomas, 1915-1968.
Passivity and abuse of authority. [n.p., 1962?]
6p. 28cm.
1. Lepp, Ignace, 1909-   The Christian failure.
KyU, NUC 67-50400

M93
Merton, Thomas, 1915-1968.
Peace and protest. [n.p.] 1965.
5p. 28cm.
1. Peace. 2. Nonviolence.
KyU, NUC 67-47238

M94
Merton, Thomas, 1915-1968.
Two articles by Thomas Merton. The root of war [and] red or dead: the anatomy of a cliche. [Nyack, N.Y., Fellowship Publications, 196]
11p. 23cm.
Cover title.
1. War. 2. Communism. I. Fellowship Publications.
MoU

M95
Meyer, Hershel D.
History and conscience: the case of Howard Fast. New York, Anvil-Atlas Publishers, 1958.
63p. 21cm.
1. Fast, Howard Melvin, 1914-   I. Anvil-Atlas Publishers.

CLU, MH, WHi-L, NN, NNC, CU,
OClW, ICU, DLC 58-31267, KU-J,
M258

M96
Meyer, Hershel D.
  The Krushchev report and the
  crisis in the American left.
  Brooklyn, Independence Publishers [1956]
  111p. 20cm.
  1. Khrushchev, Nikita Sergeevich,
  1894-   The anatomy of terror.
  2. Communist Party of the United
  States of America.
  NN, CtY, NIC, WaU, IEN, CU, MH,
  KU-J, DLC 57-38157

M97
Meyer, Karl.
  Through effective tax resistance:
  a fund for mankind. [New York,
  War Tax Resistance, 1970?]
  [4]p. 28cm.
  Caption title.
  Reprinted from Catholic Worker,
  Oct.-Nov., 1969 and Jan. 1970.
  1. Tax evasion. 2. Government,
  Resistance to. I. War Tax Re-
  sistance.
  KU-RH

M98
Meyer, Philip.
  A survey of attitude of Detroit
  negroes after the riot of 1967.
  Detroit, Detroit Urban League
  [1967]
  1. Negroes--Detroit. 2. Detroit
  --Riots, 1967.
  WHi-L

M99
Meyers, George.
  Appalachia U.S.A.; a study in
  poverty. [New York, Publishers
  New Press, 196]
  15p. illus. 20cm.
  Cover title.
  1. Appalachian Mountains, South-
  ern--Econ. condit. 2. Poor--Ap-
  palachian Mountains, Southern.
  3. Coal mines and mining--Appal-
  achian Mountains, Southern.
  I. Publishers New Press.
  KU-RH

M100
Meynor, Robert B.
  Bomb shelters will not save us.
  [Woodmont, Conn., Promoting
  Enduring Peace, 1960]
  6p.
  Caption title.
  Reprinted from Coronet, Sept.
  1960.
  1. Atomic bomb shelters.
  I. Promoting Enduring Peace.
  WHi-L

M101
Miami Interracial Action Institute.
  Summary and evaluation. New
  York, Congress of Racial Equal-
  ity [1959]
  21p. 22cm.
  Cover title.
  1. Negroes. I. Congress of
  Racial Equality.
  MiU

M102
Michaels, Sheila.
  The archetypal woman. New
  York, The Feminists [1969?]
  4p. 28cm.
  Caption title.
  1. Woman--History and condi-
  tion of women. I. Feminists.
  KU-RH, WHi-L

M103
Michigan Committee Against
    Apartheid.
  Apartheid in action in South
  Africa. [n.p., 196 ?]
  [2] leaves. 28cm.
  Caption title.
  1. South Africa--Race question.
  MiU

M104
Mickleson, Karen.
  Proposal to members of RSU.
  [Berkeley? 1969?]
  [2]p. 36cm.
  Caption title.
  1. Radical Student Union.
  2. Student movements--Berkeley,
  Calif.
  CU-B

M105
Midwest Conference on Socialist
    Youth, University of Chicago,
    1958.
    Report. [Chicago?] Socialist
    Youth Committee of Chicago [1958]
    16p. 28cm.
    Cover title.
    1. Socialism. 2. Student move-
    ments--Middle States. I. Soc-
    ialist Youth Committee of
    Chicago.
    MiU

M106
Milani, Don.
    Self-defense. Montreal, Our
    Generation [196]
    23p. (A WRI publication)
    1. Pacifism. I. Our Generation.
    NNU-T

M107
The Militant.
    Israel and the Arabs; Militant
    readers debate the mideast con-
    flict. [New York, Merit Pub-
    lishers, 1969]
    23p. illus. 28cm.
    Cover title.
    1. Zionism. 2. Israel-Arab
    War, 1967. I. Merit Publishers.
    KU-RH, MiU

M108
Miller, Dorothy.
    Danville, Virginia. [Atlanta,
    Student Nonviolent Coordinating
    Committee, 1963]
    [15]p. illus. 22cm.
    Cover title.
    1. Negroes--Danville, Va.
    2. Danville, Va.--Race question.
    I. Student Nonviolent Coordina-
    ting Committee.
    CU-B, WHi-L, MiU, NUC 67-10048

M109
Miller, Mike.
    The place of student politics in
    the university. [n.p., Slate?
    1961]
    [2]p. 28cm.
    Caption title.
    1. Student movements--Berkeley,
    Calif. I. Slate.
    WHi-A

M110
Miller, Ruthann.
    In defense of the women's move-
    ment. Articles by Ruthann Mil-
    ler, Mary-Alice Waters [and]
    Evelyn Reed. [New York, Path-
    finder Press, 1970]
    15p. 22cm.
    Cover title.
    1. Woman--Rights of women.
    I. Waters, Mary-Alice, jt. auth.
    II. Reed, Evelyn, jt. auth.
    III. Pathfinder Press.
    KU-RH, MiU, CU-B

M111
Miller, S.M.
    Dropouts: a political problem.
    [Nashville?] Southern Student
    Organizing Committee [1963?]
    4p.
    Cover title.
    Reprinted from Integrated Edu-
    cation, Aug. 1963.
    1. Students. 2. Education.
    3. Dropouts. I. Southern Stu-
    dent Organizing Committee.
    WHi-L

M112
Miller, William Robert, comp.
    Bibliography of books on war,
    pacifism, nonviolence and re-
    lated studies. Rev. ed. Nyack,
    N.Y., Fellowship of Reconcil-
    iation, 1961.
    36p.
    1. War--Bibl. 2. Pacifism--
    Bibl. I. Fellowship of Recon-
    ciliation.
    WHi-L

M113
Miller, William Z.
    The S.L.P. and its double
    "moral" standard. [n.p., 1970]
    [2]p. 28cm.
    Caption title.
    1. Socialist Labor Party.
    CU-B

M114
Millet, Kate.
    Sexual politics. Boston, New
    England Free Press [1968?]
    12p. 22cm.
    Cover title.

1. Woman--Rights of women.
I. New England Free Press.
KU-RH

M115
Mills, C. Wright.
  Letter to the new left. [New
York, Students for a Democratic
Society, 196]
  [10]p. 22cm.
  1. Student movements. I. Stu-
dents for a Democratic Society.
  CU-B

M116
Mills, C. Wright.
  An open letter to the new left
from C. Wright Mills. New York,
Students for a Democratic Society [196]
  8p. 28cm.
  Cover title.
  1. Student movements. I. Students for a Democratic Society.
  KU-RH

M117
Mills, C. Wright.
  Open letter to the new left from
C. Wright Mills. [Montreal.
Our Generation, 196]
  10p.
  Cover title.
  Reprinted from Studies on the
Left.
  1. Student movements. I. Our
Generation.
  NNU-T

M118
Mills, C. Wright.
  An open letter to the new left
from C. Wright Mills. Toronto,
Research, Information and Publications Project, Student Union
for Peace Action, 1965.
  9p. 28cm.
  Cover title.
  1. Student movements. I. Student Union for Peace Action.
  WHi-A

M119
The Milwaukee statement. [Mil-
waukee, Milwaukee Fourteen
Defense Committee, 196]

folder. illus. 23x11cm.
  1. Vietnamese conflict, 1961-
1975. 2. Government, Resistance to. I. Milwaukee Fourteen
Defense Committee.
  MoU

M120
Minnis, Jack.
  The care and feeding of power
structures. Boston, New England Free Press [196]
  9p. 21cm.
  Cover title.
  1. Business and politics.
  2. Corporations. 3. Negroes--
Civil rights. 4. Power (Social science) I. New England
Free Press.
  KU-RH

M121
Minnis, Jack.
  The care and feeding of power
structures. [Chicago, Students for a Democratic Society,
196]
  8p. 22cm.
  1. Power (Social science)
  2. Business and politics.
  3. Corporations. I. Students
for a Democratic Society.
  CU-B, WHi-L, MiU

M122
Minnis, Jack.
  The care and feeding of power
structures. [Nashville, Sou-
thern Student Organizing Com-
mittee, 196]
  7p. 28cm.
  Cover title.
  1. Power (Social science)
  I. Southern Student Organizing
Committee.
  MoU

M123
Minnis, Jack.
  The care and feeding of power
structures. New York, Distributed by Students for a Democratic Society, Educational
Research and Action Project
[196]
  7p. 28cm.

Cover title.
1. Power (Social science)
I. Students for a Democratic Soc-
iety. Education Research and
Action Project.
KU-RH, WHi-A

M124
Minnis, Jack.
  The care and feeding of power
  structure revisited. [Louis-
  ville, Southern Conference Educational Fund, c1967]
  [20]p. 22cm.
  Cover title.
  1. Power (Social science)
  2. Corporations. 3. Business
  and politics. I. Southern Conference Educational Fund.
  KU-RH

M125
Minnis, Jack.
  The care and feeding of power
  structures revisited. [Louis-
  ville, Ky., Southern Conference
  Educational Fund, c1967]
  30p. 22cm. (Organizers Library
  series)
  1. Negroes--Civil rights.
  2. Business and politics.
  3. Corporations. 4. Power (Social science) I. Southern Conference Educational Fund.
  MoU, WHi-L

M126
Minnis, Jack.
  A chronology of violence and
  intimidation in Mississippi
  since 1961. [n.p., 1961]
  19p. 28cm.
  1. Negroes--Mississippi.
  2. Mississippi--Race question.
  3. Violence.
  WHi-A

M127
Minnis, Jack.
  Lowndes County freedom organization; the story of the development of an independent political movement on the county
  level. [Louisville, Southern
  Conference Educational Fund,
  c1967]

13p. illus. 28cm.
Cover title.
1. Negroes--Lowndes Co., Ala.
2. Lowndes, Co., Ala.--Race
question. I. Southern Conference Educational Fund.
KU-RH, MoU

M128
Mintz, Norbett L.
  The Cuba "episode" and the
  American press: April 9-23,
  1961. [New York, Liberation,
  1961]
  15p.
  Cover title.
  1. U.S.--For. rel.--Cuba.
  2. Cuba--For. rel.--U.S.
  3. Cuba--History--Invasion,
  1961. 4. Press. I. Liberation.
  MiU

M129
Mississippi Freedom Democratic
    Party.
  Background papers on the Missis-
  sippi Freedom Democratic Party.
  Washington [196]
  [7] leaves. 28cm.
  Cover title.
  1. Negroes--Mississippi.
  2. Mississippi--Race question.
  WHi-A

M130
Mississippi Freedom Democratic
    Party.
  Challenge of the Mississippi
  Freedom Democratic Party.
  [Jackson, Miss., 1964?]
  4p. 28cm.
  Caption title.
  1. Democratic Party. 2. Negroes
  --Mississippi. 3. Mississippi--
  Race question.
  WHi-A

M131
Mississippi Freedom Democratic
    Party.
  The convention challenge and
  the freedom vote. [n.p., 1964]
  10p. 28cm. (Freedom primer
  no. 1)
  Cover title.
  1. Democratic Party. National

Convention, Atlantic City, 1964.
2. Negroes--Civil rights.
WHi-A

M132
Mississippi Freedom Democratic
    Party.
The freedom vote and right to
vote. [n.p., 1964]
9p. 28cm. (Freedom primer no.
2)
Cover title.
1. Mississippi--Race question.
2. Negroes--Mississippi.
WHi-A

M133
Mississippi Freedom Democratic
    Party.
Mississippi challenge--progress
report and future action.
[Washington, 1965]
6p. 36cm.
Caption title.
1. Mississippi--Race question.
2. Negroes--Civil rights.
WHi-A

M134
Mississippi Freedom Democratic
    Party.
The Mississippi Freedom Democratic Party. [Jackson, Miss.,
196]
26p. 28cm.
Cover title.
1. Democratic Party. Mississippi.
2. Mississippi--Race question.
3. Negroes--Mississippi.
WHi-A

M135
Mississippi Freedom Democratic
    Party.
The Mississippi Freedom Demo-
cratic Party. New York, Distri-
buted by Students for a Democra-
tic Society and Young Christian
Students [196]
6p. 28cm.
Cover title.
1. Negroes--Civil rights.
2. Mississippi--Race question.
I. Students for a Democratic
Society. II. Young Christian
Students.
WHi-A

M136
Mississippi Freedom Democratic
    Party.
A primer for delegates to the
Democratic National Convention
who haven't heard about the
Mississippi Freedom Party.
[n.p., 1964?]
17p. illus.
Cover title.
1. Democratic Party. National
Convention, Atlantic City, 1964.
2. Mississippi--Race question.
3. Negroes--Mississippi.
WHi-L, MiU

M137
Mississippi Freedom Democratic
    Party.
The right to vote and the congressional challenge. [n.p.,
196]
11p. 28cm.
Cover title.
1. Voting. 2. Negroes--Civil
rights.
WHi-A

M138
Mississippi violence vs. human
    rights. [Atlanta? Distribu-
    ted by Committee for the Dis-
    tribution of the Mississippi
    Story, 1963]
15p.
1. Mississippi--Race question.
2. Negroes--Mississippi.
I. Committee for the Distribution of the Mississippi Story.
WHi-L

M139
Missouri Peace Study Institute.
 A program proposal of the
Missouri Study Institute.
[n.p., 196]
22 leaves. 28cm.
Cover title.
1. Peace.
KU-RH

M140
Mitchell, H.L.
The Southern Tenant Farmer's
Union. Nashville, Southern
Student Organizing Committee
[196]

5p. 28cm.
Cover title.
Reprinted from New South Student,
Ap. 1968.
1. Agricultural laborers--South-
ern States. 2. Southern Tenant
Farmer's Union. I. Southern Stu-
dent Organizing Committee.
MoU

M141
Mitchell, Henry.
   Discrimination within the college,
   by Henry Mitchell. A case study
   in job discrimination, by Skip
   Robinson. [Madison? Liberal
   Study Group, 196]
   3, 7 leaves. 28cm.
   Cover title.
   1. Negroes--Education. 2. Ne-
   groes--Employment. 3. Negroes--
   Champaign, Ill. 4. Champaign,
   Ill.--Race question. I. Liberal
   Study Group. II. Robinson, Skip,
   jt. auth.
   WHi-A

M142
Mitchell, Juliet.
   Women: the longest revolution.
   Boston, New England Free Press
   [196]
   11-36p. 22cm.
   Cover title.
   Reprinted from New Left Review,
   Nov./Dec. 1966.
   1. Woman--Rights of women.
   I. New England Free Press.
   KU-RH

M143
Mitchell, Juliet.
   Women: the longest revolution.
   San Francisco, Bay Area Radical
   Education Project [196]
   27p. 28cm.
   Cover title.
   1. Woman--Rights of women.
   I. Bay Area Radical Education
   Project.
   CU-B

M144
Mizell, M. Hayes.
   Federal programs to promote em-
   ployment and development in

rural communities. Atlanta,
   Ga., Southern Regional Council
   [196]
   15p.
   1. Rural conditions. I. Southern Regional Council.
   CaU, NUC 66-94925

M145
Monk, Richard.
   Patriotic working class revol-
   utionaries. [n.p., 1969?]
   [1] leaf. 28cm.
   Caption title.
   1. Labor and laboring classes.
   WHi-L

M146
Monsonis, James.
   The Albany movement: an example
   of the civil rights movement.
   [n.p.] Students for a Democratic
   Society for the Liberal Study
   Group [1962?]
   16p. 36cm.
   Cover title.
   1. Albany, Ga.--Race question.
   2. Negroes--Albany, Ga.
   3. Negroes--Civil rights.
   I. Students for a Democratic
   Society. II. Liberal Study
   Group.
   MiU

M147
Montgomery, Jim.
   South cannot overtake U.S. per
   capita income. [Nashville]
   Southern Student Organizing
   Committee [1966?]
   2p.
   Reprinted from Atlanta Consti-
   tution, Nov. 30, 1966.
   1. Southern States--Econ. condit.
   I. Southern Student Organizing
   Committee.
   WHi-L

M148
Monthly review (New York, 1949-
)
   China shakes the world again,
   by Charles Bettelheim [and
   others] With an editorial by
   Leo Huberman [and] Paul M.
   Sweezy. New York, Monthly

Review Press [1959?]
64p.   23cm.
1. China (People's Republic of
China, 1949-   )--Econ. condit.
2. Communes (China)   I. Bettelheim, Charles.   I. Huberman, Leo,
1903-   II. Sweezy, Paul
Marlor, 1910-
CSt-H, MiU, MoU, MnU, NN, NIC,
InU, DLC 60-26927

M149
Monthly review (New York, 1949-
)
The criminal invasion plan.
[New York, Monthly Review, 1961]
48p.   22cm.
Cover title.
Contents--The commitment of the
intellectual, by Paul A. Baran.
1. Cuba--History--Invasion, 1961
--Foreign opinion.   I. Baran,
Paul A.
CSt-H, NUC 67-56926

M150
Monthly review (New York, 1949-
)
Cuba and communism [by] J.P.
Morray.   Articles by Che Gue-
vara, Paul A. Baran, Fidel Cas-
tro, Mark Schleifer.   New York,
1961.
94p.   22cm.
Special issue on Monthly review,
July-Aug. 1961.
1. Communism--Cuba.   I. Morray,
Joseph P., 1916-   II. Gue-
vara, Ernesto, 1920-1967.
III. Baran, Paul A.   IV. Castro,
Fidel, 1927-
FU, NUC 66-19913

M151
Monthly review (New York, 1949-
)
The Kennedy doctrine.   [New York,
Monthly review, 1961]
49-96p.   22cm.
Cover title.
Vol. 13, no. 2; June 1961.
Contents--The truth about Cuba,
by Leo Huberman, and Letter to
the United Nations, by Lazaro
Cardenas.
1. Cuba--History--Invasion,

1961--Foreign opinion.   I. Cardenas, Lazaro, Pres. Mexico,
1895-   II. Huberman, Leo,
1903-
CSt-H, NUC 67-52152

M152
Monthly review (New York, 1949-
)
Notes on inflation and the dol-
lar.   Boston, New England Free
Press [1970?]
12p.   21cm.
Cover title.
Reprinted from Monthly review,
Mar. 1970.
1. Inflation (Finance)   2. U.S.
--Econ. condit.   I. New England
Free Press.
KU-RH

M153
Monthly review (New York, 1949-
)
The split in the capitalist
world; socialist world.   By
Paul M. Sweezy and Leo Huberman
[editors]   New York, Monthly
Review Press, 1963.
38p.   22cm.   (Monthly review
pamphlet series no. 22)
1. World politics--1955-
I. Sweezy, Paul Marlor, 1910-
         II. Huberman, Leo,
1903-
DLC 63-19861

Moody, Kim
see
Moody, Kimberly

M154
Moody, Kimberly.
The American working class in
transition.   [New York] International Socialists [196]
44, viip.   28cm.
Cover title.
1. Labor and laboring classes.
2. Socialism.   I. International
Socialists.
KU-RH

M155
Moody, Kimberly.
The American working class in

transition. [New York, International Socialists; New England
Free Press, 196]
22p. 28cm.
Cover title.
1. Labor and laboring classes.
2. Negroes--Employment. 3. Socialism. I. New England Free
Press. II. International Socialists.
KU-RH

M156
Moody, Kimberly.
  ERAP, ideology, and social
  change. [Baltimore? 196]
  6 leaves. 28cm.
  Caption title.
  1. Labor and laboring classes.
  2. Students for a Democratic
  Society. Economic Research and
  Action Project.
  WHi-L

M157
Moody, Kimberly.
  Organizing the poor whites.
  Nashville, Southern Student Or-
  ganizing Committee [196]
  5p. 28cm.
  Cover title.
  1. Organization. 2. Poor.
  I. Southern Student Organizing
  Committee.
  MiU, WHi-L

M158
Moody, Kimberly.
  Toward the working class: a
  position paper for the new left,
  by Kim Moody, Fred Eppsteiner &
  Mike Flug, together with why the
  working class? by Hal Draper.
  [Berkeley, Independent Socialist
  Committee, c1966]
  19p. 22cm.
  Cover title.
  1. Labor and laboring classes.
  2. Student movements. I. Epp-
  steiner, Fred, jt. auth.
  II. Flug, Mike, jt. auth.
  III. Draper, Hal. IV. Indepen-
  dent Socialist Committee.
  CU-B, MiU

M159
Moody, Kimberly.
  Vietnam: a revolutionary alternative. [Chicago] American Socialist Organizing Committee
  [196]
  [4]p. 28cm.
  Cover title.
  1. Vietnamese conflict, 1961-
  1975. I. American Socialist
  Organizing Committee.
  WHi-L

M160
Moon, Henry Lee.
  Negroes in the U.S.--1968.
  [New York? NAACP? 1968?]
  2 leaves. 36cm.
  Caption title.
  1. Negroes--Civil rights.
  I. National Association for the
  Advancement of Colored People.
  KU-RH

M161
Moore, Charles.
  Student economic welfare and
  the unionization of university
  employees, a discussion paper
  by Charles Moore, with supplementary comments by Charles Van
  Tassel. [n.p.] Students for a
  Democratic Society for the Liberal Study Group [196]
  5 leaves. 28cm.
  Cover title.
  1. Student employment.
  2. Trade-unions. 3. Universities and colleges. I. Van Tassel, Charles. II. Students for
  a Democratic Society. III. Liberal Study Group.
  MiU

M162
Moore, Edward Le Roy.
  The last best hope of Earth.
  [San Diego, Peace Research
  Society, 1961]
  47 [1]p. 22cm.
  1. Peace. I. Peace Research
  Society, San Diego.
  RPB, NUC 65-34491

M163
Moos, Elizabeth.
  Higher education in the Soviet
  Union. [New York, National
  Council of American-Soviet Friend-
  ship, 1956]
  32p. 22cm.
  Cover title.
  1. Education--Russia. I. Nat-
  ional Council of American-Soviet
  Friendship.
  ViU, NIC, PPD, PPiU, CU, OrCS,
  NcGW, IU, DLC 56-14692, CSSR

M164
Moos, Elizabeth.
  Soviet education: achievements
  and goals. New York, National
  Council of American-Soviet
  Friendship, 1967.
  127p. illus. 23cm.
  1. Education--Russia--1945-
  I. National Council of American-
  Soviet Friendship.
  MiU, KU-RH

M165
Moos, Elizabeth.
  Soviet education, 1970. New
  York, National Council of Ameri-
  can-Soviet Friendship, 1970.
  63p. illus. 22cm.
  1. Education--Russia. I. Nat-
  ional Council of American-Soviet
  Friendship.
  KU-RH

M166
Morgan, Nigel.
  The case for a Canadian water
  policy; a reply to the U.S. plan
  to take over Canada's water resources. [Toronto, Progress
  Books, 1966]
  38p. illus.
  Cover title.
  1. Water--Pollution. 2. Water--
  Laws and legislation--Canada.
  3. U.S.--Relations (general)
  with Canada. 4. Canada--Relat-
  ions (general) with the U.S.
  I. Progress Books.
  MiU

M167
Morin, Jacques Ivan.

What is equality of two nations?
  Toronto, Research, Information,
  and Publications Project, Student Union for Peace Action
  [196]
  5p. 28cm.
  Cover title.
  1. French in Canada. I. Student Union for Peace Action.
  WHi-A

M168
Morland, John Kenneth.
  Lunch-counter desegregation in
  Corpus Christi, Galveston and
  San Antonio, Texas. Atlanta,
  Southern Regional Council, 1960.
  21 [3]p. 28cm.
  Cover title.
  1. Negroes--Texas. 2. Texas--
  Race question. I. Southern
  Regional Council.
  WHi-A

M169
Morland, John Kenneth.
  Token desegregation and beyond.
  Atlanta, Southern Regional Coun-
  cil; Anti-Defamation League,
  1963.
  vii, 27p. 23cm.
  1. Negroes--Civil rights.
  2. Segregation in education.
  I. Southern Regional Council.
  II. Anti-Defamation League.
  NjR, ICU, CtY-D, WHi-L,
  NUC 65-73624

M170
Morray, J.P.
  The real issues at Geneva: the
  strategy for disarmament. [New
  York, New World Review, 1962?]
  7p. 22cm.
  Reprinted from New World Review,
  July 1962.
  1. Disarmament. I. New World
  Review.
  KU-J

M171
Morris, George, 1903-
  American labor, which way? New
  York, New Century Publishers,
  1961.
  159p. 21cm.

1. Labor and laboring classes.
2. Trade-unions. I. New Century
Publishers.
CLU, GU, WHi-L, NcU CU, RPB, IEN,
OkU, NIC, ICU, DLC 61-16148.

M172
Morris, George, 1903-
Labor and the menace of Goldwat-
erism. [New York, Publishers
New Press, 1964]
23p. illus.
1. Goldwater, Barry Morris, 1909-
     2. Labor and laboring
classes. 3. Anti-communist movements. I. Publishers New Press.
MiEM, WHi-L, NUC 67-44783

M173
Morris, George, 1903-
Labor unity: what AFL-CIO merger
means for workers. [New York,
New Century Publishers, 1955]
15p.
1. Labor and laboring classes.
2. American Federation of Labor
and Congress of Industrial Organizations. I. New Century
Publishers.
CSSR, WHi-L, M404

M174
Morris, George, 1903-
Outlook for a new labor advance.
[New York, New Press Publishers,
196]
30p. 21cm.
1. Labor and laboring classes.
2. Negroes--Civil rights.
3. Peace. I. New Press Publishers.
KU-RH

M175
Morris, George, 1903-
The USSR today: 50 years of socialism. [New York, New Outlook
Publishers, 1967]
31p. 23x10cm.
1. Russia. I. New Outlook Publishers.
MiU, CU-B

M176
Morris, George, 1903-
What I saw in--the Soviet Union
today. New York, New Century

Publishers, 1959.
64p.
1. Russia--Descr. & travel.
I. New Century Publishers.
M406, KU-J

M177
Morris, Leslie.
Labor-farmer political action.
[Toronto, Progress Books, 1959]
23p.
1. Labor and laboring classes--
Canada. 2. Farmers--Canada.
I. Progress Books.
CaOTU, NUC 67-16767

M178
Morris, Leslie.
New jobs through new markets;
how the cold war causes unemployment. [Toronto, Progress
Books for the Communist Party
of Canada, 1962]
28p.
Cover title.
1. World politics--1955-
2. Unemployed--Canada. 3. Can-
ada--Commercial policy.
I. Communist Party of Canada.
CaOTU, NUC 67-15618

M179
Morris, Leslie.
Where do we go from here?
[Toronto, Progress Books, 1962]
23p. 13cm.
1. Communist Party of Canada.
IaU, NUC 67-14766

M180
Morris, Mark.
How to demonstrate, be tried,
go to jail and stop the war in
Vietnam: a practical guide to
nonviolent direct action. [San
Francisco, Peace & Gladness
Press for the Committee for Non-
violent Action, West, 196]
12 [4] leaves. 28cm.
1. Vietnamese conflict, 1961-
1975. 2. Government, Resist-
ance to. 3. Nonviolence.
I. Peace & Gladness Press.
II. Committee for Nonviolent
Action, West.
CU-B

M181
Morris, Mark.
   Why draft repeal? Answers to
   questions about military conscrip-
   tion. Foreword by Dr. George
   Wald. [Philadelphia, National
   Peace Literature Service, Ameri-
   can Friends Service Committee,
   1969?]
   32p. illus. 22cm.
   1. Military service, Compulsory.
   I. Wald, George. II. Friends,
   Society of. American Friends
   Service Committee.
   KU-RH

M182
Morris, Stuart.
   Pacifism and conscientious ob-
   jection. Philadelphia, Peace
   Literature Service, American
   Friends Service Committee, 1963.
   [4]p. 22cm.
   Cover title.
   1. Conscientious objectors.
   2. Pacifism. I. Friends, Society
   of. American Friends Service
   Committee.
   KU-RH

M183
Morse, Elsa Peters.
   The key to world peace and plenty. With an introduction by Holland Roberts. [San Francisco,
   Summit Press, 1960]
   96p. 22cm.
   1. Socialism. 2. Peace. I. Summit Press.
   KU-J, CLU, NN, OOxM, PPD, NcU,
   NIC, CSt, NcD, IU, DLC 60-8383

M184
Mortimer, Wyndham.
   The Soviet auto workers. [De-
   troit, Global Books, 196]
   8p. 28cm.
   At head of title: Wyndham Morti-
   mer meets.
   1. Automobile industry workers--
   Russia. I. Global Books.
   MiU

M185
Morton, Joseph.
   How the cradle of liberty was

robbed; the awful truth about a
law to muzzle people and leash
unions. [New York, New Century
Publishers, 1955]
15p.
Cover title.
1. Anti-communists movements.
I. New Century Publishers.
MiU, KU-J

M186
The Moscow-Peking dispute and the
   4th International, "the Chin-
   ese and Trotskyists form a
   bloc" [by] Izvestia. Reply
   to Isvestia by P. Frank of
   the 4th International. For-
   ward to Lenin not back to
   Stalin, by E. Germain. [Tor-
   onto, Workers Vanguard? 1963]
   32p. 22cm.
   Cover title.
   1. China (People's Republic of
   China, 1949-   )--For. rel.--
   Russia. 2. Russia--For. rel.--
   China (People's Republic of
   China, 1949-   ) 3. Fourth
   International. I. Frank,
   Pierre. II. Germain, Ernest.
   MoU

M187
Moscow trials in New Orleans, by
   a defendant. [New Orleans,
   Spartacist League, 1967]
   9 leaves. 28cm.
   Caption title.
   1. Committee to End the War in
   Vietnam, New Orleans. 2. Pro-
   gressive Labor Party. 3. Stu-
   dents for a Democratic Society.
   I. Spartacist League.
   WHi-L

M188
Moseley, George.
   Tibet: tradition vs. reform.
   Ann Arbor, Radical Education
   Project [196]
   5p. 28cm.
   Cover title.
   Reprinted from Far Eastern Eco-
   nomic Review, Oct. 7, 1965.
   1. Tibet--Soc. condit.
   2. China (People's Republic of
   China, 1949-   )--For. rel.--

Tibet.   I. Radical Education Project.
MoU

M189
Moseley, George.
  Tibet: tradition vs. reform.
  Toronto, Research, Information
  and Publications, Student Union
  for Peace Action [196]
  5p. 28cm.
  Cover title.
  1. Tibet--Soc. condit.
  2. China (People's Republic of
  China, 1949-   )--For. rel.--
  Tibet. I. Student Union for
  Peace Action.
  WHi-A

M190
The Movement.
  Black Panther sisters talk about
  women's liberation. [Boston,
  New England Free Press, 1970?]
  4p. illus. 28cm.
  Cover title.
  Reprinted from The Movement,
  Sept. 1969.
  1. Woman--Rights of women.
  2. Negroes. I. New England Free
  Press.
  MiU

M191
The Movement.
  Cultural revolution in China.
  [Chicago, Students for a Demo-
  cratic Society, 1969]
  22p. 22cm.
  Cover title.
  Contents--An interview with
  Chris Milton.
  1. China (People's Republic of
  China, 1949-   )--Intellectual
  life. I. Students for a Demo-
  cratic Society. II. Milton,
  Chris.
  WHi-A

M192
The Movement.
  Don't mourn--organize. [Chicago,
  Students for a Democratic Soc-
  iety, 1968]
  35p. illus.
  Cover title.

1. Students for a Democratic
Society. Economic Research and
Action Project. 2. Poor.
3. Labor and laboring classes.
I. Students for a Democratic
Society.
WHi-L

M193
The Movement.
  Interview on the cultural re-
  volution with Chris Milton, a
  participant. Boston, New Eng-
  land Free Press [1970?]
  7p. illus. 21cm.
  Cover title.
  Reprinted from the Movement,
  Feb. 1969.
  1. China (People's Republic of
  China, 1949-   )--Intellec-
  tual life. I. New England Free
  Press. II. Milton, Chris.
  KU-RH

M194
The movement and the workers.
  [Seattle, C. Van Lydegraf,
  196]
  23p. illus. 22cm.
  Cover title.
  1. Student movements. 2. Labor
  and laboring classes. I. Van
  Lydegraf, Clayton.
  MoU, WHi-L

M195
Movement for a Democratic Military.
  Free the Fort Ord 40,000. [n.
  p., 1970?]
  [12]p. 22cm.
  Cover title.
  1. Soldiers. 2. Civil rights.
  3. Vietnamese conflict, 1961-
  1975.
  CU-B

M196
Movement for a Democratic Society.
  Welfare: the exterminating
  angel: a radical view. [n.p.,
  196]
  [8]p. 22cm.
  Cover title.
  1. Public welfare.
  WHi-L

M197
Movement for a Democratic Society,
   Springfield, Mass.
  Welcome to Springfield: a Mass.
  Mutual property, by Springfield
  area Movement for a Democratic
  Society. [Springfield, Mass.,
  Movement Workshop, 1969]
  22p. illus. 22cm.
  Cover title.
  1. Massachusetts Mutual Life In-
  surance Company. 2. Springfield,
  Mass.--Econ. condit.
  KU-RH, WHi-L

M198
Movement for Nonviolent Revolution.
  You don't gotta. [Palo Alto,
  Calif., 196]
  folder. 22x10cm.
  Cover title.
  1. Military service, Compulsory.
  KU-RH

M199
Movement Liberation Front.
  A radical defense handbook.
  [Detroit, Radical Education Pro-
  ject, 1970]
  [13]p. illus. 28cm.
  Cover title.
  1. Defense (Criminal procedures)
  I. Radical Education Project.
  KU-RH

M200
Movement Liberation Front.
  A radical defense handbook.
  [San Francisco, 196]
  [12]p. 28cm.
  Cover title.
  1. Law enforcement. 2. Defense
  (Criminal procedures)
  CU-B

M201
Movimento Popular de Libertacao
   de Angola.
  Report of the MPLA to UN Committee on Decolonization.
  [Seattle] Liberation Support
  Committee [1970?]
  55p. 22cm.
  Cover title.
  1. Portugal--Relations (general)
  with Angola. 2. Angola--Pol.

& govt. I. Liberation Support
Committee.
CU-B

M202
Mower, A. Glenn.
  "But--you can't trust the Russians!" Philadelphia, American
  Friends Service Committee,
  Peace Education Program, 1960.
  31p. 23cm.
  1. Russia--Foreign policy.
  2. Communism. I. Friends, Society of. American Friends Service Committee.
  KU-RH

M203
Mstislavskii, Pavel Sergeevich.
  Living standards in the U.S.S.
  R. [n.p.] National Council of
  American-Soviet Friendship
  [1964]
  11p. illus.
  Reprinted from New World Review, July 1964.
  1. Russia--Econ. condit.--
  1945-   I. National Council
  of American-Soviet Friendship.
  InU, NUC 65-70845

M204
Mull, Brenda.
  Blue Ridge: the history of our
  struggle against Levi-Strauss.
  Boston, New England Free Press
  [196]
  11p. 28cm.
  Cover title.
  1. Levi-Strauss & Co. 2. Labor
  and laboring classes--Blue Ridge,
  Ga. I. New England Free Press.
  WHi-L, KU-RH

M205
Mull, Brenda.
  Blue Ridge: the history of our
  struggle against Levi Strauss.
  Nashville, Southern Student Or-
  ganizing Committee [196]
  11p. 28cm.
  Cover title.
  1. Levi-Strauss & Co. 2. Labor
  and laboring classes--Blue
  Ridge, Ga. I. Southern Student
  Organizing Committee.
  MoU

M206
Muller, Hermann J.
  Radiation damage and the avoid-
  ance of war. Yellow Springs, O.,
  American Humanist Association
  [1957?]
  [8]p. 28cm.
  Caption title.
  1. Radiation. 2. Atomic weapons
  and disarmament. I. American
  Humanist Association.
  KU-RH

M207
Munis, Grandizo.
  What policy for revolutionists--
  Marxism or ultra-leftism? By
  Grandizo Munz and James P. Can-
  non. New York, Merit Publishers
  [1969]
  64p. 22cm.
  1. Socialist Workers Party.
  2. Socialism. I. Cannon, James
  Patrick, 1890-   , jt. auth.
  II. Merit Publishers.
  KU-RH

M208
Munk, Michael.
  The new left. [New York, Nat-
  ional Guardian, 196]
  22p. illus. 14x21cm.
  Cover title.
  1. Youth--Political activity.
  I. National Guardian.
  KU-RH

M209
Muse, Benjamin.
  Louisville. [Atlanta, Southern
  Regional Council] 1964.
  45p. (Special report)
  1. Louisville--Race question.
  2. Negroes--Louisville. I. Southern Regional Council.
  WHi-L

M210
Muse, Benjamin.
  Memphis. [Atlanta, Southern
  Regional Council, 1964?]
  49p.
  1. Memphis--Race question.
  2. Negroes--Memphis. I. Southern Regional Council.
  WHi-L

M211
Muste, Abraham John, 1885-
  Conscription and conscience.
  Philadelphia, American Friends
  Service Committee [n.d.]
  9p.
  Cover title.
  1. Military service, Compulsory.
  I. Friends, Society of. Ameri-
  can Friends Service Committee.
  NIC

M212
Muste, Abraham John, 1885-
  Cuba: an analysis of American
  and Soviet policy. [New York,
  War Resisters League, 1963?]
  [8]p. 23x10cm.
  1. Cuba--For. rel.--U.S.
  2. U.S.--For. rel.--Cuba.
  3. Cuba--For. rel.--Russia.
  4. Russia--For. rel.--Cuba.
  I. War Resisters' League.
  FU, NUC 66-17636

M213
Muste, Abraham John, 1885-
  Factors affecting work for peace
  today; a summarization of five
  lectures delivered at the annual
  Conference of the Episcopal pacifist fellowship at Seabury
  house, Greenwich, Conn., Aug.
  27-30, 1957. [New York, Episcopal Pacifist Fellowship,
  1957]
  16p. 22cm.
  1. Peace. I. Episcopal Pacifist Fellowship.
  NN

M214
Muste, Abraham John, 1885-
  Getting rid of war. [New York,
  War Resisters League, 1959]
  12p.
  1. Disarmament. 2. Peace.
  3. U.S.--Military policy.
  I. War Resisters League.
  WHi-L

M215
Muste, Abraham John, 1885-
  Getting rid of war. [Philadel-
  phia, American Friends Service
  Committee, 1959?]

12p. 22cm.
Reprinted from Liberation, Mar.
1959.
1. U.S.--For. rel.--Russia.
2. Russia--For. rel.--U.S.
3. Peace. I. Friends, Society
of. American Friends Service
Committee.
WHi-A

M216
Muste, Abraham John, 1885-
It is our job; a report and
appeal from A.J. Muste. New
York, Committee for Nonviolent
Action [196]
[2]p. 28cm.
Cover title.
1. U.S.--For. rel.--Cuba.
2. Cuba--For. rel.--U.S.
3. Peace. I. Committee for Nonviolent Action.
WHi-A

M217
Muste, Abraham John, 1885-
The meaning of Albany. [New
York, Committee for Nonviolent
Action, 196]
[2]p. 28cm.
Caption title.
1. Georgia--Race question.
2. Negroes--Albany, Ga.
I. Committee for Nonviolent
Action.
KU-RH

M218
Muste, Abraham John, 1885-
Of holy disobedience. [2d. ed.]
Canterbury, N.H., Greenleaf
Books [1968]
1v (unpaged) 28cm.
Cover title.
1. Pacifism. 2. Government, Re-
sistance to. I. Greenleaf Books.
MoU, KU-RH

M219
Muste, Abraham John, 1885-
The primacy of peace. Toronto,
Research, Information and Publication Project, Student Union
for Peace Action, 1965.
9p. 28cm.
Reprinted from Liberation.
1. Peace. 2. Nonviolence.

3. Civil rights. I. Student
Union for Peace Action.
WHi-A

M220
Muste, Abraham John, 1885-
Saints for this age. [Walling-
ford, Pa., Pendle Hill, 1962]
24p. 20cm. (Pendle Hill pamphlet no. 124)
1. Christian life. I. Pendle
Hill.
NN, MH-AH, MsU, DLC 62-21962

M221
Muste, Abraham John, 1885-
Statement by Rev. A. J. Muste
on his support of Herbert
Aptheker for Congress. [Brook-
lyn, Independent Citizens Committee to Elect Herbert Aptheker Congressman, 196]
[4]p. illus. 22cm.
1. Aptheker, Herbert, 1915-
         I. Independent Citizens
Committee to Elect Herbert
Aptheker Congressman.
KU-RH

M222
Muste, Abraham John, 1885-
A strategy for the peace move-
ment. [Nyack, N.Y.] Fellowship
of Reconciliation [1962?]
5-[8]p. 28cm.
Caption title.
Reprinted from Liberation,
June 1962.
1. Peace. I. Fellowship of
Reconciliation.
WHi-A

M223
Muste, Abraham John, 1885-
Total war or total pacifism?
New York, Fellowship of Recon-
ciliation [n.d.]
12p. 23cm.
1. Peace. 2. Pacifism. 3. War.
I. Fellowship of Reconciliation.
MH-AH

M224
Muste, Abraham John, 1885-
Where are we now? American
radicalism and the impact of

recent Soviet developments.
[New York, Liberation, 1956?]
16p. 20cm.
Cover title.
1. Socialism. I. Liberation.
WHi-L, NUC 65-45500

M225
Myers, Robin.
   Black builders; a job program
   that works. The story of the
   Joint Apprenticeship Program of
   the Workers Defense League and
   with the A. Philip Randolph Edu-
   cational Fund, by Robin Myers
   and Thomas R. Brooks. New York,
   League for Industrial Democracy
   [196]
   136p. 28cm.
   1. Negroes--Employment.
   I. Brooks, Thomas R., jt. auth.
   II. League for Industrial Demo-
   cracy. III. Workers Defense
   League. Joint Apprenticeship
   Fund. IV. Randolph (A. Philip)
   Educational Fund.
   NNU-T

M226
Myers, Robin.
   Louisiana story, 1964. The sugar
   system and the plantation workers.
   [New York, National Advisory Committee on Farm Labor, 196]
   40p. 22cm.
   1. Agricultural laborers--Louis-
   iana. I. National Advisory Committee on Farm Labor.
   WHi-A

M227
Myerson, Michael.
   ILGWU: fighting for lower wages.
   Boston, New England Free Press
   [1970?]
   51-55p. illus. 28cm.
   Cover title.
   Reprinted from Ramparts.
   1. International Ladies' Gar-
   ment Workers' Union. I. New
   England Free Press.
   KU-RH

M228
Myerson, Michael.
   Student political action and
   the administration. [n.p. Slate?
   1961?]
   [2]p. 28cm.
   Caption title.
   1. Universities and colleges--
   Administration. 2. Student
   movements. I. Slate.
   WHi-A

M229
Myerson, Michael.
   The United States' war in
   Vietnam. San Francisco, W.E.B.
   DuBois Clubs of America, 1965.
   28p. 28cm.
   Cover title.
   1. Vietnamese conflict, 1961-
   1975. I. DuBois (W.E.B.)
   Clubs of America, 1965.
   CU-B

‡
N
‡

N.O.W.
   see
National Organization for Women.

N1
Nader, Ralph.
   Who speaks for the consumer?
   Introduction by Paul Jennings.
   [New York, League for Industrial
   Democracy, 196]

12p. illus. 23cm.
1. Consumer protection. I. League for Industrial Democracy.
II. Jennings, Paul.
KU-RH, NNU-T

M2
Nadler, Eugene B.
   Organizational consequences for
   CORE's changing mission. [n.p.,

196]
9 leaves. 28cm.
Caption title.
1. Congress of Racial Equality.
2. Negroes--Civil rights.
KU-RH

N3
Naison, Mark.
  The Southern Tenants Farmers'
  Union and the C.I.O. Boston,
  New England Free Press [196]
  [36]-55p. 22cm.
  Cover title.
  Reprinted from Radical America,
  Sept./Oct. 1968.
  1. Southern Tenants Farmers'
  Union. 2. Congress of Industrial
  Organization. 3. Agricultural
  laborers--Southern States.
  I. New England Free Press.
  KU-RH

N4
National Action Research on the
    Military Industrial Complex.
  Weapons for counterinsurgency.
  [Philadelphia, 1970]
  104p. illus. 28cm. (Local
  research action guide no. 1)
  Cover title.
  1. U.S.--Military policy.
  2. Government, Resistance to.
  3. Vietnamese conflict, 1961-
  1975. 4. Military research.
  KU-RH, CtU

N5
National Advisory Committee on
    Farm Labor.
  The case for the domestic farm
  worker. New York [1965]
  [16]p. 22cm.
  Cover title.
  1. Agricultural laborers.
  WHi-L, WHi-A

N6
National Advisory Committee on
    Farm Labor.
  Farm labor organizing, 1905-
  1967: a brief history. New
  York, 1967.
  68 [1]p. illus. 23cm.
  1. Agricultural laborers--His-
  tory.

KU-RH, CU-B, LU, MoU, DLC, WU,
NUC 68-56910

N7
National Advisory Committee on
    Farm Labor.
  The grape strike. [New York,
  1966]
  35p. illus. 22cm.
  Cover title.
  1. Agricultural laborers--Calif.
  --Delano. 2. Mexicans in the
  U.S. 3. National Farm Workers
  Association.
  WHi-L, WHi-A

N8
National Assembly for Democratic
    Rights, New York, 1961.
  Reports and proceedings. [New
  York, 1962?]
  32p. illus. 28cm.
  Cover title.
  1. Internal security. 2. Civil
  rights.
  MiU

N9
National Association for the
    Advancement of Colored People.
  Black studies primer. [New
  York, 196]
  [12]p. 16x10cm.
  Cover title.
  1. Negroes--Civil rights.
  KU-RH

N10
National Association for the Ad-
    vancement of Colored People.
  The day they changed their
  minds. [New York, 1962]
  [12]p. illus. 22cm.
  Cover title.
  1. Student movements. 2. Ne-
  greos--Civil rights.
  WHi-A, KU-RH

N11
National Association for the Ad-
    vancement of Colored People.
  Does your congressman represent
  you? A voter's guide. [New
  York, 1964]
  22p. 20cm.
  Cover title.

1. Negroes--Civil rights.
2. Negroes--Politics ans suffrage.
KU-RH

N12
National Association for the Ad-
    vancement of Colored People.
  The Jim Crow school--North and
  West. [New York, 1962]
  11p. 22cm.
  Cover title.
  1. Negroes--Education.
  MiU

N13
National Association for the Ad-
    vancement of Colored People.
  NAACP: an American organization.
  [New York, 1959]
  11p. 29cm.
  Cover title.
  1. Communism. 2. Internal
  security. 3. Negroes--Civil
  rights.
  KU-RH

N14
National Association for the Ad-
    vancement of Colored People.
  NAACP: 60 years in the fight for
  freedom. [New York, 1969]
  14p. 23cm.
  Cover title.
  1. Negroes--Civil rights.
  2. Civil rights--History.
  KU-RH

N15
National Association for the Ad-
    vancement of Colored People.
  Speeches by the leaders; the
  March on Washington for Jobs and
  Freedom, August 28, 1963. New
  York [196]
  [16]p. illus. 28cm.
  1. Negroes--Civil rights.
  2. March on Washington for Jobs
  and Freedom.
  KU-RH

N16
National Association for the Ad-
    vancement of Colored People.
  Target for 1963: goals of the
  fight for freedom. [New York,
  1961]

15p. 21cm.
Cover title.
1. Negroes--Civil rights.
KU-RH

N17
National Association for the Ad-
    vancement of Colored People.
  This is the NAACP. [New York,
  1968]
  [8]p. 23x10cm.
  Cover title.
  1. Negroes--Civil rights.
  KU-RH

N18
National Association for the Ad-
    vancement of Colored People.
  "Your future rests in your
  hands." [New York, 196]
  [16]p. illus. 26cm.
  Cover title.
  1. Negroes--Employment.
  KU-RH

N19
National Association for the Ad-
    vancement of Colored People.
    Housing Dept.
  Urban renewal or urban removal.
  [New York, 1959?]
  [4]p. 28cm.
  Cover title.
  1. Urban renewal.
  WHi-A

N20
National Association for the Ad-
    vancement of Colored People.
    Labor Dept.
  The negro wage-earner and apprenticeship training programs:
  a critical analysis with recommendations. New York [196]
  60p. 28cm.
  1. Negroes--Employment.
  WHi-A

N21
National Association for the Ad-
    vancement of Colored People.
    Labor Dept.
  Racism within organized labor:
  a report of five years of the
  AFL-CIO, 1955-1960. New York,
  [1961?]

13 leaves. 28cm.
Cover title.
1. Trade-unions. 2. Negroes--
Employment.
MiU, WHi-L

N22
National Association for the Advancement of Colored People.
   Legal Defense and Educational
   Fund.
A report on services to the
people of the United States by
the Legal Defense Fund, 1940-
1970. New York [1970]
1. Negroes--Civil rights.
2. Law.
MiU

N23
National Association for the Ad-
   vancement of Colored People.
   Legal Defense and Educational
   Fund.
The tragic gap, between civil
rights law and its enforcement.
[New York, 196]
30p. illus. 15x23cm.
Cover title.
1. Negroes--Civil rights.
KU-RH

N24
National Association for the Ad-
   vancement of Colored People.
   New York branch. Anti-Crime
   Committee.
Report of the Anti-Crime Commit-
tee of the New York branch of
NAACP. New York [1969]
11p. 23x10cm.
Cover title.
1. Negroes--Civil rights.
2. Crime and criminals--Harlen,
New York (City)
KU-RH

N25
National Association for the Ad-
   vancement of Colored People.
   Special Contribution Fund.
Night of terror: Houston, U.S.A.
[New York, 1968]
[8]p. illus. 14x22cm.
Cover title.
1. Texas. Southern University,

Houston. 2. Negroes--Civil
rights. 3. Police--Texas--Hous-
ton. 4. Houston--Race question.
KU-RH

N26
National Committee Against Discrimination in Housing.
The impact of housing patterns
on job opportunities; an interim
report on where people live and
where the jobs are, with an introduction by Kenneth B. Clark.
New York [1968]
x, 38p. illus., maps.
1. Negroes--Housing. 2. Discrimination in housing.
WHi-L

N27
National Committee for a Political
   Settlement in Vietnam/Negoti-
   ate Now.
Do we seek to stop killing--or
just "Vietnamize" it? New York
[1970]
folder. 22x10cm.
Cover title.
1. Vietnamese conflict, 1961-
1975.
CU-B

N28
National Committee for a Sane
   Nuclear Policy.
Documents on the test ban negotiations. [n.p., 196]
4 leaves. 28cm.
1. Atomic weapons and disarmament.
WHi-A

N29
National Committee for a Sane
   Nuclear Policy.
The necessity for a comprehen-
sive test-ban treaty. [n.p.]
1964.
4 leaves. 28cm.
Caption title.
1. Atomic weapons and disarmament.
WHi-A

N30
National Committee for a Sane

Nuclear Policy.
Policy statement on South Vietnam. [New York, 196]
2 leaves. 28cm.
Caption title.
1. Vietnamese conflict, 1961-
1975.
WHi-A

N31
National Committee for a Sane
   Nuclear Policy.
What is the National Liberation
Front of South Vietnam? New
York, 1965.
6 leaves. 28cm.
Cover title.
1. South Viet Nam National Front
for Liberation.
WHi-L

N32
National Committee for a Sane
   Nuclear Policy.
Which way in Vietnam? [New York,
196]
folder. 22cm.
Cover title.
1. Vietnamese conflict, 1961-
1975.
WHi-L

N33
National Committee for the Albany
   Defendants.
Upside-down justice: the Albany
cases. [Prepared in cooperation
with the Southern Educational
Fund. Albany, Ga., 196 ?]
9p. illus. 22cm.
Cover title.
1. Negroes--Albany, Ga.
2. Albany, Ga.--Race question.
I. Southern Conference Education-
al Fund.
KU-RH

N34
National Committee for the Repeal
   of the McCarran Act.
What you need to know about the
McCarran act. Chicago [196]
94p. 22cm.
1. U.S. Laws, statutes, etc.
Internal Security Act of 1950.
2. Internal security. 3. Com-

munist Party of the United
States of America.
KU-RH, MiEM, N14

N35
National Committee of Black
   Churchmen.
The national black referendum
on Vietnam. [New York] 1970.
6 leaves. 28cm.
Caption title.
1. Vietnamese conflict, 1961-
1975. 2. Negroes.
MoU

N36
National Committee of Black
   Churchmen.
Organizer's kit for the national black referendum on Vietnam.
[n.p., 1970?]
6 leaves. 28cm.
Cover title.
1. Vietnamese conflict, 1961-
1975. 2. Public welfare.
MoU

N37
National Committee to Abolish the
   House Un-American Activities
   Committee.
The 89th Congress & the abolition of HUAC. A progress report
dedicated to Aubery W. Williams,
1890-1965. Los Angeles [1965?]
32p. illus. 28cm.
Cover title.
1. U.S. Congress. House.
Committee on Un-American Activities. 2. U.S. 89th Cong.
1st. sess., 1965.
KU-RH

N38
National Coordinating Committee to
   End the War in Vietnam.
Organizing a Vietnam protest
committee prepared by the Information Committee of the University of Wisconsin CEVN. Madison [196]
22 [6]p. 28cm.
Cover title.
1. Vietnamese conflict, 1961-
1975.
WHi-L

N39
National Coordinating Committee to
    End the War in Vietnam.   Inter-
    national Secretariat.
The international protest movement against American intervention in the war in Vietnam. Berkeley, Vietnam Day Committee
[1966]
42p. 28cm.
1. Vietnamese conflict, 1961-
1975.
WHi-L, CU-B

N40
National Coordinating Committee to
    End the War in Vietnam.   Viet-
    nam Day Committee, Berkeley.
Attention all military personnel. [Berkeley, 1965]
[2]p. 36cm.
Caption title.
1. Vietnamese conflict, 1961-
1975.
CU-B

N41
National Coordinating Committee to
    End the War in Vietnam.   Viet-
    nam Day Committee, Berkeley.
A reply to your "open letter to
faculty participant in the Vietnam Day Committee."
8 leaves. 28cm.
Caption title.
1. Vietnamese conflict, 1961-
1975. 2. Student movements--
Berkeley, Calif.
CU-B

N42
National Coordinating Committee to
    End the War in Vietnam.   Viet-
    nam Day Committee, Berkeley.
Vietnam. [Berkeley, 1966?]
32p. 22cm.
Caption title.
1. Vietnamese conflict, 1961-
1975.
CU-B

N43
National Coordinating Committee to
    End the War in Vietnam.   Viet-
    nam Day Committee, Berkeley.
Why we sit-in. [Berkeley, 1966?]

2p. 28cm.
Caption title.
1. Vietnamese conflict, 1961-
1975. 2. Government, Resistance
to.
CU-B

N44
National Coordinating Committee to
    End the War in Vietnam.   Viet-
    nam Day Committee, Berkeley,
    Anti-Draft Committee.
Proposed anti-draft program
from the VDC Anti-Draft Committee. [Berkeley? 1965?]
[1] leaf. 28cm.
Caption title.
1. Military service, Compulsory.
CU-B

N45
National Coordinating Committee to
    End the War in Vietnam.   Viet-
    nam Day Committee, Berkeley.
    International Committee.
Twenty four years after Pearl
Harbor and the Japanese anti-
war movement. [Berkeley, 1965]
2p. 28cm.
Caption title.
1. Vietnamese conflict, 1961-
1975. 2. Japan--For. rel.--
U.S.
CU-B

N46
National Council of American-
    Soviet Friendship.
Addresses delivered at the rally
for peace and friendship. [New
York, 1968]
19p.
Cover title.
1. U.S.--For. rel.--Russia.
2. Russia--For. rel.--U.S.
WHi-L

N47
National Council of American-
    Soviet Friendship.
American-Soviet facts. New
York [1964]
19p. 21cm.
Reprinted from New World Review,
Oct. 1964.
1. U.S.--Relations (general)

with Russia.   2. Russia--Relations
(general) with the U.S.
CSt-H, NUC 67-11717

N48
National Council of American-
    Soviet Friendship.
  Bomb testing: rising level of
  dangerous radioactivity. [n.p.,
  1957]
  10 leaves.
  1. Atomic weapons and disarmament.   2. Radioactivity--Physio-
  logical effect.
  NNC

N49
National Council of American-
    Soviet Friendship.
  Cultural relations, U.S.A.--U.S.
  S.R., 1957. New York [1957]
  25p.   (American Soviet facts)
  1. U.S.--Relations (general)
  with Russia. 2. Russia--Relat-
  ions (general) with the U.S.
  MH

N50
National Council of American-Sov-
    iet Friendship.
  U.S.A. welcomes Soviet farmers.
  New York [1955]
  61p. illus. 23cm.
  1. Agriculture.
  KU-J, DLC 56-1957

N51
National Council of American-Sov-
    iet Friendship.
  USSR, your questions answered.
  [New York, 1957]
  39p.
  Cover title.
  1. Russia--Pol. & govt.--1945-
        2. Russia--Econ. condit.
  --1945-
  NNC, NN, NcD, PPD

N52
National Council to Repeal the
    Draft.
  An all-volunteer army of the
  poor and black. [Washington,
  1970]
  folder. 9x22cm.
  Caption title.

1. Military service, Compulsory.
2. Negroes. 3. Poverty.
KU-RH

N53
National Council to Repeal the
    Draft.
  An all-volunteer 'professional'
  army? [Washington, 1970]
  folder. 22x9cm.
  Caption title.
  1. Military service, Compulsory.
  KU-RH

N54
National Council to Repeal the
    Draft.
  An analysis of the Gates Commission report, by an ad hoc
  committee of citizens. A response to the President's Commission on an All-volunteer
  Armed Force. [Washington,
  1970]
  [16]p. 22cm.
  Cover title.
  1. Military service, Compulsory.
  2. U.S. President's Commission
  on All-volunteer Armed Force.
  I. Gates, Thomas Sovereign,
  1906-
  KU-RH

N55
National Council to Repeal the
    Draft.
  The case for draft repeal in
  1970: a study of the current
  situation. [Washington, 1970?]
  [16]p. 22cm.
  Cover title.
  1. Military service, Compulsory.
  KU-RH

N56
National Council to Repeal the
    Draft.
  An eighteen month program for
  draft repeal. [Washington,
  1970?]
  9p. 22x9cm.
  Cover title.
  1. Military service, Compulsory.
  KU-RH

N57
National Council to Repeal the
    Draft.
  End all wars like Vietnam. End
  the draft. [Washington, 1969?]
  folder. illus. 22x10cm.
  Cover title.
  1. Military service, Compulsory.
  2. Vietnamese conflict, 1961-
  1975.
  KU-RH

N58
National Council to Repeal the
    Draft.
  The feasibility of ending the
  draft in 1971. [Washington,
  1971]
  [12]p. illus. 22x10cm.
  Caption title.
  1. Military service, Compulsory.
  KU-RH

N59
National Council to Repeal the
    Draft.
  A guide to organizing for the
  draft repeal. Washington [1970]
  13p. 28cm.
  Cover title.
  1. Military service, Compulsory.
  KU-RH

N60
National Labor Service.
  The people take the lead; a record of progress in civil rights:
  1948 to 1957. [New York, 1957]
  39p. 23cm.
  Cover title.
  1. Negroes--Civil rights.
  NN

N61
National Labor Service.
  Your rights...under state and
  local fair employment practice
  laws. [New York, 1956]
  32p. 23cm.
  Cover title.
  Second printing.
  1. Negroes--Civil rights.
  CtY-L

National Lawyers Guild
  see also
Bay Area National Lawyers Guild.

N62
National Lawyers Guild.
  Citizens' guide to the 1964
  civil rights act. [Detroit]
  1965.
  28p.
  1. Civil rights.
  CLL

N63
National Lawyers Guild.
  Project Mississippi--an account
  of the National Lawyers Guild
  program of legal assistance to
  civil rights workers in Mississippi: summer 1964. [Detroit,
  1964?]
  16p. illus.
  Cover title.
  1. Mississippi--Race question.
  2. Law enforcement--Mississippi.
  3. Lawyers.
  MiU, CLL, C

N64
National Lawyers Guild. Commit-
    tee to Assist Southern Lawyers.
  Civil rights & liberties hand-
  book: pleadings & practice.
  [Editor: Ann Faga Ginger] Ber-
  keley, Calif., Civil Rights
  Handbook, 1963-
  1v. (loose-leaf) illus. 30cm.
  1. Civil rights. I. Ginger,
  Ann Fagan, ed.
  CU, DLC 63-5180

N65
National Lawyers Guild. Commit-
    tee to Assist Southern Lawyers.
  Civil rights and liberties hand-
  book: pleadings and practice.
  Ann Fagan Ginger, editor. Ber-
  keley, c1967.
  2v. (loose-leaf)
  1. Civil rights. I. Ginger,
  Ann Fagan, ed.
  OkU, NUC 70-15123

N66
National Lawyers Guild. Inter-
    national Law Committee.
  American foreign policy and the
  rule of law. [n.p., 1966]
  [29]p. 22x9cm.
  1. U.S.--Foreign policy.
  2. Law.

MiU-L, MnU-L, WHi-L, C, GU,
NUC 70-29926

N67
National Lawyers Guild. Inter-
    national Law Committee.
The policy of the United States
intervention in the affairs of
the Dominican Republic--unilat-
eral vs. adherence to treaty ob-
ligations and principles of international; memorandum of law
prepared by International Law
Committee of the National Lawyers Guild, Robert Schmorleitz,
chairman. Detroit, National
Lawyers Guild [1968?]
11p. 23cm.
1. Dominican Republic--Relations
(general) with the U.S. 2. U.S.
--Relations (general) with Dominican Republic.
C, NUC 69-95291

N68
National Lawyers Guild. Inter-
    national Law Committee.
A summary of disarmament documents 1945-1962. San Francisco,
National Lawyers Guild, International Law Committee, Subcommittee on Disarmament [1963?]
iv, 171p. 23cm.
Cover title.
1. Disarmament.
MH-L, DLC 64-406

N69
National Mobilization Committee to
    End the War in Vietnam.
Fact sheet on Vietnam: March 13,
1969. New York [1969?]
3 leaves. 28cm.
Caption title.
1. Vietnamese conflict, 1961-
1975.
KU-RH

N70
National Mobilization Committee to
    End the War in Vietnam.
Inauguration, Chicago indictments,
anti-war directions: a mobilization report. [New York, 1969?]
[3]p. 28cm.
Caption title.

1. Youth--Political activity.
2. Vietnamese conflict, 1961-
1975.
KU-RH

N71
National Mobilization Committee to
    End the War in Vietnam.
Mobilization report. New York
[196]
7 [1]p. illus. 23cm.
Caption title.
Partial contents--The Mobilization & the movements, by Dave
Dellinger.
1. Vietnamese conflict, 1961-
1975. 2. Youth--Political activity. I. Dellinger, Dave.
KU-RH

National Organization for Women.
xNOW

N72
National Organization for Women.
Abortion counseling information.
Rev. [New York, 1969]
2p. 28cm.
1. Abortion.
MoU

N73
National Organization for Women.
    Education Committee.
Token learning: a study of women's higher education in America. [New York, 1968]
57p. 28cm.
1. Education of women. 2. Wo-
man--Rights of women.
WHi-L

N74
National Service Board for Reli-
    gious Objectors.
Conscientious objectors and the
draft. [Washington, 196]
folder (8p.) 22x9cm.
1. Conscientious objectors.
KU-RH

N75
National Service Board for Reli-
    gious Objectors.
Questions & answers on the clas-
sification and assignment of

conscientious objectors.   Rev.
ed. Washington, 1969.
35p. illus. 23x10cm.
Cover title.
1. Conscientious objectors.
KU-RH, MoU

N76
National Service Board for Reli-
     gious Objectors.
Statement of religious bodies on
the conscientious objector.
[Rev. ed.] Washington [1963]
62p. 21cm.
1. Conscientious objectors.
KU-RH

N77
National Service Board for Reli-
     gious Objectors.
Statements of religious bodies
on the conscientious objector,
compiled by the National Service
Board for Religious Objectors.
[5th ed. Edited by Robert C.
Heath] Washington [1967]
59p. 21cm.
1. Conscientious objectors.
MoU

N78
National Service Board for Reli-
     gious Objectors.
Statements of religious bodies
on the conscientious objector,
compiled by the National Service
Board for Religious Objectors.
[6th ed. Edited by P. Wayne
Wisler and J. Harold Sherk]
Washington [1968]
68p. 21cm.
1. Conscientious objectors.
MoU

N79
National Service Board for Reli-
     gious Objectors.
Who is a conscientious objector?
[Washington, 196]
folder (8p.) 22x9cm.
1. Conscientious objector.
KU-RH

N80
National Student Christian Feder-
     ation.

Working paper on Latin America.
[New York, 196]
6 leaves. 28cm.
Caption title.
1. Latin America--Soc. condit.
WHi-A

N81
National Student Christian Feder-
     ation. Committee on Race.
Report. [New York? 196]
6 leaves. 28cm.
Caption title.
1. U.S.--Race question. 2. Ne-
groes--Civil rights.
WHi-A

N82
National Student Christian Feder-
     ation. Latin American Con-
     cern Committee.
Report. [New York? 196]
6 leaves. 28cm.
Caption title.
1. Latin America--Relations
(general) with the U.S. 2. U.
S.--Relations (general) with
Latin America.
WHi-A

N83
National Student Movement.
The National Student Movement:
national prospectus [and] data
on project cities. New York,
Students for a Democratic Soc-
iety [196]
14p. 28cm.
Cover title.
1. Negroes--Civil rights.
I. Students for a Democratic
Society.
WHi-A

N84
National Welfare Rights Organi-
     zation.
...about the National Welfare
Rights Organization. Washington [1970?]
[4]p. 28cm.
Cover title.
1. Public welfare.
KU-RH

N85
National Welfare Rights Organiza-
    tion.
  A brief history of the National
  Welfare Rights Organization.
  Washington [196]
  [4]p. 28cm.
  Cover title.
  1. Public welfare.
  KU-RH

N86
National Welfare Rights Organiza-
    tion.
  Don't buy Sears. [Washington,
  196]
  [4]p. 28cm.
  Cover title.
  1. Sears, Roebuck and Company.
  KU-RH

N87
National Welfare Rights Organiza-
    tion.
  Goals of the National Welfare
  Rights Organization. Washington
  [1968?]
  [8]p. 28cm.
  Cover title.
  1. Public welfare.
  KU-RH

N88
National Welfare Rights Organiza-
    tion.
  How NWRO works. Washington
  [196]
  [6]p. illus. 28cm.
  Cover title.
  1. Public welfare.
  KU-RH

N89
National Welfare Rights Organiza-
    tion.
  NWRO's guaranteed adequate in-
  come plan. [Washington, [1970?]
  [8]p. 28cm.
  Cover title.
  1. Public welfare. 2. Poverty.
  KU-RH, WHi-A

N90
National Welfare Rights Organiza-
    tion.
  Rights you should know. Wash-

ington [1970]
  [4]p. 28cm.
  Cover title.
  1. Public welfare.
  KU-RH

N91
National Welfare Rights Organiza-
    tion.
  School lunch program bill of
  rights. [Washington, 1969?]
  6p. 28cm.
  1. Child welfare.
  KU-RH

N92
National Welfare Rights Organiza-
    tion.
  Some ideas on how to raise [dol-
  lars] for your WRO. [n.p.,
  1969?]
  [14]p. 15x22cm.
  Cover title.
  1. Poverty. 2. Welfare economics.
  KU-RH

N93
National Welfare Rights Organiza-
    tion.
  Welfare and riots. Washington,
  1968.
  [4]p. 28cm.
  Cover title.
  1. Riots. 2. Public welfare.
  KU-RH

N94
National Welfare Rights Organiza-
    tion.
  Welfare bill of rights. Washington [1970?]
  5p. 28cm.
  Cover title.
  1. Public welfare. 2. Legal
  assistance to the poor.
  KU-RH

N95
National Welfare Rights Organiza-
    tion.
  The welfare WIP program and
  you. Washington [1969?]
  [4]p. 28cm.
  Cover title.
  1. Public Welfare.
  KU-RH

N96
Neal, Fred Warner.
    False concepts in foreign policy.
    [Woodmont, Conn., Promoting En-
    during Peace, 1969]
    [2]p. 28cm. (No. 143)
    Caption title.
    Reprinted from The Progressive,
    June 1969.
    1. U.S.--Foreign policy.
    I. Promoting Enduring Peace.
    KU-RH

N97
Neal, Fred Warner.
    War and peace, and the problem
    of Berlin: Claremont summer ses-
    sion convocation lecture, July
    20, 1961. [Chevy Chase, Md.,
    F.F. Fodor, 1961]
    13p. 28cm.
    Cover title.
    1. Berlin question (1945-   )
    NIC, NUC 63-52248

N98
Neal, Fred Warren.
    War and peace and the problem of
    Berlin. [New York, Marzani &
    Munsell, 196]
    13p. 23cm.
    Cover title.
    1. Berlin question (1945-   )
    I. Marzani and Munsell.
    KU-J

N99
Nearing, Helen.
    Our right to travel, by Helen
    and Scott Nearing. Harborside,
    Me., Social Science Institute
    [196]
    24p. 22cm. (Social science
    pamphlet 3)
    Cover title.
    1. Passports. 2. Travel.
    3. Civil rights. I. Nearing,
    Scott, 1883-   I. Social
    Science Institute.
    MiU, NNC-L, NN, DLC

N100
Nearing, Helen.
    USA today; reporting extensive
    journeys and first-hand obser-
    vations, commenting on their

meaning, and offering conclus-
ions regarding present-day
trends in the domestic and
foreign affairs of the United
States. By Helen & Scott
Nearing. Harborside, Me.,
Social Science Institute, 1955.
254p. 22cm.
1. U.S.--Soc. condit. I. Nearing, Scott, 1883-   , jt. auth.
I. Social Science Institute.
CU, NjN, PPT, PP, NN, OOxM,
PSC, ViU, IaU, WaU, KU, DLC
55-12158

N101
Nearing, Scott, 1883-
    Cuba and Latin America: eyewit-
    ness report on the Continental
    Congress for Solidarity with
    Cuba. Harborside, Me., Social
    Science Institute, 1963.
    36p. (Social science pamphlet,
    5)
    1. Cuba--For. rel.--Latin Amer-
    ica. 2. Latin America--For.
    rel.--Cuba. 3. Continental
    Congress for Solidarity with
    Cuba, Niteroi, Brazil, 1963.
    I. Social Science Institute.
    MH, NUC 70-15876

N102
Nearing, Scott, 1883-
    Cuba and Latin America: eyewit-
    ness report on the Continental
    Congress for Solidarity with
    Cuba. New York, New Century
    Publishers, 1963.
    36p. 20cm.
    1. Cuba--For. rel.--Latin Amer-
    ica. 2. Latin America--For.
    rel.--Cuba. 3. Continental
    Congress for Solidarity with
    Cuba, Niteroi, Brazil, 1963.
    I. New Century Publishers.
    MiU, FU, NUC 65-82075

N103
Nearing, Scott, 1883-
    Economic crisis in the United
    States. Harborside, Me. [196]
    24p. (Social Science Institute.
    Social science pamphlet, 4)
    1. U.S.--Econ. condit. I. Soc-
    ial Science Institute.
    MH, NUC 63-52254

N104
Nearing, Scott, 1883-
  Socialism in practice; the trans-
  formation of East Europe. New
  York, New Century Publishers,
  1962.
  104p. 22cm.
  1. Communism--Europe, Eastern.
  I. New Century Publishers.
  KU-J, MH, DLC 63-584

N105
Nearing, Scott, 1883-
  Soviet education. [Harborside,
  Me., 1959?]
  30p. illus. 22cm. (Political
  Science Institute. Social science
  pamphlet no. 2)
  1. Education--Russia. I. Soc-
  ial Science Institute.
  MeBa CaBVaU, P, NbU, IU, MoU,
  NN, DLC 59-47548

N106
Nearing, Scott, 1883-
  Soviet education: what does it
  offer to America? [San Francisco, American Russian Institute,
  1959?]
  30 [2]p. illus. 24cm.
  1. Education--Russia. I. American Russian Institute.
  RPB, NcGW, CLSU, KU, CSSR

N107
Needham, Joseph, 1900-
  The past in China's present; a
  cultural, social, and philoso-
  phical background for contem-
  porary China. [New York] Far
  East Reporter [196]
  38p. map. 22cm.
  Cover title.
  Reprinted from Arts and Sciences
  in China, London.
  1. China--Civilization--History.
  I. Far East Reporter.
  CSt-H, NUC 68-57914

N108
Negrin, Su.
  A graphic notebook on feminism.
  [New York, Times Change Press,
  1970]
  60 [4]p. illus. 18cm.
  1. Woman--Rights of women.

I. Times Change Press.
CtU

N109
Nell, Edward J.
  Automation and the abolition of
  the market. [New York, Movement for a Democratic Society,
  196]
  27p. 22cm. (MDS pamphlet 2)
  Reprinted from New Left Notes,
  Aug. 7, 1967.
  1. Cybernetics. 2. Markets.
  3. Commerce. I. Movement for a
  Democratic Society.
  MoU

N110
Nelson, Truman John, 1912-
  People with strength: the story
  of Monroe, N.C. [New York,
  Committee to Aid the Monroe Defendants, 1963]
  37p. 22cm.
  Cover title.
  1. Williams, Robert Franklin,
  1925-   2. Negroes--Monroe,
  N.C. 3. Monroe, N.C.--Race
  question. I. Committee to Aid
  the Monroe Defendants.
  KU-RH, NcU, WHi-L, NUC 64-49166

N111
Neto, Agostinho.
  A message to companions in the
  struggle. [Oakland] Liberation
  Support Movement [1970?]
  19p. illus. 22cm.
  Cover title.
  1. Mozambique. 2. Angola.
  3. Portuguese in Angola.
  4. Movimento Popular de Libertacao de Angola. I. Liberation
  Support Movement.
  MiU, CU-B

N112
Neufeld, Russ, ed.
  GI counseling. [New York, New
  York Regional SDS, 196]
  33 [14]p. 22cm.
  Cover title.
  1. Soldiers. I. Students for
  a Democratic Society, New York
  Regional.
  MoU

N113
New England Committee for Nonvio-
    lent Action.
  Don't buy war. Voluntown, Conn
  [197]
  [1] leaf. 28cm.
  Caption title.
  1. Taxation. 2. Tax evasion.
  KU-RH

N114
New England Committee for Nonvio-
    lent Action.
  Statements of draft resisters.
  Voluntown [1967]
  1v. (unpaged) 28cm.
  1. Military service, Compulsory.
  CU-B

N115
New England Committee for Nonvio-
    lent Action.
  Training program in nonviolent
  action, July 1-September 1, 1962.
  New London, Conn. [1962]
  [5]p. 28cm.
  1. Nonviolence.
  KU-RH

N116
The new fascist danger. [New York,
    New Century Publishers, 1962]
  15p.
  "Editorial from World Marxist
  Review, April, 1962."
  1. Anti-communist movements.
  I. New Century Publishers.
  I. World Marxist Review.
  MiEM, NUC 67-96629

N117
New Left Notes.
  Two GIs in the struggle. [Chi-
  cago, Students for a Democratic
  Society, 196]
  folder (7p.) illus. 23cm.
  Cover title.
  Interview with Dave Kline and
  Guy Smith, conducted in Jan.
  1969.
  1. U.S. Army. Military Life.
  2. Soldiers. I. Kline, Dave.
  II. Smith, Guy. III. Students
  for a Democratic Society.
  KU-RH

N118
New Mobilization Committee.
  They order us to remain silent
  in the face of injustice; the
  case of Martha Allen and Mike
  Honey,...issued by New Mobili-
  zation [and others. Louisville,
  Ky., Southern Conference Edu-
  cational Fund, 1970]
  folder. 22x9cm.
  Cover title.
  1. Allen, Martha. 2. Honey,
  Mike. 3. Civil rights--Ken-
  tucky. I. Southern Conference
  Educational Fund.
  KU-RH

N119
New Mobilization Committee to End
    the War in Vietnam.
  Organizing for civil disobedience. Washington [196]
  15p. 28cm.
  1. Government, Resistance to.
  WHi-A

N120
New University Conference.
  Black liberation. [Chicago,
  1970]
  34p. illus. 28cm.
  Cover title.
  "A special edition of the New
  University Conference news let-
  ter, edited by Judy Nissman
  Taylor."
  1. Negroes--Civil rights.
  I. Taylor, Judy Nissman, ed.
  KU-RH

N121
New University Conference.
  But why should I join a national organization? [Chicago,
  1970?]
  4p. illus. 28cm.
  Caption title.
  1. Student movements.
  KU-RH

M122
New University Conference.
  Crisis paper: electoral politics and change. [Chicago,
  c1970]

[4]p. 28cm.
Caption title.
1. Politics, Practical. 2. Social change. 3. Elections.
KU-RH

N123
New University Conference.
  Crisis paper: recession, inflation, and politics. [Chicago,
  1970]
  [2]p. 36cm.
  Caption title.
  1. U.S.--Econ. condit. 2. Inflation (Finance) 3. U.S.--Pol.
  & govt.--1969-
  KU-RH

N124
New University Conference.
  Crisis paper: violence, nonviolence, & change. [Chicago,
  1970]
  [4]p. 28cm.
  Caption title.
  1. Violence (Law). 2. Nonviolence. 3. Social change.
  KU-RH

N125
New University Conference.
  How Harvard rules women. [Chi-
  cago? 1970]
  77p. illus.
  1. Woman--Rights of women.
  2. Education of women. 3. Harvard University.
  WHi-L

N126
New University Conference.
  Open up the schools: political
  perspective I [and II] draft.
  Chicago [1970?]
  [12]p. 28cm.
  Caption title.
  1. Universities and colleges.
  2. Education.
  KU-RH

N127
New University Conference.
  People's peace treaty. Chicago
  [1970?]
  24p. illus. 28cm.
  Cover title.

1. Vietnamese conflict, 1961-
1975--Peace.
KU-RH

N128
New University Conference.
  The student rebellion. [Chi-
  cago, 1969]
  [4]p. 28cm.
  Caption title.
  1. Student movements. 2. Radicalism.
  KU-RH

N129
New University Conference.
  Women's caucus perspective
  [adopted at the national convention of the New University
  Conference, June 1969. Chicago,
  c1970]
  4p. illus. 28cm.
  Cover title.
  1. Woman--Rights of women.
  KU-RH

N130
New University Conference. Tea-
    cher Organizing Project.
  Classes and schools: a radical
  definition for teachers. [Chi-
  cago, c1970]
  13p. 28cm.
  Cover title.
  1. Teachers. 2. Education.
  3. Radicalism.
  KU-RH

N131
New York Ad Hoc Committee for the
    Support of the Mississippi
    Freedom Democratic Party.
  Organizing manual; Mississippi
  Freedom Democratic Party chal-
  lenge. [New York? 196]
  6p. [1] leaf. 28cm.
  Cover title.
  1. Mississippi Freedom Democra-
  tic Party.
  WHi-A

New York City Spartacist League.
see also
Bay Area Spartacist League.
Spartacist League.

Campus Spartacist Club, Berkeley,
   Calif.
Philadelphia Spartacist League.

N132
New York City Spartacist League.
  Fight back. [New York, 1969]
  [2]p. 28cm.
  Caption title.
  1. Labor and laboring classes--
  New York (City) 2. New York
  (City)--Econ. condit.
  CU-B

N133
New York City Spartacist League.
  Where is 65 being taken? [New
  York, 1969]
  2p. 28cm.
  Caption title.
  1. Retail, Wholesale and Depart-
  ment Store Union, District 65.
  CU-B

N134
New York Committee to Free Angela
   Davis.
  A political biography of Angela
  Davis. [Highland Park, Mich.,
  Michigan Committee to Free An-
  gela Davis, 1970?]
  9p. 22cm.
  Cover title.
  1. Davis, Angela, 1944-
  I. Michigan Committee to Free
  Angela Davis.
  MiU

N135
New York Committee of Students for
   Peace in Vietnam.
  The North Vietnamese position
  on negotiations. New York, New
  York Committee of Students for
  Peace in Vietnam and Students
  for a Democratic Society, New
  York Region [196]
  2p. 28cm. (Vietnam factsheet 2)
  Caption title.
  1. Vietnamese conflict, 1961-
  1975. I. Students for a Demo-
  cratic Society, New York Region.
  WHi-L

N136
New York Committee of Students for

   Peace in Vietnam.
  Policy statement. [New York,
  196]
  [1] leaf. 36cm.
  Caption title.
  1. Vietnamese conflict, 1961-
  1975.
  WHi-L

N137
New York Peace Information Center.
  U.S. agencies, corporations, organizations and institutions en-
  gaged in programs of research
  relevant to issues of war and
  peace. [Ross Flanagan and Donald McKelvey, editors] New
  York [1965]
  15p.
  1. Peace--Societies, etc.--Dir-
  ect. I. Flanagan, Ross.
  II. McKelvey, Donald.
  MiU, NUC 69-123292

N138
New York Revolutionary Union.
  The student movement: history,
  prospects, & tasks. [New York,
  197 ?]
  12p. illus. 28cm.
  Cover title.
  1. Student movements--New York
  (City)
  NNU-T

N139
Newberry, Mike.
  The cruel and unusual punish-
  ment of Henry Winston. New
  York, Harlem Committee to Free
  Henry Winston [196]
  23p. port. 19cm.
  1. Winston, Henry. 2. Negroes
  --Civil rights. 3. Communism.
  I. Harlem Committee to Free
  Henry Winston.
  KU-RH, WHi-L

N140
Newberry, Mike.
  The fascist revival; the inside
  story of the John Birch Society.
  New York, New Century Publishers, 1961]
  47p. 19cm.
  1. John Birch Society. 2. Anti-

communist movements. 3. Fascism.
I. New Century Publishers.
WHi-L, CSt-H, NN, IaU, NUC 63-
55758

N141
Newberry, Mike.
Goldwater-ism. New York, Marzani & Munsell [1964]
64p. illus. 22cm.
1. Goldwater, Barry Morris, 1909-
        2. Fascism. I. Marzani
and Munsell.
KU-RH, DLC

N142
News & Letters.
Black mass revolt [a statement
by the News & Letters committees]
Detroit, 1967.
23p. 28cm.
1. Negroes--Civil rights.
MoU, MiU, WHi-L, MB, NUC 71-86151

N143
News & Letters.
8 to 3: high school prison notes.
[Detroit?] News & Letters and
Radical Student Union [1970?]
25p. 28cm.
Cover title.
1. Student movements. 2. High
schools. I. Radical Student
Union.
MiU, KU-RH

N144
News & Letters.
Freedom riders speak for them-
selves. [Detroit, 1961]
62p. illus.
Cover title.
1. Negroes--Civil rights.
WHi-A

N145
News & Letters.
Notes on women's liberation: we
speak in many voices. Detroit
[1970]
86p. illus. 23cm.
Cover title.
1. Woman--Rights of women.
KU-RH

N146
News & Letters.
Notes on women's liberation: we
speak in many voices. [Detroit,
1970]
75p.
1. Woman--Rights of women.
WHi-L, MiU-H

N147
News & Letters. Convention, 1960.
On war and peace. [Detroit,
News & Letters] 1960.
14p. 28cm.
Cover title.
1. Socialism. 2. Peace.
3. U.S.--Foreign policy.
MiU

N148
News & Letters. National Editorial Board.
American civilization on trial;
the negro as touchstone of history. Detroit, 1963.
34p. illus. 26cm.
At head of title: 100 years
after the emancipation procla-
mation.
1. Negroes--Civil rights.
KU-RH, MoU, NNC, DLC, WHi-L,
MH, LNHT, NNU-T

N149
News & Letters. National Editorial Board.
American civilization on trial;
black masses as vanguard, with
a new section: black caucuses
in the unions. [3d. expanded
edition. Detroit, News & Letters, 1970]
40p.
Cover title.
"A statement by the National
Editorial Board of News & Letters."
1. Negroes--Civil rights.
2. Trade-unions.
MiU

N150
News & Letters. Women's Liberation Committee.

Who we are. Detroit [196]
[2]p. 28cm.
Caption title.
1. Woman--Rights of women.
WHi-L

N151
Newton, Huey P.
  Essays from the Minister of Defense. [San Francisco? 1968]
  22p. 22cm.
  1. Black Panther Party.
  MB, NUC 70-103626

N152
Newton, Huey P.
  Essays from the Minister of Defense. [n.p., 1968]
  23p. 22cm.
  1. Black Panther Party. 2. Ne-
  groes--Civil rights.
  WHi-L, MiU, CU-B

N153
Newton, Huey P.
  The genius of Huey P. Newton,
  Minister of Defense, Black Pan-
  ther Party. Intro. by Eldridge
  Cleaver. [San Francisco, Mini-
  ster of Information, Black Pan-
  ther Party, 1970?]
  31p.
  Cover title.
  1. Negroes--Civil rights.
  I. Black Panther Party.
  WHi-L, MiU

N154
Newton, Huey P.
  Huey Newton talks to The Move-
  ment about the Black Panther
  Party, cultural nationalism,
  SNCC, liberals and white revol-
  utionaries. [Boston, New Eng-
  land Free Press, 1969?]
  14p. illus. 22cm.
  Reprinted from The Movement,
  Aug. 1968.
  1. Black Panther Party. 2. Ne-
  groes--Civil rights. 3. Student
  Nonviolent Coordinating Committee.
  I. New England Free Press.
  II. The Movement.
  KU-RH

N155
Newton, Huey P.
  Huey Newton talks to the move-
  ment about the Black Panther
  Party, cultural nationalism,
  SNCC, liberals and white revol-
  utionaries. [Chicago, Students
  for a Democratic Society, 1968]
  14p. illus., port. 22cm.
  1. Negroes--Civil rights.
  2. Black Panther Party. 3. Stu-
  dent Nonviolent Coordinating
  Committee. I. The Movement.
  II. Students for a Democratic
  Society.
  NIC, MoU, NNU-T, NUC 70-5441

N156
Newton, Huey P.
  Huey's message to revolution-
  ary people's constitutional
  convention plenary session
  September 5, 1970, Philadelphia,
  Pa. [n.p., Black Panther Party,
  1970]
  [4]p. illus.
  Cover title.
  1. Negroes--Civil rights.
  I. Black Panther Party.
  NNU-T

N157
Newton, Huey P.
  Message from Huey: taped in
  prison. [n.p., 196]
  3p. 28cm.
  Caption title.
  1. Vietnamese conflict, 1961-
  1975. 2. Youth--Political activity. 3. Negroes--Civil
  rights.
  KU-RH

N158
Nicholas, Martin.
  Vietnamese and American freedom.
  [Nashville] Southern Student
  Organizing Committee [196]
  5p. 28cm.
  Cover title.
  1. Vietnamese conflict, 1961-
  1975. I. Southern Student
  Organizing Committee.
  WHi-L, MiU

N159
Nicolaus, Martin.
    The contradiction of advanced
    capitalist society and its resol-
    ution. Ann Arbor, Radical Edu-
    cation Project [196]
    10p. 28cm.
    Cover title.
    1. Capitalism. 2. Labor and
    laboring classes. I. Radical
    Education Project.
    MiU, WHi-L, CU-B

N160
Nicolaus, Martin.
    The contradiction of advanced
    capitalist society and its re-
    solution. Boston, New England
    Free Press [196]
    10p. 28cm.
    Cover title.
    1. Capitalism. 2. Socialism.
    3. Hippies. I. New England Free
    Press.
    KU-RH

N161
Nicolaus, Martin.
    The iceberg strategy: universi-
    ties and the military-industrial
    complex. Ann Arbor, Radical
    Education Project [196]
    6p. 28cm.
    Cover title.
    1. U.S.--Military policy.
    2. Military research. 3. Busi-
    ness and politics. 4. Univer-
    sities and colleges. I. Radical
    Education Project.
    MoU, KU-RH, WHi-L

N162
Nicolaus, Martin.
    Ruling-class sociology. San
    Francisco, Bay Area Radical Edu-
    cation Project [196]
    4 leaves. 28cm.
    Cover title.
    1. Power (Social science)
    2. Sociology. I. Bay Area Radi-
    cal Education Project.
    CU-B

N163
Nicolaus, Martin.
    The unknown Marx: the contempor-

ary relevance of Marx. [Boston,
New England Free Press, 196]
[84]-110p. 22cm.
Cover title.
Reprinted from New Left Review,
Mar/Ap 1968.
1. Marx, Karl, 1818-1883.
2. Socialism. I. New England
Free Press.
KU-RH

N164
The nine for peace. [n.p., Resis-
    tance, c1968]
    [13]p. illus.
    1. Vietnamese conflict, 1961-
    1975. I. Resistance.
    WHi-L

N165
Nolan, David.
    The peace called war; Lyndon
    Johnson's poverty program.
    [Nashville, Southern Student
    Organizing Committee, 196]
    5p. 28cm.
    Reprinted from New South Stu-
    dent, Feb. 1967.
    1. Poverty. 2. U.S. Office of
    Economic Opportunity. I. Sou-
    thern Student Organizing Com-
    mittee.
    MoU, MiU

N166
Nolan, David.
    Two commentaries on "wars" on
    poverty [by] David Nolan [and]
    Edouard Smith. [Montreal, Our
    Generation, 196]
    3-15p.
    Caption title.
    1. Poor--Canada. I. Our Gene-
    ration. II. Smith, Edouard,
    jt. auth.
    NNU-T

N167
Nolan, David.
    The university of the status
    quo. Nashville, Southern Stu-
    dent Organizing Committee [1966]
    7p. 28cm.
    Cover title.
    1. Universities and colleges.
    2. Student movements. I. Sou-

thern Student Organizing Committee.
WHi-L, CU-B

N168
Nolan, David.
  Vietnam: the myth and reality
  of American policy. Nashville,
  Southern Student Organizing
  Committee, 1967.
  9p. 28cm.
  Cover title.
  1. Vietnamese conflict, 1961-
  1975. I. Southern Student Or-
  ganizing Committee.
  CU-B, WHi-L, KU-RH

N169
Norden, Eric.
  American atrocities in Vietnam.
  [New York] 1966.
  15p. illus.
  Reprinted from Liberation, Feb.
  1966.
  1. Vietnamese conflict, 1961-
  1975--Atrocities.
  WHi-L

N170
Norden, Eric.
  American atrocities in Vietnam.
  [New York, Liberation] c1966.
  19p. illus. 28cm.
  Caption title.
  Reprinted from Liberation, Feb.
  1966.
  1. Vietnamese conflict, 1961-
  1975--Atrocities. I. Liberation.
  MiU, MoU

N171
Norman, Andrew R.
  A program for industrial democracy. [n.p., League for Industrial Democracy? 1961]
  3 leaves. 28cm.
  Caption title.
  1. U.S.--Pol. & govt.--1959-
  2. Students for a Democratic
  Society. I. League for Industrial Democracy.
  WHi-L

N172
North, Joseph.
  Cuba: hope of a hemisphere. New

York, International Publishers
[1961]
95p. 21cm.
1. Cuba--Pol. & govt.--1933-
1959. 2. Cuba--Pol. & govt.--
1959-   3. Castro, Fidel,
1927-   I. International
Publishers.
ICU, IU, NcD, WU, NNC, NjP,
NIC, CLU, MiU, MH, DS, N178,
DLC 61-10116

N173
North, Joseph.
  Cuba's revolution: I saw the
  people's victory. [New York,
  New Century Publishers, 1959]
  23p.
  Cover title.
  1. Cuba--History--1959-
  I. New Century Publishers.
  CtY, NN, MiU, KU-J

N174
North, Joseph.
  William Z. Foster: an appre-
  ciation. New York, International Publishers [c1955]
  48p. 20cm.
  1. Foster, William Zebulon,
  1881-   I. International
  Publishers.
  MiU, KU-J, DLC 56-188

N175
North American Congress on Latin
  America.
  Mexico 1968: a study of domination and repression. [New
  York, 1968?]
  50p. illus., maps. 28cm.
  1. Student movements--Mexico.
  2. Mexico--Econ. condit.
  3. Mexico--Pol. & govt.
  MoU, CSt-H, KU-RH

N176
North American Congress on Latin
  America.
  N.A.C.L.A. research methodology
  guide. New York [1968?]
  18p. 28cm.
  Cover title.
  Reprinted from Viet-Report.
  1. Military research. 2. Uni-
  versities and colleges.

3. Imperialism.
MoU, KU-RH

N177
North American Congress on Latin
    America.
  NACLA research methodology guide.
  [New York, 1970]
  72p. illus. 28cm.
  1. Imperialism. 2. Police.
  3. Labor and laboring classes.
  4. Corporations. 5. Military
  research. 6. Universities and
  colleges. 7. Religion. 8. Political parties.
  KU-RH, DLC

N178
North American Congress on Latin
    America.
  Subliminal warfare: the role of
  Latin American studies. [New
  York, c1970]
  63p. illus. 28cm.
  1. Latin American studies.
  2. Imperialism. 3. U.S.--Rela-
  tions (general) with Latin America. 4. Universities and colleges.
  MoSW, KU-RH

N179
North American Congress on Latin
    America.
  Who rules Columbia? [New York,
  1968]
  36p. illus., map. 28cm.
  1. Columbia University. 2. Student movements--Columbia University.
  MoU, NIC, NUC 72-68410

N180
North American Congress on Latin
    America, San Francisco.
  The Debray case. [San Francisco,
  Sponsored by U.S. Committee for
  Justice to Latin American Poli-
  tical Prisoners, 196]
  7 [2] leaves. 28cm.
  1. Bolivia--Pol. & govt.
  2. Debray, Regis. I. U.S.
  Committee for Justice to Latin
  American Political Prisoners.
  WHi-L

N181
Northern California Guardian
    Committee.
  Why the Huey case. [San Fran-
  cisco, 1968?]
  8p. 24cm.
  1. Newton, Huey P. 2. Negroes
  --Civil rights. 3. Peace and
  Freedom Party.
  CU-B

N182
Northern civil rights proposal.
    [n.p., Students for a Demo-
    cratic Society, 196]
  2 leaves. 28cm.
  Caption title.
  1. Negroes--Civil rights.
  I. Students for a Democratic
  Society.
  WHi-A

N183
Northern Student Movement.
  The city. NSM--working papers;
  campus conference fall 1963.
  [n.p., 1963]
  5, [1] leaves. [5]p. 28cm.
  1. Cities and towns. 2. Detroit.
  MiU

N184
Northern Student Movement.
  The civil rights movement: where
  are we now? NSM--working papers;
  campus conference fall 1963.
  [n.p., 1963]
  [11]p. 28cm.
  1. Negroes--Civil rights.
  2. Student movements.
  MiU

N185
Northern Student Movements.
  Confronting the ghetto: the
  northern student approach. New
  York [1963]
  3 leaves. [10]p. 28cm.
  1. Negroes--Civil rights.
  2. Cities and towns. 3. Student
  movements. 4. Slums.
  WHi-A

N186
Northern Student Movement.

Confronting the ghetto: the
Northern Student Movement approach. New York [196]
[2] leaves., 3p. [2] leaves.
28cm.
Cover title.
1. Poor. 2. Cities and towns.
3. Negroes--Housing. 4. Student
movements. 5. Slums.
MiU

N187
Northern Student Movement.
    Crisis in black and white. A con-
    ference on myth and reality in
    the civil rights movement. Con-
    ference journal. [New Haven?
    1963?]
    [5] leaves. [20]p. [6] leaves.
    28cm.
    Cover title.
    Partial contents--Movements and
    the political arena, by Steve
    Max; Dropouts: a political pro-
    blem, by S.M. Miller; Civil
    rights and the northern ghettos:
    whose existential crisis, by
    Nat Hentoff; The economics of
    racism, by Michael Harrington.
    1. Negroes--Civil rights.
    I. Max, Steve, jt. auth. II. Har-
    rington, Michael, jt. auth.
    III. Hentoff, Nat, jt. auth.
    WHi-A

N188
Northern Student Movement.
    Employment. NSM--working papers;
    campus conference fall 1963. [n.
    p., 1963?]
    [12]p. 28cm.
    Cover title.
    1. Negroes--Employment.
    MiU

N189
Northern Student Movement.
    Northern Student Movement. [n.
    p., 1963]
    2 leaves. 28cm.
    Caption title.
    1. Student movements. 2. Negroes
    --Civil rights.
    WHi-A, KU-RH

N190
Northern Student Movement.
    Northern Student Movement.
    [n.p., 1963]
    3 leaves. 28cm.
    Caption title.
    1. Student movements. 2. Ne-
    groes--Civil rights.
    MiU

N191
Northern Student Movement.
    The Northern Student Movement--
    national prospectus--data on
    project cities. New York, Stu-
    dents for a Democratic Society
    [196]
    14p. 28cm.
    Cover title.
    1. Cities and towns. 2. Neg-
    roes--Civil rights. I. Students
    for a Democratic Society.
    MiU

N192
Northern Student Movement.
    Northern Student Movement pre-
    sents crisis in black and white.
    A conference on myth and reality
    in the civil rights movement.
    Conference journal. [n.p.,
    196]
    [50] leaves. 28cm.
    Cover title.
    1. Negroes--Civil rights.
    MiU

N193
Northern Student Movement.
    Summer tutorials--1962. New
    Haven [1962]
    20 leaves. 28cm.
    Cover title.
    1. Negroes--Education. 2. Har-
    lem, New York (City) 3. Phila-
    delphia--Race question.
    WHi-A

N194
Nossiter, Bernard.
    The new folklore of capitalism.
    New York, Distributed by Stu-
    dents for a Democratic Society
    [196]
    6p. 28cm.

Cover title.
Reprinted from The Progressive,
Sept. 1962.
Contents--Selection from The
Paper Economy, by David T. Baze-
lon.
1. Business ethics. 2. Business
and politics. 3. Capitalism.
I. Bazelon, David T., jt. auth.
II. Students for a Democratic
Society.
CU-B, MiU, WHi-L, KU-RH

N195
Notes and proposals for the coming
    convention of the Communist
    Party, submitted by a group of
    communist intellectuals, Jan.
    4, 1957. [n.p., 1957]
9 leaves. 36cm.
Caption title.
1. Communism. 2. Communist
Party of the United States of
America.
NIC, NUC 63-83025

N196
Notes from the first years. [New
    York, New York Radical Women,
    1968]
[33]p.
Cover title.
1. Woman--Rights of women.
I. New York Radical Women.
WHi-L

N197
Notes from the Second Year.
    Women's liberation; major writ-
    ings of the radical feminist.
    [New York, c1970]
126p. illus. 28cm.
Cover title.
1. Woman--Rights of women.
WHi-L, KU-RH

N198
Novack, George Edward.
  Genocide against the Indians;
  its role in the rise of U.S.
  capitalism. [New York, Pathfinder Press, 1970]
31p. 22cm.
Cover title.
1. Indians of North America--
Government relations. 2. Capi-

talism. I. Pathfinder Press.
MiU, KU-RH

N199
Novack, George Edward.
  How can the Jews survive? A
  socialist answer to Zionism.
  [New York, Merit Publishers,
  1969]
22p.
Cover title.
1. Zionism. 2. Jews. 3. Near
East--Pol. & govt. I. Merit
Publishers.
MiU

N200
Novack, George Edward.
  How can the Jews survive? A
  socialist answer to Zionsim.
  [New York, Pathfinder Press,
  1970]
22p. 18cm.
Cover title.
1. Zionism. 2. Socialism.
3. Jews. I. Pathfinder Press.
KU-RH

N201
Novack, George Edward.
  The long view of history, by
  William F. Warde [pseud.]
  [New York] Pioneer Publishers
  [1960]
64p. 18cm. (Pioneer pocket
library no. 8)
1. History. 2. Socialism.
I. Pioneer Publishers.
KU-RH, DLC 60-1455rev.

N202
Novack, George Edward.
  The long view of history. [2d.
  ed. New York, Merit Publishers,
  1969]
63p. 19cm.
1. History. 2. Socialism.
I. Merit Publishers.
MoU

N203
Novack, George Edward.
  Marxism versus neo-anarchist
  terrorism. [New York, Pathfinder Press, 1970]
15p. 22cm.

1. Students for a Democratic
Society. 2. Socialism. 3. Anarchism and anarchists. I. Pathfinder Press.
MiU

N204
Novack, George Edward.
  Moscow vs. Peking: the meaning of
  the great debate, by William F.
  Warde [pseud.] Appendix: complete text of the Chinese criti-
  cism of the program of American
  Communist Party. New York, Pioneer Publishers [1963?]
  30p. 21cm.
  Reprinted from The Militant.
  1. Communism. 2. China (People's
  Republic of China, 1949-   )--
  For. rel.--Russia. 3. Russia--
  For. rel.--China (People's Republic of China, 1949-   ) 4. Communist Party of the United States
  of America. I. Pioneer Publishers.
  KU-RH, MoU

N205
Novack, George.
  Revolutionary dynamics of women's
  liberation. [New York, Merit
  Publishers, 1969]
  22p. 22x9cm.
  Cover title.
  Reprinted from the Militant,
  Oct. 17, 1969.
  1. Woman--Rights of women.
  I. Merit Publishers.
  CU-B, MiU, KU-RH

N206
Novack, George Edward.
  The understanding of history:
  two essays, by George Novack.
  [New York, Merit Publishers,
  1967]
  39p. 22cm.
  Cover title.
  1. History. 2. Socialism.
  I. Merit Publishers.
  MiDW, KU-RH, MiU, NUC 69-83147

N207
Novack, George Edward.
  Uneven and combined development
  in history. New York, Pioneer

Publishers [1965]
59p. 20cm.
1. U.S.--History. 2. Capitalism. 3. Sociology. I. Pioneer
Publishers.
MiU

N208
Novack, George Edward.
  Uneven and combined development
  in history. [3d. ed. New York,
  Merit Publishers, 1966]
  59p. 22cm.
  1. U.S.--History. 2. Socialism.
  I. Merit Publishers.
  MoU, KU-RH

N209
Novack, George Edward.
  Who will change the world? The
  new left and the views of C.
  Wright Mills. Introduction by
  John Riddell. Toronto, YSF Publications [196]
  35p. 21cm.
  1. Student Union for Peace Action. 2. Socialism in Canada.
  3. Student movements--Canada.
  4. Peace. 5. Mills, C. Wright.
  I. Young Socialist Forum.
  II. Riddell, John.
  MoU, KU-RH

N210
Nunez, Carlos, 1941-
  The Tupamaros: urban guerrillas
  of Uruguay. [New York, Times
  Change Press, 1970]
  48p. 18cm.
  Reprinted from Tricontinental,
  Jan./Feb. 1969.
  1. Movimiento de Liberacion
  Nacional (Tupamaros) 2. Guer-
  rillas--Uruguay. I. Times
  Change Press.
  CtU

N211
Nyack Conference on Unemployment
    and Social Change, Nyack, N.Y.
    1963.
  Working papers for Nyack conference on unemployment and social
  change. New York, Students for
  a Democratic Society [1963?]
  [18]p. 28cm.

Cover title.
1. U.S.--Econ. condit. 2. Unemployed. 3. Negroes--Civil rights.
4. Automation. I. Students for
a Democratic Society.
MiU

N212
Nyack Conference on Unemployment
    and Social Change, Nyack, N.Y.,
    1963.
Working papers [by Stanley Arono-
witz and others] New York, Stu-

dents for a Democratic Society
and its Economic Research and
Action Project [1963]
16p.
Cover title.
1. U.S.--Econ. condit. 2. Unemployed. 3. Automation.
4. Negroes--Civil rights.
I. Students for a Democratic
Society. Economic Research
and Action Project.
WHi-L

O

O1
O'Brien, James.
    America the beautiful: an essay
    on Daniel Boorstin and Louis
    Hartz. Ann Arbor, Radical Edu-
    cation Project [196]
    9p. 22cm.
    Cover title.
    1. U.S.--History. 2. Hartz,
    Louis, 1919-   The liberal
    tradition in America. 3. Boor-
    stin, Daniel Joseph, 1914-
    The genius of American politics.
    I. Radical Education Project.
    KU-RH, MoU, WHi-L

O2
O'Brien, James.
    A history of the new left, 1960-
    1968. Boston, New England Free
    Press [1969?]
    30 [2]p. 28cm.
    Caption title.
    Reprinted from Radical America,
    1968.
    1. Student movements--History.
    I. New England Free Press.
    WHi-L, KU-RH, MoU

O3
Ochs, David.
    Suggested SDS projects in for-
    eign policy. [n.p., 1965]
    3p. 28cm. (SDS national con-
    vention--working paper)

Caption title.
At head of title: "1965 SDS
National Convention--working
paper."
1. U.S.--Foreign policy.
I. Students for a Democratic
Society. National Convention,
1965.
KU-RH

O4
O'Connor, Harvey, 1897-
    For abolition of the inquisi-
    tional committee of Congress.
    [New York, Emergency Civil
    Liberties Committee? 1957?]
    16p. 22cm.
    Cover title.
    1. U.S. Congress. House.
    Committee on Un-American Acti-
    vities. 2. Legislative investi-
    gations. I. Emergency Civil
    Liberties Committee.
    MiU, WHi-L, DLC, MH, KU-J

O5
O'Connor, James.
    The meaning of economic imper-
    ialism. Detroit, Radical Edu-
    cation Project [1970?]
    24p. 28cm.
    Cover title.
    Reprinted from O'Connor's Cor-
    porate capital.
    1. Capitalism. 2. Imperialism.
    I. Radical Education Project.
    ICU, KU-RH

O6
O'Connor, Lynn.
  Defining reality. [New York,
  Redstockings, 196]
  [4]p. illus. 28cm.
  Caption title.
  1. Woman--Rights of women.
  I. Redstockings of the Women's
  Liberation Movement.
  MoU

O7
Ofari, Earl, ed.
  The black book, edited by Earl
  Ofari [and] composed by Judy
  Davis. [Detroit] Radical Edu-
  cation Project [1970?]
  30p. illus. 14cm.
  1. Negroes. 2. DuBois, William
  Edward Burghardt, 1868-1963.
  3. Fanon, Frantz. 4. Little,
  Malcolm, 1925-1965. I. Radical
  Education Project.
  KU-RH, WHi-L

O8
Ofari, Earl.
  Black liberation (cultural &
  revolutionary nationalism) Ann
  Arbor, Radical Education Project
  [196]
  8 [1]p. illus. 28cm.
  Cover title.
  1. Negroes--Civil rights.
  I. Radical Education Project.
  MoU, MiU

O9
Ofari, Earl.
  Black liberation--cultural and
  revolutionary nationalism. [Rev.
  Detroit, Radical Education Pro-
  ject, 1970]
  [15]p. illus. 22cm.
  Cover title.
  1. Negroes--Civil rights.
  I. Radical Education Project.
  MiU

O10
Ogden, Alan.
  University reform, platform
  statement. Nashville, Southern
  Student Organizing Committee
  [196]
  3p. 28cm.

  1. Virginia. University.
  2. Student movements. I. Southern Student Organizing Committee.
  MoU, WHi-L

O11
Oglesby, Carl.
  Democracy is nothing if it is
  not dangerous. [n.p., Students
  for a Democratic Society, 196]
  [2]p. 28cm.
  Caption title.
  Reprinted from the Peacemaker.
  1. Students for a Democratic
  Society. I. Students for a
  Democratic Society.
  CU-B, KU-RH, MiU-H

O12
Oglesby, Carl.
  "Let us shape the future".
  [Ithaca, N.Y., Glad Day Press,
  196]
  [4]p. port. 28cm.
  Caption title.
  Speech was delivered at the
  Nov. 27, 1965, March on Wash-
  ington to End the War in Viet-
  nam.
  Reprinted from Liberation, Jan.
  1966.
  1. Vietnamese conflict, 1961-
  1975. 2. Liberalism. I. Glad
  Day Press.
  KU-RH

O13
Oglesby, Carl.
  "Let us shape the future".
  [Los Angeles, Students for a
  Democratic Society, 196]
  [6]p. illus. 28cm.
  Caption title.
  Reprinted from Liberation, Jan.
  1966.
  1. U.S.--Pol. & govt.--1963-
        2. Students for a Demo-
  cratic Society.
  MiU-H

O14
Oglesby, Carl.
  "Let us shape the future".
  [New York? Liberation? 1966?]
  folder. 28cm.

Reprinted from Liberation, Jan.
1966.
1. Students for a Democratic Society. I. Liberation.
CU-B

O15
Oglesby, Carl.
  Notes on a decade ready for the
  dustbin. [New York, Liberation,
  1969?]
  13p. illus. 28cm.
  Cover title.
  1. Student movements--History.
  I. Liberation.
  MiU

O16
Oglesby, Carl.
  That bright and necessary day of
  peace [by Carl Oglesby and Todd
  Gitlin. n.p., SDS Prep. Office,
  1965]
  2p. 28cm.
  Caption title.
  1. Vietnamese conflict, 1961-
  1975. 2. U.S.--Military policy.
  I. Gitlin, Todd, jt. auth.
  II. Students for a Democratic
  Society.
  KU-RH, WHi-A

O17
Oglesby, Carl.
  Trapped in a system. Ann Arbor,
  Radical Education Project [196]
  12p. 22cm.
  Cover title.
  Reprinted from Monthly Review,
  Jan. 1966.
  Contents--A complete text of a
  talk delivered by Carl Oglesby
  at March on Washington, November
  27, 1965.
  1. Vietnamese conflict, 1961-
  1975. 2. U.S.--Pol. & govt.--
  1963-   3. Liberalism.
  I. Radical Education Project.
  MoU, KU-RH

O18
Oglesby, Carl.
  Trapped in a system. [Chicago,
  Students for a Democratic Soc-
  iety, 1965]
  [6]p. illus. 22cm.

Cover title.
1. U.S.--Pol. & govt.--1963-
       2. Liberalism. 3. Social
change. I. Students for a Democratic Society.
WHi-L, CU-B

O19
Oglesby, Carl.
  Trapped in a system. [Chicago,
  Students for a Democratic Soc-
  iety, 196]
  [8]p. 22cm.
  Cover title.
  1. Vietnamese conflict, 1961-
  1975. 2. U.S.--Pol. & govt.--
  1963-   3. Liberalism.
  I. Students for a Democratic
  Society.
  WHi-A

O20
Oglesby, Carl.
  U.S. imperialism and South
  Africa. [Goleta, Calif., Santa
  Barbara Resistance, c1969]
  9p.
  Cover title.
  1. Imperialism. 2. U.S.--Rela-
  tions (general) with South
  Africa. 3. South Africa--Rela-
  tions (general) with the U.S.
  WHi-L

O21
Oglesby, Carl.
  The Vietnam war: world revolution and American containment.
  [n.p.] 1965.
  [46]p. 28cm.
  Cover title.
  1. U.S.--Foreign policy.
  2. Underdeveloped areas.
  3. Revolutions. 4. Vietnamese
  conflict, 1961-1975.
  WHi-A

O22
Oglesby, Carl.
  The Vietnam war: world revolution and the American containment. [n.p.] S.D.S., 1965.
  22, 6, 16, [2]p. 28cm.
  Cover title.
  1. Vietnamese conflict, 1961-
  1975. 2. U.S.--Foreign policy.

I. Students for a Democratic
Society.
KU-RH, WHi-A

023
Oglesby, Carl.
  The Vietnam war: world revolu-
  tion and American containment.
  [n.p., Students for a Democratic
  Society?] 1965.
  [48]p.   28cm.
  Cover title.
  1. Vietnamese conflict, 1961-
  1975.   2. U.S.--Foreign policy.
  I. Students for a Democratic
  Society.
  MiU

024
Oglesby, Carl.
  The Vietnam war: world revolution
  and American containment. [Law-
  rence, Kan., Kansas University
  Students for a Democratic Society]
  1965.
  45p.   28cm.
  1. Vietnamese conflict, 1961-
  1975.   2. U.S.--Foreign policy.
  I. Students for a Democratic Society, University of Kansas.
  MiU

025
Okinawa Prefecture Council Against
    Atomic and Hydrogen Bombs.
  Okinawa white paper. Woodmont,
  Conn., Promoting Enduring Peace
  [196]
  4p.   28cm.
  Caption title.
  1. Okinawa--Pol. & govt.   2. U.
  S.--For. rel.--Japan.   3. Japan
  --For. rel.--U.S.   I. Promoting
  Enduring Peace.
  KU-RH

026
Olden, Herman.
  U.S. over Latin America [by]
  Herman Olden in collaboration
  with Labor Research Association.
  [New York] International Pub-
  lishers [1955]
  63p.   illus. 21cm.
  1. Latin America--Econ. condit.
  I. International Publishers.
  KU-J, DLC 55-3874

027
Ole Mole.
  So what are we complaining
  about? A collection of women's
  articles from the Old Mole.
  [Cambridge, Bread and Roses,
  1970]
  48p.   illus., facsim.
  Cover title.
  1. Woman--Rights of women.
  I. Bread and Roses.
  WHi-L

028
Olinick, Michael.
  The campus press. [n.p., Distributed by Students for a
  Democratic Society, 1962]
  13p.   28cm.
  Cover title.
  1. Universities and colleges.
  2. Newspapers.   I. Students for
  a Democratic Society.
  WHi-A, KU-RH

029
Olson, Jon.
  A plan for the post-revolution-
  ary society. [Haleixa, Hawaii
  Free People's Press, 196]
  13p.   26cm.
  Cover title.
  1. Socialism.   2. Revolutions.
  I. Hawaii Free People's Press.
  KU-RH

030
On-the-job oppression of working
    women: a collection of arti-
    cles. Boston, New England
    Free Press [196]
  [9]p.   illus. 28cm.
  Cover title.
  1. Woman--Rights of women.
  I. New England Free Press.
  KU-RH

031
One, two, three...many SDS's
    (a symposium) [by] Paul Glus-
    man, David Horowitz [and] Todd
    Gitlin. [Cicero, Ill., John-
    ny Appleseed Patriotic Publi-
    cations, c1969]
  [7]p.   28cm.
  Cover title.
  Reprinted from Ramparts.

1. Students for a Democratic Society. I. Glusman, Paul. II. Horowitz, David. III. Gitlin,
Todd. IV. Johnny Appleseed Patriotic Publications.
KU-RH

O32
Ontario Federation of Labour.
  Notes on poverty. Toronto, Re-
  search, Information and Publica-
  tions Project, Student Union for
  Peace Action [196]
  7p. 28cm.
  Cover title.
  Excerpts from Poverty in Canada
  published by the Ontario Feder-
  ation of Labour.
  1. Poor--Ontario. I. Student
  Union for Peace Action.
  WHi-A

O33
Operation Freedom.
  Helping across the south. [Cin-
  cinnati, 1966?]
  [4]p. illus. 28cm.
  Caption title.
  1. Negroes--Civil rights.
  KU-RH

O34
Oppenheimer, Martin.
  Alienation or participation: the
  sociology or participatory democracy. [Chicago] Students for
  a Democratic Society, 1966.
  7p. illus.
  Cover title.
  1. Student movements. 2. Democracy. I. Students for a Democratic Society.
  WHi-L

O35
Oppenheimer, Martin.
  Disarmament and the war on pov-

erty. [Philadelphia] National
Peace Literature Service Publication from American Friends
Service Committee [1964]
11p. 22cm.
Cover title.
1. Disarmament. 2. Poverty.
3. U.S. Office of Economic
Opportunity. I. Friends, Society of. American Friends Service Committee.
WHi-A

O36
Oppenheimer, Martin.
  Participative techniques of
  social integration. [Montreal,
  Our Generation, 196]
  10p.
  Caption title.
  At head of title: Radical vigi-
  lance.
  1. Social change. I. Our
  Generation.
  NNU-T

O37
Our Generation.
  Editorial statement on Quebec.
  [Montreal, 196]
  12 leaves. illus.
  Caption title.
  1. Quebec.
  NNU-T

O38
Our Generation.
  Radicals in professions: selected papers [presented at
  the Radicals in the Profession
  Conference. Ann Arbor? Radical Education Project, c1967]
  62p. 23cm.
  1. Radicalism. 2. Professions.
  I. Radical Education Project.
  MoU, WHi-A, WHi-L

‡
P
‡

P1
PLP: a critique. [Detroit] Radi-

cal Education Project [196]
13p. illus. 21cm.

Cover title.
Reprinted from the Old Mole.
1. Progressive Labor Party.
I. Old Mole. II. Radical Educa-
tion Project.
MoU, KU-RH

P2
Pacific Studies Center.
  Black Monday. Boston, New England Free Press [1970?]
  18-23p. illus. 28cm.
  Cover title.
  Reprinted from Ramparts.
  1. Negroes--Employment. 2. Construction workers. I. New England Free Press.
  KU-RH

P3
Pacific Studies Center.
  Indonesia: the making of a neo-
  colony. [Boston, New England
  Free Press, 196]
  10 [1]p. illus. 28cm.
  Cover title.
  1. Indonesia. I. New England
  Free Press.
  MiU

P4
Pacific Studies Center.
  Strike at GM: articles on General Motors Corporation and its
  adversaries. [East Palo Alto,
  Calif.] 1970.
  28p. illus. 28cm.
  Cover title.
  1. General Motors Corporation.
  2. Automobile industry workers.
  3. Strikes and lockouts.
  WHi-L, KU-RH

P5
Paff, Joe.
  Position of farm workers in soc-
  ial and labor legislation. [n.
  p., Slate? 1961?]
  [2]p. 28cm.
  Caption title.
  1. Agricultural laborers.
  I. Slate.
  WHi-A

P6
Palestine National Liberation

Movement.
  Towards a democratic state in
  Palestine. [Detroit, Radical
  Education Project, 1970]
  13 [2]p. 22cm.
  Cover title.
  Contribution to World Confer-
  ence on Palestine, 2d, 1970.
  1. Palestine. 2. Near East--
  Pol. & govt. I. Radical Edu-
  cation Project.
  MiU

P7
Palmer, L.F.
  Out to get the Panthers. Wood-
  mont, Conn., Promoting Enduring
  Peace [1969?]
  [4]p. 28cm.
  Caption title.
  Reprinted from The Nation,
  July 28, 1969.
  1. Black Panther Party. I. Pro-
  moting Enduring Peace.
  KU-RH

P8
Palo Alto Tenants' Union.
  Up against the bulldozers; de-
  velopment in Palo Alto. [Palo
  Alto, Calif.? 1970?]
  44p. 22cm.
  Cover title.
  1. Palo Alto, Calif.--Pol. &
  govt. 2. Cities and towns--
  Planning--Palo Alto, Calif.
  KU-RH

P9
Pankey, Kay.
  Some mighty morning: the legacy
  of Dr. W.E.B. DuBois. San Fran-
  cisco, W.E.B. DuBois Clubs of
  America, 1964.
  10p. 22cm.
  1. Negroes. 2. DuBois, William
  Edward Burghardt, 1868-1963.
  I. DuBois (W.E.B.) Clubs of
  America.
  WHi-A, CU-B

P10
Pantaleone, Joseph.
  Uni-variety; the new practical
  solution to man's greatest crisis. A manifesto for the sal-

vation, the preservation and the
unlimited future progress of all
mankind. Trenton, N.J., United
World Movement, 1961.
13p. 23cm.
Cover title.
1. International organization.
I. United World Movement.
KU-RH

P11
Pantaleone, Joseph.
The urgent need for inter-group
cooperation in the present crisis
(an appeal for immediate action).
Trenton, N.J., United World Move-
ment [1958]
5p. 24cm.
Cover title.
1. International organization.
I. United World Movement.
KU-RH

P12
Pape, Arthur.
How the university fails society.
Toronto, Research, Information
and Publications Project, Student
Union for Peace Action, 1966.
4p. 28cm.
Cover title.
1. Universities and colleges.
2. Education. I. Student Union
for Peace Action.
WHi-A

P13
Pappenheim, Fritz.
Alienation in American society.
New York, Monthly Review Press
[c1967]
32p. 22cm. (Monthly review
pamphlet series, no. 28)
1. Alienation (Social psychology)
I. Monthly Review Press.
MiU, DLC 67-15593

P14
Pardun, Robert.
Election year campaign [by Robert Pardun and others. n.p.,
1968]
[3]p. 28cm.
Caption title.
1. Students for a Democratic
Society. 2. Presidents--Election

--U.S.--1968. 3. Politics,
Practical.
WHi-L

P15
Pardun, Robert.
Election year campaign [by Rob-
ert Pardun and others. Rev.
n.p., 1968]
6p. 28cm.
Caption title.
1. Students for a Democratic
Society. 2. Presidents--Elec-
tion--U.S.--1968. 3. Politics,
Practical.
WHi-L

P16
Pardun, Robert.
Internal education: chapter
structure. [n.p., 1967?]
3p. 28cm.
Caption title.
1. Students for a Democratic
Society.
KU-RH

P17
Park, L.C.
Canadian neocolonialism in Latin
America [by] L.C. Park [and] F.
W. Park. Toronto, Research,
Information, and Publications
Project of Student Union for
Peace Action [196]
11p. 28cm.
Cover title.
1. Latin America--Relations
(general) with Canada. 2. Can-
ada--Relations (general) with
Latin America. 3. Latin Amer-
ica--Pol. & govt. I. Student
Union for Peace Action.
II. Park, F.W., jt. auth.
KU-RH

P18
Parker, Jerry.
Discussion paper on developing
areas. [n.p., Student Peace
Union, 1964]
3p. 28cm.
Caption title.
At head of title: SPU National
Convention, June 1964.
1. Underdeveloped areas.

I. Student Peace Union. National
Convention, 1964.
CU-B

P19
Parker, Michael.
  Proposed program statement. [n.
  p., Student Peace Union, 1964]
  4p. 28cm.
  Caption title.
  1. U.S.--Pol. & govt.--1963-
  2. U.S.--Foreign policy.
  I. Student Peace Union.
  CU-B

P20
Parker, Michael.
  Resolution: fight racism in the
  white working class. [Berkeley,
  Calif.? ISC?; Students for a
  Democratic Society: 196]
  [4]p. 28cm.
  Caption title.
  1. Labor and laboring classes.
  2. Negroes--Civil rights.
  3. Race discrimination. 4. Radicalism. I. Independent Socialist
  Club. II. Students for a Democratic Society.
  KU-RH

P21
Parker, Michael.
  The social sciences and racism
  [by] Mike Parker [and] Jack
  Bloom. [Berkeley] Independent
  Socialist [196]
  6p. 28cm.
  Cover title.
  1. Jensen, Arthur. 2. Negroes.
  3. Intelligence levels--Negroes.
  4. Education. I. Bloom, Jack,
  jt. auth. II. Independent Socialist.
  CU-B

P22
Parker, Robert.
  Proposed high school pamphlet:
  draft...2. [Chicago, Student
  Peace Union, 196]
  15 leaves. 28cm.
  Caption title.
  1. Student movements. 2. Peace.
  I. Student Peace Union.
  KU-RH, CU-B

P23
Parker, Robert.
  SPU high school handbook.
  [Chicago, Student Peace Union,
  196]
  Cover title.
  1. Student movements. 2. High
  schools. I. Student Peace
  Union.
  CU-B

P24
Parker, William.
  Homosexuals and employment.
  [San Francisco?] Corinthian
  Foundation, 1970.
  33p. 22cm.
  1. Homosexuality. I. Corinthian
  Foundation.
  MiU

P25
Parodi, Pierre.
  The use of poor means in helping
  the third world; with an appendix on nutrition in the poor
  countries. Translated by Elizabeth Gravalos Marshall. [1st
  ed. South Acworth, N.H., Greenleaf Books, 1970]
  42p. 22cm.
  Cover title.
  1. Underdeveloped areas. 2. Nutrition. I. Greenleaf Books.
  KU-RH, MiU

P26
Parris, Bob.
  Vietnam and civil rights; two
  papers: a talk with Bob Paris
  from Southern Patriot. Should
  civil rights workers take a
  stand, Howard Zinn from the
  SNCC Voice. Nashville, Southern Student Organizing Committee
  [196]
  2, 5p. 28cm.
  Cover title.
  1. Vietnamese conflict, 1961-
  1975. 2. Negroes--Civil rights.
  I. Southern Patriot. II. Zinn,
  Howard, jt. auth. III. Southern Student Organizing Committee.
  MoU

P27
Parsons, Howard L.
  The young Marx and the young
  generation. [Toronto, Horizons,
  1968]
  60p. 22cm.
  Cover title.
  1. Socialism. 2. Youth--Politi-
  cal activities. 3. Marx, Karl,
  1818-1883.
  MoU

P28
Patterson, William L.
  Ben Davis: crusader for negro
  freedom and socialism, with a
  chronology and bibliography of
  the life and writings of Benjamin J. Davis prepared by Dr.
  Oakley C. Johnson. New York,
  New Outlook Publishers, 1967.
  48p. 22cm.
  1. Negroes--Civil rights.
  2. Communism. 3. Davis, Benjamin Jefferson, 1903-1964.
  I. Johnson, Oakley C. II. New
  Outlook Publishers.
  MiU

P29
Peace Action Center.
  An appeal to our fellow citizens:
  no more nuclear weapons testing.
  Washington [196]
  [4]p. 22cm.
  Caption title.
  1. Peace. 2. Atomic weapons and
  disarmament.
  KU-RH

P30
Peace Action Center.
  An appeal to our fellow citizens:
  stop preparing germ weapons; be-
  gin a world health center at
  Fort Detrick. Washington [196]
  [4]p. 22cm.
  Caption title.
  1. Biological warfare.
  KU-RH

P31
Peace Action Center.
  An appeal to people of the United
  States and the Soviet Union on
  behalf of the human family.

Washington [196]
[4]p. 22cm.
Caption title.
1. Peace. 2. Atomic weapons.
KU-RH

P32
Peace Action Center.
  Bomb tests kill people. Washington [196]
  [4]p. 22cm.
  Caption title.
  1. Atomic weapons and disarmament.
  KU-RH

P33
Peace Action Center.
  Can we learn from the Cuban
  crisis? [Washington, 196]
  [4]p. 22cm.
  Caption title.
  1. U.S.--For. rel.--Russia.
  2. Peace. 3. U.S.--Military
  policy.
  KU-RH

P34
Peace Action Center.
  Turn toward peace; a disarmed
  world community under the reign
  of law. Washington [196]
  [4]p. 22cm.
  Caption title.
  1. Disarmament. 2. Internationalism.
  KU-RH

P35
Peace Action League, Victoria.
  Canada seeks a way out. [Vic-
  toria, B.C., 196]
  4p. 28cm.
  Caption title.
  1. Vietnamese conflict, 1961-
  1975. 2. Canada--Relations
  (general) with the U.S.
  WHi-A

P35a
Peace Activities Coordinating
    Council.
  Peace Activities Coordinating
  Council presents a cooperative
  program for the stimulation of
  peace thinking and activity.

[Los Angeles, 196 ?]
[4]p. 21cm.
Caption title.
1. Peace.
KU-RH

P36
Peace and Freedom Movement.
  The battle of Berkeley. [Berke-
  ley? 1968?]
  [1] leaf. 28cm.
  Caption title.
  1. Law enforcement--Berkeley,
  Calif.
  CU-B

P37
Peace and Freedom Movement.
  Black liberation and white rac-
  ism. [Berkeley, Calif., 1968?]
  [4]p. 22cm.
  Caption title.
  1. Negroes--Civil rights.
  CU-B

P38
Peace and Freedom Movement. Alameda County Steering Committee.
  King is dead. [n.p., 1968?]
  [1] leaf. 36cm.
  Caption title.
  1. King, Martin Luther, 1929-
  1968.
  CU-B

P39
Peace and Freedom Movement. Labor
  Committee.
  Why workers should support Huey
  Newton. [n.p., 1968?]
  [2]p. 28cm.
  Caption title.
  1. Labor and laboring classes.
  2. Newton, Huey P.
  CU-B

P40
Peace and Freedom Movement. Radical Caucus.
  Statement of PFM Radical Caucus.
  [n.p., 1968?]
  [2]p. 36cm.
  Caption title.
  1. Peace and Freedom Party.
  CU-B

P41
Peace and Freedom Movement of
  California.
  An end to futility: build a
  real alternative. [Berkeley?
  1969?]
  4p. 22cm.
  Caption title.
  1. Democratic Party. 2. U.S.--
  Pol. & govt.--1963-
  3. McCarthy, Eugene J. 1916-
  CU-B

P42
Peace and Freedom Party.
  Peace & Freedom Party platform.
  [New York? 1968?]
  10p. 22cm.
  Cover title.
  "Platform passed at Peace and
  Freedom Party membership con-
  vention, Nov. 1968."
  KU-RH

P43
Peace and Freedom Party. Alameda
  County. Convention, 1969.
  Purpose and Program Committee.
  A program for survival. [n.p.]
  1969.
  5 leaves. 28cm.
  1. Social change. 2. U.S.--Pol.
  & govt.--1969-
  CU-B

P44
Peace and Freedom Party. Ecology
  Action.
  What is peace, what is freedom.
  [Abany, Calif.? 1968?]
  [12]p. 28cm.
  Cover title.
  1. Environmental policy.
  CU-B

P45
Peace and Freedom Party. Syracuse, N.Y.
  [PFP disorientation handbook.
  Syracuse, 196]
  15p. illus. 28cm.
  1. Negroes--Civil rights.
  2. Police. 3. Vietnamese conflict, 1961-1975.
  KU-RH

P47
Peacemaker.
  Handbook on nonpayment of war
  taxes. [1st. ed. Cincinnati,
  1963]
  52p.
  1. Tax evasion. 2. Conscientious
  objectors.
  MiU, NUC 65-82462

P48
Peacemaker.
  Handbook on non-payment of war
  taxes. 2d. ed. Raymond, N.H.,
  Peacemaker Movement, 1966.
  42p.
  Cover title.
  1. Tax evasion. 2. Conscientious
  objectors.
  WHi-L, MiU, NUC 66-86409

P49
Peacemaker.
  Handbook on nonpayment of war
  taxes. [3d. ed. South Acworth,
  N.H., Greenleaf Books, 1970]
  49p. 28cm.
  Cover title.
  1. Tax evasion. 2. Conscientious
  objectors. I. Greenleaf Books.
  KU-RH, MoU

P50
Peacemaker.
  Thinking about destruction of
  draft files. [Cincinnati? 1969]
  [2]p. 28cm.
  Caption title.
  Reprinted from Peacemaker, Dec.
  6, 1969.
  1. Government, Resistance to.
  2. Military service, Compulsory.
  KU-RH

P51
Peattie, Lisa.
  Reflections on advocacy planning.
  Ann Arbor, Conference on Radi-
  cals in the Professions, 1967.
  8 [1]p. 28cm.
  1. Poor. 2. Cities and town--
  Planning. I. Conference on Radi-
  cals in the Professions.
  MiU-H

P52
Peck, James.
  Cracking the color line; non-
  violent direct action methods
  of eliminating racial discrim-
  ination. [New York, CORE, 1960]
  24p. illus. 23cm.
  1. Negroes--Civil rights.
  I. Congress of Racial Equality.
  WHi-L, OrU, CLU, IU, RPB, MiU,
  NcU, OO, NcD, KU, KU-J, CU-B,
  DLC 60-1071

P53
Peck, James.
  Cracking the color line; nonviolent direct action methods
  of eliminating racial discrimination [New York, Congress of
  Racial Equality, 196]
  32p. illus.
  Cover title.
  1. Negroes--Civil rights.
  2. Nonviolence. I. Congress of
  Racial Equality.
  WHi-A

P54
Peck, James, ed.
  Sit ins; the student report.
  [New York, CORE, 196]
  [16]p. 22cm.
  Cover title.
  1. Student movements. 2. Ne-
  groes--Civil rights. I. Con-
  gress of Racial Equality.
  WHi-A, CU-B

P55
Peck, James.
  Underdogs vs upperdogs. Canterbury, N.H., Greenleaf Books
  [1969]
  105p. illus. 28cm.
  Cover title.
  1. Conscientious objectors.
  2. Negroes--Civil rights.
  3. Government, Resistance to.
  I. Greenleaf Books.
  MiU, KU-RH

P56
Pelletier, Wilfred.
  Childhood in an Indian village.

Boston, New England Free Press
[1969?]
6-22p. illus. 21cm.
Cover title.
Reprinted from This Magazine is
About Schools, Sp. 1969.
1. Indians of North America--Edu-
cation. I. New England Free
Press.
MiU, KU-RH

P57
Pelton, Richard.
  Life in these United States; in-
  flation: what it is, how it
  works. Boston, New England Free
  Press [1970?]
  26-[34]p. 28cm.
  Cover title.
  Reprinted from PL, June 1970.
  1. Socialism. 2. U.S.--Econ.
  condit. 3. Inflation (Finance)
  4. Capitalism. I. New England
  Free Press.
  KU-RH, MiU

P58
Pelton, Richard.
  Who really rules America? Boston, New England Free Press
  [1970]
  16-36p. 28cm.
  Cover title.
  At head of title: Highly concen-
  trated finance capital controls
  even the largest corporations.
  Reprinted from PL, Feb. 1970.
  1. U.S.--Econ. condit. 2. U.S.--
  Pol. & govt. 3. Corporations.
  4. Finances.
  KU-RH

P59
Penner, Jacob.
  The crisis in municipal government. [Toronto, Communist Party
  of Canada, 1960]
  24p. 13cm.
  1. Municipal government--Canada.
  2. Local taxation--Canada.
  I. Communist Party of Canada.
  NN, CaOTU, NUC 65-102525

P60
People Against Racism.
  The myth of Negro progress.

[Detroit? 196]
6p. 28cm.
Caption title.
1. Negroes--Econ. condit.
2. Negroes--Health and hygiene.
WHi-L, KU-RH

P61
People Against Racism.
  Racism in the United States--an
  introduction. Detroit [196]
  17p. 28cm.
  Cover title.
  1. Negroes--Civil rights.
  MoU, KU-RH

P62
People Against Racism.
  Repression in America. Detroit
  [1969?]
  8p. 28cm.
  Caption title.
  Revised edition.
  1. Negroes--Civil rights.
  2. Law enforcement.
  KU-RH

P63
People Against Racism.
  Repression in America; a background paper prepared by People
  Against Racism for conference
  on "law, order, & the white
  backlash". [Detroit? 196]
  31p. 28cm.
  Cover title.
  1. Police. 2. Negroes--Civil
  rights.
  KU-RH

P64
People Against Racism.
  The war in Vietnam is a racist
  war. [Detroit, 196]
  14p. 28cm.
  Caption title.
  At head of title: PAR preliminary statement on the war in
  Vietnam.
  1. Vietnamese conflict, 1961-
  1975. 2. Negroes--Civil rights.
  3. Race discrimination.
  WHi-L, KU-RH

P65
People Against Racism.

What is relevant research for an
anti-racist organization? [De-
troit? 196]
[8]p. 28cm.
Cover title.
1. Negroes--Civil rights.
KU-RH

P66
People Against Racism, Detroit
    Area.
    A collection of racist myths
about I. Africa and Africans,
II. the peculiar institution,
III. the Civil War, IV. reconstruction, V. reunion and reaction. Ferndale, Mich. [196]
11, 13, 5, 18p. 6 leaves, 28cm.
Cover title.
1. Negroes--Civil rights.
2. Slavery in the U.S.
KU-RH

P67
People's Coalition.
    On liberating occupied minds.
[Berkeley? 196]
10p. 22cm.
Cover title.
1. Universities and colleges.
2. U.S.--Foreign policy.
CU-B

P68
People's peace treaty. [Chicago,
1970?]
[2]p. 28cm.
Caption title.
1. Vietnamese conflict, 1961-
1975.
KU-RH

P69
People's peace treaty. [Chicago,
    New University Conference, etc.,
    1970?]
[2]p. 28cm.
Caption title.
1. Vietnamese conflict, 1961-
1975. I. New University Conference.
KU-RH

P70
People's Press.
    Cops are hired to enforce the

laws. [Detroit, Radical Education Project, 1970?]
[7]p. illus. 22cm.
Cover title.
1. Police. I. Radical Education
Project.
KU-RH

P71
People's Press.
    Don't carry more than you can
eat, or how to survive a little
bit longer than you will if you
keep on doing what you're doing
right now. [San Francisco,
196]
6 [2]p. illus.
Cover title.
1. Police. 2. Law enforcement.
MiU

P72
Pepper, Claude, 1900-
    An American policy for peace; a
program for big three unity and
American-Soviet friendship.
[New York] National Council of
American-Soviet Friendship
[195]
15p. 14x22cm.
Cover title.
1. U.S.--Foreign policy.
I. National Council of American-
Soviet Friendship.
WHi-L, NUC 65-86665

P73
Perdew, John.
    The Los Angeles rebellion of
1965. [Atlanta? 1965]
5p. 28cm.
Caption title.
1. Negroes--Los Angeles.
2. Los Angeles--Race question.
KU-RH

P74
Perdew, John.
    Mississippi legislature: old
wine in new bottles. [Atlanta,
1965]
6p. 28cm.
Caption title.
1. Mississippi--Race question.
WHi-A

P75
Perelman, Michael.
  Misuse of land. [Berkeley, Ecology Action Education Institute,
  1969?]
  [2]p. 28cm.
  Caption title.
  1. Land. 2. Environmental policy.
  I. Ecology Action Educational Institute.
  KU-RH

P76
Perelman, Michael.
  Text delivered by Mike Perelman
  of Berkeley Ecology Action at
  UNESCO conference, November 25,
  1969. Berkeley, Distributed by
  Ecology Action Educational Institute [1969]
  [2]p. 28cm.
  Caption title.
  1. Environmental policy. 2. Pollution. I. Ecology Action Educational Institute.
  KU-RH

P77
Perelson, Ira.
  For a collective and anti-imperialist struggle against the draft
  [by Ira Perelson, Jeff Gordon,
  Chris Pendergast. n.p., 1968]
  4p. 28cm.
  Caption title.
  1. Military service, Compulsory.
  2. Students for a Democratic
  Society. I. Gordon, Jeff, jt.
  auth. II. Pendergast, Chris,
  jt. auth.
  WHi-L

P78
Perez, Dorothy.
  Working with JOIN for a democra-
  tic movement [by] Dorothy Perez,
  Alonzo Brown and Sam Assmar.
  Prepared for the Cleveland Com-
  munity People's Conference. [n.
  p., 196]
  2, 5, 3p. 28cm.
  Cover title.
  1. Jobs or Income Now Community
  Union. I. Brown, Alonzo, jt.
  auth. II. Assmar, Sam, jt. auth.
  WHi-A

P79
Perlman, Fredy.
  The reproduction of daily life.
  [Kalamazoo, Mich., Black & Red,
  1969]
  20p.
  Cover title.
  1. Socialism. 2. Capitalism.
  I. Black & Red.
  WHi-L

P80
Perlmutter, Nathan.
  We don't help blacks by hurting
  whites. New York, League for
  Industrial Democracy [c1968]
  [8]p. 28cm. (Looking forward
  no. 14)
  Cover title.
  1. Negroes--Civil rights.
  I. League for Industrial Demo-
  cracy.
  NNU-T, WHi-L, KU-RH

P81
Perlo, Victor.
  Fuera la bota militar se Santo
  Domingo. [New York, New Outlook
  Publishers, 1965]
  35p. 20cm.
  Translation of Marines in Santo
  Domingo.
  1. Dominican Republic--For. rel.
  --U.S. 2. U.S.--For. rel.--
  Dominican Republic. I. New Out-
  look Publishers.
  TxU, NUC 67-1064

P82
Perlo, Victor.
  How the Soviet economy works,
  an interview with A.I. Mikoyan,
  First Deputy Prime Minister of
  the U.S.S.R. New York, International Publishers [1961]
  63p. 21cm.
  1. Russia--Economic policy--
  1959-   2. Russia--Econ.
  condit.--1955-   I. Mikoian,
  Anastas Ivanovich, 1895-
  I. International Publishers.
  InU, NN, NNC, KyU, MiU, MnU,
  IU, RPB, DLC 61-16824

P83
Perlo, Victor.

Marines in Santo Domingo. [New
York, New Outlook Publishers,
1965]
31p. illus. 20cm.
Cover title.
1. Dominican Republic--For. rel.
--U.S. 2. U.S.--For. rel.--Dom-
inican Republic. I. New Outlook
Publishers.
KU-RH, WHi-L, TxU, CLSU

P84
Perlo, Victor.
  The Vietnam profiteers. [New
  Outlook Publishers, 1966]
  47p. 20cm.
  1. Profiteering--Vietnam.
  2. Vietnamese conflict, 1961-
  1975--Economic aspects. I. New
  Outlook Publishers.
  MiU, MnU, MB, DLC 67-1271, NBuU

P85
Perlo, Victor.
  Why the Vietnamese people are
  winning. [New York, Center for
  Marxist Education, 1970?]
  [2]p. 28cm.
  Caption title.
  Reprinted from Daily World, Feb.
  3, 1970.
  1. Vietnamese conflict, 1961-
  1975. I. Center for Marxist
  Education.
  CU-B

P86
Peslikis, Irene.
  Resistance to consciousness.
  Cambridge, Distributed by Female
  Liberation [1970?]
  [1] leaf. 28cm.
  Caption title.
  1. Woman--Rights of women.
  I. Female Liberation.
  KU-RH

P87
Peslikis, Irene.
  Resistance to consciousness.
  [New York, Redstockings, 196]
  2p. 28cm.
  Caption title.
  1. Woman--Rights of women.
  I. Redstockings of the Women's
  Liberation Movement.
  MoU

P88
Petersen, Arnold, 1885-
  Bourgeois socialism; its rise
  and collapse in America. New
  York, New York Labor News Co.,
  1963.
  208p. 18cm.
  1. Thomas, Norman. 2. Socialist Party (U.S.) 3. Debs,
  Eugene Victor, 1855-1926.
  4. Socialist Labor Party.
  I. New York Labor News Co.
  KU-RH

P89
Petersen, Arnold, 1885-
  Capital and labor. New York,
  New York Labor News Co., 1959.
  80p. illus. 19cm.
  Cover title.
  1. Labor and laboring classes.
  I. New York Labor News Co.
  MiU

P90
Petersen, Arnold, 1885-
  Capitalism is doomed; socialism
  is the hope of humanity. New
  York, New York Labor News Co.
  [1961]
  30p. 19cm.
  "Third printing."
  1. Socialism. 2. U.S.--Pol. &
  govt. 3. Capitalism. 4. De
  Leon, Daniel, 1852-1914.
  I. New York Labor News Co.
  KU-RH

P91
Petersen, Arnold, 1885-
  Constitution of the United
  States: founding of the bour-
  geois republic. New York, New
  York Labor News Co., 1959.
  93p. facsims., port. 20cm.
  1. U.S. Constitution. 2. U.S.
  --Pol. & govt. I. De Leon,
  Daniel, 1852-1914. II. New
  York Labor News Co.
  KU, NB, NUC 68-50418, CU-B

P92
Petersen, Arnold, 1885-
  Daniel De Leon: social archi-
  tect. Brooklyn, New York Labor
  News Co., 1966.

59p. illus. 19cm.
1. De Leon, Daniel, 1852-1914.
MU, NUC 68-62772

P93
Petersen, Arnold, 1885-
  Inflation of prices or deflation
  of labor? New York, New York
  Labor News Co., 1961.
  32p. 18cm.
  "Fifth printing."
  1. Inflation (Finance) 2. Socialism. 2. Socialist Labor Party. I. New York Labor News Co.
  KU-RH

P94
Petersen, Arnold, 1885-
  Karl Marx and Marxian science.
  Brooklyn, New York Labor News
  Co., 1967.
  191p. 19cm.
  1. Marx, Karl, 1818-1883. I. New
  York Labor News Co.
  CU-B

P95
Petersen, Arnold, 1885-
  Marxism vs. Soviet despotism.
  New York, New York Labor News
  Co., 1958.
  52p. illus. 19cm.
  1. De Leon, Daniel, 1852-1914.
  2. Socialism. I. New York Labor
  News Co.
  WU, CLU, NN, CU-B, DLC 58-4142

P96
Petersen, Arnold, 1885-
  Marxism vs. Soviet despotism.
  New York, New York Labor News
  Co., 1959.
  50p. 19cm.
  "Second printing."
  1. Lenin, Vladimir Il'ich, 1870-
  1924. 2. De Leon, Daniel, 1852-
  1914. 3. Communism--Russia.
  I. New York Labor News Co.
  KU-RH

P97
Petersen, Arnold, 1885-
  Proletarian democracy vs. dic-
  tatorship and despotism. New
  York, New York Labor News Com-
  pany, 1955.

63p. 19cm.
1. Socialism. 2. Despotism.
I. New York Labor News Co.
CU-B

P98
Petersen, Arnold, 1885-
  War why? [New York, New York
  Labor News Co., 1962]
  61p. 18cm.
  "Seventh printing."
  1. War. 2. Capitalism. I. New
  York Labor News Co.
  KU-RH

P99
Petran, Tabitha.
  Zionism: a political critique.
  [Boston, New England Free
  Press, 196]
  20p. maps. 22cm.
  Cover title.
  1. Zionism. 2. Israel. 3. Pal-
  estine. 4. Jewish-Arab rela-
  tions. I. New England Free
  Press.
  KU-RH

P100
Petras, James.
  What is happening in Peru? [By]
  James Petras & Nelson Rimensny-
  der. Boston, New England Free
  Press [1970?]
  15-28p. 22cm.
  Cover title.
  Reprinted from Monthly Review,
  Feb. 1970.
  1. Peru--Pol. & govt. I. Rimen-
  snyder, Nelson, jt. auth.
  I. New England Free Press.
  MiU

P101
Phelan, Lana Clarke.
  Abortion laws: the cruel fraud.
  San Francisco, Society for Hu-
  man Abortion [1968?]
  6p. 28cm.
  Cover title.
  "Speech presented at California
  Conference on Abortion in Santa
  Barbara on February 10, 1968."
  1. Abortion. 2. Society for
  Human Abortion.
  CU-B

P102
Phelan, William D.
  The authoritarian prescription.
  [Philadelphia, American Friends
  Service Committee, 1969]
  7p. 28cm.
  Cover title.
  At head of title: Nixon's 'sou-
  thern' strategy.
  Reprinted from The Nation, Nov.
  3, 1969.
  1. U.S.--Pol. & govt.--1969-
  2. Republican Party--Southern
  strategy. I. Friends, Society
  of. American Friends Service
  Committee.
  KU-RH

P103
Phelps, Linda.
  Mirror, mirror...fashion, beauty,
  and woman's liberation. [Kansas
  City, Mo., Women's Liberation,
  1969?]
  [2] leaves. 28cm.
  Cover title.
  1. Woman--Rights of women.
  KU-RH

P104
Phelps, Linda.
  [untitled. Kansas City, Mo.?
  1969?]
  4 leaves. 28cm.
  1. Woman--Rights of women.
  KU-RH

P105
Philadelphia Resistance.
  Resistance programs '69. [Phila-
  delphia, 1969?]
  [4]p. illus. 22cm.
  Cover title.
  1. Military service, Compulsory.
  2. Government, Resistance to.
  KU-RH

Philadelphia Spartacist League.
  see also
Spartacist League
Bay Area Spartacist League
Campus Spartacist Club, Berkeley,
  Calif.
New York City Spartacist League.

P106
Philadelphia Spartacist League.
  Which road for SDS? [Philadel-
  phia, 1968]
  [4]p. 28cm.
  Caption title.
  1. Students for a Democratic
  Society.
  WHi-L

P107
Pickus, Robert.
  The ABM and a world without
  war, by Robert Pickus, with
  editorial assistance of David
  Lure. [Berkeley? World Without
  War Council, 1969]
  iv, 86p.
  1. Antimissile missiles. 2. U.
  S.--Military policy. I. World
  Without War Council.
  WHi-L

P108
Pickus, Robert.
  To end war; a citizen's intro-
  duction, ideas, books, organi-
  zations, by Robert Pickus and
  Robert Woito. Berkeley, World
  Without War Council [1969?]
  14 leaves. 28cm.
  Cover title.
  1. War. 2. Peace. I. World
  Without War Council. II. Woito,
  Robert S., jt. auth.
  KU-RH

P109
Pickus, Robert.
  Vietnam Day--Berkeley. Speech
  delivered...at Vietnam rally,
  May 21, 1965...[Berkeley? 1965?]
  7p. 28cm.
  1. Vietnamese conflict, 1961-
  1975. I. National Coordinating
  Committee to End the War in
  Vietnam. Vietnam Day Committee,
  Berkeley.
  CU-B

P110
Piercy, Marge.
  The grand coolie damn. [Boston,
  New England Free Press, 1970?]
  14p. illus. 21cm.

Reprinted from Leviathan, Nov.
1969.
1. Woman--Rights of women.
2. Radicalism. I. New England
Free Press.
KU-RH

P111
Pierpoint, Robert Joe.
New stage in the longshore strug-
gle. New York, Workers Defense
League [196]
67-71p. 22cm.
Cover title.
Reprinted from New Politics.
1. International Longshoremen's
and Warehousemen's Union.
2. Longshoremen. I. Workers
Defense League.
KU-RH

P112
Pillsbury, Peter W.
Some thoughts on white supremacy
and the church. Detroit, People
Against Racism, 1968.
6p. 28cm.
Caption title.
1. Race discrimination. 2. Ne-
groes--Civil rights. 3. Religion
and sociology. 4. Church and
race problems. 5. Indians of
North America. I. People Against
Racism.
KU-RH, WHi-L

P113
Pittman, Margrit.
Sense and nonsense about Berlin,
by Margrit and John Pittman [New
York, New Century Publishers,
1962]
60p. 19cm.
1. Berlin question (1945-   )
I. Pittman, John, jt. auth.
II. New Century Publishers.
MiU

P114
Plekhanov, Georgii Vallentinovich,
    1856-1918.
The bourgeois revolution: the
political birth of capitalism.
Translated by Henry Kuhn. New
York, New York Labor News Co.,
1955.

31p. 19cm.
1. France--History--Revolution.
2. Capitalism. I. New York
Labor News Co.
KU-RH

P115
Poinsett, Alex.
Thirteen years after 1954. [New
York, Committee of 100, 196]
[12]p. illus.
Cover title.
1. Negroes--Civil rights.
I. Committee of 100.
MiU

P116
Polianskii, Dmitrii Stepanovich.
The Russian Federation, by
Smitri S. Polyansky. New York,
Crosscurrents Press [1960]
48p. illus. ports. 22cm.
[Documents of current history,
no. 17]
1. Russia--Descr. & trav.
I. Crosscurrents Press.
NNC, ICU, MH, DLC

P117
Polin, Charlotte.
Why North Viet-Nam is being
combed. [n.p., 196]
5p. 28cm.
Caption title.
1. Vietnamese conflict, 1961-
1975.
KU-RH

P118
Polites, Bernice.
In memory of my father. [New
York, American Committee for
Protection of Foreign Born,
1967]
folder. illus. 22x9cm.
Cover title.
1. Emigration and immigration.
I. American Committee for Pro-
tection of Foreign Born.
KU-RH

P119
Political Action for Peace, New
    England Committee.
Platform for 1962 elections.
[Cambridge, 1962]

folder. 21x10cm.
Cover title.
1. Disarmament. 2. Peace. 3. U.
S.--Pol. & govt.--1963-
KU-RH

P120
Political Affairs.
  Communism and religion [by Gus
  Hall and others.] New York, 1966.
  97p. 21cm.
  Political Affairs; theoretical
  journal of the Communist Party,
  U.S.A., XLV (July, 1966)
  1. Communism and religion.
  I. Hall, Gus.
  MH-AH, NUC 67-57773

P121
Political Affairs.
  The ideological struggle in the
  American left. New York, New
  Century Publishers, 1963.
  22p. 19cm.
  "An editorial article reprinted
  from Political Affairs, August
  1963."
  1. Communism. 2. Socialism.
  3. Liberalism. I. New Century
  Publishers.
  KU-RH, MiU, WHi-L

P122
Political and armed struggle.
    [Washington, Middle East and
    Information Project, 196]
  47p. 22cm.
  Cover title.
  1. Jewish-Arab relations.
  2. Palestine National Liberation
  Movement. 3. Near East--Pol. &
  govt. I. Middle East Research
  and Information Project.
  KU-RH

P123
Pollack, Norman, 1933-
  Southern populism. Nashville,
  Southern Student Organizing Com-
  mittee and New England Free Press
  [196]
  [4]p. 28cm.
  Cover title.
  1. Populist Party. 2. Negroes--
  Civil rights. I. New England
  Free Press. II. Southern Student

Organizing Committee.
KU-RH

P124
Pollard, Vickie.
  They almost seized the time, by
  Vickie Pollard & Donna Keck.
  [Detroit, Radical Education
  Project, 1970?]
  13p. illus. 22cm.
  Cover title.
  1. Woman--History and condition
  of women. I. Radical Education
  Project. II. Keck, Donna, jt.
  auth.
  MiU

P125
Poor black women; including birth
    control pills and black child-
    ren, a statement by the Black
    Unity (Peekskill, N.Y.); a
    response, by black sisters;
    poor black women, by Patricia
    Robinson. [Boston, New Eng-
    land Free Press, 196]
  [4]p. 28cm.
  Caption title.
  1. Negroes. 2. Woman--Rights
  of women. 3. Poverty. I. Robinson, Patricia, jt. auth.
  II. New England Free Press.
  KU-RH

P126
Poor People's Campaign.
  Statement of purpose. [n.p.,
  1968?]
  Caption title.
  1. Poverty. 2. Negroes--Civil
  rights.
  CU-B

P127
Pope, Danny.
  Chester, Pa.: a case study in
  community organizations, by
  Danny Pope [and others. n.p.,
  196]
  5p. 28cm.
  Caption title.
  1. Chester, Pa. 2. Poor--Ches-
  ter, Pa. 3. Negroes--Chester,
  Pa.
  WHi-L

P128
Pope, Danny.
  Chester, Pa.: a case study in
  community organization, by Danny
  Pope [and others] New York, Distributed by Students for a Democratic Society; Economic Research
  and Action Project [196]
  5p. 28cm.
  Cover title.
  1. Community organization.
  2. Chester, Pa.--Pol. & govt.
  3. Negroes--Chester, Pa. I. Students for a Democratic Society.
  Economic Research and Action
  Project.
  WHi-A, KU-RH, CU-B

P129
Pope, Denis.
  Democracy in the university.
  Ann Arbor, Radical Education
  Project [1965?]
  12p. 28cm.
  Cover title.
  1. Democracy. 2. Universities
  and colleges. I. Radical Edu-
  cation Project.
  MiU

P130
Pope, Richard K.
  Democracy and the university.
  Ann Arbor, Radical Education
  Project [196]
  8p. 28cm.
  Cover title.
  1. Democracy. 2. Universities
  and colleges. I. Radical Edu-
  cation Project.
  NNU-T

P131
Pope, W.H.
  Let Canada lead; a new defense
  policy, by Major W.H. Pope MC
  and the Defense Research Committee of the Combined Universities Campaign for Nuclear Disarmament. Montreal [1960?]
  16p. 22cm. (Discussion pamphlet)
  Cover title.
  1. Disarmament. 2. Canada--Mili-
  tary policy. I. Combined University Campaign for Nuclear
  Disarmament. Defense Research

Committee.
  KU-RH

P132
Popper, Walt.
  The Thursday group: a history
  and analysis. Ann Arbor, Con-
  ference on Radicals in the
  Professions, 1967.
  4p. 28cm.
  Cover title.
  1. Education. 2. Teachers.
  I. Conference on Radicals in
  the Professions.
  MiU-H

P133
Posey, Barbara Ann.
  Why I sit in. [New York, National Association for the Advancement of Colored People,
  1960]
  [4]p. 22cm.
  Cover title.
  1. Negroes--Civil rights.
  I. National Association for
  the Advancement of Colored
  People.
  WHi-A

P134
Potter, Paul.
  The intellectual as an agent of
  social change. [n.p.] Liberal
  Study Group [196]
  7p. 28cm.
  Cover title.
  1. Intellectuals. 2. Social
  change. I. Liberal Study
  Group.
  MiU

P135
Potter, Paul.
  The intellectual as an agent of
  social change. [n.p., S.D.S.?
  1963?]
  7p. 28cm.
  Cover title.
  1. Intellectuals. 2. Social
  change. I. Students for a
  Democratic Society.

P136
Potter, Paul.
  The intellectual as an agent of

social change. New York, Students
for a Democratic Society and its
Economic Research and Action Project [1963?]
7p.
Cover title.
1. Student movements. 2. Intellectuals. 3. Social change.
I. Students for a Democratic Society. Economic Research and Action Project.
WHi-A

P137
Potter, Paul.
  The new radical encounters the
  university. San Francisco, Students for a Democratic Society
  [196]
  7p. 28cm.
  Cover title.
  1. Student movements. I. Students for a Democratic Society.
  MiU

P138
Potter, Paul.
  Research and education in community action projects. Chicago,
  Students for a Democratic Society [196]
  9p. 28cm.
  Cover title.
  1. Community organization.
  2. Education. I. Students for
  a Democratic Society.
  CU-B, MiU

P139
Potter, Paul.
  Research and education in the
  community action project. New
  York, Students for a Democratic
  Society and its Economic Research
  and Action Project [196]
  9p. 28cm.
  Cover title.
  1. Community organization.
  I. Students for a Democratic Soc-
  iety. Economic Research and Ac-
  tion Project.
  WHi-A

P140
Potter, Paul.
  SDS and foreign policy. [n.p.,

1965]
  [1] leaf. 28cm.
  Caption title.
  At head of title: "1965 nation-
  al convention--working paper."
  1. U.S.--Foreign policy.
  I. Students for a Democratic
  Society. National Convention,
  1965.
  WHi-A

P141
Potter, Paul.
  [Speech delivered on April 17,
  1965 during the march on Washington to end the war in Vietnam. Chicago, Students for a
  Democratic Society, 196]
  [8]p. 20cm.
  1. Vietnamese conflict, 1961-
  1975. I. Students for a Democratic Society.
  KU-RH

P142
Potter, Paul.
  The university and the cold war.
  [n.p.] Liberal Study Group
  [196]
  7p. 28cm.
  Cover title.
  1. Universities and colleges.
  2. U.S.--For. rel.--Russia.
  2. Russia--For. rel.--U.S.
  Liberal Study Group.
  MiU

P143
Potter, Paul.
  The university and the cold war.
  Chicago, Students for a Democra-
  tic Society [196]
  10p. 22cm.
  Cover title.
  1. Universities and colleges.
  2. U.S.--For. rel.--Russia.
  3. World politics--1955-
  I. Students for a Democratic
  Society.
  KU-RH, CU-B

P144
Potter, Paul.
  The university and the cold war.
  [Los Angeles, Students for a
  Democratic Society, 1964?]

7p. 28cm.
Cover title.
1. Universities and colleges.
2. U.S.--Foreign policy. I. Students for a Democratic Society.
MiU-H

P145
Potter, Paul.
The university and the cold war.
New York, Students for a Democratic Society and its Peace Research and Education Project
[196]
7p. 28cm.
Cover title.
1. Universities and colleges.
2. U.S.--For. rel.--Russia.
3. Russia--For. rel.--U.S.
I. Students for a Democratic Society. Peace Research and Education Project.
WHi-A

P146
Power, power, who's got the power?
    (A primer in military law) from
    the Potemkin Bookshop. [Boston, New England Free Press,
    196]
[20]p. 14cm.
Cover title.
1. Military law. I. New England Free Press.
KU-RH

P147
Preliminary report on the grape
    strike. [n.p., Students for a
    Democratic Society? 196]
8p. 28cm.
Caption title.
1. Chavez, Cesar Estrada.
2. Strikes and lockouts--Vineyard laborers--Calif. 3. National Farm Workers Association. I. Students for a Democratic Society.
KU-RH

P148
Presbyterian Service Committee for
    Religious Objectors.
To be a conscientious objector.
    [Rev. Philadelphia, 1968.]
[8]p. 19cm.
Cover title.

1. Conscientious objectors.
KU-RH

P149
Price, Judith.
Politics of violence. [n.p.,
1970?]
[1] leaf. 28cm.
Caption title.
1. Woman--Rights of women.
2. Marriage.
KU-RH

P150
Price, Margaret (Walzen)
The Negro and the ballot in the
South. Atlanta, Southern Regional Council, 1959.
83p. tables. 23cm.
1. Negroes--Politics and suffrage. 2. Voters, Registration of--Southern States. I. Southern Regional Council.
MnU, MiU, NcU, CU, NjP, DLC 60-1006

P151
Price, Margaret (Walzem)
The negro voter in the South.
Atlanta, Southern Regional
Council [1967?]
2, 55p. tables. 23cm.
1. Negroes--Southern States.
2. Voting--Southern States.
I. Southern Regional Council.
MH-L, ViU, ICU, NN, GU, MsU,
AAP, TxDaM

P152
Price, Margaret (Walzem)
Neighborhoods, where human relations begin. Atlanta, Southern Regional Council, 1967.
44p.
1. Negroes--Philadelphia.
2. Negroes--Washington, D.C.
3. Negroes--Baltimore. I. Southern Regional Council.
DHUD, PPULC NjP, NUC 68-69148

P153
Price, Margaret (Walzem)
Toward a solution of the sit-in
controversy. Atlanta, Southern
Regional Council, 1960.
20p. 28cm.

Cover title.
1. Negroes--Civil rights.   I. Southern Regional Council.
WHi-A

P154
Price, William A.
  SNCC charts a course; an inter-
view with Stokely Carmichael, by
William A. Price. [New York,
National Guardian, 196]
  11p. illus.
  Cover title.
  1. Student Nonviolent Coordina-
ting Committee. 2. Negroes--
Civil rights.   I. Carmichael,
Stokely.   II. National Guardian.
MiU

P155
Pritchard, William A.
  Italy--"tragedy or farce." [n.
p., 1970]
  4p. 28cm.
  Caption title.
  1. Italy--Pol. & govt. 2. Soc-
ialism--Italy.
  CU-B

P156
Pritt, D.N.
  Land reform in China. [New York,
New World Review, 1957?]
  23p. 22cm.
  Cover title.
  Reprinted from New World Review,
January 1957.
  1. Land--China (People's Republic
of China, 1949-   ) I. New
World Review.
  KU-J

P157
Progressive Labor Party.
  Black and white construction
workers divided by the bosses.
Boston, New England Free Press
[1970]
  50-55p. 28cm.
  Cover title.
  Reprinted from PL, Feb. 1970.
  1. Labor and laboring classes.
  2. Negroes--Civil rights.   I. New
England Free Press.
  MiU

P158
Progressive Labor Party.
  Black liberation. [Brooklyn,
196]
  75 [3]p. illus. 28cm.
  Cover title.
  1. Negroes--Civil rights.
  NNU-T, MiU

P159
Progressive Labor Party.
  Build a base in the working
class. [Brooklyn, 1969]
  81p. illus. 22cm.
  Includes a report and speech by
Milton Rosen.
  1. Labor and laboring classes.
  I. Rosen, Milton.
  KU-RH

P160
Progressive Labor Party.
  Don't be a sucker. [New York,
1967?]
  [24]p. 16cm.
  Cover title.
  1. Negroes--Civil rights.
  CU-B

P161
Progressive Labor Party.
  Fight police terror; smash
racism. [Brooklyn, 196]
  14p. 28cm.
  Cover title.
  1. Police. 2. Negroes--Civil
rights.
  CU-B

P162
Progressive Labor Party.
  Get the U.S. out of Vietnam
now. Vote Nakashima for state
assembly 69th A.D. [Brooklyn,
196]
  29p. illus. 28cm.
  Cover title.
  1. Vietnamese conflict, 1961-
1975.
  NNU-T

P163
Progressive Labor Party.
  Latest ruling class mechanism
of cooption. [Brooklyn, 1969?]

[2] leaves. 28cm.
Caption title.
1. Peace and Freedom Party.
CU-B

P164
Progressive Labor Party.
  National Committee report of the
  Progressive Labor Party on our
  position on China. [n.p., 1970?]
  9 leaves. 28cm.
  Caption title.
  1. China (People's Republic of
  China, 1949-   )
  NNU-T

P165
Progressive Labor Party.
  A plan for black liberation (articles by the Progressive Labor
  Party) [Brooklyn, 196]
  75p. illus. 28cm.
  Cover title.
  1. Labor and laboring classes.
  2. Negroes--Civil rights.
  3. Socialism.
  WHi-L

P166
Progressive Labor Party.
  Progressive Labor Party trade
  union program. [New York, 1966]
  58p. illus.
  Cover title.
  1. Trade-unions. 2. Labor and
  laboring classes.
  WHi-L

P167
Progressive Labor Party.
  Rank-and-file caucuses for
  workers' power in trade unions.
  [Brooklyn, 1970?]
  14p. 21x11cm.
  1. Trade-unions.
  CU-B

P168
Progressive Labor Party.
  Road to revolution; the outlook
  of the Progressive Labor Movement. New York, 1964.
  126p. 20cm.
  1. Revolutions.
  NNU-T

P169
Progressive Labor Party.
  Students and revolution; what is
  the Progressive Labor Party.
  [Brooklyn, 196]
  36p. illus. 18cm.
  1. Student movements. 2. Revolutions.
  NNU-T

P170
Progressive Labor Party.
  Those who are guilty are going
  to pay. [New York, 196]
  [8]p. 17cm.
  Caption title.
  1. Johnson, Eric.
  CU-B

P171
Progressive Labor Party.
  Vietnam and the ruling class.
  [Berkeley, 1966?]
  [2]p. 28cm.
  Caption title.
  1. Vietnamese conflict, 1961-
  1975.
  CU-B

P172
Progressive Labor Party.
  Vietnam: defeat U.S. imperialism. [Brooklyn, 196]
  71p. illus. 28cm.
  Cover title.
  1. Vietnamese conflict, 1961-
  1975.
  NNU-T

P173
Progressive Labor Party.
  Vietnam; people's war or negotiations? [Brooklyn, 196]
  56 [1]p. illus. 28cm.
  Cover title.
  1. Vietnamese conflict, 1961-
  1975.
  NNU-T

P174
Progressive Labor Party.
  Who is really guilty? LBJ,
  Yorty, General Motors. John
  Harris arrested for "criminal
  syndicalism". Los Angeles

[1966?]
[1] leaf. 28cm.
Caption title.
1. Harris, John. 2. Negroes--
Civil rights.
CU-B

P175
Progressive Labor Party. Black
    Liberation Commission.
Black liberation--now! [Harlem,
N.Y., 196]
24p. illus.
Cover title.
1. Negroes--Civil rights.
MiU, WHi-L

P176
Progressive Labor Party. Black
    Liberation Commission.
Notes on black liberation. New
York [1965?]
25 [4]p. 28cm.
Cover title.
Reprinted from Progressive Labor,
Oct. 1965.
1. Negroes--Civil rights.
NNU-T, CU-B, MiU, CU-B

P177
Progressive Labor Party. Black
    Liberation Commission.
The revolt in Watts and the com-
ing battle. New York [196]
[4]p. illus. 28cm.
Cover title.
1. Negroes--Los Angeles. 2. Los
Angeles--Riots.
MiU, NNU-T

P178
Progressive Labor Party. Educa-
    tion Committee.
We must rule the school. [New
York, 1967]
[36]p. illus.
Cover title.
1. New York (City)--Public
schools. 2. Negroes--Education.
WHi-L, NNU-T

P179
Progressive Labor Party. Harlen
    Branch.
The plot against black America.
[Brooklyn, 196]

14 [1]p. illus. 28cm.
Cover title.
1. Police. 2. Negroes--Civil
rights.
CU-B, NNU-T, WHi-L

P180
Progressive Labor Party. National
    Committee.
Build a base in the working
class. [Brooklyn, 1969?]
81p. 22cm.
Cover title.
1. Labor and laboring classes.
2. Social classes.
MiU

P181
Progressive Labor Party. Student
    Club, Berkeley, Calif.
Escalation at home. [Berkeley,
1966?]
[1] leaf. 36cm.
Caption title.
1. Student movements--Berkeley,
Calif. 2. National Coordinating
Committee to End the War in
Vietnam. Vietnam Day Committee,
Berkeley.
WHi-L

P182
Progressive Labor Party. Student
    Collective.
Students and revolution; what
is the Progressive Labor Party.
[New York, 196]
36p. illus.
Cover title.
1. Student movements.
WHi-L

P183
Progressive Labor Party. Trade
    Union Division.
Progressive Labor Party union
program. Brooklyn [1965?]
16p. 28cm.
Cover title.
1. Trade-unions.
CU-B

P184
Progressive Labor Party. Trade
    Union Division.
Progressive Labor Party trade

union program. [Brooklyn, 1966]
58p. 17cm.
Cover title.
1. Trade-unions.
CU-B

P185
Progressive Workers Movement of
    Canada.
Conference statement of the Progressive Workers Movement. [n.
p., 196]
[3]p. 36cm.
Caption title.
1. U.S.--Foreign policy. 2. Can-
ada--For. rel.--U.S.
WHi-A

P186
Promoting Enduring Peace.
  Insights into the problem of
  Viet Nam. [Woodmont, Conn.,
  196]
  [2]p. 28cm.
  Caption title.
  1. Vietnamese conflict, 1961-
  1975.
  KU-RH

P187
Promoting Enduring Peace.
  Let us make peace in Vietnam.
  [Woodmont, 196]
  [12]p. 22cm.
  Caption title.
  1. Vietnamese conflict, 1961-
  1975.
  KU-RH

P188
Promoting Enduring Peace.
  Religion speaks for peace: official pronouncements of major religious bodies. Woodmont, Conn.,
  195]
  47p. 18cm.

1. Peace. 2. Religion.
KU-RH

P189
Prospectus for the Mississippi
    freedom summer, [n.p., 196]
  7 leaves. 28cm.
  Caption title.
  1. Mississippi--Race question.
  2. Negroes--Mississippi.
  KU-RH

P190
Provisional Defense Committee.
  What happened on June 15? [New
  York, 195]
  12p.
  Cover title.
  1. Disarmament. 2. Pacifism.
  3. Civilian defense.
  MoU

P191
Provisional Student Civil Liber-
    ties Coordinating Committee.
  Report on HUAC hearings on Cuba,
  Sept. 12-13, 1963. [Washington,
  1963]
  4 leaves. 28cm.
  Caption title.
  1. Student movements. 2. U.S.
  Congress. House. Committee on
  Un-American Activities.
  WHi-A

P192
Puerto Rican Youth Movement.
  Puerto Rico: a colony of the
  United States. [Boston, New
  England Free Press, 1969?]
  14p. illus. 28cm.
  Cover title.
  At head of title: Viva Puerto
  Rico libre.
  1. Puerto Rico--Relations (gen-
  eral) with the U.S. 2. Puerto
  Rico--Pol. & govt.
  KU-RH

‡
Q
‡

Q1
Que, Don Zuan.
  Sick of the war, Say so. Chicago, Catholic Worker [1966?]
  [1] leaf. 36cm.
  Caption title.
  1. Vietnamese conflict, 1961-
  1975.
  CU-B

Q2
Queens Committee to End the War in
    Vietnam.
  Why we are running an independent campaign for congress.
  [Flushing, N.Y., 196]
  Caption title.
  1. U.S.--Pol. & govt. 2. Vietnamese conflict, 1961-1975.
  WHi-L

Q3
Questions and alternatives for the

sciences. [Madison, 196]
[12]p. 22cm.
Cover title.
1. Student movements. 2. Research. 3. Science.
WHi-A

Q4
Questions facing Progressive Labor. Also James Weinstein and
    the revolt against anti-theory.
    [New York, Bulletin of International Socialism, 1967?]
i, 25 [2]p.
1. Socialism. 2. Progressive
Labor Party. 3. Weinstein,
James, 1926-   4. Russia--
Foreign policy. 5. China--Foreign policy. I. Bulletin of
International Socialism.
WHi-L

‡
R
‡

R1
Rader, Gary.
  A statement, by Gary Rader, the
  Green Beret who burned his draft
  card. [Chicago, Chicago Area
  Draft Resisters, 1967]
  5p. 28cm.
  Caption title.
  1. Vietnamese conflict, 1961-
  1975. 2. Military service, Compulsory. I. Chicago Area Draft
  Resisters.
  CU-B

R2
Radical Arts Troup, Berkeley,
    Calif.
  Reserve liberal training corps
  (a play) and suggestions for
  building a guerrilla theatre
  group. Boston, Students for a
  Democratic Society, and New

England Free Press [1970?]
[4]p. 28cm.
Caption title.
Reprinted from New Left Notes,
July 30 and August 14, 1969.
1. Theater and society. I. Students for a Democratic Society.
II. New England Free Press.
MiU, KU-RH

Radical Education Project
  see also
Bay Area Radical Education Project.

R3
Radical Education Project.
  Fight racism; on racism and the
  movement. Ann Arbor [196]
  42p. illus. 28cm. (REP topical literature packet 3)
  Cover title.
  1. Negroes--Civil rights.
  MiU

R4
Radical Education Project.
  Radical Education Project [Ann
  Arbor, 1966]
  19p. 28cm.
  Cover title.
  1. Youth--Political activity.
  CU-B, WHi-L

R5
Radical Education Project.
  The Radical Education Project:
  an introduction and an invita-
  tion. [Ann Arbor, 1966?]
  7p. 28cm.
  Caption title.
  1. Youth--Political activity.
  MiU-H

R6
Radical Education Project.
  Revolutionary youth movement--to-
  wards unity of theory and practice. Ann Arbor [196]
  40 [1]p. illus. 28cm. (REP
  topical literature packet 4)
  Cover title.
  1. Student movements.
  MiU

R7
Radical Student Union.
  On strike; close Standard Oil
  down!· [Berkeley? 1969?]
  [2]p. 36cm.
  Caption title.
  1. Standard Oil Company
  CU-B

R8
Radical Student Union.
  Radical Student Union. [Berke-
  ley, 1969?]
  [4]p. 21cm.
  Caption title.
  1. Student movements.
  CU-B, KU-RH

R9
Radical Student Union.
  Strike chronology. [Berkeley]
  1969.
  4p. 41cm.
  Caption title.
  1. Negroes. 2. Mexicans in the
  U.S. 3. California. University,

Berkeley. 4. Student movements--
Berkeley, Calif.
  CU-B

R10
Radical Student Union.
  The uses of U.C. Berkeley research. [Berkeley, c1969]
  56p. 28cm.
  Cover title.
  1. Research--California.
  2. California. University.
  CU-B

R11
Radical Student Union.
  Vietnam. [Berkeley, 1969?]
  folder. 29cm.
  1. Vietnamese conflict, 1961-
  1975.
  CU-B

R12
Radical Student Union. Labor
  Committee.
  Dow on strike. [Berkeley?
  1969?]
  [1] leaf. 36cm.
  1. International Chemical Work-
  ers Union, Local 23, Pittsburg,
  Calif. 2. Dow Chemical Company.
  CU-B

R13
Radical Student Union. Labor
  Committee.
  J.I. Case vs the people. [Ber-
  keley, 196]
  [1] leaf. 36cm.
  Caption title.
  1. Case (J.I.) Company, Racine,
  Wis.
  CU-B

R14
Radical study guide. [Cambridge,
  Mass] Africa Research Group
  [1969]
  38p. 28cm.
  Cover title.
  1. Africa--Bibl. I. Africa
  Research Group.
  KU-RH

R15
Radicalesbians.

The woman identified woman.   [n.
p., c1970]
[2]p.   28cm.
Caption title.
1. Lesbianism.
CU-B

R16
Radio Free People.
  Initial statement of Radio Free
  People. [Brooklyn] 1968.
  2 leaves. 28cm.
  Caption title.
  WHi-L

R17
Ramparts.
  In the shadow of Dallas; a primer on the assassination of President Kennedy. [San Francisco,
  196]
  120p. 21cm.
  Cover title.
  1. Kennedy, John Fitzgerald,
  Pres. U.S., 1917-1963--Assassin-
  ation.
  WHi-L, KU-RH

R18
Ramparts.
  Mississippi eyewitness: the
  three civil rights workers--how
  they were murdered. [Menlo
  Park, Calif., E.M. Keating,
  c1964]
  63p. illus.
  "Special issue of Ramparts Magazine."
  1. Mississippi--Race question.
  2. Goodman, Andrew. 3. Schwer-
  ner, Michael. 4. Chaney, James.
  5. Negroes--Mississippi.
  WHi-L

R19
Ramparts.
  A special Ramparts report: Southeast Asia. [n.p., c1965]
  30p. illus. 28cm.
  1. Vietnamese conflict, 1961-
  1975.
  WHi-A

R20
Ramparts.
  Vietnam primer. [San Francisco,

196]
97p. illus. 21cm.
Cover title.
1. Vietnamese conflict, 1961-
1975. 2. U.S.--Military policy.
KU-RH

R21
Randolph (A. Philip) Institute.
  A "freedom budget" for all
  Americans: a summary. New York,
  1967.
  24 [1]p. illus. 21cm.
  Foreword by Martin Luther King.
  1. Poor. 2. Public welfare.
  I. King, Martin Luther, 1929-
  1968.
  MiU

R22
Randolph (A. Philip) Institute.
  A "freedom budget" for all
  Americans; budgeting our resources, 1966-1975 to achieve
  freedom from want. New York,
  1966.
  84p. illus. 22cm.
  1. Poor. 2. Public welfare.
  MiU

R23
Ransom, David.
  The Berkeley mafia and the In-
  donesian massacre. [New York,
  Glad Day Press, 1970?]
  [39-49]p. illus. 28cm.
  Caption title.
  Reprinted from Ramparts, Oct.
  1970.
  1. California. University.
  NNU-T

R24
Ransom, Robert, 1944-1968.
  Letters from a dead GI. [New
  York, Clergy and Laymen Concern-
  ed About Vietnam, 1969?]
  folder. 28cm.
  Cover title.
  1. Vietnamese conflict, 1961-
  1975. I. Clergy and Laymen
  Concerned About Vietnam.
  KU-RH

R25
Rapoport, Anatol.

Have the intellectuals a class
interest? [Montreal, Our Generation, 196]
31-49p.
Cover title.
1. Intellectuals. 2. Social
classes. I. Our Generation.
NNU-T

R26
Rapoport, Roger.
  Labor in an affluent society,
  collection of articles by Roger
  Rapoport [and others] Ann Arbor,
  Radical Education Project [196]
  14p. 28cm.
  Cover title.
  1. Labor and laboring classes.
  I. Radical Education Project.
  WHi-L

R27
Rapoport, Roger.
  Labor in an affluent society, a
  collection of articles by Roger
  Rapoport [and others] Boston,
  New England Free Press [196]
  14p. 28cm.
  Cover title.
  1. Labor and laboring classes.
  I. New England Free Press.
  KU-RH

R28
Raskin, Marcus.
  Deterrance and reality, by Marcus Raskin and Arthur Waskow.
  [n.p., 1961]
  172 leaves. 29cm.
  "Originated in a staff report on
  defense policy to congressman
  Robert W. Kastenmeier."
  1. Deterrence (Strategy) 2. U.
  S.--Military policy. 3. Atomic
  warfare. I. Waskow, Arthur, jt.
  auth.
  DLC 61-33481

R29
Raskin, Marcus.
  A diplomatic alternative, by
  Marcus G. Raskin and Bernard B.
  Fall. Berkeley, Turn Toward
  Peace [196]
  4p. 28cm.
  Caption title.

Reprinted from New York Review
of Books, Sept. 16, 1965.
1. Vietnamese conflict, 1961-
1975. I. Fall, Bernard B.,
1926-1967. I. Turn Toward
Peace.
CU-B

R30
La raza! Why a chicano party?
  Why chicano studies? By
  Roger Alvarado [and others.
  New York, Pathfinder Press,
  1970]
  15p. 22cm. (A Merit pamphlet)
  Cover title.
  1. Mexicans in the U.S. I. Al-
  varado, Roger. II. Pathfinder
  Press.
  KU-RH

R31
Reaven, Debbie.
  The battle of Berkeley: from
  mass struggle to sell-out [by
  Debbie Reaven and others. n.
  p., 1969?]
  16 [2]p. 28cm.
  Cover title.
  1. Students for a Democratic
  Society. 2. Radical Student
  Union. 3. Revolutionary Union.
  4. Berkeley, Calif.--Riots,
  1969. 5. Student movements--
  Berkeley, Calif.
  WHi-L, KU-RH

R32
Reaven, Debbie.
  The battle of Berkeley: from
  mass struggle to sell-out [by
  Debbie Reaven and others. n.p.,
  Students for a Democratic Soc-
  iety, 196]
  17 [1]p. 28cm.
  Cover title.
  1. Student movements--Berkeley,
  Calif. 2. Berkeley, Calif.--
  Riots, 1969. 3. Radical Stu-
  dent Union. 4. Students for a
  Democratic Society. 5. Radical
  Student Union. I. Students for
  a Democratic Society.
  KU-RH

R33
Record, Jane Cassels.
  The red-tapping of Negro protest.
  [New York] National Association
  for the Advancement of Colored
  People, 1957.
  325-333p. 22cm.
  Cover title.
  Reprinted from American Scholar.
  1. Anti-communist movements.
  2. Negroes--Civil rights. I. Na-
  tional Association for the Ad-
  vancement of Colored People.
  WHi-A

R34
Redding, Louis.
  Louisville travesty, with a pre-
  face by Harvey O'Connor. [New
  York, Emergency Civil Liberties
  Committee, 1955]
  24p. ports.
  Cover title.
  1. Negroes--Louisville.
  2. Louisville--Race question.
  I. Emergency Civil Liberties
  Committee. II. O'Connor, Harvey.
  WHi-L

R35
Redstockings of the Women's Lib-
    eration Movement.
  Redstockings manifesto. [New
  York, 1969]
  [2]p. 28cm.
  Caption title.
  1. Woman--Rights of women.
  MoU

R36
Reed, Evelyn.
  The myth of women's inferiority.
  [Boston, New England Free Press,
  196]
  [58]-66p. 28cm.
  Cover title.
  Reprinted from The Fourth Inter-
  national, spring 1954.
  1. Woman--History and condition
  of women. I. New England Free
  Press.
  KU-RH

R37
Reed, Evelyn.
  Problems of women's liberation;

a Marxist approach. [New York,
Merit Publishers, 1969]
63p. 22cm.
Cover title.
1. Woman--History and condition
of women. I. Merit Publishers.
CU-B, WHi-L, DLC 77-97800

R38
Reeves, Thomas C.
  Let us repeal the draft now!
  Washington, National Council to
  Repeal the Draft [1969]
  3p. 28cm.
  Caption title.
  1. Military service, Compulsory.
  I. National Council to Repeal
  the Draft.
  KU-RH

R39
Reeves, Thomas C.
  Statement. Testimony submitted
  for the Subcommittee on Administrative Practice and Procedure
  of the Committee on the Judiciary of the United States Senate. [Washington, National
  Council to Repeal the Draft,
  1970?]
  9p. 28cm.
  Caption title.
  1. Military service, Compulsory.
  I. National Council to Repeal
  the Draft.
  KU-RH

R40
Regnary, Thomas E.
  Love and violence. [New York,
  Episcopal Peace Fellowship,
  196]
  folder (8p.) 22x9cm.
  Caption title.
  1. Peace. I. Episcopal Peace
  Fellowship.
  KU-RH

R41
Reints, John.
  A draft law primer; an introduction to rights and procedures
  under the draft law. Revised to
  include new court decisions and
  administrative rulings. [Nyack,
  N.Y.] Fellowship Publications

[1970]
23p. 23x10cm.
Cover title.
1. Military service, Compulsory.
I. Fellowship Publications.
KU-RH, WHi-A

R42
Religious Freedom Committee.
  Abolish congressional inquisition.
  Stop violations of religious freedom. [New York, 1958?]
  29p. 22cm.
  Cover title.
  1. U.S. Congress. House. Committee on Un-American Activities.
  2. Religious liberty.
  KU-J, MiU

R43
A report by four Canadians on Cuba
    as they saw it. Toronto, Fair
  Play for Cuba Committee [1963]
  31p. 22cm.
  1. Cuba--Descr. & trav. I. Fair
  Play for Cuba Committee.
  MoU

R44
Research Organization Cooperative,
    San Francisco.
  Basta ya! The story of las
  siete de la raza. [San Francis-
  co, 1970?]
  [38]p. illus. 26cm.
  Cover title.
  1. Mexicans in the U.S. 2. San
  Francisco--Race question.
  MiU, KU-RH

R45
Research Organization Cooperative,
    San Francisco.
  Strike at Frisco State! The
  story behind it. [San Francisco,
  1969]
  37p. illus. 28cm.
  Cover title.
  1. California. State College,
  San Francisco. 2. Student move-
  ment--San Francisco.
  KU-RH

R46
Research Organizing Cooperative,
    San Francisco.

To get a good job, get a good
  education. [Detroit, Radical
  Education Project, 1969?]
  17p. 22cm.
  1. Education.
  MiU

R47
Resist.
  Resist draft counselor's kit.
  [Cambridge, Mass., 196]
  1v. (unpaged) 28cm.
  1. Military service, Compulsory.
  MoU

R48
Resist the draft, Nov. 14. [n.p.,
    Liberation Press, 196]
  [4]p. 22cm.
  Cover title.
  1. Military service, Compulsory.
  CU-B

R49
Resistance.
  "The first step in the procurement of military manpower is
  registration." [San Francisco?
  1969?]
  [12]p. illus. 22cm.
  Cover title.
  1. Military service, Compulsory.
  KU-RH

R50
Resistance.
  Men of draft age. Fresno,
  Calif. [196]
  [1] leaf. illus. 28cm.
  Caption title.
  1. Military service, Compulsory.
  KU-RH

R51
Resistance.
  The Resistance; where it's at;
  where it's going. Chicago,
  Chicago Area Draft Resisters
  [196]
  5p. 28cm.
  Cover title.
  1. U.S. Selective Service Sys-
  tem. 2. Conscientious objectors.
  I. Chicago Area Draft Resisters.
  KU-RH

R52
Resistance.
  You don't gotta. [Los Angeles,
  196]
  folder. 22x10cm.
  Cover title.
  1. Military service, Compulsory.
  KU-RH

R53
Resistance. [n.p., 196]
  [4]p. illus. 22cm.
  1. U.S. Selective Service System. 2. Military service, Compulsory.
  KU-RH

R54
The responsibility of investiga-
  ting commissions. [Philadel-
  phia, Philadelphia Resistance,
  1970?]
  [2]p. 28cm.
  Caption title.
  1. Black Panther Party. 2. Hampton, Fred, 1948-1969. 3. Pol-
  ice--Illinois--Chicago. I. Philadelphia Resistance.
  CU-B

R55
Revolution and U.S. aggression.
  [Refuting Bundy by observer]
  Boston, New England Free Press
  [196]
  [4]p. illus. 28cm.
  Cover title.
  1. Bundy, William Puttman, 1917-
      2. Imperialism. 3. U.S.
  --For. rel.--Asia. I. New Eng-
  land Free Press.
  MoU, KU-RH

R56
Revolutionary Marxist students in
  Poland speak out, 1964-1968
  [by] Jacek Kuron and [others.
  New York, Merit Publishers,
  1968]
  96p. 22cm.
  Cover title.
  Contents--Open letter to mem-
  bers of the University of Warsaw
  Sections of the United Polish
  Workers Party and the Union of
  Young Socialists, by J. Kuron

and K. Modzelewski.--Reply to
the Control Commission of the
United Polish Workers Party, by
A. Zambrowski.--An open letter
to Wladyslaw Gomulka and the
Central Committee of the Polish
Workers Party, by I. Deutscher.
  1. Poland--Pol. & govt.--1945-
      2. Poland--Econ. condit.
  --1945-   3. Student move-
  ments--Poland. I. Merit Publishers. II. Kuron, Jacek.
  DLC 68-8837

R57
Revolutionary quotations from the
  thoughts of Uncle Sam. Ci-
  cero, Ill., Johnny Appleseed
  Patriotic Publications [1969]
  xi, 113p. 14cm.
  1. Radicalism. 2. Revolutions.
  I. Johnny Appleseed Patriotic
  Publications.
  MoU, KU-RH, DLC 74-5070

R58
Revolutionary youth movement.
  [Berkeley? Radical Student
  Union, 1969]
  5 leaves. 28cm.
  Caption title.
  1. Students for a Democratic
  Society. 2. Student movements.
  I. Radical Student Union.
  CU-B

R59
Revolutionary youth movement: toward unity of theory and practice. Ann Arbor, Radical
  Education Project [1969]
  40 [1]p. illus. 28cm. (REP
  topical literature packet 4)
  Cover title.
  1. Student movements. I. Radical Education Project.
  MoU

R60
Revueltas, Jose, 1914-
  The youth movement and the
  alienation of society. [New
  York] Merit Publishers [1969]
  34p. 18cm.
  Cover title.
  At head of title: From a Mexi-

can prison.
1. Student movements--Mexico.
2. Mexico--Soc. condit. I. Merit Publishers.
KU-RH

R61
Richards, D.A.
33 steps to a better understanding of humanism and your life
values; an inventory of religious beliefs. [Yellow Springs,
O.] American Humanist Association, 1962.
[12]p. 22x10cm. (AHA publication no. T-2)
Cover title.
1. Humanism. I. American Humanist Association.
KU-RH

R62
Richardson, Beulah.
A black woman speaks of white
womanhood. [New Orleans, South-
ern Female Rights Union, 1970?]
5p. 28cm.
Caption title.
1. Women, Negro. 2. Negroes.
I. Southern Female Rights Union.
KU-RH

R63
Richardson, Channing Bulfinch,
   1917-
The Federation of Rhodesia and
Nyasaland: the future of a dilemma [by] Channing Richardson
[and others. New York] American Committee on Africa [1959]
38p. 22cm. (Africa today pamphlets, 4)
Cover title.
1. Rhodesia and Nyasaland--Pol.
& govt. 2. Rhodesia and Nyasa-
land--Native races. I. American
Committee on Africa.
MH, NIC, TxU, MiU, KU-RH

R64
Richardson, F.O.
The GI's handbook on military
injustice; why rank and file GIs
need an organization of their
own, by F.O. Richardson, with an
introduction by Pvt. Andrew

Stapp. New York, American Servicemen's Union, 1967.
39p. illus. 22cm.
1. Soldiers. 2. U.S. Army--
Military life. I. Stapp, Andrew. II. American Servicemen's
Union.
KU-RH, WHi-L

R65
Ridenour, Ron.
The fire this time. [Los An-
geles] W.E.B. DuBois Club [1965]
14p.
1. Los Angeles--Riots, 1965.
2. Negroes--Los Angeles.
I. Leslie, Anne, jt. auth.
II. Oliver, Victor, jt. auth.
I. DuBois (W.E.B.) Clubs of
America.
WHi-L

R66
Ridgeway, James.
One million abortions; "it's
your problem, sweetheart".
[Berkeley, Campus Sexual Free-
dom Forum, 196]
[4]p. 22cm.
Caption title.
1. Abortion. 2. Campus Sexual
Freedom Forum, Berkeley, Calif.
KU-RH

R67
Ridgeway, James.
Para-real estate: the handing
out of resources. [Ithaca,
N.Y., Glad Day Press, 1970?]
[29]-33p. illus. 28cm.
Caption title.
1. Environmental policy.
2. Natural resources. I. Glad
Day Press.
NNU-T

R68
Riessman, Frank, 1924-
A comparison of two social action approaches: Saul Alinsky
and the new student left. New
York, Congress of Racial Equality, 1965.
9 leaves.
1. Student movements. 2. Alinsky, Saul David, 1909-

I. Congress of Racial Equality.
NNC, NUC 68-18508

R69
Riessman, Frank, 1924-
  New careers; a basic strategy
  against poverty. Introduction
  by Michael Harrington. [New
  York, A. Philip Randolph Educational Fund, 1967?]
  27p. (A. Philip Randolph Educational Fund, 2)
  1. Poverty. 2. Vocational education. I. Randolph (A. Philip)
  Educational Fund. II. Harrington,
  Michael.
  WHi-L

R70
Rifkin, Bernard.
  How literature can help the re-
  volutionary. 2d rev. ed. [New
  York? Committee for Political
  Studies?] 1967.
  15 leaves. 28cm.
  Cover title.
  1. Politics in literature.
  2. Revolutions. 3. Art. I. Com-
  mittee for Political Studies.
  KU-RH

R71
Rifkin, Bernard.
  How the workers can fight against
  taxes; a suggested model of the
  kind of class battle the United
  States workers will have to fight
  in order to defend their living
  standards and to gain revolutionary experience. 2d. rev. ed.
  [New York? Committee for Political Studies? [1967]
  25 leaves. 28cm.
  Cover title.
  1. Sales tax. 2. Labor and
  laboring classes. I. Committee
  for Political Studies.
  KU-RH

R72
Rifkin, Bernard.
  How to build revolutionaries; a
  discussion of the problems of
  training people for the United
  States revolution. 2d rev. ed.
  [New York? Committee for Politi-

cal Studies?] 1967.
21p. 28cm.
Cover title.
1. Revolutions. I. Committee
for Political Studies.
KU-RH

R73
Rifkin, Bernard.
  How to fight and win the workers; a discussion of the best
  methods to use in winning the
  United States people for revolutionary mass struggle. 2d.
  rev. ed. [New York? Committee
  for Political Studies?] 1967.
  30 leaves. 28cm.
  Cover title.
  1. Revolutions. 2. Labor and
  laboring classes. I. Committee
  for Political Studies.
  KU-RH

R74
Rifkin, Bernard.
  An introduction to Marxism-
  Leninism; a study guide prepar-
  ed for students of United States
  revolutionary problems. [New
  York? Committee for Political
  Studies? 1969?]
  13 leaves. 28cm.
  Cover title.
  1. Socialism. 2. Revolutions.
  I. Committee for Political
  Studies.
  KU-RH

R75
Rifkin, Bernard.
  The position of the Jews in
  American society. [New York?
  Committee for Political Studies?
  196 ?]
  147 [20] leaves. 28cm.
  1. Jews. I. Committee for Pol-
  itical Studies.
  KU-RH

R76
Rifkin, Bernard.
  Winning the battle of ideas; a
  discussion of some of the ideological problems involved in
  the building of a United States
  revolutionary movement. 2d.

rev. ed. [New York? Committee
for Political Studies?] 1967.
25 leaves. 28cm.
Cover title.
1. Revolutions. 2. Socialism.
I. Committee for Political
Studies.
KU-RH

R77
Ring, Harry.
How Cuba uprooted race discrim-
ination. Introduction by Richard
Gibson. [New York, Pioneer Pub-
lishers, 1961]
15p. 22cm.
Cover title.
1. Race discrimination--Cuba.
2. Cuba--Race question. 3. Cuba
--Pol. & govt.--1959-
I. Pioneer Publishers. II. Gib-
son, Richard.
LNHT, MoU, LaU, FU, CU-B,
NUC 63-37451

R78
Ring, Harry.
How Cuba uprooted race discrim-
ination. [2d. ed. New York]
Merit Publishers [1969]
15p. 22cm.
Cover title.
1. Race discrimination--Cuba.
2. Cuba--Race question. 3. Cuba
--Pol. & govt.--1959-
I. Merit Publishers.
KU-RH

R79
Ring, Harry.
Move to derail Mobe into multi-
issue morass. [New York? The
Militant? 1969?]
[2]p. 36cm.
Caption title.
At head of title: Retreat from
mass antiwar action.
1. New Mobilization Committee to
End the War in Vietnam.
2. Peace--Societies, etc.
3. Vietnamese conflict, 1961-
1975. I. The Militant.
KU-RH

R80
Rioux, Marcel.

Youth in the contemporary world
and in Quebec. [Montreal] Our
Generation [196]
5-29 leaves.
Caption title.
1. Youth--Quebec. I. Quebec.
II. Our Generation.
NNU-T

R81
Rivera, Alice de.
Jumping the track. [Boston,
New England Free Press, 1970]
[2]p. 28cm.
Caption title.
1. Education--New York (State)--
New York (City). 2. Woman--
Rights of women. 3. Education
of women. I. New England Free
Press.
KU-RH, MiU

R82
Robbins, Jhan.
"Why didn't they hit back?"
[New York, Congress of Racial
Equality, 1963?]
folder. 28cm.
1. Negroes--Civil rights.
2. Nonviolence. 3. Dickerson,
Eddie. I. Congress of Racial
Equality.
CU-B

R83
Robbins, Richard.
The future of negro colleges.
Nashville, Southern Student Organizing Committee [196]
[4]p. 28cm.
Cover title.
Reprinted from New South Student, April 1966.
1. Negroes--Education. 2. Universities and colleges. I. Southern Student Organizing Committee.
MiU, MoU

R84
Robert Scheer for Congress.
Draft platform. [Berkeley,
1966?]
4 leaves. 28cm.
Cover title.
1. Scheer, Robert.
CU-B

R85
Robert Scheer for Congress Committee.
  The record of Jeffery Cohelan; a
  work paper of the Scheer for Congress Committee. Berkeley [1966?]
  20p. 36cm.
  Cover title.
  1. Cohelan, Jeffery. 2. Califor-
  nia--Pol. & govt.--1963-
  CU-B

R86
Roberts, Adam.
  Non-violent defense. [Montreal,
  Our Generation, 196]
  76-80 leaves.
  Caption title.
  At head of title: alternatives
  to nuclear policies.
  1. Nonviolence. 2. Pacifism.
  I. Our Generation.
  NNU-T

R87
Roberts, Holland.
  Behind the Berlin wall. [New
  York, New World Review, 1962]
  folder. 22cm.
  Caption title.
  Reprinted from New World Review,
  Nov. 1962.
  1. Berlin question (1954-   )
  I. New World Review.
  KU-J

R88
Roberts, Paula.
  In favor of tubal ligation. [n.
  p., People's Free Medical Clinic,
  1970?]
  3 leaves. 36cm.
  Caption title.
  1. Birth control. 2. Woman--
  Rights of women. I. People's
  Free Medical Clinic.
  KU-RH

R89
Robinson, Cedric.
  Campus civil rights groups and
  the administration. [Berkeley?
  Slate? 1961]
  [2]p. 28cm.
  Caption title.
  1. Civil rights. 2. Student
  movements. 3. Universities and

colleges--Administration.
  I. Slate.
  WHi-A

R90
Robinson, Skip.
  Job discrimination. [n.p.,
  Slate? 1961?
  6p. 28cm.
  Caption title.
  1. Negroes--Champaign, Ill.
  2. Champaign, Ill.--Race quest-
  ion. I. Slate.
  WHi-A

R91
Roca, Blas.
  The road to socialism. [New
  York] Fair Play for Cuba Commit-
  tee [196]
  [6]p.
  Cover title.
  1. Socialism in Cuba. 2. Cuba
  --Pol. & govt.--1959-
  I. Fair Play for Cuba Committee.
  MiU

R92
Roche, John Pearson, 1923-
  Testimony of John P. Roche on
  behalf of Americans for Democratic Action, before subcommittee
  number five of the House Judiciary Committee, Tuesday, May 28,
  1963...[n.p., 1963]
  8 leaves. 36cm.
  Caption title.
  Reproduced from typewritten
  copy.
  1. Civil rights. I. Americans
  for Democratic Action.
  MH-L

R93
Rodeny, Walter.
  West Africa and the Atlantic
  slave-trade. [Cambridge, Afri-
  ca Research Group, 196]
  27p. 22cm. (Reprint 6)
  Cover title.
  1. Slave-trade. I. Africa
  Research Group.
  MiU

R94
Roe, Charlotte.

The rise and fall of American
women. New York, Young People's
Socialist League [196]
12p.
1. Woman--History and condition
of women. I. Young People's
Socialist League.
WHi-L

R95
Roebuck, Don.
U.S. ownership and control of
Canadian industry. Toronto,
Research, Information, and Pub-
lications Project of Student
Union for Peace Action [196]
11p. 28cm.
1. U.S.--Relations (general)
with Canada. 2. Corporations--
Canada. I. Student Union for
Peace Action.
WHi-A

R96
Romano, Paul.
The American worker, by Paul
Romano and Ria Stone. Detroit
[Facing Reality Publishing Com-
mittee, c1969]
ii, 70p. 21cm.
1. Labor and laboring classes.
I. Stone, Ria, jt. auth.
II. Facing Reality Publishing
Committee.
MiU

R97
Romano, Paul.
Life in the factory. Boston,
New England Free Press [1969?]
40p. 22cm.
1. Labor and laboring classes.
I. New England Free Press.
KU-RH

R98
Rony, Vera.
Davey Crockett in Little Egypt.
Nashville, Tenn., Southern Student Organizing Committee [c1969]
15p. 28cm.
Cover title.
1. Murray Ohio Company. 2. Labor and laboring classes--Law-
renceburg, Tenn. I. Southern

Student Organizing Committee.
MoU, WHi-L

R99
Rose, Mary Ellen.
Freedom of the campus press.
[n.p. Slate? 1961]
[2]p. 28cm.
Caption title.
1. Liberty of the press.
2. Newspapers. I. Slate.
WHi-A

R100
Rose, Sharon.
Palestine, by Sharon Rose and
Cathy Tackney. [Washington,
Middle East Research and Infor-
mation Project, 1970?]
[6]p. 28cm.
Caption title.
Reprinted from Off Our Backs,
Oct. 15, 1970.
1. Near East--Pol. & govt.
2. Palestine. 3. Jewish-Arab
relations. I. Tackney, Cathy,
jt. auth. II. Middle East Re-
search and Information Project.
KU-RH

R101
Rosebury, Celia.
Black liberation or trial: the
case of Huey Newton. Berkeley,
Bay Area Committee to Defend
Political Freedom, 1968.
19p. 26cm.
1. Newton, Huey P. 2. Negroes--
Civil rights. 3. Black Panther
Party. I. Bay Area Committee
to Defend Political Freedom.
CU-B, MiU

R102
Rosen, Milton.
Build a base in the working
class [by Milton Rosen and Progressive Labor Party, National
Committee. New York, Progressive Labor Party, 1969]
81p. 22cm.
1. Socialism. 2. Labor and
laboring classes. I. Progressive Labor Party. National
Committee.
WHi-L

R103
Rosen, Sumner.
  Liberals and reality. New York,
  Students for a Democratic Society [196]
  6p. 28cm.
  Cover title.
  "A shorter version of this essay
  originally appeared as an article
  in Liberation."
  1. U.S.--Pol. & govt.--1959-
          2. Labor and laboring
  classes. 3. Liberalism. I. Students for a Democratic Society.
  WHi-L, KU-RH, CU-B

R104
Rosenshine, Daniel.
  Resolution on Vietnam. [n.p.,
  Student Peace Union, National
  Convention, 1964]
  [1] leaf. 28cm.
  Caption title.
  1. Vietnamese conflict, 1961-
  1975. I. Student Peace Union.
  National Convention, 1964.
  CU-B

R105
Rosenthal, Steven J.
  Vietnam study guide & annotated
  bibliography. Chicago, Students
  for a Democratic Society [196]
  6p. 28cm.
  Cover title.
  1. Vietnamese conflict, 1961-
  1975--Bibl. I. Students for a
  Democratic Society.
  NNU-T

R106
Rosenthal, Steven J.
  Vietnam study guide and annotated
  bibliography. Chicago, Students
  for a Democratic Society [196]
  [10]p. 28cm.
  Cover title.
  1. Vietnamese conflict, 1961-
  1975--Bibl. I. Students for a
  Democratic Society.
  WHi-L

R107
Ross, Bob.
  Notes on the welfare state.
  Chicago, Students for a Democra-

tic Society [1966]
  [8]p. 28cm.
  Cover title.
  Reprinted from Liberation, Mar.
  1966.
  1. Public welfare. I. Students
  for a Democratic Society.
  MiU-H

R108
Ross, Bob.
  Notes on the welfare state.
  Chicago, Students for a Democra-
  tic Society [196]
  7 [1]p. illus. 28cm.
  Cover title.
  1. Public welfare. I. Students
  for a Democratic Society.
  NNU-T, CU-B, KU-RH

R109
Ross, Bob.
  The United States National Student Association: a policy critique. New York, Students for
  a Democratic Society [196]
  6 [2]p. 28cm.
  Cover title.
  1. United States National Student Association. 2. Students.
  I. Students for a Democratic
  Society.
  MiU, WHi-A, WHi-L, NUC 69-49198

R110
Ross, Bob.
  Whose welfare? Notes on pover-
  ty and the welfare state. Chi-
  cago, Students for a Democratic
  Society for the Liberal Study
  Group [1965?]
  13p. 28cm.
  Cover title.
  1. Public welfare. 2. Poverty.
  I. Students for a Democratic
  Society. II. Liberal Study
  Group.
  WHI-A

R111
Ross, Bob.
  Whose welfare? Notes on the
  welfare state. Rev. ed. Chicago, Students for a Democratic
  Society, 1966.
  11p. 28cm.

1. Public welfare. 2. Poverty.
I. Students for a Democratic
Society.
CU-B

R112
Ross, Paul L.
  Preventive detention in American
  concentration camps. [New York,
  Citizens Committee for Constitu-
  tional Liberties, 1969?]
  [8]p. 22cm.
  Cover title.
  Reprinted from Guild Practition-
  er, winter, 1969.
  1. Concentration camps. 2. In-
  ternal security. I. Citizens
  Committee for Constitutional
  Liberties.
  KU-RH

R113
Rossa, Della.
  Why Watts exploded: how the
  ghetto fought back. [Los Angeles, Los Angeles Local, Socialist Workers Party, 1966]
  21p. illus. 22cm.
  Cover title.
  1. Los Angeles--Riots, 1965.
  2. Negroes--Los Angeles.
  I. Socialist Workers Party, Los
  Angeles.
  CU-B, MiU, WHi-L, NUC 70-12614

R114
Rossa, Della.
  Why Watts exploded: how the
  ghetto fought back. [New York,
  Merit Publishers, 1969]
  21p. 22cm.
  Cover title.
  1. Los Angeles--Riots, 1965.
  2. Negroes--Los Angeles.
  I. Merit Publishers.
  KU-RH

R115
Rossman, Michael.
  An alternative proposal for
  November 20. [Berkeley? Vietnam Day Committee? 1965]
  4p. 28cm.
  Caption title.
  1. Vietnamese conflict, 1961-
  1975. I. National Coordinating

Committee to End the War in
Vietnam. Vietnam Day Committee,
Berkeley.
CU-B

R116
Rothstein, Richard.
  E.R.A.P. and how it grew. Bos-
  ton, New England Free Press
  [196]
  13 [2]p. 22cm.
  Cover title.
  1. Students for a Democratic
  Society. Economic Research and
  Action Project. 2. Jobs or In-
  come Now Community Union.
  I. New England Free Press.
  MoU, KU-RH

R117
Rothstein, Richard.
  JOIN organizes city poor. Ann
  Arbor, Students for a Democra-
  tic Society [196]
  3 leaves. 28cm.
  Caption title.
  1. Poverty. 2. Jobs or Income
  Now Community Union. 3. Cities
  and towns. I. Students for a
  Democratic Society.
  WHi-A

R118
Rothstein, Richard.
  A short history of ERAP. [Chi-
  cago? 1966?]
  4p. 28cm.
  Caption title.
  1. Students for a Democratic
  Society. Economic Research and
  Action Project.
  WHi-A

R119
Rouissi, Boualam.
  Che Guevara on Africa [inter-
  view by Boualam Rouissi and
  Josie Fanon. Toronto, Fair Play
  for Cuba Committee, 196]
  8p. 22cm.
  Cover title.
  1. Africa. 2. Revolutions--La-
  tin America. I. Fanon, Josie,
  jt. auth. II. Guevara, Ernesto,
  1920-1967. III. Fair Play for
  Cuba Committee.
  MiU

R120
Roussopoulos, Dimitrios.
  The student syndrome. Toronto,
  Research, Information and Publications Project, Student Union
  for Peace Action, 1965.
  12p. 28cm.
  Cover title.
  1. Student movements. I. Student Union for Peace Action.
  WHi-A

R121
Roussopoulos, Dimitrios.
  What is the new radicalism?
  [Montreal, Our Generation, 196]
  15-26 leaves.
  Caption title.
  1. Radicalism. 2. Student move-
  ments. I. Our Generation.
  NNU-T

R122
Rowen, James.
  The case against ROTC. Madison,
  Madison Students for a Democra-
  tic Society, Student Moratorium
  Committee, 1969.
  9p. 28cm.
  Cover title.
  1. U.S. Army. Reserve Officers'
  Training Corps. I. Students for
  a Democratic Society, Madison.
  II. Student Moratorium Committee,
  Madison.
  WHi-L

R123
Rowntree, John.
  The political economy of youth
  (youth as a class) [by] John and
  Margaret Rowntree. Ann Arbor,
  Radical Education Project [196]
  36p. 22cm.
  Cover title.
  Reprinted from Our Generation,
  v. 6, no. 1-2.
  1. Youth--Political activity.
  I. Rowntree, Margaret, jt. auth.
  II. Radical Education Project.
  WHi-L

R124
Rowntree, John.

The political economy of youth
(youth as a class) [by] John and
Margaret Rowntree. Commentary
by Edgar Z. Friedenberg [and]
Marcel Rioux. [Montreal, Our
Generation, 196]
42p.
Cover title.
1. Youth--Political activity.
I. Friedenberg, Edgar Zodiag,
1921-   II. Rioux, Marcel.
III. Rowntree, Margaret, jt.
auth. IV. Our Generation.
NNU-T

R125
Rowntree, John.
  Youth as a class [by] John &
  Margaret Rowntree. Nashville,
  Southern Student Organizing
  Committee [196]
  23, vp. 28cm.
  Cover title.
  1. Youth. 2. Student movements.
  I. Southern Student Organizing
  Committee. II. Rowntree, Mar-
  garet, jt. auth.
  MoU

R126
Roy, Manabandra Nath, 1893-
  A Marxist analysis of Chinese
  history--the foundation of the
  traditional culture--structure
  of Chinese society--foreign ag-
  gression. Toronto, Research,
  Information, and Publications
  Project, Student Union for Peace
  Action [196]
  15p. 28cm.
  Cover title.
  1. China--History. I. Student
  Union for Peace Action.
  WHi-A

R127
Roy, Manabandra Nath, 1893-
  A Marxist interpretation of
  Chinese history. Boston, New
  England Free Press [196]
  [13]-25, [76]-128p. 21cm.
  Cover title.
  Reprinted from Roy's Revolution
  and counterrevolution in China.

1. China--History. I. New England Free Press.
MoU, KU-RH

R128
Royall, Norman N.
  Vietnam: vital interest or tra-
  gic mistake? America must decide!
  [Des Moines, American Friends
  Service Committee, 1969]
  ii, 36p. 22cm.
  Cover title.
  1. Vietnamese conflict, 1961-
  1975. I. Friends, Society of.
  American Friends Service Com-
  mittee.
  MoKU, NUC 6949163, KU-RH, MoU

R129
Roysher, Martin.
  The march as a political tactic.
  [n.p., Students for a Democratic
  Society, 196]
  [3] leaves. 28cm.
  Caption title.
  1. March on Washington to End
  the War in Vietnam, April 1965.
  2. Vietnamese conflict, 1961-
  1975. I. Students for a Democratic Society.
  KU-RH

R130
Roysher, Martin.
  The march as a political tactic
  [by Martin Roysher and Charles
  Capper. n.p., 196]
  3 leaves. 28cm.
  Caption title.
  1. March on Washington to End
  the War in Vietnam, April 1965.
  2. Students for a Democratic
  Society. I. Capper, Charles,
  jt. auth.
  WHi-A

R131
Rubbo, Sydney D.
  Thou shalt not poison. [Volun-
  town, Conn., Distributed by
  Committee for Nonviolent Action,
  196]
  [2]p. illus. 28cm.
  Caption title.
  1. Vietnamese conflict, 1961-
  1975. 2. Biological warfare.

I. Committee for Nonviolent
Action.
KU-RH

R132
Rubenstein, Dale Ross.
  How the Russian revolution
  failed women. Boston, New Eng-
  land Free Press [1970?]
  30 [1]p. 28cm.
  Cover title.
  1. Women in Russia. I. New
  England Free Press.
  MiU

R133
Rubin, Jerry.
  Statement to HUAC. [n.p., 1966]
  [2]p. 36cm.
  Caption title.
  1. Vietnamese conflict, 1961-
  1975.
  CU-B

R134
Rubin, Jerry.
  Proposal for the future of the
  National Coordinating Committee
  [signed by Jerry Rubin, Berkeley Vietnam Day Committee. n.
  p., 196]
  6 leaves. 36cm.
  Caption title.
  1. National Coordinating Committee to End the War in Vietnam.
  WHi-L

R135
Rubin, Mike.
  An Israeli worker's answer.
  [New York, Committee to Support
  Middle East Liberation] 1970.
  23p. 22cm.
  1. Israel-Arab War, 1967.
  2. Israel--Foreign policy.
  I. Committee to Support Middle
  East Liberation.
  KU-RH, CU-B

R136
Rubin, Mike.
  An Israeli worker's answers
  [New York] Committee to Support
  Middle East Liberation [1969]
  21p. 22cm.

Cover title.
1. Israel-Arab War, 1967.
2. Arabs.   3. Near East--Pol. &
govt.   I. Committee to Support
Middle East Liberation.
MiU

R137
Rudwick, Elliott M.
   The unequal badge; negro police-
   men in the south.   Atlanta, Southern Regional Council, 1962.
   14p.
   1. Police--Southern States.
   2. Negroes--Southern States.
   I. Southern Regional Council.
   WHi-L

R138
Russell, Bertrand Russell 3d earl,
   1872-
   The myth of American "freedom".
   Passaic, N.Y., Minority of One
   [c1963]
   folder.   21x8cm.
   Cover title.
   1. Internal security.   2. Civil
   rights.   I. Minority of One.
   KU-RH

R139
Russell, Maud.
   China in today's world: "economic failure"?   "Opposing peaceful coexistence"?   "Isolated"?
   "Threat to Asian neighbors"?
   [New York, Far East Reporter,
   196]
   54p.   21cm.
   1. China (People's Republic of
   China, 1949-   )--Foreign opinion.   I. Far East Reporter.
   NIC, CSt-H, NUC 68-25660

R140
Russell, Maud, comp.
   Medicine and public health in
   the People's Republic of China.
   [New York, Far East Reporter,
   196 ?]
   24p.   21cm.
   1. Medicine, State--China (People's Republic of China, 1949-
)   2. Hygiene, Public--
   China (People's Republic of
   China, 1949-   )   I. Far East

Reporter.
NIC, CSt-H, NUC 68-25743

R141
Russell, Maud.
   New people in new China; some
   personal glimpse of people in
   China.   [New York, Far East Re-
   porter, 196]
   48p.   illus., map.   21cm.
   1. China (People's Republic of
   China, 1949-   )--Soc. condit.
   I. Far East Reporter.
   NIC, CSt-H, NUC 68-25537

R142
Russell, Maud.
   Urban people's communes in
   China.   [New York, Far East
   Reporter, 1960]
   24p.   map.
   Cover title.
   1. Communes (China)   I. Far
   East Reporter.
   CLU, NIC, NUC 69-17881

R143
Russell, Maud.
   Whiter India?   [New York] Far
   East Reporter [1963?]
   28p.   21cm.
   Cover title.
   1. India--Pol. & govt.--1947-
        2. India--Foreign policy.
   I. Far East Reporter.
   CSt-H, MiU, NUC 68-80629

R144
Russell, Maud.
   Why do Chinese "refugees" escape
   to Hongkong?   By Maul Russell
   and Anna Louise Strong.   [New
   York, Far East Reporter, 196]
   15p.   21cm.
   1. Hongkong--Soc. condit.
   2. Refugees, China (People's
   Republic of China, 1949-   )
   I. Far East Reporter.
   II. Strong, Anna Louise.
   NIC, CSt-H, NUC 68-22383

R145
Russia (1923-   U.S.S.R.)
   The Soviet Union proposes peaceful co-existence; the end of the
   cold war, banning of atomic ar-

358   THE AMERICAN LEFT

maments, strict international control and inspection progressive
disarmament. The full text of
proposals submitted to the United
Nations on May 10, 1955. New
York, National Council of American-Soviet Friendship [1955?]
12p. 20cm.
Cover title.
1. Disarmament. 2. Atomic weapons and disarmament. I. National Council of American-Soviet
Friendship.
KU-J

R146
Russia (1923-   U.S.S.R.)
  Statement of the Soviet government, Sept. 21, 1963. Reply to
a statement of a Chinese government spokesman, Sept. 1, 1963
New York, Crosscurrents Press
[c1963]
  1. Russia--For. rel.--China
(People's Republic of China,
1949-   ) 2. China (People's
Republic of China, 1949-   )--
For. rel.--Russia. I. Crosscurrents Press.
DLC 64-22725

R147
Rustin, Bayard, 1910-
  The alienated. [Washington,
International Labor Press Assoc.,
196]
9p.
  1. Youth. 2. Negroes.
WHi-L

R148
Rustin, Bayard, 1910-
  The anatomy of frustration.
New York [Anti-Defamation League
of B'nai B'rith] 1968.
unpaged. illus.
  1. Jews. 2. Negroes--Civil
rights.
WHi-L

R149
Rustin, Bayard, 1910-
  From protest to politics: the
future of civil rights movement.
New York, League for Industrial
Democracy [1965?]

[8]p. 28cm. (Looking forward
no. 1)
Cover title.
Reprinted from Commentary, Feb.,
1965.
  1. Negroes--Civil rights.
  2. U.S.--Pol. & govt.--1963-
          I. League for Industrial
Democracy.
WHi-L, NNU-T, KU-RH

R150
Rustin, Bayard, 1910-
  The report of the National Advisory Commission on Civil Disorders: an analysis. New York,
A. Philip Randolph Institute
[1968?]
16p. 28cm.
  1. Riots. 2. Negroes--Civil
rights. I. Randolph (A. Philip)
Institute.
CU-B

R151
Rustin, Bayard, 1910-
  "Right to work" laws--a trap for
America's minorities. [New
York] A. Philip Randolph Insti-
tute [196]
15p. 16cm.
Cover title.
  1. Labor and laboring classes.
  2. Right to labor. 3. Minor-
ities. 4. Negroes--Employment.
I. Randolph (A. Philip) Insti-
tute.
KU-RH, WHi-L

R152
Rustin, Bayard, 1910-
  Three essays. [New York] A.
Philip Randolph Institute, 1969.
23p.
  1. Negroes. 2. Randolph (A.
Philip) Institute.
WHi-L

R153
Rustin, Bayard, 1910-
  The Watts "manifesto" & the
McCone report. New York, Lea-
gue for Industrial Democracy
[1966]
[8]p. 28cm.
Cover title.

Reprinted from Commentary, Mar.
1966.
1. Negroes--Civil rights. 2. Los
Angeles--Race question. I. League for Industrial Democracy.
KU-RH, NNU-T

R154
Rustin, Bayard, 1910-
   A way out of the exploding
   ghetto. New York, A. Philip
   Randolph Institute, c1967.
   11p. illus.
   Cover title: which way out?
   1. Negroes--Civil rights.
   2. Slums. I. Randolph (A. Philip) Institute.
   WHi-L

R155
Rustin, Bayard, 1910-
   Which way out? [New York, Lea-
   gue for Industrial Democracy,

1967?]
11p. illus. 22cm. (Looking
forward no. 9)
Cover title.
1. Negroes--Civil rights.
2. Slums. I. League for Industrial Democracy.
NNU-T

R156
Rustin, Bayard, 1910-
   A word to black students. [New
   York, A. Philip Randolph Insti-
   tute, 1970?]
   6p.
   Reprinted from Dissent, Nov
   Dec. 1970.
   1. Students. 2. Negroes--
   Education. I. Randolph (A.
   Philip) Institute.
   WHi-L

✜
S
✜

SANE
   see
National Committee for a Sane Nu-
      clear Policy.

S1
SDS in the northwest. [n.p., 196]
   [3] leaves. 36cm.
   Caption title.
   1. Students for a Democratic
   Society.
   CU-B

SNCC
   see
Student Nonviolent Coordinating
      Committee.

S2
SNCC speaks for itself. Ann Arbor,
      Radical Education Project
   [196]
   12p. 28cm.
   Cover title.
   1. Brown, H. Rap. 2. Student
   Nonviolent Coordinating Commit-

tee. 3. Negroes--Civil rights.
I. Radical Education Project.
CU-B

S3
Sachs, Patricia, ed.
   The Black Panthers. Editor:
   Patricia Sachs, text by J. Alvin
   Kugelmass. New York, Universal
   Publishing and Distributing
   Corporation, c1969.
   1v. (unpaged) illus., ports.
   28cm.
   1. Black Panther Party.
   I. Kugelmass, J. Alvin.
   KU-RH

S4
Sade, Jannie.
   History of the equality issue
   in the contemporary women's
   movement. New York, The Feminists [1969]
   3 leaves. 28cm.
   Caption title.
   1. National Organization

for Women. 2. Woman--History
and condition of women. I. Feminists.
WHi-L

S5
Salisbury, Harrison Evans, 1908-
  The urgent question that domin-
  ates the Asian heartland today is
  will there be war between Russia
  and China? [Woodmont, Conn.,
  Promoting Enduring Peace, 1969?]
  [4]p. 28cm. (No. 150)
  Caption title.
  Reprinted from New York Times
  Magazine, July 27, 1969.
  1. Russia--For. rel.--China
  (People's Republic of China,
  1949-   ) 2. China (People's
  Republic of China, 1949-   )--
  For. rel.--Russia. I. Promoting
  Enduring Peace.
  KU-RH

S6
Samual Mabry Defense Committee
    Against Police Brutality.
  Patrolman brutally assaults
  purple heart veteran. [New York,
  196]
  [4]p. 22cm.
  Caption title.
  1. Mabry, Samual. 2. Police--
  New York (State)--New York (City)
  3. Law enforcement--New York
  (City)
  WHi-A

S8
San Francisco Legal Defense
    Committee.
  Insanity in the courts; the
  story of the mass bust trials of
  the San Francisco State strikers.
  [San Francisco, 196]
  10p. 14x22cm.
  1. Student movements--San Francisco. 2. California. State
  College, San Francisco.
  CU-B

S9
San Francisco's housing market--
    open or closed? Civil rights
    inventory of San Francisco.
    [San Francisco, Council for

Civic Unity of San Francisco,
196]
47p. 22cm.
1. Negroes--San Francisco.
2. San Francisco--Race question.
I. Council for Civic Unity of
San Francisco.
KU-RH

S10
San Jose Peace Center.
  To end the war join in the work
  of the San Jose Peace Center.
  San Jose, Calif. [196]
  folder.
  Cover title.
  1. Vietnamese conflict, 1961-
  1975.
  WHi-A

S11
Sanchez-Mazas, Miguel.
  Spain in chains, a report on
  political repressions in Franco
  Spain. [New York, Veterans of
  the Abraham Lincoln Bridge,
  1959?]
  32p. port. 22cm.
  1. Spain--Hist.--1939-
  2. Political rights, Loss of--
  Spain. I. Veterans of the Abraham Lincoln Brigade.
  KU-RH

S12
Sanders, Helen.
  The churches and social change.
  New York, Distributed by Stu-
  dents for a Democratic Society
  and Young Christian Students
  for the Liberal Study Group
  [196]
  5p. 28cm.
  Cover title.
  1. Church and social problems.
  2. Religion. 3. Social change.
  I. Students for a Democratic
  Society. II. Young Christian
  Students. III. Liberal Study
  Group.
  WHi-A

S13
Santa Anna, Julio de.
  Economic situation of the third
  world: proposals for the solu-

tion of its problems. A speech
delivered by Julio de Santa Anna
to the Third All-Christian Peace
Assembly--Prague, March 31-April
5, 1968. [n.p., 196]
8 [1]p. 28cm.
Caption title.
1. Poverty. 2.World politics--
1965-   I. All-Christian
Peace Assembly, Prague, 3d, 1968.
KU-RH

S14
Sarachild, Kathie.
  Consciousness raising and intui-
tion. [New York, Redstockings of
the Women's Liberation Movement]
1968.
[3]p. 28cm.
Caption title.
1. Woman--Rights of women.
I. Redstockings of the Women's
Liberation Movement.
KU-RH

S15
Sargeant, Jay.
  The moraturium is a cover, not
a solution, by Jay Sargeant, Fred
Gordon, Cheyney Ryan. [Chicago,
Students for a Democratic Soc-
iety, 196]
Caption title.
1. Vietnamese conflict, 1961-
1975. I. Gordon, Fred, jt. auth.
II. Ryan, Cheyney, jt. auth.
III. Students for a Democratic
Society.
CU-B

S16
Satin, Mark Ivor, 1946-   ed.
  Manual for draft-age immigrants
to Canada. 2d ed. Toronto,
Toronto Anti-draft Programme,
1968.
87p. 21cm.
1. Military service, Compulsory.
2. Emigration and immigration
law--Canada. I. Toronto Anti-
draft Programme.
KU-RH

S17
Satin, Mark Ivor, 1946-   ed.
  Manual for draft-age immigrants

to Canada. 2d. ed. Toronto,
House of Anansi, 1968.
128p.
Sponsored by the Toronto Anti-
Draft Programme.
1. Military service, Compulsory.
2. Emigration and immigration
law--Canada.
WHi-L

S18
Saunders, George.
  Rebels and bureaucrats: Soviet
conflicts as seen in Solzhenitsyn's 'Cancer ward'. [New York,
Merit Publishers, 1969]
59p. 18cm.
1. Solzhenitsyn, Aleksandr
Isaevich, 1918-   Cancer
ward. I. Merit Publishers.
KU-RH

S19
Save Our Schools, New Orleans.
  Our stake in New Orleans
schools: a study of education
and economics. New Orleans,
1960.
18 leaves. 28cm.
Cover title.
1. Negroes--Education. 2. New
Orleans--Race question.
CU-B

S20
Savio, Mario.
  An end to history. Nashville,
Southern Student Organizing
Committee [196]
3 leaves. 28cm.
Cover title.
1. Student movements. 2. Uni-
versities and colleges. 3. Ci-
vil rights. I. Southern Stu-
dent Organizing Committee.
CU-B

S21
Savio, Mario.
  The Free Speech Movement and
the Negro revolution, by Mario
Savio, Eugene Walker, Raya Dun-
ayevskaya. Detroit, News and
Letters, 1965.
53p. illus. 23cm.
"Includes also Robert Moses on

Education in the South and Inside
Sproul Hall: an eyewitness account of the arrest of 800 students, by Joel L. Pimsleur.
1. Student movements--Berkeley,
Calif. 2. Negroes--Civil rights.
3. Free Speech Movement. I. Walker, Eugene, jt. auth. II. Dunayevskaya, Raya, jt. auth.
III. Moses, Robert, jt. auth.
IV. News and Letters.
KU, MoU, MH, WHi-L, ICU, KU-RH,
ODW, DLC, NUC 69-11134

S22
Sax, Joseph L.
  Civil disobedience: the law is
  never blind. [Philadelphia,
  American Friends Service Commit-
  tee, c1968]
  folder (5p.) illus. 22cm.
  Caption title.
  Reprinted from Saturday Review,
  Sept. 28, 1968.
  1. Government, Resistance to.
  I. Friends, Society of. Ameri-
  can Friends Service Committee.
  KU-RH

S23
Saxe, Lan Thi.
  U.S. air war against Vietnam.
  [New York, Aid to Vietnamese to
  U.S. Bombings, 196]
  8p. 28cm.
  Caption title.
  1. Vietnamese conflict, 1961-
  1975. I. Aid to Vietnamese
  Victims of U.S. Bombings.
  CU-B, KU-RH

S24
Schechter, Dan.
  The CIA is an equal opportunity
  employer, by Daniel Schechter,
  Michael Ansara & David Kolodney.
  [Cambridge, Mass.] Africa Research Group [196]
  [2] 25-33p. 28cm. (Reprint 4)
  Cover title.
  Reprinted from Ramparts.
  1. U.S. Central Intelligence
  Agency. 2. Africa--Pol. & govt.
  --1960-   3. U.S.--Relations
  (general) with Africa. I. Ansara, Michael, jt. auth. II. Ko-

lodney, David, jt. auth.
III. Africa Research Group.
KU-RH, MoU

S25
Scheer, Robert.
  The winner's war. Berkeley,
  Scheer for Congress [1966?]
  [4]p. 22cm.
  Cover title.
  1. Vietnamese conflict, 1961-
  1975. I. Scheer for Congress.
  CU-B

S26
Schesch, Adam.
  An outline history of Vietnam.
  [Madison? 1965?]
  42p. 28cm.
  Cover title.
  1. Vietnamese conflict, 1961-
  1975. 2. Vietnam--History.
  WHi-A, MoU

S27
Schesch, Adam.
  An outline of Vietnam, prepared
  by Adam Schesch and Frances
  Prevas for the University of
  Wisconsin Student/Faculty Committee to End the War in Vietnam. Madison, National Coordinating Committee to End the War
  in Vietnam, 1965.
  35p. 28cm.
  Cover title.
  1. Vietnamese conflict, 1961-
  1975. 2. Vietnam--History.
  I. Prevas, Frances, jt. auth.
  II. National Coordinating Committee to End the War in Vietnam.
  WHi-L

S28
Schesch, Adam.
  Vietnam: an outline history
  [prepared by Adam Schesch and
  Frances Prevas for the University of Wisconsin Student/
  Faculty Committee to End the War
  in Vietnam. Madison? 196]
  55p.
  Cover title.
  1. Vietnam--History. 2. Viet-

namese conflict, 1961-1975.
I. Prevas, Frances, jt. auth.
WHi-A

S29
Schesch, Adam.
  Who are the Vietcong? [Woodmont,
  Promoting Enduring Peace, 196]
  [4]p. 28cm.
  Caption title.
  Reprinted from The Progressive.
  1. Viet Cong. 2. Vietnamese
  conflict, 1961-1975. I. Promo-
  ting Enduring Peace.
  KU-RH

S30
Schiff, Paul M.
  The Schiff papers. [Ann Arbor?
  196]
  [18]p.
  Cover title.
  1. Student movements--Ann Arbor,
  Mich.
  WHi-L

S31
Schiffrin, Andre.
  The student movement in the '50s:
  a reminiscence. Boston, New En-
  gland Free Press [196]
  6p. 28cm.
  Cover title.
  Reprinted from Radical America,
  May-June 1968.
  1. Student League for Industrial
  Democracy. 2. Student movements
  --History. I. New England Free
  Press.
  MoU, MiU, KU-RH

S32
Schleifer, Marc.
  A letter from Havana [Toronto,
  Fair Play for Cuba Committee,
  196]
  4 [2]p. 22cm.
  Cover title.
  Reprinted from The Nation,
  April 27, 1964.
  1. Cuba. I. Fair Play for Cuba
  Committee.
  MiU

S33
Schoenbrum, David.

Vietnam and beyond. Testimony
presented before the Senate Foreign Relations Committee, May 13,
1970. [Ithaca, N.Y., Glad Day
Press, 1970?]
12p. 28cm.
Cover title.
1. Vietnamese conflict, 1961-
1975. I. Glad Day Press.
NNU-T

S34
Scholarship, Education and De-
    fense Fund for Racial Equality.
  How to raise money for community
  action. [New York, 196]
  23p.
  1. Community organization.
  WHi-L

S35
Scholarship, Education and De-
    fense Fund for Racial Equality.
  Your welfare rights: New Jersey
  residents handbook of information. [New York] 1967.
  40p. illus.
  1. Public welfare--New Jersey.
  WHi-L

S36
Schrader, Emmie.
  Poor whites and the movement.
  Nashville, Southern Student Or-
  ganizing Committee [196]
  3 leaves. 28cm.
  Cover title.
  1. Poor--Mississippi. 2. Mis-
  sissippi--Race question.
  I. Southern Student Organizing
  Committee.
  WHi-L, MiU

S37
Schuman, Frederick Lewis, 1904-
  Why a department of peace?
  [Beverly Hills, Calif., Another
  Mother for Peace, c1969]
  28p. 23cm.
  1. Peace. I. Another Mother
  for Peace.
  CSt-H, NUC 70-96313

S38
Schuman, Frederick Lewis, 1904-
  Why a department of peace?

[2d. ed. Beverly Hills, Calif.,
Another Mother for Peace, c1969]
56p. 23cm.
1. Peace. 2. U.S.--Pol. & govt.
--1963-   I. Another Mother
for Peace.
CU-B, KU-RH

S39
Schwartz, Rosalind.
 Notes from the lower class. New
 York, The Feminists [196]
 [2] leaves. 28cm.
 Caption title.
 1. Jews. 2. Woman--Rights of
 women. I. Feminists.
 WHi-L

S40
Schwartz, Rosalind.
 Notes from the working class: a
 Jewish woman speaks her mind.
 New York, The Feminists [196]
 3p. 28cm.
 Caption title.
 1. Woman, Jewish. 2. Woman--
 Rights of women. I. Feminists.
 KU-RH

S41
Scott, Jack.
 Second look at Cuba. Toronto,
 Fair Play for Cuba [1963]
 28p. 22cm.
 Reprinted from Vancouver Sun
 from May 28 to June 7, 1963.
 1. Cuba. I. Fair Play for Cuba
 Committee.
 MoU, MiU, DLC, CaBViP

S42
Scott, Lawrence.
 A call to repentance for a change
 of heart. For a new direction
 [by Lawrence Scott and Wilmer
 Young. n.p., 1962?]
 [2]p. 28cm.
 Caption title.
 1. Pacifism. 2. Disarmament.
 I. Young, Wilmer, jt. auth.
 KU-RH

S43
Scott, Lawrence.
 The communist issue in the peace
 movement of America. [n.p.,

196]
4p. 28cm.
Caption title.
1. Peace--Societies, etc.
2. Communism.
KU-RH

S44
Scott, Peter Dale.
 Air America; flying the U.S.
 into Laos. Boston, New England
 Free Press [1970?]
 7p. illus. 28cm.
 Cover title.
 Reprinted from Ramparts, Feb.
 1970.
 1. Air America, Inc. 2. Laos--
 For. rel.--U.S. 3. U.S. Cen-
 tral Intelligence Agency.
 I. New England Free Press.
 KU-RH

S45
Scott, Peter Dale.
 Cambodia: why the generals won.
 [Ithaca, N.Y., Glad Day Press,
 1970?]
 11p. illus. 28cm.
 Cover title.
 Reprinted from New York Review
 of Books, June 18, 1970.
 1. Cambodia. I. Glad Day Press.
 NNU-T

S46
Scott, Peter Dale.
 Laos, Nixon, and the CIA.
 [Ithaca, N.Y., Glad Day Press,
 1970?]
 10 [2]p. illus. 28cm.
 Cover title.
 Reprinted from New York Review
 of Books, Ap. 9, 1970.
 1. Laos--For. rel.--U.S. 2. U.
 S.--For. rel.--Laos. 3. U.S.
 Central Intelligence Agency.
 I. Glad Day Press.
 NNU-T

S47
Scott, Stanley, 1921-
 Metropolitan problems and pro-
 grams for state action. [San
 Francisco, Calif., Americans
 for Democratic Action, State
 Policy Committee, 1962]

[24]p.
1. Metropolitan areas. I. Americans for Democratic Action.
MH-PA, NUC 65-42397

S48
Scull, David H.
    Loyalty, oaths, and conscience.
    Richmond, Ind. [etc.] Board on
    Peace and Social Concerns, The
    Five Years Meetings of Friends
    [etc.] 1961.
    folder (6p.) 23x10cm.
    1. Loyalty oaths. 2. Patriotism.
    KU-RH

S49
Seale, Bobby.
    Message from Bobby Seale on
    harassment of Connecticut State
    Panthers. [n.p., 1970?]
    [1] leaf. 36cm.
    Caption title.
    1. Black Panther Party. 2. Ne-
    groes--Connecticut. 3. Connect-
    icut--Race question.
    CU-B

S50
Search for peace in the Middle
    East. Philadelphia, American
    Friends Service Committee [1970]
    vii, 75p. 23cm.
    1. Jewish-Arab relations.
    I. Friends, Society of. American
    Friends Service Committee.
    DLC 72-17074

S51
Seattle Group.
    About the Seattle Group. [Sea-
    ttle, 196]
    [8]p.
    Cover title.
    1. Anarchism and anarchists--
    Seattle.
    MiU

S52
Seattle Post Intelligencer.
    Seattle women speak out. Seat-
    tle, Radical Women, 1970.
    [14] leaves. 28cm.
    Cover title.
    A reprint from Seattle Post In-
    telligencer series on the woman's

liberation movement.
    1. Woman--Rights of women.
    I. Radical Women.
    WHi-L

S53
Seattle Radical Women.
    Program and structure. Seattle
    [1969]
    10 leaves. 28cm.
    Caption title.
    1. Woman--Rights of women.
    WHi-L

S54
Seattle Women's Liberation. Abor-
    tion Committee.
    1 out of 4; an abortion primer.
    [Seattle, 1970]
    20p.
    Cover title.
    1. Abortion.
    WHi-L

S55
Seattle Youth for Peace in Vietnam.
    Statement by Seattle Youth for
    Peace in Vietnam on the recent
    harassment of the W.E.B. DuBois
    Clubs by the U.S. government and
    others. Seattle [196]
    [1] leaf. 28cm.
    Caption title.
    1. DuBois (W.E.B.) Clubs of
    America.
    WHi-A

S56
Seaver, Ben.
    Should the draft be dropped?
    Washington, National Council to
    Repeal the Draft [1970?]
    4p. 28cm.
    Caption title.
    1. Military service, Compulsory.
    I. National Council to Repeal
    the Draft.
    KU-RH

S57
Seeley, John.
    The Berkeley issue in time and
    place. [Montreal] Our Genera-
    tion [196]
    6 [1]p. illus. 22cm.
    Cover title.

1. Student movements--Berkeley,
Calif. 2. Education--Canada.
2. Universities and colleges--
Canada. I. Our Generation.
NNU-T

C58
Selsam, Howard, 1903-
    Ethics and progress; new values
    in a revolutionary world. New
    York, International Publishers
    [1965]
    126p. 18cm.
    1. Ethics. 2. Social changes.
    I. International Publishers.
    DLC 65-16395

S59
Serviceman's Link to Peace.
    Chronology of events surrounding
    the Fort Jackson eight. Washing-
    ton [196]
    7 [2]p. 28cm.
    Caption title.
    1. Soldiers.
    WHi-L

S60
Severn, Jill.
    Women and draft resistance: re-
    volution in the revolution. Sea-
    ttle, Radical Women [1968]
    [3]p. 28cm.
    Caption title.
    1. Military service, Compulsory.
    2. Woman--Rights of women.
    I. Radical Women.
    WHi-L

S61
Sexton, Brendan.
    "Middle class" workers and the
    new politics. New York, League
    for Industrial Democracy [1969?]
    [8]p. 24cm. (Looking forward
    no. 15)
    Cover title.
    Reprinted from Dissent, May-
    June 1969.
    1. Trade-unions. 2. Labor and
    laboring classes. 3. Social
    classes. 4. Liberalism. I. Lea-
    gue for Industrial Democracy.
    KU-RH, MiU, NNU-T

S62
Sexual Freedom League.
    Statement of position. [Berke-
    ley, Calif., 196]
    14p.
    Cover title.
    1. Sex.
    WHi-L

S63
Shachtman, Max, 1903-
    Two views on the Cuban invasion.
    [Oakland, Calif., H. Draper,
    1961]
    16p. 29cm.
    Cover title.
    1. Cuba--History--Invasion, 1961.
    I. Draper, Hal.
    NcD, NUC 66-50325

S64
Shackleton, N.A.
    The war-making potential of
    communist China. Toronto, Re-
    search, Information and Publi-
    cations Project, Student Union
    for Peace Action [196]
    8p. 28cm.
    Cover title.
    1. China (People's Republic of
    China, 1949-   )--Military
    policy. I. Student Union for
    Peace Action.
    WHi-A

S65
Shapiro, Peter.
    San Francisco State, by Peter
    Shapiro and Bill Barlow. San
    Francisco, Bay Area Radical
    Education Project [1969?]
    15 leaves. 28cm.
    Cover title.
    Reprinted from Leviathan.
    1. Student movement--San Fran-
    cisco. 2. California. State
    College, San Francisco. I. Bay
    Area Radical Education Project.
    II. Barlow, Bill, jt. auth.
    CU-B

S66
Sharp, Gene.
    The need for a substitute for
    war. [Montreal] Our Genera-

tion [196]
50-[57]p.
Caption title.
At head of title: Conflict and
struggle.
1. War. I. Our Generation.
NNU-T

S67
Shaw, Robert, comp.
  Questions for the administration.
  [Washington, 1966]
  [4]p. 28cm.
  Caption title.
  Reprinted from Concern, Nov. 1,
  1966.
  1. Vietnamese conflict, 1961-
  1975.
  KU-RH

S68
Sheak, Bob.
  The center of power in St. Louis,
  interlocking directorates, and
  the United Fund. [St. Louis]
  RAP, 1970.
  [20]p. illus. 28cm.
  Cover title.
  1. St. Louis, Mo.--Pol. & govt.
  2. Corporations--St. Louis.
  3. United Fund. I. RAP.
  KU-RH

S69
Sheehan, Neil.
  Not a dove, but no longer a hawk.
  [New York, National Committee for
  a Sane Nuclear Policy, 1966]
  [5] leaves.
  Reprinted from New York Times.
  1. Vietnamese conflict, 1961-
  1975. I. National Committee for
  a Sane Nuclear Policy.
  WHi-L

S70
Shelley, Martha.
  Steppen Fetchit woman. [n.p.,
  1970?]
  4 leaves. 28cm.
  Cover title.
  1. Homosexuality.
  CU-B

S71
Shephard, David A.E.

Chemical and biological warfare:
some implications for society.
Victoria, Canada, The Jim Lawson Memorial Fund [196]
8p. 28cm.
Caption title.
1. Biological warfare. I. Jim
Lawson Memorial Fund.
KU-RH

S72
Shero, Jeffery.
  Bulletin proposal. [n.p., 1965]
  3p. 28cm.
  Caption title.
  At head of title: 1965 SDS nat-
  ional convention--working paper.
  1. Students for a Democratic
  Society. Bulletin. I. Stu-
  dents for a Democratic Society.
  National Convention, 1965.
  WHi-A, KU-RH

S73
Shero, Jeffery.
  M.D.S.--Movement for a Democra-
  tic Society. [n.p., 1965]
  3p. 28cm.
  Caption title.
  At head of title: 1965 SDS na-
  tional convention--working paper.
  1. Movement for a Democratic
  Society. I. Students for a De-
  mocratic Society. National
  Convention, 1965.
  KU-RH, WHi-A

S74
Sherry, Gerard E.
  Civil liberties Catholic concern. Landale, Calif., Catholic Council on Civil Liberties
  [196]
  [3]p.
  Cover title.
  1. Civil rights. I. Catholic
  Council on Civil Liberties.
  MiU

S75
Shields, Art.
  Unemployment: the wolf at the
  door. [New York, New Century
  Publishers, 1958]
  22p.
  1. Socialism. 2. Unemployed.

I. New Century Publishers.
MiU, S172

S76
Shiller, Edward.
Report of the research director
of the Baltimore Research and
Action Project to the Economic
Research and Action Project.
[Baltimore?] 1964.
11 leaves. 28cm.
Cover title.
1. Baltimore--Econ. condit.
2. Poor--Baltimore. I. Students
for a Democratic Society. Economic Research and Action Project.
WHi-A

S77
Shoup, David M.
The new American militarism.
Woodmont, Conn., Promoting En-
during Peace [1969?]
folder. 22cm.
Caption title.
Reprinted from Atlantic Monthly.
1. U.S.--Military policy.
I. Promoting Enduring Peace.
KU-RH

S78
Shumm, Lawrence.
A revolutionary perspective for
the anti-war movement, by Lawrence Schumm and Clara Kaye.
[n.p., 196]
2 leaves. 28cm.
Caption title.
1. Vietnamese conflict, 1961-
1975. I. Kaye, Clara, jt. auth.
WHi-A

S79
Shu-tse, Peng.
Behind China's "great cultural
revolution", by Peng Shu-tse
[and others. New York, Pathfinder Press, 1970]
63p. 22cm.
Cover title.
1. China (People's Republic of
China, 1949-   )--Social conditions. 2. China (People's
Republic of China, 1949-   )--
Pol. & govt. I. Pathfinder

Press.
KU-RH

S80
Sibley, Mulford Quickert.
Unilateral initiatives and disarmament; a study and commentary. [Philadelphia, Peace
Literature Service of the American Friends Service Committee,
c1962]
64p. 21cm. (Beyond deterrence
series)
1. Disarmament. I. Friends,
Society of. American Friends
Service Committee.
NcD, MH, DS, MoU, MH, DLC 64-
56023, WHi-L

S81
Siebert, Bill.
The war in Vietnam and the
American economy; who pays; who
pays; who profits? [By Bill
Siebert and others. Ithaca,
N.Y., Glad Day Press, 1970?]
23p. 28cm.
Cover title.
1. Vietnamese conflict, 1961-
1975. I. Glad Day Press.
NNU-T

S82
Siegel, Leonard.
Guide to draft counseling.
[Palo Alto? Stanford Anti-Draft
Union, 1968?]
8p. 28cm.
Caption title.
1. Military service, Compulsory.
I. Stanford Anti-Draft Union.
WHi-L

S83
Siff, David.
Imperialism on campus. [Madi-
son? 196]
[3]p. 28cm.
1. Military research. 2. Universities and colleges.
WHi-L

S84
Simon, Jean.
Desegregation. Labor's stake
in the fight for Negro equal-

ity. [New York, Pioneer Publishers, 1955]
16p.
Cover title.
1. Labor and laboring classes.
2. Negroes--Civil rights. I. Pioneer Publishers.
MiU

S85
Simpson, Charlie.
  Kennedy's cultural center is a
  leopard--skin pillbox hat. Ann
  Arbor, Radical Education Project
  [196]
  8p. illus. 22cm.
  Cover title.
  Reprinted from Caw.
  1. Popular culture. I. Radical
  Education Project.
  MoU

S86
Sinclair, John.
  Ten years for two joints. [Ann
  Arbor, Youth International Par-
  ty; White Panthers, 1969]
  8p.
  Cover title.
  1. Narcotics. 2. White Panther
  Party. I. Youth International
  Party. II. White Panther Party.
  WHi-L

S87
Singleton, Fred.
  Two articles on Yugoslavia [by]
  Fred Singleton [and others. Bos-
  ton, New England Free Press,
  196]
  1v. (various pagings) 22cm.
  Cover title.
  Reprinted from New Left Review,
  no. 18, and Monthly Review,
  Mar. 1964.
  1. Socialism in Yugoslavia.
  2. Yugoslavia--Pol. & govt.
  3. Labor and laboring classes--
  Yugoslavia. I. New England Free
  Press.
  KU-RH

S88
Situationist International.
  The decline and the fall of the
  "spectacular" commodity-economy.

[New York, 1965?]
[8]p. 22cm.
Cover title.
1. Negroes--Civil rights.
2. Riots.
WHi-L, CU-B

S89
Situationist International.
  On the poverty of student life.
  A consideration of its economic,
  political, sexual, psychological
  and notable intellectual aspects
  and of a few ways to cure it.
  1st American ed. New York 1967.
  36p. 22cm.
  Cover title.
  1. Student movements. 2. Students.
  MiU, WHi-A

S90
Situationist International.
  On the poverty of student life
  [translated from French by Sit-
  uationist International. New
  York, 196]
  21p. 22cm.
  Cover title.
  1. Student movements--Strasbourg
  Universite.
  CU-B

S91
Situationist International.
  Ten days that shook the university. [New York, 196]
  25p. 22cm.
  Cover title.
  1. Student movements--Stras-
  bourg Universite.
  WHi-A, CU-B

S92
Situationist International.
  Watts uprising '65. [Mountain
  View? SRAF Print Co-op, 196]
  [16]p. 22cm.
  Cover title.
  1. Negroes--Los Angeles.
  2. Los Angeles--Riots. 3. Ana-
  rchism and anarchists. I. SRAF
  Print Co-op.
  MiU

S93
Six statements: peace in America.
   [n.p., Peace & Liberation Commune Press, 196]
   [12]p. 28cm.
   Cover title.
   1. Military service, Compulsory.
   2. Government, Resistance to.
   I. Peace & Liberation Commune
   Press.
   CU-B

S94
Slate.
   The big myth. [Berkeley, Calif.,
   1961?]
   [16]p. 28cm.
   Cover title.
   1. Students movements--Berkeley,
   Calif.
   MiU

S95
Slate.
   Slate platform; ASUC general
   election spring 1962. [Berkeley?
   1962]
   [7]p. 21cm.
   Cover title.
   1. Student movements--Berkeley,
   Calif. 2. California, University.
   MiU

S96
Slate. Summer Conference, 1962.
   The negro in America--working
   papers. [n.p., 1962]
   35 [14]p. 28cm.
   Cover title.
   Partial contents--Northern school
   segregation, by Frederick D.
   Smith; The negro and organized
   labor, by Doug Brown; Negro farm
   workers and human rights, by
   Hank Anderson; Automation, education, and delinquency, by Carl
   Werthman.
   1. Negroes--Civil rights. 2. Agricultural laborers. 3. Labor
   and laboring classes.
   WHi-A

S97
Slater, R. Giuseppi.
   The earth belongs to the people:

ecology and power. [Research &
text by R. Giuseppi Slater and
others. San Francisco, Peoples
Press, c1970]
   45p. illus. 28cm.
   Cover title.
   1. Pollution. 2. Ecology.
   I. Peoples Press.
   KU-RH

S98
Smash ROTC. [n.p., 1970?]
   10p. 22cm.
   Cover title.
   1. U.S. Army. Reserve Officer's
   Training Corps.
   CU-B

S99
Smedberg, Mike.
   Duke trustees & labor. Nashville, Southern Student Organizing Committee [196]
   9p. 28cm.
   Cover title.
   1. Duke University, Durham, N.
   C. 2. Labor and laboring
   classes--Duke University, Durham, N.C.
   MoU

S100
Smiley, Glenn E.
   Nonviolence in Latin America: a
   first-hand report. [Nyack, N.
   Y.? Fellowship Publications?
   1968?]
   [2]p. 36cm.
   Caption title.
   Reprinted from Fellowship,
   Sept. 1968.
   1. Nonviolence. 2. Latin Ameri-
   ca--Pol. & govt. I. Fellowship
   Publications.
   KU-RH

S101
Smith, Bill.
   Court-martial turned around;
   Pvt. M. Smith charges military
   harassment. [New York, American Servicemen's Union, 1970]
   24p. illus. 22cm.
   1. Soldiers. I. American Servicemen's Union.
   KU-RH

S102
Smith, Charles L.
  Prisoner release: work furlough
  and conjugal visits, a biblio-
  graphy compiled from the files of
  the Institute of Governmental
  Studies, University of Califor-
  nia, Berkeley by Charles L.
  Smith. [San Francisco, Friends
  Committee on Legislation, n.d.]
  2 leaves.
  1. Prisoners--Bibl. I. Friends
  Committee on Legislation, San
  Francisco.
  ICU, NUC 68-6136

S103
Smith, Charles L.
  Police review boards, a biblio-
  graphy compiled from assorted
  materials gathered by the staff
  of the Institute of Governmental
  Studies [University of Califor-
  nia. San Francisco, Friends
  Committee on Legislation, 1965]
  3 leaves.
  1. Police--Bibl. I. Friends
  Committee on Legislation, San
  Francisco.
  ICU, NUC 68-5897

S104
Smith, Edouard.
  Quebec: a historical overview.
  [Montreal, Our Generation, 196]
  13-33 leaves.
  Caption title.
  1. Quebec--History. I. Our
  Generation.
  NNU-T

S105
Smith, Jessica, 1895-
  The American people want peace;
  a survey of public opinion. New
  York, S.R.T. Publications, 1955.
  47p. 20cm.
  1. Peace. 2. U.S.--For. rel.--
  1945-   3. World politics--
  1955-
  DLC 56-20989

S106
Smith, Jessica, 1895-
  Hungary in travail. [New York,
  New Century Publishers, 1956]

23p.
  Reprinted from New World Review, Dec. 1956.
  1. Hungary--Pol. & govt.
  2. Hungary--History--Revolution,
  1956. 3. Communism--Hungary.
  I. New Century Press.
  MiEM, NUC 68-19624

S107
Smith, Jessica, 1895-
  Soviet democracy, and how it
  works. All photos from Sovfoto.
  New York, National Council of
  American-Soviet Friendship,
  1969.
  96p. illus., ports. 22cm.
  (Half century series)
  Reprinted from New World Review,
  Jan.-July, 1967.
  1. Russia--Pol. & govt.--1953-
     I. New World Review.
  II. National Council of Ameri-
  can-Soviet Friendship.
  DLC 73-7423, KU-RH

S108
Smith, Jessica, 1895-
  What rearming Germany means.
  [New York, New World Review,
  1955]
  23p. 21cm.
  Cover title.
  Reprinted from New World Review,
  Jan. 1955.
  1. Germany (Federal Republic,
  1949-   )--Military policy.
  I. New World Review.
  MiU, NNJef, CSSR

S109
Smith, John, pseud.
  Birch putsch plans for 1964, by
  John Smith [pseud.] as told to
  Stanhope T. McReady. [n.p.]
  Domino Publications, 1963.
  95p. 14cm.
  1. Welch, Robert Henry Winborne,
  1899-   2. John Birch Soc-
  iety. I. Domino Publications.
  II. McReady, Stanhope T.
  KU-RH

S110
Smith, Lee.
  Political and legal defense.

[n.p., 1970?]
2p. 28cm.
Caption title.
At head of title: Young Socialist Alliance position paper.
1. Justice, Administration of.
2. Student movements. I. Young
Socialist Alliance.
KU-RH

S111
Smith, Robert Freeman.
  Social revolution in Latin Ameri-
  ca: the role of U.S. aid. Boston,
  New England Free Press [196]
  [637]-649p. 22cm.
  Cover title.
  Reprinted from International Af-
  fairs (London), Oct. 1965.
  1. U.S.--Relations (general) with
  Latin America. 2. Revolutions--
  Latin America. 3. Latin America
  --Soc. condit. I. New England
  Free Press.
  MoU, WHi-L

S112
Smith, Walker C.
  Sabotage: its history, philosophy
  & function. [Chicago, Black Swan
  Press, 196]
  32p. 17cm.
  Cover title.
  1. Sabotage. 2. Strikes and
  lockouts. 3. Capitalism.
  4. Labor and laboring classes.
  I. Black Swan Press.
  KU-RH

S113
Snow, Edgar, 1905-
  War and peace in Vietnam. New
  York, Marzani & Munsell [1963]
  [680]-707p. 23cm.
  1. Vietnam--History. I. Marzani
  and Munsell.
  WHi-L

S114
Sobell Committee.
  The facts in the Rosenberg-Sobell
  case, 1950-1964. [New York,
  1964?]
  8p. ports.
  Cover title.
  1. Justice, Administration of.

  2. Sobell, Morton. 3. Rosenberg, Julius, 1918-1953. 4. Rosenberg, Ethel (Greenglass),
  1916-1953.
  WHi-L

S115
Sober, Richard.
  30 [cents] for what? By Rich-
  ard Sober, Paul Milkman, and
  Leif Johnson. [New York] New
  York Labor Committee and the
  Joint Committee on Transit,
  1969.
  23p. 22cm.
  Cover title.
  1. Subways--New York (City)
  I. Milkman, Paul, jt. auth.
  II. Johnson, Leif, jt. auth.
  III. New York Labor Committee.
  IV. Joint Committee on Transit.
  KU-RH

S116
Socialist Committee of Correspon-
    dence.
  The Cameron resignation documents. New York [196]
  47 leaves. 28cm.
  Cover title.
  1. Cameron, Bruce. 2. Socialist Labor Party.
  CU-B

S117
Socialist Committee of Correspon-
    dence.
  The truth about the section
  Palo Alto. New York [1967?]
  [28] leaves. 28cm.
  Cover title.
  1. Socialist Labor Party.
  CU-B

S118
Socialist Committee of Correspon-
    dence.
  United States out of Vietnam
  now; smash imperialism! [New
  York, 196]
  [2]p. 28cm.
  Caption title.
  1. Vietnamese conflict, 1961-
  1975. 2. Imperialism.
  KU-RH

S119
Socialist Labor Party.
  Angry, frightened over Vietnam?
  Then read this. [Brooklyn, 1965?]
  [4]p. 22cm.
  Caption title.
  1. Vietnamese conflict, 1961-
  1975.
  KU-RH

S120
Socialist Labor Party.
  Automation crisis: how safe is
  your job? [Brooklyn, 1964?]
  [4]p. 23cm.
  Caption title.
  1. Automation.
  KU-RH

S121
Socialist Labor Party.
  Greatest robbery in history: the
  exploitation of wage-labor.
  [Brooklyn, 196]
  [4]p. illus. 28cm.
  Caption title.
  1. Labor and laboring classes.
  2. Capitalism.
  KU-RH

S122
Socialist Labor Party.
  His strike is your concern.
  [Brooklyn, 196]
  [4]p. 23cm.
  1. Strikes and lockouts.
  KU-RH

S123
Socialist Labor Party.
  How to build a sane world.
  [Brooklyn, 1955?]
  [4]p. 23cm.
  Caption title.
  At head of title: a do-it-your-
  self plan for labor.
  1. Socialism.
  KU-RH

S124
Socialist Labor Party.
  The majority wants peace, but.
  [Brooklyn, 1969?]
  folder. 18x19cm.
  Caption title.
  1. Vietnamese conflict, 1961-

1975. 2. U.S.--Military
policy.
KU-RH

S125
Socialist Labor Party.
  The 1956 platform of the Social-
  ist Labor Party: peace, plenty,
  freedom. [New York, 1956]
  [4]p. ports. 23cm.
  Caption title.
  WHi-L

S126
Socialist Labor Party.
  Not black power, not white power, but worker's power. [Brook-
  lyn, 1968?]
  [4]p. 23cm.
  1. Negroes--Employment. 2. Labor and laboring classes.
  KU-RH

S127
Socialist Labor Party.
  Peace is possible. [New York,
  1960?]
  [4]p. 22cm.
  Caption title.
  1. Peace.
  KU-RH

S128
Socialist Labor Party.
  Politicians promise and things
  get worse. Why? [Brooklyn,
  1968]
  [4]p. 22cm.
  Caption title.
  1. Socialism. 2. Politics,
  Practical.
  KU-RH

S129
Socialist Labor Party.
  The promise of socialism.
  [Brooklyn, 1960?]
  [4]p. 23cm.
  Caption title.
  1. Socialism.
  KU-RH

S130
Socialist Labor Party.
  Race prejudice, why? Who bene-
  fits from it? [Brooklyn, 1957]

[4]p. 23cm.
Caption title.
1. Race discrimination.
KU-RH

S131
Socialist Labor Party.
  Rightism is American fascism.
  [New York, 1962?]
  [4]p. 22cm.
  1. Fascism. 2. John Birch Society. 3. Anti-communist movements.
KU-RH

S132
Socialist Labor Party.
  Socialism: champion of civilized
  principles. [Brooklyn, 1965?]
  [4]p. 22cm.
  Caption title.
  1. Socialism.
KU-RH

S133
Socialist Labor Party.
  Socialism--its meaning and pro-
  mise. [Brooklyn, 196]
  [4]p. 23cm.
  Caption title.
  1. Socialism.
KU-RH

S134
Socialist Labor Party.
  Socialism versus Soviet despot-
  ism. [Brooklyn, 1958?]
  [4]p. 22cm.
  Cover title.
  1. Communism--Russia. 2. Russia
  --Pol. & govt.
KU-RH

S135
Socialist Labor Party.
  Socialist industrial unionism.
  [Brooklyn, 1957?]
  [4]p. illus. 28cm.
  Caption title.
  1. Socialism.
KU-RH

S136
Socialist Labor Party.
  Socialist Labor Party: position
  & program. Brooklyn [196]

folder. 22x10cm.
Cover title.
1. Socialism.
KU-RH

S137
Socialist Labor Party.
  This is prosperity? [Brooklyn,
  196]
  folder. 18cm.
  Caption title.
  1. U.S.--Econ. condit.--1961-
        2. Inflation (Finance)
KU-RH

S138
Socialist Labor Party.
  Vietnam: understanding vs.
  emotion. Do demonstrations have
  value? [Brooklyn, 1966?]
  [4]p. 23cm.
  Caption title.
  1. Vietnamese conflict, 1961-
  1975. 2. Government, Resistance to.
KU-RH

S139
Socialist Labor Party.
  War and unemployment: capitalism the cause; socialism the
  solution. New York, New York
  Labor News Co., 1958.
  14p.
  1. Socialism. 2. War--Economic
  aspects.
MH-IR, NN

S140
Socialist Labor Party.
  War why? [Brooklyn, 1960?]
  [4]p. 22cm.
  Caption title.
  1. War. 2. Capitalism. 3. Soc-
  ialism.
KU-RH

S141
Socialist Labor Party.
  What causes war? [Brooklyn,
  1958?]
  [4]p. 22cm.
  Caption title.
  A letter from editor of the
  Weekly People published in the
  Daily News of McKeesport, Pa.

1. War.   2. Capitalism.
KU-RH

S142
Socialist Labor Party.
 What is socialism? Answering
 questions most frequently asked.
 New York, New York Labor News
 Co., 1958.
 45p. illus. 18cm.
 Sixteenth printing.
 1. Socialism.
 WHi-L

S143
Socialist Labor Party.
 What is socialism? Answering
 questions most frequently asked.
 New York, New York Labor News
 Co., 1962.
 45p. 18cm.
 "Nineteenth printing."
 1. Socialism. I. New York
 Labor News Co.
 KU-RH

S144
Socialist Labor Party.
 What is socialism? Answering
 questions most frequently asked.
 New York, New York Labor News
 Co., 1963.
 45p. 19cm.
 1. Socialism.
 CU-B

S145
Socialist Labor Party.
 Which would you choose? Capit-
 alism, state despotism, or real
 socialism. [Brooklyn, 1963?]
 [4]p. 28cm.
 Cover title.
 1. Capitalism. 2. Communism--
 Russia. 3. Socialism.
 KU-RH

S146
Socialist Labor Party.
 Who speaks for socialism?
 [Brooklyn, 1956?]
 [4]p. 22cm.
 Caption title.
 1. Socialism. 2. Socialist
 Workers Party. 3. Socialist
 Party (U.S.)
 KU-RH

S147
Socialist Labor Party.
 Young people have good reason
 to rebel. [Brooklyn, 196]
 folder. 18cm.
 Caption title.
 1. Youth--Political activity.
 2. Socialism.
 KU-RH

S148
Socialist League for Industrial
   Government.
 Society in crisis; a DeLeonist
 appraisal. [Menlo Park, Calif.,
 etc., 196]
 4p. 28cm.
 Caption title.
 1. Socialism. 2. U.S.--Econ.
 condit.
 KU-RH

Socialist Party-Social Democratic Federation
 see also
Socialist Party (U.S.)

S149
Socialist Party-Social Democra-
   tic Federation.
 Socialist platform 1960. [New
 York, 1960?]
 21p. 22cm.
 1. Socialism.
 KU-RH, WHi-L, DLC 61-1217

S150
Socialist Party-Social Democratic
   Federation.
 Unity convention, January 18-
 19, 1957, New York, minutes.
 [New York, 1957]
 8p.
 1. Socialism.
 MH-PA

S151
Socialist Party-Social Democratic
   Federation.
 A way forward; political realignment in America, political
 declaration of the 1960 national convention. [New York, 1960]
 8p. 22cm.
 1. Socialism. 2. U.S.--Pol. &
 govt.--1961-
 KU-RH, DLC 61-2776

Socialist Party (U.S.)
see also
Socialist Party-Social Democratic
Federation

S152
Socialist Party (U.S.)
The crisis in higher education.
New York [1969]
[7]p.   28cm.
Cover title.
1. Universities and colleges.
CU-B

S153
Socialist Party (U.S.)
Nixon and Wallace must be de-
feated; appeal to reason--'68
elections.   [New York, 1968?]
8p.   28cm.
Cover title.
1. Nixon, Richard Milhous,
Pres U.S., 1913-   2. Wallace, George Corley, 1919-
3. Presidents--U.S.--Election--
1968.
CU-B

S154
Socialist Party (U.S.)
A Nixon decade or a new era of
social progress? Statement by
the Socialist Party, U.S.A. and
the Young People's Socialist League. New York [1970]
12p.   23x10cm.
At head of title: The challenge
of the 1970 elections.
1. Nixon, Richard Milhous, Pres.
U.S., 1913-   2. U.S.--Pol.
& govt.--1969-   I. Young
People's Socialist League.
KU-RH

S155
Socialist Party (U.S.)
Robot revolution: the implications of automation.   [New York]
Socialist Society, USA, Pennsylvania, 1955.
47p.   illus. 23cm.
1. Automation.
IU

S156
Socialist Party (U.S.)

The Socialist Party looks at
the war on poverty. [New York,
196]
2p.   28cm.
Caption title.
1. Poverty. 2. U.S.   Office of
Economic Opportunity.
KU-RH

S157
Socialist Party (U.S.)
Socialist Party, U.S.A., for a
mass movement of the democratic
left. [New York, 196]
folder. 21x9cm.
Cover title.
1. Socialism.
KU-RH

S158
Socialist Party (U.S.)
Socialist platform, 1964.   [New
York, 1964]
30p.   22cm.
Cover title.
1. Socialism.
KU-RH

S159
Socialist Party (U.S.)
Socialist platform, 1966.   New
York [1966?]
65p.   28cm.
Cover title.
1. Socialism.
CU-B

S160
Socialist Party (U.S.)
A socialist program for the
seventies. New York [1970?]
16p.   28cm.
Cover title.
1. Socialism. 2. U.S.--Pol. &
govt.--1969-
KU-RH

S161
Socialist Party (U.S.)
Some questions and answers on
democratic socialism.   [New
York, c1965]
14p.
1. Socialism.
WHi-L

S162
Socialist Party (U.S.)
  To build a better world: the 1962
  socialist platform. New York
  [1962?]
  28p. 22cm.
  1. Socialism. 2. U.S.--Pol. &
  govt.--1963-
  KU-RH, CU-B

S163
Socialist Party (U.S.)
  To build a democratic left. [New
  York, 1968]
  24p. 23cm.
  Cover title.
  At head of title: 1968 platform:
  Socialist Party, U.S.A.
  1. Socialism.
  CU-B, KU-RH

S164
Socialist Party (U.S.) Washington.
  Some perspectives for the anti-
  war movement [by Socialist Party
  of Washington State and Student
  Peace Union. Seattle, Wash.,
  196]
  [2]p. 28cm.
  Cover title.
  1. Vietnamese conflict, 1961-
  1975. I. Student Peace Union,
  Seattle, Wash.
  KU-RH

S165
Socialist Society, U.S.A. Debs
  Centennial Committee.
  Eugene Victor Debs (1855-1955):
  the centennial year. [New York]
  1956.
  53p.
  1. Debs, Eugene Victor, 1855-
  1926.
  CtY, UU, DLC, ICU, PP, MB, MnU,
  MiDW, OrU, LNHT, CSaT, WHi-L

S166
Socialist Workers California
  Campaign.
  Capitalism fouls things up.
  Vote socialist workers. [Berke-
  ley? 1970?]
  [4]p. 21cm.
  Cover title.
  1. Capitalism.
  CU-B

S167
Socialist Workers California
  Campaign.
  The status of women: a socialist
  approach. [San Francisco? 1970?]
  [4]p. 28cm.
  Caption title.
  1. Woman--Rights of women.
  CU-B

Socialist Workers Campaign
  Committee
  see also
Socialist Workers Party. Campaign Committee.

S168
Socialist Workers Campaign
  Committee.
  The socialist candidates in 68:
  Fred Halstead for president;
  Paul Boutelle for vice president.
  [New York, 1968]
  folder. illus. 22x9cm.
  Cover title.
  1. Socialist Workers Party.
  2. Halstead, Fred. 3. Boutelle,
  Paul.
  KU-RH

S169
Socialist Workers Campaign
  Committee.
  Vote Socialist Workers in 68.
  [New York, 1968]
  folder. illus. 22x9cm.
  Cover title.
  1. Socialist Workers Party.
  KU-RH

S170
Socialist Workers Party.
  The class-struggle road to negro equality. [New York] Pioneer Publishers [1957]
  22 [1]p. illus. 21cm.
  1. Negroes--Civil rights.
  I. Pioneer Publishers.
  LNHT

S171
Socialist Workers Party.
  Election platform. [New York,
  1964]
  11p. 21cm.
  Caption title.

1. U.S.--Pol. & govt.--1963-
CU-B

S172
Socialist Workers Party.
   Freedom now; new stage in the
   struggle for Negro emancipation.
   [Text of resolution adopted by
   the 1963 convention of the Soc-
   ialist Workers Party. New York,
   Pioneer Publishers, 1963]
   23p. 23cm.
   1. Negroes--Civil rights.
   I. Pioneer Publishers.
CSt-H, KU-RH, WHi-L, NUC 70-70085

S173
Socialist Workers Party.
   A summary of the Socialist
   Workers Party 1968 national cam-
   paign. [New York? 1968]
   14p. 28cm.
   Cover title.
   1. U.S.--Pol. & govt.--1969-
WHi-L

S174
Socialist Workers Party.
   Vote for socialism in 1956.
   [New York, 1956?]
   15p. ports.
   Cover title.
   1. Socialism. 2. U.S.--Pol. &
   govt.--1953-1961.
WHi-L

S175
Socialist Workers Party.
   Vote socialist, Berkeley city
   elections. [Berkeley, 1969]
   folder. 22x9cm.
   Cover title.
   1. Socialism. 2. Berkeley,
   Calif.--Pol. & govt.
CU-B

S176
Socialist Workers Party. Cam-
   paign Committee.
   What is wrong with the Peace and
   Freedom Party: a socialist view.
   [New York, 1968?]
   12 [4]p. illus.
   Cover title.
   1. Peace and Freedom Party.
WHi-L

S177
Socialist Workers Party. National Committee.
   Revolution in Hungary and the
   crisis of Stalinism. [New
   York] Pioneer Publishers [1957]
   34p. 22cm.
   1. Socialism. 2. Hungary--His-
   tory--Revolution, 1956.
   I. Pioneer Publishers.
LNHT

S178
Socialist Workers Party. Nation-
   al Convention, 1967.
   The case for a black party, in-
   troduction by Paul Boutelle.
   [New York, 1968]
   22p. illus. 21cm.
   Cover title.
   1. Negroes--Politics and suf-
   frage. 2. Political parties.
   I. Boutelle, Paul.
CSt-H, KU-RH, CU-B, WHi-L,
NUC 70-39165

S179
Socialist Workers Party. National Convention, 1969.
   A transitional program for black
   liberation. [New York, Pathfinder Press, 1970]
   13p. 28cm.
   Cover title.
   1. Negroes--Civil rights.
   I. Pathfinder Press.
KU-RH

S180
Socialist Workshop, San Francisco.
   Women's liberation, revolution,
   the class struggle. San Francisco [196]
   11, 15, 7p.
   1. Socialism. 2. Woman--Rights
   of women. 3. Social classes.
WHi-L

S181
Socialist Youth Conference.
   Call for a new revolutionary
   socialist youth organization.
   [Seattle, 196]
   3p. 28cm.
   Signed by Lawrence Shumn and
   others.

1. Socialism.   2. Youth--Politi-
cal activity.   I. Shumn, Lawrence.
WHi-A

S182
Society for Individual Rights.
  The armed services & homosexuality. [San Francisco, 196]
  [12]p. 22cm. (Essays on Homosexuality, essay no. 1)
  1. H⸴mosexuality.   2. U.S. Army.
  Military life.
  MiU

S183
Solnit, Albert.
  Deliberate depopulation of whole
  areas: a protest. Nashville,
  Southern Student Organizing
  Committee [196]
  6p. 28cm.
  Reprinted from the Mountain
  Eagle (Whitesburg, Ky.) Aug. 4,
  1965.
  1. Environmental policy--Ken-
  tucky. 2. Kentucky--Econ. condit. I. Southern Student Organizing Committee.
  MoU, WHi-L

S184
Sorel, Jules.
  Education for revolt; radical
  teachers in American schools.
  Ann Arbor, Conference on Radicals in the Professions, 1967.
  4p. 28cm.
  1. Teachers.   2. Education.
  3. Radicalism.   I. Conference on
  Radicals in the Professions.
  MiU-H

S185
Sostre, Martin Gonzales, 1923-
  Letters from prison, a compilation of Martin Soster's correspondence from civic country jail
  ..., prepared by the Philosophi-
  cal Society, State University of
  New York at Buffalo...in cooperation with the Martin Sostre Defense Committee. [Buffalo, 1969]
  75p. 24cm.
  1. Negroes--Civil rights.
  CU-B

S186
South Viet Nam National Front for
    Liberation.
  Political program of South Vietnam National Liberation Front.
  [Philadelphia? Reprinted by American Friends Service Committee,
  1969?]
  26p.
  Cover title.
  1. Vietnam--Pol. & govt.
  I. Friends, Society of. American Friends Service Committee.
  UU, NUC 71-110261

S187
South Viet Nam National Front for
    Liberation.
  Political programme of the
  South Vietnam National Front
  for Liberation. [Chicago, Stu-
  dents for a Democratic Society,
  196]
  16p. 22cm.
  Cover title.
  1. Vietnam--Pol. & govt.
  I. Students for a Democratic
  Society.
  WHi-A

S188
South Viet Nam National Front for
    Liberation.
  Political programme of the
  South Vietnam National Front
  for Liberation. Nashville,
  Southern Student Organizing
  Committee [196]
  17p. 28cm.
  "Introduction by Tom Gardner."
  1. Vietnam--Pol. & govt.
  I. Southern Student Organizing
  Committee. II. Gardner, Tom.
  MoU

S189
South Viet Nam Provisional Revo-
    lutionary Government.
  PRG 7 point peace proposal.
  [New York] U.S. Committee to
  Aid the N.L.F.-S.V.N. [196]
  [1] leaf. 28cm.
  Caption title.
  1. Vietnamese conflict, 1961-
  1975--Peace. I. U.S. Commit-
  tee to Aid the National Liber-

ation Front-South Viet Nam.
KU-RH

S190
South Vietnam. [n.p., 1968?]
56p. illus. 15cm.
Stamped on verso t.p. U.S. Committee to Aid the National Liberation Front of South Vietnam,
New York.
1. Vietnamese conflict, 1961-
1975. I. U.S. Committee to Aid
the National Liberation Front of
South Vietnam.
NN, NUC 72-24920

S191
Southern Africa. [Cambridge,
   Mass., Africa Research Group,
   197 ?]
12p. illus. 28cm.
1. Africa, South--Pol. & govt.
2. U.S.--Relations (general) with
Africa, South. I. Africa Research Group.
KU-RH

S192
Southern Africa: a smuggled account
   from a guerrilla fighter.
   [Cambridge, Africa Research
   Group, 1969?]
[4]p. map. 28cm.
Caption title.
1. African National Congress.
2. Africa, South--Race question.
I. Africa Research Group.
MoU, KU-RH

S193
Southern Africa Committee.
Sharpeville and after: suppres-
sion and liberation in southern
Africa. [Prepared by Southern
Africa Committee, U.M.C. and the
American Committee of Africa.
New York, American Committee on
Africa, 196]
[12]p. illus., map. 22cm.
Cover title.
1. Africa, South--Race question.
I. American Committee on Africa.
KU-RH

S194
Southern Christian Leadership

Conference.
Citizenship workbook. [Atlanta,
196]
32p. 28cm.
Cover title.
1. Negroes--Civil rights.
CU-B

S195
Southern Christian Leadership
   Conference.
SCLC. [Atlanta, 1967]
[8]p.
1. Negroes--Civil rights.
WHi-A

S196
Southern Committee on Political
   Ethics.
The Wallace labor records.
[Washington, 1968?]
13 [3]p. illus. 28cm.
Cover title.
1. Labor and laboring classes.
2. Wallace, George Corley,
1919-
KU-RH

S197
Southern Conference Educational
   Fund, Louisville.
Appalachia: case study in
repression. [Louisville, 1970?]
5p. illus. 22x28cm.
Cover title.
1. Kentucky--Pol. & govt.
2. Poor--Appalachian Mountains.
3. Appalachian Mountains--Econ.
condit. 4. Civil rights--Appal-
achian Mountains.
KU-RH

S198
Southern Conference Educational
   Fund, Louisville.
Appalachia: case study in repression. [Louisville, 196]
7p. illus. 22x28cm.
Cover title.
1. Coal mines and mining--
Kentucky--Pike Co. 2. Civil
rights--Appalachian Mountains.
3. Poor--Appalachian Mountains.
4. Appalachian Mountains--Econ.
condit.
MoU

S199
Southern Conference Educational
    Fund, Louisville.
An enemy of the people; how the
draft is used to stop movements
for social change. [Louisville,
1969]
[12]p. illus. 22cm.
1. Military service, Compulsory.
2. Negroes--Civil rights. 3. Col-
lins, Walter. 4. Mulloy, Joe.
MoU, KU-RH, WHi-L

S200
Southern Conference Educational
    Fund, Louisville.
A letter to the people of Kentucky. [Louisville, Ky., 196]
[4]p. 28cm.
Caption title.
1. Negroes--Kentucky. 2. Ken-
tucky--Race question.
KU-RH

S201
Southern Conference Educational
    Fund, Louisville.
A new day begun: the SCEF program for the new period in the
South. [Louisville, 1966?]
folder.
Cover title.
1. Negroes--Southern States.
2. Southern States--Race question.
MiU

S202
Southern Conference Educational
    Fund, Louisville.
There are 40 million white people in the South; who will organize them? [Louisville, 196]
folder. illus. 18x9cm.
1. Southern States--Pol. & govt.
2. Organization.
MoU

S203
Southern Conference Educational
    Conference, Louisville.
Voices from the white South.
[Louisville, 1969?]
[8]p. illus. 22cm.
Cover title.
1. Poor--Southern States.

2. Southern States--Econ. condit.
KU-RH, MoU

S204
Southern Conference Educational
    Fund, Louisville.
Where we stand. Resolutions
adopted by the board of direct-
ors of the Southern Conference
Educational Fund. [Louisville,
1970]
[4]p. 28cm.
Caption title.
1. U.S.--Pol. & govt.--1969-
2. Civil rights. 3. Woman--
Rights of women.
KU-RH

S205
Southern Conference Educational
    Fund, New Orleans.
Give decency a chance in the
south. [New Orleans, 196]
folder. illus. 23x9cm.
1. Negroes--Civil rights.
KU-RH

S206
Southern Conference Educational
    Fund, New Orleans.
How legislative inquisitions
stifle integration and social
progress. [New Orleans, 1960]
20p. illus. 21cm.
1. Governmental investigations.
2. Social change. 3. Negroes--
Civil rights.
NIC, NN, DLC

S207
Southern Conference Educational
    Fund, New Orleans.
"My beliefs and my associations
are none of the business of this
committee." [New Orleans,
196 ?]
20p. illus. 22cm.
Cover title.
1. Negroes--Civil rights. 2. U.
S. Congress. House. Committee on Un-American Activities.
MiU, NcD, NUC 66-56114

S208
Southern Conference Educational
    Fund, New Orleans.

To the platform committee of the
1956 national convention: we, the
undersigned citizens of the
South, wish to stress the need
for firm federal action in the
field of civil rights... [New
Orleans? 1956]
broadsides.
Includes blank for signatures to
petition, cover letter, self-ad-
dressed return envelope.
1. Negroes--Civil rights.
I. Democratic Party. National
Convention, Chicago, 1956.
ViU

S209
Southern Female Rights Union, New
   Orleans.
Southern Female Rights Union for
female liberation. New Orleans
]1969?]
[2]p. 28cm.
Caption title.
1. Woman--Rights of women.
KU-RH

S210
   Southern Regional Council.
Augusta, Georgia and Jackson
State University; Southern epi-
sodes in a national tragedy.
[Atlanta] 1970.
x, 76p.
1. Negroes--Augusta, Ga.
2. Augusta, Ga.--Race question.
LN, DLC, NIC, MsU, NcU,
NUC 71-28527

S211
Southern Regional Council.
A city slum--poor people and
problems, a report on an attempt
to build a community around local self-interest issues in a
southern city. Atlanta, Ga.
[1966?]
[26]p.
1. Poor--Atlanta. 2. Atlanta--
Race question. 3. Negroes--At-
lanta. 4. Slums.
WHi-L

S212
Southern Regional Council.
   The continuing crisis: an

assessment of the new racial
tensions in the south. Atlanta, Southern Regional Council [and] American Jewish Committee, Institute of Human Relations, 1966.
40p. 23cm.
1. Southern States--Race question. 2. Negroes--Southern
States.
KU-RH

S213
Southern Regional Council.
Cooperative, credit unions,
and poor people. Atlanta, 1966.
16, vip. (Special report)
1. Poor--Southern States.
2. Cooperative societies.
3. Credit.
WHi-L

S214
Southern Regional Council.
The Delta prisons: punishment
for profit [by William J. Far-
mar] Atlanta [1968]
23 [2]p. 28cm. (Special report)
1. Prisons--Arkansas. 2. Pri-
sons--Louisiana. 3. Prisons--
Mississippi. I. Farmar, William J.
CSaT, MU, WHi-L, PPULC, Wa, CSt,
DLC 70-18269

S215
Southern Regional Council.
Dual justice in the courts--un-
concerned community. [Atlanta,
1966]
iii, 12 [4] leaves.
1. Justice, Administration of.
2. Negroes--Civil rights.
WHi-L

S216
Southern Regional Council.
The freedom ride, May 1961.
[Atlanta] 1961.
12, iv leaves. 28cm.
1. Negroes--Civil rights.
WHi-A

S217
Southern Regional Council.
Ghetto in your town. Atlanta

[1967]
19p. illus. 23cm. (Urban plan-
ning project publication no. 3)
Prepared by John A Brown and C.
Bron Cleveland.
Cover title: Slum ghettos in your
town.
1. Slums. 2. Poverty. I. Brown,
John A. II. Cleveland, C. Bron.
NNC, NUC 71-28627

S218
Southern Regional Council.
  Housing for negroes in Atlanta,
  Georgia. [Atlanta, 1959]
  9p.
  1. Negores--Housing. 2. Negroes
  --Atlanta.
  WHi-L

S219
Southern Regional Council.
  Hungry children. [Atlanta,
  1967]
  27 leaves. (Special report)
  1. Hunger. 2. Children--Care
  and hygiene. 3. Child welfare.
  WHi-L

S220
Southern Regional Council.
  Law enforcement in Mississippi.
  [Atlanta] 1964.
  35, vp. 28cm.
  1. Mississippi--Race question.
  2. Law enforcement--Mississippi.
  WHi-A

S221
Southern Regional Council.
  Lawlessness and disorder; fourteen years of failure in southern school desegregation. [At-
  lanta, 1968?]
  iii, 58p. 28cm. (Special report)
  1. Negores--Southern States.
  2. Negroes--Education.
  CtY, InU, CST-L, ICU, AAP,
  DLC 75-16521, WHi-L

S222
Southern Regional Council.
  Neighborhood stabilization: a
  program. [Atlanta] 1966.
  1p., 12 (20 leaves. 28cm.

(Special report)
1. Neg oes--Housing.
MH-L, WHi-L, NUC 66-91199

S223
Southern Regional Council.
  On the national crisis: a
  statement. [Atlanta] 1967.
  7p. 28cm.
  Cover title.
  1. Riots. 2. Negroes--Civil
  rights.
  KU-RH

S224
Southern Regional Council.
  The price we pay [for discrim-
  ination] prepared by Barbara
  Patterson and other staff members of the Southern Regional
  Council and the Anti-defamation
  League. [Atlanta] 1964.
  44p. 22cm.
  1. Negroes--Civil rights.
  2. Southern States--Race question. 3. Southern States--Econ.
  condit. I. Patterson, Barbara.
  II. Anti-defamation League.
  NjP, DHHF, NUC 65-60396

S225
Southern Regional Council.
  Public assistance in the South.
  [Atlanta] 1966.
  16, xiip. 28cm. (Special re-
  port)
  1. Public welfare--Southern
  States.
  WHi-L, DLC 67-8177

S226
Southern Regional Council.
  Public assistance: to what end?
  [Atlanta] 1967.
  41p. illus. 28cm. (Special
  report)
  1. Public welfare.
  WHi-L, InU, GASC, DLC 76-274708

S227
Southern Regional Council.
  The question for Jacksonville.
  Atlanta, 1964.
  14 leaves. 28cm. (Report L-47)
  Caption title.
  1. Jacksonville, Fld.--Race

question. 2. Negroes--Jackson-
ville, Fld.
MiU

S228
Southern Regional Council.
  Race makes the difference; an
  analysis on sentence disparity
  among black and white offenders
  in Southern prisons. [Atlanta]
  1969.
  iii, 16p. illus.
  1. Prisoners--Southern States.
  2. Negroes--Southern States.
  3. Law enforcement--Southern
  States.
  WHi-L

S229
Southern Regional Council.
  Racial discrimination in the
  southern federal courts. [At-
  lanta] 1965.
  11p. 28cm.
  1. Southern States--Race question. 2. Law enforcement--South-
  ern States. 3. Negroes--South-
  ern States.
  WHi-A, WHi-L

S230
Southern Regional Council.
  A report on school desegration
  for 1960-61. [Atlanta, 196]
  38p. illus.
  Cover title.
  1. Negroes--Education. 2. Edu-
  cation--Southern States.
  WHi-L

S231
Southern Regional Council.
  School desegregation: old problems under a new law. Atlanta,
  1965.
  23p. map, facsims., tables.
  28cm. (Special report)
  1. Education--Southern States.
  2. Negroes--Education.
  MH-L, MiU, WHi-L, NUC 66-92736

S232
Southern Regional Council.
  School desegregation: the first
  six years. [Atlanta, 1960]
  35p. 23cm.

Cover title.
1. Negroes--Education.
2. Segregation in education.
WHi-A

S233
Southern Regional Council.
  School desegregation 1966:
  the slow undoing. Atlanta,
  1966.
  i, 46p. illus. 28cm.
  1. Segregation in education.
  GA, WHi-L, DLC 75-21826, MH-L

S234
Southern Regional Council.
  Some general observation in the
  Negro community of Little Rock,
  Arkansas. Atlanta, 1958.
  13p.
  1. Negroes--Little Rock, Ark.
  2. Little Rock, Ark.--Race
  question.
  GAU, NUC 67-87112

S235
Southern Regional Council.
  A status study of Negro employment and training opportunities
  in four southern cities; Houston, Atlanta, Chattanooga, and
  Miami. Atlanta, 1961.
  14p.
  1. Negroes--Employment.
  2. Houston--Race question.
  3. Atlanta--Race question.
  4. Chattanooga, Tenn.--Race
  question. 5. Miami, Fld.--Race
  question.
  GAU, NUC 67-86520

S236
Southern Regional Council.
  The student protest movement: a
  recapitulation. [Atlanta] 1961.
  16 leaves. 28cm.
  1. Student movements--Southern
  States. 2. Negroes--Civil
  rights.
  WHi-L, WHi-A

S237
Southern Regional Council.
  The student protest movement,
  winter 1960. Rev. Atlanta,
  1960.

xxv leaves. 28cm.
1. Student movements--Southern
States. 2. Negroes--Civil rights.
WHi-A

S238
Southern Regional Council.
  Waiting room practices in 21
  southern cities. [Atlanta]
  1959.
  12 leaves.
  1. Negroes--Southern States.
  2. Segregation in transportation
  --Southern States.
  WHi-L, GAU, NUC 67-86362

S239
Southern Regional Council.
  What happened in the South?
  Atlanta, 1964.
  15 leaves.
  1. Elections--Southern States.
  2. Presidents--U.S.--Election--
  1964. 3. Negroes--Politics and
  suffrage.
  MiU, NUC 66-90680

S240
Southern Regional Council. Voter
  Education Project (1966-   )
  Black elected officials in the
  Southern States. Atlanta [1969]
  iii, 24p. 28cm.
  Cover title.
  1. Negroes--Politics and suf-
  frage. 2. Southern States--Pol.
  & govt.
  WHi-L, NUC 70-18652

S241
Southern Regional Council. Voter
  Education Project (1966-   )
  How to conduct a registration
  campaign. [Atlanta, 1967]
  20p. illus. 23cm.
  Cover title.
  1. Voters, Registration of.
  2. Negroes--Politics and suffrage.
  GU, GAT, NcD, WHi-L, DLC 73-4701

S242
Southern Regional Council. Voter
  Education Project (1966-   )
  Know your Georgia government.
  [Atlanta, 1967?]
  23p. illus.

Cover title.
1. Georgia--Pol. & govt.
2. Local government--Georgia.
3. Municipal government--Geor-
gia.
McSM, NUC 71-26494

S243
Southern Regional Council. Voter
  Education Project (1966-   )
  Voter registration in the south:
  summer 1966. [Atlanta, 1966]
  unpaged.
  1. Negroes--Southern States.
  2. Southern States--Pol. & govt.
  --1963-   3. Voters, Registration of--Southern States.
  WHi-L

S244
Southern Student Organizing Com-
  mittee.
  Alcorn 1966: an incident. Nash-
  ville [1966?]
  Cover title.
  1. Student movements--Mississip-
  pi. 2. Alcorn Agricultural and
  Mechanical College, Alcorn,
  Miss.
  WHi-L

S245
Southern Student Organizing Com-
  mittee.
  Bylaws. [Nashville, 196]
  3 leaves. 28cm.
  WHi-A

S246
Southern Student Organizing Committee.
  Emigration to Canada; legal
  notes for draft age men.
  [Nashville, 196]
  [10]p.
  Cover title.
  1. Emigration and immigration
  law--Canada.
  WHi-L

S247
Southern Student Organizing Com-
  mittee.
  Florida peace tour, Feb. 23-
  April 7, 1967. [Nashville?
  1967]

iii, 21p.
1. Vietnamese conflict, 1961-1975.
2. Peace.
WHi-L

S248
Southern Student Organizing
    Committee.
Proposal of organization.
[Nashville, 1964?]
7 leaves. 28cm.
Caption title.
1. Student movements--Southern
States.
WHi-A

S249
Southern Student Organizing
    Committee.
Prospectus: 1967-68. Nashville
[1967?]
19, vi, ii, ii, iii leaves.
28cm.
1. Student movements--Southern
States.
WHi-L

S250
Southern Student Organizing
    Committee.
Southern Student Organizing Com-
mittee. [Nashville? 1964?]
[42]p. 28cm.
Cover title.
1. Student movements--Southern
States.
WHi-A

S251
Southern Student Organizing
    Committee.
We'll take our stand. Nashville,
1964.
2 leaves. 28cm.
Caption title.
1. Student movements--Southern
States.
WHi-A

S252
Southern Student Organizing
    Committee.
Women's liberation bibliography.
Nashville [1969]
14p. 28cm.
1. Woman--Rights of women--Bibl.
NcD, NUC 71-84742

S253
Southern Student Organizing Com-
    mittee. Executive Committee.
A resolution concerning SDS's
role in the south and the rela-
tionship between SDS and the
Southern Student's Organizing
Committee. [Austin, Tex.? 1964]
[6]p. 28cm.
Caption title.
1. Students for a Democratic
Society. 2. Southern States--
Race question. 3. Student move-
ments--Southern States.
WHi-A

S254
Southern Student Organizing Com-
    mittee. University of Vir-
    ginia Chapter.
An open letter to David Rocke-
feller on apartheid and the
Chase Manhattan Bank. [Char-
lottesville, 196]
[2]p. 28cm.
Caption title.
1. Southern Africa--Race quest-
ion. 2. Chase Manhattan Bank,
New York.
KU-RH

S255
Southwide Conference of Black
    Elected Officials, Atlanta,
    1968.
Conference proceedings. [At-
lanta, 1969]
62p. illus., ports. 28cm.
Cover title.
Conference sponsored by the
Voter Education Project, South-
ern Regional Council.
1. Negroes--Politics and suf-
frage. I. Southern Regional
Council. Voter Education Pro-
ject (1966-   )
TU, LLafS, TNJ, MiU, NiC, KMK,
MU, NjP, NBC, CSt, GU, MoSW, IU,
DLC 73-21173

S256
Spalding, Karen.
Peru: the military managers.
[San Francisco? Leviathan?
1969]
[7]p. 28cm.
Cover title.

Reprinted from Leviathan, July/
August 1969.
1. U.S.--Relations (general) with
Peru. 2. Peru--Pol. & govt.
I. Leviathan.
KU-RH

S257
Spannaus, Ed.
  For better action: less talk,
  more action [by Ed Spannaus and
  Steve Fraser. New York? NY SDS
  Labor Committee? 196]
  4p. 28cm.
  Caption title.
  1. Negroes--Education. 2. Stu-
  dent movements. I. Students for
  a Democratic Society, New York.
  Labor Committee. I. Fraser,
  Steve, jt. auth.
  KU-RH

S258
Spannaus, Ed.
  Radicals in social work. Ann
  Arbor, Conference on Radicals
  in the Professions, 1967.
  4p. 28cm.
  Cover title.
  1. Social work as a profession.
  2. Public welfare. 3. Radicalism.
  I. Conference on Radicals in the
  Professions.
  MiU-H

S259
Spannaus, Ed.
  Who pays for poverty? By Ed
  Spannaus and Paul Gallagher.
  Boston, New England Free Press
  [196]
  [4]p. 28cm.
  Caption title.
  Reprinted from Viet-Report, sum-
  mer 1968.
  1. Poverty. 2. U.S.--Econ. con-
  dit. I. Gallagher, Paul, jt.
  auth. II. New England Free
  Press.
  MoU, KU-RH

S260
Sparks, Selma.
  A Harlem mother's nightmare; the
  story of six Harlem youths who
  face possible death for a crime

they did not commit. [New York,
Committee to Defend Resistance
to Ghetto Life, 196]
7p. illus. 28cm.
Cover title.
1. Negroes--Harlem, New York
(City) 2. Law enforcement--Har-
lem, New York (City) 3. Police
--New York (State)--Harlem, New
York (City) I. Committee to
Defend Resistance to Ghetto
Life.
KU-RH

S261
Spartacist.
  Cuba and Marxist theory. [New
  York, 1966]
  1v. 28cm. (Marxist bulletin,
  no. 8)
  Cover title.
  1. Cuba--History. 2. Social-
  ism in Cuba.
  WHi-L

S262
Spartacist.
  Expulsion from the Socialist
  Workers Party. [New York,
  1965?]
  2v (110 leaves) (Marxist bulletin, no. 4)
  Cover title.
  Documents on the exclusion of
  revolutionary tendency supporters.
  1. Socialist Workers Party.
  WHi-L

S263
Spartacist.
  In defense of a revolutionary
  perspective. A statement of
  basic position by the revolutionary tendency. Presented to
  the June 1962 plenary meeting
  of the SWP National Committee.
  New York [196]
  19 leaves. 28cm. (Marxist bulletin, no. 1)
  Cover title.
  1. Socialist Workers Party.
  WHi-L

S264
Spartacist.

The Leninist position on youth-
party relations. [New York,
196]
28 leaves. 28cm. (Marxist bulletin, no. 7)
Cover title.
1. Socialist Workers Party.
2. Young Socialist Alliance.
WHi-L

S265
Spartacist.
The nature of the Socialist
Workers Party--revolutionary or
centrest? New York [1965]
vi, 166 leaves. 28cm. (Marxist
bulletin, no. 2)
Cover title.
1. Socialist Workers Party.
WHi-L

S266
Spartacist. Texas Organizing
   Committee.
Free the Cuban Trotskyists: an
appeal to Prime Minister Fidel
Castro for restoration of social-
ist standards of democracy in
Cuba. [Houston, 196]
3 leaves. 28cm.
1. Cuba--Pol. & govt.--1959-
      2. Political prisoners--
Cuba. 3. Socialism in Cuba.
WHi-A

Spartacist League.
see also
Campus Spartacist Club, Berkeley,
   Calif.
New York City Spartacist League.
Philadelphia Spartacist League.
Bay Area Spartacist League.

S267
Spartacist League.
The Black Panthers--yes. Peace
& Freedom--no. New York, 1968.
[1] leaf. 36cm.
Caption title.
1. Peace and Freedom Party.
2. Black Panther Party.
CU-B

S268
Spartacist League.
Don't be fooled. [New York,

1968]
2p. 28cm.
Caption title.
1. Workers League. 2. Socialist Workers Party.
CU-B

S269
Spartacist League.
New York City school strike;
beware liberal union busters.
[New York, 1968]
2p. 36cm.
Caption title.
1. Education--New York (State)
--New York (City) 2. United
Federation of Teachers.
CU-B

S270
Spartacist League.
"We don't believe in free
speech here". New York, 1969.
[1] leaf. 36cm.
Caption title.
1. Progressive Labor Party.
CU-B

S271
Spartacist Socialist Club.
Come to the march prepared to
defend yourself. [Berkeley?
1965?]
[2]p. 28cm.
Caption title.
1. Pacifism. 2. National Coor-
dinating Committee to End the
War in Vietnam. Vietnam Day
Committee, Berkeley.
CU-B

S272
Speak truth to power; a Quaker
search for an alternative to
violence. [Philadelphia?]
American Friends Service Committee [1955]
71p.
1. Pacifism. 2. U.S.--Foreign
policy. I. Friends, Society
of. American Friends Service
Committee.
WHi-L

S273
Spector, Morgan.

A sense of the body resolution
[by Morgan Spector, Jeff Segal,
Neil Buckel. n.p., 1968?]
3p. 28cm.
Caption title.
1. Students for a Democratic
Society. I. Segal, Jeff, jt.
auth. II. Buckel, Neil, jt.
auth.
WHi-L

S274
Spencer, Jean.
Draft of SDS peace project pro-
posal. [n.p., 196]
5 leaves. 28cm.
Caption title.
1. Peace. 2. Students for a
Democratic Society.
WHi-A

S275
Spencer, Scott.
Johnson's skirmish with poverty
[by Scott Spencer, Robert Brown,
and David Komatsu. Chicago,
Young People's Socialist League,
196]
13p. 28cm.
Caption title.
1. Poverty. 2. U.S. Office of
Economic Opportunity. I. Brown,
Robert, jt. auth. II. Komatsu,
David, jt. auth. III. Young
People's Socialist League.
MiU

S276
Springfield Women's Liberation.
The way we see it. [n.p., 197 ?]
18p. illus. 28cm.
Cover title.
1. Woman--Rights of women.
WHi-L, KU-RH

S277
Stallings, Frank H.
Atlanta and Washington; racial
differences in academic achieve-
ment. Atlanta, Southern Regional Council, 1960.
unpaged.
1. Segregation in education.
2. Negroes--Education. I. Southern Regional Council.
GAU, NUC 66-61469

S278
Stanfield, J. Edwin.
In Memphis: more than a garbage
strike. [Atlanta, Southern
Regional Council, 1968]
49p. 28cm. (Special report)
1. Memphis--Race question.
2. King, Martin Luther, 1924-
1968. I. Southern Regional
Council.
WHi-A, WHi-L

S279
Stanfield, J. Edwin.
In Memphis: tragedy unaverted.
Atlanta, Southern Regional
Council, 1968.
14p. 29cm.
"Supplement to special report
[of the Southern Regional Coun-
cil] of March 22, 1968."
1. Memphis--Riots, 1968.
2. Negroes--Memphis. I. Southern Regional Council.
DLC 70-284615

S280
Stanford, John W.
Open letter to president John
F. Kennedy. [San Antonio, 1963]
[5] leaves. 28cm.
Caption title.
1. U.S. Laws, statutes, etc.
Subversive Activities Control
Act of 1950. 2. Internal se-
curity. 3. Communism. 4. Ken-
nedy, John Fitzgerald, Pres. U.
S., 1917-1963.
KU-RH

S281
Stanford Biology Study Group.
The destruction of Indochina;
a legacy of our presence. Stanford, Calif. [1970]
8p. illus. 26cm.
1. Biological warfare. 2. Vietnamese conflict, 1961-1975.
WHi-L, KU-RH

S282
Stanford Radical Caucus.
Fire and sandstone: the last
radical guide to Stanford [by
Stanford Radical Caucus and
New Left Project. Stanford,

Calif., 1970?]
46p. illus. 28cm.
1. Stanford University. 2. Student movements--Stanford University. 3. Palo Alto, Calif.--Pol. & govt. I. New Left Project.
KU-RH

S283
Stapp, Andy.
Black marines against the brass, interview with William Harvey and George Daniels. Interview by Andy Stapp. Introduction by Shirley Jolls. [New York, American Servicemen's Union, 1969]
19p. illus. 22cm.
1. Vietnamese conflict, 1961-1975. 2. Soldiers. 3. Negroes--Civil rights. I. Harvey, William. II. Daniels, George. III. Jolls, Shirley. IV. American Servicemen's Union.
KU-RH, WHi-L

S284
Stavenhagen, Rodolfo.
Seven erroneous theses about Latin America. Boston, New England Free Press [196]
25-37p. 22cm.
Reprinted from New University Thought, v. 4, no. 4; winter 1966/67.
1. Latin America--Pol. & govt. 2. Latin America--Econ. condit. I. New England Free Press.
MoU, KU-RH

S285
Steel, Ronald.
Letter from Havana. San Francisco, Clergy and Laymen [and] Radical Education Project [196]
7 leaves. 28cm.
1. Cuba--Descr. & trav. I. Radical Education Project.
CU-B

S286
Steel, Ronald.
Letter from Oakland: the Panthers. [Washington, New Mobilization Committee to End the War in Vietnam, 1969?]

[9]p. 28cm.
Caption title.
Reprinted from New York Review of Books, Sept. 11, 1969.
1. Black Panther Party. I. New Mobilization Committee to End the War in Vietnam.
KU-RH

S287
Steering Committee Against Repression.
An appeal for justice by the Steering Committee Against Repression. [Atlanta, 196]
[2]p. 28cm.
Caption title.
1. King, Martin Luther, 1929-1968. 2. Brown, H. Rap. 3. Negroes--Civil rights.
KU-RH

S288
Stein, Buddy.
The Scheer campaign [by] Buddy Stein and David Wellman. Ann Arbor, Radical Education Project [196]
[62]-77p. 22cm.
Reprinted from Studies on the Left, Jan./Feb. 1967.
1. California--Pol. & govt.--1963-   2. Scheer, Robert. I. Radical Education Project. II. Wellman, David, jt. auth.
MoU

S289
Stein, Buddy.
The Scheer campaign [by] Buddy Stein and David Wellman. Boston, New England Free Press [196]
[62]-77p. 22cm.
Reprinted from Studies on the Left, Jan./Feb. 1967.
1. Scheer, Robert. 2. California--Pol. & govt.--1963-
I. Wellman, David, jt. auth. II. New England Free Press.
KU-RH

S290
Stein, Pattie.
Pattie's paper. [n.p., 1969?]
[8]p. 28cm.

Cover title.
1. Education.   2. Student movements.
KU-RH

S291
Stein, Sue.
  Statement by Sue Stein, Harold
  Jacobs [and] Bettina Apthekar.
  [Berkeley, 1966?]
  [2] leaves.
  Caption title.
  1. Student movements.   I. Jacobs,
  Harold, jt. auth.   II. Apthekar,
  Bettina, jt. auth.
  WHi-A

S292
Steinberg, David.
  Farm and migrant workers in America.   [n.p.] Students for a
  Democratic Society for the Liberal Study Group, 1962.
  8 leaves.   36cm.
  Cover title.
  1. Negroes--Employment.   2. Mexicans in the U.S.   3. Migrant labor.   4. Agricultural laborers.
  I. Students for a Democratic Society.   II. Liberal Study Group.
  WHi-A

S293

Stembridge, Jane.
  Freedom school notes.   Nashville, Southern Student Organizing Committee [196]
  4p.   28cm.
  Cover title.
  1. Negroes--Education.   2. Work-
  study Institute, Waveland, Miss.
  I. Southern Student Organizing
  Committee.
  MoU, WHi-L

S294
Stembridge, Jane.
  Freedom school notes.   Nashville,
  Southern Student Organizing Com-
  mittee, and New England Free
  Press [196]
  [3]p.   28cm.
  Cover title.
  1. Work-study Institute, Wave-
  land, Miss.   2. Negroes--Educa-

tion.   I. Southern Student Or-
ganizing Committee.   II. New
England Free Press.
MoU, KU-RH

S295
Sterling, Pete.
  CORE Housing Committee research
  report, prepared by Pete Sterling, Herb Oberlander, Sam Gorovitz.   York? CORE? 1963]
  12 leaves.   28cm.
  Caption title.
  1. Negroes--Housing.   I. Congress of Racial Equality.
  Housing Committee.   II. Oberlander, Herb, jt. auth.
  III. Gorovitz, Sam, jt. auth.
  CU-B

S296
Stern, Roger.
  The university: a construct.
  [n.p., 1965]
  2p.   28cm.
  Caption title.
  At head of title: 1965 SDS
  national convention--working
  papers.
  1. Universities and colleges.
  I. Students for a Democratic
  Society. National Convention,
  1965.
  WHi-A, KU-RH

S297
Stewart, Joffre.
  Some implications of non-
  violence in the Montgomery re-
  sistance movement.   [n.p.,
  1961]
  [4]p.   22cm.
  Caption title.
  Reprinted from Balanced Living,
  Dec. 1961.
  1. Nonviolence.   2. Montgomery,
  Ala.--Race question.   3. Ne-
  groes--Montgomery, Ala.
  WHi-A, CU-B, MiU

S298
Stone, Jeremy J.
  How the arms race works.   Woodmont, Conn., Promoting Enduring Peace [1969?]
  [2]p.   28cm.   (No. 142)

Caption title.
Reprinted from Progressive, june
1969.
1. U.S.--Military policy. 2. U.
S. Dept. of Defense. 3. Arma-
ments. I. Promoting Enduring
Peace.
KU-RH

S299
Stop the Draft Week, University of
    California, Berkeley.
    Crisis report number two. [Ber-
    keley, Campus Stop the Draft
    Week and Movement Against Politi-
    cal Suspensions, 196]
    8p. 28cm.
    1. Student movements--Berkeley,
    Calif.
    CU-B

S300
Stop the Draft Week Defense Fund.
    The Oakland seven. [Oakland,
    Calif., 196]
    [12]p. 22cm.
    Cover title.
    1. Military service, Compulsory.
    2. Vietnamese conflict, 1961-
    1975. 3. Government, Resistance
    to.
    WHi-A

S301
Stop the Draft Week Defense Fund.
    The Oakland seven. [Oakland,
    Calif., 1968]
    [8]p. 22cm.
    Cover title
    1. Vietnamese conflict, 1961-
    1975. 2. Military service, Com-
    pulsory. 3. Government, Resist-
    ance to.
    CU-B

S302
Stover, F.W.
    The truth about the farm betray-
    als: a 1968 appraisal. Des
    Moines, Ia., The Farmers Assoc-
    iation [1968?]
    32p. illus. 22cm.
    Cover title.
    1. Agriculture--Economic aspects.
    2. Peace. I. Farmers Association.
    KU-RH

S303
Strauss, Anselm L.
    Medical ghettos. Ann Arbor,
    Radical Education Project,
    c1967.
    6 [1]p. illus. 28cm.
    Cover title.
    Reprinted from Trans-action,
    May 1967.
    1. Medical care. 2. Poverty.
    I. Radical Education Project.
    MoU

S304
Strauss, Anselm L.
    Medical ghettos. Nashville,
    Southern Student Organizing
    Committee [c1967]
    9p. 28cm.
    Cover title.
    1. Medical care. 2. Poverty.
    I. Southern Student Organizing
    Committee.
    MoU

S305
Strauss, Ed, ed.
    The black flag of anarchy.
    [Woodstock, Vt., 1968]
    56p. 22cm.
    Cover title.
    1. Anarchism and anarchists.
    WHi-A, MiU

S306
Strike.
    Students in revolt. [Cleveland,
    196]
    13p. 28cm.
    Cover title.
    1. Student movements--Ohio.
    WHi-A

S307
Strong, Anna Louis, 1885-
    The rise of the Chinese   ople's
    communes. Ann Arbor, Radical
    Education Project [196]
    34p. 18cm.
    Cover title.
    1. Communes (China) 2. China
    (People's Republic of China,
    1949-   )--Rural conditions.
    I. Radical Education Project.
    MoU

S308
Strong, Anna Louise.
  The rise of the Chinese people's
  communes. Toronto, Research,
  Information, and Publications
  for Student Union for Peace Action [196]
  10p. 28cm.
  1. Communes (China) 2. China
  (People's Republic of China,
  1949-   )--Rural conditions.
  I. Student Union for Peace Action.
  WHi-A

S309
Strong, Anna Louise, 1885-
  The rise of the people's communes
  in China. [1st ed.] New York,
  Marzani and Munsell, 1960.
  95p.
  1. Communes (China) 2. China
  (People's Republic of China,
  1949-   )--Rural conditions.
  I. Marzani and Munsell.
  MiU, NNC, FU, TxU, NUC 65-91102

S310
Student Association to End the War
    In Vietnam.
  Ottawa's complicity in Vietnam.
  [Toronto, 196]
  14p. 22cm.
  1. Canada--For. rel.--Vietnam.
  2. Vietnamese conflict, 1961-
  1975.
  MiU

S311
Student Civil Liberties Coordina-
    ting Committee.
  The attack on South Confer-
  ence Educational Fund: a report.
  [Washington, D.C., 196]
  7p. 28cm.
  1. U.S. Congress. House.
  Committee on Un-American Activi-
  ties. 2. Southern Conference
  Educational Fund.
  WHi-A, MiU

S312
Student Civil Liberties Coordina-
    ting Committee.
  Attack on Y.S.A. at Indiana
  University. [Washington, 196]
  8p. 28cm.
  1. Internal security. 2. Young

Socialist Alliance. 3. Anti-
communist movements--Indiana.
4. Student movement--Indiana.
WHi-A

S313
Student League for Industrial
    Democracy.
  The Student League for Industrial Democracy. [New York,
  1960?]
  [4]p. 22cm.
  1. Student movements.
  WHi-A

S314
Student Mobilization Committee
    to End the War in Vietnam.
  The student mobs. [Washington,
  1970?]
  [4]p. illus. 28cm.
  1. Vietnamese conflict, 1961-
  1975. 2. Student movements.
  KU-RH

S315
Student Mobilization Committee
    to End the War in Vietnam.
  National Conference, 1970.
  Third world people unite
  against the war. [Washington,
  1970?]
  [2]p. illus. 28cm.
  1. Underdeveloped areas.
  2. Vietnamese conflict, 1961-
  1975.
  MiU-H

S316
Student Mobilization Committee
    to End the War in Vietnam.
  National Conference, 1970.
  Women unite against the war.
  [Washington, 1970]
  [2]p. illus. 28cm.
  1. Woman. 2. Vietnamese con-
  flict, 1961-1975.
  MiU-H

S317
Student Nonviolent Coordinating
    Committee.
  Black power, a reprint of a
  paper by the SNCC Vine City
  Project, 1966. Nashville,
  Southern Student Organizing
  Committee [196]
  7p. 28cm.

1. Negroes--Civil rights. I. Southern Student Organizing Committee.
MoU, MiU

S318
Students Nonviolent Coordinating
    Committee.
Black power. SNCC speaks for
itself; a collection of state-
ments and interviews. Boston,
New England Free Press [196]
9p. 28cm.
Cover title.
Contents--Statement, by Stokely
Carmichael--Statement, by H. Rap
Brown--Interview with H. Rap
Brown.
1. Negroes--Civil rights.
I. Carmichael, Stokely.
II. Brown, H. Rap.   III. New
England Free Press.
KU-RH

S319
Student Nonviolent Coordinating
    Committee.
Brief memorandum on federal civil
rights authority. Atlanta [196]
4p. 28cm.
1. Negroes--Civil rights.
CU-B

S320
Student Nonviolent Coordinating
    Committee.
A chronology of violence and
intimidation in Mississippi
since 1961. [Atlanta, 1964?]
19p. illus.
1. Negroes--Mississippi.   2. Mis-
sissippi--Race question.   3. Vio-
lence--Mississippi.
WHi-L, NUC 71-817777

S321
Student Nonviolent Coordinating
    Committee.
Federal prosecution & civil
rights in Albany, Georgia. [New
York, 196]
[4]p. 21cm.
1. Albany, Ga.--Race question.
2. Negroes--Albany, Ga.
KU-RH

S322
Student Nonviolent Coordinating
    Committee.
Freedom school poetry. [Com-
piled by Nancy Cooper] Foreword by Langston Hughes. Atlanta, 1965 [c1966]
47p. 21cm.
1. American poetry--Negro authors. 2. Negroes--Civil rights
--Poetry. I. Hughes, Langston,
1902-
DLC 65-19797

S323
Student Nonviolent Coordinating
    Committee.
The general condition of the
Alabama Negro. Atlanta, 1965.
28p. map, tables.
1. Negroes--Alabama. 2. Ala-
bama--Race question.
GAU, NUC 67-92134

S324
Student Nonviolent Coordinating
    Committee.
The general condition of the
Mississippi Negro. Atlanta,
1963.
18p. tables.
1. Negroes--Mississippi.
2. Mississippi--Race question.
GAU, NUC 67-92543

S325
Student Nonviolent Coordinating
    Committee.
Genocide in Mississippi. [At-
lanta, 196]
12p. 28cm.
1. Mississippi--Race question.
2. Negroes--Civil rights.
WHi-A

S326
Student Nonviolent Coordinating
    Committee.
Mississippi: a colony of Stan-
dard Oil and Sears, Roebuck.
Atlanta, 1965.
5p. 28cm.
Caption title.
1. Sears, Roebuck and Company.
2. Standard Oil Company of
California. 3. Mississippi--

Race question.
KU-RH

S327
Student Nonviolent Coordinating
    Committee.
Mississippi: subversion of the
right to vote. [Atlanta, 196]
17p. illus. 22cm.
Cover title.
1. Mississippi--Race question.
2. Negroes--Mississippi.
WHi-A, WHi-L

S328
Student Nonviolent Coordinating
    Committee.
Mississippi summer project.
[Atlanta, 196]
folder, illus. 22x9cm.
Cover title.
1. Mississippi--Race question.
2. Negroes--Mississippi.
CU-B, MiU

S329
Student Nonviolent Coordinating
    Committee.
1967 calendar.   [Atlanta, 196]
unpaged.
WHi-L

S330
Student Nonviolent Coordinating
    Committee.
A primer for delegates to the
Democratic national convention
who haven't heard about the Mississippi Freedom Democratic Party. [n.p., 1965?]
[8] leaves. 28cm.
Cover title.
1. Mississippi Freedom Democratic Party. 2. Democratic Party.
3. Negroes--Mississippi.
WHi-A

S331
Student Nonviolent Coordinating
    Committee.
Program outline for campus
friends of SNCC groups. Atlanta [196]
[7] leaves. 28cm.
Caption title.

1. Negroes--Civil rights.
MoU

S332
Student Nonviolent Coordinating
    Committee.
SNCC. [Atlanta, 196]
folder.
Cover title.
WHi-A

S333
Student Nonviolent Coordinating
    Committee.
SNCC programs for 1965. Atlan-
ta [1965]
4 leaves. 28cm.
Caption title.
1. Negroes--Civil rights.
WHi-A

S334
Student Nonviolent Coordinating
    Committee.
Selected articles on the integration movement in the South,
reprinted from Look, Saturday
Evening Post, SNCC, and Selma
Times-Journal. Atlanta, 1963.
1v.
1. Negroes--Civil rights.
2. Southern States--Race question.
ODW, NUC 66-30395

S335
Student Nonviolent Coordinating
    Committee.
Testimony of the Student Nonviolent Coordinating Committee
before the House Judiciary
subcommittee [no.] 5 on H.R.
6400. [n.p., 1965]
[3]p. 28cm.
Caption title.
1. Negroes--Civil rights.
WHi-A

S336
Student Nonviolent Coordinating
    Committee.
Testimony of the Student Nonviolent Coordinating Committee
before the House Judiciary Committee, Tuesday, May 28, 1963.

Atlanta [196]
54 [9] leaves. 36cm.
1. Negroes--Civil rights.
WHi-A

S337
Student Nonviolent Coordinating
   Committee.
We want the vote. [New York,
196]
folder.
Cover title.
1. Negroes--Civil rights.
2. Voting--Southern States.
WHi-A

S338
Student Nonviolent Coordinating
   Committee.
What would it profit a man: a
report on Alabama. [Atlanta, 196]
[8]p. 22cm.
Cover title.
1. Alabama--Race question.
2. Negroes--Alabama.
CU-B

S339
Student Nonviolent Coordinating
   Committee.
You can help. [Atlanta, 196]
13p. 28cm.
Cover title.
1. Negroes--Civil rights.
WHi-A, MoU

S340
Student Nonviolent Coordinating
   Committee. Legal Committee.
Report on federal prosecution of
civil rights workers in Albany,
Georgia. [San Francisco? Bay
Area Friends of SNCC, 196]
18p. 28cm.
Cover title.
1. Negroes--Albany, Ga. 2. Al-
bany, Ga.--Race question.
I. Bay Area Friends of SNCC.
WHi-A

S341
Student Nonviolent Coordinating
   Committee. Summer Program
   Committee.
SNCC summer 1965. [Atlanta,
1965]

folder.
Cover title.
WHi-A

S342
Student Peace Union.
Beyond Vietnam. [New York,
196]
[2]p. illus. 28cm.
Caption title.
1. Vietnamese conflict, 1961-
1975.
MiU-H, CU-B, KU-RH

S343
Student Peace Union.
Constitution, 1962-63. [Chica-
go, 196]
[2]p. 28cm.
KU-RH

S344
Student Peace Union.
Introducing SPU. [Chicago,
196]
folder. illus. 22x10cm.
KU-RH

S345
Student Peace Union.
An introduction. [New York,
196]
folder. illus. 22x10cm.
KU-RH

S346
Student Peace Union.
1964 revised program state-
ment--draft. [n.p., 1964]
8 leaves. 28cm.
Caption title.
1. U.S.--Pol. & govt.--1959-
        2. U.S.--Foreign policy.
CU-B

S347
Student Peace Union.
Organizer's handbook. [Chica-
go? 196]
[30] leaves. 28cm.
Cover title.
WHi-A

S348
Student Peace Union.
Organizers' handbook. [New

York, 196]
[2] leaves. [19]p. 28cm.
Caption title.
CU-B

S349
Student Peace Union.
  Peace books; Student Peace Union
  compilation of recommended read-
  ings on peace and related topics.
  [New York, 196]
  19p. 22cm.
  Cover title.
  1. Peace--Bibl.
  CU-B

S350
Student Peace Union.
  Proposed program statement. [n.
  p., 196]
  [5]p. 28cm.
  Caption title.
  1. U.S.--Foreign policy. 2. U.
  S.--Pol. & govt.--1959-
  CU-B

S351
Student Peace Union.
  Resolution on the draft. New
  York [196]
  1 leaf. 36cm.
  Caption title.
  1. Military service, Compulsory.
  CU-B

S352
Student Peace Union.
  Rough draft of students speak
  for peace day pamphlet. Chicago
  [19]61.
  [1] leaf. 28cm.
  Caption title.
  1. Peace. 2. U.S.--Foreign policy.
  CU-B

S353
Student Peace Union.
  SPU statement of unity in the
  student peace movement. Chicago,
  1961.
  [1] leaf. 28cm.
  Caption title.
  1. Student movements.
  CU-B

S354
Student Peace Union.
  Short bibliography. [Chicago,
  1963]
  20p. 22cm.
  Cover title.
  1. Peace--Bibl. 2. Disarmament
  --Bibl.
  CU-B, KU-RH

S355
Student Peace Union.
  [Statement of purpose, etc.
  Chicago, 196]
  folder. 22x10cm.
  KU-RH

S356
Student Peace Union.
  Statement on foreign policy;
  the 1963-64 convention of the
  Student Peace Union. [Chicago,
  196]
  [4]p. 28cm.
  Caption title.
  1. U.S.--Foreign policy.
  2. Disarmament.
  KU-RH

S357
Student Peace Union.
  Students speak for peace.
  [Chicago, 196]
  [2]p. 22cm.
  Caption title.
  1. Atomic weapons and disarma-
  ment.
  CU-B

S358
Student Peace Union.
  The tragedy of Vietnam [by]
  Student Peace Union [and]
  Students for a Democratic
  Society. Chicago [196]
  [1] leaf. 28cm.
  Caption title.
  1. Vietnamese conflict, 1961-
  1975. I. Students for a
  Democratic Society.
  KU-RH

S359
Student Peace Union.
  Viet Nam. [Chicago, Student
  Peace Union and Students for a

Democratic Society, 196]
[2]p. illus. 22cm.
1. Vietnamese conflict, 1961-
1975. I. Student for a Democratic Society.
CU-B

S360
Student Peace Union.
  Vietnam: a documentation of disaster. [Washington?] 1963.
[14]p. 28cm.
Cover title.
1. Vietnamese conflict, 1961-
1975.
KU-RH, CU-B

S361
Student Peace Union.
  Vietnam: errors and lessons.
[New York, 1965?]
[2]p. 28cm.
Caption title.
1. Vietnamese conflict, 1961-
1975.
CU-B

S362
Student Peace Union.
  Vietnam, what's happening? [New
York, 196]
[2]p. 28cm.
1. Vietnamese conflict, 1961-
1975.
CU-B, KU-RH

S363
Student Peace Union.
  Why we protest. [Chicago, 196]
[2]p. 22cm.
Caption title.
1. U.S.--Foreign policy.
CU-B

S364
Student Peace Union. Caucus for
  Effective Action.
  Resolution on electoral action.
[n.p., 1964?]
2p. 28cm.
Caption title.
1. U.S.--Pol. & govt.--1963-
2. Elections. 3. Presidents--
U.S.--Election--1964.
CU-B

S365
Student Peace Union. Convention,
  1963-64.
  Statement on foreign policy.
[Chicago, 1964?]
Caption title.
1. U.S.--Foreign policy.
CU-B

S366
Student Peace Union. National
  Convention, 1961.
  Program statement of the 1961
National Convention of the
Student Peace Union. [Chicago,
1961]
[2]p. 28cm.
Caption title.
1. Disarmament.
CU-B, KU-RH

S367
Student Peace Union. National
  Convention, 1961.
  Program statement of the 1961
National Convention of the
Student Peace Union. [Chicago,
1961]
4p. 28cm.
Caption title.
1. Disarmament. 2. Negroes--
Civil rights.
KU-RH

S368
Student Peace Union. National
  Convention, 1962.
  Minutes of the Student Peace
Union National Convention,
April 27-29, 1962, Antioch
College, Yellow Springs, Ohio.
[n.p., 1962]
[19]p. 28cm.
Caption title.
KU-RH

S369
Student Peace Union. National
  Convention, 1963.
  Civil rights, a statement by
the 1963 National Convention
of the Student Peace Union.
[Chicago, 1963?]
folder. 20cm.
1. Negroes--Civil rights.
CU-B

S370
Student Peace Union. National
    Council.
  Berlin: a statement by Student
  Peace Union National Council.
  Chicago, 1961.
  2p. 28cm.
  Caption title.
  1. Berlin question (1945-   )
  KU-RH

S371
Student Peace Union. National
    Council.
  India and China--statement by
  the National Council of the SPU.
  [n.p., 196]
  [2]p. [3] leaves.
  Caption title.
  1. India--For. rel.--China (People's Republic of China, 1949-
) 2. China (People's Rep-
  ublic of China, 1949-   )--For.
  rel.--India.
  CU-B

S372
Student Peace Union. National
    Council.
  Vietnam. [New York, 1965]
  [2]p. 28cm.
  Caption title.
  1. Vietnamese conflict, 1961-
  1975.
  MiU-H

S373
Student Peace Union. National
    Secretary.
  National secretary's report.
  [Chicago] 1962.
  4p. 28cm.
  KU-RH

S374
Student Peace Union. National
    Steering Committee.
  Civil liberties statement. [n.
  p., 196]
  [1] leaf. 28cm.
  Caption title.
  1. Civil rights.
  CU-B

S375
Student Peace Union. National
    Steering Committee.
  Cuba: a statement of the Nat-
  ional Steering Committee of the
  Student Peace Union. [Chicago,
  1962]
  [2]p. 28cm.
  Caption title.
  1. Cuba.
  KU-RH, CU-B

S376
Student Peace Union. National
    Steering Committee.
  Nuclear testing, statement by
  the SPU National Steering Committee. Chicago, 1961.
  [1] leaf. 28cm.
  Caption title.
  1. Atomic weapons and disarmament. 2. Atomic bomb--Testing.
  KU-RH, CU-B

S377
Student Peace Union, University
    of Kansas.
  Alternatives; KU-SPU policy
  statement and public appeal.
  [Lawrence, 196]
  [2]p. 28cm.
  Caption title.
  CU-B

S378
Student Peace Union, University
    of Kansas.
  SPU and the mass society.
  [Lawrence, 1964?]
  [2] leaves. 28cm.
  Caption title.
  At head of title: 1964 SPU
  convention.
  1. U.S. Army. Reserve Offi-
  cers' Training Corps. 2. Stu-
  dent movements--Lawrence, Kan.
  CU-B

S379
The student revolt, an analysis
    by a Socialist Labor Party
    faculty member of the Uni-
    versity of California. [n.
    p., Section Washtenaw County,
    Michigan Socialist Labor Par-
    ty, 196]
  5p. 28cm.
  Caption title.

1. Student movements. 2. Social-
list Labor Party.
MiU-H

S380
Student Union for Peace Action.
  Vietnam. [Toronto, 196]
  17, 5 leaves. 28cm.
  Cover title.
  1. Vietnamese conflict, 1961-
  1975.
  WHi-A

S381
Student Union for Peace Action.
  Research, Information and
  Publication Project.
  Coming to Canada? Toronto [196]
  7p. 28cm.
  1. Emigration and immigration
  law--Canada.
  MiU-H

S382
Students for a Democratic Society.
  Action against American economic
  support of apartheid. [New York,
  1965]
  11p. 22cm.
  Cover title.
  1. South Africa--Race question.
  2. Chase Manhattan Bank, New
  York. 3. U.S.--Relations (general) with South Africa.
  WHi-A, KU-RH

S383
Students for a Democratic Society.
  Action against apartheid. [New
  York, 196]
  folder.
  Cover title.
  1. Chase Manhattan Bank, New
  York. 2. South Africa--Race
  question.
  WHi-A

S384
Students for a Democratic Society.
  America and the new era. New
  York [196]
  30p. 28cm.
  Cover title.
  Prepared at the Students for a
  Democratic Society convention,
  June 1963.

1. U.S.--Pol. & govt.--1963-
        2. U.S.--Foreign pol-
  icy.
  KU-RH, MiU

S385
Students for a Democratic Society.
  American involvement in South
  Africa: a web of power. New
  York, 1965.
  5 [2] leaves. 28cm.
  Cover title.
  1. U.S.--Relations (general)
  with South Africa. 2. South
  Africa--Relat-ons (general) with
  the U.S. 3. Chase Manhattan
  Bank, New York.
  WHi-A

S386
Students for a Democratic Society.
  American involvement in South
  Africa: a web of power. New
  York [196]
  5 [3]p. 28cm.
  Cover title.
  1. U.S.--Foreign economic relations. 2. U.S.--Relations
  (general) with South Africa.
  3. South Africa--Relations (general) with the U.S.
  MiU, KU-RH

S387
Students for a Democratic Society.
  Bring the war home. [Chicago,
  1969?]
  folder (8p) illus. 22cm.
  Cover title.
  1. U.S.--Pol. & govt.--1963
  2. Vietnamese conflict, 1961-
  1975.
  KU-RH

S388
Students for a Democratic Society.
  A call to all students to march
  on Washington to end the war in
  Vietnam April 17, 1965. New
  York [1965]
  [1] leaf. 28cm.
  Caption title.
  1. Vietnamese conflict, 1961-
  1975. 2. March on Washington
  to End the War in Vietnam,
  April 1965.
  WHi-A

S389
Students for a Democratic Society.
  Civil liberties and the McCarran
  act, a joint statement by Students for a Democratic Society
  and Campus Americans for Democratic Action. New York [196]
  6p. 28cm.
  Cover title.
  1. Internal security. 2. Civil
  Rights. 3. U.S. Laws, statutes,
  etc. Internal Security Act of
  1950. I. Campus Americans for
  Democratic Action.
  WHi-A, KU-RH

Students for a Democratic Society.

  see also
Students for a Democratic Society.
  National Convention, 1959.

S391
Students for a Democratic Society.
  Constitution. Boston [1970?]
  [4]p. 22cm.
  Cover title.
  KU-RH

S392
Students for a Democratic Society.
  Constitution. New York [1964]
  [5]p. 28cm.
  Caption title.
  Originally adopted in June 1962.
  Amended in June 1963 and in
  June 1964.
  WHi-L, NUC 66-30362

S393
Students for a Democratic Society.
  Constitution. [Amended in con-
  vention, June 1963] New York
  [1963]
  4p. 28cm.
  Caption title.
  KU-RH

S394
Students for a Democratic Society.
  Constitution. [Amended in convention, June 1964] Chicago
  [1964?]

  [4]p. 28cm.
  Caption title.
  KU-RH

S395
Students for a Democratic Society.
  Constitution revisions & gener-
  al comments. New York, 1962.
  5, 5 [6]p. 28cm.
  Caption title.
  Contents--Draft constitution,
  1962--Aims and purposes of
  SDS: some comments--Comments on
  manifesto drafts: excerpts from
  mail received.
  WHi-A

S396
Students for a Democratic Society.
  Democracy or the draft. [Los
  Angeles, 196]
  [2]p. 28cm.
  Caption title.
  1. Military service, Compulsory.
  MiU-H

S397
Students for a Democratic Society.
  The draft: what it is, how to
  stay out, how to fight it.
  Hell no! [Chicago, 1969]
  12p. illus. 22cm.
  Cover title.
  1. Military service, Compulsory.
  KU-RH, CU-B

S398
Students for a Democratic Society.
  Ecology: pollution means profit.
  [Boston, 1970]
  22p. illus. 28cm.
  Cover title.
  1. Environmental policy.
  2. Zero Population Growth.
  3. Pollution.
  KU-RH

S399
Students for a Democratic Society.
  Elections. [Chicago, 1968]
  folder. illus. 23cm.
  Cover title.
  1. U.S.--Pol. & govt.--1963-
          2. Presidents--U.S.--
  Election--1968.
  KU-RH

S400
Students for a Democratic Society.
  Excerpts from the Port Huron
  statement. [Chicago, 196]
  13p. 21cm.
  Cover title.
  KU-RH

S401
Students for a Democratic Society.
  Fight against racism; a national
  SDS strategy. [Berkeley? 1969?]
  6p. 28cm.
  Cover title.
  1. Negroes--Civil rights.
  CU-B

S402
Students for a Democratic Society.
  Fight racism! Articles from SDS'
  experience in fighting racism on
  campus and supporting black
  workers' action. [Boston, 1969?]
  28p. illus. 21cm.
  1. Negroes--Civil rights.
  KU-RH, NcWsW, NUC 73-43113

S403
Students for a Democratic Society.
  Guide to conscientious objection.
  [Chicago, 1966]
  12p.
  1. Military service, Compulsory.
  WHi-L

S404
Students for a Democratic Society.
  Immigration to Canada as an alternative to the draft. Nashville, Southern Student Organizing Committee [196]
  7 [6]p.
  Cover title.
  1. Military service, Compulsory.
  2. Emigration and immigration
  law--Canada. I. Southern Student Organizing Committee.
  WHi-L, NUC 70-34212

S405
Students for a Democratic Society.
  Immigration to Canada as an al-
  ternative to the draft. San
  Francisco [196]
  8p. 28cm.
  Cover title.

  1. Military service, Compulsory.
  2. Emigration and immigration
  law--Canada.
  CU-B

S406
Students for a Democratic Society.
  Imperialism: the main enemy of
  the people of the world. [Chi-
  cago? 1969?]
  [4]p. illus. 46cm. (Educational packet)
  Caption title.
  Contents--excerpts from Imperialism: the highest stage of
  capitalism, by Lenin--Excerpts
  from Long live the victory of
  the people's war, by Lin Pao.
  1. Imperialism. 2. U.S.--For-
  eign policy.
  KU-RH

S407
Students for a Democratic Society.
  Insurgent's handbook. [Madison?
  1969]
  5 [2]p. illus.
  1. Vietnamese conflict, 1961-
  1975. 2. Student movements.
  WHi-L

S408
Students for a Democratic Society.
  An introduction. [Chicago,
  196]
  folder (7p.) illus. 23cm.
  Cover title.
  MoU

S409
Students for a Democratic Society.
  Introductory paper for education conference, December, 1967.
  [n.p., 1967]
  6p. 28cm.
  Caption title.
  1. Student movements.
  KU-RH

S410
Students for a Democratic Society.
  A letter to young Democrats.
  New York [196]
  [3] leaves. 28cm.
  Cover title.
  1. Democratic Party.
  MiU

S411
Students for a Democratic Society.
  March on Washington. [Chicago,
  1965?]
  [1] leaf. 28cm.
  Caption title.
  1. March on Washington to End
  the War in Vietnam, April 1965.
  2. Vietnamese conflict, 1961-
  1975.
  WHi-A

S412
Students for a Democratic Society.
  Movement fund-raising guide.
  [Chicago? 1966?]
  8p.
  1. Fund raising.
  WHi-L

S413
Students for a Democratic Society.
  National Viet Nam examination.
  [Chicago, 196]
  [4]p. 28cm.
  Caption title.
  1. Vietnamese conflict, 1961-
  1975.
  KU-RH

S414
Students for a Democratic Society.
  National Vietnam examination.
  [Chicago] Students for a Demo-
  cratic Society and Inter-univer-
  sity Committee for Debate on
  Foreign Policy [1966?]
  [4]p. 28cm.
  Caption title.
  1. Vietnamese conflict, 1961-
  1975.
  CU-B

S415
Students for a Democratic Society.
  Occupation troops out. [Chica-
  go, 1969?]
  folder (8p.) illus. 23cm.
  Cover title.
  1. U.S.--Military policy.
  2. U.S.--Foreign policy.
  KU-RH

S416
Students for a Democratic Society.
  Plight of jobless miners. [New

York, 196]
  folder. illus. 22x10cm.
  Cover title.
  1. Miners--Appalachian Mountains.
  2. Appalachian Mountains--Soc.
  condit.
  KU-RH

S417
Students for a Democratic Society.
  Policy for action against the
  Chase Manhattan Bank (draft)
  [n.p., 196]
  [2] leaves. 28cm.
  Caption title.
  1. Chase Manhattan Bank, New
  York. 2. Africa, South--Race
  question.
  KU-RH

S418
Students for a Democratic Society.
  The Port Huron statement. [New
  York, 196]
  52p. 28cm.
  KU-RH

S419
Students for a Democratic Society.
  The Port Huron statement of the
  Students for a Democratic Soc-
  iety. [New York, 1962?]
  64p. 28cm.
  Caption title.
  WHi-A

S420
Students for a Democratic Society.
  Possibilities for the graduate.
  [Chicago, 196]
  3p. 22cm.
  Cover title.
  1. Military service, Compulsory.
  WHi-L

S421
Students for a Democratic Society.
  A radical union of students.
  [Chicago, 196]
  folder. illus. 21x10cm.
  KU-RH

S422
Students for a Democratic Society.
  Readings on poverty, with an
  introduction by Ken McEldowney.

[n.p., 196]
8p. 28cm.
Cover title.
Partial contents--Our invisible
poor, by Dwight MacDonald.
1. Poverty. I. McEldowney, Ken.
II. MacDonald, Dwight.
WHi-A

S423
Students for a Democratic Society.
Resistance and repression.
[Chicago, 1968?]
folder. 22x9cm.
Cover title.
1. Government, Resistance to.
2. Spock, Benjamin McLane, 1903-
        3. Raskin, Marcus G.
4. Coffin, William Sloane.
5. Goodman, Mitchell. 6. Ferber,
Michael.
CU-B

S424
Students for a Democratic Society.
Revolutionary youth. [Chicago,
1969?]
[4]p. illus. 46cm. (Educa-
tional packet)
Caption title.
Partial contents--This orienta-
tion of the youth movement, by
Chairman Mao.
1. China (People's Republic of
China, 1949-   )--Pol. & govt.
2. Youth--Political activity.
KU-RH

S425
Students for a Democratic Society.
SDS anti-draft statement, passed
at the December 28, 1966 meeting
of SDS national council. [New
York, Fellowship of Reconcilia-
tion, 196]
2p. 28cm.
Caption title.
1. Military service, Compulsory.
I. Fellowship of Reconciliation.
MoU

S426
Students for a Democratic Society.
SDS educational packed on self
determination. [Chicago? 1969?]
[4]p. illus. 46cm.

Caption title.
1. Vietnamese conflict, 1961-
1975. 2. Self-determination,
National.
KU-RH

S427
Students for a Democratic Society.
SDS national resolution on wo-
men. Boston, New England Free
Press [1969?]
[3]p. 28cm.
Cover title.
1. Woman--Rights of women.
I. New England Free Press.
KU-RH, MoU

S428
Students for a Democratic Society.
SDS work-in 1968: towards a
worker-student alliance. [Chi-
cago, 1969?]
31p. illus. 22cm.
Cover title.
1. Labor and laboring classes.
2. Student movements.
MoU, CU-B, WHi-L, NUC 73-34993

S429
Students for a Democratic Society.
Selected bibliography on civil
rights in the north. Columbus,
O., Students for a Democratic
Society for the Liberal Study
Group, 1962.
5p. 28cm.
Caption title.
1. Negroes--Civil rights--Bibl.
KU-RH

S430
Students for a Democratic Society.
Stop the festival of thieves
Monday, Sept. 15-19. [n.p.,
1969]
folder. 29cm.
Cover title.
1. Business and politics.
2. Corporations. 3. Underdeveloped areas.
CU-B

S431
Students for a Democratic Society.
The struggle against racism in
America. [Chicago, 1969?]

[4]p. illus. 46cm. (Educat-
ional packet)
Caption title.
Contents--Excerpts from Black
reconstruction, by W.E.B. DuBois
--Excerpts from The origins of
black nationalism: revolutionary
and reactionary, by Bill McAdoo
--Basis of white supremacy, by
Noel Ignatin.
1. Negroes--Civil rights.
KU-RH

S432
Students for a Democratic Society.
  Students for a Democratic Soc-
  iety. [Chicago, 196]
  folder. 22x10cm.
  Cover title.
  KU-RH

S433
Students for a Democratic Society.
  Students for a Democratic Society, an organization committed
  to: racial equality, disarmament,
  jobs and abundance, civil liberties, liberal education. New
  York [196]
  folder. 22x10cm.
  Cover title.
  KU-RH

S434
Students for a Democratic Society.
  Tenant housing manual. [Chicago,
  University of Illinois, Chicago
  Circle, c1966]
  50p.
  1. Housing.
  WHi-L

S435
Students for a Democratic Society.
  Thousands support GE workers.
  [Boston, 1969?]
  [2]p. 28cm.
  Caption title.
  1. General Electric Company.
  2. Vietnamese conflict, 1961-
  1975. 3. Labor and laboring
  classes.
  WHi-L

S436
Students for a Democratic Society.

Tuition's not the main issue.
[San Francisco, 1967?]
[2]p. 28cm.
Caption title.
1. Universities and colleges--
California. 2. Student move-
ments--California.
CU-B

S437
Students for a Democratic Society.
  Turn your guns around. [Chicago,
  1969?]
  folder (7p.) illus. 22cm.
  Cover title.
  1. U.S.--Military life. 2. Soldiers. 3. Vietnamese conflict,
  1961-1975.
  KU-RH

S438
Students for a Democratic Society.
  U.S. imperialism and Vietnam:
  an economic view. [n.p., 1970?]
  6p. 28cm.
  Caption title.
  1. Vietnamese conflict, 1961-
  1975.
  CU-B

S439
Students for a Democratic Society.
  U.S. imperialism and Vietnam:
  an economic view. [Boston,
  1970?]
  13p. illus. 22cm.
  1. Vietnamese conflict, 1961-
  1975. 2. Imperialism. 3. U.S.
  --Relations (general) with
  Vietnam.
  KU-RH

S440
Students for a Democratic Society.
  U.S. out of Southeast Asia.
  ROTC must go! [n.p., 1970?]
  10p. 22cm.
  Cover title.
  1. Vietnamese conflict, 1961-
  1975. 2. U.S. Army. Reserve
  Officers' Training Corps.
  3. Universities and colleges.
  CU-B

S441
Students for a Democratic Society.

Vietnam: no mistake. [Boston]
1970.
46p. illus. 28cm.
1. Vietnamese conflict, 1961-
1975. 2. U.S.--Pol. & govt.--
1959-
CU-B, KU-RH

S442
Students for a Democratic Society.
  Wanted for exploitation, racism
  and murder! Columbia, the boss.
  Ally with campus workers. [Bos-
  ton, 1970?]
  23p. illus. 28cm.
  Cover title.
  1. Student movements. 2. Labor
  and laboring classes.
  KU-RH

S443
Students for a Democratic Society.
  Who are the bombers? Often the
  rulers! [Boston, 1970?]
  10p. illus. 28cm.
  Cover title.
  1. Students for a Democratic
  Society. Revolutionary Youth
  Movement. 2. Radicalism.
  KU-RH

Students for a Democratic Society.
  Working papers for Nyack conference.
  see also
Aronowitz, Stanley.
  Working papers for Nyack conference.

S444
Students for a Democratic Society.
  Working papers for Nyack conference on unemployment and social
  change. New York [1963]
  8 [3]p. 28cm.
  Cover title.
  1. Poverty. 2. Social change.
  MiU

S445
Students for a Democratic Society,
  Baltimore.
  The John Hopkins Univ., who
  serves it and how. [Baltimore?
  1969]
  [30]p.

1. John Hopkins University.
WHi-L

Students for a Democratic Society.
  Berkeley Chapter.
  see also
Students for a Democratic Society.
  University of California,
  Berkeley.

S446
Students for a Democratic Society,
  Berkeley Chapter.
  SDS banned. [Berkeley? 1970?]
  [2] leaves. 36cm.
  Caption title.
  CU-B

Students for a Democratic Society.
  Economic Research and Action
  Project.
  xEconomic Research and Action
  Project.

S447
Students for a Democratic Society.
  Economic Research and Action
  Project.
  Announcing summer programs.
  [Ann Arbor, 196]
  folder. illus. 22x10cm.
  Cover title.
  KU-RH

S448
Students for a Democratic Society.
  Economic Research and Action
  Project.
  Appalachian summer project:
  preliminary prospectus. [Ann
  Arbor] 1964.
  4p. 28cm.
  Caption title.
  1. Appalachian Mountains.
  MiU

S449
Students for a Democratic Society.
  Economic Research and Action
  Project.
  ERAP fall program; report to the
  national council. Ann Arbor
  [196]
  6p. 28cm.
  Cover title.

1. Student movements.   2. Poverty.
WHi-L, MiU, WHi-A

S450
Students for a Democratic Society.
   Economic Research and Action
   Project.
Economic Research and Action Pro-
ject--an introduction.   [Ann Ar-
bor, 196]
3 leaves.   28cm.
Caption title.
WHi-A, KU-RH

S451
Students for a Democratic Society.
   Economic Research and Action
   Project.
[The economics of equality.   Ann
Arbor., 196]
folder.   illus.   23x11cm.
1. Negroes--Civil rights.
2. Poverty.
KU-RH

S452
Students for a Democratic Society.
   Economic Research and Action
   Project.
Fall program to the national
council.   Ann Arbor, [196]
4p.   28cm.
Cover title.
KU-RH

S453
Students for a Democratic Society.
   Economic Research and Action
   Project.
An introductory statement.
[Ann Arbor, 196]
4p.   28cm.
Cover title.
KU-RH

S454
Students for a Democratic Society.
   Economic Research and Action
   Project.
A movement of many voices.   [Ann
Arbor, 196]
[28]p.   illus.   22cm.
Cover title.
1. Student movements.   2. Pov-
erty.   3. Community organization.

4. Jobs or Income Now Community
Union.
KU-RH, CU-B, WHi-A

S455
Students for a Democratic Society.
   Economic Research and Action
   Project.
Prospectus for Newark organizing
--research project.   [Ann Arbor,
196]
4 leaves.   28cm.
Caption title.
1. Newark, N.J.--Race question.
2. Poor--Newark, N.J.
WHi-A

S456
Students for a Democratic Society.
   Economic Research and Action
   Project.
Summer 1964: project reports.
A compendium of reports of 6
summer projects sponsored by
the Economic Research and Action
Project of Students for a Demo-
cratic Society.   [Swarthmore,
Pa.] 1965.
2v.   28cm.
Cover title.
Contents--v. 1. An interracial
movement of the poor--Baltimore
report--Boston report--v.
2. Chester report--Newark re-
port--Philadelphia report--
Trenton report.
1. Poverty.   2. Negroes--Econ.
condit.
PSC, PPULC, NUC 69-68279

S457
Students for a Democratic Society.
   Economic Research and Action
   Project.
Trenton, New Jersey: report of
the ERAP summer project, 1964.
New York [1964?]
[6]p.   28cm.
Cover title.
1. Trenton, N.J.--Econ. condit.
2. Poor--Trenton, N.J.
WHi-A

S458
Students for a Democratic Society.
   Educational Conference, Mid-

Atlantic Area, Washington, 1962.
Working papers. [n.p., 196]
[32]p. 28cm.
Cover title.
Partial contents--The ability to
face whatever comes, by Tom Hayden.
1. U.S.--Foreign policy. 2. Capitalism. 2. U.S.--Pol. & govt.
--1959-   I. Hayden, Thomas.
MiU-H

Students for a Democratic Society.
    JOIN Community Union.
see
Jobs or Income Now Community Union.

S459
Students for a Democratic Society.
    Labor Committee.
Convention report. New York,
1969.
4p. 44cm.
Caption title.
1. Students for a Democratic
Society. National Convention,
1969.
MoU

S460
Students for a Democratic Society.
    Labor Committee.
The copper blitz on organized
labor. [n.p., 196]
8p. 36cm.
Caption title.
1. Trade-unions. 2. Copper
industry and trade.
CU-B

S461
Students for a Democratic Society.
    Labor Committees. National
    Caucus.
The third American revolution;
draft political program of the
National Caucus of SDS Labor
Committees. [New York? 196]
30p. (Campaigner supplement)
1. Socialism. 2. U.S.--Econ.
condit.
WHi-L

S462
Students for a Democratic Society.
    Louis Lingg Memorial Chapter.

Proposed resolution on the
counter-revolutionary nature
of the English language.
[Cicero, Ill.? Johnny Apple-
seek Patriotic Publications?
1969?]
4p. 28cm.
Caption title.
1. Languages--Political aspects.
I. Johnny Appleseed Patriotic
Publications.
KU-RH, CU-B

S463
Students for a Democratic Society.
    Madison.
The CIA: who was that military
dictator I see ja with? [Madi-
son? 1967?]
7 [1]p.
Cover title.
1. U.S. Central Intelligence
Agency.
WHi-L

S464
Students for a Democratic Society.
    Madison.
A student handbook. [Madison,
1967?]
33p.
Cover title.
1. Student movements.
WHi-L

S465
Students for a Demcoratic Society.
    Madison.
A student handbook. [Madison?
196]
28p. 22cm.
Cover title.
1. Student movements.
MiU

S466
Students for a Democratic Society,
    Madison. WDRU Anti-Imperial-
    ist Research and Action Pro-
    ject.
Business as usual, social uses
of the university. Madison
[196]
12p.
Cover title.
1. Wisconsin. University.

2. Universities and colleges.
WHi-L

S467
Students for a Democratic Society,
   Massachusetts Institute of
   Technology. War Research Sub-
   committee.
M.I.T. and the welfare state.
[Cambridge, 196]
22p. 22cm.
Cover title.
1. Military research. 2. Massa-
chusetts Institute of Technology.
WHi-A

S468
Students for a Democratic Society.
   National Convention, 1959.
Constitution (as amended by the
national convention, June 12, 13,
1959)
[n.p., 1959]
5 leaves. 28cm.
Caption title.
WHi-A

S469
Students for a Democratic Society.
   National Convention, 1962.
Constitution. New York, 1962.
5p. 28cm.
Caption title.
WHi-A

S470
Students for a Democratic Society.
   National Convention, 1963.
America and the new era. Chi-
cago [196]
23p. 28cm.
Cover title.
1. U.S.--Pol. & govt.--1963-
CU-B

S471
Students for a Democratic Society.
   National Convention, 1969.
Resolutions passed at the SDS
convention. Boston, New England
Free Press [1969]
7 [1]p. illus. 28cm. (Docu-
ments on SDS and the split)
Caption title.
Reprinted from New Left Notes
and Fight to Win.

Partial contents--The movement
must serve the people; the
schools can't, by Jeff Gordon.
1. Woman--Rights of women.
2. Negroes--Civil rights.
I. Gordon, Jeff. I. New England Free Press.
KU-RH

S472
Students for a Democratic Society.
   National Convention, 1969.
SDS on the split at the conven-
tion. [Boston] New England Free
Press [1969]
[4]p. 28cm. (Documents on SDS
and the split)
Reprinted from New Left Notes,
June 30, 1969.
Caption title.
Contents--Statement on the walk-
out. RYM walks out, by John
Pennington.
1. Students for a Democratic
Society. Revolutionary Youth
Movement. I. Pennington, John.
II. New England Free Press.
KU-RH

S473
Students for a Democratic Society.
   National Council.
Anti-draft resolution, adopted
December 28, 1966. [Berkeley,
Calif.? 1966?]
[2]p. 26cm.
Caption title.
1. Military service, Compulsory.
MiU

S474
Students for a Democratic Society.
   National Council.
National council meeting working
papers. [New York, 1963]
[40]p. 28cm.
Cover title.
WHi-A

S475
Students for a Democratic Society.
   National Council.
Resolution on SNCC. [Chicago?
1966]
[1] leaf. 28cm.
Caption title.

1. Student Nonviolent Coordinating Committee.
KU-RH

S476
Students for a Democratic Society.
    National Council.
Resolution on SNCC. [New York?]
1966.
1p.
1. Student Nonviolent Coordinating Committee. 2. Negroes--
Civil rights.
WHi-L

S477
Students for a Democratic Society.
    National Council.
SDS national resolution on wo-
men. Boston, New England Free
Press [1969?]
[3]p. 28cm.
Cover title.
1. Woman--Rights of women.
I. New England Free Press.
KU-RH

S478
Students for a Democratic Society.
    National Council.
SDS resolution on electoral
action. Chicago [1966]
3 leaves. 28cm.
Caption title.
1. Politics, Practical.
WHi-L

S479
Students for a Democratic Society.
    National Executive Committee.
Relationship between SDS and
LID. New York, 1962.
28p. 28cm.
Cover title.
1. League for Industrial Demo-
cracy.
CU-B

S480
Students for a Democratic Society.
    National Executive Committee.
Relationship between SDS and
LID. New York, 1962.
25 leaves. 28cm.
Cover title.
1. League for Industrial Demo-

cracy.
WHi-A

S481
Students for a Democratic Society,
    New York. Labor Committee.
The rape of the LIRR. [New
York, 196]
16p. 22cm.
Cover title.
1. Long Island Railroad Company.
KU-RH

S482
Students for a Democratic Society,
    New York Region.
Work-in: a national SDS summer
project. [New York, 196]
[2]p. 36cm.
Caption title.
WHi-L

S483
Students for a Democratic Society,
    New York Region. Vietnam Or-
    ganizing Project.
The myth of an independent South
Vietnam. [New York, 196]
5 leaves. 28cm. (Vietnam fact
sheet 1)
1. Vietnam--Pol. & govt.
2. Vietnamese conflict, 1961-
1975.
WHi-L

S484
Students for a Democratic Society,
    Northern California.
Fight police terror! [Berke-
ley? 1969?]
[1] leaf. 28cm.
Caption title.
1. Police. 2. Black Panther
Party.
CU-B

S485
Students for a Democratic Society,
    Northern California.
No mortorium on fighting imper-
ialism--support G.E. strikers
(or who are you kidding Wayne
Morse?) [Berkeley? 1969]
[2]p. 36cm.
Caption title.
1. Imperialism. 2. General

Electric Company.
CU-B

S486
Students for a Democratic Society.
    Peace Research and Education
    Project.
Peace in the college curriculum:
a resource kit. Ann Arbor (196)
7p. 28cm.
Cover title.
1. Peace. 2. Education--Curri-
cula.
NNU-T

S487
Students for a Democratic Society.
    Peace Research and Education
    Project.
Peace in the college curriculum--
a resource kit. New York [196]
7p. 28cm.
1. Peace. 2. Education--Curri-
cula.
MiU, WHi-A

S488
Students for a Democratic Society.
    Peace Research and Education
    Project.
South Africa: voices of the vic-
tims. Ann Arbor [196]
18p. 28cm.
Cover title.
1. South Africa--Race question.
WHi-A

S489
Students for a Democratic Society.
    Peace Research and Education
    Project.
Toward an effective peace program on campus. Ann Arbor
[1964?]
8p. 28cm.
Cover title.
1. Peace. 2. Student movements.
CU-B, WHi-A

S490
Students for a Democratic Society.
    Peace Research and Education
    Project, Boston.
Boston PREP: a summer report.
Ann Arbor [196]
15p. 28cm.

Cover title.
1. Boston--Econ. condit.
2. Poor--Boston.
WHi-A

S491
Students for a Democratic Society.
    Peace Research and Politics
    Office.
Towards an effective peace program on the campus. Ann Arbor,
1962.
[7]p. 28cm.
Caption title.
1. Peace. Education--Curricula.
WHi-A

S492
Students for a Democratic Society.
    Political Education Project.
The 1964 presidential campaign.
[n.p., 1964]
[4]p. 28cm.
Cover title.
1. Goldwater, Barry Morris,
1909-   2. Presidents--U.S.
--Election--1964. 3. U.S.--
Pol. & govt.--1963-
WHi-A

S493
Students for a Democratic Society.
    Political Education Project.
PEP report to the national
council of SDS. [n.p., 1964?]
4p. 28cm.
Caption title.
WHi-A

S494
Students for a Democratic Society.
    Rank and File Caucus.
Towards a new perspective: a
rank and file upsurge (adopted
as a working paper by the Rank
and File Caucus formed at the
SDS convention, June 1969) [n.
p., 1969?]
11 leaves. 28cm.
1. Progressive Labor Party.
2. Students for a Democratic
Society. National Convention,
1969.
MoU

S495
Students for a Democratic Society.
    Revolutionary Youth Movement.
RYM SDS on the split at the con-
vention. Boston, New England
Free Press [1969?]
[3]p. 28cm.
Cover title.
Reprinted from RYM New Left
Notes, June 25, 1969.
1. Students for a Democratic
Society, National Convention,
1969. I. New England Free
Press.
KU-RH

S496
Students for a Democratic Society.
    Revolutionary Youth Movement.
Weatherman. Boston, New England
Free Press [1969?]
13p. illus. 28cm. (Documents
on SDS and the split)
Cover title.
Reprinted from New Left Notes,
June 18, 1969.
1. Negroes--Civil rights.
2. Youth--Political activity.
I. New England Free Press.
KU-RH

S497
Students for a Democratic Society,
    San Francisco.
An introduction to Students for
a Democratic Society: democracy.
San Francisco [1966?]
[4]p. 28cm.
Cover title.
MiU

S498
Students for a Democratic Society,
    San Francisco Regional Office.
An introduction to Students for
a Democratic Society. [San
Francisco, 1966?]
[4]p. 28cm.
Cover title.
CU-B

S499
Students for a Democratic Society,
    Swarthmore College Chapter.
Chester, Pa.: jobs, freedom now;
community organization in the

other America [submitted by the
Swarthmore College Chapter of
SDS, in collaboration with the
Committee for Freedom Now of
Chester...and the Swarthmore
Political Action Club] New York,
Distributed by Students for a
Democratic Society [196]
10, 2p. 28cm.
Cover title.
1. Poor--Chester, Pa. 2. Ne-
groes--Chester, Pa. 3. Chester,
Pa.--Econ. condit.
KU-RH, WHi-L

S500
Students for a Democratic Society.
    University Committee.
Report of the SDS University
Committee, June 28-30, 1965.
[n.p., 1965]
[4]p. 28cm.
Caption title.
1. Student movements. 2. Uni-
versities and colleges.
KU-RH

Students for a Democratic Society,
    University of California,
    Berkeley.
see also
Students for a Democratic Society,
    Berkeley Chapter.

S501
Students for a Democratic Society,
    University of California,
    Berkeley.
Fight racist U.C. bosses!
[Berkeley? 1969?]
[2]p. 28cm.
Caption title.
1. California. University,
Berkeley. 2. Student movements
--Berkeley, Calif.
CU-B

S502
Students for a Democratic Society,
    University of California,
    Berkeley.
Keep Yank. [Berkeley? 1969]
[8]p. 22cm.
Cover title.
1. Yank, Ronald. 2. California.
University, Berkeley.
CU-B

S503
Students for a Democratic Society,
    University of California,
    Berkeley.
  Program for action; build the
  campus worker-student alliance,
  fight fascism, smash ROTC. [Ber-
  keley? 1969?]
  11p. 22cm.
  Cover title.
  1. Negroes--Civil rights.
  2. Labor and laboring classes.
  3. U.S. Army. Reserve Officers'
  Training Corps.
  CU-B

S504
Students for a Democratic Society,
    University of California,
    Berkeley.
  SLAP: student-labor action project. [Berkeley, 196]
  [4]p. 28cm.
  1. Labor and laboring classes.
  2. Student movements.
  CU-B

S505
Students for a Democratic Society,
    University of California,
    Berkeley.
  Vietnam: mistake or economic
  necessity? [Berkeley? 1970?]
  [4]p. 36cm.
  Caption title.
  1. Vietnamese conflict, 1961-
  1975. 2. Imperialism.
  CU-B

S506
Students for a Democratic Society,
    University of California,
    Berkeley.
  What happen to the Panther con-
  ference? [Berkeley? 1969?]
  [2]p. 28cm.
  Caption title.
  1. Conference for a United Front
  Against Fascism. 2. Black Pan-
  ther Party.
  CU-B

S507
Students for a Democratic Society,
    University of California,
    Berkeley.

What is racism? [Berkeley?
1969?]
  [8]p. 22cm.
  Cover title.
  1. California. University,
  Berkeley--Race question. 2. Ne-
  groes--Berkeley, Calif.
  CU-B

S508
Students for a Democratic Society,
    University of California,
    Berkeley. Labor Committees.
  For a meaningful alliance with
  workers. [Berkeley? 1968?]
  [1] leaf. 28cm.
  Caption title.
  1. Standard Oil Company.
  2. Labor and laboring classes.
  CU-B

S509
Students for a Democratic Society,
    University of California,
    Berkeley. Labor Committees.
  What should the movement do this
  summer? [Berkeley? 1968?]
  [1] leaf. 36cm.
  1. Student movements.
  CU-B

S510
Students for a Democratic Society,
    University of California,
    Berkeley. Monday Night Caucus.
  End crisis politics, build a
  movement. [Berkeley? 1968?]
  [2]p. 28cm.
  1. Student movements.
  CU-B

S511
Students for a Democratic Society,
    University of California,
    Berkeley. University War
    Complicity Committee.
  Dow--one of many. [Berkeley?
  196]
  [2]p. 36cm.
  Caption title.
  1. Dow Chemical Company.
  2. Vietnamese conflict, 1961-
  1975.
  CU-B

S512
Students for a Democratic Society,
    University of California,
    Berkeley. Worker-Student Al-
    liance Committee.
SDS build a campus worker student
alliance. [Berkeley, 1969?]
[4]p. 22cm.
1. Labor and laboring classes.
CU-B

S513
Students for a Democratic Society,
    University of California,
    Los Angeles.
SDS-VDC speeches. [Los Angeles,
1966?]
[4]p. 21cm.
Cover title.
1. Vietnamese conflict, 1961-
1975.
CU-B

S514
Students for a Democratic Society,
    University of Chicago.
Position on selective service.
[Chicago, 196]
[4]p. 22cm.
Caption title.
1. Military service, Compulsory.
2. U.S. Selective Service Sys-
tem.
CU-B

S515
Students for a Democratic Society,
    University of Kansas.
Vietnam resolution. [Lawrence,
1965]
2p. 28cm.
Caption title.
1. Vietnamese conflict, 1961-
1975.
KU-RH

S516
Students for a Democratic Society,
    University of Texas.
Prospectus for a Texas student
program. [Austin? 196]
[3]p. 28cm.
Caption title.
1. Student movements--Texas.
WHi-A

S517
Students for a Democratic Society.
    University of Washington.
Vietnam, democracy and the
draft [Seattle? 1966]
[4]p. 28cm.
Caption title.
1. Democracy. 2. Vietnamese
conflict, 1961-1975. 3. Military service, Compulsory.
WHi-A

Students for a Democratic Society.
    Worker-Student Alliance Cau-
    cus.
xWorker-Student Alliance Caucus.

S518
Students for a Democratic Society.
    Worker-Student Alliance Cau-
    cus.
The Worker-Student Alliance cau-
cus. [Boston, New England Free
Press, 1970?]
[4]p. 28cm. (Documents on SDS
and the split)
Caption title.
Contents--The Student-Labor
Action Project proposal.
1. Labor and laboring classes.
2. Student movements. I. Stu-
dents for a Democratic Society.
Student-Labor Action Project.
II. New England Free Press.
KU-RH

S519
Students for a Democratic Society.
    Worker-Student Alliance Cau-
    cus, Columbia University.
Statement of the Columbia Uni-
versity Worker-Student Alliance
Caucus on the demands raised by
the Columbia S.D.S. leadership.
[New York, 1969?]
5p. 36cm.
Caption title.
1. Columbia University. 2. Ne-
groes--Education.
KU-RH

S520
Students for Positive Action.
    Declaration of academic freedom

& student's rights. [Manhattan,
Kan.? 196]
[3] leaves. 28cm.
Caption title.
1. Student movements--Manhattan,
Kan. 2. Teaching, Freedom of.
KU-RH

S521
Suall, Irwin.
  The American ultras; the extreme
  right and the military-industrial
  complex. New York, New America
  [1962]
  65p. 23cm.
  1. Anti-communist movements.
  2. Communism. I. New America.
  IU, MiU, KU-RH, DLC 62-1461

S522
Suall, Joan.
  Socialist Party report, 1969.
  [n.p., 1969]
  2p. 36cm.
  Caption title.
  1. Socialist Party (U.S.)
  WHi-L

S523
Suffield Peace Manifestation Com-
    mittee.
  Hymns, Suffield Peace Manifes-
  tation, July 5, 1964. Grand
  Forks, B.C. [1964?]
  26p. 22cm.
  Cover title.
  1. Peace.
  KU-RH

S524
Sung, Kim Il.
  Today Vietnam, tomorrow Korea?
  An interview with Kim Il Sung.
  New York, World View Publishers
  [1970]
  1v. (unpaged) 22cm.
  1. Korea Democratic(People's
  Republic, 1948-   )--For. rel.
  --U.S. 2. U.S.--For. rel.--
  Korea Democratic(People's Re-
  public, 1948-   ) I. World
  View Publishers.
  KU-RH

S525
Susan, Barbara.

About my consciousness raising.
[New York, Redstockings? 1969]
4p. 28cm.
Caption title.
1. Woman--Rights of women.
I. Redstockings of the Women's
Liberation Movement.
MoU

S526
Sutherland, Elizabeth.
  The cat and mouse game. [Atlan-
  ta, Student Nonviolent Coordinating Committee, 196]
  [2]p. 36cm.
  Caption title.
  1. Negroes--Civil rights.
  2. Mississippi--Race question.
  3. Council of Federated Organizations. I. Student Nonviolent
  Coordinating Committee.
  WHi-A

S527
Swabeck, Arne.
  The split in the Socialist
  Party. When theory collides
  with fact let's rewrite history;
  a book review. [Boston, New
  England Free Press, 1970?]
  [25]-38p. illus. 28cm.
  Caption title.
  1. Weinstein, James, 1926-
  The decline of socialism in
  America. 2. Socialist Party
  (U.S.) I. New England Free
  Press.
  MiU, KU-RH

S528
Swanky, Ben.
  National identity or cultural
  genocide? A reply to Ottawa's
  new Indian policy. [Toronto,
  Progress Books, 1970?]
  38p.
  Cover title.
  1. Indians of North America--
  Canada. 2. Indians of North
  America--Government relations.
  I. Progress Books.
  MiU

S529.
Swann, Bob.
  Prison: the inner life. Volun-

town, Conn., New England Commit-
tee for Nonviolent Action [196]
[1] leaf. 28cm.
Caption title.
1. Prisons. 2. Negroes. I. New
England Committee for Nonviolent
Action.
CU-B

S530
Swann, Marjorie.
Decade of nonviolence; through
the years with the New England
CNVA. Voluntown, Conn., New
England Committee for Nonviolent
Action [1970]
8p. illus. 28cm.
Cover title.
1. Nonviolence. 2. Government,
Resistance to. 3. New England
Committee for Nonviolent Action.
KU-RH

S531
Swann, Marjorie.
Why non-cooperation? An interpretation of noncooperation with
police, courts and jails. [Vol-
untown, Conn., New England Committee for Nonviolent Action,
196]
2p. 36cm.
Caption title.
1. Government, Resistance to.
I. New England Committee for
Nonviolent Action.
KU-RH

S532
Sweezy, Paul Marlor, 1910-
Can the ruling class shape his-
tory? Boston, New England Free
Press [1969]
9p. 22cm.
Cover title.
Reprinted from Monthly Review,
Ap. 1969.
1. Vietnamese conflict, 1961-
1975. I. New England Free Press.
KU-RH

S533
Sweezy, Paul Marlor, 1910-
Marx and the proletariat. Boston, New England Free Press
[1969?]
25-42p. 22cm.

Cover title.
Reprinted from Monthly Review,
Dec. 1967.
1. Proletariat. 2. Socialism.
3. Capitalism. I. New England
Free Press.
KU-RH

S534
Sweezy, Paul Marlor, 1910-
Marxian socialism. Power elite
or ruling class? New York,
Monthly Review Press, 1956.
32p. (Monthly review pamphlet
series, 13)
Reprinted from Monthly Review.
1. Mills, C. Wright. 2. Soc-
ialism. I. Monthly Review
Press.
MH, MiU

S535
Sweezy, Paul Marlor, 1910-
The merger movement; a study
in power [by] Paul Sweezy [and]
Harry Magdoff. Boston, New
England Free Press [1969?]
18p. 22cm.
Cover title.
Reprinted from Monthly Review,
June 1969.
1. Corporations. 2. Consoli-
dation and merger of corpora-
tions. I. Magdoff, Harry, jt.
auth. II. New England Free
Press.
MiU, KU-RH

S536
Sweezy, Paul Marlor, 1910-
The split in the capitalist
world [and] socialist world,
by Paul M. Sweezy and Leo
Huberman. New York, Monthly
Review Press, 1963.
38p. 22cm. (Monthly Review
pamphlet series, no. 22)
1. World politics--1955-
I. Huberman, Leo, 1903-
II. Monthly Review Press.
KU-RH

S537
Sweezy, Paul Marlor, 1910-
The theory of U.S. foreign
policy [by] Paul M. Sweezy [and]
Leo Huberman. New York, Mon-

thly Review Press, 1960.
31p. 22cm. (Monthly Review pamphlet series, no. 17)
"Reprinted from Monthly Review,
September, October, November
1960."
1. U.S.--For. rel.--1945-
2. U.S.--Foreign economic relations. I. Huberman, Leo, 1903-
    jt. auth. I. Monthly Review
Press.
MH, DS, MiU, InU, CLSU, NNC-L,
NcU, DLC 60-53539

S538
Sweezy, Paul Marlor, 1910-
  Thoughts on the American system,
  with emphasis on the contradic-
  tion between the national ruling
  class and city rulers. Boston,
  New England Free Press [1969?]
  13p. 21cm.
  Cover title.
  Reprinted from Monthly Review,
  Feb. 1969.
  1. U.S.--Pol. & govt.--1963-
  2. Power (Social science)
  3. Nixon, Richard Milhous, Pres.
  U.S., 1913-   4. Vietnamese
  conflict, 1961-1975. I. New
  England Free Press.
  KU-RH, MiU

S539
Sweezy, Paul Marlor, 1910-
  Towards a critique of economics.
  Boston, New England Free Press
  [1970?]
  9p. 28cm.
  Cover title.
  Reprinted from Monthly Review,
  Jan. 1970.
  1. Economics. 2. Socialism.
  I. Monthly Review Press.
  MiU

S540
Sweezy, Paul Marlor, 1910-
  What you should know about Suez,
  by P.M. Sweezy and L. Huberman.
  [New York, Monthly Review Press,
  1956]
  24p. (Monthly Review pamphlet
  series, 12)
  Reprinted from Monthly review,
  Oct. 1956.

  1. Suez Canal. I. Huberman,
  Leo, 1903-   jt. auth.
  I. Monthly Review Press.
  MH, MiU

S541
Swomley, John M.
  Amnesty: the record and the
  need. [New York, Clergy and
  Laymen Concerned About Vietnam,
  1969?]
  8p. 22cm.
  Cover title.
  Reprinted from National Catholic
  Reporter, Jan. 1, 1969.
  1. Military service, Compulsory.
  2. Amnesty. I. Clergy and Lay-
  men Concerned About Vietnam.
  KU-RH

S542
Swomley, John M.
  The national service proposal.
  [San Francisco, American Friends
  Service Committee, Northern
  California Regional Office,
  1967?]
  [4]p. 28cm.
  Caption title.
  Reprinted from The Christian
  Century, Jan. 11, 1967.
  1. Military service, compulsory.
  I. Friends, Society of. Ameri-
  can Friends Service Committee.
  KU-RH

S543
Swomley, John M.
  The peacetime draft. Nyack, N.
  Y., Fellowship of Reconcilia-
  tion, 1968.
  6p. 28cm. (Current issues)
  Caption title.
  1. Military service, Compulsory.
  I. Fellowship of Reconciliation.
  KU-RH

S544
Swomley, John M.
  Twenty-five years of conscription. [San Francisco? American Friends Service Committee?
  c1967?]
  8p. 28cm.
  Caption title.
  Reprinted from Christian Century,

Ap. 12, 1967.
1. Military service, Compulsory.
I. Friends, Society of. American Friends Service Committee.
KU-RH

S545
Swomley, John M.
   Twenty-five years of conscrip-
tion. San Francisco, American
Friends Service Committee,
Northern California Regional
Office [1967]
   [4]p. 28cm.
   Caption title.
   1. Military service, Compulsory.
I. Friends, Society of. Ameri-
can Friends Service Committee.

Northern California Regional
Office.
KU-RH

S546
Swomley, John M.
   Why the draft should go. [Phi-
ladelphia, Distributed by
National Peace Literature Ser-
vice, American Friends Service
Committee, 196 ?]
   fol er (5p) 27x10cm.
         title.
   1. Military service, Compulsory.
I. Friends, Society of. Ameri-
can Friends Service Committee.
KU-RH

☦
T
☦

T1
Tabata, I.B.
   The freedom struggle in South
Africa presidential address de-
livered at the first national
conference of the African's
People's Democratic Union of
Southern Africa, April 1962, in
Cape Town. [New York] Alexander
Defense Committee, 1965.
   23p. 22cm.
   1. South Africa--Pol. & govt.
2. South Africa--Race question.
3. Labor and laboring classes--
South Africa. I. Alexander De-
fense Committee.
MoU, MiU

T2
Tabor, Michael "Cetewayo".
   Capitalism plus dope equals
genocide. [Boston, New England
Free Press, 197]
   11p. illus. 21cm.
   Cover title.
   1. Narcotics. 2.Capitalism.
3. Negroes--Econ. condit.
4. Black Panther Party. I. New
England Free Press.
KU-RH

T3
Tabor, Michael "Cetewayo".
   Capitalism plus dope equal
genocide. [New York?] Black
Panther Party [1970?]
   11p.
   Cover title.
   1. Narcotics. 2. Negroes--
Econ. condit. 3. Black Pan-
ther Party. 4. Capitalism.
I. Black Panther Party.
WHi-L

T4
Tabor, Michael "Cetewayo".
   Capitalism plus dope equals
genocide. [San Francisco,
Black Panther Party, 196]
   10 [4]p. 28cm.
   Cover title.
   1. Narcotics. 2. Capitalism.
3. Negroes--Econ. condit.
4. Black Panther Party.
I. Black Panther Party.
MiU

T5
Tabor, Michael "Cetewayo".
   The plaque: capitalism + dope =
genocide. [New York, Committee to Defend the Panther 21,

1970?]
[4]p. illus.
Caption title.
1. Narcotics. 2. Negroes--Econ.
condit. 3. Black Panther Party.
4. Capitalism. I. Committee to
Defend the Panther 21.
NNU-T

T6
Tabor, Ron.
  SDS and the student movement.
  [New York? Independent Socialist
  Club? 196]
  6p. 28cm.
  Caption title.
  1. Students for a Democratic
  Society. 2. Student movements.
  I. Independent Socialist Club.
  MiU

T7
Tarmy, Elaine.
  Civil rights discussion paper.
  [Chicago? Student Peace Union?
  196]
  2 leaves. 28cm.
  Cover title.
  1. Negroes--Civil rights.
  I. Student Peace Union.
  CU-B

T8
Tatum, Arlo.
  So you would fight if this coun-
  try were attacked? Philadelphia,
  Central Committee for Conscien-
  tious Objectors [196]
  [1] leaf. 28cm.
  Caption title.
  1. Conscientious objectors.
  I. Central Committee for Con-
  scientious Objectors.
  KU-RH

T9
Tatum, Arlo.
  So you would have fought Hitler?
  Philadelphia, Central Committee
  for Conscientious Objectors
  [1968?]
  [1] leaf. 28cm.
  Caption title.
  1. Pacifism. 2. Hitler, Adolf,
  1889-1945. I. Central Committee
  for Conscientious Objectors.
  KU-RH

T10
Tax, Meredith.
  Woman and her mind: the story
  of daily life. [Cambridge,
  Mass., Bread and Roses; New
  England Free Press, c1970]
  20p. illus. 28cm.
  Cover title.
  1. Woman--History and condition
  of women. I. Bread and Roses.
  II. New England Free Press.
  MiU, KU-RH

T11
Taylor, Charles.
  Image and reality; China from
  within. San Francisco, Peace
  Literature Service, American
  Friends Service Committee
  [196]
  [1] leaf., [4]p. illus. 28cm.
  Caption title.
  Reprinted from The Nation,
  Oct. 4, 1965.
  1. China (People's Republic
  of China, 1949-   ) I. Fri-
  ends, Society of. American
  Friends Service Committee.
  KU-RH

T12
Teachers Defense Committee.
  The courage to be free. A
  statement by teachers in Los
  Angeles now under subpoena to
  appear before September, 1959,
  hearings of the House Committee
  on Un-American Activities.
  [Los Angeles, 1958]
  7p. 22cm.
  Cover title.
  1. Teachers--Los Angeles.
  2. U.S. Congress. House.
  Committee on Un-American Activities.
  MiU

T13
Teachers for Integrated Schools.
  Hearts and minds. [Chicago]
  1962.
  15p.
  Cover title.
  1. Negroes--Education.
  WHi-A

T15
Temporary Organizing Committee for
    a New Marxist-Leninist Youth
    Organization.
  Open admission: a proposal to the
  SDS convention. [n.p., 1969?]
  18p. 22cm.
  Cover title.
  1. Students. 2. Universities
  and colleges--Admission. 3. Ne-
  groes--Education. I. Students
  for a Democratic Society. National Convention, 1969.
  WHi-L

T16
Tenny, Gerry.
  Towards a new perspective, a
  rank and file upsurge. [Chica-
  go? 1969?]
  13p. 28cm.
  Caption title.
  1. Students for a Democratic
  Society.
  WHi-L

T16a
Their morals and ours; Marxist ver-
    sus liberal views on morality.
    Four essays, by Leon Trotsky,
    John Dewey [and] George Novack.
    New York, Merit Publishers
    [1969]
  80p. 22cm.
  Contents.--Introduction, by G.
  Novack--Their morals and ours,
  by L. Trotsky--The moralists and
  sycophants against Marxism, by
  L. Trotsky--Means and ends, by
  J. Dewey--Liberal morality, by
  G. Novack.
  1. Communist Ethics. 2. Liber-
  alism. 3. Moral conditions.
  I. Trotskii, Lev, 1879-1940.
  II. Dewey, John, 1859-1952.
  Means and ends. III. Novack,
  George Edward. Liberal morality.
  IV. Merit Publishers.
  KU-RH, DLC 76-518362

T17
Theobald, Robert.
  Cybernation and human rights.
  [New York, Liberation, 1964?]
  folder.
  Reprinted from Liberation, Aug.

1964.
1. Cybernetics. 2. Social
change. 3. Automation. 4. Civil rights. I. Liberation.
WHi-L

T18
Theobald, Robert.
  The cybernation revolution.
  Nashville, Southern Student Organizing Committee [1964]
  14p.
  address delivered to the 52d.
  annual conference of the Council of the Southern Mountains,
  April 7, 1964.
  1. Cyvernetics. 2. Poverty.
  3. Automation. I. Southern
  Student Organizing Committee.
  WHi-L

T19
Thomas, Norman.
  Democratic socialism, a new
  appraisal. New York, Post War
  World Council [1963]
  47p. 22cm.
  1. Socialism. I. Post War
  World Council.
  MiU

T20
Thomas, Norman.
  Speech by Norman Thomas [at the]
  Socialist Party Conference on
  Poverty and Unemployment, Wash-
  ington, D.C., April 18, 1964.
  [New York? 1964?]
  7 leaves. 28cm.
  Caption title.
  1. Poverty. 2. Employment
  (Economic theory) I. Socialist
  Party (U.S.)
  KU-RH

T21
Thomas, Norman.
  A straight forward letter from
  Norman Thomas to you and other
  people who want to do something
  about racial injustice. [New
  York? Scholarship, Educational
  and Defense Fund for Racial
  Equality, 1967?]
  [4]p. port.
  Caption title.

1. Negroes--Civil rights.
I. Scholarship, Education and
Defense Fund for Racial Equality.
WHi-L

T22
Thomas, Norman.
  Why socialism? [New York? 196]
  4p. 28cm.
  Caption title.
  1. Socialism.
  KU-RH

T23
Thomas, Richard.
  United States economic involvement in South Africa. [New York,
  American Committee on Africa,
  1966]
  10 leaves. 28cm.
  1. South Africa--Race question.
  2. U.S.--Relations (general)
  with South Africa. I. American
  Committee on Africa.
  KU-RH

T24
Thomas, Trevor.
  This life we take: a case against
  the death penalty. [San Francis-
  co] Friends Committee on Legislation [196]
  34p. 22cm.
  1. Capital punishment. I. Friends Committee on Legislation,
  San Francisco.
  MiU

T25
Thompson, Daniel C.
  The case for integration. [At-
  lanta] Southern Regional Council
  [1961]
  11p. 23cm.
  Caption title.
  1. Negroes--Civil rights.
  I. Southern Regional Council.
  WHi-A

T26
Thompson, Robert.
  Report of Robert Thompson on
  the 12 party declaration and 64
  party peace manifesto made at
  the national executive committee,
  CPUSA, December 22, 1957. [n.
  p., 1957]

6 leaves. 36cm.
Caption title.
1. Communism. 2. Twelve Party
Declaration and Sixty-four Party Peace Manifesto. I. Communist Party of the United States
of America.
KU-J

T27
Thompson, Sir Robert Grainger
    Ker, 1916-
  On the Communist Party [some
  problems and perspectives] New
  York, Labor Committee, Commun-
  ist Party, New York State [195]
  [8]p. port. 22cm.
  Speech delivered at the Carne-
  gie Music Hall in New York City.
  1. Communism. I. Communist
  Party of the United States of
  America. New York (State).
  Labor Committee.
  NcD, NUC 70-22229

T28
Thorman, Donald J.
  Catholics and civil liberties.
  [Omaha, Catholic Council on
  Civil Liberties, 196]
  [6]p. port. 22cm.
  At head of title: An interview
  with the Dean of Notre Dame Law
  School.
  1. O'Meara, Joseph. 2. Civil
  rights. 3. Catholics. I. Ca-
  tholic Council on Civil Libert-
  ies.
  KU-RH, MiU

T29
Thorson, Joseph T.
  "A non-nuclear role for Canada."
  [Toronto, Canadian Campaign for
  Nuclear Disarmament, 196]
  [12]p. 23x10cm.
  1. Atomic weapons. 2. Disarma-
  ment. I. Canadian Campaign for
  Nuclear Disarmament.
  KU-RH

T30
Thurston, Linda.
  Birth control, abortion, vener-
  eal disease. Revised May 1970
  for the Resist high school kit.
  Cambridge, Resist, 1970.

11p. 28cm.
Cover title.
1. Birth control.   2. Abortion.
3. Venereal diseases. I. Resist.
KU-RH

T31
Timberg, Thomas.
  On "neo-colonialism". [n.p.,
  Distributed by Liberal Study
  Group, 196]
  4p. 28cm.
  1. Colonization. I. Liberal
  Study Group.
  WHi-A

T32
Tishman, Mark.
  Racial oppression and working-
  class politics [by Mark Tishman,
  Joel Salinger and John Sebesta,
  n.p., 196]
  6p. 36cm.
  Caption title.
  1. Students for a Democratic
  Society. 2. Spartacist League.
  3. Labor and labor classes.
  4. Negroes--Civil rights.
  1. Salinger, Joel, jt. auth.
  II. Sebesta, John, jt. auth.
  CU-B

T33
Tobis, David.
  The Central American Common Market: the integration of underde-
  velopment. Cambridge, Mass.,
  American Friends Service Committee [1970?]
  12p. 28cm.
  Caption title.
  Reprinted from NACLA newsletter,
  v. 3, no. 9; Jan. 1970.
  1. Central American Common Market. 2. U.S.--Relations (general) with Central America.
  3. Central America--Econ. condit.
  I. Friends, Society of. American Friends Service Committee.
  KU-RH

T34
Tocsin.
  Tocsin: a student organization
  at Harvard University and Rad-
  cliffe College. [n.p., 196]

[2]p. 28cm.
Caption title.
1. Student movements--Boston.
WHi-L

T35
Toivo, Toivo Hermann ja.
  "South Africa has robbed us of
  our country". [New York, Afri-
  ca Defense and Aid Fund of the
  American Committee on Africa,
  196]
  [12]p. 20cm.
  Cover title.
  1. South Africa--Pol. & govt.
  2. South Africa--Race question.
  I. American Committee on Africa.
  Africa Defense and Aid Fund.
  KU-RH

T36
Tornquist, Elizabeth.
  "Over 30". Nashville, Southern
  Student Organizing Committee
  [196]
  [3]p. 28cm.
  Cover title.
  1. Youth--Political activity.
  I. Southern Student Organizing
  Committee.
  WHi-L, MoU

T37
Touma, Emile.
  About the idea of a Palestinian
  state. [New York, New Outlook
  Publishers, 1970]
  15p. 22cm.
  Cover title.
  1. Near East--Pol. & govt.
  2. Palestine. I. New Outlook
  Publishers.
  MiU

T38
Tournour, Gene.
  Henry Winston meets Angela
  Davis. [New York, Communist
  Party, U.S.A., 1970?]
  6p.
  Cover title.
  Reprinted from the Daily World.
  1. Davis, Angela, 1944-
  2. Winston, Henry. I. Commun-
  ist Party of the United States
  of America.
  WHi-L

T39
Toward a post-scarcity society:
    the American perspective and
    S.D.S. [n.p., 1969]
  10p. 28cm. (Radical decentra-
  list project resolution no. 1)
  1. Students for a Democratic
  Society.
  WHi-L

T40
Towards a Quaker view of sex, by
    a group of British Friends;
    and is the problem really sex?
    by Gene Hoffman. New York,
    Students for a Democratic
    Society [196]
  10, 2p. 28cm.
  Cover title.
  Reprinted from Liberation, sum-
  mer 1963.
  1. Sex. I. Students for a Demo-
  cratic Society. II. Hoffman,
  Gene, jt. auth.
  WHi-L, KU-RH

T41
Towe, Bill.
  Who runs the schools? Nashville,
  Southern Student Organizing Committee [196]
  9p. 28cm.
  1. Education. 2. Universities
  and colleges. I. Southern Student Organizing Committee.
  MoU

T42
Toynbee, Arnold Joseph, 1889-
  America needs an agonizing reappraisal. [Nashville, Southern
  Student Organizing Committee
  [1965?]
  4p.
  Cover title.
  1. U.S.--Foreign policy. I. Southern Student Organizing Committee.
  WHi-L

T43
Trainor, Kate.
  Grass roots work and the main-
  stream. New York, Distributed by
  Students for a Democratic Society
  and Young Christian Students for

the Liberal Study Group [1964]
5p. 28cm.
Cover title.
1. Social change. 2. Student
movements. I. Students for a
Democratic Society. II. Young
Christian Students. III. Liberal Study Group.
WHi-A

T44
The Tripoli program; program of
    the Algerian revolution [ad-
    opted by the National Revol-
    utionary Council...of the Na-
    tional Liberation Front (FLN)
    at its June, 1962 conference
    held in Tripoli, Libya. [Tor-
    onto, Workers Vanguard Pub-
    lishing Association, 1963]
  20p. 28cm.
  Cover title.
  1. Algeria--Pol. & govt.
  2. Jabhat al-Tahrir al-Qawmi.
  I. Workers Vanguard Publishing
  Association.
  MoU

T45
Trotskii, Lev., 1879-1940.
  The Chinese revolution; pro-
  blems and perspectives. New
  York, Merit Publishers [1969]
  23p. 28cm.
  "2d. edition."
  Cover title.
  1. Communism--China. 2. China--
  Pol. & govt.--1912-1937.
  I. Merit Publishers.
  KU-RH

T46
Trotskii, Lev, 1879-1940.
  The Chinese revolution; pro-
  blems and perspectives. New
  York, Pioneer Publishers, 1957.
  22p. (Bulletin of Marxist stu-
  dies, no. 1)
  1. Communism--China. 2. China-
  -Pol. & govt.--1912-1937.
  I. Pioneer Publishers.
  ICU

T47
Trotskii, Lev, 1879-1940.
  The death agony of capitalism

and the tasks of the Fourth
International: the transitional
program. [New York, Pathfinder
Press, 1970]
46p. 22cm.
Cover title.
1. Socialism. 2. Capitalism.
3. Fourth International.
I. Pathfinder Press.
KU-RH

T48
Trotskii, Lev, 1879-1940.
  Fascism; what it is; how to fight
  it. New York, Pioneer Publishers
  [1962]
  42p. 22cm.
  Cover title.
  Introduction by Robert Chester.
  1. Fascism. I. Chester, Robert.
  II. Pioneer Publishers.
  MiU, KU-RH

T49
Trotskii, Lev, 1879-1940.
  Fascism: what it is, how to fight
  it. Rev. compilation [by George
  Lavan Weissman. New York, Merit
  Publishers, 1969]
  31p. 24cm.
  Cover title.
  1. Fascism. I. Weissman, George
  Lavan. II. Merit Publishers.
  TNJ, MiU, NUC 70-87876

T50
Trotskii, Lev, 1879-1940.
  Fascism; what it is; how to fight
  it. A revised compilation. [New
  York, Pathfinder Press, 1970]
  31p. 22cm.
  Cover title.
  1. Fascism. I. Pathfinder Press.
  KU-RH

T51
Trotskii, Lev, 1879-1940.
  If America should go Communist.
  New York, Pioneer Publishers
  [1957]
  21p. 18cm. (Pioneer pocket
  library no. 7)
  Reprinted from Liberty Magazine,
  Mar. 23, 1935.
  1. Communism. I. Pioneer Pub-
  lishers.
  KU-RH, WHi-L, LNHT, TxU

T52
Trotskii, Lev, 1879-1940.
  Leon Trotsky on black nation-
  alism and self-determination.
  [Edited, with introduction,
  by George Breitman. New York,
  Pathfinder Press, c1970]
  63p. 22cm.
  Cover title.
  1. Black nationalism. 2. Ne-
  groes--Civil rights. I. Breit-
  man, George. II. Pathfinder
  Press.
  WHi-L, KU-RH

T53
Trotskii, Lev, 1879-1940.
  Leon Trotsky on Engels and Kaut-
  sky. [1st ed. New York, Merit
  Publishers, 1969]
  30p. 22cm.
  Cover title.
  1. Engels, Frederick, 1820-
  1895. 2. Kautsky, Karl, 1854-
  1938. 3. Socialism. I. Merit
  Publishers.
  MiU, KU-RH

T54
Trotskii, Lev, 1879-1940.
  Leon Trotsky on labor party.
  Stenographic report of discus-
  sion held in 1938 with leaders
  of Socialist Workers Party.
  With introduction: the struggle
  for an American labor party.
  [New York] Bulletin Publications
  [196]
  20p. illus. 28cm.
  Cover title.
  1. Labor and laboring classes.
  2. Socialism. 3. Congress of
  Industrial Organizations.
  4. American Federation of Labor.
  I. Bulletin Publications.
  MiU, KU-RH

T55
Trotskii, Lev, 1879-1940.
  Leon Trotsky on the Jewish
  question. [Intro. by Peter
  Buch. New York, Pathfinder
  Press, 1970]
  31p. 22cm.
  1. Jewish question. I. Buch,
  Peter. II. Pathfinder Press.
  KU-RH, DLC 76-17209

T56
Trotskii, Lev, 1879-1940.
  Leon Trotsky on the Kirov assassination. New York, Pioneer Publishers [1956]
  31p. 18cm. (Pioneer pocket
  library 3)
  1. Communism--Russia. 2. Kirov,
  Sergei Mironovich, 1886-1934.
  I. Pioneer Publishers.
  KU-RH

T57
Trotskii, Lev, 1879-1940.
  Leon Trotsky on the labor party
  in the United States. [New York,
  Merit Publishers, 1969]
  35p. 22cm.
  Cover title.
  1. Labor and laboring classes.
  2. Socialism. 3. American Federation of Labor. 4. Congress
  of Industrial Organizations.
  I. Merit Publishers.
  KU-RH, WHi-L

T58
Trotskii, Lev, 1879-1940.
  Leon Trotsky on the suppressed
  testament of Lenin. [New York,
  Pathfinder Press, 1970]
  47p. 19cm.
  Cover title.
  "Third edition."
  1. Lenin, Vladimir Il'lich,
  1870-1924. I. Pathfinder Press.
  KU-RH

T59
Trotskii, Lev, 1879-1940.
  Leon Trotsky on the trade unions.
  With preface by Farrell Dobbs.
  New York, Merit Publishers [1969]
  80p. 22cm.
  A collection of articles, inclu-
  ding an interview.
  1. Trade-unions and communism.
  I. Dobbs, Farrell. II. Merit
  Publishers.
  DLC 75-92904

T60
Trotskii, Lev, 1879-1940
  The negro question in America.
  [n.p., 1967?]
  66p.

Edited by James Wechsler.
  Caption title.
  1. Negroes--Civil rights.
  2. U.S.--Race question.
  I. Wechsler, James
  NcU, NUC 70-33504

T61
Trotskii, Lev, 1879-1940.
  Problems of civil war. [New
  York, Pathfinder Press, c1970]
  23p. 22cm.
  Cover title.
  1. Revolutions. 2. Civil wars.
  I, Pathfinder Press.
  MiU, KU-RH

T62
Trotskii, Lev, 1879-1940.
  Stalinism and bolshevism; concerning the historical & theoretical roots of the Fourth
  International. [New York, Pathfinder Press, 1970]
  29p. 22cm.
  Cover title.
  1. Fourth International.
  2. Communism. I. Pathfinder
  Press.
  KU-RH

T63
Trotskii, Lev, 1879-1940.
  What is the permanent revolution?
  Three concepts of the Russian
  revolution. [New York, Distri-
  buted by Spartacist, 1965]
  [14]p. 22cm.
  1. Revolutions. 2. Russia--
  History--Revolution, 1917-1921.
  I. Spartacist.
  MiU

T64
Trotskii, Lev, 1879-1940.
  Women and the family. [New
  York, Pathfinder Press, 1970]
  47p. 22cm.
  Cover title.
  1. Family. 2. Woman. I. Path-
  finder Press.
  KU-RH

T65
Trow, Prof.
  Student and campus politics.

[Berkeley? Slate, 1959?]
6p.   28cm.
Caption title.
Speech given by Prof. Trow at
the Slate Summer Retreat, Aug.
1959.
1. Student movements. I. Slate.
WHi-A

T66
Trumbo, Dalton, 1905-
The devil in the book. [Los
Angeles, California Emergency
Defense Committee, 1956]
42p., 1 leaf. 21cm.
"First printing, May, 1956."
1. Communism--California.
I. California Emergency Defense
Committee.
MH-L, IEN, KU-J, CSSR

T67
The truth about George Wallace.
[Louisville, Southern Confer-
ence Educational Fund, 1968?]
[6]p. illus. 28cm.
Cover title.
1. Wallace, George Corley, 1919-
I. Southern Conference
Educational Fund.
KU-RH

T68
Tucker, R.S.
The case for socialized medicine.
[Rev. New York, The Call Asso-
ciation, 1963]
36p. 24cm.
Cover title.
1. Medicine, State. I. Call
Association.
WHi-L, WHi-A, KU-RH

T69
The Tupamaros; urban guerilla warfare in Uruguay. [New York,
Liberated Guardian, 1970?]
49p. illus.
1. Guerillas--Uruguay. I. Liberated Guardian.
NNU-T, MiU

T70
Turadzhev, Vladimir Konstantino-
vich, 1932-
The main Soviet aim: a society

of abundance. New York, Crosscurrents Press [1962]
37p. illus. 22cm. (Documents
of current history, no. 24)
1. Russia--Econ. condit--1955-
I. Crosscurrent Press.
DLC 62-17674

T71
Turn Toward Peace.
American initiatives in a turn
toward peace. New York [196 ?]
folder. 21x9cm.
Cover title.
1. U.S.--Military policy.
2. Russia--For. rel.--U.S.
3. Peace.
KU-RH

T72
Turn Toward Peace. Youth Committee.
Our cold war society; the student search for alternatives.
New York, 1964.
9p. 28cm.
Caption title.
1. U.S.--Military policy.
2. Peace. 3. Social change.
4. Student movements.
KU-RH

T73
Turner, Les.
How to be a good communist.
Seattle, Pacific Northwest
Progressive Labor Party [196]
[1] leaf. 28cm.
Caption title.
1. Communism. I. Progressive
Labor Party, Pacific Northwest.
WHi-A

T74
Tyler, Gus.
Can anyone run a city? [New
York, League for Industrial
Democracy, 1970?]
[4]p. illus. 28cm.
Cover title.
Reprinted from Saturday Review,
Nov. 8, 1969.
1. Municipal government.
I. League for Industrial Demo-
cracy.
MiU

T75
Tyner, Jarvis.
  War, racism, the movement: as we
  see it. [New York] W.E.B. DuBois
  Clubs of America [1968]
  23p. illus. 22cm.
  Cover title.

1. Vietnamese conflict, 1961-
1975. 2. Negroes--Civil rights.
3. Student movements. I. DuBois
(W.E.B.) Clubs of America.
WHi-L, KU-RH

‡

U

‡

U1
Ulmer, Al.
  Cooperatives and poor people in
  the South. [Atlanta, Southern
  Regional Council] 1969.
  31p. 28cm.
  1. Poor--Southern States.
  2. Cooperative marketing of farm
  produce. 3. Southern States--
  Econ. condit. I. Southern Regional Council.
  KU-RH

U2
Union committeemen and wildcat
    strikes. [Detroit? Corres-
    pondence Publishing Co., 1955]
  23p. 22cm. (Correspondence
  pamphlet 1)
  1. Automobile industry workers.
  2. Strikes and lockouts. 3. International Union, United Automobile, Aircraft and Agricultural Implement Workers of America.
  4. Zupan, Johnny. I. Correspondence Publishing Company.
  MiU

U3
Union for Democratic Action Edu-
    cational Fund.
  ABM. Washington, c1969.
  20p. 42cm.
  Cover title.
  1. Antimissile missiles.
  2. Militarism.
  KU-RH

U4
United Federation of Teachers.
    Teacher's Freedom Party.
  The lie that is American educa-
  tion; a critique of and program

for all schools. New York [196]
27 leaves. 28cm.
Cover title.
1. Education.
WHi-A

U5
United Federation of Teachers.
    Teacher's Freedom Party.
The New York City teacher's
strike or the U.F.T. comes of
age. Rev. [New York, 196]
15 leaves. 28cm.
Cover title.
1. New York (City)--Public
schools. 2. Education--New
York (State)--New York (City).
WHi-A

U6
U.S.--China relations: revolu-
    tion and aggression, by Ob-
    server. Toronto, Research,
    Information, and Publications
    Project, Student Union for
    Peace Action [196]
4p. 28cm.
Cover title.
Reprinted from (Peking) People's
Daily, February 20, 1966.
1. Bundy, William Puttman,
1917-   2. U.S.--For. rel.
--China (People's Republic of
China, 1949-   ) 3. China
(People's Republic of China,
1949-   )--For. rel.--U.S.
I. Student Union for Peace
Action.
WHi-A

U7
U.S. Committee to Aid the
    National Liberation Front

of South Vietnam.
Personalities of the liberation
movement of South Vietnam. [n.
p., 196]
13p. 28cm.
1. South Viet Nam National Front
for Liberation--Biography.
WHi-L

U8
U.S. Committee to Aid the Nation-
    al Liberation Front of South
    Vietnam.
Structure of the National Liber-
ation Front of South Vietnam.
[New York], 196]
8p. 28cm.
Cover title.
1. South Viet Nam Front for Li-
beration.
WHi-L

U9
U.S. Festival Committee.
Report on Helsinki World Youth
Festival, July 28-Aug. 6, 1962.
New York [1962?]
49p. illus. 28cm.
1. Youth--Political activity.
I. World Festival of Youth and
Students for Peace and Friend-
ship. Helsinki, 1962.
KU-RH

U10
U.S. imperialism and Vietnam; an
    economic view. [From PL Bos-
    ton news] Boston, New England
    Free Press [1970?]
18p. 28cm.
Cover title.
1. Vietnamese conflict, 1961-
1975. I. Progressive Labor
Party. II. New England Free
Press.
KU-RH

U11
U.S. Selective Service System.
Channeling; this is an unedited,
official Selective Service System memorandum. [n.p., the Resistance, 196]
[8]p. illus. 22cm.
Cover title.
1. Military service, Compulsory.

II. Resistance.
KU-RH

U12
U.S. Selective Service System.
Selective service memorandum
on channeling. Nashville,
Southern Student Organizing
Committee [196]
5 [2]p. 28cm.
Cover title.
1. Military service, Compulsory.
I. Southern Student Organizing
Committee.
CU-B

U13
U.S. Supreme Court.
The Watkins decision of the
United States Supreme Court,
June 17, 1957. An historic
rebuke to the Committee on Un-
American Activities of the House
of Representatives. [New York,
Emergency Civil Liberties Committee, 1957?]
35, 17p. 22cm.
Cover title.
1. U.S. Congress. Committee
on Un-American Activities.
2. Internal security. I. Emergency Civil Liberties Committee.
KU-RH

U14
United Veterans for Freedom.
United Veterans for Freedom:
summary of purposes, proposals,
programs, budget. [Philadel-
phia, 1968?]
[30] 5 leaves.
1. Veterans. 2. Negroes--Soc.
condit.
WHi-L

U15
Universal national service. [Des
    Moines, American Friends Ser-
    vice Committee, 1968]
[4]p. 28cm.
Caption title.
Reprinted from Center Diary: 15.
1. Military service, Compulsory.
I. Friends, Society of. Ameri-
can Friends Service Committee.
KU-RH

U16
The university and the war: re-
    search guide. [Nashville,
    Southern Student Organizing
    Committee [196]
3 [9]p. 28cm.
Cover title.
1. Biological warfare. 2. Chemical warfare. 3. Military research. 4. Universities and
colleges. I. Southern Student
Organizing Committee.
WHi-L, MiU

U17
University of Michigan Student
    Employees' Union.
    Toward equal educational oppor-
tunity--a UMSEU statement of
policy and alternative financial
programs. [Ann Arbor, 1965?]
5 leaves. 28cm.
Caption title.
1. Student movements--Ann Arbor,
Mich.
WHi-A

U18
Up against your own wall, by
    Mathew, liberated artist,
    Trans-love energi. [Detroit?
    196]
3 leaves. 28cm.
Caption title.

1. Newspapers--Detroit.
2. Police--Michigan--Detroit.
3. Sinclair, John.
MiU-H

U19
The urban school crisis; an antho-
    logy of essays [by] Maurice R.
    Berube [and others] with an
    intro. by Irving Howe. New
    York, League for Industrial
    Democracy [and] United Fed-
    eration of Teachers, AFL-
    CIO, 1966.
80p. illus. 24cm.
1. Education, Urban. I. Berube,
Maurice R. II. Howe, Irving.
III. League for Industrial Demo-
cracy. IV. United Federation of
Teachers.
N, OCL, IU, NjP, NcD, NNU-T,
NUC 68-72791

U20
Utgoff, Dima.
    SMC proposal. [n.p., 1970?]
3p. 28cm.
Caption title.
1. Student Mobilization Committee to End the War in Vietnam.
2. Vietnamese conflict, 1961-
1975.
KU-RH

V

V1
Valentine, Paul.
    Look out liberals: Wallace power
gonna get you! Nashville, Southern Student Organizing Committee [196]
5p. 28cm.
Cover title.
1. Wallace, George Corley, 1919-
        2. Ku-Klux Klan. I. Sou-
thern Student Organizing Committee.
MoU

V2
Valenzuela, Arthur A.
    Latin America: continent in
revolution. [n.p.] Distributed
...by Liberal Study Group, 1963.
4p. 28cm.
Cover title.
1. Revolutions--Latin America.
2. Latin America--Pol. & govt.
I. Liberal Study Group.
WHi-A, WHi-L, MiU

V3
Vanauken.
 Freedom for movement girls--now.
 Nashville, Southern Student Organizing Committee [1969]
 6p. 28cm.
 Cover title.
 1. Woman--Rights of women.
 2. Student movements. I. Southern Student Organizing Committee.
 NcD, MoU, NUC 72-8909

V4
Vancouver Committee to Aid American
   War Objectors.
 Renuniciation of U.S. citizen-
 ship. [Rev. Des Moines, Ameri-
 can Friends Service Committee,
 1968]
 5p. 28cm.
 Caption title.
 1. Military service, Compulsory.
 2. Expatriation. I. Friends,
 Society of. American Friends
 Service Committee.
 KU-RH

V5
Vaneigem, Raoul.
 The totality for kids, translated from the French by Christopher Gray and Philippe Vissac.
 [New York, Situationist International, 196]
 30p. 22cm.
 Cover title.
 1. Student movements. 2. Radicalism. 3. Power (Social
 science) I. Situationist International.
 CU-B, MiU

Van Lydegraf, Clayton
 see
Lydegraf, Clayton Van

V6
Varela, Mary E.
 Catholic students and political
 involvement. [n.p.] Distributed for the Liberal Study Group
 by Students for a Democratic
 Society [1962]
 4p. 28cm.
 Cover title.
 1. Catholics. 2. Student move-

ments. I. Liberal Study Group.
 II. Students for a Democratic
 Society.
 WHi-A

V7
Varela, Mary E., ed.
 Something of our own, part 1.
 [Jackson, Miss., 1967]
 24p. illus. 28cm.
 1. Negroes--Batesville, Miss.
 MiU

V8
Varela, Mary E., ed.
 Something of our own, Part II.
 Jackson, Miss., c1965.
 23p. illus. 28cm.
 1. Negroes--Batesville, Miss.
 2. Batesville (Miss.) Farmers
 Co-op.
 MiU

V9
Vatuk, Ved Prakash.
 British Guiana. New York,
 Monthly Review Press, 1963.
 36p. 22cm. (Monthly Review
 pamphlet series, no. 21)
 1. British Guiana. I. Monthly
 Review Press.
 NNU-T, KU-RH, DLC 63-12517

V10
Vernon, Robert.
 The black ghetto, preface by
 Rev. Albert B. Cleage, Jr.,
 intro. by James Shabazz. [New
 York, Pioneer Publishers, 1964]
 26p.
 Cover title.
 1. Negroes. 2. Slums. 3. Lit-
 tle, Malcolm, 1925-1965.
 4. Capitalism. 5. Harlem, New
 York (City) I. Pioneer Publi-
 shers. II. Shabazz, James.
 III. Cleage, Albert B.
 WHi-A

V11
Vernon, Robert.
 The black ghetto. Preface by
 Rev. Albert B. Cleage, Jr.
 Introduction by James Shabazz.
 [Expanded ed. New York, Merit
 Publishers, 1968]

31p.
Cover title.
1. Slums. 2. Negroes--Econ. condit. 3. Little, Malcolm, 1925-
1965. 4. Capitalism. 5. Harlem,
New York (City) I. Merit Publishers. II. Shabazz, James.
III. Cleage, Albert B.
WHi-L

V12
Vernon, Robert.
Watts and Harlem; the rising revolt in the black ghettos, by
Robert Vernon and George Novack.
[New York] Pioneer Publishers
[1965]
15p. illus.
Cover title.
Reprinted from The Militant,
1964-1965.
1. Los Angeles--Riots. 2. Harlem, New York (City)--Riots.
3. Negroes--Civil rights.
I. Novack, George Edward, jt.
auth. II. Pioneer Publishers.
MiU, WHi-L, CU-SB, NUC 71-3406

V13
Vesters, Mike.
Two European views on the cold
war: Berlin. Why not recognize
the status quo? by Mike Vester.
A Hungarian proposal for depol-
arization by Geza Ankerl and
Laszlo Huszara. [n.p.] Distri-
buted by Students for a Democra-
tic Society for the Liberal
Study Group [196]
10, 3 [1]p. 28cm.
Cover title.
1. World politics--1955-
2. Berlin question (1945-
I. Ankerl, Geza, jt. auth.
II. Huszara, Laszlo, jt. auth.
III. Liberal Study Group.
IV. Students for a Democratic
Society.
WHi-A

V14
Vietnam and the future of the
American empire. [New York,
Clergy and Laymen Concerned
About Vietnam, 1969?]
15p. 28cm.

Caption title.
1. Vietnamese conflict, 1961-
1975. I. Clergy and Laymen Concerned About Vietnam.
KU-RH

Vietnam Day Committee.
see
National Coordinating Committee
to End the War in Vietnam.
Vietnam Day Committee, Berkeley.

V15
Vietnam peace proposals. [Editor:
Robert S. Woito. Berkeley,
Calif., World Without War
Council, 1967]
52p. 23cm.
1. Vietnamese conflict, 1961-
1975. I. World Without War
Council. II. Woito, Robert S.
DLC 67-9049

V16
Vietnam Research Incorporated.
Blood money: a study of war
contracts. 2d. ed. Edited by
Dick Meier. [n.p., National
Coordinating Committee to End
the War in Vietnam? 196]
[12]p. 28cm.
Cover title.
1. War--Economic aspects.
2. Military research.
I. Meier, Dick, ed. II. Nat-
ional Coordinating Committee to
End the War in Vietnam.
WHi-L

V17
Vietnam Research Incorporated.
The facts on the South Vietnamese "free elections" (Sept.
11, 1966) [n.p., 1966?]
12p. 28cm.
Cover title.
1. Vietnam--Pol. & govt.
WHi-L

V18
Vietnam Summer.
Vietnam Summer. Cambridge,
Mass. [1967?]
5 leaves. 28cm.
Caption title.

1. Vietnamese conflict, 1961-
1975.
KU-RH

V19
Villarejo, Don.
  Stock ownership and the control
  of corporations. Ann Arbor,
  Radical Education Project [196]
  33-62p. 22cm.
  Cover title.
  Reprinted from New University
  Thought, autumn 1961 & winter 1962.
  1. Stockholders. 2.Corporations.
  I. Radical Education Project.
  MoU, WHi-L

V20
Villarejo, Don.
  Stock ownership and the control
  of corporations. Boston, New
  England Free Press [196]
  64p. 22cm.
  Cover title.
  Reprinted from New University
  Thought, autumn 1961 and winter
  1962.
  1. Stockholders. 2. Corpora-
  tions. I. New England Free
  Press.
  MiU, KU-RH

V21
Virginia Student Civil Rights
    Committee.
  A project for Virginia's black
  belt. [Hampton, Va.?] 1965.
  14 [14] leaves. 28cm.
  1. Student movements--Virginia.
  2. Negroes--Virginia.
  WHi-A

V22
Vogt, Carol.
  A radical teacher in a white
  working class community. Ann
  Arbor, Conference on Radicals
  in the Professions, 1967.
  7p. 28cm.
  Cover title.
  1. Teachers. 2. Radicalism.
  3. Education. I. Conference on
  Radicals in the Professions.
  MiU-H

V23
Voice of Women/La Voix des
    Femmes.
  Fourth draft--constitution and
  by-laws of Voice of Women/La
  Voix des Femmes. [Toronto, 196]
  10p. 36cm.
  Caption title.
  1. Woman. 2. Peace.
  KU-RH

V24
Voice Political Party--Students
    for a Democratic Society,
    Ann Arbor.
  The Black Panther Party is
  under attack. [Ann Arbor,
  1968?]
  [2]p. 28cm.
  Caption title.
  1. Black Panther Party.
  MiU-H

V25
Voice Political Party--Students
    for a Democratic Society,
    Ann Arbor.
  "End to poverty week". [Ann
  Arbor, 196]
  3 leaves. 28cm.
  Caption title.
  1. Poverty.
  MiU

V26
Voice Political Party--Students
    for a Democratic Society,
    Ann Arbor.
  Repression in Czechoslovakia.
  [Ann Arbor, 1968]
  [2]p. 28cm.
  Caption title.
  1. Czechoslavak Republic--Pol.
  & govt.
  MiU

V27
Voice Political Party--Students
    for a Democratic Society,
    Ann Arbor.
  Voice platform. [Ann Arbor?
  1963?]
  9p. 28cm.
  Cover title.
  1. Civil rights. 2. U.S.--Econ.

condit. 3. U.S.--Foreign policy.
4. University and colleges.
WHi-A, MiU

V28
Von Hoffman, Nicholas.
  Finding and making leaders.
  Nashville, Southern Student Or-
  ganizing Committee [196]
  12p. 28cm.
  Cover title.
  1. Student movements. 2. Lead-
  ership. 3. Social change.
  I. Southern Student Organizing
  Committee.
  MoU

V29
Von Hoffman, Nicholas.
  Finding and making leaders.
  New York, Students for a Demo-
  cratic Society and its Economic
  Research and Action Project
  [196]
  12p. 28cm.
  Cover title.
  1. Student movements. 2. Social

change. I. Students for a Democratic Society. Economic Research and Action Project.
WHi-A

V30
Von Hoffman, Nicholas.
  Finding and making leaders.
  San Francisco, Students for
  a Democratic Society [196]
  14p. 28cm.
  Cover title.
  1. Student movements.
  2. Social change. I. Students
  for a Democratic Society.
  CU-B

V31
Von Hoffman, Nicholas.
  On organizing the ghetto.
  [Montreal, Our Generation,
  [196]
  10p.
  Cover title.
  1. Slums. I. Our Generation.
  NNU-T

W

W1
Wachtel, Howard M.
  An insight into economic plan-
  ning. [n.p.] Campus Division,
  Americans for Democratic Action
  for the Liberal Study Group
  [1962]
  4 [1] leaf. 36cm.
  Cover title.
  1. U.S.--Econ. policy. I. Ameri-
  cans for Democratic Action.
  Campus Division. II. Liberal
  Study Group.
  WHi-A, MiU

W2
Walborn, Judy.
  Japan between two worlds: island
  democracy or imperialisms lackey?
  New York, Students for a Democratic Society and its Peace Research and Education Project [196]

15p. 28cm.
Cover title.
1. Japan--Pol. & govt. I. Stu-
dents for a Democratic Society.
Peace Research and Education
Project.
NNU-T, WHi-A

W3
Wald, George.
  A generation in search of a
  future. Woodmont, Conn., Pro-
  moting Enduring Peace [1969?]
  [4]p. port. 27cm.
  Cover title.
  1. U.S.--Military policy.
  I. Promoting Enduring Peace.
  KU-RH

W4
Walker, Charles C.
  Organizing for nonviolent

direct action.   [Cheyney, Pa.,
1961]
31p.   23cm.
1. Nonviolence.
CU-B, WHi-A

W5
Walker, Charles C.
Peacekeeping: 1969, a survey and
evaluation prepared for Friends
Peace Committee. [Philadelphia,
1969]
28p.   23x10cm.
1. Peace.   2. United Nations.
KU-RH

W6
Walker, Eugene.
American youth revolt: 1960-
1969.   Detroit, News & Letters,
1969.
8p.   28cm.
"Youth report to News & Letters
Plenum."
1. Youth--Political activity.
I. News & Letters.
MiU

W7
Walker, Eugene.
France, spring 1968.   Masses in
motion; ideas in flow; an eyewitness critical report.   Detroit, News & Letters [1968?]
10p.   28cm.   (News & Letters
youth pamphlet number 1)
1. Student movements--France.
2. Strikes and lockouts--
France.   I. News & Letters.
MoU, KU-RH, MiU, MiU-H

W8
Waller, Joseph.
Remember, Patrick Henry was a
racist.   [n.p., 196]
[8]p.   21cm.
1. Negroes--Civil rights.
2. Little, Malcolm, 1925-1965.
WHi-L

W9
Waller, Shirley.
History of the international
socialist youth movement to
1929, prepared by Shirley
Waller, edited by Tim Wohlforth.

New York, Young Socialist Forum
[196]
vi, 31 leaves.   28cm.
1. Socialism.   2. Communism.
3. Youth--Political activity.
I. Young Socialist Forum.
II. Wohlforth, Tim, ed.
MiU

W10
Wallis, W.Allen.
Abolish the draft.   Washington,
National Council to Repeal the
Draft [1969?]
[1] leaf.   28cm.
Reprinted from Science, Jan.
17, 1969.
1. Military service, Compulsory.
I. National Council to Repeal
the Draft.
KU-RH

W11
Walls, Dwayne E.
The chickenbone special.   At-
lanta, Southern Regional Council,
1970.
44p.   (Leadership series no. 2)
1. Population transfers.
I. Southern Regional Council.
DHUD, DLC, NcU, ViRUt, MH,
NUC 71-6199

W12
Walls, Dwayne E.
Fayette County, Tennessee:
tragedy and confrontation.
[Atlanta] Southern Regional
Council, 1969.
ii, 36p.   28cm.   (Special
report)
1. Fayette Co., Tenn.--Race
question.   2. Negroes--Fayette
Co., Tenn.   I. Southern Region-
al Council.
ICU, GAT, NIC, TNJ, MH, WHi-L,
McU, IEds, DHUD, TxU, MsU,
AAP, DLC 79-13835

W13
Walter, Nicholas.
About anarchism.   [Montreal]
Our Generation [1969]
5-36p.
Reprinted from Anarchy.
1. Anarchism and anarchists.

I. Our Generation.
NNU-T

W14
Walter, Robert H.K.
  The sounds of protest. [Berke-
  ley, Slate, 196]
  16p. 22cm.
  1. U.S. Congress. House. Committee on Un-American Activities.
  2. Student movements. I. Slate.
  MiU

W15
Walters, Robert.
  Where do we go from here? [New
  York, Students for a Democratic
  Society] 1961.
  7 leaves. 28cm.
  Caption title.
  1. Student movements. I. Stu-
  dents for a Democratic Society.
  WHi-A

W16
Walzer, Ken.
  A seminar on radicalism in American History, by Ken Walzer
  and Dennis Gregg. Ann Arbor,
  Radical Education Project,
  c1967]
  [11]p. 28cm. (Study guide
  no. 5)
  Caption title.
  1. Radicalism. I. Gregg, Dennis, jt. auth. II. Radical Education Project.
  MoU, WHi-L, NNU-T

W17
Wang, K.P.
  Mineral wealth and industrial
  power; communist's China's boast
  begin to come true. Toronto,
  Research, Information and Pub-
  lications Project for Student
  Union for Peace Action [196]
  10 [2]p. illus. 28cm.
  Cover title.
  1. Mines and mineral resources--
  China (People's Republic of
  China, 1949-   ) 2. China
  (People's Republic of China,
  1949   )--Industries.
  I. Student Union for Peace
  Action.
  MoU, WHi-A

W18
War Corporation.
  The human question and the final
  solution. [New York, 196]
  [2]p. 28cm.
  Caption title.
  1. War.
  CU-B

W19
War Resisters League.
  G.I. or C.O.? [New York, 196]
  [8]p. 23x10cm.
  At head of title: Which will
  it be.
  1. Military service, Compulsory.
  2. Conscientious objectors.
  KU-RH, WHi-A, CU-B

W20
War Resisters League.
  Hang up on war. [San Francisco,
  1970?]
  [8]p. 22cm.
  Caption title.
  1. Taxation. 2. Government,
  Resistance to.
  CU-B

W21
War Resisters League.
  Resist war taxes. [San Francisco, 196]
  [4]p. 22cm.
  1. Government, Resistance to.
  2. Tax evasion.
  CU-B

W22
War Resisters League.
  Techniques of war tax resist-
  ance. [San Francisco, 196]
  [20]p. 22cm.
  1. Tax evasion. 2. Government,
  Resistance to.
  KU-RH

W23
War Resisters League.
  Uptight with the draft? [New
  York, 1967]
  [12]p. 22x10cm.
  1. Military service, Compulsory.
  CU-B

W24
War Resisters League.
  The way to war tax resistance.

[San Francisco, 1970?]
folder. 23x11cm.
Cover title.
1. Government, Resistance to.
2. Tax evasion.
CU-B

W25
War Resisters League.
  We protest our dirty war in South
  Viet-Nam. [New York, 196]
  [4]p. 23x10cm.
  Caption title.
  1. Vietnamese conflict, 1961-
  1975.
  KU-RH

W26
War Resisters League.
  What can I do to end this war?
  [New York, 1967]
  folder. 22x10cm.
  Cover title.
  1. Vietnamese conflict, 1961-
  1975.
  KU-RH, CU-B

W27
War Resisters League.
  What is the War Resisters
  League? New York [196]
  2 [1] leaves. 28cm.
  Caption title.
  1. Peace--Societies, etc.
  CU-B, KU-RH

W28
War Resisters League.
  Work sheet for summer action.
  [New York, 1968]
  [4]p. 28cm.
  1. Vietnamese conflict, 1961-
  1975. 2. Negroes--Civil rights.
  CU-B

W29
Warburg, James P.
  Foreign policy and Judo-Christ-
  ian morality. An address to
  the Baltimore annual conference
  of the Methodist Church at Western Maryland College, Westmins-
  ter, Maryland on June 5, 1958.
  [Philadelphia? American Friends
  Service Committee? 196]
  14p. 22cm.

Cover title.
1. U.S.--Foreign policy.
2. Ethics. I. Friends, Society of. American Friends
Service Committee.
KU-RH

W30
Warburg, James P.
  Toward a strategy of peace; an
  election year guide for responsible citizens. New York, Current Affairs Press [1964]
  72p. 22cm.
  Cover title.
  1. U.S.--Foreign policy.
  2. Peace. I. Current Affairs
  Press.
  KU-RH, WHi-A

W31
Warburg, James P.
  Turning point toward peace, a
  non-partisan study to help the
  independent voter in supporting
  a positive American program for
  peace. New York, Current Affairs Press [1955?]
  56p. 28cm.
  Cover title.
  At head of title: a challenge
  to candidates.
  1. Peace. 2. U.S.--Foreign policy. I. Current Affairs Press.
  WHi-A

W32
Ward, Harry Frederick, 1873-
  The story of American-Soviet
  relations, 1917-1959. New
  York, National Council of
  American-Soviet Friendship,
  1959.
  95p. 22cm.
  1. U.S.--For. rel.--Russia.
  2. Russia--For. rel.--U.S.
  I. National Council of American-
  Soviet Friendship.
  MiU, KU-J, WHi-L, MoSW, OrU,
  IaU, MH, DLC 60-1295

W33
Ward, Richard.
  South Viet-nam: background to
  war, by Richard Ward and Arnold
  Lockshin. [n.p.] May 2 Commit-

tee for Peace in Viet-nam [1964]
12p. 28cm.
Cover title.
1. Vietnam--History. 2. Vietna-
mese conflict, 1961-1975.
I. Lockshin, Arnold, jt. auth.
II. May 2 Committee for Peace in
Viet-nam.
WHi-L

Warde, William F., pseud.
  see
Novack, George Edward.

W34
Warner, Tom.
  Electoral action, the Fulbright-
  Morse opposition, and the anti-
  war movement. [n.p., 196]
  [4]p. 36cm.
  Caption title.
  1. U.S.--Pol. & govt.--1963-
  2. Vietnamese conflict, 1961-
  1975. 3. Fulbright, James William, 1905-   4. Morse, Wayne
  Lyman, 1900-
  WHi-A

W35
Warnock, John W.
  Why I am anti-American. [Winni-
  peg, Canadian Dimension, 196]
  [2]p. 28cm.
  Caption title.
  Reprinted from Canadian Dimen-
  sion Magazine, v. 5, no. 1.
  1. U.S.--Pol. & govt. 2. U.S.--
  Econ. condit. I. Canadian Di-
  mension.
  MoU, KU-RH

W36
Warren, Earl, 1891-
  "I do not think the court's
  action can be justified", dissenting opinion of...Earl Warren
  in the McCarran Act decision.
  [New York, Citizens' Committee
  for Constitutional Liberties,
  1961]
  23p. 20cm.
  Cover title.
  1. Communist Party of the United
  States of America. 2. Internal
  security. I. Citizens' Committee for Constitutional Liberties.
  KU-RH, WHi-L, MiU

W37
Warren, Susan.
  Formosa (Taiwan) [New York]
  Far East Reporter [196]
  11p. 21cm.
  1. Formosa--History--1945-
  NIC, NUC 68-27893

W38
Warren, Susan.
  The real Tibet. New York, Far
  East Reporter, 1959.
  32p. illus. 21cm.
  1. Tibet. I. Far East Reporter.
  KU-J

W39
Warren, Susan.
  Report from UN: the China debate; a reporter's eyewitness
  account. [New York, Far East
  Reporter, 196]
  20p. 21cm.
  1. United Nations. 2. China
  (People's Republic of China,
  1949-   )
  NIC, CSt-H, NUC 68-24582

W40
Warrior, Betsy.
  Abortion--a women's decision
  or the law's [n.p., 1970?]
  [1] leaf. 28cm.
  Caption title.
  1. Abortion. 2. Woman--Rights
  of women.
  KU-RH

W41
Warrior, Betsy.
  Females and welfare. [Boston,
  New England Free Press, 196]
  [2]p. 28cm.
  Caption title.
  1. Public welfare. 2. Woman--
  Rights of women. I. New Eng-
  land Free Press.
  KU-RH

W42
Warrior, Betsy.
  The "protection" hoax. [Boston,
  Female Liberation, 1970?]
  [2]p. 28cm.
  Caption title.
  1. Woman--Rights of women.
  I. Female Liberation.
  KU-RH

W43
Warrior, Betsy.
  The quiet ones. [n.p., 1970?]
  [1] leaf. 28cm.
  Caption title.
  1. Woman--Rights of women.
  2. Poverty.
  KU-RH

W44
Waskow, Arthur I.
  How to prevent a program. Nashville, Southern Student Organizing Committee [196]
  6p. 28cm.
  Cover title.
  1. Riots. 2. Negroes--Civil
  rights. I. Southern Student Organizing Committee.
  MiU

W45
Waskow, Arthur I.
  A memo for Art Waskow on a new
  South African program. [n.p.,
  Students for a Democratic Soc-
  iety? 196]
  [3]p. 28cm.
  Caption title.
  1. Chase Manhattan Bank, New
  York. 2. South Africa--Race
  question. I. Students for a
  Democratic Society.
  KU-RH

W46
Waskow, Arthur I.
  The new student movement.
  [Montreal, Our Generation,
  196]
  52-64p.
  Caption title.
  1. Student movements. I. Our
  Generation.
  NNU-T

S47
Waskow, Arthur I.
  Unintended war: a study and commentary in the beyond deterrence
  series. [Philadelphia, American
  Friends Service Committee, 1962]
  64p. (Beyond deterrence series)
  1. Atomic warfare. 2. Deterrence (Strategy) 3. Military
  policy. I. Friends, Society of.

American Friends Service Committee.
DS

W48
Waters, Mary Alice.
  G.I.'s and the fight against
  war, introduction by Fred Hal-
  stead. [New York, Young Soc-
  ialist, 1967]
  31p. illus. 22cm.
  Cover title.
  1. Soldiers. 2. War and morals.
  I. Halstead, Fred. I. Young
  Socialist.
  MiU, WHi-L, KU-RH

W49
Waters, Mary Alice.
  Maoism in the U.S.: a critical
  history of the Progressive La-
  bor Party. [New York, Young
  Socialist Alliance, 1969]
  23p. illus. 28cm.
  Cover title.
  1. Progressive Labor Party.
  I. Young Socialist Alliance.
  KU-RH, WHi-L

W50
Waters, Mary Alice.
  The politics of women's liber-
  ation today. [New York, Path-
  finder Press, 1970]
  23p. 22x9cm.
  Cover title.
  1. Woman--Rights of women.
  I. Pathfinder Press.
  MiU, KU-RH

W51
Watson, John.
  To the point...of production,
  an interview with John Watson
  [by the Fifth Estate] Detroit,
  Radical Education Project
  [1969]
  9p. illus. 28cm.
  Cover title.
  Reprinted from The Movement,
  July 1969.
  1. Negroes--Employment.
  2. League of Revolutionary
  Black Workers. 3. Automobile
  industry workers. I. Fifth
  Estate. II. Radical Education

Project.
KU-RH

W52
Watson, John.
To the point of production, an
interview with John Watson of
the League of Revolutionary
Black Workers [by the Fifth Es-
tate] Boston, New England Free
Press [1969?]
22p. 22cm.
Cover title.
Reprinted from the Movement,
July 1969.
1. Negroes--Employment. 2. Auto-
mobile industry workers.
3. League of Revolutionary Black
Workers. 4. Trade-unions.
I. Fifth Estate. II. New England
Free Press.
MiU

W53
Watson, John.
To the point of production. An
interview with John Watson of the
League of Revolutionary Black
Workers [by the Fifth Estate]
San Francisco, Bay Area Radical
Education Project [196]
21p. 22cm.
Cover title.
1. Negroes--Civil rights.
2. League of Revolutionary Black
Workers. I. Fifth Estate.
II. Bay Area Radical Education
Project.
CU-B

W54
Watters, Pat.
Brunswick. [Atlanta, Southern
Regional Council] 1964.
94p. 28cm. (Special report)
1. Negroes--Brunswick, Ga.
2. Brunswick, Ga.--Race quest-
ion. I. Southern Regional
Council.
MiU

W55
Watters, Pat.
Charlotte. [Atlanta, Southern
Regional Council] 1964.
91p.

1. Charlotte, N.C.--Race question. 2. Negroes--Charlotte, N.
C. I. Southern Regional Council.
GAU, CSt, TxFTC, NUC 67-60620

W56
Watters, Pat.
Encounter with the future.
Atlanta, Southern Regional
Council, 1965.
34p. 23cm.
1. Negroes--Civil rights.
I. Southern Regional Council.
NcD, NUC 66-45535

W57
Watters, Pat.
Events at Grangeburg; a report
based on study and interviews
in Orangeburg, South Carolina,
in the aftermath of tragedy,
by Pat Watters and Weldon Rougeau. [Atlanta, Southern Regional Council] 1968.
ii, 42p. 28cm. (Special report)
1. Orangeburg, S.C.--Riot,
1968. 2. Negroes--Orangeburg,
S.C. I. Rougeau, Weldon, jt.
auth. I. Southern Regional
Council.
FU, NcRS, CSaT, ScCleU, NN,
MsSM, LU, MH, TNJ, PPULC, GU,
DLC 75-25281, WHi-L

W58
Watters, Pat.
In Memphis: one year later, by
Pat Watters with J. Edwin Stan-
field. [Atlanta] Southern
Regional Council, 1969.
37p. 28cm. (Special report)
1. Memphis--Race question.
2. King, Martin Luther, 1929-
1968. 3. Negroes--Memphis.
I. Stanfield, J. Edwin.
I. Southern Regional Council.
WHi-L, NcD, NUC 71-54706

W59
We accuse; a powerful statement
of the new political anger
in America, as revealed in the
speeches given at the 36-hour
"Vietnam Day" protest in Ber-

keley, California. [Berkeley]
Diablo Press [1965]
100p. 18cm.
Organized by the Vietnam Day
Committee.
1. U.S.--For. rel.--1963-
2. Vietnamese conflict, 1961-
1975. I. National Coordinating
Committee to End the War in Vietnam. Vietnam Day Committee, Berkeley.
MoU, DLC 66-784

W60
We burned every hut! Americans at
    war. Woodmont, Conn., Promo-
    ting Enduring Peace [1967?]
[1] leaf. 28cm.
Caption title.
Reprinted from the Akron Beacon
Journal, Mar. 27, 1967.
1. Vietnamese conflcit, 1961-
1975--Atrocities. I. Promoting
Enduring Peace.
KU-RH

W61
Webb, Lee.
The anti-war movement from protest to radical politics, by
Lee Webb and Paul Booth. Chicago, Students for a Democratic
Society, 1965.
12 leaves. 28cm.
Cover title.
1. Student movements. 2. Radicalism. 3. Vietnamese conflict,
1961-1975. I. Booth, Paul, jt.
auth. II. Students for a Democratic Society.
WHi-L

W62
Webb, Lee.
Bibliography on the American
economy. New York, Students
for a Democratic Society and
its Economic Research and Action
Project [196]
3p. 28cm.
Cover title.
1. U.S.--Econ. condit--Bibl.
I. Students for a Democratic
Society. Economic Research and
Action Project.
WHi-L, MiU, KU-RH

W63
Webb, Lee.
Bibliography on the American
economy. Rev. ed. New York,
Students for a Democratic Soc-
iety [1965?]
5p. 28cm.
Cover title.
1. U.S.--Econ. condit.--Bibl.
I. Students for a Democratic
Society.
WHi-L, KU-RH

W64
Webb, Lee.
Churches and the war. Chicago,
Students for a Democratic Soc-
iety [196]
7p. 28cm.
Cover title.
1. Vietnamese conflict, 1961-
1975. 2. War and religion.
I. Students for a Democratic
Society.
WHi-L

W65
Webb, Lee.
How to research the Democratic
Party. Nashville, Southern
Student Organizing Committee
[196]
13p. 28cm.
Cover title.
1. Democratic Party. 2. U.S.--
Pol. & govt.--1959-
I. Southern Student Organizing
Committee.
MoU

W66
Webb, Lee.
Sources for research. [n.p.,
Students for a Democratic
Society? 1966?]
[7]p. 28cm.
Caption title.
1. Labor and laboring classes--
Bibl. I. Students for a Demo-
cratic Society.
KU-RH

W67
Weber, Alice.
The Memorial Library. Madison,
Wis., Students for a Democratic

Society.
WHi-L, NUC 71-2618

W68
Webster, Ted.
  War tax resistance: individual
  witness or community movement?
  New York, Distributed by War Tax
  Resistance [1970]
  19p. 22cm.
  Cover title.
  1. Tax evasion. 2. Government,
  Resistance to. I. War Tax Re-
  sistance.
  KU-RH

W69
Wegman, David.
  A radical doctor and the dil-
  emmas of medical practice. Ann
  Arbor, Conference on Radicals in
  the Professions, 1967.
  3p. 28cm.
  Cover title.
  1. Physicians. 2. Medical care.
  3. Radicalism. I. Conference on
  Radicals in the Professions.
  MiU-H

W70
Weik, Mary Hays.
  "Hot spots" in prospect for
  America; nuclear plans for Chi-
  cago and the Connecticut River
  Valley. [New York, Committee to
  End Radiological Hazards, c1967]
  4 [1] leaf. 28cm.
  Cover title.
  1. Atomic power-plants--Illin-
  ois. 2. Atomic power-plants--
  Connecticut. I. Committee to
  End Radiological Hazards.
  WHi-A

W71
Weik, Mary Hays.
  The pollution of waterways by
  atomic waste. New York, Committee to End Radiological Hazards
  [1967]
  [15] leaves.
  1. Pollution. 2. Atomic energy.
  I. Committee to End Radiological
  Hazards.
  WHi-A

W72
Weik, Mary Hays.
  Shadow over America. [Rev.
  New York, c1958, 1960]
  15p. 22cm.
  Cover title.
  1. U.S. Laws, statutes, etc.
  Internal Security Act of 1950.
  MiU

W73
Weik, Mary Hays.
  The story nobody prints; a report on conditions around U.S.
  atomic plants. New York, Committee to End Radiological
  Hazards, c1965.
  16p. 28cm.
  1. Atomic energy. 2. Radio-
  activity--Physciological effect. I. Committee to End
  Radiological Hazards.
  KU-RH

W74
Weiner, Sam.
  Ethics and American unionism
  and the path ahead for the
  working class. [New York,
  Libertarian League, 1958]
  24p. 22cm.
  1. Trade-unions. 2. Labor and
  laboring classes. 3. Anarchism and anarchists. I. Libertarian League.
  MiU, KU-RH

W75
Weiner, Sam.
  The labor party illusion. [New
  York, Libertarian League, 1961]
  14p. 16cm.
  Cover title.
  1. Labor and laboring classes.
  2. Anarchism and anarchists.
  I. Libertarian League.
  MiU, KU-RH

W76
Weinstein, James, 1928-
  Notes on the need for a socialist party. [n.p., Students for
  a Democratic Society, 1967]
  50-61p.
  Cover title.

1. Socialism.   I. Students for a
Democratic Society.
WHi-L

W77
Weinstock, Nathan.
  The truth about Israel and Zionism, by Nathan Weinstock and
  Jon Rothschild.   [New York, Pathfinder Press, c1970]
  15p.   22cm.
  Cover title.
  1. Israel--Pol. & govt. 2. Zionism.   I. Rothschild, John, jt.
  auth.   I. Pathfinder Press.
  MiU

W78
Weinstone, William.
  Starobin's views on the perspect-
  tives of the new period. [n.p.]
  1957.
  3 leaves.   36cm.
  Caption title.
  1. Daily worker.   2. Communist
  Party of the United States of
  America.   3. Starobin, Joseph
  Robert, 1913-
  KU-J

W79
Weir, Stanley.
  A new era of labor revolt; on
  the job vs. official unions.
  Berkeley, Independent Socialist
  Club, 1966.
  26p.   28cm.
  1. Labor and laboring classes.
  2. Trade-unions.   I. Independent
  Socialist Club.
  CU-B

W80
Weir, Sanley.
  A new era of labor revolt; on
  the job vs. official unions.
  New York, Independent Socialist
  Clubs of America, 1968.
  32p.   28cm.
  1. Labor and laboring classes.
  2. Trade-unions.   I. Independent
  Socialist Clubs of America.
  MiU

W81
Weir, Stanley.

U.S.A.--the labor revolt.   Ann
Arbor, Radical Education Project
[1969?]
279-296, 465-473p.   22cm.
Cover title.
Reprinted from International
Socialist Journal, April & June
1967.
1. Labor and laboring classes.
2. Trade-unions.   I. Radical
Education Project.
MoU, WHi-L, KU-RH

W82
Weir, Stanley.
  U.S.A.--the labor revolt.   Boston, New England Free Press
  [196]
  279-296, 467-473p.   22cm.
  Cover title.
  Reprinted from Socialist International.
  1. Labor and laboring classes.
  2. Trade-unions.   I. New England Free Press.
  KU-RH

W83
Weisberg, Barry.
  The politics of ecology. [Bos-
  ton, New England Free Press,
  1970]
  [4]p.   28cm.
  Caption title.
  Reprinted from Liberation,
  Jan. 1970.
  1. Pollution.   2. Ecology.
  I. New England Free Press.
  KU-RH

W84
Weiss, Max.
  The meaning of the XXth Con-
  gress of the Communist Party
  of the Soviet Union.   New York,
  New Century, 1956.
  40p.
  Report to a meeting of the
  National Committee, CPUSA,
  April 1956.
  1. Kommunisticheskaia partiia
  Sovetskogo Soiuza. 20. S"ezd,
  Moscow, 1956.   2. Communism--
  Russia. 1. New Century Pub-
  lishers.   II. Communist Party
  of the United States of America.
  MiU, NNJef OrU, CSSR, KU-J, W109

W85
Weiss, Max.
  Report by Max Weiss to national
  committee meeting, April 29, 1956.
  [n.p., 1956]
  15 leaves. 36cm.
  Caption title.
  1. Khrushchev, Nikita Sergeevich,
  1894-   2. Kommunisticheskaia partiia Sovetskogo Soiuza.
  20. S"ezd, Moscow, 1956.
  KU-J

W86
Weissman, Aaron, 1922-
  The best years of their lives.
  [New York, New Century Publish-
  ers, 1955]
  15p. 19cm.
  Cover title.
  1. U.S.--Military policy.
  2. Military service, Compulsory.
  I. New Century Publishers.
  KU-RH

W87
Weissman, Aaron, 1922-
  What's behind juvenile delin-
  quency? [New York, New Century
  Publishers, 1955]
  15p. illus. 19cm.
  1. Juvenile delinquency. I. New
  Century Publishers.
  NN, NNJef, DLC 55-57990

W88
Weissman, Stephen.
  Freedom and the university, by
  Stephen Weissman and Doug Tut-
  hill. Chicago, Students for a
  Democratic Society [1966]
  [7]p. 28cm.
  Cover title.
  1. Student movements. 2. Uni-
  versities and colleges. I. Stu-
  dents for a Democratic Society.
  II. Tuthill, Doug, jt. auth.
  MiU, MiU-H, CU-B, WHi-A

W89
Weissman, Stephen.
  Freedom in the university. Los
  Angeles, Students for a Demo-
  cratic Society [196]
  8p. 28cm.
  Cover title.

  1. Student movements. 2. Universities and colleges.
  MiU-H

W90
Weissman, Stephen.
  The Vietnamization of Latin
  America, by Steve Weissman and
  John Gerassi. [Berkeley, North
  American Congress on Latin
  America, 196]
  [26]p. 22cm.
  1. Latin America--For. rel.--U.
  S. 2. U.S.--For. rel.--Latin
  America. I. North American
  Congress on Latin America.
  II. Gerassi, John, jt. auth.
  WHi-L

W91
Weissman, Stephen.
  Why the population bomb is a
  Rockefeller baby. [Ithaca,
  N.Y., Glad Day Press, 1970?]
  43-47p. illus. 28cm.
  Cover title.
  1. Population. I. Glad Day
  Press.
  NNU-T

W92
Weisstein, Naomi.
  Kinde, kuche, kirche as scien-
  tific law; psychology constructs
  the female. Boston, New England Free Press [196]
  7 [2]p. 28cm.
  Cover title.
  1. Woman. 2. Psychology.
  I. New England Free Press.
  MoU, KU-RH

W93
Weistein, Jacob J.
  Vietnam and a clergyman's
  conscience. New York, Clergy
  and Laymen Concerned About
  Vietnam [196]
  [1] leaf. 28cm.
  Caption title.
  1. Vietnamese conflict, 1961-
  1975. I. Clergy and Laymen
  Concerned About Vietnam.
  KU-RH

W94
Wellman, David.

Putting-on the poverty program.
Ann Arbor, Radical Education Pro-
ject [1969?]
52-66p. illus. 28cm.
Cover title.
Reprinted from Steps, no. 2.
1. Public welfare. 2. Negroes--
Employment. 3. Poverty. I. Ra-
dical Education Project.
MoU, KU-RH

W95
Wells, Lyn.
American women: their use and
abuse. Nashville, Southern
Student Organizing Committee and
New England Free Press [1969?]
16p. 28cm.
Cover title.
1. Woman--History and condition
of women. I. Southern Student
Organizing Committee. II. New
England Free Press.
WHi-L, KU-RH, MoU

W96
Welsh, David.
Building Lyndon Johnson. [Bos-
ton? New England Free Press?
196]
54-64p. 28cm.
Cover title.
Reprinted from Ramparts.
1. Johnson, Lyndon Baines,
Pres. U.S., 1908-1973. 2. Brown
& Root, inc., Houston. I. New
England Free Press.
KU-RH, WHi-L

W97
Welsh, David.
Clark Clifford; attorney at war,
by David Welsh and David Horowitz. Boston, New England Free
Press [196]
[44-50]p. 28cm.
Cover title.
Reprinted from Ramparts.
1. Business and politics.
2. Clifford, Clark McAdams,
1906-   I. Horowitz, David,
jt. auth. II. New England Free
Press.
KU-RH

W98
Weltner, Charles Longstreet.

John Willie Reed; an epitaph.
Atlanta, Southern Regional
Council, c1969.
40p. illus. 26cm. (Leadership series number 1)
1. Reed, John Willie. 2. Ne-
groes--Civil rights. 3. Southern States--Race question.
I. Southern Regional Council.
KU-RH

W99
Wertham, Fredric.
Is so much violence in films
necessary? [Nyack, N.Y. Fel-
lowship Publications, 196]
[4]p. 22cm.
Caption title.
Reprinted from the Journal of
the Producers Guild of America,
Dec. 1967.
1. Violence in mass media.
I. Fellowship Publications.
KU-RH

W100
Wesley, David.
Hate groups and the Un-American
Activities Committee. [New
York, Emergency Civil Liberties
Committee, 1961]
15p. 22cm.
1. U.S. Congress. House.
Committee on Un-American Acti-
vities. 2. Subversive acti-
vities. I. Emergency Civil
Liberties Committee.
OrU, NUC 67-24361

W101
Wesley, David.
Hate groups and the Un-American
Activities Committee. [2d ed.
rev.] New York, Emergency
Civil Liberties Committee [1962]
18p. 22cm.
Cover title.
1. U.S. Congress. House.
Committee on Un-American Acti-
vities. 2. Subversive acti-
vities. I. Emergency Civil
Liberties Committee.
WHi-L, WHi-A, MiU, KU-RH

W102
West, Don.

People's cultural heritage in
Appalachia. [Huntington, W.Va.,
Appalachian Movement Press, 196]
[12]p. illus. 22cm.
Cover title.
1. Culture. 2. Appalachian Moun-
tains--Soc. condit. I. Appalachian Movement Press.
NNU-T

W103
West, Don.
  Robert Tharin: biography of a
mountain abolitionist. [Hunting-
ton, W.Va., Appalachian Movement
Press, 196]
24p.
Cover title.
1. Tharin, Robert. I. Appalachian Movement Press.
NNU-T

W104
West, Don.
  Romantic Appalachia, or poverty
pays if you ain't poor. Pipe-
stem, W.Va., Appalachian South
Folklife Center [196]
[8]p.
1. Poor--Appalachian Mountains.
I. Appalachian South Folklife
Center.
NNU-T

W105
West, Don.
  A time for anger. [Huntington,
W.Va., Appalachian Movement
Press, 196]
(unpaged) 22cm.
Cover title.
I. Appalachian Movement Press.
NNU-T

W106
West Side Welfare Rights Organiza-
  tion, Louisville.
Kentucky welfare rights handbook.
Louisville, 1970.
27p. 28cm.
1. Public welfare--Kentucky.
WHi-L

W107
What about Christians in China?
  The YWCA; as reported by a

Canadian YWCA visitor. [New
  York, Far East Reporter, 196]
16p. illus. 21cm.
1. Christianity--China (People's
Republic of China, 1949-   )
2. Young Women's Christian Association. I. Far East Reporter.
NIC, CSt-H, NUC 73-12421

W108
Wheelwright, Edward Lawrence.
  Colonialism in Asia--past and
present. San Francisco, Bay
Area Radical Education Project
[196]
17p. 22cm.
Cover title.
Reprinted from Eastern Horizon,
v. 8, no. 1 & 2.
1. Asia--Pol. & govt. 2. Asia--
Colonization. I. Bay Area Radi-
cal Education Project.
CU-B

W109
Wheelwright, Edward Lawrence.
  The cultural revolution in China.
San Francisco, Bay Area Radical
Education Project [c1967]
17p. 22cm.
Cover title.
Reprinted from Monthly Review,
May 1967.
1. China (People's Republic of
China, 1949-   )--Intellectual
life. I. Bay Area Radical Edu-
cation Project.
CU-B

W110
Wheelwright, Edward Lawrence.
  Impressions of the Chinese econ-
omy. San Francisco, Bay Area
Radical Education Project [196]
16p. 22cm.
Cover title.
Reprinted from Eastern Horizon,
v. 5; no. 6 & 7.
1. China (People's Republic of
China, 1949-   )--Econ. condit.
I. Bay Area Radical Education
Project.
CU-B

W111
When the southern vote was counted;

an analysis of the impact of
the negro vote in the south
on the 1964 election, produced
by Political Education Project
associated with Students for a
Democratic Society. New York
[1964?]
7p. 28cm.
Cover title.
1. Southern States--Pol. & govt.
--1963-   2. Negroes--Poli-
tics and suffrage. 3. Negroes
--Southern States. I. Students
for a Democratic Society. Political Education Project.
MiU

W112
Where it's at; a research guide
   for community organization.
   Boston, New England Free Press
   [196]
95p. 28cm.
Cover title.
1. Community organization. II.
New England Free Press.
Whi-L

W113
White, Geoffrey.
   The student revolt at Berkeley.
   [New York, Spartacist, 1965?]
[6]p. illus. 24cm.
Caption title.
Reprinted from Spartacist, May-
June 1965.
1. Student movements--Berkeley,
Calif. 2. Free Speech Movement.
I. Spartacist.
MiU, WHi-L

W114
White Panther Party.
   White Panther 10 point program,
   July 4, 1969. [Ann Arbor, White
   Panther/Trans-love Tribe, 1969?]
[8]p. 22cm.
Cover title.
1. Radicalism.
MiU-H

W115
Who plans America? An animation
   film for the Peace & Freedom
   Movement. [Berkeley? 196]
9 leaves. 28cm.

Cover title.
1. Business and politics. 2.
U.S.--Pol. & govt.--1963-
I. Peace and Freedom Movement.
CU-B

W116
Why female liberation? [n.p.,
   196]
[1] leaf. 36cm.
Caption title.
1. Woman--Rights of women.
KU-RH

W117
Wicker, Roger A.
   Black Mountain College: an ex-
   periment in education. Nash-
   ville, Southern Student Organ-
   izing Committee [196]
8p. 28cm.
Cover title.
1. Black Mountain College, Black
Mountain, N.C. 2. Rice, John
Andrew. 3. Education--North
Carolina--Black Mountain. I.
Southern Student Organizing
Committee.
MoU

W118
Wiener, Carolyn L.
   San Francisco and the Un-Amer-
   ican Activities Committee.
   [San Francisco, Northern Cali-
   fornia Chapter, Americans for
   Democratic Action, 196]
12p. 22cm.
Cover title.
1. U.S. Congress. House.
Committee on Un-American Activ-
ities. 2. Student movements--
California. I. Americans for
Democratic Action, Northern
California Chapter.
MiU

W119
Wilcox, Laird M.
   Position paper on exclusionism
   and totalitarianism. [Lawrence,
   Kansas Free Press, 1965]
[3]p. 22cm.
"Distributed to the December
conference of the Students for
a Democratic Society in Urbana,

Ill."
1. Totalitarianism. 2. Students
for a Democratic Society. I.
Kansas Free Press.
KU-RH

W120
Wiley, Brad.
  Historians & the new deal. Mad-
  ison, Madison Students for a
  Democratic Society [196]
  17p. 22cm.
  Cover title.
  1. U.S.--Pol. & govt.--1933-1945.
  2. Historians, American. I.
  Students for a Democratic Soci-
  ety, Madison.
  KU-RH, WHi-L, MoU

W121
Wiley, Peter.
  Vietnam and the Pacific rim stra-
  tegy. [Boston, New England Free
  Press, 1969?]
  21p. illus. 21cm.
  Cover title.
  Reprinted from Leviathan, June
  1969.
  1. U.S.--Foreign policy. 2.
  Vietnamese conflict, 1961-1975.
  I. New England Free Press.
  KU-RH

W122
Wiley, Peter.
  Vietnam and the Pacific rim strategy. San Francisco, Bay Area
  Radical Education Project [196]
  16p. 22cm.
  Cover title.
  1. Vietnamese conflict, 1961-
  1975. 2. U.S.--For. rel.--Asia.
  3. Asia--For. rel.--U.S. I.
  Bay Area Radical Education Project.
  CU-B

W123
Wilkerson, Cathy.
  Draft resistance program: March
  1968 N.C. [submitted by Cathy
  Wilkerson, Robert Pardun, Carl
  Davidson. n.p., 1968]
  3p. 28cm.
  Caption title.
  1. Students for a Democratic

Society. 2. Military service,
Compulsory. I. Pardun, Robert,
jt. auth. II. Davidson, Carl,
jt. auth.
WHi-L

W124
Wilkerson, Cathy.
  Rats, washtubs and block organ-
  izations. New York, Distribu-
  ted by Students for a Democra-
  tic Society [196]
  5p. 28cm.
  Cover title.
  1. Community organization. 2.
  Poverty. I. Students for a
  Democratic Society.
  KU-RH, CU-B, WHi-A

W125
Wilkerson, Cathy.
  Woman; the struggle for liberation: an introduction. [Wash-
  ington, D.C., D.C. Region Students for a Democratic Society
  and Washington Women's Liberation, 196]
  21 [2]p. illus. 22cm.
  Cover title.
  1. Woman--Rights for women. I.
  Students for a Democratic Society, D.C. Region. II. Washington (D.C.) Women's Liberation.
  MiU

W126
Wilkerson, Doxey Alphonso, 1905-
  The people versus segregated
  schools. [New York, New Century Publishers, 1955]
  15p.
  Cover title.
  1. Negroes--Education. 2. Segregation in education. I. New
  Century Publishers.
  MiU, NNJef, CtY, W191

W127
Wilkins, Roy.
  Negro history or mythology;
  the "black heritage series"
  controversy. [New York, Association for the Advancement of
  Colored People, 1969]
  11p. 22cm.

"An exchange of correspondence
between Roy Wilkins...and officials of WCBS-TV, in New York."
1. Negroes--Civil rights. 2.
Negroes--History. I. National
Association for the Advancement
of Colored People.
KU-RH

W128
Wilkinson, Frank.
And now the bill come due.
[n.p., 196]
[2]p. 36cm.
Caption title.
Reprinted from Frontier, Oct.
1965.
1. Negroes--Housing. 2. Negroes
--Los Angeles. 3. Los Angeles--
Race question. 4. Los Angeles--
Riots, 1965.
KU-RH

W129
Will we use the plague as a weapon?
[Cambridge, Mass., Massachu-
setts Political Action for
Peace and American Friends
Service Committee, 196]
[16]p. illus. 16cm.
1. Biological warfare. I. Massa-
chusetts Political Action for
Peace. II. Friends, Society of.
American Friends Service Commit-
tee.
KU-RH

W130
Williams, Jim.
Haber's critique of the N.C. reflections of a southern hillbilly
SDS'er [n.p., 196]
2p. 28cm.
1. Students for a Democratic Society. 2. Haber, Robert Alan.
WHi-L

W131
Williams, Jim.
The march on Frankfort; a study
in protest-organization. New
York, Political Education Project, Students for a Democratic
Society [196]
8p. 28cm.
1. Negroes--Frankfort, Ky.

2. Kentucky--Race question.
I. Students for a Democratic
Society. Political Education
Project.
WHi-A, KU-RH

W132
Williams, Jim.
The new left today--or two years
of the "new era". [n.p., 1965]
4p. 28cm.
Caption title.
At head of title: SDS national
convention--working paper.
1. U.S.--Foreign policy. 2.
U.S.--Econ. condit. 3. Student
movements. I. Students for a
Democratic Society. National
Convention, 1965.
WHi-A, KU-RH

W133
Williams, Jim.
Students, labor and the South.
Nashville, Southern Student
Organizing Committee [1965?]
5, 2p. 28cm.
1. Labor and laboring classes--
Southern States. 2. Student
movements--Southern States.
3. Trade-unions. I. Southern
Student Organizing Committee.
WHi-L, MoU

W134
Williams, Maxine.
Black women's liberation, by
Maxine Williams and Pamela
Newman. [New York, Pathfinder
Press, 1970]
15p. 22cm.
1. Woman--Rights of women.
2. Women, Negro. I. Newman,
Pamela, jt. auth. II. Pathfind-
er Press.
MiU

W135
Williams, Robert F.
Black power, speech by Robert
F. Williams at mass rally in
Peking on Aug. 8, 1966. [San
Francisco, Global Views, 196]
8p.
Cover title.
1. Negroes--Civil rights. I.

Global Views.
MiU

W136
Williams, Robert F.
Listen, brother. New York, World
View Publishers [1968]
40p. illus. 22cm.
1. Negroes--Civil rights. 2.
Soldiers. I. World View Pub-
lishers.
CU-B, MiU

W137
Willis, Ellen.
"Consumerism" and women. Cam-
bridge, Mass., Distributed by
Cell 16, Female Liberation
[1970?]
5p. 28cm.
Caption title.
1. Consumers. 2. Woman--Rights
of women. I. Female Liberation.
Cell 16.
KU-RH

W138
Willis, Ellen.
"Consumerism" and women. [New
York, Redstockings of the Women's
Liberation Movement, 196]
4 [2]p. 28cm.
Caption title.
1. Woman--Rights of women. 2.
Consumers. I. Redstockings of
the Women's Liberation Movement.
MoU

W139
Willis, Ellen.
Whatever happen to women? Noth-
ing--that's the trouble. A report on the new feminism. New
York, Redstockings [196]
[2]p. 28cm.
1. Woman--Rights of women. I.
Redstockings of the Women's Liberation Movement.
MoU

W140
Wilson, Edwin H.
Humanism: a fourth faith. [Yel-
low Springs, O., American Humanist Association, 196]
[8]p. 22x10cm. (AHA publication

no. 216)
Cover title.
1. Humanism. I. American Humanist Assoc tion.
KU-RH

W141
Wilson, Page Huidekoper.
Through the looking glass dark-
ly, a political fantasy; [a
day with President Garry Bold-
water. Washington, c1963]
22p. 22cm.
1. U.S.--Pol. & govt.--1963-
2. Goldwater, Barry Morris,
1900-   I. American for
Democratic Action.
DLC 64-5000

W142
Wilson, Robert Anton.
Lysander Spooner, with excerpts
from the Con[sti]tution of no
authority. [Mountain View,
Calif., SRAF Print Co-op] 1970.
[13]p. 22cm. (SRAFlet)
Cover title.
1. Spooner, Lysander, 1808-1888.
2. Anarchism and anarchists.
I. SRAF Print Co-op.
MiU

W143
Windmiller, Marshall.
Scholars and soldiers; a crisis
of values. [Philadelphia]
American Friends Service Committee [1967?]
folder (6p.) 31x10cm.
Caption title.
Reprinted from The Nation, Dec.
18, 1967.
1. Vietnamese conflict, 1961-
1975--Peace. 2. Universities
and colleges. I. Friends, Society of. American Friends
Service Committee.
KU-RH

W144
Windoffer, Melba.
Women who work. Seattle, Seat-
tle Radical Women [196 ?]
8p. 28cm.
Cover title.
Reprinted from International

Socialist Review, summer, 1962.
1. Woman--Employment. 2. Equal
pay for equal work. I. Seattle
Radical Women.
WHi-L

W145
Winkler, Ilene.
  Women workers: the forgotten
  third of the working class.
  [New York] International Social-
  ist [196]
  18, 3p. 28cm.
  Cover title.
  1. Woman--Rights of women. 2.
  Labor and laboring classes. 3.
  Socialism. I. International
  Socialist.
  KU-RH

W146
Winston, Henry.
  Black Americans and the Middle-
  East conflict. [New York, New
  Outlook Publishers, 1970]
  14p. 22cm.
  Cover title.
  1. Negroes. 2. Near East--Pol.
  & govt. I. New Outlook Publish-
  ers.
  MiU

W147
Winston, Henry.
  Build the Communist Party: the
  party of the working class.
  New York, New Outlook Publishers,
  1969.
  30p.
  1. Communism. 2. Communist Party of the United States of America. I. New Outlook Publishers.
  WHi-L

W148
Winston, Henry.
  Negro--white unity. Key to full
  equality, negro representation,
  economic advance of labor, black
  and white. [New Outlook Publishers, 1967]
  31p. 20cm.
  Cover title.
  1. Negroes--Civil rights. I.
  New Outlook Publishers.
  KU-RH, CSSR, MiU, WHi-L

W149
Winston, Henry.
  New colonialism--U.S. style.
  [2d. ed. New York, New Outlook
  Publishers, 1965]
  30p. map. 20cm.
  Cover title.
  1. U.S.--Foreign policy. 2.
  Colonization. I. New Outlook
  Publishers.
  WHi-L, MiU, CLSU

W150
Winters, Stanley B.
  Urban renewal and civil rights.
  New York, Students for a Demo-
  cratic Society and Economic Re-
  search and Action Project
  [196]
  13 [3]p. 28cm.
  Cover title.
  1. Urban renewal. 2. Negroes--
  Civil rights. I. Students for
  a Democratic Society. Economic
  Research and Action Project.
  CU-B

W151
Wisconsin Draft Resistance Union.
  What is guerrilla theatre, any-
  way? A summer with the Wisconsin Draft Resistance Union car-
  avan. [Madison, Wis., 196]
  24p. illus. 22cm.
  Cover title.
  1. Theater.
  MoU

W152
Wisconsin Draft Resistance Union.
  Wisconsin Draft Resistance Un-
  ion. Madison [196]
  20p.
  Cover title.
  1. Military service, Compulsory.
  WHi-L

W153
Wittman, Carl.
  A gay manifesto. [San Francis-
  co, 1970?]
  [14]p. 22cm.
  Cover title.
  1. Homosexuality.
  MiU

W154
Wittman, Carl.
   In a psychiatric ward.   [Los
   Angeles, Students for a Democra-
   tic Society, 196]
   4p.   28cm.
   Caption title.
   1. Psychiatric hospitals.   I.
   Students for a Democratic Soci-
   ety.
   MiU

W155
Wittman, Carl.
   Refugees from Amerika: a gay manifesto.   [Berkeley, Calif., Committee of Concern for Homosexuals, 1970?]
   [11]p.   28cm.
   Caption title.
   1. Homosexuality.   I. Committee
   of Concern for Homosexuals.
   KU-RH

W156
Wittman, Carl.
   Seminar on Marxism.   New York,
   Students for a Democratic Soci-
   ety [196]
   17p.   28cm.
   Cover title.
   1. Marx, Karl, 1818-1883.   2.
   Socialism.   I. Students for a
   Democratic Society.
   MiU

W157
Wittman, Carl.
   Students and economic action.
   New York, Students for a Demo-
   cratic Society [196]
   8p.   28cm.
   Cover title.
   1. Student movements--Chester,
   Pa.   2. Poor--Chester, Pa.   3.
   Negroes--Econ. condit.   I. Stu-
   dents for a Democratic Society.
   WHi-A, MiU, WHi-L, NNU-T

W158
Wittman, Carl.
   Waves of resistance.   Los Angeles, Supporters of Resistance
   [196]
   6p.   28cm.
   Caption title.

Reprinted from Liberation Magazine.
   1. Military service, Compulsory.
   I. Supporters of the Resistance.
   KU-RH

W159
Wofford, Harris.
   A lawyer's case for civil diso-
   bedience.   [Chicago, Student
   Peace Union, 1961?]
   [4] leaves.   28cm.
   Caption title.
   1. Lawyers.   2. Government,
   Resistance to.   I. Student
   Peace Union.
   CU-B

W160
Wohlforth, Tim.
   Black nationalism & Marxist
   theory.   [New York, Labor Publications, 1970]
   35p.   21cm.   (Bulletin pamphlet
   series 1)
   Cover title.
   1. Socialism.   2. Socialist
   Workers Party.   3. Black nationalism.   I. Labor Publications.
   WHi-L, KU-RH

W161
Wohlforth, Tim.
   The new nationalism and the
   negro struggle.   [New York,
   Bulletin Publications, 196 ?]
   24p.
   Cover title.
   1. Socialist Workers Party.
   2. Nationalism.   3. Negroes--
   Civil rights.   4. Socialism.
   I. Bulletin Publications.
   MiU

W162
Wohlforth, Tim.
   Open letter to SNCC.   San Fran-
   cisco, Bulletin of Internation-
   al Socialism [1966?]
   [2]p.   36cm.
   Caption title.
   1. Negroes--Civil rights.   2.
   Student Nonviolent Coordinating
   Committee.   I. Bulletin of In-
   ternational Socialsim.
   CU-B

W163
Wohlforth, Tom.
  Revolt on the campus: the stu-
  dent movement in the 1930's.
  [New York, Young Socialist Forum,
  1960]
  25 leaves. 28cm.
  Cover title.
  1. Student movement--History. I.
  Young Socialist Forum.
  MiU

W164
Wohlforth, Tim.
  The struggle for Marxism in the
  United States. [New York, Bul-
  letin Publications, 196]
  74p. illus. 25cm.
  Cover title.
  1. Socialism. 2. Communism. I.
  Bulletin Publications.
  WHi-L, KU-RH

W165
Wolfe, Robert.
  Imperialism: an exchange. American imperialism and the peace
  movement [by] Robert Wolfe. Soc-
  ialism--the sustaining menace
  [by] Ronald Aronson. Ann Arbor,
  Radical Education Project [196]
  29-61p. 22cm.
  Cover title.
  Reprinted from Studies on the
  Left, v. 6, no. 3.
  1. Imperialism. 2. U.S.--Foreign
  policy. 3. Socialism. 4. Anti-
  communist movements. 4. Vietnamese conflict, 1961-1975. I.
  Aronson, Ronald, jt. auth. II.
  Radical Education Project.
  MoU

W166
Wolfe, Robert.
  Imperialism: an exchange. Ameri-
  can imperialism and the peace
  movement [by] Robert Wolfe.
  Socialism--the sustaining menace
  [by] Ronald Aronson. Boston,
  New England Free Press [196]
  [28]-61p. 22cm.
  Cover title.
  Reprinted from Studies on the
  Left, May-June 1966.
  1. Anti-communist movements.

  2. Vietnamese conflict, 1961-
  1975. 3. U.S.--Foreign policy.
  I. Aronson, Ronald, jt. auth.
  I. New England Free Press.
  KU-RH

W167
Wolff, Peter.
  Civil liberties during the Vietnamese war. [n.p., 1966?]
  [5] leaves. 28cm.
  Caption title.
  1. Civil rights. 2. Vietnamese
  conflict, 1961-1975.
  MiU-H

W168
Wolfson, Alice.
  Women vs health industry; health
  care may be hazardous to your
  health. [Detroit, Radical Ed-
  ucation Project, 197 ?]
  3 [1]p. illus. 28cm.
  Cover title.
  Reprinted from Up from Under.
  1. Woman--Health and hygiene.
  I. Radical Education Project.
  MiU

W169
Womack, Marcella.
  Women in society or "a women's
  place is in the home" or "women
  are allright, if they are kept
  in their place". [n.p., 1969?]
  5 leaves. 28cm.
  Cover title.
  1. Woman--History and condition
  of women. 2. Woman--Rights of
  women.
  KU-RH

W170
Women and socialism: women in the
  liberation struggle--an over-
  view. Ma Bell has fleas--and
  a lot of angry workers.
  Boston, New England Free Press
  [1970?]
  40p. illus. 28cm.
  Cover title.
  Reprinted from Red Papers 3.
  1. Woman--Rights of women. 2.
  American Telephone and Telegraph
  Company. I. New England Free
  Press.
  MiU

W171
Women for Peace. Radiation Com-
    mittee.
  Radiation. [Berkeley, Calif.,
  196]
  18p. 22cm.
  Cover title.
  1. Radioactivity. 2. Atomic
  weapons and disarmament.
  KU-RH

W172
Women Strike for Peace, Washington,
  D.C.
  A nuclear test ban; what are the
  risks? [Washington, 196]
  7p. illus. 23cm.
  Cover title.
  1. Atomic weapons and disarma-
  ment.
  KU-RH

W173
Women Strike for Peace, Washington,
  D.C.
  The question of civil defense.
  [Washington, 196]
  [8]p. illus. 15x23cm.
  Cover title.
  1. Atomic warfare. 2. Civilian
  defense.
  KU-RH

W174
Women Strike for Peace, Washington,
  D.C.
  So many great things have been
  said. [Washington, 1962?]
  [20]p. illus. 28cm.
  Cover title.
  1. Woman. 2. Peace. 3. U.S.
  Congress. House. Committee on
  Un-American Activities.
  KU-RH

W175
Women Strike for Peace, Washington,
  D.C. Disarmament Committee.
  The story of disarmament, 1945-
  1963. Washington, c1962.
  80p. illus. 28cm.
  1. Disarmament.
  KU-RH, DLC 62-21482

W176
Women--the struggle for freedom.

  Boston, New England Free
  Press [1969?]
  [1] leaf. 51x36cm.
  Caption title.
  Reprinted from the Black Dwarf,
  Jan. 10, 1969.
  1. Woman--Rights of women. I.
  New England Free Press.
  KU-RH

W177
Women's Counseling Service.
  Abortion: a women's decision--
  a women's right. [Minneapolis,
  1970?]
  folder. 22cm.
  Caption title.
  1. Abortion. 2. Woman--Rights
  of women.
  KU-RH

W178
Women's International League for
    Peace and Freedom.
  Civil rights U.S.A. [Philadel-
  phia, 1966?]
  folder. 23x11cm.
  Cover title.
  1. Civil rights.
  MoU

W179
Women's International League for
    Peace and Freedom.
  Danger to mankind: chemical and
  biological warfare, a series of
  statements by prominent scientists. Philadelphia [1968]
  14p. 21cm.
  Cover title.
  1. Chemical warfare. 2. Biological warfare.
  MoU, KU-RH

W180
Women's International League for
    Peace and Freedom.
  Have you thought what the draft
  means in your life? [San Jose,
  196]
  folder. 22x12cm.
  Caption title.
  1. Military service, Compulsory.
  KU-RH

454 THE AMERICAN LEFT

W181
Women's International League for
    Peace and Freedom.
  Pioneering the future. A chron-
  ical of fifty years of the Wo-
  men's International League for
  Peace and Freedom. [Philadel-
  phia, 1965[
  [7]p. 24cm.
  Cover title.
  WHi-L, NUC 67-28675

W182
Women's International League for
    Peace and Freedom.
  Our patriotic duty to dissent.
  [Philadelphia, 196]
  folder. 22x9cm.
  Cover title.
  1. Dissenters.
  KU-RH, MoU

W183
Women's International League for
    Peace and Freedom.
  Recommendations for national
  action. Excerpts from the re-
  port of the National Advisory
  Commission on Civil Disorders.
  Philadelphia [1968]
  7 [1]p. 23x11cm.
  Cover title.
  1. Negroes--Civil rights. I.
  U.S. National Advisory Commis-
  sion on Civil Disorders.
  MoU

W184
Women's International League for
    Peace and Freedom. Minneapo-
    lis branch. Childhood Educa-
    tion Committee.
  "Let's train them for peace"--a
  study and action kit on toys of
  violence. Philadelphia [196]
  42p. 28cm.
  Cover title.
  1. Toys. 2. Violence.
  KU-RH

W185
Women's International League for
    Peace and Freedom. United
    States Section.
  Principles and policies; a blue-
  print for peace and freedom as

adopted by the annual meeting
  of the U.S. section, WILF, June
  1969. [Philadelphia, 1969]
  folder (7p.) 22x10cm.
  Cover title.
  1. Peace.
  KU-RH

W186
Women's Liberation.
  The politics of "free" love:
  forced fornication. Boston,
  Distributed by Female Libera-
  tion [1969?]
  [1] leaf. 28cm.
  Caption title.
  1. Woman--Rights of women. I.
  Female Liberation.
  KU-RH

W187
The women's street theater. [San
    Francisco, People's Press,
    1970?]
  (unpaged) 41cm.
  Cover title.
  1. Woman. I. Peoples Press
  KU-RH

W188
Wood, Myrna.
  We may not have much, but
  there's a lot of us? Detroit,
  Radical Education Project
  [1970?]
  8 [1]p. illus. 28cm.
  Cover title.
  Reprinted from Leviathan.
  1. Woman--Rights of women.
  I. Radical Education Project.
  KU-RH

W189
Woodcock, George.
  What is anarchism? [New York,
  Libertarian League, 19]
  8p.
  Cover title.
  1. Anarchism and anarchists.
  I. Libertarian League.
  MiU

W190
Woodward, Comer Vann, 1908-
  Civil rights: the movement re-
  examined. Three essays by C.

Van Woodward, Paul Feldman,
Bayard Rustin, with an introduc-
tion by A. Philip Randolph.
[New York, A. Philip Randolph
Education Fund, 1967?]
48p. illus.
1. Negroes--Civil rights.
I. Feldman, Paul, jt. auth.
II. Rustin, Bayard, 1910-
jt. auth. III. Randolph, Asa
Philip, 1889-   IV. Randolph
(A. Philip) Education Fund.
WHi-L

W191
The Worker.
  The crucial issues facing man-
  kind. New York, 1963.
  16p. illus. 45x29cm.
  A supplementary issue of The
  Worker, July 28, 1963.
  1. Kommunisticheskaia partiia
  Sovetskogo Soiuza. TSentral'nyi
  Komitet. II. Chung-kuo kung
  ch'an tang. Chung yang wei yuan
  hui.
  NIC, NUC 67-33898

W192
The Worker.
  A selection of drawings from The
  Worker, 1924-1960. [Foreword
  by Joseph North] New York
  [1961?]
  unpaged. (chiefly illus.)
  1. Caricatures and cartoons.
  2. American wit and humor, Pic-
  torial. I. North, Joseph.
  MiU, NUC 67-31087

Worker-Student Alliance Caucus.
  see
Students for a Democratic Society.
  Worker-Student Alliance Caucus.

W193
Workers Defense League.
  The case of the anti-Franco sail-
  ers. [New York, 1961]
  6 leaves. 28cm.
  Caption title.
  1. Spain--Pol. & govt.
  WHi-A

W194
Workers Defense League.

Not only to preserve the past
but to enrich the future. [New
York, 196]
[8]p.
Cover title.
1. Workers Defense League.
WHi-A

W195
Workers for a Democratic Society,
  San Diego.
  What's happened to Workers for
  a Democratic Society (San Diego).
  [n.p., 1969]
  4p. 28cm.
  Caption title.
  1. Students for a Democratic
  Society. 2. Progressive Labor
  Party.
  WHi-L

W196
Workers for People's Democracy.
  Hayakawa panders to campus radicals. [San Bruno, Calif.,
  1970]
  3 leaves. 28cm.
  Caption title.
  1. Labor and laboring classes.
  2. Student movements--San Francisco.
  CU-B

W197
Workers for People's Democracy.
  What American workers know about
  the "doomsday theory". [San
  Bruno, Calif., 196]
  [2]p. 28cm.
  Caption title.
  1. Capitalism. 2. Labor and
  laboring classes.
  CU-B

W198
Workers League.
  Open letter to SMC, submitted
  by Workers League. [New York,
  1970]
  [2]p. 36cm.
  Caption title.
  1. Student Mobilization Committee to End the War in Vietnam.
  2. Socialist Workers Party.
  3. Vietnamese conflict, 1961-
  1975.
  KU-RH

W199
Workers World.
  Counter-revolution in Czechoslovakia; an account of the attempt
  to restore capitalism under
  cover of "liberal reform." New
  York, World View Publishers
  [1968]
  51p. 24cm.
  1. Czechoslovak Republic.
  2. Russia--For. rel.--Czechoslo-
  vak Republic. I. World View
  Publishers.
  KU-RH

W200
Workshop in Nonviolence, Charlot-
    tesville, Va.
  "No more war! War never again!"
  [Charlottesville, Va., 196]
  [3]p. 36cm.
  Caption title.
  1. Vietnamese conflict, 1961-
  1975.
  KU-RH

W201
World Committee for a World Con-
    stitutional Convention.
  A call to all peoples and all
  national governments of the
  earth. Denver [1963]
  [4]p. 22cm.
  Cover title.
  1. International organization.
  KU-RH

W202
World Federalist of Canada, Vic-
    toria Branch. Special Study
    Group in Viet Nam.
  The facts about the war in Viet
  Nam. 2d. ed. Victoria, 1965.
  8p. 28cm.
  Cover title.
  1. Vietnamese conflict, 1961-
  1975.
  WHi-L

W203
World Socialist Party.
  Our declaration of principles.
  [Boston, 1970?]
  folder. 22cm.
  Caption title.
  1. Socialism.
  KU-RH

W204
World Student Christian Federa-
    tion.
  The banks and apartheid. [An
  open letter to the member student Christian movements of
  the World Student Christian
  Federation. New York? University Christian Movement? 196]
  [16]p. 29cm.
  Cover title.
  1. Banks and banking. 2. Africa, South--Race question.
  3. Student movements.
  KU-RH

W205
World Without War Council.
  Conscience and war; questions
  and readings to help you clarify your choices. Berkeley
  [196]
  [7] leaves. 28cm.
  Caption title.
  1. Conscientious objectors.
  2. Military service, Compulsory.
  CU-B

W206
World Without War Council, North-
    ern California.
  Vietnam peace proposals.
  [Berkeley, 1967?]
  52p. 23cm.
  Cover title.
  1. Vietnamese conflict, 1961-
  1975
  CU-B

W207
World Without War Council.
    Northern California.
  Why we counsel conscientious
  objectors. Berkeley [196]
  7 leaves. 28cm.
  Caption title.
  1. Conscientious objectors.
  2. Military service, Compulsory.
  CU-B

W208
Wynner, Edith.
  The federal idea. Glencoe,
  Campaign for World Government
  [c1960]

12p. 21cm.
Cover title.
1. International organization.

‡
Y
‡

Y1
Yale, David R.
  Ecology and revolution. [Chica-
  go, New University Conference,
  c1970]
  21p. 28cm.
  Cover title.
  1. Pollution. 2. Revolutions.
  3. Capitalism. I. New University Conference.
  KU-RH

Y2
Young, Andrew.
  These questions have been asked:
  does Martin Luther King, Jr.
  have the right? The qualifica-
  tions? The duty? To speak out
  on peace. [n.p., SCLC, 196]
  [8]p. 23cm.
  1. King, Martin Luther, 1929-
  1968. 2. Vietnamese conflict,
  1961-1975. I. Southern Christian Leadership Council.
  KU-RH

Y3
Young, Joe.
  U.S. aggression in Vietnam and
  Canada's complicity. [Toronto,
  Canadian Vietnam Newsletter,
  196]
  12p. 22cm.
  1. Canada--For. rel.--Vietnam.
  2. Vietnamese conflict, 1961-
  1975. I. Canadian Vietnam Newsletter.
  MiU

Y4
Young, Nigel.
  Nonviolence and revolutionary
  change. Address to the annual
  meeting of the Women's Inter-
  national League for Peace and
  Freedom, April, 1968, Berkeley,
  California. [Berkeley, Women's

I. Campaign for World Government.
KU-RH

International League for Peace
and Freedom, 1968]
  7p. 28cm.
  Caption title.
  1. Nonviolence. 2. Revolutions.
  I. Women's International League
  for Peace and Freedom.
  CU-B

Y5
Young, Ron.
  The draft: reform or repeal?
  Washington, National Council
  to Repeal the Draft [1970?]
  5p. 28cm.
  Caption title.
  1. Military service, Compulsory.
  I. National Council to Repeal
  the Draft.
  KU-RH

Y6
Young People's Socialist League.
  The American scene. Chicago
  [196]
  6p. 28cm.
  Cover title.
  1. Socialism. 2. U.S.--Pol.
  & govt.--1963-
  CU-B

Y7
Young People's Socialist League.
  Constitution of the Young
  People's Socialist League.
  [New York, 1962]
  [8]p. 28cm.
  Caption title.
  1. Socialism.
  KU-RH

Y8
Young People's Socialist League.
  The defense of man. [New York,
  196]
  4p. illus. 44cm.
  Caption title.

At head of title: an introduction to democratic socialism.
1. Socialism.
KU-RH

Y9
Young People's Socialist League.
  The lesson of Vietnam; the need
  for a democratic foreign policy.
  [Berkeley, 196]
  7p. 22cm.
  Cover title.
  1. Vietnamese conflict, 1961-
  1975.
  CU-B

Y10
Young People's Socialist League.
  The 1968 election. For intelligent student political action
  against the growing threat of:
  racism, reaction, repression.
  [New York, 1968]
  4p. 22cm.
  Caption title.
  1. U.S.--Pol. & govt. 1963-
  2. Socialism. 3. Presidents--
  U.S.--Election--1968.
  CU-B

Y11
Young People's Socialist League.
  The politics of pollution. New
  York [196]
  [1] leaf. 32cm.
  Caption title.
  1. Pollution.
  KU-RH

Y12
Young People's Socialist League.
  Sit-ins continue: freedom riders:
  an offensive for democracy.
  [New York, 1961?]
  6p.
  Cover title.
  1. Negroes--Civil rights.
  2. Student movements.
  WHi-L

Y13
Young People's Socialist League.
  Socialism as problem and ideal;
  an annotated reading list.
  [New York, 1962?]
  [16]p. 22cm.

Cover title.
1. Socialism.--Bibl.
CU-B

Y14
Young People's Socialist League.
  Socialist ideals and American
  reality; an approach to building a democratic socialist
  youth movement in the United
  States. [New York, 1966?]
  [14]p. 28cm.
  Cover title.
  1. Student movements. 2. Socialism.
  CU-B

Y15
Young People's Socialist League.
  Socialist song book. [3d. ed.
  New York, 1964]
  68p. 28cm.
  Cover title.
  KU-RH

Y16
Young People's Socialist League.
  Support the UAW strikers.
  New York [196]
  [1] leaf. 36cm.
  Caption title.
  1. International union, united
  automobile, aircraft and agri-
  cultural implement workers of
  America. 2. Strikes and lock-
  outs--Automobile industry.
  KU-RH

Y17
Young People's Socialist League.
  Towards peace: a statement on
  foreign policy. [New York,
  1961?]
  10p. 22cm.
  Cover title.
  1. U.S.--Foreign policy.
  2. Peace
  CU-B

Y18
Young People's Socialist League.
  What is the Young People's
  Socialist League? [New York,
  196]
  folder.
  1. Socialism.
  WHi-L

Y19
Young People's Socialist League.
  Where we stand: the political
  views of the YPSL left wing.
  American scene and political
  action. [Chicago, 196]
  [2]p. 28cm.
  1. Youth--Political activity.
  KU-RH

Y20
Young People's Socialist League,
    Austin, Tex.
  Towards the building a revolu-
  tionary party in America, state-
  ment of YPSL-Austin and YPSL-
  Cornell. [n.p., 196]
  3p. 36cm.
  Caption title.
  1. Socialism. 2. Revolutions.
  I. Young People's Socialist
  League, Cornell.
  KU-RH

Y21
Young People's Socialist League.
    Norman Thomas Chapter.
  The democratic left: an open
  letter to liberal students.
  [Berkeley, 196]
  11p. 22cm.
  Cover title.
  1. Student movements. 2. Social-
  ism.
  CU-B

Y22
Young People's Socialist League.
    Norman Thomas Chapter.
  Electricity, socialization and
  democratic economy. [Berkeley,
  196]
  6p.
  1. Pacific Gas and Electric Co.
  2. Public utilities.
  WHi-L

Y23
Young People's Socialist League.
    Norman Thomas Chapter.
  The lesson of Vietnam; the need
  for a democratic foreign policy.
  [Berkeley, 196]
  7p.
  1. U.S.--Foreign policy. 2.
  Vietnamese conflict, 1961-1975.
  WHi-L

Y24
Young People's Socialist League.
    Philadelphia Chapter.
  The view from Philadelphia:
  perspective. [Philadelphia,
  1963?]
  3 leaves. 28cm.
  Caption title.
  1. Socialism.
  KU-RH

Y25
Young People's Socialist League
    and Democratic Socialism.
  The politics of pollution.
  New York [1970?]
  [1] leaf. 32cm.
  Caption title.
  1. Environmental policy.
  CU-B

Y26
Young Socialist Alliance.
  For independent political
  action in 1964. Berkeley
  [1964]
  7p. 28cm.
  Cover title.
  1. Presidents--U.S.--Election--
  1964. 2. Socialism. 2. U.S.--
  Pol. & govt.--1963-
  CU-B

Y27
Young Socialist Alliance.
  Introducing the Young Social-
  ist Alliance. [New York, 1968]
  63p. 28cm.
  Cover title.
  1. Socialism.
  CU-B

Y28
Young Socialist Alliance.
  Join the Young Socialist Alli-
  ance. [New York, 196]
  folder. illus. 21x9cm.
  Cover title.
  1. Socialism.
  KU-RH

Y29
Young Socialist Alliance.
  An open letter to U.S. students
  from the YSA. [New York, 1970?]
  [4]p. 28cm.
  Caption title.

1. Student movements.   2. Hoover,
John Edgar, 1895-1972.
KU-RH

Y30
Young Socialist Alliance.
Socialists and the war in Viet-
nam; an open letter to the Du-
Bois Clubs. New York, 1966.
6p. 28cm.
Caption title.
1. Vietnamese conflict, 1961-
1975. 2. Socialism. 3. DuBois
(W.E.B.) Clubs of America.
KU-RH

Y31
Young Socialist Alliance, Ann
   Arbor.
Documented fact sheet on Vietnam.
[Ann Arbor, 1966?]
[7]p. 28cm.
Cover title.
1. Vietnamese conflict, 1961-
1975.
MiU-H

Y32
Young Socialist Alliance. National Executive Committee.
YSA program for the campus revolt. [New York, 196]
[4]p. 28cm.
1. Student movements.
KU-RH

Y33
Young Socialist Alliance. National Executive Committee.
YSA program for the student revolt. [New York, 196]
[4]p. 28cm.
Caption title.
1. Student movements. 2. Socialism.
KU-RH

Y34
Young Socialist for Halstead and
   Boutelle.
Join Young Socialist for Halstead
and Boutelle. [New York, 1968?]
folder. 22x10cm.
Cover title.
1. Socialism. 2. Halstead, Fred.
3. Boutelle, Paul. 4. Socialist

Workers Party.
KU-RH

Y35
Young Socialist for Halstead and
   Boutelle.
Young Socialist for Halstead
and Boutelle. [New York, 1968?]
folder. 22x9cm.
Cover title.
1. Socialism. 2. Halstead,
Fred. 3. Boutelle, Paul.
4. Socialist Workers Party.
KU-RH

Y36
Young Socialist League.
Aid the Vietnamese revolution.
Ithaca, N.Y., 1965.
[1] leaf. 36cm.
Caption title.
1. Vietnamese conflict, 1961-
1975.
WHi-L

Y37
Young Socialist League.
Socialists aid the Vietnamese
revolution. [Ithaca, N.Y.,
1966]
2p. 36cm.
Caption title.
1. Vietnamese conflict, 1961-
1975. 2. South Viet Nam National Front for Liberation.
WHi-L

Y38
Young Socialist League.
Which road for socialist youth?
Reformism or revolutionary
socialism? [Berkeley, Calif.,
Young Socialist Forum for] the
Young Socialist [1959]
iv, 51 leaves. 28cm. (Young
Socialist educational bulletin
2)
Cover title.
1. Socialism. 2. Revolutions.
3. Student movements. I. Young
Socialist Forum.
MiU

Y39
Young Workers' Liberation League,
   Ann Arbor.

Black-white unity brings BAM victory. [Ann Arbor? 1970?]
[4]p. 28cm.
Caption title.
1. Black Action Movement. 2. Ne-
groes--Ann Arbor, Mich.
MiU-H

Y40
Young Workers' Liberation League
  of Ohio.
End the war in Vietnam--end
racism. Cleveland [1970?]
[1] leaf. 28cm.
Caption title.
1. Vietnamese conflict, 1961-
1975. 2. Race discrimination.
KU-RH

Y41
Youth Against War and Facism.
  The only answer to the Vietnam
war. New York [196]
[4]p. 28cm.
Caption title.
1. Vietnamese conflict, 1961-
1975.
CU-B

Y42
Youth Against War and Fascism,

Z

Z1
Zahn, Gordon Charles, 1918-
  An alternative to war. [New
York] Council on Religion and
Industrial Affairs [c1963, 1967]
32p. 23cm.
1. Pacifism. 2. War and reli-
gion. 3. Passive resistance to
government.
MoU, DLC

Z2
Zahn, Gordon Charles, 1918-
  Vietnam and the just war. [Ny-
ack, N.Y., Catholic Peace Fellow-
ship, 196]
[4]p. 28cm.
Caption title.
Reprinted from Worldview, Dec.

West Coast Branch.
"The Indonesia coup--in the
light of Bunker's strange re-
quest". [n.p., 196]
5p. 28cm.
Caption title.
1. U.S.--For. rel.--Indonesia.
2. Indonesia--For. rel.--U.S.
CU-B

Y43
Youth Against War and Facism.
  Women's Caucus.
International women's day 1970.
[New York, 1970]
4p. illus. 42cm.
Caption title.
1. Woman--Rights of women.
KU-RH

Y44
Youth Committee for Peace and De-
  mocracy in the Middle East.
For peace and democracy in the
Middle East. New York [196]
[1] leaf. 36cm.
Caption title.
1. Near East--Pol. & govt.
2. Israel-Arab War, 1967.
CU-B

1965.
1. Vietnamese conflict, 1961-
1975. I. Catholic Peace Fellowship.
KU-RH

Z3
Zelman, Annette.
  Teaching "about communism" in
American public schools. Pref.
by Roland F. Gray. New York,
Published for A.I.M.S. by Human-
ities Press [1965]
vi, 74p. 23cm. (American Institute for Marxist Studies.
Research report no. 1)
1. Communism--Study and teaching. I. American Institute
for Marxist Studies.
DLC 65-16702

Z4
Zeluck, Steve.
  The UFT strike; a blow against
  teachers unions. New York,
  Peace and Freedom Party [196]
  [12]p. 22cm. (Southern Manhattan Peace and Freedom pamphlet
  no. 1)
  Cover title.
  Reprinted from New Politics,
  v. 7, no. 1
  1. United Federation of Teachers.
  2. Teachers--New York (City).
  I. Peace and Freedom Party.
  NNU-T

Z5
Zetlin, Maurice.
  Labor in Cuba: Castro and Cuba's
  communists, two articles by Mau-
  rice Zeitlin. [Toronto, Fair
  Play For Cuba Committee, 1962?]
  12p. 22cm.
  Cover title.
  Reprinted from The Nation, Oct.
  20, 1962 and Nov. 3, 1962.
  1. Labor and laboring classes--
  Cuba. 2. Communism--Cuba.
  I. Fair Play for Cuba Committee.
  MiU

Z6
Zhukov, Viktor.
  Gains in the Soviet standard of
  living under the seven-year plan.
  New York, International Arts and
  Sciences Press [c1959]
  64p. illus. 22cm.
  1. Russia--Economic policy--
  1959-   I. International
  Arts and Sciences Press.
  MoSW, NcU, CSSR

Z7
Zinn, Howard, 1922-
  Albany. [Atlanta, Southern Regional Council] 1962.
  34p. 28cm.
  1. Albany, Ga.--Race question.
  2. Negroes--Albany, Ga.
  I. Southern Regional Council.
  WHi-A

Z8
Zinn, Howard, 1922-
  Dow shalt not kill. [Washington,

Liberation News Service; New
Media Project, [1967]
4p. 28cm. (LNS reprint no.
1)
Caption title.
1. Dow Chemical Company.
2. Vietnamese conflict, 1961-
1975. I. Liberation News Service. II. New Media Project.
KU-RH

Z9
Zinn, Howard, 1922-
  Dow shalt not kill. Nashville,
  Southern Student Organizing
  Committee [196]
  7, 2p. 28cm.
  Cover title.
  Contents.--Dow over all, By Bob
  Schwartz.
  Reprinted from New South Stu-
  dent, Dec. 1967.
  1. Dow Chemical Company.
  2. Vietnamese conflict, 1961-
  1975. I. Southern Student Or-
  ganizing Committee.
  MoU

Z10
Zinn, Howard, 1922-
  Schools in context: the Mississippi idea. [Atlanta, Student
  Nonviolent Coordinating Committee, 1964?]
  10p.
  Cover title.
  1. Free schools--Mississippi.
  2. Negroes--Education. I. Student Nonviolent Coordinating
  Committee.
  WHi-L

Z11
Zinn, Howard, 1922-
  A speech for LBJ. [Ithaca,
  N.Y., Glad Day Press, 196]
  6p.
  Cover title.
  Reprinted from Zinn's Vietnam;
  the logical withdrawal.
  1. Vietnamese conflict, 1961-
  1975. 2. Johnson, Lyndon
  Baines, Pres. U.S., 1908-1973.
  WHi-L

Z12
Zionism and the Arab revolution:
    the myth of progressive Israel
    [by Peter Buch and Israeli So-
    cialist Organization. New
    York, Young Socialist Alliance,
    1968]
31p. 28cm.
Cover title.
1. Israel-Arab War, 1967.
2. Israel--Pol. & govt. 3. Jewish-Arab relations. I. Buch,
Peter. II. Israeli Socialist
Organization. III. Young Socialist Alliance.
MoU

Z13
Zippert John.
  Rural community organization.
Nashville, Southern Student Or-
ganizing Committee [1966?]
7p.
Cover title.
1. Community organization.
2. Farmers. 3. Rural conditions.
I. Southern Student Organizing
Committee.
WHi-L

Z14
Zorin, Valerian Aleksandrovich,
    1902-
  Disarmament problem must be set-
tled. Address to UN disarmament
sub-committee on March 18.
[n.p., 1957]
12p.
1. Disarmament.
DS

Z15
Zverev, Arsenii Grigor'evich.

The Soviet standard of living;
social benefits. [New York,
International Arts and Sciences
Press, c1959]
32p. illus., map. 22cm.
Cover title.
1. Russia--Soc. condit.--1945-
2. Russia--Social policy.
I. International Arts and Sci-
ences Press.
IU, CLU, MoSW, KU, McU, ViU,
CLSU, CSSR

Z16
Zweig, Michael.
  Eastern Kentucky in perspective
[prepared for the Hazard Confer-
ence. n.p., Committee for Min-
ers and Economic Research and
Action Project of Students for
a Democratic Society, 1964]
4p. 28cm.
Caption title.
1. Poor--Kentucky. 2. Kentucky
--Econ. condit. I. Committee
for Miners. II. Students for a
Democratic Society. Economic
Research and Action Project.
WHi-A, MiU

Z17
Zweig, Michael.
  The radical in the academic
world. Ann Arbor, Conference
on Radicals in the Professions,
1967.
6p. 28cm.
Cover title.
1. Radicalism. 2. Teachers.
3. Universities and colleges.
I. Conference on Radicals in
the Professions.
MiU-H

Index

Another Mother for Peace,
  G112, S37, S38.
Ansara, Michael, S24.
Anthropology, A4.
Anti-communist movements,
  A11, A57, B204, C144, D170,
  E30, G106, G163, H217, J80,
  L164, M172, M185, N116,
  N140, R33, S521, W165, W166.
Anti-communist movements--
  California, A12.
Anti-communist movements--
  Indiana, S312.
Anti-communist movements--
  Kentucky, K50.
Anti-Defamation League, M169,
  S224.
Antimissile missiles, B126,
  C355, F83, P107, U3.
Antisemitism, H121.
Antisemitism--Russia, A147,
  L166.
Anvil-Atlas Publishers, M95.
Appalachian Committee for
  Full Employment, G96.
Appalachian Mountains, D104,
  S448.
Appalachian Mountains--Econ.
  condit., B259, B261, C98,
  C99, F27, S197, S198.
Appalachian Mountains--
  History, C377.
Appalachian Mountains--Race
  question, A136.
Appalachian Mountains--Soc.
  condit., S416, W102.
Appalachian Mountains, South-
  ern--Econ. condit., M99.
Appalachian Movement Press,
  H105, W102, W103, W105.
Appalachian South Folklore
  Center, W105.
Aptheker, Bettina, S291.
Aptheker, Herbert, 1915-
  G163, M221.
Arabs, R136.
Armaments, S298.
Aronson, Ronald, W165, W166.
Arrest (Police methods),
  B272.
Art, D142, M42, R70.
Art--Appalachian Mountains,
  F27.
Art and society, F27.
Artificial satellites,
  Russian, A158.

Asia, K53, L76.
Asia--Colonization, W108.
Asia--For. rel.--U.S., J77,
  W122.
Asia--Pol. & govt., A170,
  W108.
Asia, Southwestern--Pol.
  & govt., K95.
Assassination, M62.
Assmar, Sam, P78.
Atheism, J72.
Atlanta--Race question, C346,
  S211, S235.
Atomic bomb--Testing, S376.
Atomic bomb shelters, M56,
  M100.
Atomic energy, W71, W73.
Atomic power, F116.
Atomic power-plants--Con-
  necticut, W70.
Atomic power-plants--Illi-
  nois, W70.
Atomic warfare, G58, H208,
  H233, R28, W47, W173.
Atomic warfare--Moral and
  religious aspects, E24.
Atomic warfare and society,
  H51.
Atomic weapons, A17, A18,
  C37, C138, C202, F34, F114,
  P31, T29.
Atomic weapons and disarma-
  ment, A8, B268, C237, C244,
  E24, F33, K69, L30, M206,
  N28, N29, N48, P29, P32,
  R145, S357, S376, W171,
  W172.
Augusta, Ga.--Race question,
  S210.
Authoritarianism, A178.
Automation, B113, B216, B219,
  D80, H124, K32, N211, N212,
  S120, S155, T18, T17.
Automation--Social aspects,
  L165.
Automobile industry and
  trade, C3.
Automobile industry and
  trade--Latin America, F49.
Automobile industry and
  trade--Mexico, F49.
Automobile industry workers,
  B33, C3, G69, E19, I24,
  J12, J20, P4, U2, W52,
  W51.
Automobile industry workers--

Sedition, C273.
Segal, Jeff, S273.
Segregation in education, B6,
  C213, F186, M169, S232,
  S233, S277, W126.
Segregation in transportation
  --Southern States, S238.
Self-determination, Nation-
  al, S426.
Sex, A173, A174, A177, A178,
  K103, K109, S62, T40.
Shabazz, James, V10, V11.
Shahn-ti Sena Publishers,
  C202.
Shakespeare, William, 1564-
  1616--Political and social
  views--Bibliography, F82.
Shields, Art, L79.
Shils, Edward Albert, 1911-
  , H5, H6.
Shimkin, David, K48.
Shumn, Lawrence, S181.
Simon Fraser University, A7.
Sinclair, John, U18.
Situationist International,
  C121, V5.
Slate, M109, M228, P5, R89,
  R90, R99, T65, W14.
Slave-trade, R93.
Slavery in the U.S., A152,
  G27, G28, P66.
Slavery in the U.S.--Insur-
  rections, etc., J27.
Slums, D121, D147, N185,
  N186, R154, R155, S211,
  S217, V10, V11, V30.
Smith, Edouard, N166.
Smith, Guy, N117.
Smith, Howard Worth, 1883-
  , E26.
Smith, Louise Pettibone,
  L155.
Smoler, Barry, C203.
Sobell, Morton, A71, E6,
  H162, S114.
Sobukwe, Robert Mangaliso,
  A86, A87.
Social change, B144, C177,
  C253, C373, D53, F179,
  F200, G137, H9, H98, H144,
  H145, H146, H150, J61, L11,
  L46, L56, L154, M75, Mc31,
  N122, N124, O18, O36, P43,
  P134, P135, P136, S12, S58,
  S206, S444, T17, T43, T72,
  V28, V29, V30.

Social classes, A143, B153,
  C162, H87, H90, H153, M80,
  M81, P180, R25, S61, S180.
Social classes--Africa, A118,
  L66.
Social classes--Quebec, D171.
Social Science Institute,
  N99, N100, N101, N103,
  N105.
Social work as a profession,
  S258.
Socialism see also Indepen-
  dent Socialists; Indepen-
  dent Socialist Clubs of
  America; Freedom Socialist
  Party.
Socialism, A68, A124, A150,
  B14, B20, B38, B100, B112,
  B184, B185, B186, B187,
  B191, B192, B265, C14, C15,
  C22, C27, C28, C31, C32,
  C72, C238, C240, C305,
  C380, C381, D45, D46, D47,
  D48, D49, D50, D51, D52,
  D53, D54, D55, D56, D57,
  D58, D59, D61, D62, D79,
  D93, D125, D126, D130,
  D131, D132, D152, D160,
  D173, D182, D183, E37,
  F94, F95, F98, F101, F118,
  F124, F125, F140, F206,
  G22, G69, G70, H70, H73,
  H87, H99, H115, H116, H119,
  H121, H123, H122, H169,
  H176, H219, H225, H226,
  H229, I7, I11, I20, I21,
  I23, J21, J25, J31, J70,
  J71, K29, K88, K110, K126,
  L1, L7, L50, L80, L81, L84,
  L161, L171, M26, M27, M28,
  M29, M31, M46, M105, M154,
  M155, M183, M207, M224,
  Mc32, Mc33, Mc37, N147,
  N160, N163, N200, N201,
  N203, N206, N207, N208, O29,
  P27, P57, P79, P90, P93,
  P79, P90,
  P95, P97, P121, P165, Q4,
  R74, R76, R102, S75, S123,
  S128, S129, S132, S133,
  S135, S136, S139, S140,
  S142, S143, S144, S145,
  S146, S147, S148, S149,
  S150, S151, S157, S158,
  S159, S160, S161, S162,
  S163, S174, S175, S177,

About the Editor

Ned Kehde, associate archivist at the University of Kansas, received an M.A. in history and an M.A. in library science from the University of Missouri. He is coeditor of *Access* and has published articles on pamphleteering and the American left and right in such journals as *American Libraries* and *Missouri Library Association Quarterly*.

DATE DUE